P9-EDF-416

Fourth Edition

INTRODUCTION TO SECURITY

OPERATIONS AND MANAGEMENT

P. J. Ortmeier, Ph.D.
Grossmont College

PEARSON

Boston   Columbus   Indianapolis   New York   San Francisco   Upper Saddle River
Amsterdam   Cape Town   Dubai   London   Madrid   Milan   Munich   Paris   Montreal   Toronto
Delhi   Mexico City   São Paulo   Sydney   Hong Kong   Seoul   Singapore   Taipei   Tokyo

Vice President and Executive Publisher: Vernon Anthony
Senior Acquisitions Editor: Eric Krassow
Assistant Editor: Tiffany Bitzel
Editorial Assistant: Lynda Cramer
Media Project Manager: Karen Bretz
Director of Marketing: David Gesell
Marketing Manager: Cyndi Eller
Senior Marketing Coordinator: Alicia Wozniak

Production Manager: Holly Shufeldt
Creative Director: Jayne Conte
Cover Designer: Suzanne Duda
Cover Illustration/Photo: Fotolia
Full-Service Project Management/Composition: Chitra Ganesan/PreMediaGlobal
Printer/Binder: Courier Companies, Inc.

Pearson Education LTD.
Pearson Education Australia PTY, Limited
Pearson Education Singapore, Pte. Ltd
Pearson Education North Asia Ltd
Pearson Education, Canada, Ltd
Pearson Educación de Mexico, S.A. de C.V.
Pearson Education–Japan
Pearson Education Malaysia, Pte. Ltd

Library of Congress Cataloging-in-Publication Data
Ortmeier, P. J.
    Introduction to security : operations and management / P.J. Ortmeier. — 4th ed.
       p. cm.
    Includes bibliographical references and index.
    ISBN-13: 978-0-13-268295-4
    ISBN-10: 0-13-268295-8
  1. Private security services—Management. 2. Buildings—Security measures. 3. Industries—Security measures. 4. Corporations—Security measures. 5. Security systems. 6. Computer security. I. Title.
    HV8290.O78 2012
    363.28'9068—dc23

2011041118

10 9 8 7 6 5 4 3 2 1

ISBN-10: 0-13-268295-8
ISBN-13: 978-0-13-268295-4

To Jacob, Luke, Kelly, Marcus, Yasmin, Blake, and Keira

BRIEF CONTENTS

CONTENTS

PREFACE

Gratified by the positive response to previous editions of this book, I wrote *INTRODUCTION TO SECURITY: Operations and Management,* fourth edition, to address security operations and management in the post–9/11 era. The book is designed to meet the need for a comprehensive yet concise and efficient introduction to security or security management text. Published originally as *Security Management: An Introduction,* this fourth edition retains, reinforces, and expands on topics addressed in previous editions. Additions and modifications enhance rather than compromise the integrity of the book's predecessors.

The book is balanced between introductory protection concepts and security management principles and practices. It is organized into a logical sequence, enhancing its flow and consolidating similar topics. In addition, the book's scope is expanded significantly to address subjects identified through extensive research and by numerous reviewers. Faculty, students, and practitioners provided valuable input as well. New to the fourth edition are the following:

- "Security Spotlight" and "A Quick Survey" features within each chapter
- An appendix listing websites offering additional information
- The latest statistics on key trends including security profession salaries and types of crime
- Expanded and up-to-date coverage of terrorism, women in security, and retail loss prevention
- New examples and analysis as available to illustrate key themes such as security technology advances and investigative techniques
- Expanded and new end-of-chapter interactive case studies
- Added headings to serve as signposts for readers.

The book has been adopted for use in traditional and online lower and upper division undergraduate as well as graduate introduction to security, business, and security management courses. It is also a useful reference for security personnel. Practitioners working within specific security venues can also use the book to familiarize themselves with other applications in the security industry.

Every attempt was made to capture the essence of introductory and advanced loss prevention concepts and best practices. The book is unique because it presents operational tactics and management strategies as well as an overview of the security field. It highlights the multitude of security-related subjects, avoids unnecessary discussion, balances the business and legal orientations of security services, and addresses security from public as well as private perspectives. The book also identifies and explores more than 20 security environments, applications, and services, and it examines issues encountered within these areas.

Those pursuing an ASIS International Certified Protection Professional (CPP) designation will discover that this book is a must read when preparing for the CPP examination. A CPP recipient stated that the book presents a systematic approach to the broad array of data contained within the scope of security management. The CPP declared that the book "contains a significant amount of information tested on the CPP examination" and it serves as a "guide" and "confidence builder" for the exam.

Reviewers refer to the book as excellent, balanced, well rounded, and efficient in identifying and explaining the significant topics in the security arena. They also indicate that the book presents valuable information for the frontline manager as well as the student of security management. About the book, one reviewer commented that the fundamentals of security management are rarely so well articulated.

ORGANIZATION OF THE BOOK

The book is divided into five major parts. Part I introduces the reader to security's role in society. Chapter 1 presents a brief history and overview of security services. Chapter 2 addresses threats to safety and security. Chapter 3 focuses on the legal aspects of public and private security operations.

Part II addresses security's essential functions. Chapter 4 focuses on *physical security*. Chapter 5 presents *personnel security*, emphasizing the need for ethical leadership at all levels of the organization. *Information, communications*, and *computer security* are the subjects of Chapter 6.

Part III focuses on security management principles and practices. Chapter 7 emphasizes the need for risk assessment, security surveys, and planning. Chapter 8 addresses the implementation and administration of action plans selected. Chapter 9 discusses civil and criminal investigations, competitive and criminal intelligence operations, and the importance of reports.

Part IV examines specific security applications and solutions to security problems. Chapters 10 and 11 identify and explore numerous security specialties. Chapter 12 is devoted entirely to homeland security issues.

Part V explores security trends and challenges. Career opportunities are highlighted in Chapter 13 and the future of security services is studied in Chapter 14.

Each chapter begins with a set of learning objectives and ends with a summary, a list of key terms, discussion questions and exercises, and a case-study activity (Your Turn) to enhance critical thinking and knowledge acquisition. New to this edition are several interactive pedagogical features added to each chapter: "Security Spotlight" focuses readers' attention on a particular topic or theme within the chapter and invites them to investigate further or apply their understanding of the topic to their own situation. "A Quick Survey" is a brief poll related to a particular theme or topic within the chapter. Readers respond to the survey and explore several brief questions for thought related to it. A glossary of terms is provided. The appendices also include a correlation of the ASIS symposia topics with the book's contents, a sample safety and security survey instrument, and a new chapter-by-chapter list of websites at which readers can learn more about topics of interest. Numerous additional sources of information on the topics discussed are presented throughout the text.

ACKNOWLEDGMENTS

I wish to express my deepest appreciation to the many people who provided support and assistance during the development of the fourth edition of this book. Gratitude is extended to my editorial consultant, Laurie Keller Johnson, and to my many friends at Pearson Prentice Hall who assisted with this project over the years, including but certainly not limited to Tim Peyton, Eric Krassow, Lynda Cramer, Alicia Kelly, JoEllen Gohr, Kathleen Sleys, Tiffany Bitzel, Jessica Sykes, Adam Kloza, Alicia Wozniak, and Holly Shufeldt, and to senior production manager Chitra Ganesan and copyeditor Nivasini Karthikeyan for their keen eyes, professionalism, and dedication. A thank you is also extended to Deanna Hook, Gloria Aldaba, and David Mehlhoff for their assistance with the preparation of the manuscript.

I also appreciate the valuable contributions made by the reviewers of the previous editions: Jamie A. Latch, Remington College; Patrick Patterson, Remington College; Charles Green, Remington College; Jerome Randall, University of Central Florida; Richard Hill, University of Houston-Downtown; Dimitrius A. Oliver, Ph.D., Holly Dersham-Bruce, Dawson Community College, Glendive, MT; Stephen Jones, University of Maryland, College Park, MD; Sean Gabbidon, Penn State University, Middletown, PA; Neal Strehlow, Fox Valley Technical College, Appleton, WI; Donald Jenkins, Central Community College, Grand Island, NE; Michael Moberly, Southern Illinois University, Carbondale, IL; Charles Biggs, Oakland City University, Oakland City, IN; Terrance Hoffman, Nassau Community College, Garden City, NY; and Kevin Peterson, Innovative Protection Solutions LLC, Herndon, VA.

Finally, I wish to express my heartfelt gratitude to my family, friends, and colleagues for their encouragement and patience.

ABOUT THE AUTHOR

P. J. Ortmeier holds bachelor's and master's degrees in criminal justice and a Ph.D. in educational leadership with an emphasis in public safety training and development. He is a U.S. Army veteran, a former police officer, and a former vice president of United Security Systems, Incorporated. Ortmeier developed and implemented numerous courses and degree programs in law enforcement, corrections, security management, and public safety. Currently, he is the chair of the 1,400-student Administration of Justice Department at Grossmont College in the San Diego suburb of El Cajon, California.

Ortmeier is the author of *Public Safety and Security Administration, Policing the Community: A Guide for Patrol Operations,* and *Introduction to Law Enforcement and Criminal Justice* as well as several articles appearing in journals such as *Police Chief, The Law Enforcement Executive Forum, California Security, Police and Security News,* and *Security Management.* With Edwin Meese III, former attorney general of the United States, Ortmeier coauthored *Leadership, Ethics, and Policing: Challenges for the 21st Century.* He also coauthored *Crime Scene Investigation: A Forensic Technician's Field Manual* with Tina Young as well as *Police Administration: A Leadership Approach* with Joseph J. Davis, a retired New York police captain. Ortmeier's publications focus on police field services, security operations, forensic science, professional career education, management, leadership, and competency development for public safety personnel.

Ortmeier is a member of the Academy of Criminal Justice Sciences, the International Association of Chiefs of Police, the International Public Safety Leadership Development Consortium, the California Association of Administration of Justice Educators, ASIS International, and the American Society of Criminology. His current interests include homeland defense, forensic science, and the development of leadership skills and career education pathways for public safety and security professionals.

The author encourages and solicits comments regarding the book as well as suggestions for future editions. The author is also available to provide technical assistance to any faculty person who adopts this text for a course. The author may be contacted directly at:

P. J. Ortmeier, Ph.D.
Coordinator, Administration of Justice
Grossmont College
8800 Grossmont College Drive
El Cajon, CA 92020

PART ONE

Introduction: Security's Role in Society

The three chapters constituting Part I introduce readers to security's role in society. Chapter 1 presents a brief history and overview of security services and discusses regulation of the security industry and professional certification and education programs. Chapter 2 addresses the wide range of threats to safety and security, from accidents, human error, and fire to natural disasters, civil liability, and numerous manifestations of crime. Chapter 3 focuses on the legal aspects of public and private security operations, including the judicial process, a variety of types of law, and laws regarding search and seizure.

CHAPTER 1

History and Overview

LEARNING OBJECTIVES

After completing this chapter, the reader should be able to

- articulate the theoretical foundation for security.
- compare and contrast public law enforcement with private policing.
- describe the goals of security management.
- outline and describe the history of security services.
- demonstrate knowledge of the essential elements of security.
- describe the different types of security organizations.
- evaluate the roles of the security manager.
- discuss the importance of regulation of the security industry.
- evaluate professional certification and education programs for security personnel.

THE CONTEXT FOR SECURITY

Theoretical Foundation

Societies were slow to create protections for their individuals and groups. However, as the concepts of territoriality and personal property developed, human beings became more concerned with the protection of persons and property. As societies became more complex, unwritten behavioral rules and, ultimately, written laws were developed and formalized to proscribe (forbid) and prescribe (encourage) specific types of human behavior. Eventually, private and public security systems were created to deter potential offenders, enforce societal rules and laws, and provide protection for persons and property (Purpura, 2003; Simonsen, 1998).

The theoretical foundation for **security** is based on several behavioral assumptions, or beliefs about human behavior. First, individuals choose pleasure over pain and often make inappropriate decisions in search of gratification. Second, individuals commit crime when conditions

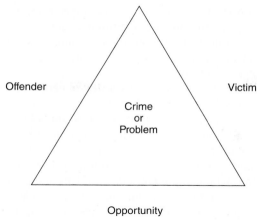

FIGURE 1–1   Crime (or Problem) Triangle

exist that promote suitable targets of opportunity and the influence of social control is lacking. Third, although crime will exist to some degree in any society regardless of social controls, the opportunity for crime can be reduced through manipulation of the environment. Fourth, in addition to the threat of criminal behavior, numerous human activities and natural phenomena create situations through which great harm may occur if appropriate prevention and intervention strategies are not implemented (American Society for Industrial Security, 1998; Crowe, 2000; Hancock & Sharp, 2004; Hess & Wrobleski, 2009). Security is intended to provide these prevention and intervention strategies.

The theoretical foundation for security may also be viewed from the standpoint of the crime (or problem) analysis triangle (see Figure 1–1). The triangle offers a simple mechanism to visualize and analyze crime, disorder, and potentially harmful events. Because all three elements (sides) of the triangle must be present for a crime or harmful event to occur, the elimination of any one of the three elements may prevent the crime, solve the problem, or mitigate harm caused by an event. If a potential victim implements measures to eliminate or reduce the opportunity for a crime to occur, the crime may be prevented. Improved locks and lighting, for example, can harden a target (victim) and reduce a potential burglar's opportunity to commit a burglary without detection.

Defining Security's Role

Since the terrorist attacks of September 11, 2001, security has moved from the periphery to the center, with government, private organizations, and individual citizens placing more emphasis on the need for security. However, even before the horrific events of 9/11, the level of support for security from senior management in many organizations was increasing. Corporate executives realized that effective security protects the ultimate bottom line: that is, survival of the organization.

Security services today are sophisticated and complex and virtually defy a simple definition. In a sense, security is a concept in search of a definition. As an occupation, **security management** is multifaceted and interdisciplinary. Security involves the use of criminal and civil law, investigations, business management, policy formulation, psychology, sociology, and technology to protect persons and property. Contemporary security operations often focus on diverse areas such as fraud, disaster recovery and business continuity, energy management, fire prevention and protection, Internet and information protection, preemployment screening, executive protection, counterterrorism, business intelligence, environmental safety and crime, substance abuse, and workplace violence prevention.

Security is involved and interacts with every aspect of personal, organizational, and group life. Individuals strive to be safe and secure. Private businesses and corporations seek to prevent loss and protect property and human assets. Societies and political entities seek protection. Security operations include or collaborate with elements of the criminal justice system. Security cooperates with law enforcement in the crime prevention effort, interacts with the judicial system to assist in prosecution, and may, through a trend toward privatization of certain correctional services, be involved in the staffing and management of jails and prisons. In some areas, security's mission includes protection from hazardous materials, fire safety, and firefighting through industrial fire brigades. Security operations may also be used to generate revenue through the sale of products and services (Harowitz, 2003; Ortmeier & Meese, 2010; Peak & Glensor, 2008; Simonsen, 1998).

SECURITY SPOTLIGHT

Think about your typical day. In what respects is security being provided to you during each part of your day? For example, as you leave your home, drive to school or work, shop at a store or online, or go out for the evening with family or friends, what forms of security are in place in each of those settings and during each of those activities?

Security's Impact

The singularly most important and conspicuous purpose of security is that of protector or guardian. As the guardian against harm to people, property, and information, security is a service function with a tremendous impact. However, security's value may be difficult to measure or quantify. Therefore, security's impact may be determined more appropriately by what does not happen, rather than by what does.

Security may add value to an organization by aggressively seeking cost reduction initiatives. Security managers may cut costs through entrepreneurial ventures and articulation arrangements with other security service providers. Collaborative business arrangements and consortiums are formed to increase efficiency and reduce expenses. In Washington, DC, five independent high-rise building management groups entered into an agreement to share services provided by a third-party vendor. Hospitals share services, including security services, with other hospitals. Multiple facilities with proprietary (in-house) alarm and video surveillance systems can collaborate to create a single central station to share in the cost or can charge member organizations for the service. Large facilities can utilize security personnel, instead of mailroom staff, to provide internal mail and delivery services, thus adding value to the organization by cutting delivery costs while increasing patrol activity (Colling, 2001; Dalton, 1995; Ortmeier & Davis, 2012).

Security involves government, nonprofit, and for-profit institutions. In an organizational sense, security is a function and responsibility that is woven increasingly throughout the operation of all public agencies and private institutions. As a function within an organization, security may be defined as a public or private service-related activity that provides personnel and equipment and creates policies and procedures designed to prevent or reduce losses caused by criminal action as well as by noncriminal events resulting from human error, emergencies, human-caused and natural disasters, and business intelligence collection by competitors.

In the past, security's image usually reflected a poorly trained individual who earned near minimum wage and guarded a gate or patrolled a business at night. Most contemporary security personnel, however, are much more sophisticated. Security personnel are used for emergency response, access control, deterrence, investigations, and persons and property protection. They monitor and operate security equipment utilized for access control, surveillance, fire protection, and patrol activities. Security managers are called upon to establish policies and procedures for disaster recovery, emergency management, fire prevention, security education, loss prevention, and asset protection. Ultimately, the goals of security promote a safe and secure environment and prevent loss. The result is maximum return on the investment of public or private capital. An organization's management is legally and morally responsible for the safety and security of people and property. If an organization has a security problem, it has a management problem. Security involves all those activities and objectives designed to meet asset protection goals to ensure that security problems do not materialize (Bratton, 2011; Dempsey, 2011; Kakalik & Wildhorn, 1971; Sennewald, 2003; Simonsen, 1998).

As the crime rate in the United States increased during the mid-twentieth century and law enforcement resources became increasingly strained, the public police were unable to effectively police private property. Additionally, many organizations realized that human and property assets required more protection. As a result, the security profession grew at an extremely rapid rate. In 1970, the number of security personnel in the United States, approximately 500,000, was about the same as the number of **public law enforcement** officers (Cunningham, Strauchs, & Van Meter, 1990). By 1991, the number of police officers increased to 580,000, while security personnel increased to 1.5 million. By 2000, the number of police officers increased to over 600,000, while security personnel numbered approximately 2 million. By 2012, police officers were estimated at 680,000, while security personnel numbered over 2 million. Currently, expenditures for security services are almost twice that of public law enforcement. Clearly, security services are the primary protective service in the United States (Fagin, 2007; Ortmeier & Davis, 2012; Siegel & Senna, 2008).

The Contemporary Security Environment

The security environment depends on several factors. Every enterprise differs in its mission, in its culture, and in the way it conducts internal as well as external affairs. This difference is a result of a culture emanating from organization's history, personnel, and interrelationships. Organizational ethics also play an important role in the development of the security environment. Some organizations have very strict policies regarding personnel behavior, while others do not. In addition, private enterprises generate rules, regulations, and standards of conduct that form the foundation for a private justice system. These **private justice systems** codify and implement certain levels of punishment for misbehavior, much like criminal codes define and punish individuals for violation of societal rules. The security environment also depends on the relationship between security and public safety personnel. In the past, the relationship between public law enforcement and corporate security was often strained due to the low quality of some security personnel and the fact that many **private police** forces engaged in a protective function that many in public law enforcement believed fell under the purview of public policing.

Another compounding factor involves the relationship between security personnel and the organization being protected. Many security employees are contract workers provided by third parties. Following a trend in American business, numerous organizations are replacing some of their proprietary employees with contract workers. Loyalty to the organization, therefore, often remains with the contractor rather than with the site being protected. Finally, a major challenge for security management in the electronic age is the protection of proprietary information for the organization it services. Competitive pressures, foreign and domestic, combined with the ability to invade an institution or country electronically, pose enormous threats to national security and business enterprises.

In spite of any shortcomings within the security environment, the future seems relatively unlimited for the security profession and for individuals who choose security services as an occupation. Among other factors, constraints on public law enforcement budgets are likely to continue and necessitate increased use of private police (security) services. Security's positive impact in the modern world is without question. As security concepts are integrated into organizations, leaders are becoming more aware of the importance of security's value and contribution to the enterprise (American Society for Industrial Security, 1998; Dalton, 2003; Schmalleger, 2010).

Exciting career opportunities also exist in the security field (Harr & Hess, 2006). Salaries for security managers are generally competitive with those received in other professions. The results of a salary survey conducted in 1999 by the publisher of a security trade journal indicated that the average salary for security management personnel ranged from $30,000 to over $150,000 annually (Access Control & Security Systems Integration, 1999). A salary survey conducted in 2002 indicated that the highest average business-sector security manager salaries are earned in information technology ($109,105), followed by security professionals employed in the utilities and energy industry ($103,636) (Anderson, 2002). By 2007, the average annual salary for security professionals reached $117,000 (Moran, 2007). The salary for chief security officer (CSO) positions in large multinational organizations was expected to reach $400,000 annually (Lohr, 2002). By 2006, the salary range for CSOs reached $199,000–$294,000 (Scalet, 2006). In 2010, the median compensation for security professionals in the United States was $93,000, a 6 percent increase from 2009; those who held a **Certified Protection Professional (CPP)** certification earned a median salary of $118,000 (ASIS International, 2010).

Based on the growth in the number of people employed as well as the increase in compensation levels, it is apparent that career opportunities and salaries are excellent for those interested in security services. Additional information on career opportunities is presented in Chapter 13.

SECURITY SPOTLIGHT

Identify an individual who works in security services, perhaps at your school, at your place of employment, or in your community. Determine whether this person would be willing to talk with you for a few moments about security work. If so, consider asking the individual questions such as What attracted you to security as a profession? What do you enjoy most about the work? What do you enjoy least?

SECURITY: A BRIEF HISTORY

Ancient Traditions

In early times, protection of persons and property was the responsibility of individuals, clans, or tribes. Social control was maintained through custom, and redress of grievances was handled informally by the individual or group. In 2100 B.C., customs were codified for the first time through the efforts of Hammurabi, the king of Babylon (site of present-day Iraq). The **Code of Hammurabi** represented the first written laws designed to prescribe the responsibilities of the individual to the group. The Code also specified a predictable punishment for each offense, thus reducing the possibility of barbarous and capricious punishment at the hands of revenge-seeking victims. In 1500 B.C., Egypt created a judiciary system, and in 1400 B.C., Amenhotep, pharaoh of Egypt, developed customs houses and marine patrols.

English Common Law

After the Norman Conquest in 1066 A.D., England developed a system of county (shire) government through which the king appointed a law officer (reeve) to act as the magistrate for each county. Thus, the shire reeve, forerunner of the **sheriff**, was created and authorized by the king to make arrests. The shire reeve could deputize a posse to seek out criminals and enforce the common law of England.

The eleventh-century Norman Period also marked the beginning of an English court system. These courts formed a rudimentary criminal justice system. Decisions by judges became binding as precedent for future cases of a similar nature, thus establishing the foundation for the English common law. In 1215, the Magna Carta created by King John guaranteed basic civil rights to freeborn people. In 1285, the Statute of Winchester established a day-and-night watch for walled cities. Individuals took turns as nonpaid night watchmen in the community.

In the late 1600s and early 1700s, the industrial revolution dramatically transformed economic and social conditions. Villages became cities and crime increased. In response, the central government in England passed additional laws. The Highwayman Act of 1692 made provisions for **thief takers**, forerunners of the bounty hunters, who were compensated for capturing thieves and recovering stolen property. The law backfired because thief takers themselves stole property and sought the reward for its recovery. In response to the corrupt thief taker system, Henry Fielding, chief magistrate of the court on Bow Street in London, established a small group of salaried thief takers, known as the Bow Street Runners, to capture criminals. The unit's strategy was to arrive at the crime scene as quickly as possible, usually by running, to capture the criminal.

The American Experience

The criminal justice system in the United States developed primarily from the English common law structure. Most of the original American colonies were settled by the English. Thus, the colonists simply transplanted the laws of England onto American soil. As in England, the sheriff was the primary legal official. When the American colonies became a nation after the Revolutionary War, many states continued to observe English common law.

In the United States, as well as in the world, the development of a formalized police service was slow. Historians trace the beginnings of police departments to Detroit in 1801 and Cincinnati in 1803, and the first national investigative agency to the U.S. Post Office in 1828. However, it is London, England, which is credited with the creation of the first full-time paid

Sir Robert Peel, 1788–1850. Peel's efforts led to the passage of the Metropolitan Police Act in 1829, creating the first recognizable police force. *(Photo courtesy of Library of Congress.)*

public police department in the world. Largely as the result of the efforts of **Sir Robert (Bobbie) Peel**, the British Parliament passed the **Metropolitan Police Act** on September 9, 1829. The Act authorized the establishment of the London police force.

Boston created the first formal police department in the United States in 1838. New York City followed suit in 1844, San Francisco in 1847, and Dallas in 1856. At the federal level, an investigative arm was formed in the U.S. Treasury Department in 1864, and the Border Patrol was created in the U.S. Justice Department in 1882. However, public policing in the United States remained fragmented, decentralized, and often corrupt. Therefore, the security business in the United States grew rapidly to fill the void created by the limitations of public law enforcement.

On the American frontier, police services were provided primarily by county or city sheriffs, constables, and marshals. Lacking assistants, sheriffs and marshals were authorized to deputize citizens and form posses when necessary. When police officials were not available, citizens often formed vigilante groups and enforced laws themselves. Most vigilantes administered

Allan Pinkerton, 1819–1884.
(Photo courtesy of Library of Congress.)

justice fairly. Others, however, enforced their own concepts of law, without regard to justice or due process.

Private policing (security) flourished during this period. In 1850, Henry Wells and William Fargo established two cargo companies. American Express operated east of the Missouri River, and Wells Fargo operated west of the Missouri River. In 1851, **Allan Pinkerton** established the first national private security and investigations company in the United States. The Pinkertons provided private police service to the railroads, offered detective services, and functioned as the intelligence arm of the Union Army during the Civil War. In 1853, August Pope patented one of the first burglar alarms. In 1858, Edwin Holmes introduced the first central station burglar alarms. In the same year, Washington Perry Brinks introduced the first armored carriages for the transportation of money and valuables.

Although public and private police agencies proliferated throughout the 1800s and early 1900s, policing remained primarily a local function controlled at the municipal level. Most police agencies were adjuncts of local political machines. Private police remained prominent until the early twentieth century. Former law enforcement officers began to enter the security services arena. In 1909, a former director of the U.S. Department of Justice's Bureau of Investigation formed the William J. Burns International Detective Agency.

Between 1929 and 1939, private security employment declined as a result of the Great Depression. Between 1940 and 1945, due to the need to protect the United States' infrastructure and military and industrial facilities during World War II, the use of private security increased. After World War II, professionalism in law enforcement and private security grew because many returning veterans, who had acquired military police experience during and immediately after the war, selected police work and private security as occupations. In 1954, George Wackenhut, a retired FBI agent, formed the Wackenhut Corporation, an enterprise that became another one of the largest private security companies in the United States.

In 1955, a group of security professionals formed the **American Society for Industrial Security (ASIS)**, which was later renamed ASIS International. Today, ASIS International's membership exceeds 35,000, making it the world's largest organization of security professionals. Dedicated to protecting the people, property, and information assets of a diverse group of private and public organizations, its members include management professionals who formulate security policy and direct security programs in a wide range of businesses, industries, and government operations.

In 1965, a national commission was established to investigate the nature and extent of crime in the United States and develop recommendations for the improvement of the criminal justice system. The President's Commission on Law Enforcement and Administration of Justice, commonly referred to as the President's Crime Commission, issued its report in 1967 and recommended improvements in law enforcement, courts, and corrections services. In response to the President's Crime Commission report, Congress enacted the Omnibus Crime Control and Safe Streets Act in 1968 and budgeted billions of dollars to fight crime and make improvements in the administration of justice. Among its provisions, the Act established the **Law Enforcement Assistance Administration (LEAA)** in the U.S. Department of Justice. The LEAA was responsible for administering federal grant programs to local, county, and state governments to establish and improve police training programs and upgrade equipment and facilities. A major portion of the money was set aside for the **Law Enforcement Education Program (LEEP)**. LEEP provided grants and interest-free loans to preservice as well as in-service law enforcement personnel to attend college. Colleges and universities throughout the country were also eligible for federal funding that enabled them to establish education programs in law enforcement and criminal justice. Although no longer in existence, the LEAA and the LEEP helped to launch an era of professionalism in the public police service. However, virtually all of the federal funding was directed toward improvement of the criminal justice system with a significant portion of the funds allotted to public law enforcement. Professionalism of private-sector security services lagged because government funding was not available for training and education of private protection service personnel.

The Omnibus Crime Control and Safe Streets Act of 1968 also led to the creation of the National Institute of Law Enforcement and Criminal Justice, which later became the National Institute of Justice (NIJ). As an organization that still exists, the NIJ continues to provide financial support for criminal justice–related research efforts. Many of these research efforts address crime prevention, yet most of the financial support is directed toward local government crime-fighting efforts. Although the vast majority of crime prevention efforts and expenditures occur in the private sector, few government dollars are available for private prevention research efforts.

Despite the federal effort and marked improvements in the quality and quantity of police services, the crime rate continued to increase between 1968 and the early 1970s. In response, the National Commission on Criminal Justice Standards and Goals was formed. One of the Commission's last reports, the **Task Force Report on Private Security**, was published in 1976. For the first time, a national commission recognized private security as an essential ingredient to public safety. The Task Force, through its report, recommended that the private sector be encouraged to improve the nature and quality of security services and complement the law enforcement community in its efforts to fight crime. Thus, the Task Force Report and other developments during the 1970s created an environment in which security services began to assume a more direct role in the crime-fighting and prevention effort. During the last quarter of the twentieth century, the security industry continued to grow rapidly due to increasing concern over crime and the limited availability of law enforcement resources. By 2012, security personnel outnumbered law enforcement personnel by at least three to one (American

Society for Industrial Security, 1998; Barlow, 2000; Collins, Ricks, & Van Meter, 2000; Fagin, 2007; Fennelly, 2004; Gaines & Miller, 2011; Ortmeier, 2006; Ortmeier & Davis, 2012; Siegel & Senna, 2008).

PRIVATE POLICE AND PUBLIC LAW ENFORCEMENT

As the private police (private security) arena continues to grow, its relationship with public law enforcement continues to evolve. The growth of private security during the 1970s and 1980s was identified as a major source of friction between private security services and public law enforcement. The public police, having enjoyed a dominant position in the provision of protective services, foresaw an erosion of their "turf" to private security. Additionally, the public police's view of security as inferior was often reinforced because security personnel lacked adequate training (Cunningham, Strauchs, & Van Meter, 1990). However, many experts today recognize that the private and public sectors can assist each other (Craighead, 2009; Ross, 2012). Indeed, as early as 1976, the Task Force Report on Private Security promoted private/public collaboration and recommended that private security and public law enforcement work together in a complementary, rather than competitive, relationship to prevent crime and disorder. Still, major distinctions exist between the private and public policing sectors.

Private policing, or private security as it is known today, evolved gradually over a period of years. Currently, private police (security) personnel and operations provide most of the nonpublic police protective services in the United States. As time progresses, more public police services are likely to be privatized. Unlike the majority of public police services, security includes a multitude of specialties located in government as well as business and industry. Since security is both multidisciplinary and interdisciplinary, the contemporary security manager must draw upon several disciplines in an effort to prevent loss and protect tangible, intangible, and human assets. Security's authority is also quite distinct from that of public law enforcement. Except for some government operatives and a few privately financed security persons with statutorily mandated public police powers, the security person is concerned primarily with the welfare of a private client or group. Public law enforcement, on the other hand, is a function of the executive branch of government. Thus, public police officers are compensated entirely through public funds generated from tax revenues, grants, and other public sources. The publicly paid police officer is concerned primarily with the welfare of the general public. The **roles of public law enforcement** are to keep the public peace, maintain order, police public property, and respond to and investigate reported crimes on public and private property. The public police have no authority to enforce a private organization's policies and procedures.

Estimates of the number of separate and distinct law enforcement jurisdictions in the United States range from 17,500 (Gaines & Miller, 2011) to 20,000–25,000 (Inciardi, 2010). This includes agencies of national (federal), state, county, and local governments. **National law enforcement agencies**, for the most part, have broad territorial jurisdiction and narrow subject matter jurisdiction. This means that federal agents generally have the authority to operate anywhere in the United States or its territories but are statutorily limited in the types of laws they may enforce. They do not have general police powers because the U.S. Constitution limits the authority of the national government.

In the aftermath of 9/11, the U.S. Department of Homeland Security (DHS) was created by the Homeland Security Act of 2002 (U.S. Congress, 2002). The DHS represents the largest transformation of the national government since President Harry S. Truman merged the branches of the armed forces in 1947 to create the U.S. Department of Defense. On March 1,

2003, 180,000 employees in 22 separate federal agencies throughout several departments of government became part of the DHS. The primary mission of the DHS is to consolidate and better coordinate national (federal) efforts to combat terrorism and protect the United States against other threats to the homeland. Besides providing a better coordinated defense for the United States, the DHS maintains liaison with state and local governments as well as the private sector (U.S. Department of Homeland Security, 2003; White, 2012). Additional information regarding the DHS, its organizational functions, and the federal agencies it consumed is discussed in Chapter 12.

Most public policing in the United States is not a national function. Rather, it is the responsibility of state, county, and local governments, where the jurisdiction of law enforcement agencies is the opposite of federal agencies. Whereas federal agencies have very broad territorial jurisdiction, **state, county, and local law enforcement agencies** have very narrow territorial jurisdiction. Their authority is generally confined to the boundaries of the municipality, county, or state. However, police agencies confined within state boundaries have very broad subject matter jurisdiction. They have general police powers and enforce a wide variety of state and local laws. They are usually the first responders to emergency and disaster scenes, including those caused by acts of terrorism.

State agencies include the **state police** and **highway patrol**. Some states have one or the other, while a few states have both. Where both types of agencies exist within the state, the state police are generally responsible for policing state government property and providing executive protection for the governor. The primary responsibility for state highway patrol agencies is traffic law enforcement. Highway patrols function as the state police in states that do not have a separate state police agency. The Texas Rangers are credited with being the first form of state police organization. Many states also operate a form of state bureau of investigation. Often an

The Texas Rangers are credited with being the first form of state police in the United States.
(Photo courtesy of Steve Adamson/Shutterstock.com.)

arm of a state's department of justice, a state bureau investigates major, multijurisdictional, and organized crimes.

Historically, the chief law enforcement officer in a county is the sheriff. The sheriff and the sheriff's deputies provide public law enforcement services throughout the county and may, in some jurisdictions, staff county jails. The sheriff usually patrols rural and unincorporated areas of the county as well as municipalities that do not have a police department.

Local, or municipal, police departments provide police service to villages, towns, and cities. These agencies generally confine themselves to the city limits and are led by a chief who is politically appointed by the mayor, city council, city manager, or a police commission. In some cities, the police chief is provided with civil service protection.

In addition to national, state, county, and local police, other law enforcement (public police) agencies have been created for special or limited purposes. Airport, school, university, transit, port authority, and public housing police agencies are examples of special purpose agencies. Limited purpose agencies are often restricted in the types of public laws they can enforce. Alcohol beverage control, parks and recreation, conservation, fish and game, and Native American tribal police are examples of agencies with limited police powers.

Despite the differences between the private and public policing sectors in the primary duties and responsibilities (generally, private versus public interests), the relationship between the sectors has evolved positively since the 1980s. ASIS International and the International Association of Chiefs of Police (IACP) have joined forces through Operation Cooperation, a call to action that encourages public law enforcement and private security professionals to work together. The impetus for partnership creation is the growth in security services coupled with the success of community policing in forging alliances with citizen groups. Activities associated with Operation Cooperation include networking, information and resource sharing, crime prevention, training, joint operations, and the development and promotion of state and federal legislation of mutual interest (Operation Cooperation, 2001).

Since the terrorist attacks of 9/11, public law enforcement–private security partnerships have been viewed as critical to preventing terrorism-related activities. The private sector owns and protects most of the nation's infrastructure and public law enforcement collects threat information regarding infrastructure. Further, the public police are not experts on specific site security. Thus, to effectively protect the nation's infrastructure, the public and private sectors must work collaboratively. Working alone, neither of the sectors possesses the necessary resources to protect the nation's infrastructure (U.S. Department of Justice, Bureau of Justice Assistance, 2005a).

Cooperative relationships between and among private security organizations, government operations, and public law enforcement demonstrate a growing trend toward **private/public interdependence**. Joint public and private ventures, investigations, emergency planning efforts, and crime prevention programs, and the privatization of some public police services are mutually advantageous. They are illustrative of a trend toward maximization of private and public security resources (Anderson, 2010; Barlow, 2000; Fischer & Green, 2008; Fischer & Janoski, 2000; Ortmeier & Meese, 2010; Ross, 2012).

Some public police agencies have multiplied their capabilities by establishing collaborative relationships with private security. Many security companies possess technology and resources that surpass those of their local police agency counterparts. Private security personnel can also assist the police by collecting and forwarding information and extending surveillance activities beyond that which can be conducted by police agencies. Information collection and surveillance can provide critical intelligence to assist with community policing and counterterrorism efforts.

The vital role of private security in crime prevention efforts should not be overlooked by the public police. The security professional may be the one person in society who has the

Benefits of Law Enforcement–Security Partnerships

Public law enforcement and security service providers have much to gain from working together.

Law enforcement can

prepare private security to assist in emergencies.

coordinate efforts to safeguard the nation's critical infrastructure.

obtain free training and services.

gain additional personnel and expertise.

use the private sector's specialized knowledge and advanced technology.

obtain evidence in criminal investigations.

gather better information about incidents (through reporting by security staff).

reduce the number of calls for service.

Security service providers can

coordinate plans with the public sector regarding evacuation, transportation, and food services during emergencies.

gain information from law enforcement regarding threats and crime trends.

develop relationships so private practitioners know whom to contact when they need help or want to report information.

build law enforcement understanding of corporate needs (e.g., confidentiality).

enhance law enforcement's respect for the security field (U.S. Department of Justice, Bureau of Justice Assistance, 2005a).

knowledge and technology to effectively prevent crime. Since the resources of the public police are limited, it is in the best interests of public safety for police agencies to initiate cooperative efforts with the private sector to increase the quantity and improve the quality of crime prevention services (Lyman, 2010; Meese & Ortmeier, 2004; National Advisory Commission on Criminal Justice Standards and Goals, 1976).

Twelve Keys to Successful Public–Private Security Partnerships

- Common goals.
- Common tasks.
- Knowledge of participating agencies' capabilities and missions.
- Well-defined projected outcomes.
- A timetable for implementation and evaluation.
- Education/training for all involved.
- A tangible purpose.
- Clearly identified persons in charge (leadership).
- Operational planning.
- Agreement on how to proceed.
- Mutual commitment to provide necessary resources.
- Assessment (evaluation) and reporting of results (U.S. Department of Justice, Bureau of Justice Assistance, 2005a).

SECURITY: ESSENTIAL FUNCTIONS

The management of security operations may be categorized according to the security functions performed. These functions include the essential elements of **physical security**, **personnel security**, and **information security (INFOSEC)** (see Figure 1–2). *Physical security* refers to tangible objects, such as walls, fences, locks, and building design, that promote the protection of persons and property. It also includes lighting, surveillance and alarm systems, and security personnel devoted to access control activities. The physical safety and security requirements for persons and property are balanced with operational needs and the aesthetic qualities required in the environment. Good physical security protects a facility and its people. It can affect a potential criminal offender's perception of a possible crime target.

The protection of electronic systems from loss due to accidents, natural disasters, or unauthorized access is another function of physical security. Computer systems, data, software, transmission lines, airwave frequencies, voice communications, electronic mail, and Internet servers must be protected. Revolutionary changes in technology have radically changed the nature of business and the environment in which business and government operate. As a result, special attention must focus on the protection of these systems. Security measures must also be designed and implemented to protect the operation itself. In other words, an organization's processes must be protected. Without redundant systems, such as backup power supplies, temporary inactivity may occur in a critical stage of the operation, resulting in expensive downtime.

Personnel security involves the protection of persons associated with the organization as well as protection from individuals who might harm the organization. Protection of employees, customers, and guests is inherent in the security function. Unique strategies may be required to protect dignitaries, corporate officers, and celebrities. Personnel security also involves hiring the right people and maintaining their integrity. It includes the utilization of an effective preemployment screening process as well as policies and procedures to reduce the opportunity and motive for employee theft and poor productivity.

Information security is the third leg of the security management triad. Other than death or injury to a person, the greatest single threat to any individual, agency, institution, or nation is the loss of intellectual property or proprietary and confidential information. All stages of the information cycle must be protected. The methods used in the creation, processing, storage, retrieval, transmission, dissemination, and disposition of information in any form must be secured. The level of protection required at each stage depends on the information's value to the organization, the ability of an outsider to duplicate the information, and the potential harm that could result if the information is acquired by the wrong individuals, organizations, or nations.

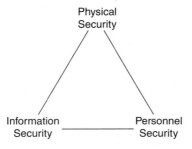

FIGURE 1–2 The Security Triad

Other elements of security management, often considered subsets of physical, personnel, and information security, include **technical security** and **operations security (OPSEC)**. Usually associated with protection against technical threats such as electronic eavesdropping and computer hacking, *technical security* is used to describe the development and implementation of counter-measures identified in risk assessments and security surveys. The principles of technical security involve understanding the threat, predicting the likelihood the threat will become an actual loss event, projecting the impact the loss will have on the enterprise, and preventing the loss if possible.

Operations security is the process utilized to deny potential adversaries information about capabilities and/or intentions by identifying, controlling, and protecting evidence of the planning and execution of sensitive activities. It is used to analyze operations and identify vulnerabilities from an adversary's perspective. OPSEC strategies also evolve from a risk assessment or security survey. OPSEC is the process used to protect critical information by changing or concealing indicators that might disclose the information protected. OPSEC may also be used to refer to all measures designed to protect the operation through which information proceeds. Sometimes OPSEC is used to refer to administrative countermeasures, such as procedural controls and policies, designed to complement physical security measures (American Society for Industrial Security, 1998; Dempsey, 2011; OPSEC Professionals Society, 2007; Pitorri, 1998; Simonsen, 1998).

SECURITY ORGANIZATIONS

An important consideration for any security manager is the decision relating to how the security operations should be structured and who will perform security-related tasks. Proprietary (in-house) personnel may be used, or a contract service (outside vendor) may provide security services or personnel for a fee. Some security operations use a combination of proprietary and contract services. Still others may prefer to blend or merge the security operation with another department within the parent organization.

Contract Security Services

In contrast to a proprietary security program, which is controlled directly by the protected organization, a firm that provides security services to other organizations for a fee is referred to as a **contract security service**. Virtually any security function can be performed by a contract service. Security services provided under contract include personnel, patrol, alarm systems, armored delivery, consultants, executive protection, preemployment screening, drug testing, and investigative services. With respect to investigations alone, contractors may provide services and specialties in areas such as criminal defense, personal injury, surveillance, expert testimony, workers' compensation and insurance fraud, hazardous waste disposal, undercover operations, trademark infringement, stalking prevention, and personal protection.

The component of the contract service industry that experienced the most growth in the past 25 years is the uniformed security personnel business. Downsizing by many U.S. corporations during the 1980s and early 1990s resulted in layoffs for many proprietary security personnel. Many of these security officers were replaced with less expensive contract officers. Additionally, as governmental budgets stabilized (or in some cases, decreased) and the fear of crime and terrorism increased, many organizations began to employ contract security firms to protect personnel and reduce liability by creating a safer workplace.

The trend toward personnel outsourcing and the use of temporary employment services in the United States has created tremendous demand for contract security services. From a consumer

The use of uniformed contract security personnel increased in recent years.
(Photo courtesy of Wackenhut Corporation.)

standpoint, there are advantages as well as disadvantages to the use of a contract service, particularly the employment of security personnel. Some of the advantages include the following:

- ***Lower cost.*** Expenses can be as much as 20 percent lower than proprietary services, not counting the costs associated with benefit packages (health insurance, retirement, vacation, etc.).
- ***Administrative unburdening.*** The contractor is responsible for hiring, training, equipping, scheduling, supervising, evaluating, and terminating employees.
- ***Flexibility.*** As personnel needs change, the number of contracted personnel required can be increased or decreased easily.
- ***Fewer direct personnel problems.*** Problem contract employees may be replaced through a phone call to the contractor. Problems associated with unionized employees, wrongful termination lawsuits, and unemployment benefits are reduced or eliminated.
- ***Objectivity.*** Contract employees are likely to be more objective and less susceptible to collusion with nonsecurity employees of the host company or agency.

The disadvantages associated with the use of contract security personnel include higher attrition, inadequate training, and the contractor's failure to conduct thorough background investigations on employees. Ultimately, outsourcing security personnel and services is a management decision that should not be taken lightly. Careful consideration should be given to the needs of the organization. Cheaper is not necessarily better. If a contract service is used, the host organization should specify the qualifications, training, wage, supervision, and evaluation requirements in the contract.

Proprietary Security

Security organizations that function within and for a parent agency, business, or institution are referred to as **proprietary security** or *in-house security*. These security units provide services similar to those offered by contract providers. However, in proprietary security, personnel are employees of the organization where they actually work and are not under contract through a third-party agency or business. Some of the advantages include the following:

- Higher quality. Personnel are generally paid more. This may result in a higher quality of personnel.
- Loyalty to the organization and site where employed.
- Low attrition. Higher pay and benefits promote retention. In some contract organizations, the turnover rate may approach 300 percent.
- Stability. Where a stable workforce, with knowledge of the facility and its personnel, is an important consideration, a contract guard service is not recommended.
- More direct control and supervision over the security force.
- High morale and motivation (Canton, 2003; Fischer & Green, 2008; Maurer, 2000b).

The disadvantages associated with the employment of proprietary security personnel include generally higher costs, lengthy disciplinary and termination procedures, and the administrative burden associated with human resource management.

Hybrid Security Organizations

Some organizations employ contract as well as proprietary personnel and benefit from the advantages of both. A **hybrid security organization** employs a permanent proprietary security staff as well as contract security personnel to supplement in-house operations. Many large businesses, for example, employ a behind-the-scenes in-house security staff. They also employ contract personnel to monitor surveillance equipment, screen visitors, and patrol parking structure.

The Virtual Security Organization

Some agencies and businesses do not have distinct security departments. They may have a **virtual security organization** through which the security function is integrated with the entire operation or merged with another department, such as human resources, health and safety, environmental services, or risk management. Economic conditions and budgetary constraints associated with consolidation and efficiency may force integration of a security component with another operational unit within an organization. Actually, as a function, security crosses departmental lines anyway. Security should be an integral part of every facet of the enterprise (Anderson, 2010; Kovacich & Halibozek, 2003; Ortmeier, 1999).

A QUICK SURVEY

Which of the following types of security organizations is used by the educational institution you are currently attending or the organization where you are currently employed?

- Contract security services
- Proprietary security
- Hybrid security organization
- Virtual security organization

In your view, what are the advantages offered by the type of security organization your school or workplace uses? What are the disadvantages?

ROLES OF THE SECURITY MANAGER

Since security management is a multifaceted occupation, the **roles of the security manager** are varied. The security manager simultaneously assumes managerial, administrative, preventive, and investigative roles and responsibilities.

As a *manager*, the security professional is responsible for selecting, training, scheduling, supervising, and evaluating security personnel. The manager is responsible for issues related to productivity, morale, compensation, well-being, and professional growth of security personnel as well as safety and security indoctrination and training of all employees. Employee attitudes and expectations toward authority are changing. Workforce diversity is commonplace and workplace violence has become a major issue. Organizations are also requiring higher productivity and improvements in the quality of output.

In the role of an *administrator*, the security professional is responsible for the establishment of security's organizational vision, mission, goals, and objectives. The security administrator must create a vision for the security operation as well as administer the day-to-day operations of the department. This involves planning, financial control, public relations, and community liaison activities. Security managers have become risk managers. They must anticipate, analyze, and protect an organization from virtually every conceivable threat, from liability to terrorism.

As a primary *prevention officer* of an organization, the security manager is ultimately responsible and accountable for prevention of loss from any source. It is the manager's responsibility to recognize and appraise hazards, and initiate action to reduce or remove the risk of loss. A high number of arrests for crimes committed on the premises is not a good measure for security program effectiveness. The measure of the best security program is how many crimes are prevented.

When a loss does occur, the security manager must become an *investigator* and determine the cause. Conducting background investigations on prospective employees and auditing the site to ensure that security measures are working are also part of the investigative function.

The security manager is not a police officer. Security management and public policing are not synonymous. The language of the security manager is the language of business, loss prevention, and asset protection, not law enforcement. Similarities between public policing and security in the actual functions performed often end with appearance and structure. Although security personnel are involved in the detection and investigation of crime and the arrest of suspected criminal offenders, most of a security person's time is spent on preventive efforts to reduce losses from noncriminal sources. In fact, former law enforcement officers do not always make the best security managers. Individuals and organizations that employ security personnel prefer individuals with specialized training, education, and experience in security services rather than in law enforcement. Security management and business skills, such as planning, accounting, budgeting, public relations, and value-added contribution techniques, are not taught in police academies. In a study conducted by the author, consumers of security services as well as security professionals preferred management candidates who possessed knowledge of security and skills in general business practices, personnel management, labor relations, planning, threat assessment, and policy formulation. Much less emphasis was placed on criminal law enforcement skills. In the post-9/11 environment, security knowledge and business skills remain important, with increased emphasis placed on intelligence (information gathering) capabilities and investigative skills (Burstein, 1996; Fischer & Green, 2008; Harowitz, 2003; Johnson, 2005; Maurer, 2000a; Ortmeier, 1996b).

The security manager simultaneously assumes managerial, administrative, preventive, and investigative roles and responsibilities.
(Photo courtesy Vadym Drobot/Shutterstock.com.)

REGULATION OF THE SECURITY INDUSTRY

Although security operations and personnel are employed in public as well as private environments, most regulatory recommendations and initiatives have focused primarily on the private security industry. This has been due, in large measure, to the general lack of minimum selection, training, compensation, and employee retention standards for private-sector security personnel. The need for minimum standards and regulatory oversight has also been cited in several research studies. The first major research study of the private security industry in the United States was conducted by the Rand Corporation in the early 1970s. Funded through a grant from the U.S. Department of Justice, Rand researchers discovered poor training of, and abuses of authority by, private security officers. The Rand report noted that the typical private security officer of the 1970s was an undereducated, untrained, very poorly paid, undersupervised, aging white male. The Rand report solutions to private security's personnel problems focused on licensing security businesses and registration of security officers (Kakalik & Wildhorn, 1971, 1972; Purpura, 2003).

From 1972 to 1977, the Private Security Advisory Council (PSAC) produced advisory reports for the LEAA. Through the LEAA, the PSAC published model state statutes for licensing burglar alarm companies and security officers, a code of ethics for security operations and management personnel, standards for armored car and armed courier services, guidelines outlining the scope of authority for security personnel, and areas of the public police–private security conflict (U.S. Department of Justice, Private Security Advisory Council to the Law Enforcement Assistance Administration, 1977).

In 1976, the Task Force on Private Security of the National Advisory Commission on Criminal Justice Standards and Goals determined that the security industry was significantly underregulated and its protective services function was underestimated. The Task Force Report recommended minimum training and regulation standards. The Task Force on Private Security represented the first national effort to set standards and goals for the regulation of the security industry. The Task Force Report stated that virtually every aspect of society was in some way affected by private security. Specifically, the Task Force placed emphasis on licensing security businesses; uniform minimum security personnel selection, training, and registration standards; codes of ethics and conduct; increased cooperation with the public police; improvement of security alarms and other crime prevention systems; state regulation; and continuing professional education and training (National Advisory Commission on Criminal Justice Standards and Goals, 1976).

Subsequent to the publication of the Task Force Report, the U.S. Department of Justice, through the LEAA, funded two studies of the private security industry. The results of these studies, the Hallcrest Report (1985) and the **Hallcrest Report II** (1990), reaffirmed the need for training and regulation of the security industry. The Hallcrest Report II contained numerous findings, recommendations, and forecasts relative to private security. The Report addressed general and economic crime; selected crime concerns, including unethical business practices and terrorism; the dimensions of protection; security personnel issues; security services and products; comparisons of public police and private security; and future research needs (Cunningham & Taylor, 1985; Cunningham, Strauchs, & Van Meter, 1990).

The need for minimum regulatory standards may be apparent to some. After all, the security industry fulfills a vital function, and security personnel are responsible for the protection of persons and property. In many cases, security officers carry lethal weapons and exercise authority over others, and the potential consequences of negligent behavior are great. Nevertheless, regulation of the industry has been slow in its development. Viewed primarily as a state function, comprehensive regulation of the industry is not common, and mandatory minimum training standards are not required in several states. In some states, a person could be employed as an armed security officer although no background check, training, or licensing is required.

Although uniform minimum standards are lacking and only about half of all states require training, approximately 80 percent of the states have some form of legislation that regulates and licenses security personnel and organizations. However, most existing laws focus on contract rather than proprietary security services. Training requirements also vary. Some state training programs are consistent with the minimum standard recommended by the 1976 Task Force Report on Private Security. The Task Force recommended a minimum of 8 hours of formal preassignment training coupled with an additional 32 hours of in-service training, 16 hours of which could be supervised on-the-job training (Hall, 2003; National Advisory Commission on Criminal Justice Standards and Goals, 1976; Nemeth, 2005; Ross, 2012).

In California, contract personnel are required to complete an 8-hour preassignment course on security officer powers to arrest. Armed contract personnel must complete an additional 24 hours of firearms training through which the trainee must achieve an 85 percent minimum score on a written test and a qualifying score on a firearms range skills test. Additional instruction and licensing are required for contract security personnel who wish to possess a baton or a chemical weapon.

Since January 1, 2003, security personnel subject to licensing in California can no longer operate with a temporary 120-day license while a criminal history verification is being conducted. A licensee can be employed as a contract security officer only after the criminal history check is completed and the registration credential is issued by the state's Bureau of Security and Investigative Services. Effective July 1, 2004, preassignment training for licensed security personnel increased from 3 to 8 hours. Sixteen additional hours of training on specified subjects must be completed within 30 days of beginning work, with another 16 hours of training completed within the first 6 months of employment. Effective January 2005, license holders are also required to complete 8 hours of refresher training/continuing education each calendar year (California Bureau of Security and Investigative Services, 2003). For licensing requirements in other states, readers are advised to consult laws in their respective jurisdictions.

The first federal government effort to regulate the security industry commenced with the introduction of a bill by former vice president Al Gore when he was a senator from Tennessee. If passed, the bill would have required minimum standards for proprietary and contract security personnel working in U.S. government operations. Subsequent initiatives by Congressmen Matthew Martinez (D, OK) in 1992 and Don Sundquist (R, TN) in 1993, and Senator John Edwards (D, NC) in 2003 did not result in the passage of any federal law regulating the industry.

A Private Security Officer Quality Assurance Act was considered by the U.S. Congress. Commonly referred to as the Barr-Martinez/DeWine bill, the proposal required authorization to function as a private security officer. Under the Act, applicants for licensure would have been required to submit fingerprints routed to the FBI by a state clearinghouse for a criminal history check. Results of the check would be forwarded by the FBI to the state regulatory agency that has licensing authority over the applicant.

The National Association of Security Companies (NASCO) endorsed the Private Security Officer Quality Assurance Act. In addition, the National Association of Security and Investigative Regulators (NASIR), founded in 1993, was formed in response to the need for regulators to share information and address common concerns. NASIR's membership includes representatives from more than 30 of the 40 states that regulate private security in some form.

On April 2, 2003, U.S. Senator Carl Levin (D, MI) introduced a bill, the Private Security Officer Employment Act of 2003, to permit review of FBI criminal history records of applicants for private security officer employment. Cosponsored by Senators Lamar Alexander (R, TN), Joseph Lieberman (D, CT), Mitch McConnell (R, KY), and Charles Schumer (D, NY), the bill was read twice and referred to the Senate's Committee on the Judiciary. As part of the Intelligence Reform Bill, President George W. Bush signed the **Private Security Officer Employment Authorization Act of 2004** into law on December 17, 2004. Under the Act, employers may conduct criminal history checks of applicants for, and holders of, positions in which the primary duty is to perform security services, including positions held by contract and proprietary security personnel.

The Private Security Officer Employment Authorization Act program is completely voluntary. Employers may, if they choose and if the applicant or employee consents, send fingerprints or other positive identification to a state identification bureau as well as the FBI. Employers do not have direct access to the results of the criminal history search. However, employers are provided with enough information to make an informed employment decision. The program is supported financially through user fees.

Although some form of regulation may be necessary in the security industry, there is disagreement with respect to the form it should take. The recent emphasis on states' rights, deregulation, and less governmental interference with private industry may delay the development of uniform regulatory and training standards for private security well into the twenty-first century. At least one security consultant intimates that various states use licensing requirements more as a source of revenue than as a means to screen and qualify applicants. Further, the consultant recommends that the industry regulate itself because employers, not the state, are ultimately responsible for the quality of personnel (Sennewald, 2003). However, uniform minimum selection, training, and licensing standards for security personnel are unlikely without some form of state or federal legislation mandating such standards.

PROFESSIONAL CERTIFICATION AND EDUCATION PROGRAMS

In spite of the lack of uniform governmental standards for the regulation of the security industry, organizations within the industry, as well as private and public instructional providers, have voluntarily developed certification, training, and education programs. Diligent efforts on the part of ASIS International led to the development of a professional code of ethics and the CPP program. To acquire the CPP designation, the candidate must meet minimum experience and education criteria and pass a professional certification examination. The program focuses on security management and is administered by a professional certification board under the auspices of ASIS International. Additional certification programs offered by ASIS International include the Physical Security Professional (PSP) and the Professional Certified Investigator (PCI) designations.

Similar efforts to improve the quality of security personnel have been articulated through programs developed by the International Foundation of Protective Officers (focusing primarily on security officers), International Association of Hospital Security, Academy of Security Educators and Trainers, International Association of Professional Security Consultants, and International Association of Computer Systems Security.

The Loss Prevention Foundation offers two training and certification programs: Loss Prevention Qualified (LPQ) and Loss Prevention Certified (LPC). The LPQ certification is designed for entry-level retail loss prevention personnel. The LPQ program focuses on the retail environment, business practices, and basic loss prevention techniques. The LPC program offers advanced education for and certification of retail loss prevention managers and executives. The LPC program focuses on leadership, advanced business practices, operations, crisis management, and supply chain management (The Loss Prevention Foundation, 2007).

Very few security education programs existed until the late 1970s. Since that time, associate, baccalaureate, and master's degree programs have been developed at several colleges and universities. Some of these programs prospered, while others were eliminated due to low enrollments. Those that prospered maintain a close working relationship with security companies and executives in responsible charge of the security function in private corporations and public agencies. The key to successful security education programs lies in the strong linkages between instructional providers and the employer-consumer. Academic program advisory committees, made up of representatives from employer groups, function as recommending bodies and monitor instructional programs to ensure quality competency development that meets the contemporary needs of those who employ security personnel.

One of the criticisms leveled against many security education programs is that faculty tend to be former law enforcement officers who have little experience in, or formal education related to, prevention and business management techniques. Most law enforcement efforts are directed toward apprehending an offender after a crime has been committed. Security education program faculty should have training, education, and experience with the provision of security services or the management of security operations. Another criticism relates to the placement of academic security programs within higher education institutions. Most are housed in criminology departments or are adjuncts to law enforcement and criminal justice programs. Since security is a business-related function, academic programs might be more appropriately placed in colleges of business (American Society for Industrial Security, 1998; Chuvala & Fischer, 1991; Longmore-Etheridge, 2000). Alternatively, security education programs and students located in criminal justice–related academic departments would benefit from articulation of security subjects with business subjects. Students majoring in security management might also be allowed to include appropriate business courses in their degree programs.

Education as well as certification programs are important ingredients to professionalism. Education programs assist individuals with acquisition of the philosophy and knowledge specific to a discipline. A legitimate certification program ensures that members of a profession are competent to practice in the field. The contemporary security manager can no longer survive simply with a high school diploma and 20 years' experience in the military or public law enforcement (Johnson, 2005; Simonsen, 1998). Many professional career development and lifelong learning opportunities exist today, and they are available through a variety of mediums. A complete list of security education and certification programs is beyond the scope of this book. However, additional information regarding such programs may be obtained by contacting ASIS International.

Information regarding specific training, education, and certification programs may be obtained by contacting ASIS International at www.asisonline.org.

Summary

The theoretical foundation for security is based on several assumptions, not the least of which is the belief that many losses can be prevented and that criminal behavior may be deterred through appropriate security-related activities. Numerous intentional and unintentional hazards threaten people, property, and information. Security's mission is to prevent these hazards from materializing.

Although their histories are intertwined, private security and public law enforcement differ greatly in approaches and focus. Security services focus on prevention of loss from any source, while the public police react primarily to reported crimes and public disorder. Security is provided through contract services, proprietary, and hybrid security organizations, and virtually through other elements of an enterprise.

The security manager simultaneously assumes the roles of a manager, administrator, prevention person, and investigator. Although a national quality control standard for security personnel does not exist at this time, numerous states and many professional security organizations have developed statutes and standards for regulating security services. The professional groups as well as colleges and universities also provide security-related training and education programs.

Key Terms

American Society for Industrial Security (ASIS)
Certified Protection Professional (CPP)
Code of Hammurabi
contract security service
Hallcrest Report II
highway patrol
hybrid security organization
information security (INFOSEC)

Law Enforcement Assistance Administration (LEAA)
Law Enforcement Education Program (LEEP)
Metropolitan Police Act
national law enforcement agencies
operations security (OPSEC)
Peel, Sir Robert
personnel security

physical security
Pinkerton, Allan
private justice system
private police
private/public interdependence
Private Security Officer Employment Authorization Act of 2004
proprietary security
public law enforcement

roles of public law enforcement	sheriff	Security
roles of the security manager	state, county, and local law	technical security
security	enforcement agencies	thief takers
security management	state police	virtual security organization
security services	Task Force Report on Private	

Discussion Questions and Exercises

1. Discuss the theoretical foundation for security and the reasons for the tremendous growth in security services.
2. Compare the authority of the public police with that of private security.
3. List and describe the goals of security management.
4. Describe the development of security services.
5. What are the essential elements of security?

6. List and describe the types of security organizations.
7. The security manager functions in several roles. Identify and describe each of these roles.
8. Why are certification and education programs important for the security profession?
9. What are the security personnel licensing and training requirements in your jurisdiction?

YOUR TURN: Forging Law Enforcement–Security Partnerships

Crime can be reduced and the impact of disasters can be minimized through effective partnerships between public law enforcement and security personnel. Yet the success of any partnerships depends on "four Cs"—*communication, cooperation, coordination,* and *collaboration.*

Think about the following situation: In the business district of a city, commercial burglaries are on the rise. Burglars have been breaking into corporate offices and merchants' stores, stealing everything from computers and office furniture to appliances, clothing, and pharmaceuticals. How would you advise local police and corporate security personnel to join forces to address the burglary problem?

Discuss what would need to happen in order for the local police and corporate security personnel to *communicate* with one another effectively, to *cooperate* toward mutually important objectives, to *coordinate* their decisions and actions, and to *collaborate* on developing effective solutions to the problem. As you consider these issues, remember the keys to successful public–private security partnerships that you learned about earlier in this chapter. Draw on those keys as you formulate your thoughts.

CHAPTER 2

Threats to Safety and Security

LEARNING OBJECTIVES

After completing this chapter, the reader should be able to

- identify and describe threats to safety and security.
- discuss the nature and importance of unintentional threats against an organization.
- discuss the importance of accident prevention.
- describe the fire triangle and classifications of fire.
- distinguish between natural and environmental disasters and civil disorder.
- analyze factors that create civil liability.
- demonstrate knowledge of substance abuse prevention, intervention, and treatment strategies.
- discuss the nature and extent of crime.
- list and describe types of crime.
- evaluate crime prevention strategies.

INTRODUCTION

Numerous threats and hazards jeopardize the safety and security of people, property, and information. Some threats involve the ability or an expression of intent to harm or destroy. Other threats are inadvertent (unintentional), yet they pose a source of danger. A materialized threat can emanate either intentionally or unintentionally from a human agent or from a natural cause. A fire, for example, can result from arson activity (intentional) or through an accident or natural phenomenon (unintentional). Loss prevention and asset protection strategies in the security arena must often focus on potential harm that could emanate from a variety of sources, such as accidents, human error, fire, natural and environmental disasters, civil liability, substance abuse, civil disorder, and crime. Thus, security personnel are generally concerned with a wide variety of potential threats and hazards.

ACCIDENTS

An **accident** is an unfortunate event caused unintentionally by a human agent. A majority of accidents result from carelessness or failure to have or enhance safety rules. In addition to the possibility of personal injury or death, direct costs associated with these events include increases in insurance premiums and worker's compensation claims. Indirect costs include lost productivity. Accidents resulting in medical emergencies can occur at any time, and employees should be trained to respond properly.

To assist in the creation of a safe work environment, Congress passed the **Occupational Safety and Health Act** in 1970. The Act established the Occupational Safety and Health Administration (OSHA) and outlined specific requirements for employers. The Act imposes upon an employer a general duty to provide a work environment that is free from recognized hazards that are causing, or are likely to cause, serious bodily injury or death to employees. In addition to the general duty, an employer must comply with specific OSHA-promulgated safety rules. The Act also prohibits any employer from discriminating against or discharging an employee who exercises rights under the Act. More specifically, employers must know and comply with OSHA regulations and standards; eliminate hazards and provide a safe and healthy work environment; establish a record-keeping and reporting system covering all work-related injuries, deaths, and illnesses; conduct periodic safety and health inspections and correct any hazards found; allow OSHA to inspect their facilities; provide protective equipment; keep workers informed of their rights, the company's safety record, and safety standards; develop and enforce safety and health standards; and provide safety training for employees. Thankfully, workplace injuries and fatalities seem to be declining. For example, the total recordable nonfatal occupational injury and illness incidence rate among private industry employers declined to 3.6 cases per 100 workers in 2009—its lowest level since 2003 when North American Industry Classification System (NAICS)-based estimates from the Survey of Occupational Injuries and Illnesses were first published (U.S. Department of Labor, Bureau of Labor Statistics, 2010a). Moreover, fatal work injuries are down 26 percent since 2006 (U.S. Department of Labor, Bureau of Labor Statistics, 2010b).

Enforcement of the Act may involve OSHA inspections and citations of employers for breach of the general duty; breach of specific safety and health standards; or failure to document incidents, maintain appropriate records, or conspicuously post notices required under the Act. The penalties for violations of the Act can be both civil and criminal (Mann & Roberts, 2009). Initially, the cost of OSHA compliance can be considerable. Strategically, however, the cost of organizational operations can be reduced significantly because accidents, long-term illnesses, and deaths resulting in liability are decreased. Thus, sick time, medical claim costs, and wrongful death suits are reduced or eliminated. The security element of an organization is often responsible for OSHA regulation enforcement and compliance, as well as for employee training.

HUMAN ERROR

Losses may occur mistakenly and unintentionally through **human error**. Inaccurate record keeping and the inadvertent discard of valuables are commonplace. Shrinkage (loss of assets) within a retail organization, for example, is not always the result of internal or external criminal action. Merchandise may be inadvertently under-rung at a cash register. Damaged merchandise may be discarded without proper documentation, and defective merchandise may be destroyed when it could be returned to the manufacturer for credit. Thus, human error can increase the cost of operations (Davies, 2007; Fay, 2000).

One study examined employee misunderstanding and its financial impact on 400 businesses with more than 5,000 employees in the United Kingdom and the United States. According to the study's findings, as much as 23 percent of employees do not understand at least one critical aspect of their job. On average, businesses with 100,000 employees are each losing $46.5 million per year, while the estimated overall cost to U.S. and U.K. businesses is roughly $28 billion (*Counting the cost of employee misunderstanding*, 2008).

FIRE

Few events can cause as much personal injury or property damage as a fire. Approaches to fire safety include strategies for **fire prevention** as well as **fire protection** and suppression. Fire prevention refers to policies and practices that focus on preventing a fire from occurring. Fire protection involves minimizing personal injury and damage to property after a fire starts.

The three components of the **fire triangle** are heat, fuel, and oxygen. The components must be present in appropriate amounts and under specific conditions for a fire to occur. Prevention strategies involve control of the fire triangle. Fuel and oxygen are usually present. In addition, numerous heat sources are available to complete the fire triangle and ignite the fuel. Prevention strategies are designed to limit fuel and heat exposure. Flammable materials (fuel) should not be stored or placed near heat sources. Ignition resistant firewalls can prevent the spread of fire between adjacent occupancies. Heat sources, such as cigarettes, can be reduced or eliminated. Fire prevention also involves training and education of individuals as well as organizations as to the nature, extent, and realities of fire and its prevention. **Products of combustion** include flame, heat, smoke, and invisible toxic gases. Fire suppression involves control and elimination of the products of combustion. Limiting exposure to all products of combustion is extremely critical to human life. Exposure to flame and heat may cause serious injury and death within a very short period of time. Smoke obscures vision and exit routes. Toxic gases displace life-sustaining oxygen, and most fire deaths result from the inhalation of these gases.

The **classification of fire** is determined in accordance with the type of combustibles involved.

Class A: ordinary combustibles such as paper and wood

Class B: flammable liquids such as gasoline

Class C: electrical

Class D: combustible metals

After a fire starts, suppression strategies are used to minimize the damage and spread of fire. These strategies include the use of personnel and fire protection and suppression equipment such as alarms, extinguishers, sprinkler systems, and firefighting equipment. Strategies also include the use of fire escapes, exit routes, evacuation procedures, and fire doors to help contain the fire (National Fire Protection Association, 2008).

Fire can be devastating. Consider these notorious fires that have struck counties in California alone in recent decades:

- June 1990, Santa Barbara—641 structures destroyed
- October 1991, Oakland-Berkeley Hills—2,900 structures destroyed
- October 1993, Laguna—330 structures destroyed
- November 1993, Malibu, Topanga Canyon—323 structures destroyed

Wildfires pose major threats.
(Photo courtesy of Fred Funke/Prentice Hall College Library.)

- October 2003, San Diego—2,820 structures destroyed
- October 2007, San Bernardino—272 structures destroyed
- November 2008, Los Angeles—604 structures destroyed (California Department of Forestry and Fire Protection, 2009).

Destruction of property aside, fire also poses a tremendous threat to life safety. In some cases, loss of human life and personal injury can be unimaginable. On February 20, 2003, a fire broke out during the rock band Great White's concert in The Station nightclub in West Warwick, Rhode Island. Pyrotechnics (fireworks) used during the band's performance inside the club ignited combustible interior building materials. Within minutes, flames engulfed the club. Most concert-goers were unaware that the flames were not part of the show. Subsequently, 99 people died and nearly 200 more were injured in a frantic struggle to escape the aging wood frame building. The West Warwick fire was the deadliest nightclub fire in the United States since the Beverly Hills Supper Club fire in Southgate, Kentucky, killed 165 in 1977 (Zuckerman, 2003).

In late October, 2003, three major wildfires in the California county of San Diego killed 16 people, including a firefighter, and destroyed nearly 2,500 homes and businesses. One of the fires, designated the Cedar Fire, was the largest in California history. It consumed almost 300,000 acres in less than 3 days. The Cedar Fire's origin was traced to a lost hunter who lit fires to alert rescuers of his location ("End in sight," 2003).

In October 2006, a wildfire set by an arsonist in Riverside County, California, consumed nearly 40 square miles and resulted in the deaths of four federal firefighters. On June 18, 2007, nine firefighters from Charleston, South Carolina, died while combating a fire at a furniture store. The Charleston deaths represented the largest loss of life for firefighters in a single event since 340 firefighters died in New York City as a result of the terrorist attacks of September 11, 2001. During the summer of 2007, numerous wildfires throughout the West, including fires in California, Arizona, Nevada, Idaho, Oregon, and South Dakota, consumed tens of thousands of acres. In October 2007, wildfires again ravaged Southern California. The wildfires covered over 500,000 acres, displaced nearly 1 million residents, destroyed over 2,000 homes, and killed several people.

NATURAL DISASTERS

A **natural disaster** involves any sudden, extraordinary misfortune in nature. Types of natural disasters include tornadoes, earthquakes, hurricanes, forest fires, landslides, tsunamis, coastal erosion, floods, storms, and extreme temperatures. Any natural disaster can result in injuries, death, and property loss. One particularly horrific example is the Indian Ocean tsunami that struck on December 26, 2004. The tsunami, triggered by an undersea earthquake, resulted in huge losses, including an estimated 174,000 deaths and 108,000 persons reportedly missing ("Tsunami toll updated," 2005). On March 11, 2011, an 8.9-magnitude undersea earthquake caused a 13-foot tsunami to hit Japan, killing and injuring thousands of people. An estimated 14,000 were missing (Foster, 2011).

The best way to mitigate risks of such losses is to develop contingency plans in advance of any natural disaster. These plans should involve an assessment of the potential risk, prioritization of tasks necessary to prevent or reduce losses, preparation for various disaster scenarios, and a plan to recover from the disaster (Haddow & Bullock, 2010). Additional information on natural disasters and responses to them is presented in Chapter 12.

ENVIRONMENTAL DISASTERS

An **environmental disaster** includes events associated with and exposure to hazardous materials, diseases, conventional and nuclear power failures, mine explosions, and gas or oil line or water main breaks. The Gulf of Mexico Deepwater Horizon drilling rig explosion on April 20, 2010, and subsequent major oil spill is an especially appalling example. The explosion aboard the British Petroleum–financed oil rig left 11 workers dead and precipitated the largest offshore oil spill in U.S. history. The disaster sharpened focus on the safety of offshore drilling and oil production (Banerjee, 2011).

Sometimes referred to as technological or human-caused disasters, environmental disasters also include nuclear accidents, terrorist incidents, and the use of nuclear, biological, chemical, or radiological weapons (Haddow & Bullock, 2010). Hazardous materials emergencies require extreme care due to the volatile nature of most toxic gases, chemicals, liquids, and corrosive materials. Failure of utilities may also be life-threatening, and backup systems and procedures should be preplanned. Additional information on environmental disasters and responses to them is presented in Chapter 12.

CIVIL LIABILITY

Civil liability has become a major concern for public as well as private organizations and institutions. Simply stated, civil liability may occur when a person is harmed or injured through the action or inaction of another. Huge jury awards and out-of-court settlements have been granted to plaintiffs who file and prove claims of sexual harassment, unsafe environments, negligence, wrongful death, defects in design, manufacture and packaging, failure to warn, invasion of privacy, use of excessive force, personal injury, violations of civil rights, and conspiracy to defraud. Incidents that precipitate these claims involve intentional or unintentional wrongs, failure to protect, and failure to exercise a reasonable standard of care.

Plaintiffs often sue for **punitive damages** as well as **compensatory damages**. Juries assign punitive damages to punish the respondent in a lawsuit, thus sending a strong message of disapproval. Compensatory damages are designed to compensate the petitioner for actual losses incurred. The large non–class-action lawsuit jury awards in 2000 alone exemplified a trend toward multimillion dollar compensatory and punitive damage assessments.

- A $341.7 million judgment against the Iranian government was awarded to former Associated Press reporter Terry Anderson, who was held hostage by Iranian-supported terrorists in Lebanon for 7 years.
- $328 million was awarded to the parents of 10-year-old Jeffrey Curley of Cambridge, Massachusetts, against the two men who were convicted of raping and murdering Jeffrey.
- $327 million was awarded to the families of a young couple killed in Israel in 1996 by Iranian-backed terrorists. The judgment was the second largest award against the Iranian government in 2000.
- $268.7 million was awarded to the family of a teenager who died from an overdose of medication after an operation.
- $268.6 million was awarded to a South Dakota woman who was seriously injured and widowed by a driver under the influence of drugs.
- A $240 million judgment against the Disney Corporation was awarded to two men who claimed Disney stole their idea for a sports complex.
- $113.5 million was awarded to the family of a murdered woman after the woman's husband tried to obtain money from the deceased woman's trust fund.
- A $111.5 million judgment against Bear Stearns Company was awarded to a multimillionaire who lost $300 million in high-risk currency futures trading.
- $105 million was awarded to the father of a man who was sexually molested by a South Carolina school teacher decades earlier.
- A $105 million judgment against Bridgestone-Firestone was awarded to a man who was seriously injured when a tire-rim assembly system broke during a tire change. (Sukiennik, 2001).

However, the punitive damages award landscape is changing. Regarding blockbuster punitive damages awards (at least $100 million), as of the end of 2008, there had been 100 such awards with an average value of $3 billion. The U.S. Supreme Court decision in *State Farm v. Campbell* suggested a single digit upper bound on the punitive damages/compensatory damages ratio, which reduced the annual number of blockbuster awards (Del Rossi & Viscusi, 2009).

Liability may arise from situations and events associated with errors and omissions, as well as claims of wrongful termination, workplace violence, and sexual harassment. In many cases, liability attaches to an incident even though an individual is not at fault or did not intend any harm, which is referred to as **strict liability**. In other cases, organizations or third parties may be held liable for the actions of others with whom they have a relationship, which is called **vicarious liability**. Avoiding, reducing, or mitigating liability involves the development of a comprehensive plan to prevent incidents that create liability and to take action to limit liability once an incident occurs. Appropriate strategies involve adequate physical and information security as well as a human resource management plan that includes proper selection, training, supervision, and discipline; policy review and revision; and legal support. Liability can also be transferred, to some degree, through the purchase of appropriate amounts of liability insurance (Canton, 2003;

Cheeseman, 2010). Examples of the negative impact of liability as well as policies and procedures designed to mitigate liability are presented throughout this book.

SUBSTANCE ABUSE

Substance abuse refers to the inappropriate ingestion of toxic and controlled substances into the human body. Substance abuse has become increasingly costly in both economic and human terms. According to the U.S. Department of Health and Human Services, drug use among 12- to 17-year-olds increased dramatically and drug abuse in the workplace became more common during the 1990s. The 2010 annual report of the U.S. government's Substance Abuse and Mental Health Services Administration mentioned that the use of illegal drugs rose 9 percent in 2009, the highest level in nearly a decade. This increase was fueled by a substantive increase in marijuana use as well as abuse of ecstasy and methamphetamine ("Use of illegal drugs up 9 percent in 2009," 2010). A majority of drug addicts in the United States may be employed full-time ("Most drug abusers have steady jobs," 1999; "Picture of drug use by young mixed," 2000). This situation creates serious problems for society, employers, and individuals.

Chemical abuse is pervasive and far-reaching. It accounts for a large proportion of present-day criminal law violations, and it places a tremendous strain on the criminal justice system. It is often a contributing factor in many types of crimes, including burglary, robbery, smuggling, theft, and murder. In fact, 1,800 recently reported robberies of pharmacies were attributed to perpetrators seeking drugs (Goodnough, 2011). Drug law violations clog courtrooms, and drug-related convictions crowd corrections programs and facilities. Substance abuse may lead to even greater destructive consequences than other so-called victimless crimes. Lost productivity, wasted human potential, disease, violence, fragmented families, and economic loss are but a few of the negative consequences of chemical abuse (Schmalleger, 2010).

Commonly abused substances include alcohol, prescription drugs, hallucinogens, amphetamines (stimulants), depressants, and tranquilizers that are swallowed; phencyclidine (PCP), cocaine base, and cannabis (marijuana) products that are inhaled; heroin, which is injected; and methamphetamine and cocaine hydrochloride that may be snorted or injected. The **symptoms of substance abuse** include significant changes in personal appearance, sudden and irrational flare-ups, unusual degrees of activity or inactivity, as well as sudden and dramatic changes in discipline and job performance. Physically, the abuser may have dilated pupils or may wear sunglasses at inappropriate times. The abuser may have needle marks or razor cuts, or may wear long sleeves to hide such marks. Borrowing money, stealing, and frequent association with known substance abusers or dealers are also strong indicators.

A person exhibiting the symptoms of hallucinogen use, such as lysergic acid diethylamide (LSD), peyote, and psilocybin, may have dilated pupils, sweat excessively, hallucinate, and have increased respiratory and heart rates. The symptoms associated with PCP use often include high pain tolerance, great physical strength, hallucinations, unpredictability, aggressive and extremely violent behavior, excessive sweating, drowsiness, nystagmus (involuntary movement of the eyes), paranoia, confusion, blank stares, muscle rigidity, unusual gait or convulsions, and a possible chemical odor on the breath or body. Symptoms of stimulant use, such as cocaine, amphetamines, or methamphetamine, include restlessness, talkativeness, trembling, dilated pupils, sleeplessness, hyperactivity, and increased respiratory and heart rates. Finally, symptoms of depressant use, such as barbiturates, sedatives, or tranquilizers, include slurred speech, poor coordination, unsteadiness, intoxicated behavior with no odor of alcoholic beverages, nystagmus, and decreased respiratory and heart rates.

SECURITY SPOTLIGHT

Visit your local hospital or medical center, and ask whether you can speak with someone there about trends the organization is seeing in substance abuse problems in the area. For example, is the number of emergency room visits owing to drug overdoses increasing or decreasing? What types of illegal substances are most often the culprits behind these visits? Likewise, interview the head of a local drug-addiction treatment program, and ask that person to describe trends regarding substance abuse gleaned from participants' experiences in the program. (Of course, reassure your interviewee that all participants will remain anonymous.)

Public substance abuse prevention and treatment strategies include programs such as Drug Abuse Resistance Education (DARE) for juveniles and law enforcement's emphasis on drug law enforcement and interdiction ("Truth, DARE, and consequences," 1998). The DARE program and law enforcement, by themselves, have had little appreciable impact on reducing illicit drug use. One study indicated that the impact of each dollar spent in drug treatment produces approximately the same results as $7 spent for law enforcement. Government efforts to reduce illicit drug use apparently have the greatest impact when treatment and law enforcement strategies are used conjunctively (Mishra, 1998; National Institute on Drug Abuse, 2007; Rand Corporation, 1999).

On November 7, 2000, California voters overwhelmingly approved Proposition 36, a measure designed to divert many drug offenders from the criminal justice system into treatment programs. Under the law, those convicted of illegal drug possession for the first or second time, as well as some drug-related parole violators, are referred to treatment rather than receive a criminal justice sanction. This law does not apply to drug dealers. The law represents an experimental shift away from drug law enforcement toward treatment and rehabilitation (Ainsworth, 2000).

Learn more about substance abuse prevention and treatment through the National Institute on Drug Abuse at www.nida.nih.gov.

Private strategies include prevention and treatment programs sponsored by health care organizations, private rehabilitation facilities, and employer-sponsored employee assistance programs. Appropriate employer responses to substance abuse involve a written and communicated company policy, documentation of incidents of abuse in the workplace, and employer interventions through counseling, treatment, probation, and termination. Currently, private employers have no legal right to intervene unless the substance abuse affects job performance and safety. Drug testing in the workplace is increasing, although the legality of such testing has yet to be firmly established. Local statutes and case law should be reviewed, and a legal opinion obtained prior to implementing or modifying any drug-testing program.

When legal and authorized, tests to detect drug use can be conducted on various human biological specimens. Testing for alcohol is typically conducted by obtaining a breath, blood, or saliva sample. However, when a person is monitored following treatment for alcoholism, and abstinence is expected, urine may be tested. Testing for drugs other than alcohol is typically conducted using urine samples although some employers prefer hair samples. Employers regulated by federal testing programs may use only urine samples for drug testing. U.S. Department of Transportation regulations require breath testing for alcohol.

Consistent with applicable laws, employers may test applicants and employees for alcohol or drugs in one or more of the following situations:

- during an annual physical
- before promotions or transfers
- before assigned to—or routinely while in—positions involving security, safety, or access to money
- after accidents
- when previous drug use is made public
- following treatment
- when referred by management through just cause or reasonable suspicion
- on a random basis

The only methodology for drug testing approved by the U.S. Department of Health and Human Services is urinalysis. Urinalysis involves screening urine for the presence of drug metabolites. The procedure is relatively simple and inexpensive. Samples with positive results are subjected to a more accurate but expensive confirmation procedure known as gas chromatography/ mass spectrometry (GC/MS). No adverse personnel action should ever be taken before completing the two-step procedure.

Most employers contract with vendors that perform drug testing. If drug testing is conducted, employers must balance legal liabilities due to lawsuits (brought by rejected applicants or employees who refuse the test or are discharged or disciplined for positive test results) with the well-being of customers, clients, fellow employees, and members of the general public who may be injured or affected by a drug-using employee. Settlements in the former category are usually in the low thousands of dollars, while those in the latter are often in the millions.

Court rulings and verdicts find an increasing number of organizations responsible for the actions of employees while working under the influence of alcohol or drugs. Some courts have declared that liability exists when employers do nothing or act inappropriately in the face of clear evidence of drug and/or alcohol abuse in the workplace (U.S. Department of Justice, Drug Enforcement Administration, 2007).

For more information about substance abuse and its prevention and treatment, contact the U.S. Drug Enforcement Administration at www.dea.gov.

UNTREATED MENTAL DISORDER

A **mental disorder** (mental illness) is a psychological pattern that is generally associated with a defect or disease of the individual's mind. It causes a disability that may affect an individual's behavior patterns in ways that are not part of one's normal development or culture. Mental disorders are common in the United States. Within any given year, nearly 25 percent of adults and slightly over 20 percent of children are diagnosable for one or more mental disorders. While mental disorder appears to be widespread among the population, the main burden (or threat) emanates from about 6 percent of those who suffer from a debilitating mental illness (National Institute of Mental Health, 2011).

Left untreated, a mental disorder may pose a threat to safety and security. It has been alleged that Jared Loughner, born September 10, 1988, killed 6 people, including U.S. District Court Judge John Roll, and wounded 14 others, including Congresswoman Gabrielle Giffords, during a gathering outside a Safeway store in Tucson, Arizona, on January 8, 2011. Although Loughner was indicted on criminal charges by a federal grand jury in Tucson on January 19, 2011, many allege that the precipitating factor behind the shootings by Loughner was his untreated mental disorder (Abcarian, Reston, & Hennessy-Fiske, 2011).

> Learn more about mental disorder types, symptoms, diagnosis, and treatment through the National Institute of Mental Health at www.nimh.nih.gov/index.shtml.

CIVIL DISORDER

Civil disorder occurs when an individual or a group disrupts the normal peace and tranquility of a community or the operations of a business or organization. The perpetrator's activities may be legal or illegal. Strikes and labor disputes, demonstrations, special events such as sports activities, concerts, parades, and riots are all examples of civil disturbances. In 2010, demonstrations and riots broke out in France and the United Kingdom after those governments announced austerity measures designed to combat the debt crisis plaguing numerous European nations. Ratings agency Moody's predicted uprisings in the United States as well should it initiate similar measures ("Top agency warns austerity riots could hit America," 2010).

Although most civil disorder events are peaceful, a nonviolent group could become violent if conditions conducive to violence exist. The potential for property loss, injuries, and death is tremendous. For example, the Los Angeles riot that occurred subsequent to the acquittal of police officers involved in the Rodney King incident in 1992 began as a demonstration. It became a riot and resulted in over $1 billion in losses, with 10,000 businesses destroyed, at least 1,300 injuries, and 44 deaths. The damage and casualties were greater than that which occurred during the Watts Riot in Los Angeles in 1965 and the Detroit riots in 1967 ("Path of destruction," 1992).

Even joyous events sometimes transform into disastrous riots. On June 19, 2000, hundreds of celebrators threw rocks, set fires, and looted subsequent to the Los Angeles Laker's National Championship basketball victory. Two police vehicles were destroyed by fire and several businesses were vandalized and looted. As recently as a 2006 game for the ULEB Cup (Europe's second-tier basketball league) in Belgrade, several fans of Red Star's rival Partizan arrived to cheer for the visiting Greek squad. A brawl erupted that swiftly turned into a riot, with participants throwing flares—a particularly dangerous move in an enclosed arena featuring a wooden floor and plastic seats. Hundreds of fans streamed onto the court, and many hurled their stadium seats into the air or at their fellow rioters. Six people were injured ("Seven of history's most terrifying sports riots," 2009). As with natural disasters, contingency plans should be developed to deal with civil disorder and minimize property loss and casualties.

Although much has changed since the early days of labor unrest, a potential problem for many organizations involves labor disputes, including strikes (work stoppages) and protests over workplace conditions. While the number of major work stoppages and the number of employees involved have declined, such events can still occur and present significant challenges. In 2009, there were five major strikes and lockouts involving 1,000 or more workers in the United States

(U.S. Department of Labor, Bureau of Labor Statistics, 2010c). When planning is inadequate and responses inappropriate, the stage for disaster is set. The organization is often faced with millions of dollars in losses, negative publicity, and consumer disillusionment with the organization. As evidenced by the history of labor unrest, merely assigning security personnel to the entrances of the organization's facility is not enough. A comprehensive labor dispute contingency plan is essential and must contain several possible courses of action. The strategy should include liaison with public law enforcement, appropriate security personnel, vulnerability assessments, evidence collection, intelligence operations, and good media relations.

Preestablished liaison with and commitment from law enforcement and other public safety agencies ensures response if demonstrators engage in illegal activities. Adequate, well-trained security personnel can deescalate conflict through self-restraint and are not intimidated by demonstrators. Regular vulnerability assessments of the facility, homes of employees, distribution points, and off-site meeting facilities are a necessity.

During a strike, labor unions often claim unfair labor practices on the part of management. Organizations should document the illegal activities of strikers through the use of audio and video tape, still photographs, and personal affidavits. The documentation can be used as a defense in subsequent litigation stemming from the unfair labor practices claims. Intelligence operations at local gathering places outside the facility can assist management and security personnel to anticipate problem situations.

Media relations are also important. Liaison should be established with news organizations, and managers should be trained on how to respond to media inquiries. Finally, management and security personnel should avoid confrontations with the disputants that might create long-lasting resentments. In most cases, union workers will resume employment when the labor dispute is settled. Tensions between management and union workers can taint labor relations in the future (Taylor, 2000).

Civil disorder may result from peaceful demonstrations as well as riots
(Photo courtesy of arindambanerjee/Shutterstock.com.)

CRIME

Although a majority of most security personnel time is spent addressing noncriminal matters, crime prevention and the detection of criminal activity are major security concerns. All types of crime are potential threats. However, security personnel most often deal with the prevention and detection of crimes involving theft (larceny), burglary, trespassing, vandalism, embezzlement, computer crime, substance abuse, assault, robbery, and various forms of fraud and economic crime. Studies indicate a large number of employees steal from employers, resulting in losses of billions of dollars each year.

Crime is a complex concept, and an inclusive definition of crime is often difficult due to the competing theories about what causes it. In addition, behavior that is codified as criminal today may not be criminal tomorrow. The public's perception and attitudes toward criminal behavior also change over time. Property crime offenders were severely punished at one time and, in some cases, as severely as violent offenders. Today, most property crime offenders are treated much less severely than their violent criminal counterparts (Brown, Esbensen, & Geis, 2007; Fuller, 2012; Siegel, 2010; Slater, 2000).

Scope of Crime

In 1929, the attorney general of the United States and the FBI were authorized by Congress to develop and implement a uniform system for the collection and dissemination of crime statistics. The system was built upon the recommendations of earlier efforts by the International Association of Chiefs of Police (IACP). The system was designed to identify major crime trends by comparing seven crimes included in Part I of the **Uniform Crime Report (UCR)** contained in *Crime in the United States*. Part I, or **Index crimes**, included the violent crimes of murder, forcible rape, robbery, and aggravated assault as well as the so-called nonviolent crimes of burglary, larceny, and auto theft. These offenses represented the types of crime most likely to be reported to the police. In 1979, arson was added to the Index crimes list. Crimes not listed in Part I were included in Part II of the UCR. The UCR includes information regarding the crime rate based on the number of reported crimes per 100,000 population.

Crime statistics included in the UCR are supplied to the FBI voluntarily by law enforcement agencies. Initially, approximately 400 agencies reported their crime statistics to the FBI. By 1971, approximately 8,000 of the estimated 20,000 law enforcement agencies in the United States reported crimes. Today, nearly 17,000 agencies submit crime reports. Because police officers rarely observe a crime when it occurs, law enforcement agencies rely on citizens and victims to report criminal activity (U.S. Department of Justice, Federal Bureau of Investigation, 2007).

According to reported statistics, the crime rate began to increase significantly in the 1960s. Campus unrest, anti–Vietnam War protests, urban riots, and the increase in the number of young men in the population contributed to the increase in the crime rates. Crime rates in the United States reached a peak in 1980 and began a slow decline in 1981 (U.S. Department of Justice, Bureau of Justice Statistics, Office of Justice Programs, 1997). Factors contributing to the decline have been attributed to tougher sentences, community policing, and a decline in the number of men in the Index crime–prone age group of 14 to 24 (Dorning, 2000; "Is LA's crime honeymoon over?" 2000). However, with the potential increase in the number of males in their late teens and early 20s on the horizon, many experts began predicting that the crime rate would rise again (Arner, 2000a). Additionally, if certain negative political, social, and economic conditions develop, some experts predict a dramatic increase in both violent and property crimes (Fuller, 2012). Crime rates have fluctuated. For example, statistics for the mid-2000s indicated that violent crime was rising

TABLE 2–1	Percent Changes in Crime, 2006–2010								
Years	Violent crime	Murder	Forcible rape	Robbery	Aggravated assault	Property crime	Burglary	Larceny	Auto theft	Arson
2007/2006	−1.8	−1.1	−6.1	−1.2	−1.7	−2.6	−1.3	−2.1	−7.4	−9.7
2008/2007	−3.5	−4.4	−3.3	−2.2	−4.1	−2.5	−0.8	−1.2	−12.6	−5.6
2009/2008	−4.4	−10.0	−3.3	−6.5	−3.2	−6.1	−2.5	−5.3	−18.7	−8.2
2010/2009	−6.2	−7.1	−6.2	−10.7	−3.9	−2.8	−1.4	−2.3	−9.7	−14.6

Source: U.S. Department of Justice, Federal Bureau of Investigation.

(U.S. Department of Justice, Federal Bureau of Investigation, 2007). The increase may have stemmed in part from complacency; as the crime rate dropped in the 1990s and counterterrorism was emphasized subsequent to 9/11, many crime prevention and suppression strategies (such as community- and problem-oriented policing) were abandoned. However, preliminary figures gathered by the FBI during 2010 indicated that, as a whole, police agencies throughout the nation reported a decrease of 6.2 percent in the number of violent crimes brought to their attention for the first 6 months of 2010 when compared with figures reported for the same time period in 2009 (U.S. Department of Justice, Federal Bureau of Investigation, 2010). Property crimes also declined. Table 2–1, developed by the FBI, shows percent changes in various types of crimes year by year since 2006.

A major criticism of the UCR is that it includes information on crime reports submitted to the FBI voluntarily by law enforcement agencies, and all agencies do not currently report such data. In addition, police agencies are not able to report crimes that are not reported to them (Ross, 2012; Siegel & Senna, 2008). In an effort to obtain more detailed information on the nature and extent of crime in the United States, the U.S. Department of Justice has conducted victimization surveys since 1972. The major purpose of the surveys is to uncover unreported crimes and the reasons for not reporting. The results of the early victimization surveys reported twice as much overall crime than was reported in the UCR's statistics, with theft-related offenses four times higher than official records. Burglary was the most commonplace reported crime. Reasons given for not reporting included a victim's perception that nothing would be accomplished, the incident was not serious enough for police attention, and fear of reprisal. More recent surveys have indicated that only about 40 percent of all crime and 20 percent of all theft-related crimes were reported to the police (U.S. Department of Justice, Bureau of Justice Statistics, Office of Justice Programs, 1997; U.S. Department of Justice, Office of Justice Programs, 2007).

A QUICK SURVEY

Is the overall crime rate in your area increasing or decreasing? (Hint: Use the FBI's website, www.fbi.gov, as well as resources available in your jurisdiction to identify the crime trends in your area.)

- Increasing
- Decreasing

What factors might account for the increase or decrease in crime in your area? From a security perspective, what types of crime in your area do you think are most preventable? Why?

Today, **National Crime Victimization Survey (NCVS)** information is collected by the U.S. Department of Justice's Bureau of Justice Statistics in cooperation with the U.S. Bureau of the Census. The NCVS collects data annually from a sample of approximately 50,000 households containing more than 100,000 individuals age 12 or older. The NCVS does not measure murder, kidnapping, crimes against commercial establishments, public drunkenness, drug abuse, prostitution, illegal gambling, con games, or blackmail. The NCVS is not without its critics either. There is, for example, the potential for false or exaggerated reports made by the victims to the interviewers, and no attempt is made to validate victims' claims. The UCR is still the most accurate database in terms of crimes reported to the police.

In response to criticisms of the UCR and the NCVS, the FBI introduced and began accepting crime data for the **National Incident-Based Reporting System (NIBRS)** in January 1989. The traditional UCR system required a summary of the number of occurrences of Part I offenses as well as arrest data for Part I and Part II offenses. As an alternative to summary reporting, the new enhanced UCR, or NIBRS, was developed to deal with the volume, diversity, and complexity of crime. The NIBRS requires more detailed reports. Agencies collect data regarding individual crime incidents and arrests, and submit reports detailing each incident. The incident-based reporting provides much more information.

Among the major changes introduced in NIBRS is the substitution of Part I and Part II offenses with Group A and B offenses. While existing Part I offenses focus on eight street crimes, the new Group A expands to 22 offenses and widens criminological interest to include economic crime. Detailed information is provided for each occurrence of these crimes. Included among the 52 data elements collected is information detailing the circumstances of the crime, offender characteristics, arrestee data, victim information, and offense and property data. Less detailed information is required for the 11 offenses in Group B. This group focuses generally on nonviolent and less serious offenses, such as bad checks and criminal trespass.

Other new features of the NIBRS include new offense definitions. Rape, for example, in addition to cases involving force, has been expanded to include cases in which the victim's consent was not given due to temporary or permanent mental or physical incapacity. In addition, there are new UCR codes, and all crimes occurring during the same incident are recorded. The NIBRS has also introduced a new category called crimes against society, which include gambling, prostitution, and drug sales and use. Finally, the NIBRS provides the means for distinguishing between attempted and completed crimes, and expands data on the victim–offender relationship. Although the system was intended to be fully operational by the end of 1999, states have been slow to convert to the new system. As of February 2008, 31 states had been certified to report NIBRS to the FBI (Justice Research and Statistics Association, 2008).

In 1995, the NCVS redesigned its questionnaires to include more detailed information on interaction between victim and offender, victim crime deterrence efforts, perceived effectiveness of crime deterrence efforts, bystander behavior, perceived alcohol and drug use by offenders, and suspected offender gang involvement (Ortmeier, 2002; Schmalleger, 2010).

Additional information regarding crime statistics and trends may be obtained by contacting the FBI at www.fbi.gov.

Although the overall crime rate has been declining since the early 1980s, public opinion polls indicate that citizen fear of crime remains high. Many people, for example, may keep guns in their homes as protection against nighttime intruders, although burglars rarely enter a home if it is likely to be occupied. Myths abound for many types of crime, and unrealistic fear creates a false sense of insecurity and may negatively impact the quality of life for many people.

For example, the overall rate of household burglaries has been declining since the early 1970s. Yet, burglary remains an attractive crime for the offender. The arrest rate for burglary is relatively low. A burglar evaluates potential targets based on their contents and any security measures on the premises. Two-thirds of all residential burglaries occur when no one is home. People become creatures of habit, and it is not difficult for a burglar to identify the routine of a residential target. The proportion of daytime burglaries has increased, primarily because many residences are unoccupied during regular daytime business hours. Contrary to common belief, the reported occurrence rate for many other crimes has been declining as well. The murder rate, for example, has declined fairly dramatically over the past few years (Davis, 2011; Hakim & Blackstone, 1997; U.S. Department of Justice, Federal Bureau of Investigation, 2007).

Economic Crime

Generally, an **economic crime** is defined as a violation of criminal law designed to reward an offender financially (Siegel, 2010). Organizations, businesses, governments, and other enterprises are easy targets for economic crime. Intellectual property in the form of trade secrets, copyrights, patents, client lists, financial information, and technical and strategic plans may be of interest to competitors and foreign governments. Products can be tampered with, hijacked, grey- or black-marketed, and counterfeited. Information can be acquired electronically through computers and the Internet. Technology can be acquired by reverse-engineering a product, surveillance, undercover work, hiring an employee away from a company, disingenuous contract negotiations, and bribery.

The most prevalent economic crimes involve some form of fraud. Investment fraud occurs when bogus stocks are sold. Warranty fraud takes place when merchants fraudulently claim a product is under warranty and they obtain replacement parts under a warranty exchange program. Telemarketing fraud, which involves telephone sales of high-priced, low-value items, targets the elderly and many businesses. Workers' compensation fraud resulting from faked injuries and illnesses costs businesses millions of dollars each year. As much as 10 percent of every health care dollar spent may be attributable to fraud.

Fraudulent schemes utilizing the Internet, as well as computer hacking of all types, are growing rapidly. For example, during 2009, the Internet Crime Complaint Center (IC3) website received 336,655 complaint submissions—a 22.3 percent increase over 2008 (U.S. Department of Justice, Bureau of Justice Assistance, 2010). Fraudulent checks, credit card scams, and fraudulent loans threaten financial institutions. Embezzlement, padding expense accounts, and lost production time also result in financial losses to businesses and cause a drain on the U.S. economy. Occupational fraud committed by an occupational subculture that encourages, and in some cases requires, illegal behavior of its members may account for hundreds of billions of dollars in losses to American companies annually (Coleman, 1994; U.S. Department of Justice, Federal Bureau of Investigation, 2007).

A form of economic crime that is becoming more prevalent is **identity theft**. The crime is committed when an imposter fraudulently uses another's personal identification information to obtain credit, merchandise, or services in the name of the victim. The personal identification information often stolen and used by criminals includes driver's license and social security numbers, addresses, phone numbers, and dates of birth. In some cases, the perpetrator obtains the personal information through the Internet or by accessing an organization's client account information. Other methods include theft of personal mail, eavesdropping, searching a person's trash for personal information, or simply observing the victim enter personal data on a form or at an automatic teller machine (ATM). In most cases, victims of identity theft are unaware that they are being victimized until they receive bills and invoices for goods and services they have not purchased.

A leading type of Internet-based identity theft is referred to as *phishing*. The phishing perpetrator uses email and malicious websites to gain access to personal information. Through a recent version of phishing, called *vishing*, scammers telephone the victim to obtain personal data. Additional discussion of phishing and vishing is presented in Chapter 6.

Additional information regarding identity theft, its prevention, and how to report it can be accessed on the Federal Trade Commission's website at www.ftc.gov/idtheft or on the Social Security Administration's identity theft website at www.ssa.gov/pubs/idtheft.htm.

The noted criminologist Edwin Sutherland introduced the phrase **white collar crime** and defined it as an offense committed by a person of respectability and high social status in the course of an occupation (Sutherland, 1949). Later, James Coleman (1994) expanded the definition and defined it as a violation of the law committed by a person or group of persons in the course of an otherwise respected and legitimate occupation or financial activity. White collar crime includes political corruption, bribery, illegal business practices, price-fixing, tax evasion (as compared to tax avoidance), fraud, identity theft, misrepresentation of facts that leads to financial gain, embezzlement, and other economic crime such as industrial espionage, computer-related crime, and theft of proprietary information. White collar crime accounts for a greater total financial loss to Americans than does street crime. If deaths resulting from known, yet uncorrected, workplace safety hazards were included in the statistics, white collar crime would account for a death rate that is higher than the nation's murder rate.

Perhaps the most egregious example of a form of white collar crime known as a Ponzi scheme took the form of investment advisor Bernie Madoff's defrauding of thousands of investors of billions of their dollars. The architect of a Ponzi scheme pays returns to individual investors from their own money or from money paid by subsequent investors, rather than from any actual profit earned. The scheme attracts new investors by offering returns that other investments cannot guarantee. These returns take the form of unusually high or consistent short-term returns. To perpetuate the returns that a Ponzi scheme advertises and pays, the scheme's architect must bring in an ever-increasing flow of money from investors. Madoff initiated his Ponzi scheme in the early 1990s, and in 2009, he was sentenced to 150 years in prison for the crime.

White collar crime is also a national security issue. The greatest single threat to the security of the United States today may be white collar crime, including economic crime and industrial espionage. By 2012, losses from economic crime in the United States increased to well over $100 billion. Industrial espionage agents target intellectual property such as trade secrets, financial information, corporate tactical and strategic plans, and technology. Many foreign businesses and some foreign governments are actively involved in industrial espionage against U.S. businesses (Coleman, 1994; Maras, 2012).

Case histories of economic crime depict the seriousness and magnitude of the problem. For example, in 1997, Volkswagen (VW) agreed to pay General Motors (GM) $100 million to settle a lawsuit stemming from a 4-year-old allegation that VW stole trade secrets from GM.

VW also agreed to purchase over $1 billion worth of parts from GM over a 7-year period. The settlement was one of the largest in corporate espionage history. VW did not admit any wrongdoing but acknowledged that it was possible that GM proprietary information may have been transferred when several GM executives defected to VW (Meredith, 1997).

Research on corporate espionage reveals some startling facts. For instance, of the 400 information technology professionals who participated in one recent survey, 74 percent said they knew how to circumvent security to access sensitive data, and 35 percent admitted doing so without permission. The most commonly targeted items included customer databases, email controls, and chief executive officer (CEO) passwords ("Tech gadgets help corporate spying surge in tough times," 2009).

Counterfeiting and piracy of American products cost billions of dollars in lost sales each year and threaten the brands and reputations of businesses. Generally of inferior quality, counterfeit products are purchased by unsuspecting customers who file consumer complaints against the legitimate companies when defective products are discovered. The problem impacts traditional product-based industries such as clothing, cosmetics, pharmaceuticals, beverages, and motorbikes, as well as the high-tech software, electronics, sporting goods, and entertainment companies. In some countries, counterfeiting and piracy of goods takes place in state-owned factories that have the capacity to replicate legitimately produced foreign brand products ("China's piracy plague," 2000).

In violation of copyright laws, millions of Internet users routinely duplicate copyrighted material every day. Computer software, photographs, movies, books, even cross-stitch needlework patterns are copied illegally. A South Carolina company, Pegasus Originals, which produces needlework patterns, estimated a $200,000 loss in 5 years, due largely to Internet piracy. Utilizing traditional methods, photocopies and tape recordings degrade (become less and less clear) with each copy of a copy. However, with the Internet and digital technology, every copy is of the same quality as the original. The Internet also allows for much wider distribution than a manual person-to-person format. Once an item is placed online, literally hundreds of thousands of people can download and reproduce the copyrighted item instantly.

Many cyberspace copyright infringement legal battles pit large corporations against each other. In its copyright infringement lawsuits, the music recording industry sued two large targets: MP3.com and Napster.com. MP3.com allowed Internet users to download music while Napster allowed users to exchange their digital music files with each other. On September 6, 2000, a federal judge ordered MP3.com to pay almost $250 million to the Universal Music Group for intentionally violating copyrights. The Recording Industry Association of America claimed it lost over $300 million in sales due to Napster activities (Balint, 2000).

All forms of economic and white collar crime appear to be on the rise, and fraudulent activities have been discovered in the highest echelons of some large corporations. In addition to the various methodologies previously discussed, the United States has witnessed a marked increase in corporate accounting infractions and similar financial frauds. In 2002 alone, malfeasance by many corporations and high-level executives led to criminal investigations and charges, guilty pleas, and convictions for stock manipulation and insider trading. Details about fraudulent schemes emerged from major corporations such as Enron, WorldCom, Tyco International, ImClone, Adelphia, and the accounting firm of Arthur Andersen. Many corporate executives became wealthy at the expense of employees and investors. As a result, corporate boards and executives, as well as auditing firms, face greater scrutiny, new laws, and more stringent industry standards (Foss, 2003).

Among the federal initiatives designed to safeguard corporate assets from fraudulent schemes is the Sarbanes-Oxley Act of 2002. The Act establishes specific liability for publicly traded companies and their executives if inadequate security or a lack of safeguards jeopardizes the integrity of corporate financial reporting systems or shareholder value (U.S. Securities and Exchange Commission, 2007).

Public law enforcement may be ill-equipped to combat most economic and white collar crime. Unlike most street crimes, economic crimes harm a great number of people over an extended period of time. Thus, the damage is less apparent (hidden) and often indirect. Societal reactions to economic and white collar crime are also diluted. Prison sentences are rare. More common punitive sanctions include restitution, fines, censure, and disapproval. Most of these sanctions are imposed by regulatory agencies rather than the criminal courts. Unless the offenses are made public, most economic and white collar crimes are handled internally, with corporations and organizations utilizing private disciplinary mechanisms (Siegel, 2010).

SECURITY SPOTLIGHT

Are you currently employed by an organization that competes in a particular industry (such as consumer packaged goods, computers, apparel, financial services, or any other type of industry)? If so, speak with someone in your organization who can share insights on trends in corporate espionage in your company's industry. This person may work in your organization's risk management department or some other function. Ask your interviewee to share (without jeopardizing the organization's security) steps the organization is currently taking to mitigate the risks presented by corporate (business) espionage. In addition to gaining this person's insights, conduct a little research into the subject yourself, looking for statistics and other information regarding how corporate espionage is currently affecting the industry in which your organization competes.

Organized Crime

Organized crime is defined as any relatively permanent group of individuals that systematically engage in illegal activities and provide illegal services. Organized crime is a continuous conspiratorial activity with economic gain as its primary goal. It involves the coordination of numerous persons in the planning and execution of illegal acts or the pursuit of legitimate goals through unlawful means. Organized crime's existence is maintained through the use of threats, intimidation, force, monopoly control, and corruption. Revenues from illegal activities are used to develop legitimate businesses to use as covers for more illegal activity.

The image of organized crime, often referred to as the Mafia or La Cosa Nostra, portrays people of Southern European ancestry, under the direction of a godfather, engaging in organized illegal activity. These portrayals may have been accurate in the early days, because authorities trace the beginnings of organized crime in the United States to the Prohibition Era (1919–1933) when Southern European immigrants became involved in bootlegging activities. During this period, the manufacture, distribution, and sale of alcoholic beverages in the United States were illegal. To satisfy consumers' persistent demand, the alcoholic beverage bootleggers went underground, and criminals organized. Today, organized crime crosses all ethnic and cultural lines. The groups are involved with illegal drugs, gambling, loan-sharking, prostitution, labor racketeering, intellectual property theft, stock fraud, and various other illegal activities (Albanese, 1996; Siegel, 2010).

Sometimes colloquially referred to as "the mob," organized crime group activity has expanded into the world of economic and white collar crime. An example of the mob's influence came to light in November 1997, with the arrest of 18 people who were allegedly involved with a stock price-fixing scheme. Members of the Genovese and Bonanno crime families collaborated with HealthTech International, Inc., a Mesa, Arizona, health and fitness center company, to artificially inflate the company's assets and stock prices. Through the scheme, stockbrokers convinced unwitting buyers that the company's assets were eight times their actual value. As a result, the company stock's trading value increased over 250 percent and participants in the scheme stood to gain enormous profits through the sale of the inflated stocks.

In June 2000, federal authorities raided numerous locations across the nation and arrested over 100 people in what the authorities referred to as one of the largest securities fraud cases in U.S. history. Members of New York's five organized crime families allegedly banded together in an unprecedented joint venture to scam $50 million through the stock market. In the federal indictments and criminal complaints that followed, authorities charged that gangsters recruited stockbrokers to inflate the value of companies in which the mob families had secret ownership. Through promoters, the brokers inflated the value of the stocks. Unsuspecting investors bought stock in the underfunded companies. One shell company had only $2,000 in actual assets, but was able to generate $90 million from stock sales before collapsing (G. B. Smith, 2000).

Organized crime is constantly expanding its range of illegal activities. Foreign criminal organizations, through their increasing use of computer technology, have become a direct threat to the security of the United States. Sophisticated criminal organizations can penetrate innocent computer databases, influence financial markets, and destabilize countries and entire regions of the world. In addition, international criminal organizations counterfeit money, CDs, and software; smuggle aliens, weapons, and precious gems; and kidnap and transport women and children for various forms of sexual servitude. In response, the United States created an international task force to eliminate barriers among agencies and countries that fight different types of organized crime. The interagency task force is also charged with fighting international trafficking of women and children and the smuggling of aliens ("Global crime cartels are tech-savvy, U.S. says," 2000).

Street Crime

What is commonly referred to as **street crime** includes offenses such as murder, forcible rape, robbery, aggravated assault, burglary, auto theft, larceny, and arson. These crimes are listed in Part I of the UCR, a document published annually by the FBI, as discussed earlier in this chapter. Often referred to as Index crimes, or the leading criminal indicators, the list includes serious crimes against persons and property most often reported to the police. Statistics on these crimes typically appear in the news broadcasts. The public's perception is that street crime of a felonious nature accounts for the largest percentage of crime in the United States. However, most crime in the United States is not of the street crime variety.

Most street crimes are committed by youthful offenders. Young men, teenagers to young adults, tend to commit most of the crime in the streets. Throughout the latter half of the twentieth century, juvenile gangs (groups of associates) became a major problem in urban, as well as some suburban and rural, areas. Although some gangs include adult members, most are teenagers. Specific problems associated with gangs include the use, distribution, and sale of controlled substances. Illegal drug trafficking provides an economic foundation for organized gangs. Other problematic areas include turf conflict, where rival gangs, using public areas as private space, compete for the same area. Gangs have also infiltrated businesses, the military, and a few public law enforcement agencies (Albanese, 2008; Barlow, 2000; Davenport, 2012; Newman & Kurtis, 1997).

According to one U.S. government assessment, about 1 million gang members belonging to more than 20,000 gangs were criminally active within all 50 states and the District of Columbia as of September 2008. The study also found that gang members are migrating from urban areas to suburban and rural communities, expanding the gangs' influence in most regions. The purpose of this expansion is to increase drug-distribution territories, enhance illicit revenue, recruit new members, hide from law enforcement, and escape other gangs. As a result, many suburban and rural communities are experiencing increasing gang-related crime and violence. As the study explained, criminal gangs commit as much as 80 percent of the crime in many communities. Typical gang-related crimes include alien smuggling, armed robbery, assault, auto theft, drug trafficking, extortion, fraud, home invasion robbery, identity theft, murder, and weapons trafficking (National Drug Intelligence Center, 2009).

Terrorism

Although the number of terrorist attacks declined significantly in 2002 (Dunphy, 2003), the United States, along with many other countries, finds itself immersed and preoccupied with the terrorist activities of other nations as well as of small groups and a few radical individuals (Maniscalco & Christen, 2002; U.S. General Accounting Office, 2001). Despite the magnitude of the September 11, 2001, attacks on the United States, and the salience of the attacks for Americans today, terrorism is not a new phenomenon. It has been one of the darkest features of human behavior since the beginning of recorded history. Individuals and groups have committed incredible atrocities in the name of promoting or defending a greater good. Terrorists have severely disrupted the well-being and peace of mind of everyday people, and they have destabilized entire societies (Martin, 2009). Additional information on terrorism is presented in Chapter 12.

Victimless Crime

Often referred to as public order offenses, **victimless crime** generally includes offenses in which the participants enter into the activity voluntarily. Offenses such as illegal gambling, consumption of pornography, drug use, illicit sexual behavior, public drunkenness, disorderly conduct, and vagrancy are often included in the victimless crime category. Some people suggest that many of these crimes should be decriminalized because enforcement of laws against such activity diverts public safety resources away from suppression of more serious crime, invades individuals' privacy, and sets the stage for corruption in the legal system. Others theorize that enforcement of victimless crime laws indirectly leads to other crime, such as burglary, when a drug addict steals to support a habit. Still others argue that society should retain and strictly enforce these laws. They contend that victimless crime destroys the moral fiber of society and leads to more serious offenses.

Whether one favors decriminalization or enforcement of victimless crime laws, behavior associated with such activity poses unique challenges to the security professional and business organizations. Since people engage in the behavior voluntarily, the participants often do not concede that their actions are criminal in nature, nor do they believe harm occurs as a result of their actions. Such attitudes exist in the American workforce, resulting in behaviors that threaten productivity, health, and safety.

Workplace Violence

Due to the dramatic increase in reported violence in the workplace in the late twentieth century, a new category of crime was created. **Workplace violence** is now a commonly used term defined generally as violence upon a person that occurs in the workplace. It may stem from an employment relationship, unsafe working conditions, or a relationship that exists outside the workplace. Workplace violence can occur during a robbery or other commercial crime, in employer-directed activity, in a domestic or misdirected affection situation, during a terrorist act or hate crime, or during a strike or civil disturbance (Cole & Smith, 2010; Johnson, Klehbauch, & Kinney, 1994).

Domestic Violence

Although workplace violence has generated tremendous publicity in recent years, homicides on or off the job are more closely associated with personal human relationship problems. Actually, a person is more likely to be assaulted, beaten, or killed in the individual's home by a family member or acquaintance than anywhere else or by anyone else in society. According to some state statutory provisions, domestic violence is a crime committed against an adult or fully emancipated minor. These laws apply to a present or past relationship of an intimate nature. Victims may include a present or former spouse, a cohabitant who is not an ordinary roommate, persons in dating or same-sex relationships, or a person with whom the perpetrator has had a child.

Domestic violence presents problems for organizations, since violence originating in the home and other areas outside the workplace can extend to the work site. The perpetrator of workplace violence need not be an employee. In many cases, the offender is not an employee. Either the offender enters the workplace to commit a business-related crime, such as robbery or burglary, or the offender is in some way connected to an employee. In a personal relationship, the persons involved are usually aware of the name and location of each other's employers. If the relationship deteriorates, the aggressor knows where and when to locate the victim.

There are no absolutes and no exact answers to the issues and the problems of workplace and domestic violence. However, precautionary measures can be taken. One approach is to use noninvolved third parties to mediate disputes. The mediation approach may resolve conflict well in the workplace or at home, where the disputants know each other and tensions usually build over long periods of time. Another approach focuses on company-sponsored retraining and fair hearings to thwart potential violence due to layoffs and terminations. In addition, preemployment screening tests can help identify violence-prone individuals and anger management training can help prevent workplace violence by those already employed (Craighead, 2009; Institute of Financial Management, 2011; Lynch, 2000; May, 2000). Additional policies and procedures for preventing or minimizing the damage from workplace and domestic violence are addressed in Chapter 11.

Theories of Crime Causation

This section presents a brief summary of some of the **causes of crime** and strategies for preventing criminal activity. The exact causes of crime are not actually known, although there are many different views and theories on what causes crime. The causes of crime are not explainable in specific terms or through single theories. Many theories do not account for the negative case. This phenomenon is illustrated by the individual who is exposed to the theoretical cause, but does not commit a crime. In spite of the difficulties, crime causation is generally explained in terms of psychological, sociological, physiological, economic, drug use, demographic, urbanization, cultural, and expectations theories. Theories of crime causation have emphasized numerous causes, including perpetrators' ego state, personality disorders, external forces on the individual, and physiological factors.

EGO STATE   Sigmund Freud, the father of ego-state theories, believed that an individual's personality was divided into three parts: the id, the source of all basic drives such as hunger and sex; the ego, developed during infancy and early childhood, that provides the id with a conscious avenue to acquire satisfaction of the drives; and the superego, the conscience that inhibits immediate satisfaction of the id. According to the theory, criminal behavior results from a conflict between the id and the superego. Crime occurs because the satisfaction of the basic drives is inhibited by limited avenues for success. When the desires of the id are in conflict with societal demands, impulses of the id are repressed. If the individual is unable to repress these impulses, criminal behavior may result.

PERSONALITY DISORDERS   The second set of psychological theories focus on personality disorders. A mental deficiency may promote subnormal rather than abnormal behavior. A sociopathic personality disorder may create a repressed conscience. The sociopath is hostile and aggressive on occasion and usually wants immediate satisfaction of desires. A psychotic person loses touch with reality. The criminally insane are people with psychotic personalities.

EXTERNAL FORCES   Sociological theories evaluate the impact of external forces on the individual. Thus, ecological, cultural, and social influences may contribute to delinquent behavior. Ecological influences involve the environment in which one lives or works. Cultural influences include subcultural norms of a group that contribute to crime and delinquency. Notable among cultural theories was Edwin Sutherland's theory of differential association, a theory postulating that excessive exposure to a set of values, whether the values are acceptable to society or not, reinforces behaviors consistent with those values. Other social influences that contribute to delinquent behavior include an abnormal family life as well as problems in school, work, or a recreational setting.

PHYSIOLOGICAL FACTORS   Physiological theories include those that focus on heredity, biochemicals in the human body, and anthropology. Heredity theories propose that behavior is inherited. These theories disregard the role of external forces in contributing to delinquent behavior. Biochemical theories focus on hormonal imbalances in the human body and the influences of secretions of the endocrine glands. Anthropological theories, first developed by the Italian pioneer criminologist Cesare Lombroso in the nineteenth century, correlate specific physical features with criminal behavior. According to Lombroso, unattractiveness may produce unpleasant social experiences. The socially unattractive person reacts with antisocial behavior.

OTHER FACTORS   Other theoretical causes of crime include economic theories that emphasize the role of unemployment and poverty, drug culture theories that focus on the enforcement of drug laws as high drug prices cause users to commit secondary crime to support a drug habit, and demographic theories that suggest the amount of crime depends upon the changing composition of the population (young people tend to commit most street crime). Urbanization theories postulate that more people are concentrated in smaller areas, thus causing tension. Cultural theories focus on culture conflict within a society. Expectation level theories are explained by the disparity between the rich and the poor. As the gap widens between the poor and the affluent, and the ability to become affluent diminishes, frustration among the poor grows and the poor commit crime (Brown, Esbensen, & Geis, 2007; Fuller, 2012).

In the final analysis, most crime is probably multicausal. It is difficult to isolate single causes in an individual case and treat the cause. This is very problematic for the criminal justice system because effectively dealing with the causes of crime may be beyond the control of public safety agencies. They deal with crime primarily after the fact. Thus, most crime prevention becomes an individual, familial, organizational, and community responsibility.

Crime Prevention Strategies

Crime prevention strategies include education, treatment, diversion, rehabilitation, and deterrence through law enforcement and security. Prevention of crime in organizations involves comprehensive loss prevention and asset protection tools, policies, and procedures. In addition, prevention of serious street crime, which always impacts individuals and organizations in a negative way, requires early intervention in the delinquency cycle. When one realizes that crime is caused by a complex array of risk factors, it is not difficult to understand why single-focus intervention strategies are unlikely to succeed. Crime prevention must involve comprehensive intervention approaches that address multiple risk factors. To be effective, these strategies require collaboration between and among individuals, groups, and institutions. As mentioned previously, it is extremely unlikely that a single cause contributes to delinquent or criminal behavior. Therefore, it is important that individuals, families, social services agencies, schools, public safety organizations, security professionals, and businesses work together to prevent or reduce the likelihood of criminal behavior. To date, the criminal justice system has experienced little notable success with preventing the recurrence of criminal behavior by those who have been exposed to the system. Intervention as well as deterrence through security before a crime is committed may be the best strategy for solutions to crime prevention (Bratton, 2011; Wasserman, Miller, & Cothern, 2000).

Summary

The possibility of accidents, human error, fire, natural and environmental disasters, liability, substance abuse, civil disorder, and crime pose threats to individuals, organizations, and nations. A majority of loss events caused by these threats can be prevented if adequate precautionary measures are taken. Carelessness causes most accidents, errors, and fires. The damage from natural and environmental disasters can be minimized. Liability can be mitigated. Substance abuse can be prevented and substance abusers treated. The damage from civil disorder can be decreased if adequate contingency plans are in place and activated when the need arises. Many crimes against persons and property can be prevented, and offenders quickly apprehended, if comprehensive strategies are developed to deter, deny, detect, and detain those who persist in the violation of society's criminal laws.

Key Terms

accident

causes of crime

civil disorder

civil liability

classification of fire

compensatory damages

crime

crime prevention strategies

economic crime

environmental disaster

fire prevention

fire protection

fire triangle

human error

identity theft

Index crimes

mental disorder

National Crime Victimization
    Survey (NCVS)

National Incident-Based
    Reporting System (NIBRS)

natural disaster

Occupational Safety and
    Health Act

organized crime

products of combustion

punitive damages

street crime

strict liability

substance abuse

symptoms of substance abuse

Uniform Crime Report (UCR)

vicarious liability

victimless crime

white collar crime

workplace violence

Discussion Questions and Exercises

1. Individuals, businesses, public agencies, and nations are threatened by numerous criminal and noncriminal hazards. List these hazards and describe the ramifications of each.

2. What factors tend to create liability for an organization? How might these factors be minimized?

3. Describe the types of crime security personnel encounter most often.

4. Do prevention strategies prevent crime or merely shift criminal activities to other potential victims?

YOUR TURN: Assessing Threats to Safety and Security in Your Area

Threats to safety and security take numerous forms—from accidents, human error, and fire to natural and environmental disasters, civil liability, and substance abuse to civil disorder and crime in all its many shapes. Assess and address your vulnerability to these threats by taking the following steps:

1. For your town, city, or state, research the statistics available on each of these threats. For example, consult FBI reports on various types of crimes in your area, and look for studies on the other types of threats and how the findings relate to your area.

2. Select the threat to safety and security that concerns you the most as it applies to your area. It may concern you because it is happening more frequently in your area, because you believe that your area is particularly vulnerable to that threat, or because of some other reason.

3. Formulate a strategy for addressing the threat you identified in Step 2. For instance, if the threat you identified relates to natural or environmental disasters, what kind of contingency plan or disaster-recovery strategy would you recommend to address this threat? If the threat you identified is gang-related crime, what youth programs or other strategies do you think could help mitigate this problem?

CHAPTER 3

Legal Aspects of Security

LEARNING OBJECTIVES

After completing this chapter, the reader should be able to

- describe the judicial system of the United States.
- outline the judicial process for civil as well as criminal cases.
- distinguish a tort from a crime.
- discuss types of situations conducive to tort liability.
- list and describe the essential elements of a contract.
- describe types of administrative law.
- contrast real and personal property.
- articulate the importance of employment law.
- demonstrate knowledge of labor law as it applies to security services.
- list and describe types of crime.
- evaluate incidents to determine if a crime has occurred.
- compare arrest authority of public police with private security.
- demonstrate knowledge of laws of arrest, search, and seizure.
- demonstrate appropriate attitude, appearance, demeanor, and testimonial technique for courtroom presentations.

INTRODUCTION

The legal aspects of security involve a mixture of criminal, civil, and administrative laws. Therefore, security personnel encounter relatively unique legal obligations and face a multitude of legal issues and decisions. People, physical property, and information must be protected without incurring civil liability or violating anyone's rights. Personnel matters must be dealt with in a manner consistent with existing labor laws. Security managers must enter into and audit contractual agreements. They must also prevent and investigate crime and collect and preserve evidence that may be used in a criminal prosecution.

Organizational activities must be monitored to ensure compliance with a wide array of local, state, and federal laws. Consequently, the contemporary security professional must be well versed in the law and anticipate situations in which expert legal representation is necessary. This chapter is devoted entirely to the judicial process and the legal concepts that engulf the security profession.

JUDICIAL SYSTEMS

To fully appreciate the legal considerations involved in security operations and management, one must possess knowledge of the nature of judicial systems and processes. Courts vary in their authority. In addition, procedural rules and **degrees of proof** required vary significantly between civil law and the administration of criminal justice. The judicial process in the United States is also adversarial. In a criminal case, the government, through state and federal prosecutors, must establish proof of guilt beyond a reasonable doubt. Defendants and their defense attorneys work to refute the government's case. In a civil case, a plaintiff sues a respondent to enforce an obligation or receive compensation, and the degree of proof required is much less. The adversarial process requires an impartial person (or persons) to function as a referee to ensure that the parties follow the rules. Judges and juries function as the referees. The courts shape the legal system and society in a significant way. They determine guilt, reach findings in civil cases, and issue decisions that affect the process through which criminal as well as civil cases pass.

In America, the Massachusetts Bay Colony formed a combined legislature/court in 1629 to make laws, conduct trials, and impose sentences. By 1776, all American colonies had established court systems. After the American Revolution, the colonial courts formed the foundation for state court systems. A growing population, the settlement of the West, and the movement toward urbanization led to an increase in civil lawsuits and criminal arrests by the late nineteenth century. To service the need, state legislatures and constitutions created numerous courts and a variety of court structures. The federal court system was established by the U.S. Constitution, the Federal Judiciary Acts of 1789 and 1925, and the U.S. Magistrate's Act of 1968. Throughout the twentieth century, court systems in the United States became more uniform and streamlined. Today, the federal court system has three levels, and state systems have three or four levels of courts.

There are two basic types of courts: **trial courts** and **appellate courts**. Criminal and civil trials take place in trial courts. They have original jurisdiction in these cases. Appellate courts, on the other hand, with rare exception, do not originate or try cases. They only review cases and decisions appealed to them from trial courts or lower appellate courts. Appellate courts review the **transcript** (written record) of the trial court proceeding as well as written briefs submitted by the parties in the action. The appellate court may also entertain short oral arguments from the petitioner and the respondent or their representatives. Appeals from trial courts proceed through either a state or a federal appellate review process and may culminate at the **U.S. Supreme Court**.

The judiciary in the United States operates as a dual system consisting of state and federal courts. State courts address violations of law and other legal matters pertaining to the laws of a particular state. Federal courts address violations of law as defined by the U.S. Congress. State and federal court systems operate autonomously. In some cases, both systems have concurrent jurisdiction over the same criminal activity. Robbery, for example, is a criminal law violation in every state. If a robbery is committed against a federally insured financial institution, such as a bank, the criminal activity (the robbery) is also a violation of federal law. Thus, the state government and the federal government have concurrent jurisdiction over the same case. Under such circumstances, a defendant can be tried, convicted, and sentenced in both systems without violating the Fifth Amendment's double jeopardy provision because the perpetrator committed two separate offenses. The bank robbery represents an offense against the citizens of the United States as well as an offense against the citizens of the state in which the robbery was committed.

The U.S. Constitution specifically provides for only one court, the Supreme Court of the United States. Article III, Section 1, of the Constitution reads that the judicial power of the United States shall be vested in one Supreme Court, and in such inferior courts as the Congress may from time to time ordain and establish. It was the Judiciary Act of 1789 that established other federal courts, namely the U.S. district courts and the U.S. circuit courts of appeals.

There are at least 56 separate and distinct court systems in the United States and its territories. They include the federal system, 50 state systems, and one system each in the District of

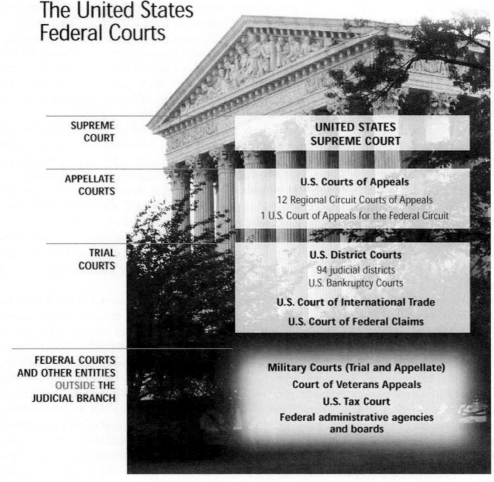

Federal courts.
(Photo courtesy of U.S. Courts.)

Columbia, Guam, Puerto Rico, the U.S. Virgin Islands, and the Northern Mariana Islands. The total number of separate courts operating within these systems exceeds 10,000.

The federal court system consists of 94 **U.S. district courts** (trial courts) situated in 13 **U.S. courts of appeals** circuits. The U.S. Supreme Court functions as an appellate court. It reviews constitutional challenges to federal and state statutes, as well as appeals from criminal and civil trial court cases brought before it through state appellate courts or one of the 13 U.S. courts of appeals. In the case of state court judgments, an appeal from a state's **court of last resort** is a matter of right when the validity of a federal statute is questioned in a state court or when a state statute is challenged because it is alleged to violate the U.S. Constitution (Cole & Smith, 2011; Fagin, 2007; President's Commission on Law Enforcement and Administration of Justice, 1967; Rutledge, 2000).

> Learn more about the federal courts through the Federal Judiciary home page located at www.uscourts.gov/about.

The U.S. Supreme Court has no authority to make a final determination in a state case. The Court may affirm (let stand) the decision of the lower court or reverse the decision and remand (return) the case to the lower court for a decision not inconsistent with the U.S. Supreme Court's opinion. If the constitutionality of the entire state court case is at issue, the charge against a defendant in a criminal case must be dismissed. If only a portion of the evidence is declared inadmissible, the state court may order a new trial based on admissible evidence only. A new trial does not violate the Fifth Amendment double jeopardy clause, since there has not been a final judgment in the case and the new trial is considered *de novo* (new), as if the original trial had not taken place.

The **intermediate appellate courts** in the federal system are the U.S. courts of appeals (see Figure 3–1). They have appellate jurisdiction over all U.S. district court decisions except under three conditions: (1) when a three-judge district court has enjoined (stopped) enforcement of a federal or state statute on grounds of unconstitutionality, and the case proceeds directly to the U.S. Supreme Court; (2) when a U.S. district court declares a federal statute unconstitutional, and the United States is a party to the action; and (3) when a case requires immediate settlement because of imperative public importance.

The U.S. district courts are the trial courts of general jurisdiction in the federal system. They have trial jurisdiction over civil actions involving copyrights, patents, postal matters, civil rights, and almost all other civil and criminal cases arising under the laws and treaties of the United States and the U.S. Constitution. They have concurrent jurisdiction with the states in criminal cases when a criminal act violates federal as well as state law. U.S. district courts have jurisdiction in civil cases in which the dollar amount in dispute is over $10,000 and the parties to the action are residents of different states.

The U.S. magistrate courts have authority to issue federal warrants, set bail, hold preliminary hearings in federal cases, and conduct summary trials for minor federal crimes in which the defendant waives the right to a trial in U.S. district court. Other specialized federal courts include the U.S. Court of Claims, which hears financial lawsuits against the United States, the U.S. Court of Customs and Patent Appeals, the U.S. Tax Court, and military and territorial courts.

State and local courts try criminal and civil cases arising out of incidents occurring within the state and cases involving violations of state and local laws. Each state has a court of last resort,

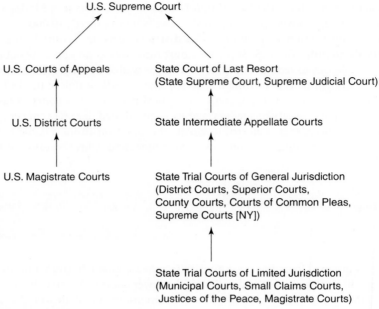

FIGURE 3–1   Court Systems

usually called the state supreme court. Appeals from these courts are taken directly to the U.S. Supreme Court, the highest court in the United States. All states also have some form of intermediate appellate court. They review decisions on appeal from state trial courts. Appeals from state intermediate appellate courts are taken to the state court of last resort.

State trial courts generally fall into two categories: general jurisdiction and limited jurisdiction. **Courts of general jurisdiction** may try any state criminal or civil case brought before it. **Courts of limited jurisdiction** are restricted in their authority. These courts adjudicate small civil claims, typically try misdemeanor cases, and conduct preliminary hearings in felony cases. If, as the result of a preliminary hearing, the court of limited jurisdiction determines that probable cause exists to hold the defendant on the felony charge, the defendant's case is transferred to the state court of general jurisdiction for arraignment and trial. Examples of courts of limited jurisdiction include municipal, juvenile, and small claims courts. Some states have merged the courts of limited jurisdiction with the courts of general jurisdiction. The merger can result in a tremendous expenditure reduction. Subsequent to a merger, the state has one trial court level, referred to as a district, county, circuit, or superior court, which assigns cases to criminal, civil, juvenile, or probate dockets, departments, or divisions.

BURDEN AND DEGREES OF PROOF

In an adversarial legal system, opposing parties in a dispute operate under varying burdens and degrees of proof. In criminal cases, a defendant is presumed innocent until proven guilty. The prosecution has the burden to proceed first with a criminal complaint and the burden of establishing guilt beyond a reasonable doubt. This is the strictest degree of proof. It does not imply a mere possible doubt, nor does it mean that guilt must be established beyond any doubt. Rather, guilt must be established in the mind of the finder of fact in such a way that the fact finder is morally certain that the defendant committed a criminal act.

Unlike criminal prosecutions, for which convictions may result in imprisonment or execution, lesser degrees of proof are required in proceedings in which one is not subject to culpability for a criminal act. Lesser degrees of proof include clear and convincing evidence, proof by a preponderance of the evidence, and *prima facie* proof. The clear and convincing standard of proof is used to establish a probability that the evidence presented is based on fact. This standard is used, for example, to determine if a juvenile under a designated age appreciated the wrongfulness of an act.

The third highest degree of proof is based on a preponderance of the evidence standard. This degree of proof is met if the evidence demonstrates a probability—at least a 51 percent likelihood—that the facts in issue are true. This standard is used in civil lawsuits.

Finally, *prima facie* (on its face) proof is the standard used to establish, through a slight showing, that the circumstances in a particular situation are as they appear. Thus, a slight showing may allow the fact finder to draw a certain conclusion, if no contradictory evidence is present. This standard, or degree, of proof is used in a preliminary hearing in the pretrial phase of a criminal prosecution (Adler, Mueller, & Laufer, 2009; Cole & Smith, 2011; Hails, 2012).

A QUICK SURVEY

With which (if any) of the following court systems do you have experience? Check all that apply.

- State trial courts of limited jurisdiction (municipal courts, small claims courts, justice of the peace, magistrate courts)
- State trial courts of general jurisdiction (district courts, superior courts, county courts, courts of common pleas, state supreme courts)
- State intermediate appellate courts
- State courts of last resort (state supreme courts, supreme judicial courts)
- U.S. magistrate courts
- U.S. district courts
- U.S. courts of appeals
- U.S. Supreme Court

If you have experience with any of these court systems, what were your impressions? Did anything about the system(s) surprise or confuse you? Explain.

THE JUDICIAL PROCESS

Criminal Cases

In a criminal case, initiation of the pretrial process is made through a physical arrest or issuance of an arrest warrant. A criminal citation is issued in lieu of an arrest for minor offenses. If arrested, the arrestee is "booked." A booking is the official recording of the arrest in the records of the arresting law enforcement agency. If the arrestee cannot be released on recognizance (ROR) without a bail hearing, and a judge is not immediately available, the arrestee may be detained in a jail for a reasonable time (about two court working days) until a first appearance before a judge. At the **first (initial) appearance**, the arrestee is informed of the charge(s), advised of rights under the Constitution, and, if possible, bail is set. In some jurisdictions, the first appearance is referred to as the arraignment on the complaint, which should not be confused with a postindictment or postinformation proceeding, called an arraignment. The first appearance is a nonadversarial proceeding.

In federal felony cases, a formal charge against the accused must be issued by a federal grand jury in the form of an **indictment**. In state cases, the prosecuting attorney may present the case to a county grand jury for possible indictment, or may file an **information**, which is a formal charge for a felony issued from the prosecuting attorney's office subsequent to a preliminary hearing. The formal charge for a misdemeanor case is usually called a criminal complaint.

Many states do not utilize a grand jury. In lieu of a grand jury proceeding, a **preliminary hearing** is conducted to determine if probable cause exists to hold the accused to answer to the charge. The preliminary hearing is an adversarial proceeding. During this hearing, the prosecution must establish a *prima facie* case, which means that on the face of the evidence presented, probable cause exists that a crime occurred and the defendant committed the offense.

If probable cause is established at the preliminary hearing, the case proceeds to the arraignment. At the **arraignment**, the accused is asked to enter a plea. The pleas available include guilty, not guilty, not guilty by reason of insanity, or no contest (*nolo contendere*). If the defendant pleads not guilty or no contest and proceeds to trial, the defense attorney usually files pretrial motions to have the charges dismissed, suppress prosecution evidence as inadmissible, discover evidence the prosecution has, or delay the trial. Motions may also be filed to change the venue (location) of the trial, consolidate multiple charges arising from a single criminal transaction, sever multiple counts or defendants, and disclose the identity and location of an informant. In many states, the arraignment occurs prior to the preliminary hearing.

If the case qualifies for, and the accused selects, a jury trial, the next step is jury selection. An initial list of potential jurors is selected from property tax records or from a list of registered voters or vehicle owners, or from the department of motor vehicle's list of those who hold driver licenses. From the initial list, a jury pool (venire) is randomly selected. Members of the jury pool receive jury duty notices and are asked to report to a court facility. From the jury pool, a jury panel of approximately 30 people is randomly selected and referred to a courtroom for trial jury selection. Members of the jury panel are interviewed by the judge, prosecution, and defense during a ***voir dire* examination** (*voir dire* means to speak the truth) to determine their suitability for service on the trial jury. Potential jurors may be excused from the jury panel for cause or due to a **peremptory challenge**. **Challenges for cause** are not limited. However, peremptory (no cause or reason need be given) challenges are limited in number, usually to 6 to 10 challenges, depending on the seriousness of the criminal charges.

After the trial jury is selected, the jury is sworn in (impaneled) and the government presents its case. During the opening statement, the prosecutor explains to the court what evidence will be presented as proof of the allegations in the complaint, indictment, or information. Subsequently, the defendant or the defendant's attorney outlines how the allegations made by the prosecutor will not be proven. Following the opening statements, the prosecution and the defense present their cases. A witness is examined directly by the side calling the witness, followed by cross-examination from the opposing party. **Impeachment** (reducing a witness' credibility) is the intended outcome of cross-examination.

When the defense rests its case, the prosecutor may offer rebuttal evidence to respond to the defendant's proof. If the prosecutor offers rebuttal evidence, the defendant may present a surrebuttal to refute the prosecutor's rebuttal evidence. States vary regarding the number and order of closing arguments. Nearly all states allow the defense to make a final argument (summation) first, followed by the prosecution. A few states permit three arguments (summaries) at the end of the trial. Where three arguments are permitted, an opening argument is made by the prosecution. The prosecutor summarizes the evidence presented, states how the evidence has satisfied the elements of the charge, and asks for a finding of guilt. This is followed by an argument from the defense. This is similar to opening argument by the prosecution, except the defense asks the court for a finding of not guilty. Finally, during a closing argument by the prosecution, the prosecutor may reply to statements in the argument made by the defense.

After all closing arguments are presented, the judge instructs the jury (if any) regarding the points of law that apply in the case. These instructions are critical to the final determination in a jury trial. As exemplified by the Charles Keating, Jr. fraud case, an appellate court may reverse a conviction if the judge's instructions are improper. Keating was convicted in 1992 in Los Angeles Superior Court of fraud involving the sale of $200 million in worthless bonds that ultimately led to the collapse of the Lincoln Savings and Loan Company. Public funds in the amount of $3.4 billion were used to keep the entire savings and loan industry from collapsing. According to the appellate court, the judge in the Keating state trial, Lance Ito (the judge in the O.J. Simpson trial), presented faulty instructions to the trial jury. Ito did not instruct the jury to consider whether Keating intended to swindle the investors (Krasnowski, 2000).

Subsequent to the judge's instructions to the jury, the jury retires to deliberate. These deliberations are not public, and the jury may be sequestered. A unanimous verdict by the jury is required in criminal cases.

If the jury's verdict is not guilty, the defendant is released. Not guilty verdicts are final. If the defendant is found guilty, the judge may order the probation department to conduct a presentence investigation. The results of the investigation assist the judge in determining the most appropriate sentence. At sentencing, the judge may impose a fine, jail or prison sentence, probation, or a suspended sentence. Due to a recent U.S. Supreme Court decision, only a trial jury can

The courts affect the legal system and society in significant ways.
(Photo courtesy of the San Diego Sheriff's Department.)

impose a death sentence. Postconviction remedies for the defendant include appeal and habeas corpus actions when all other appeal remedies are exhausted (Acker & Brody, 2004; Hails, 2012).

Civil Cases

In civil cases, a complaint (lawsuit) is initiated by a plaintiff, claiming a civil wrong committed by the respondent in the case. The respondent files an answer to the plaintiff's claim and states a defense against the complaint. A civil lawsuit is not a criminal prosecution. Therefore, neither a state's prosecuting attorney nor the U.S. attorney represents either party in a civil case.

Procedurally, a civil suit parallels, but does not replicate, a criminal proceeding. Pretrial motions requesting discovery of the opponent's information are filed by both parties. Jury selection follows a procedure similar to that which occurs in criminal cases. At trial, opening statements are made by the plaintiff (or plaintiff's counsel) and the respondent (or respondent's counsel). The plaintiff's case is presented first, followed by the respondent's case. Direct and cross-examination of witnesses is similar to criminal proceedings, although evidentiary rules, testimonial privileges, and prohibitions against admission of hearsay evidence are more relaxed. Both sides make closing statements, the judge provides instructions to the jury, and the jury deliberates to reach a verdict. Unlike criminal cases, in which unanimous verdicts are required, substantial majority verdicts are permissible in many civil cases. The function of the jury in civil lawsuits is to find, by a preponderance of evidence, for or against the plaintiff. Civil liability, rather than criminal culpability, is the issue in civil cases.

> Additional information about the judicial process as well as legal concepts and laws may be obtained through resource linkages provided by the American Bar Association at www.abanet.org.

TORT LAW

A **tort** is a civil, rather than criminal, wrong for which the law provides a remedy. Unlike a crime, which is a public wrong against society, a tort is a private wrong committed against a person or property, excluding breach of contract. The wrong, committed without just cause, must have caused physical injury, resulted in damage to an individual's property, or deprived someone of personal liberty and freedom. In some cases, an act may violate the criminal law and also provide the foundation for a tort action. In addition, a tort may be intentional (willful) or unintentional (accidental). **Intentional torts** include activities such as assault (the open threat of bodily harm against someone), battery (any harmful or offensive negligent bodily contact), wrongful death (causing another's death through negligent conduct), false imprisonment (the unlawful violation of the personal liberty of another), and fraud.

Intentional torts also include defamation of character, invasions of privacy, and misappropriation of the right to publicity. Defamation involves damaging a person's reputation by making public statements that are both false and malicious. Defamation can take the form of libel or slander. Libel includes statements in print, writing, pictures, signs, or publications that injure another person's reputation. The words can also be read aloud by a speaker or broadcast for the public to hear. Slander is speaking defamatory words intended to prejudice others against an individual, jeopardizing the person's reputation or means of livelihood. Intrusion into one's privacy or private affairs, public disclosure of private facts about a person, false publicity about a person, or using a person's name or likeness without permission are considered invasions into privacy. As a general rule, certain public officials and celebrities are unable to claim defamation of character or invasion of privacy. Because of their status, public officials and celebrities are not protected from derogatory statements, because the person making the statement is exercising the first amendment right to freedom of speech.

Employers may be sued for defamation when they provide derogatory information to a prospective employer regarding a current or former employee. Usually, the truth of the information provided is a complete defense to the lawsuit. However, even when the disclosure is truthful, statements made in a malicious or reckless manner may establish the foundation for a punitive damage award to the plaintiff (current or former employee defamed). Generally, the respondent in a defamation lawsuit will be unable to establish a defense if any of the following conditions exist:

- Actual malice on the part of the information provider is established.
- False defamatory information was published intentionally.
- False defamatory information was provided to someone who has no legitimate reason to receive it.
- False defamatory information was published recklessly, without regard to its truthfulness.
- False defamatory information was published for other than legitimate reasons.

There are situations other than employment reference inquiries that may give rise to liability for defamation. These situations include statements made in the course of an employee misconduct investigation and accusations of misconduct directed toward a customer or client of a business. Truth of the statement may be a complete defense to a defamation lawsuit. However, employers and security personnel are cautioned to refrain from making specific accusations, either verbally or in writing. Even when an adequate defense is available, the costs associated with litigating a defense can be considerable.

The tort of misappropriation of the right to publicity applies to those situations in which a person uses another living person's name or identity for commercial purposes. In the United States, people have the exclusive right to profit from the commercial use of their names and personalities during their lifetime. This is particularly true of well-known individuals and celebrities. In such cases, a plaintiff can sue for recovery of unauthorized profits acquired by the offending party, and the plaintiff can obtain an injunction against the offender to prevent unauthorized use of the plaintiff's name or identity in the future.

Unintentional torts evolve from those situations in which persons fail to exercise ordinary and prudent care and, as a result, others are injured. The accused may have failed to perform an act that a reasonable person, in similar circumstances, would do, or may have done something that a reasonable person would not do. In these situations, the actor is said to be negligent. Most professional liability suits are based on an alleged act of **negligence**. Commonly referred to as malpractice, all professional liability claims are based on improper performance of the act. Malfeasance is the performance of an act in a wrongful and unlawful manner. Misfeasance is the performance of a lawful act in a negligent manner.

Professionals can be held civilly liable if their actions or omissions meet the four requirements necessary for the legal definition of negligence: (1) The person charged with negligence owed a duty of care to the accuser (duty), (2) the provider breached the duty of care to a person (derelict), (3) the breach of the duty of care to the person was a direct cause of the person's injury (direct cause), and (4) there is a legally recognizable injury to the person (damages).

Managers and organizations may also be civilly liable for numerous personnel-related and management-related practices. Liability may be incurred when an employee is found to be negligent when acting within the scope of employment (vicarious liability). Management may be liable for negligent hiring, training, supervision, and retention, as well as for wrongful termination of personnel. Organizations and individuals may be held liable for invasion of privacy, malicious prosecution, defamation of character claims, foreseeable acts of violence, false arrest and false imprisonment, use of excessive force, and failure to protect confidential information.

The increasing number of liability-related lawsuits should be a concern for professionals in all fields, not just security. To protect themselves against criminal or civil charges, people should practice good human relations, become familiar with relevant federal and state laws, make every reasonable effort to comply with those laws, and adhere to a professional code of ethics and standards of conduct (American Society for Industrial Security, 1998; Cheeseman, 2010; Inbau, Farber, & Arnold, 1996; Seivold, 2011; Simonsen, 1998).

CONTRACT LAW

A **contract** is a legally binding voluntary agreement between two or more parties through which specific promises are made for a valuable consideration. A legally binding contract contains four basic elements: an agreement, a consideration, legal subject matter, and contractual capacity of the parties. The agreement is an offer by one party and the acceptance of that offer by another party. The offer, which relates to some present or future action, must be communicated, made in good faith and not under strain or as a joke, and clear enough to be understood by both parties, and it must define what both parties will do if the offer is accepted. An offer may be withdrawn before a valid acceptance. In addition, the acceptance must be absolute and in accordance with the terms of the offer. If the acceptance adds to or modifies conditions made in the original offer, the addition or modification constitutes a counteroffer for another contract. Mutual assent is part of the agreement and is evidenced by an offer and acceptance. For a contract to exist, both parties must agree to and fully understand the terms and conditions of the agreement.

The consideration is something of value that is bargained for as part of the agreement. When a contract is made, each party agrees to do or provide something for the other. The exchange of promises is called a consideration.

The agreement must also be for services or purposes that are legal; otherwise, they are not valid and enforceable in court. For example, a contract that provides that a manufacturer can intentionally provide a defective product for a retailer is illegal. In this case, the contract would be void. It would be set aside and treated as though it had never existed. A legally unenforceable contract should not be confused with breach of contract. Breach of contract may be charged if either party fails to comply with the terms of a legally valid contract.

The parties who enter into the agreement must also be competent and possess the capacity to enter into a contract. If any of the parties are incompetent at the time a contract is made, the agreement is voidable. The contract may be set aside or invalidated. Incompetent parties include persons under 18 years of age, or the age of majority, who are not emancipated, as well as some mentally incapacitated persons. Emancipated minors are individuals between the ages of 15 and 18 who are married, in the armed forces, or self-supporting and no longer living under the care and control of their parents or guardians. Similarly, the persons entering into the contractual agreement must be capable of fully understanding all of its terms and conditions. A person declared insane or mentally incompetent by a court may not enter into a legally binding contract. In some cases, mental incompetency extends to those under the influence of drugs or alcohol at the time the agreement is made.

Contracts may be expressed or implied. An **expressed contract** can be written or oral, but all terms of the contract are explicitly stated. An **implied contract** is unspoken and results from the actions of the parties. Conduct of the parties, rather than expressed words, create the contract.

The contract is valid if both parties understand the offer, both are competent, and the services provided are legal. State laws prescribe which contracts must be in writing to be enforced.

A promise by a third party to pay for the services of another must be in writing to be enforceable by a court. Likewise, financial arrangements must be in writing according to Regulation Z of the U.S. Consumer Protection Act of 1968. This law is also known as the Truth-in-Lending Act. Under the law, the agreement must be in writing and must contain information regarding the fees for services, amount of any down payment, date each payment is due, date of the final payment, amount of each payment, and total interest charges to be assessed. The purpose of this type of legislation is to protect consumers from fraudulent, deceptive, or hidden finance charges levied by creditors. The written agreement can also be used by creditors to collect outstanding debts.

Finally, contracts may include special clauses that stipulate liquidated damage arrangements and limitations on damages. Special clauses may also include hold-harmless and indemnification language. Hold-harmless clauses are included when one party assumes liability for another party to the contract. Indemnification clauses are included when one party agrees to reimburse the other party for expenses associated for any loss, damage, or liability claim (American Society for Industrial Security, 1998; Cheeseman, 2010; Mann & Roberts, 2009).

Although security professionals are likely to engage in numerous contractual relationships, the most probable situation involves a contract for some type of security service. Outsourcing (utilizing contracted vendors) for security services and personnel is common. Potential outsourcing situations include facility reviews, program planning, security system design and installation management, system monitoring, training, investigations, and security personnel (Maurer, 2000b).

In business and government environments, electronic mail (email) is sometimes used to negotiate and agree on contract terms. Assuming all the elements to create a contract are present, an email contract is valid and enforceable. To ensure that the contract meets a state Statute of Frauds documentation requirement, the parties to the email contract should print and retain a paper version of the electronic contract. Likewise, to overcome evidentiary problems in the event of a lawsuit, the parties should print and retain paper versions of any prior email contract negotiations. The Electronic Signature in Global and National Commerce Act, enacted by Congress and signed by the president in 2000, provides that an electronic signature has the same force and effect as a manually pen-inscribed signature on paper (Cheeseman, 2010).

Since security executives of large organizations often manage several contracts, periodic review of contractual arrangements is appropriate. In some cases, restructuring contracts can result in considerable cost savings. As an organization's operation grows through mergers and acquisitions, the decentralized approach to security service-provider agreements may not be efficient or cost effective. One major financial institution, headquartered in Pittsburgh, Pennsylvania, with 10 geographic regions spanning several states, decreased the number of contractors, obtained volume discounts, and reduced the organization's annual contracted security expenses by 9 percent. A review of existing contracts, operations, billing rates and structures, and bid solicitation procedures analysis was implemented. Surprisingly, the financial institution's management discovered that a single vendor was not the most cost-efficient solution. However, the organization was able to reduce the 14 original contractors to 4 (Mann, 1999).

Another type of contract a security professional may encounter, particularly in private industry, is a noncompete agreement. If a former employee takes critical proprietary information from the former employer to a competitor, or uses the information to start a competing enterprise, the former employer can lose trade secrets and market share. To prevent this type of knowledge transfer, employers often require employees to sign a noncompete agreement. Such agreements prohibit direct competition or knowledge transfer by the former employee.

Although the courts generally do not uphold contracts that restrict a person's ability to obtain employment, they do accept contracts designed to protect a company's legitimate business interests. Protectable business interests include trade secrets, intellectual property, and business goodwill arising from the name, location, or reputation of the company. Some courts also hold that an employee's unique skills acquired on the job are a protectable business interest.

When noncompete agreements are enforceable, the enforcement is not unlimited. The noncompete restriction is limited to a reasonable period of time, generally not more than 2 years. Most courts also restrict enforcement to the geographic area where the former employee worked and had client contact.

Noncompete agreements are upheld in most states if the contract is confined to legitimate business interests, states the irreparable harm to be suffered by disclosure, narrowly defines the scope of the restrictions to a reasonable time and place, and describes the prohibited conduct. The agreement should include a statement that lack of immediate enforcement of the agreement does not constitute a waiver, an acknowledgment by the employee that the restrictions are reasonable and necessary, and a statement that the agreement applies if the employee either resigns or is terminated.

Some companies prefer to use a nonsolicitation agreement in lieu of a noncompete agreement. Instead of completely prohibiting competition, a nonsolicitation agreement only restricts a former employee from soliciting the former employer's clients or employees.

Enforcement of noncompete or nonsolicitation agreements necessarily involves litigation through the courts. A former employer commences proceedings by obtaining a temporary restraining order (TRO), good for about 10 days, or a preliminary injunction, which remains in place until a trial determines the outcome.

Occasionally, a former employee has extensive knowledge of and experience with a former employer's operations and trade secrets and, given the nature of a new position with a competitor, it is inevitable that disclosure will take place. The former employee may have knowledge of operational and strategic plans, intellectual property, pricing structures, and other forms of proprietary information. In these situations, a former employer may ask a court to prevent a former employee from working for a direct competitor. Although not a noncompete agreement, the legal principle involved here is referred to as the *inevitable disclosure doctrine*. As with noncompete agreements, the doctrine's enforcement is not limitless, and some courts are reluctant to enforce it unless there is evidence of actual misconduct on the part of the former employee. Whether a former employer creates and seeks relief through a noncompete or nonsolicitation agreement, or through the doctrine of inevitable disclosure, state statutes and case law should be researched to determine applicability in local jurisdictions (Bland & Harkavy, 2000; Halligan, 2000; Seivold, 2011).

SECURITY SPOTLIGHT

Does the educational institution you attend or the organization that employs you have one or more contracts with external providers of security services? If so, and with the permission of the responsible person in charge, investigate one of these contracts. Is the contract an expressed contract or an implied contract? How do you know? What can you learn about the four basic elements of the contract? For example, what is the agreement, exactly? What is the consideration? Is the subject matter legal or illegal? And what is the contractual capacity of each of the parties? (Does each party have the capacity to enter a contract? Why or why not?)

ADMINISTRATIVE LAW

The branch of public law created by administrative agencies and presented in the form of rules and regulations that dictate the duties and responsibilities of individuals and organizations is referred to as **administrative law**. Administrative agencies derive their authority from state and federal statutes that authorize the agency, often referred to as a department, commission, bureau, or office, to regulate conduct involving safety, education, welfare, national security, taxation, environmental and consumer protection, transportation, communications, labor relations, commerce, and trade. Because societies are complex, countless administrative agencies have been created to regulate and control human and organizational behavior. Since the legislative process can be time consuming, legislatures pass enabling statutes that create these agencies and empower them with broad discretionary authority to formulate and implement public policy, which has the impact of law, within very short periods of time.

Administrative agencies are usually granted executive powers, such as the power to investigate and prosecute violations of statutes and administrative regulations and orders. The agency may issue an administrative subpoena for specified information. Administrative agencies may also conduct physical inspections (searches) of business and governmental premises and facilities. However, the executive powers granted to administrative agencies are subject to certain constitutional constraints. For example, administrative inspections or searches are subject to the same restrictions placed on other government agents by the Fourth Amendment to the U.S. Constitution (Cheeseman, 2010).

Although subject to judicial review, the actions of administrative agencies can disrupt daily activity and business operations if, in the minds of agency representatives, conduct does not conform to the requirements of the regulations. Security professionals must acknowledge the power and control administrative agencies retain and ensure that human and organizational behavior conforms to regulatory requirements.

PROPERTY LAW

Although property rights hold a unique position in the American society, the term *property* is not easily defined. Property includes almost every right that the law protects, except that afforded to one's personal liberty. Property rights protect lawful possession, use, and ownership. In the United States, property is a legally protected interest or group of interests, including the exclusive right of a private person to control private property, as well as the right of a political unit (city, county, state, nation) to control public property for an economic good.

Property can be tangible, such as an automobile or building to which an interest holds a possessory right or title. In contrast, intangible property does not take a physical form. Stock certificates, proprietary information, intellectual property, copyrights, and patents represent property interests that, although not physical, are legally protected by law. As technological knowledge expands more rapidly and data processing and communication systems become more sophisticated, the classifications of personal property broaden. The rise in patent applications, for example, can be explained partly by new classes of discoveries and innovations that have been granted protection.

Although the U.S. patent system has existed for over 200 years, biotech companies could not patent genetic discoveries until 1980. Patents on software were not allowed until 1981. In 1998, patent rights were expanded to include business methods. The protection and enforcement of property rights on patents of this nature are also more difficult. Since most new patents apply to intangibles such as ideas and information stored in electronic media, security is more difficult to achieve and competitors often battle over exclusive rights. Millions of Internet users routinely reproduce or misuse copyrighted material (Balint, 2000; Jones, 2000; Mann & Roberts, 2009). And the question of who is responsible for securing data stored in the "cloud" (cyberspace) is still sparking debate. For instance, in a survey of managers from large companies conducted in 2010, one in seven of the companies participating in the survey recognized that there are potential access breaches in their cloud platforms but did not know how to locate them. Respondents indicated that cloud security controls are not keeping pace with the rapidity of cloud adoption. Nearly 80 percent of those surveyed were unable to identify the chief entity responsible for protecting their company's data stored in the cloud. Even those who viewed their application and cloud service provider as accountable expressed uncertainty about their data's security ("Businesses unsure how to protect cloud data," 2010).

In some high-profile lawsuits in 2000, Amazon.com claimed its one-click ordering system patent must force Barnesandnoble.com to use two clicks. Priceline.com sued Microsoft and its Expedia subsidiary for infringement on Priceline.com's name-your-price auction model, a business methods patent (Jones, 2000). In December 2010, a district court judge dismissed a patent infringement suit brought by Microsoft cofounder Paul Allen against Apple, Facebook, Google, YouTube, AOL, eBay, Netflix, Office Depot, OfficeMax, Staples, and Yahoo. The suit claimed that these companies violated patents developed by Internal Research, a now-defunct lab funded by Allen. The patents that made up most of the claims were "Browser for Use in Navigating a Body of Information, with Particular Application to Browsing Information Represented by Audiovisual Data" and "Alerting Users to Items of Current Interest." The district court judge said that none of the alleged violations could be pursued further until Allen identified the devices infringing on the noted patents ("Judge dismisses Paul Allen's patent suit against Apple, Google, others," 2010).

The most significant distinction in property law emanates from the difference between **personal property** and **real property**. Personal property includes virtually anything, tangible or intangible, other than land and anything in it or permanently attached to it (real property, real estate). When real property, such as minerals or buildings, are extracted or removed from land, they are theoretically transformed into personal property. Important legal considerations emanate from the distinction between personal and real property. Transfer of title to personal property is relatively simple and is typically controlled by a uniform commercial code. Transfer of real property (real estate) is much more formal and includes the delivery of an instrument referred to as a deed. In some cases, an individual, political entity, or corporation (considered a "paper" person in the eyes of the law) may have a legal right to possess, rather than own, property. Renting a vehicle (personal property) or leasing a building (real property) represent contracted possessory rights rather than ownership. Under the terms of the contract, the lessee is subject to agreed-upon conditions of use, and the lessor retains ownership rights.

Whether personal or real, tangible or intangible, property can be insured, either by the owner or by the person who holds a possessory right to the property. Insurance refers to a contract of the insured within a group of contracts held by the insurer to distribute (spread) the risk, damage, or loss among a large group of contract holders. Virtually any commercial activity can be protected by insurance coverage. A business can obtain insurance to protect itself from damage or loss to tangible assets, to protect it from strict liability, intentional or unintentional torts, and negligence, or to shield itself against financial losses due to fire, death of an executive, or dishonest employees.

The concept of property is extremely important in a democratic and free society such as the United States. In a sense, property rights are almost sacred to many people. Security managers, therefore, should familiarize themselves with the nature, scope, rights, and legal consequences associated with personal and real property laws.

EMPLOYMENT LAW

Employment law covers a vast array of common law and statutory provisions that regulate the employment relationship. Employment laws include labor laws, employment discrimination laws, and laws that are created to protect employees. Originally, labor laws were created to restrict workers' efforts to unionize, strike, or picket to obtain better working conditions or higher wages. Injunctions were used in peaceful labor disputes. However, in 1932, the U.S. Congress enacted the Norris-LaGuardia Act, which withdrew federal court power to issue such injunctions in nonviolent labor disputes. More important, the Act declared that labor was free to organize and form unions without employer interference.

In 1935, Congress enacted the National Labor Relations Act. The Act outlined the federal government's support for collective bargaining and unionization. The Act also established the National Labor Relations Board, which was tasked with the responsibility to monitor and administer regulations relative to employee rights.

The Fair Labor Standards Act (FLSA) was passed by Congress in 1938. The Act forbids the use of oppressive child labor, and it established minimum wage and overtime pay for workers. Under the FLSA, an employer cannot require a nonexempt employee (nonmanagerial worker) to work more than 40 hours per week unless the employee is paid one-and-a-half times the regular pay for each hour worked over 40. In 2002, a federal trial jury in Portland, Oregon, found Wal-Mart Stores, the world's largest retailer and private employer, guilty of pressuring employees to work unpaid overtime. More than 400 current and former employees from almost two dozen Oregon Wal-Mart Stores sued the retailer for violating state and federal wage laws. More than 35 similar lawsuits were filed against Wal-Mart in 30 other states. Those suits, from New York to California, involved thousands of workers seeking millions in back pay. Other suits and complaints against Wal-Mart alleged that the company discriminated against female workers and that Wal-Mart thwarted employee efforts to unionize (Armour, 2003; "Wal-Mart loses overtime pay lawsuit," 2002).

In 1947, Congress passed the Labor-Management Relations Act, otherwise known as the Taft-Hartley Act. This law prohibits unfair union practices and amends the National Labor Relations Act to prohibit certain types of union activities.

In the area of employment discrimination law, a number of federal and state statutes prohibit discrimination in employment on the basis of gender, race, religious preference, national origin, age, or disability. Paramount among these laws is the Civil Rights Act of 1964, the Americans with Disabilities Act of 1990, and the Civil Rights Act of 1991. Additional laws afford an employee a number of job-related protections. Employees have a right to a safe and secure workplace, compensation for work-related injuries, financial security upon retirement or loss of employment, and protection against unfair dismissal from employment. The latter group of laws include the Occupational Safety and Health Act of 1970, the federal **Employee Polygraph Protection Act** of 1988, the Family and Medical Leave Act of 1993, and numerous other laws related to employee privacy, drug and alcohol testing, and workers' compensation (Cheeseman, 2010; Mann & Roberts, 2009). Additional information regarding these laws as well as examples of the legal issues associated with the employer–employee relationship are presented in Chapter 5.

Although not typically categorized under employment law, some laws are intended to protect an individual's privacy, especially laws related to the disclosure of personal information.

Employers, for example, may conduct credit history checks on prospective or current employees to determine their susceptibility to bribes or suitability for positions that provide ready access to financial assets. However, consumer credit information is protected by federal laws such as the Fair Credit Reporting Act and the Financial Modernization Act, also known as the Gramm-Leach-Bliley Act (U.S. Federal Trade Commission, 2007). In the future, the Equal Employment Opportunity Commission (EEOC) may determine that individual credit histories are an obstacle to employment in a poor economy, especially among the economically disadvantaged as well as many minorities (Anderson, 2011). Employers are cautioned to protect any personal information obtained through credit reports. Additional privacy protection information is presented in Chapter 6.

CRIMINAL LAW

Sources, Definitions, and Classifications of Crime

Sources of criminal law include the U.S. Constitution, federal statutes, state constitutions and statutes, county and municipal ordinances, judicial decisions (case law), and **common law** (law based on custom or tradition). **Statutes** and ordinances are the product of a legislative activity. Common law originated in England and formed the foundation for early U.S. law.

There is no universally accepted legal definition of crime. Generally, a crime is an offense against society. When a crime is committed, the offender commits an offense against the society that has designated the offender's behavior criminal. Therefore, if a person violates a state criminal law, the offender has harmed all the citizens of that state, regardless of who the specific victim is. When one commits a violation of the federal criminal law, the offense is committed against all the citizens of the United States.

In a more expanded form, a crime may be defined as an intentional act (*actus reus*), or omission to act, in violation of the criminal law, committed without defense or justification and punished by society as a felony, misdemeanor, violation, or infraction. The essential elements of crime include a culpable mental state, guilty mind (*mens rea*), or criminal intent (a design, resolve, or purpose of the mind), an act or omission to act, and a causal legal connection between the intent and the act itself. The *corpus delicti* (body) of a crime includes injury, loss or harm, and the existence of a criminal agent as its cause. In a criminal case, the prosecution is required to prove the elements as well as the *corpus delicti* of a crime.

Mens rea is the element of a crime that focuses on the offender's intent to commit a criminal act. Generally, a person cannot be convicted of a crime unless the act or omission involved negligence, recklessness, or knowledge, or was committed intentionally or willingly. Types of intent fall into four basic categories: general, specific, transferred, and **criminal negligence**. General criminal intent may be inferred from merely doing the act. Specific criminal intent requires a specifically intended and desired result. With transferred (constructive) intent, a person may be liable for unintended consequences, such as when A shoots at B, misses, and kills C, an unintended victim. Criminal negligence is the failure to exercise the degree of care that a reasonable and prudent person would exercise in similar circumstances. A person who operates a motor vehicle while under the influence of alcohol or drugs does so in a criminally negligent manner.

For criminal liability to attach, one must be the actual cause (cause-in-fact), as well as the proximate (legal) cause, of the events leading to the result. To be the **proximate cause** of an event, the actor can foresee (anticipate) the result. One is liable if a reasonable and prudent person can foresee the possible consequences of the act or omission. In some employer–employee relationships, the employer may also be vicariously liable for the actions of the employee when the employee commits an unlawful act within the scope of employment, even though the employer had no knowledge that the act was being committed. Some crimes, referred to as *strict*, or *absolute*, *liability* offenses, require no culpable mental state and present a significant exception to the principle that all crimes require a proximate causal connection between the act and intent. Strict liability offenses make it a crime simply to do something, regardless of the actor's intent. Such offenses are based upon the presumption that causing harm is in itself blameworthy. Corporations, as fictitious legal persons, can also be held criminally liable for the acts or omissions of their managers, agents, and employees.

Offenses are classified as felonies, misdemeanors, violations, or infractions. **Felonies** usually carry a potential penalty of a fine, over 1 year in prison, or death. **Misdemeanors** carry a potential penalty of a fine or up to 1 year in a municipal or county jail. Violations or **infractions** carry a potential penalty of a fine and are not usually punishable by imprisonment (Brody, Acker, & Logan, 2010; Cheeseman, 2010; Nemeth, 2004; Ortmeier, 2006; Siegel & Senna, 2008; Wallace & Roberson, 2012).

Specific Crimes

The type of behavior identified as criminal, as well as the name and classification given to each offense, is determined by individual jurisdictions. The federal government and each of the states have their own criminal codes. Thus, the names given to crimes and the elements of the crimes may vary. The following is an overview of several major crimes and their elements. Readers should consult their respective state criminal codes for jurisdiction-specific crimes and elements.

Learn more about criminal laws in all 50 states through Hieros Gamos Legal Directories at www.hg.org.

PRELIMINARY (PREPARATORY) CRIMES In an effort to prevent more serious crimes from occurring, virtually all jurisdictions have statutes that make preparation to engage in criminal behavior a crime in and of itself. Although the intended crime is incomplete (inchoate, unfulfilled), the acts completed in preparation for the intended crime are criminal in themselves. Often referred to as **preliminary (preparatory) crimes**, examples include the following:

- *Criminal attempt.* This crime involves an attempt to commit some other crime coupled with an act completed toward the commission of the intended crime.
- *Solicitation.* This crime involves soliciting (requesting) another to commit an intended crime. Statutes often limit **solicitation** to specific types of serious crime and sex or drug offenses.
- *Conspiracy.* This crime involves two or more persons who agree to commit any crime coupled with an overt act in furtherance of the **conspiracy**.

CRIMES AGAINST PROPERTY Offenses contained in the **crimes against property** category include those in which the victim is not present or is unaware that the crime is being committed. The typical target of these crimes is tangible or intangible property.

- *Theft (larceny).* This crime involves the intentional taking of personal property of another with the intent to permanently deprive the owner of the property. The distinction between misdemeanor (petty) and felony (grand) theft depends on the dollar value specified in the statute.

- *Vehicle theft.* This crime involves theft of a vehicle and is usually specified as grand theft, regardless of the vehicle's value.
- *Fictitious check.* This crime involves writing a no-account check or willfully, with intent to defraud, writing or delivering a check, knowing there are insufficient funds for payment in full.
- *False pretenses.* Anyone who knowingly, by false pretense or fraud, procures property of another commits the offense of false pretenses.
- *Embezzlement.* This crime involves fraudulent appropriation or unauthorized disposition of property by a person to whom the property has been entrusted.
- *Breaking and entering.* This crime involves forcible entry into a structure intended for human occupancy without the permission of the owner or lessee and destroying property of value in or around the structure.
- *Burglary.* This crime involves entry into a structure with the intent to commit a felony or steal property of any value.
- *Arson.* This crime includes those situations in which the offender willfully and maliciously sets fire to any structure, forestland, or property.
- *Forgery.* This crime involves the false making or major alteration of any document which, if genuine, would carry with it a legal obligation or responsibility.
- *Extortion (blackmail or theft by intimidation).* This crime involves withholding or obtaining property of another through the threat of some future harm.
- *Trespassing.* This crime involves a willful encroachment upon any land or building after receiving notice to the contrary by the person in lawful possession of the property.
- *Vandalism (malicious mischief).* This crime involves the malicious defacing, damaging, or destroying of another's personal or real property.

CRIMES AGAINST PERSONS **Crimes against persons** include those offenses committed by physical contact with the victim, in the presence of the victim with the victim's knowledge, or by placing the victim in fear of an immediate harm.

- *Assault.* This crime involves an attempted battery or placing someone in fear of an immediate battery.
- *Battery.* This crime involves the willful and unlawful use of force or violence on another person. Battery requires some physical contact with the victim. Several states do not differentiate between assault (conveying a threat) and battery (requiring physical contact). The designated crime of battery does not exist in these states. Rather, battery is merged within, and represents a form of, assault. Thus, the crime of battery is replaced with a more serious form (degree) of assault.
- *Domestic violence.* This crime occurs when one willfully inflicts injury upon one's spouse, the father or mother of one's child, or a cohabitant in a relationship of an intimate sexual nature. On a child, domestic violence occurs when one willfully inflicts on or permits a child to suffer unjustifiable physical pain or mental suffering, or places a child in a situation in which the child's person or health is endangered.
- *Terroristic threat (criminal threat).* This crime involves a threat to commit an act of violence or other harm. Examples include bomb threats or threatening an individual with some future physical harm.
- *Robbery.* This crime involves the felonious taking of property in the victim's presence by the wrongful use of force or fear.

- *False imprisonment.* This crime involves detaining or restricting personal liberty against the will of another.
- *Kidnapping.* This crime involves the forcible abduction of a person to another location. Taking a hostage or using a victim as a shield also constitutes kidnapping in many states.
- *Rape.* Generally, this crime involves any unconsented-to sexual penetration upon the person of another.
- *Unlawful sexual intercourse (statutory rape).* This crime involves the act of sexual intercourse with a person under the statutory age of consent who is not the spouse of the perpetrator.
- *Homicide (unlawful).* Homicide is simply defined as the killing of a human being (or fetus in some states) by another human being. Not all homicides are unlawful: Excusable homicides include accidental killings, and justifiable homicides include court-ordered executions. If a homicide is not excusable or justifiable, it is unlawful. Unlawful homicide includes the following:
  - Murder (first degree). This crime involves the intentional, willful, deliberate, or premeditated killing of a human being (or, in some states, a fetus) with malice aforethought or causing a death, which results during the commission of an inherently dangerous felony listed in the first degree murder statute (the Felony Murder Rule). Malice aforethought is expressed or implied when the killer manifests a deliberate intent to kill or when the circumstances attending the killing demonstrate an abandoned or malignant heart.
  - Murder (second degree). This crime involves an intentional, unlawful killing of a human being (or fetus) with malice aforethought but without premeditation.
  - Manslaughter (voluntary). This crime involves the intentional, unlawful killing of a human being without malice aforethought but in a fight or in the heat of passion.
  - Manslaughter (involuntary). This crime involves the unlawful killing of a human being without malice aforethought in the commission of an unlawful act not amounting to a felony or in the commission of a lawful act in an unlawful or negligent manner. Vehicular manslaughter (motor vehicle homicide) is an example of involuntary manslaughter.

OBSTRUCTION OF JUSTICE   **Obstruction of justice** offenses include those crimes that obstruct or hinder the administration of justice process.

- *Perjury.* This crime includes willful lying under oath or affirmation, or under the penalty of perjury.
- *Subordination of perjury.* This crime involves soliciting someone else to commit perjury.
- *Bribery.* This crime involves giving or offering anything of value to an official with a corrupt intent to influence any act, decision, vote, opinion, or other official function or duty of such person. Requesting or acceptance of a bribe is also a criminal offense on the part of the official.

CRIMES AGAINST CHILDREN   Many states have statutes that focus on crimes against children. Examples include child endangerment, physical abuse, lewd acts upon a child, molestation, child pornography, unlawful sexual intercourse with a child, and failure to make a report of suspected child abuse.

SEX CRIMES   In addition to the crime of rape (listed in the category of crimes against persons) and unlawful sexual intercourse (listed in crimes against children), many states, such as California, place sex-related crimes in a special category. These sex crimes include indecent exposure, sodomy, incest, failure to register as a sex offender, assault with intent to commit rape, spousal rape, and sexual battery.

CONTROLLED SUBSTANCE CRIMES   Controlled substance crimes involve acts such as the possession, sale, transportation, manufacture, furnishing, or administering of controlled substances listed in applicable state and federal statutes. These crimes include possession of drug paraphernalia and being under the influence of, or cultivating, a controlled substance. These crimes focus on narcotics, cocaine, heroin, controlled substances, amphetamines, barbiturates, and marijuana.

LIQUOR LAW VIOLATIONS   Liquor law violations include selling to, or possession by, minors under a designated age; sale and consumption during statutorily restricted hours; sale to an intoxicated person; and sale of liquor without a license.

DRIVING UNDER THE INFLUENCE   Normally found in motor vehicle codes, driving under the influence (DUI) or driving while intoxicated (DWI) statutes focus on the operation of a motor vehicle while under the influence of alcohol or drugs.

WEAPONS VIOLATIONS   The possession of certain types of weapons by ordinary citizens is prohibited by law. Crimes in this category include possession of specified handguns and long guns, certain types of knives, nunchakus, metal knuckles, and explosives. Many laws also prohibit carrying weapons concealed.

CRIMES AGAINST THE PUBLIC PEACE   **Crimes against the public peace** are those that disturb the public peace and tranquility. Crimes in this category typically include the following:

- *Disturbing the peace.* This crime includes unlawful fighting in a public place, challenging another person in a public place to a fight, maliciously and willfully disturbing another person by loud and unreasonable noise, or using offensive words in a public place that are inherently likely to produce an immediate violent reaction.
- *Unlawful assembly.* This crime involves two or more persons assembled with the intent to do an unlawful act or a lawful act in a violent manner.
- *Riot.* This crime involves two or more persons acting together without authority of law to use any force in a manner calculated to inspire terror.
- *Interference with judicial proceedings.* This crime involves offering false evidence or bribery of a judicial officer, juror, or witness.
- *Interference with law enforcement.* It is a crime in many jurisdictions to resist, delay, or obstruct a public officer, peace officer, or emergency medical technician in the course of employment (Brody, Acker, & Logan, 2010; California Commission on Peace Officer Standards and Training, 2012; California State, 2010; Davenport, 2012; Nemeth, 2004; Raymond & Hall, 1999; Simonsen, 1998; Wallace & Roberson, 2012).

SECURITY SPOTLIGHT

Select two types of crime, such as crimes against property and crimes against persons, or crimes against children and liquor law violations. Using the resources suggested in this chapter, research the laws regarding the two types of crime you selected in the state where you live. Select another state, and research that state's laws regarding the two types of crime you selected. In what ways are the two states' laws regarding these crimes similar? In what ways are they different? To what extent (if any) have they changed over the years?

LAWS OF ARREST

An arrest involves the taking of a person into custody for the purpose of answering to a criminal charge. Effecting an arrest is a risky proposition. The arresting person risks injury, possibly death, to self, the person being arrested, and others. Further, in probably no other situation is the risk of a lawsuit greater, especially when the arresting person is not a public law enforcement (peace) officer. Potential civil causes of action, not to mention criminal charges, against a non–peace officer can be extremely damaging. To avoid liability, some organizations do not allow non–peace officer personnel, such as security officers, to effect an arrest under any circumstances.

Laws of arrest differ between public peace officers and private citizens. In the vast majority of situations, security personnel operate as private citizens unless statutory authority as peace officers is granted to them. The brief discussion that follows describes the essential distinctions between peace officer and **private citizen powers to arrest**. Also included is a discussion on use of force and detention authority. State and local laws should be consulted for jurisdiction-specific powers to arrest and use of force guidelines.

A peace officer may arrest if the officer observes a felony being committed. The peace officer may also arrest for an unobserved felony if the officer has probable cause to believe that a felony was committed and that the person arrested committed it. Probable cause is established when the amount of evidence present causes a reasonable person to believe a crime has been committed. Probable cause requires more than mere suspicion but less than absolute proof. If probable cause exists and no felony crime was committed, the peace officer is protected from civil and criminal liability.

A peace officer may also arrest for a misdemeanor the officer observes. In most states, if the misdemeanor is not observed by the officer, an arrest cannot be made unless a misdemeanor arrest warrant is on file for the person arrested or an exception is noted in an applicable statute. A peace officer is protected from criminal and civil liability for false imprisonment or false arrest if the officer arrests according to legal guidelines and a subsequent investigation reveals no crime was committed.

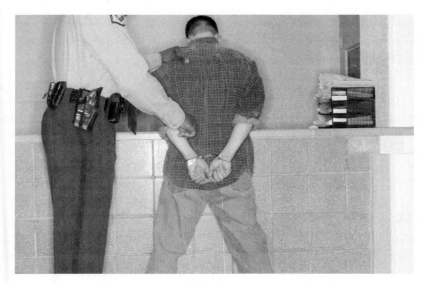

Generally, a security officer may arrest for a crime observed by the officer. (*Photo courtesy of Comstock/Thinkstock.*)

Generally, a private citizen (person not a peace officer) may arrest if the private person observes a felony being committed. For a felony not observed by the private person, an arrest can be made if the felony was, in fact, committed and the arresting person has probable cause to believe that the person arrested committed the offense. In some states, the person arrested must have, in fact, committed the felony. A private citizen may also arrest for a misdemeanor the private citizen observes. However, a private person has no authority to arrest for a misdemeanor not observed by the arresting person. Also, unlike peace officers, private citizens are not protected from criminal or civil liability due to false imprisonment or false arrest.

Although advisable, verbalizing "You are under arrest for …" is not necessary to produce an arrest situation. Actions may communicate an arrest. Restricting a person's (subject's) liberty or freedom of movement can be viewed by the courts as an arrest. If the subject reasonably believes that an arrest has taken place, whether or not arrest language is communicated, an arrest has been made. Finally, except for those private persons who may be granted limited or special public peace officer status, private citizens are not required to advise an arrestee of any rights as outlined in the Miranda admonition.

Subsequent to an arrest by a private person, the public police must be contacted and custody of the arrestee must be transferred to the police as soon as possible. In some jurisdictions, the public police cannot refuse to take custody of a subject arrested by a private person.

A person may use reasonable nondeadly force when lawfully arresting another person. If the person being arrested resists, the person making the arrest can use whatever force is reasonably necessary, including deadly force, to protect themselves or an innocent third party from serious bodily harm or death. A person may also use nondeadly force in the protection of property. The use of reasonable, nondeadly force is justifiable to protect property when the actor believes such force is immediately necessary to prevent or terminate an unlawful entry or trespass or the unlawful taking (theft) of tangible, movable property.

As part of an investigation into missing or possibly stolen company property, an employer may discuss such matters with an employee during the employee's paid work hours. Case law is divided on the issue of whether an employee may be detained during the investigative process. Obviously, nonforcible detention is permissible during work hours. An employer has the right to conduct investigations regarding conditions of employment and personnel fidelity during the course of employment. However, if force or the threat of force is used to detain the employee, the employer may be subject to a liability risk resulting from a claim of false imprisonment.

When the person being detained is not an employee, an authorized temporary detention is usually limited by statute to retail merchants and their agents. Such statutes generally allow detention for a reasonable period of time to ascertain ownership of merchandise. The phrase *retail merchants and their agents* is noteworthy. In some jurisdictions, case law suggests that contract security personnel supplied to a merchant by a vendor are not agents of a merchant within the meaning of the statute and, therefore, do not have any detention authority (Canton, 2003; Davenport, 2012; Gaines & Miller, 2011; Nemeth, 2004; Purpura, 2003; Seivold, 2011; Simonton, 1998).

EVIDENCE LAW

Evidence is used to make decisions in a judicial proceeding. Evidence includes testimony, writings, material objects, and other items presented to the human senses as proof of the existence or nonexistence of a disputed fact. The rules of evidence govern admissibility of testimony, writings, and material objects in judicial proceedings. Evidence is offered in court as an item of proof to establish a fact, to impeach a witness, to rehabilitate (support) a witness, and to assist in determining an appropriate sentence. Evidence must be relevant, competently presented, and legally obtained. Evidentiary rules are often described as the rules of exclusion because their language describes what evidence cannot be used because its use would violate a statutory or constitutional safeguard.

Sources of evidence law include the state and federal evidence code provisions regarding witness competency, the introduction of writings, privileged communications, and hearsay evidence, as well as penal (criminal) code provisions regarding accomplice testimony, invasion of privacy, and wiretapping. The U.S. Constitution, state constitutions, and case law regarding search and seizure, interrogation issues, and interpretation of evidence-related statutes are also important sources of evidence law.

Classifications of evidence include the following:

- *Testimonial.* Testimony is given by a person who has knowledge of the issues being tried in a case.
- *Documentary (writings).* This includes any documented or tangible form of communication offered as evidence in court.
- *Physical.* Examples of physical evidence include proceeds from a crime, tools (instrumentalities) of a crime, items that are illegal to possess (contraband), and physical evidence that establishes the identity of the perpetrator.
- *Demonstrative.* Examples include objects and materials such as maps, models, charts, diagrams, displays, and computer simulations that are meant to portray or enhance the meaning of evidence presented.
- *Relevant.* Evidence that has any tendency to prove or disprove a disputed fact in a case is relevant evidence.
- *Material.* Important (weighty) evidence is material evidence.
- *Admissions and confessions.* An admission is a statement by a suspect acknowledging some fact in a case. A confession is a statement by a suspect admitting liability for a crime.
- *Hearsay.* This type of evidence includes any out-of-court statement, presented in court by someone other than the original declarant, that is offered to prove the matter stated in court. Subject to certain exceptions, hearsay evidence is inadmissible.
- *Direct.* This is evidence that directly proves a fact without drawing inferences from other facts.
- *Circumstantial.* This type of evidence tends to prove a fact through inference or logical association with another fact.

Learn more about laws and legal concepts through resource linkages provided by the American Bar Association at www.abanet.org.

SEARCH AND SEIZURE

The prohibition against unreasonable search and seizure is derived from the Fourth Amendment to the U.S. Constitution. However, this prohibition applies only to governmental intrusion by public law enforcement. Searches conducted by private individuals, including private security personnel, although considered unreasonable if conducted by a public peace officer, are not subject to any judicially interpreted exclusionary rule. Thus, unreasonable searches conducted by private persons are not unconstitutional. However, private persons may be subject to a civil lawsuit for invasion of privacy.

As a general rule, public peace officers may conduct legal searches

- subject to a valid search warrant.
- incidental to a lawful arrest. This search is limited to a search of the arrestee and the area within the arrested person's immediate reach, for weapons, contraband, and means of escape.
- with consent from a person authorized to consent to the search.
- in fresh (hot) pursuit or if an exigency or public safety emergency exists.
- when items are in open (plain) view.
- of a motor vehicle when probable cause exists or the vehicle is in police custody and an inventory is necessary for safekeeping of the vehicle owner's possessions.
- for weapons on a suspicious person to protect peace officers or other prospective victims ("stop and frisk") (Acker & Brody, 2004; Hails, 2012; Nemeth, 2001; *United States v. Walker*, 2010; Wallace & Roberson, 2012).

The application of the Fourth Amendment depends upon whether the person claiming protection under the amendment can claim a justifiable, reasonable, or legitimate expectation to privacy that has been invaded by government action. Absent any established exception to the contrary, courts have held that the process of determining which warrantless searches are unconstitutional requires a balancing of the public's interests against the Fourth Amendment interests of the individual. In one landmark court case, a public hospital employee, who was aware of the hospital's policy providing for random spot inspections of packages, refused to permit inspection of a closed knapsack. The hospital's policy provided for an alternative procedure, through which an employee could check packages before entry and thereby avoid any possibility of an inspection. The appellate court ruled in favor of the hospital when it held that, in light of the public's interest in controlling pilferage from public institutions, the noncoercive search tactics used, and the availability of an alternative procedure, the individual employee's expectations of privacy were considered to be unreasonable (*Chenkin v. Bellevue Hospital Center*, N.Y.C., 1979).

A **private person's search authority** is limited. Private persons may search

- incidental to a lawful arrest. The search of the arrestee is generally limited to a search for weapons only.
- another person if an expressed or implied limited search privilege is granted through a waiver by the person subject to search.
- with the consent of the person being searched.
- to protect human life in an emergency such as a fire.
- an employee's workspace, when there is no reasonable expectation of privacy.
- an employee's locker and desk if the employer, with the employee's knowledge, retains a duplicate key. Furthermore, if an employee, after signing a waiver to search as a condition of employment, refuses to consent to a search, the refusal may provide grounds for termination when the possibility of termination is included in the waiver's language.

Conversely, if any of these circumstances are absent, a private person shall not search

- another person or their possessions without permission.
- an employee or the employee's personal possessions or workspace without uncoerced consent.
- an area where another person has exclusive dominion and control.
- a suspicious and potentially violent person unless statutory authority for a "stop and frisk" exists.
- an area retained under a lease agreement, such as a hotel room or apartment.

U.S. law recognizes each person's right to exist without unwarranted intrusion or undesired publicity. Subject to the limited exceptions previously discussed, the government does not have the right to search a business without a search warrant unless the business is regulated, such as firearms dealers, mines, and liquor stores, and case law and statutory provisions support the warrantless searches. Similarly, absent any established legal authority or well-communicated policy, private organizations cannot search a person or the person's personal workspace without subjecting itself to a tort claim for invasion of the right to privacy (Batterton, 2011; Cheeseman, 2010; Hails, 2012; Institute of Financial Management, 2011; Nemeth, 2005).

COURTROOM PRESENTATION

Attitude

Security personnel may be responsible for criminal investigations that include the identification, location, apprehension, and interrogation of criminal suspects. As a result, personnel may, because of their background and nature of their jobs, view criminal suspects negatively. Many suspects end up in court as criminal defendants. Since the security person-witness is an advocate for the prosecution, the witness may be antagonistic toward the defendant and defense counsel. However, in a court of law, the security witness should avoid favoritism. The witness should focus on an outcome that best serves the people's interest in justice. To enhance credibility, security personnel must act and speak with impartiality, dedicated to an unbiased presentation of the evidence collected in the case. Conclusions (guilty or not guilty) drawn from the evidence are the responsibility of the finder of fact, not the security person.

Appearance

One never gets a second chance to make a first impression. This is especially true in a courtroom situation. To a great extent, appearance in court may be more critical to the outcome of the case than witness testimony. Regardless of the facts in a case, juries are often influenced more by appearance than by the presentation of the facts. Defense attorneys are also well aware of the importance of appearance. The defendant may appear unkempt when arrested, but will be neat, clean, and well dressed for court appearances.

When dressing for attendance in a courtroom, security personnel should appear in professional attire. Witnesses should avoid casual or faddish clothes. Conservative dress is more appropriate. Clothes should also be color coordinated and reflect the conservative color scheme (black, grey, or dark navy blue) appreciated by most jurors. Shoes should be black and highly polished. Jewelry should be kept to a minimum and sunglasses should not be worn.

Demeanor

The security person-witness should act in a professional manner at all times when in or around a courthouse. Prosecutors, witnesses, defendants, defense attorneys, and jurors often utilize the same hallways, elevators, and restroom facilities. Witnesses should not tell jokes, discuss business, chew gum, smoke, or behave in an obnoxious or offensive manner.

When called to testify, one should walk and sit erect, avoid casual posture and crossing of legs. Both feet should be placed firmly on the floor. Hands should be placed face down on legs or closed together on the lap. Arms should not be folded. Body language communicates as much or more than the spoken word. When reciting the oath administered by the clerk or bailiff, the

When testifying in court, a witness should maintain a professional attitude, appearance, and demeanor, while responding only to questions asked and communicating facts rather than opinion. (*Photo courtesy of Comstock/Thinkstock.*)

witness should raise the right hand, upper arm parallel to the floor, fingers together, with the palm of the hand flat and facing the person administering the oath. Nervous habits must be avoided.

Testimonial Technique

Security personnel are expected to be apprehensive about testifying in court. Even seasoned actors experience stage fright and nervousness in front of a camera or audience. Unlike acting, however, the participants in a real-life courtroom are involved in an adversarial proceeding. The process as well as the opposing party can be very intimidating. Experienced witnesses still get nervous while testifying.

In a judicial proceeding, it is the responsibility of the security person to serve as a witness and communicate facts to the jury and the court. In doing so, the witness should act as natural as possible in the unnatural environment of the courtroom. Sarcasm, inappropriate or profane language, speaking out of turn or to excess, and expressing an opinion (unless as a qualified expert witness) must be avoided. If the witness is asked to repeat a vulgar statement made by the defendant, the witness should first apologize to the court for what is about to be said. The witness should listen to all that is said, and answer questions clearly, concisely, and deliberately in a voice and language that is easily heard and understood. Responses to questions should be addressed to the jury or the judge in nonjury trials. Witnesses should avoid the use of jargon or legalese. Responses should be based on the question asked. Information beyond what is called for in the response should not be volunteered. If the witness does not hear or understand a question, the witness should request that the question be repeated or clarified.

Defense attorneys will often ask tricky questions and attempt to solicit responses that are designed to reduce the credibility of the witness. This process, called impeachment, is designed to make the witness appear less believable in the mind(s) of the trier or finder of fact (judge or jury).

Before responding to any question, the witness should hesitate slightly, mentally formulate an appropriate and correct response, and truthfully reply to the question without becoming emotional. Hasty answers set the stage for mistakes. Security personnel often, and naturally, possess strong feelings toward a particular case or defendant. Defense attorneys are aware of this and will deliberately antagonize the witness. If the witness is caught in an innocent mistake, the witness should apologize, admit to the mistake, and correct the error. Respect for the truth will impress the trier (finder) of fact. If the prosecutor or defense attorney objects to a question or moves to strike a witness response, the witness should stop speaking, remain silent, and wait for the ruling and instructions from the judge.

Occasionally security personnel will be asked to demonstrate a procedure or diagram a scene to illustrate a point. Care should be exercised to ensure that the demonstration does not inflame the jury and that diagrams are clear and large enough to be viewed easily by jury members. Use of visual aids enhances presentations. However, if possible, visual aids should be preapproved by the prosecutor to avoid misrepresentation and surprises during the trial.

When excused, the witness should quietly leave the courtroom unless instructed to do otherwise. Remaining in the courtroom could have a negative impact on the jury (Guffey, 2005; Miller, 2000; Parr, 1999; Young & Ortmeier, 2011).

Summary

The judicial process in the United States is adversarial. Complex criminal and civil judicial proceedings take place in a wide variety of federal, state, and local trial and appellate courts. Prosecutors in criminal cases and plaintiffs in civil cases have a burden to proceed first. In criminal cases, a defendant can be formally charged through an indictment from a grand jury or through an information or similar complaint filed by a prosecutor. Civil actions are initiated through a complaint filed by a plaintiff. Trial juries are randomly selected initially, then proceed through a final selection during a *voir dire* (to speak the truth) examination.

A tort is an intentional or unintentional civil wrong for which the law provides a remedy. A contract is a legally binding voluntary agreement between parties. Administrative law agencies promulgate rules and regulations that prescribe duties and responsibilities of individuals and organizations. Property law focuses on possessory and ownership rights associated with real and personal property. Employment law regulates the relationship between an employer and an employee. The criminal law embodies a broad spectrum of behaviors deemed impermissible in society. Punished as felonies, misdemeanors, violations, or infractions, crimes are categorized in several ways. Paramount among the categories are crimes against property and crimes against persons. In most jurisdictions, private citizens have the authority to effect an arrest. However, the arrest authority of a private citizen differs from that of a public law enforcement officer. The rules of evidence and search and seizure place constitutional limits on the collection and admissibility of evidence. Proper attitude, appearance, demeanor, and testimonial technique are critical to effective courtroom presentations.

Key Terms

administrative law
appellate courts
arraignment
challenges for cause
common law
conspiracy
contract
court of last resort
courts of general jurisdiction
courts of limited jurisdiction
crimes against persons
crimes against property
crimes against the public peace
criminal negligence
degrees of proof
Employee Polygraph Protection Act
employment law

expressed contract
evidence
felonies
first (initial) appearance
impeachment
implied contract
indictment
information
infractions
intentional torts
intermediate appellate courts
misdemeanors
negligence
obstruction of justice
peremptory challenge
personal property
preliminary (preparatory) crimes

preliminary hearing
private citizen powers to arrest
private person's search authority
proximate cause
real property
solicitation
statutes
tort
transcript
trial courts
unintentional torts
U.S. courts of appeals
U.S. district courts
U.S. Supreme Court
voir dire examination

Discussion Questions and Exercises

1. Describe the judicial system in the United States. Include types, levels, and jurisdiction of courts in the description.
2. Compare and contrast civil with criminal pretrial and trial processes.
3. Distinguish a tort from a crime and describe types of situations that give rise to tort liability.
4. Why should a security manager, or any person nominally in charge of a loss prevention function, be familiar with contract, property, administrative, and employment law?
5. What constitutes criminal activity? In other words, what are the essential elements of a crime?
6. Compare the arrest powers of the public police with that of private security.
7. Under what circumstances may a private security person search another person? (employee workspace? another's briefcase or handbag?)
8. Under what circumstances may conversations be monitored, physically or electronically?

YOUR TURN: Researching and Writing a Case Brief

In addition to statutory law, much of the law applicable to the rules of evidence and criminal procedure is the product of judicial decisions (case law) in actual criminal cases. The ability to conduct research on case law, understand a court's reasoning for its decision, and write a synopsis (brief) of the case and the court's opinion can be very helpful to students and practitioners.

Using the following basic legal research and case brief writing guidelines, research and write a brief on a recent appellate court case of your choice.

Guidelines for Legal Research

Official and unofficial appellate court case reports contain the court majority's opinion and the dissenting opinion (if any) in individual cases. Official reports are published by the government and contain the entire text of the court case opinions. Unofficial reports are published by private companies. The following are examples of each, along with their abbreviations.

> United States Reports (U.S.)—Official report containing U.S. Supreme Court decisions.
>
> United States Supreme Court Reports—Lawyers Edition (L.Ed.). Unofficial report containing U.S. Supreme Court decisions.
>
> Federal Reporter (F. or F.Rep.)—Official report containing decisions of the 13 U.S. Courts of Appeals.
>
> California Reports (C. or Cal.)—Official report containing California Supreme Court decisions.
>
> American Law Reports (ALR)—Unofficial report containing selected appellate decisions across the United States.

A citation is used to locate a case in a law library.

Example:	Miranda v. Arizona, 384 U.S. 436 (1996).
Case name:	Miranda (appellant) v. Arizona (respondent)
Report volume number:	384
Report symbol:	U.S. (United States Reports)
Report page number:	436
Year of decision:	1966

To locate the case in a law library, proceed to the section containing the relevant reports, select the appropriate volume (numbered on the outside binder of the text), and turn to the designated page number. Learn how to access a law library online through the Law Library of Congress at www.loc.gov/law/public/law-guide.

Guidelines for Writing the Case Brief

Case briefs contain 400 words or less and usually follow a format similar to the following.

Case name and citation

Type of case—A statement describing the type of case (criminal or civil) and how the case was brought on appeal to the present appellate court.

Facts—This section contains a brief summary of the key facts of the case.

Issue(s)—This section describes the issues or questions of law the court is asked to decide. Example: Was the evidence seized illegally or unconstitutionally?

Findings—This section contains the ruling (decision, holding) of the present appellate court. The present court may affirm (agree with and let stand) the decision of the lower court or it may reverse (overturn) the lower court's decision and/or remand (send the case back) to the lower court.

Discussion—This section contains the reasons for the present court's findings based on the facts and issues presented.

PART TWO

Security Operations: Essential Functions

The chapters in this part of the book address security's essential functions. Chapter 4 focuses on *physical security*, including security of buildings, alarm systems, fire prevention and protection, and human protection systems. Chapter 5 presents *personnel security*, emphasizing the need for ethical leadership at all levels as an organization engages in personnel recruitment, selection, and management. The ASIS International Code of Ethics is provided. *Information, communications*, and *computer security* are the subjects of Chapter 6.

CHAPTER 4

Physical Security: Structural, Electronic, and Human Protection Systems

LEARNING OBJECTIVES

After completing this chapter, the reader should be able to

- describe the basics of defense.
- demonstrate knowledge of outer and inner perimeter controls.
- analyze the protective value of building exteriors and interiors.
- discuss the importance of lighting as a deterrent as well as a detection mechanism.
- demonstrate knowledge of different types of locking devices.
- list and describe types of visual assessment, surveillance, and alarm systems.
- describe the access control function of security personnel.

INTRODUCTION

Physical security is the first line of defense against a potential threat. Facility perimeters, tangible property, personnel, and information are protected using an appropriate combination of the elements of lighting, hardware, equipment, human agents, policies, and procedures. These elements form protective barriers and systems that harden the target against the potential threat.

BASICS OF DEFENSE AND LEVELS OF PROTECTION

The **basics of defense** involve the use of systems and countermeasures such as policies, procedures, people, equipment, architectural design, and strategies to prevent loss and deter, detect, deny, delay, or detain the person or agent that may cause harm to the enterprise. The basics of defense also involve the use of any combination of alarms, barriers, devices, and personnel designed to control access. The mere presence of appropriate controls may deter intruders and thus divert them from the protected area. If intruders are not deterred, controls such as alarms and surveillance systems may detect the intruder's presence. Physical security measures may also deny access. At the very least, the control system may delay access until protective personnel arrive. If all systems fail to prevent intrusion, it may be necessary (in rare circumstances) to detain a person who poses a potential threat.

The level of asset protection depends on the types of systems and countermeasures utilized. Further, the amount of protection provided depends on how the systems and countermeasures are monitored and maintained. No protection system is 100 percent defeat-proof. However, appropriate risk assessment strategies can help one visualize the level of protection that is practical and necessary.

Level 1—Minimum Protection. Designed to *impede some unauthorized external threat activity*. Includes the use of simple locks and physical barriers. Examples include using locks and simple barriers to restrict access to restrooms and stockrooms in retail stores.

Level 2—Low-Level Protection. Designed to *impede and detect some unauthorized external threat activity*. Includes the use of basic local alarms, physical barriers, security lighting, and high-security locks. Examples of settings where this level of protection would be provided include low-risk parking facilities, office buildings open to public access, and shopping centers.

Level 3—Medium Protection. Designed to *impede, detect, and assess most unauthorized external threat activity*. Includes the use of high-security physical barriers, monitored alarm systems, security personnel, and a basic communications system. Examples include perimeter protection, including chain-link fences, for elementary schools in high-crime neighborhoods, and data centers.

Level 4—High-Level Protection. Designed to *impede, detect, and assess most unauthorized external and internal threat activity*. Includes the use of perimeter alarms, surveillance systems, security personnel, advanced communications systems, access controls, high-security lighting, coordination with local public law enforcement, and formal contingency plans. Examples of settings requiring such protection include major hospitals and most government buildings.

Level 5—Maximum Protection. Designed to *impede, detect, assess, and neutralize all unauthorized external and internal threat activity*. Includes the use of on-site armed security response personnel and sophisticated alarm systems (Gigliotti & Jason, 1999; Johnson, 2005). Examples of settings requiring such protection include nuclear power facilities and courthouses.

The strategy for defense of any asset focuses on the outer perimeter and progresses through the inner perimeter, building exterior, areas within a building, and specific rooms. In this sense, countermeasures form concentric circles of protection around an asset (see Chapter 7). This layered effect provides a greater degree of protection than a single layer and does so at reasonable expense. Since several different types of countermeasures may be necessary to combat each threat, the countermeasures should complement rather than compete with each other. By utilizing design concepts embodied in the principles of crime prevention through environmental design (CPTED), countermeasures can be integrated with other facility design requirements. Thus, the initial cost of physical security measures is lowered, and the need for security retrofits is reduced (Crowe, 2000; Ortmeier & Davis, 2012).

PERIMETER CONTROLS

Perimeter controls fall into two basic categories: outer and inner controls. Outer perimeter controls focus on the neighborhood or community within which an enterprise is located. If a new facility is planned, management is well advised to conduct a site survey to determine the availability of public services, analyze crime rates, and evaluate threats from noncriminal agents and from events such as natural disasters. Natural barriers should not be discounted. In some instances, natural barriers such as streams, lakes, and rugged terrain are excellent perimeter controls. Outer perimeter controls need not be obtrusive. The perimeter control could be a clear zone. In fact, an outer perimeter that is open and clear of unnecessary obstructions may deter a would-be intruder because the intruder has nowhere to hide.

The inner perimeter includes territory or property owned or operated by the enterprise. Landscapes and parking lots fall into this category. Proper landscaping can promote safety and security while remaining aesthetically pleasing. Careful planning and design of the landscape is essential. Bushes and trees often provide hiding places for would-be intruders or predators. Parking lots should be well lit and not located in remote areas unless surveillance is possible. Perhaps the most cost effective of all security countermeasures are adequate signs, which serve as deterrents, help to create psychological barriers to human threats, and assist with pedestrian and vehicular traffic control.

BUILDING EXTERIORS AND INTERIORS

The building exterior, often referred to by architects as the *envelope*, includes the walls, doors, windows, and locking devices designed to provide exterior protection. Exterior walls should be constructed of intrusion-resistant and impact-resistant materials. This also applies to walls in common with adjoining occupancies. Access to a business can be gained easily if the common wall with an adjacent business is constructed merely of wood or metal studs and drywall, plaster, or paneling.

Exterior doors should be solidly constructed. Hinges with nonremovable pins should be located on the inside. Door frames, locks, and panels are also extremely vulnerable to attack. The frame of the door should resist prying or spreading with a crowbar. Exterior door locks should be high-quality and intrusion-resistant. Although high-quality modern door locks are pick-resistant, many can be slipped or pulled if the tools required are available. Door panels should be solid and 2 inches thick. Steel plates may be used to reinforce door interiors. Windows in door panels can be reinforced with bars or steel mesh or constructed of impact-resistant materials.

Other exterior openings larger than 96 square inches should receive special attention. Air ducts, elevator shafts, skylights, and windows should be covered with security glass or protective screening and, if possible, be alarmed. Unauthorized human intrusion into a building is often accomplished by entering through a window. The roof and main floors should be hardened and alarmed, if possible. The roof of a building is often overlooked when protection features are incorporated into building design. Usually constructed with lightweight and easily penetrated materials, a roof is rarely alarmed, and visibility of the roof is restricted. Therefore, intruders may gain access to a building through the roof without detection. Likewise, floors, especially those in multistory buildings, provide access if adequate security does not prevent access from an occupancy located below the protected enterprise.

If the interior of a building has been designed properly, activities may be assigned to functional areas based on their level of risk and vulnerability to loss. Sensitive and high-risk areas should be located deep within the building and away from the building's exterior. These areas can be target hardened with intruder-, fire-, and disaster-resistant materials as well as alarm and access control devices and personnel (Fischer & Green, 2008; Hess & Wrobleski, 2009).

LIGHTING

One of the best and least expensive security mechanisms is effective lighting. Lighting should be considered an inner as well as an outer defense. Many crimes are committed because the opportunity for detection is limited. Light increases the likelihood of detection. Continuous lighting is necessary for secured areas. Portable lights should be available for special needs. Standby or emergency lighting is used when extra light is required or electric power failures necessitate use of an alternative power and illumination source.

Perimeter lighting involves the use of streetlights, floodlights, searchlights, and Fresnel lights (which provide a long, narrow, horizontal beam without glare). Floodlights are typically used at facility boundaries to deter intruders. Parking lot and building exterior lights should be 50 feet apart and 50 feet high. Building exterior openings, doors, and windows should be illuminated also. Wiring for lights must not be exposed to damage or a possible intruder. Light fixtures should be tamper-resistant. A backup power supply or generator should be available to support emergency lights in the event of a commercial power failure.

The amount of illumination required depends on the purpose of the lighting. In operations areas such as workspaces, the amount of lighting and brightness required is usually much higher than for security purposes. Protective lighting must be of sufficient brightness to permit adequate human or technological surveillance, illuminate exit routes, identify hazards to prevent personal injury, and create a psychological barrier to unauthorized intrusion. Protective lighting must also be positioned to avoid glare that might reduce visibility for security personnel and others with authorized access to a facility.

The cost effectiveness of lighting as well as the amount of illumination and glare produced by lighting depend on the type of lamp selected. Commonly referred to as bulbs or tubes, lamps generally fall into six categories. The oldest and most common type is the incandescent lamp, which produces light by heating a filament. Although inexpensive to purchase initially, the incandescent lamp is the least efficient and most expensive in the long term because most of the energy consumed by the lamp creates heat rather than light. Mercury vapor lamps produce a strong light with a bluish cast, have a long lamp life, and can tolerate low temperatures. However, they have a long start-up time. Florescent lamps are typically of a mercury vapor type and are highly efficient. They are temperature sensitive and have limited value in cold climates. Metal halide lamps are expensive, but they depict true colors and can tolerate low temperatures. However, like mercury vapor lamps, metal halide lamps require considerable start-up and restart time. Therefore, they are not practical where continuous lighting is necessary. Frequently used in transportation environments or areas where fog is common, sodium vapor lamps emit a soft yellowish light that penetrates moisture. Produced as low-pressure or high-pressure pressure lamps, sodium vapor lamps are more efficient than mercury vapor lamps. Quartz lamps are excellent sources of illumination for perimeter control systems. They emit a very bright white light, and start-up time is short.

FENCES

Although fences typically provide minimum security, they define the perimeter, delay an intruder, channel employees and visitors to appropriate areas, and act as a platform for alarm sensors. Depending on the aesthetic qualities desired, fences may be constructed of wood, masonry, or wire. Wood, stone, brick, and masonry fences possess aesthetic qualities not typical of wire fences. However, unlike wire fences, solid barriers obstruct visibility of the area outside the fence. If concealment of inside activities to passersby is a consideration, solid walls are very effective.

Chain-link fence is the most commonly used type of fence. It requires little maintenance, is simple to erect, and provides for greater visibility than wood or masonry. To be fully effective, chain-link fences should be constructed of 11 gauge or heavier wire, at least 8 feet high, with mesh of 2 square inches or less. For maximum security effectiveness where appearance is not a concern, barbed, razor ribbon, or concertina wire may be added to the top of the 8-foot chain-link fence. The bottom of the fence can be secured to prevent lifting or crawling under by tying the lower edge of the fence to rigid metal straps. If the earth below the fence is loose or subject to erosion, the fence should be buried and secured below ground level. Culverts may be installed to prevent washouts during rainstorms.

Every opening in a perimeter barrier fence presents a potential security risk. These openings should be kept to a minimum, and access through gates should be controlled. Obviously, there should be sufficient openings to accommodate the safe and efficient movement of pedestrian and vehicular traffic. A careful analysis of needs and traffic patterns will determine how many openings are necessary. Gates may be used to secure openings when not in use. Security personnel or technical surveillance may be used to monitor open as well as secured gates.

To maintain the protective integrity of a fence, alarm sensors may be added. Electromagnetic and fiber optic cables, taut wire, and various other types of intrusion detection devices can be used for this purpose. If security personnel are available for surveillance purposes, **closed-circuit television (CCTV)** cameras (video surveillance system) can be used to monitor perimeter fencing (Fitzhenry, 2007; U.S. General Services Administration, 2011).

Chain-link fence can blend with the environment.
(Photo courtesy of Star Source International.)

LOCKS

Locking devices are used to deter the undetermined and delay the determined. Locks tend to increase the amount of time required for an intruder to gain access to a facility. Thus, locks increase the probability of detection and apprehension if used in conjunction with alarm systems and if human resources are available to respond to the affected area.

Key-operated locks are the most common. Examples include most padlocks and door locks. A notched key is inserted into a keyway containing obstacles or tumblers that can be bypassed by using the correct key. When the appropriate key is turned, a bolt, arm, or shank in the locking device is moved. In the case of a doorknob, rotating the key inside the keyway inserts or withdraws a bolt to or from a strike plate hole embedded in the door frame, thus opening or closing the lock. The lock's bolt can be a spring-loaded bolt or a deadbolt. Spring-loaded bolts (latches) automatically enter the strike when the door is closed. Deadbolts require insertion and rotation of a key or operation of a thumb latch to secure the bolt in the strike. Spring-loaded bolt locks, unless otherwise protected by a latch guard or metal plate, are easily compromised by slipping a knife or screwdriver between the door and the jamb, moving the bolt, thus releasing the spring. Deadbolt locks are not spring-loaded and require manual operation with a key. Deadbolt locks with an antiwrenching exterior collar and a minimum 1-inch throw into the strike plate hole provide the best security where key-operated locks are used.

Obviously, key control is a very important consideration with any key-based lock system. An inventory of the keys as well as a key assignment record is vital to system integrity. One major disadvantage to key-based systems surfaces when locks must be rekeyed frequently. Organizations with numerous locations or high personnel attrition may find it necessary to rekey often. The cost can be considerable. However, the expense associated with rekeying can be reduced by utilizing multiuse, instant rekeying lock systems. These systems allow up to 12 easy-to-complete key sequence changes during the life of the lock cylinder, thus reducing labor expenses associated with locksmith-assisted hardware changes. A special lock-change key is inserted into the keyway and rotated, and the cylinder is reprogrammed for a new key set.

Combination locks (dial or push-button) are often used on safes, vaults, padlocks, and vehicle doors. They cannot be picked, but can be compromised if the combination to the lock is readily available to unauthorized users. **Keypad locks** generally rely on microcomputer

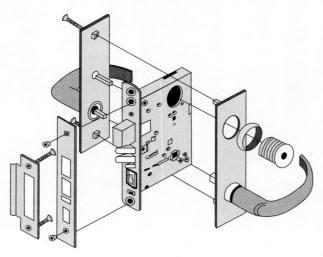

Components of a durable door locking device.
(Photo courtesy of Yale® Security Inc.)

Combination padlock.
(*Photo courtesy of Gary Ombler © Dorling Kindersley.*)

Keypad (code-operated) locks can be applied in a wide range of settings.
(*Photo courtesy of Yale® Security Inc.*)

technology and can be applied in a wide range of settings. Telephones, radios, automatic teller machines, calculators, and microwave ovens all utilize keypads to enter data and operate the device. **Electronic locks** are commonly used when control of the locking device is maintained at a location some distance from the lock. These locks are used to control gates and visitor access to businesses and apartment buildings.

A **card-operated lock** is often used to control access to restricted areas. Cards are inserted into a card reader and a minicomputer activates the locking device. A typical card-operated lock system requires the user to place a card on or near, insert a card into, or swipe a card through a reader that determines the validity of the card and releases the lock if the card is valid. Some card-key access systems also record the card number, and the date and time entry is granted. These systems make the controlled access decision based on preauthorization. They record and store access information and can summon assistance if necessary (Southerland, 2000; Tyska & Fennelly, 2000).

Sophisticated locking devices also include those that integrate *biometrics*. A **biometric system** is designed to recognize certain biological features of an individual before access to a protected area is granted. Biometric locking systems may be programmed to recognize facial features, voice patterns, an eye's retina, fingerprints, hand geometry, or the physical pressure one applies when writing a signature. It appears that biometrics may also be useful for controlling access to the Internet. For example, one researcher has developed a system that allows the identities of owners of web accounts to be verified with fingerprints rather than usernames and passwords. Users should provide their fingerprints during a one-time registration process. After they register, they can use their fingerprints to gain access to various online accounts. The system may be expanded to include palm prints and facial expressions as ways of identifying users ("Online access with a fingerprint," 2010).

One should not be lulled into a false sense of security simply because a door lock is durable. Even the strongest of locks is useless if facility personnel do not restrict access to keys (key control) or if the door or its frame is weak. Further, strong locks, doors, and framing are useless if the building construction materials that surround the protected area are weak. Building interiors with suspended (drop) ceilings and crawl spaces, for example, typically allow an intruder to bypass the door altogether. The intruder simply removes a ceiling tile in the hallway or room adjacent to the protected area and gains access to the crawl space and the protected area without entering through the secured door.

OTHER ACCESS CONTROLS

In addition to physical security mechanisms such as barriers, lighting, alarms, locks, and personnel, other tools are available to assist with access control. Relatively inexpensive, yet effective, **traffic control** and personnel identification systems can be used to restrict access. Obviously, authorized persons, including employees, must be allowed access to a facility. Retail outlets are subject to high-volume access. Even highly secure government operations may host visitors in the form of dignitaries and others with legitimate reasons for on-site access. However, through the use of concepts such as CPTED, discussed in Chapter 7, vehicular and pedestrian traffic can be routed in desirable directions to intended facility locations.

In large facilities frequented by numerous visitors, employees, or high staff attrition, consideration should be given to a **personnel identification system**. Typically, personnel identification systems include the use of color-coded, tamper-resistant identification cards, passes, or badges that indicate the level of access authorized. Although not practical in some facilities, such as retail shopping centers or entertainment venues, personnel identification systems can be effective access-control mechanisms in many facilities if the system is properly implemented and enforced. Some organizations are exploring the use of smart cards in their personnel identification systems. Such cards control employees' access to an organization's physical assets as well as computer networks. For example, employees use the cards when moving around an office building and using computers at various workstations. When an employee leaves a workstation and removes the card, this action causes the machine to lock down, preventing the risk of anyone else sitting at the person's desk and stealing sensitive information (Wagley, 2010).

SECURITY SPOTLIGHT

Do you currently use an identification card to gain access to your residence, to the educational institution you attend, or to a workplace facility where you are employed, or to use information technology systems in a facility? If so, what data are stored in the card's technology—your photo? fingerprint? a unique identification number? level of access authorized to you? If possible, speak with someone in the organization's security department to find out how this physical security system has evolved over the years. For example, has the organization adopted more sophisticated technology in its personnel identification system over time? If so, why? And how effective has the new technology proved?

Personnel identification card.
(Photo courtesy of Fargo Electronics, Inc.)

Personnel identification system equipment.
(Photo courtesy of Fargo Electronics, Inc.)

VISUAL ASSESSMENT AND SURVEILLANCE SYSTEMS

Where security personnel are limited, surveillance systems provide extra eyes and ears to the human observer. Convex mirrors are used to observe locations and blind corners that are normally unobservable. Article surveillance and antitheft systems incorporate the use of miniaturized electronic monitors and detection devices to reduce losses due to shoplifting, theft, and pilferage. Still picture, motion picture, and video cameras are used to record events. CCTV can be used for continuous monitoring of several locations simultaneously and can be connected to video recorders for future playback. **Digitization** greatly enhances CCTV, and a vast amount of information can be stored on a compact computer disk. Through digitization, an image can be converted to a computer's digital language and stored electronically.

CCTV (video surveillance) capability enhances safety and security effectiveness and efficiency in three ways. First, advances in CCTV technology offer more opportunities for

Closed-circuit television camera.
*(Photo courtesy of Panasonic Security &
Digital Imaging Company.)*

Dome camera with pan/tilt and zoom lens.
(Photo courtesy of Panasonic Security & Digital Imaging Company.)

Covert camera enclosures.
(Photo courtesy of Ultrak, Inc.)

Closed-circuit television monitor.
(Photo courtesy of Ultrak, Inc.)

integration of CCTV systems in public as well as private institutions. CCTV can be used in a wide variety of security settings. Second, CCTV operates as an extension of the human operator's eyes and ears. Although expensive to install and maintain, CCTV can generate considerable personnel cost savings because one person can monitor numerous locations simultaneously. Often coupled with time lapse recording, pinhole lenses, opaque domes, and zoom, pan, and tilt controls, CCTV increases personnel productivity and efficiency. Third, CCTV systems can provide a permanent record of an incident or event through the use of video recording.

Technological advances with CCTV have greatly enhanced surveillance capabilities. Digitization increases storage capacity, enhances high-speed communication, can compress images from four cameras into a single frame of video recording tape, and allows one person to monitor four cameras from a single four-way split screen. Some CCTV systems integrate interactive video and audio (IAVA) technology. IAVA enhances system capability because a covered area can be monitored for sight and sound. An **infrared (IR) camera** can be used for nighttime surveillance and is not inhibited by inclement weather conditions.

Many modern video security systems are linked to computer software that is programmed to identify suspicious behavior and abnormal events and notify security personnel. Video analytics software is designed to detect a wide range of abnormalities (e.g., someone falling, a package left unattended, a vehicle proceeding in the wrong direction) and notify human agents through audio or visual alarms. Using the software system greatly reduces the amount of personnel time required to monitor video in search of abnormalities (Fitzhenry, 2007; U.S. General Services Administration, 2011; Wimmer, 2000)).

Indeed, some surveillance cameras are being combined with sensors that are designed to spot potential crimes by recognizing specific behaviors such as someone raising a fist at another person or a car slowing down as it approaches a person walking along a street. The sensor alerts local police when it registers such behaviors. Officers can then zoom in on images to see whether a crime is, in fact, in progress. Computers can then be used to send the information to a laptop in the patrol car nearest the scene. The process takes only seconds ("East Orange leading the way in crime-fighting technology," 2010).

Programmable keyboard CCTV controller with touch-screen liquid crystal display.
(Photo courtesy of Ultrak, Inc.)

Digital recorder for CCTV.
(Photo courtesy of Panasonic Security & Digital Imaging Company.)

Three-dimensional (3D) graphics technology is also promising to improve surveillance systems' effectiveness by helping physical security personnel organize the ever-increasing volumes of data generated by cameras, access logs, alerts from analytics systems, and so forth. A 3D map of a facility provides a more intuitive visual framework for security personnel: They can "fly" through the virtualized facility and watch a fusion of all videos in their real locations, instead of memorizing the locations of hundreds of cameras. When locations of emergency exits and access points are included in the 3D image, security personnel have an even bigger, more useful picture. 3D also makes surveillance planning easier. Such planning typically involves diagrams of floor plans, photos, and extensive site visits. Armed with realistic 3D maps of a facility, planners can make fewer site visits—saving time and money. They can also make a more convincing business case to finance managers by using a 3D map to show how a planned upgrade of surveillance equipment would remedy gaps in coverage (Laforte, 2010).

SECURITY SPOTLIGHT

Research statistics and viewpoints on the use and effectiveness of public CCTV camera systems. Where are these systems used most often? What does the prevailing viewpoint seem to be regarding how effective they are in providing physical security? What concerns, if any, have their use raised?

ALARM SYSTEMS

An **alarm** is a communicator designed to notify a receiver of impending danger. An alarm system includes an array of interconnected parts designed to function as a unit. Alarms are not new. Geese were used by the ancient Romans in the fourth century B.C. to alert humans when an enemy approached a campsite. August Pope patented one of the first electric intrusion alarms in 1853. The device consisted of electromagnetic contacts, similar to a telegraph, that could be mounted on doors and windows and connected by wire to a battery and a bell. Today, alarm systems range from simple to complex and are used to detect fire, intrusion, medical emergencies, and other threats. They can be used to secure perimeters and buildings as well as sensitive areas within a facility. They may also be used to control energy consumption.

Every alarm system consists of three basic components: a triggering, initiating, or activation device or sensor (detector) that detects a condition; an alarm system circuit that transmits

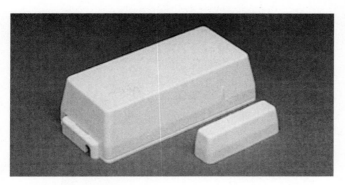

Door/window sensor.
(Photo courtesy of Interlogix, Inc.)

information; and an **annunciator** (signal) that notifies the recipient of the detected condition. **Sensors** include simple electromechanical devices that annunciate when an electric circuit is broken, pressure devices that respond to added weight or tension, photoelectric cells that activate when a light beam is interrupted, and devices activated by motion, sound, temperature, or vibration.

Passive IR sensors are designed to detect changes in heat or thermal energy. If a person with a body temperature of 98.6 degrees Fahrenheit passes through a protected room with a temperature of 70 degrees Fahrenheit, the IR sensor will detect the person's presence and activate an alarm. An **ultrasonic motion sensor** transmits extremely high (beyond a human being's audible range) sound energy that fills the volume of a protected area (e.g., room). When an object or person moves through the protected area, the motion creates a shift in the frequency of the transmitted sound energy, known as a Doppler shift. The shifted frequency is detected (sensed) by one or more receivers, and an alarm is activated. **Microwave motion sensors** are

Motion sensor.
(Photo courtesy of Interlogix, Inc.)

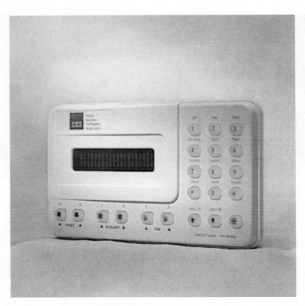

Alarm control system touchpad.
(Photo courtesy of Interlogix, Inc.)

similar in operation to ultrasonic motion sensors except that microwave systems utilize high-end radio frequencies rather than sound. Microwave sensor units transmit microwave energy and detect the energy as it is reflected from objects and returned to the transmitter/receiver unit. Except where dual or multiple sensor technologies are used simultaneously, ultrasound and microwave motion detectors have limited application due to the possibility of false alarms. However, when used in conjunction with a different type of sensor, and both sensors are required to coincidentally detect an alarm condition to signal an alarm, ultrasonic and microwave sensors can be very practical.

The **alarm system circuit** is the communication link between the sensor and the annunciator. In some cases, the circuit also connects with an audio–video recorder or communications device. A circuit communicates via wire, radio wave, electric circuit, telephone line, fiber-optic cable, microwave, satellite, or a combination of these. Advances in fiber-optic technology greatly improved materials available for alarm circuitry. Optical fiber transfers a pulsating light through a fine glass, or fiber. Optical fiber transmission has many advantages over other types of circuits. Fiber optics are low cost, safe to operate, and immune to interference from other power sources. At the end of a circuit, the annunciator notifies, or signals, a recipient that an event (intrusion, fire, medical emergency) is taking place. Annunciators include audible or silent signals, such as a light, bell, buzzer, horn, or siren, or visual text display on a computer screen.

Alarm systems fall into four basic categories. A **local alarm system**, such as a car alarm, notifies anyone who is within hearing distance. A **proprietary alarm system** is owned and operated on site by the user and requires continuous control-panel monitoring. A **public alarm system** is connected directly to a public 911 emergency dispatch center or to a local police department. A **central station alarm system**, although similar to the proprietary system, may be monitored at a remote location. Utilizing modern communications technology, a central station system can include a sensor in New York City with an annunciator in San Diego, California.

Central station systems also allow for monitoring of numerous locations simultaneously. Typically, a telephone dialer in a **central processing unit (CPU)** located at the facility where the event is occurring sends a signal through the circuit to the central station. The CPU is the brain for the system. It receives, processes, stores, and transmits information detected by the sensors. Most CPUs also have fail-safe mechanisms that notify the central station when electric power to the alarmed facility has been interrupted (National Fire Protection Association, 2007; Sweet, 2006; Trimmer, 1999; U.S. General Services Administration, 2011).

ALARM SYSTEM MANAGEMENT

An improvement in protection usually results when alarm systems are properly installed and monitored continuously. Otherwise, continuous protection can only be achieved by assigning personnel to observe the protected area. However, over time, using personnel in lieu of alarm systems is costly. Alarm systems, although expensive to purchase and install, are usually economical in the long run and provide a substantial return on the initial investment. Security professionals must recognize that alarm systems are becoming very sophisticated. The increased use of automated, personal computer (PC)-based technologies to perform critical security monitoring functions presents new challenges for the security manager. The manager must be able to effectively integrate electronic technologies into a total security management system in a way that does not conflict with an organization's operational environment. Therefore, the security manager's ability to control risk with minimal operational interference is determined by certain critical alarm systems design and integration decision-making functions: the relevance and completeness of the risk assessment, the degree of the security alarm system's applicability to the facility, the quality of the equipment selected and its installation, and how the system facilitates organizational operations. Careful planning and management of alarm systems will help avoid the costs associated with inapplicability events such as false alarms while reducing costs through integrated systems design (Gallagher & Grassie, 2000; "Sun Microsystems integrates access control worldwide," 2000; Wilberg Fitzsimons, 2000).

The first step to effective **alarm system management** involves **alarm point definition**. In other words, the points where an alarm is to be connected to the security management system must be defined (identified). The security manager must

- determine how and when the facility operates and who uses the facility.
- identify assets, threats, vulnerabilities, and security countermeasure requirements.
- develop a concept of security operations.
- integrate the concept of security operations with organizational (facility) operations.
- define and program alarm point active and inactive times.

After alarm points are identified and integrated with facility operations, the security manager can develop effective alarm response procedures. These procedures should be concise, unambiguous, consistent, and tailored to each specific alarm point, with consideration given to the time necessary for the response. Finally, alarm monitoring and response personnel must receive training consistent with the operational demands of the system. Without appropriate alarm systems management, even the best-intentioned capital investment in systems can become a nightmare for the security manager.

Access control system with CPU and components.
(Photo courtesy of Ultrak, Inc.)

Control center with video monitors.
(Photo courtesy of SONY Electronics.)

Security systems integration is advancing rapidly as the availability of new technologies provide unprecedented levels of performance and effectiveness for security systems. Experts outline at least seven trends in security systems integration:

- Standardization of operating systems is often insisted upon by information technology departments to simplify support requirements.
- Computer networks, such as local area networks (LAN), are replacing dedicated security hardware as the standard infrastructure for connecting security system components.
- Regarding card-key access and card-reader technologies, magstripe cards continue in use where cost is a consideration. However, the overwhelming choice for new card-key access

systems involves the use of proximity card technology since patents for proximity cards and card readers are about to expire and the cost should decrease considerably.

- There is greater integration of systems so that useful information can be shared, enabling more intelligent operational decisions and often reducing costs of operation.
- Video recording and transmission standards are shifting from analog to digital technology. Higher processor power as well as increased speed and memory capacity are cited as the major reasons for the shift toward digital technology.
- The demand for asset tracking capability has been heightened by an increase in thefts of small high-value items such as computer laptops. The challenge for the security manager involves the task of designing, managing, and maintaining sophisticated, large-scale security systems. Facing the challenge requires the development of new skills by security personnel.
- Real-time online access to security video recordings and associated alarm event information is increasing. Online access to video recordings of events such as alarm verifications, facility openings and closings, and officer patrols allows personnel to view activities anytime from anywhere (Coleman, 2000; Fitzhenry, 2007; Gallagher & Grassie, 2000; Sweet, 2006).

> Additional information regarding alarm systems may be obtained by contacting the Central Station Alarm Association at communications@csaaul.org or the National Burglar and Fire Alarm Association at www.alarm.org.

FIRE PREVENTION AND PROTECTION

Fire safety is probably more regulated than any other component of a safety and security program. Numerous federal, state, and local laws prescribe fire safety practices. Since fire prevention and protection principles are well established, one could assume that the application of fire safety fundamentals is very similar between and among facilities. Although similarities may exist in small facilities with common fire hazards, fire prevention and protection strategy depends primarily on the types of fire hazards present and fire exposure considerations. Through a comprehensive planning approach to fire safety, the security manager can design a fire prevention and protection program that meets the need of the facility.

Fire Prevention

Fire prevention is defined as all fire service activities that decrease incidents of uncontrolled fire. Fire prevention activities include fire department inspections, records and reports, investigations, facility plan review, hazard abatement, education, enforcement, company inspection programs, and fire information reporting systems.

The main objective of a **fire prevention inspection** is to determine if reasonable life-safety conditions exist within a given facility. Inspections are intended to identify hazards that could cause a fire or allow a fire to develop or spread. Accurate inspection documentation is an essential factor in fire prevention because inspection reports are used to enforce fire safety regulations, including those relating to violation notices, plan reviews, and issuance of permits.

Fire investigation involves fire cause determination and the investigation of criminal actions that may have contributed to a fire. Fire cause determination is important because the analysis of causes and gathered data will, over time, indicate trends in certain fire-prone areas. Moreover, the information will provide data for the development of a fire prevention program.

Facility plan review includes involvement of the public fire department during building construction. Generally, this review focuses on four areas: site plans, preliminary building plans, final building plans and specifications, and certificates for occupancy. Most sites are reviewed in conjunction with the local building, zoning, and public works departments or with authoritative state agencies. Fire officials also participate in preconstruction conferences to answer questions relating to building fire protection features, building codes, fire prevention code requirements, and other plan review processes.

If an existing facility requires an upgrade or a remodel, retrofitting the fire safety apparatus also requires special consideration and planning. The fire safety retrofit design plan should include specific elements. The plan should address applicable fire codes and standards, an identification of new fire systems arrangements, existing building characteristics and fire protection systems, a timetable for phasing in new fire safety equipment, and provision for future needs (Greene & Tappen, 2000; National Fire Protection Association, 2007; Schumacher, 2000).

How customized fire safety design principles can be incorporated with combined new construction and retrofitting is exemplified by a major project undertaken by a center for the developmentally disabled in New York State. The project added 27,000 square feet to an existing 47,000 square feet of space. In conjunction with the new construction project, the center enhanced its fire safety by expanding, upgrading, and customizing its fire alarm system. In addition to the main fire annunciator panel, three additional annunciators were located strategically throughout the facility. Anyone near one of the annunciators can view the alarm condition and take action. In lieu of traditional strobe light and blaring buzzer-type fire notification devices, strobe-only and strobe/voice notification devices were installed to minimize panic among the children in the event of a fire alarm ("Center for developmental disabilities installs access control, CCTV, fire alarms," 2000).

Fire hazard abatement involves the use of abatement codes established at the municipal level. Abatement codes focus on building, zoning, planning, electrical, plumbing, heating, air conditioning, landscaping, air pollution, and environmental protection. The codes are usually updated at 5-year intervals and are designed to correlate with the fire prevention standards of the American Insurance Association.

Fire safety education is an important ingredient to fire prevention. The two main purposes of education are fire prevention and fire reaction training. Life safety and asset protection in the event of a fire depend on good planning and proper training of employees. When a fire occurs or when a fire alarm is sounded, all occupants should react instinctively. All fire alarms should be treated as real. Plans for notification of occupants as well as firefighting and other emergency personnel are essential. Evacuation plans and routes must be developed and practiced.

Educating occupants about fire prevention and protection systems as well as evacuation procedures is critical to safety and injury prevention. Indoctrination of all new employees and periodic refresher training should be part of every employee's continuing education program. Fire prevention, reporting, and evacuation procedures, use of extinguishers, basic first aid, and fire drills should be part of every fire safety training session.

Some situations require the development and training of a private company fire unit or fire brigade. Facilities located in remote areas, away from public fire departments, may require an in-house firefighting team. Manufacturing facilities located in some foreign countries may not be located near adequate firefighting services. It may be necessary to create a company fire brigade made up of selected, well-trained employees who are competent to handle firefighting assignments. The size of a fire brigade will depend upon the location and size of a facility as well as on the nature of the fire risk.

Fire prevention enforcement encompasses the adoption and administration of fire prevention codes, enforcement procedures, and notices. Enforcement procedures involve compliance with fire permits, certificates, and licenses. Enforcement notices involve fire prevention personnel who inspect occupancies that have been issued warnings or notices of violation, red tag or condemnation notices, citations or summons, or warrants in violation of fire codes. It is the public fire inspector's duty to ensure that corrective action is taken so occupants are in compliance with all fire safety codes.

Company **fire inspection programs** include building surveys and the correction of common problems concerning life-safety conditions. They also involve locating and correcting fire hazards, and testing fire protection systems. These inspections may be conducted by company personnel. If situations are detected that need to be corrected, it is the inspector's duty to conduct all follow-up or reinspections.

Fire Protection Systems

Fire protection focuses on fire detection, containment, and suppression. It is a primary consideration during construction of new facilities as well as when upgrading existing facilities. Model building codes (statutes) and regulations for new construction have existed for many years. The codes and regulations provide for alternative methods, materials, and equipment that may be used to provide equivalent levels of safety. Performance-based fire safety design principles are used to analyze, document, and evaluate fire safety alternatives. Consultation with qualified experts and fire safety engineers is often necessary to ensure compliance with regulatory fire safety goals.

A fire progresses through four stages. In the incipient stage, invisible products of combustion (gases) are released and no smoke or heat is visible. In the smoldering stage, the products of combustion become visible as smoke. In the flame stage, an actual fire develops. Finally, in the heat stage, the temperature increases dramatically, the air expands, and the fire may become uncontrollable.

FIRE SENSORS AND ALARM SYSTEMS   Four types of fire sensors (detectors) are commonly used. They respond to the different stages of fire development. The **thermal sensor** provides the least amount of advanced warning time. It senses the heat in a protected area. Some thermal sensors are preset and respond at a specific temperature. Others, known as rate-of-rise sensors, respond to rapid increases in temperature. **IR sensors** respond to IR emissions in flame. **Photoelectric sensors**, commonly found in residences and many businesses, detect smoke in the environment. **Ionization sensors**, the most sensitive, respond to invisible products of combustion, such as toxic gases.

Fire alarm annunciators fall into two basic categories. Local annunciators sound at the location of the fire. Their purpose is to notify occupants of a residence or facility and summon help from those who are near enough to hear the alarm. Remote annunciator systems transmit the fire alarm signal to another location, such as a central station security console, 911 emergency communications center, or fire department. Remote annunciators may be monitored at some distance from the sensor location.

FIRE EXTINGUISHERS AND SPRINKLER SYSTEMS   There are six types of portable fire extinguishers. Water, fog, and foam extinguishers are effective for Class A (ordinary combustibles)

Fire sensor.
(Photo courtesy of Interlogix, Inc.)

and Class B (flammable liquid) fires. Carbon dioxide (CO_2) extinguishers are generally used on Class B and Class C (electrical) fires. Dry chemical extinguishers are designed to deal effectively with Class A, B, and C fires. Dry powder extinguishers are effective against Class D (combustible metals) fires.

Inergen fire suppression systems provide a gaseous alternative to other types of fire-extinguishing agents. They are ideal for environments that should not be exposed to water, fog, foam, dry chemical, or powder. Inergen can be applied in vaults, computer or telecommunications facilities, or any area containing sensitive electronic equipment. It is a mixture of nitrogen, argon, and CO_2 that suppresses a fire by lowering the oxygen level in the fire-affected area to a level at which combustibles will no longer burn. It is a clean, clear, nontoxic agent that allows people to breathe normally, yet it does not support combustion. In addition, Inergen is environmentally friendly. It does not deplete the ozone, and it has no global-warming potential or atmospheric lifetime.

Sprinkler systems provide one of the best-known protections against personal injury and property loss due to fire. They also provide excellent protection in high-rise buildings. Sprinkler systems use underground or overhead water pipes with sprinkler heads plugged with a metal strip that melts at a specified temperature. Properly installed and maintained sprinkler systems rarely fail to operate if there is an adequate water supply to support the system (Fireline Corporation, 2003; Gemeny, 2000; National Fire Protection Association, 2007).

To learn more about alarm systems and management through the U.S. General Services Administration, visit www.gsa.gov/portal/content/104644.

HUMAN PROTECTION SYSTEMS

People constitute the most significant protection resource. Although technology can be used to reduce security personnel requirements, hardware and high-tech devices cannot totally displace the human security agent. Monitoring, critical analysis of situations, and effective intelligent response can be accomplished only through the appropriate use of personnel. Even when alarm and surveillance systems are monitored at some remote site, such as a central station, someone (a human agent) must be in place to receive an alarm signal and respond or notify appropriate response personnel.

Security personnel take many forms. Receptionists, secretaries, janitorial and maintenance workers, supervisors, executives, retail clerks, cashiers, and operations personnel can fulfill a security function. Every person can function as a deterrent to crime and all are in a position to control access and observe and report unsafe conditions and suspicious behavior. Proper security training for all personnel expands the number of people available for loss prevention.

In all but the smallest organizations, the primary responsibility for the protective function usually rests with the facility or security manager and asset protection personnel. The security force may consist of any combination of uniformed or plainclothes protection officers, investigators, CCTV and alarm console monitoring personnel, health and safety compliance inspectors, firefighters, or emergency response specialists. The security force may be proprietary, contract, or a combination of the two. Even in organizations that have no one assigned full time to asset protection duties, someone is nominally responsible for the security function (Canton, 2003; Fischer & Green, 2008; Walsh & Healy, 1987).

As discussed previously, human beings constitute the most significant protection resource. Therefore, caution must be exercised to hire the right people, train and treat them well, and maintain their integrity. Preemployment selection procedures as well as leadership and supervision are discussed in Chapter 5. Workforce planning, training, and education of employees are discussed in Chapter 8.

People constitute the most significant protection resource.
(Photo courtesy of SONY Corporation of America.)

A QUICK SURVEY

Which of the following physical security systems is in place at the educational institution you attend or the organization that employs you? Check all that apply.

- Perimeter controls
- Walls, doors, and other elements of building exteriors and interiors
- Lighting systems
- Locks
- Visual assessment and surveillance systems
- Alarm systems
- Fire prevention and protection systems
- Human protection systems
- Other

In your view, does the facility where you attend school or where you work have adequate physical security? Why or why not? If not, what changes would you recommend?

Summary

Physical security may be defined as the use of structural, electronic, and human protection systems. The basics of defense involve the use of systems and countermeasures to control access. Outer and inner perimeter controls, natural barriers, building exteriors and interiors, lighting, fencing, locks, visual assessment, surveillance, alarm, and fire protection systems form the nonhuman elements of physical security and access control. Human protection systems include the use of security and other personnel to monitor nonhuman systems, manage the safety and security program, and take appropriate action when necessary.

Key Terms

alarm
alarm point definition
alarm system circuit
alarm system management
annunciator
basics of defense
biometric system
card-operated lock
central processing unit (CPU)
central station alarm system
closed-circuit television (CCTV)
combination locks
digitization
electronic locks

facility plan review
fire hazard abatement
fire inspection programs
fire investigation
fire prevention
fire prevention enforcement
fire prevention inspection
fire protection
fire safety education
infrared (IR) camera
ionization sensors
IR sensors
key-operated locks
keypad locks

local alarm system
microwave motion sensors
passive IR sensors
perimeter controls
perimeter lighting
personnel identification system
photoelectric sensors
proprietary alarm system
public alarm system
sensors
thermal sensor
traffic control
ultrasonic motion sensor

Discussion Questions and Exercises

1. Outline and describe the basics of physical security. Include outer and inner perimeter controls and the roles of protective lighting and locking devices in the description.
2. Compare and contrast visual assessment, surveillance, and alarm systems. What role does each fulfill?
3. Physical security and access control systems are not complete without a human resource component. Explain. Are dedicated security personnel necessary in all organizations?

YOUR TURN: Strengthening Physical Security for a Small Business Owner

Nishant Patil operates a small electronic component manufacturing business in a leased building located in an industrial park of a medium-sized city. The facility has no perimeter fencing because Patil's landlord will not permit exterior fences. Patil employs 10 full-time people who work normal daytime hours, Monday through Friday. His facility has been burglarized on three separate weekends over the past 6 months. On each occasion, small hand tools were the burglars' target. During the last burglary, the perpetrator(s) started a fire in Patil's office. The building does not have a sprinkler system. It does, however, have a local fire detection and alarm system. Fortunately, a passer-by heard the alarm on the night of the fire and contacted the fire department. Damage to the plant was minimal. The building has no intrusion detection (burglar alarm) system, and Patil has limited funds available for security-related improvements.

1. Based on the information provided, what physical security measures would you recommend to Nishant Patil? Explain your reasoning.
2. What additional information would you find helpful in developing recommendations for Patil? For example, would you want to know what time of day each burglary occurred? The layout of Patil's place of business? Information about his employees' backgrounds and financial situations? How much these and other kinds of information shape your recommendations?

CHAPTER 5

Personnel Security through Leadership and Ethics

LEARNING OBJECTIVES

After completing this chapter, the reader should be able to

- describe personnel security policies and techniques.
- outline a procedure for recruitment and selection of personnel.
- discuss the impact of legislation on human resource management.
- contrast management with leadership.
- identify leadership qualities and competencies.
- distinguish between law, policy, and ethics.
- articulate a professional code of conduct.

INTRODUCTION

Personnel security involves protection of human beings and protection from individuals who pose threats to others as well as the organization's physical and information assets. Personnel security and **personnel integrity** are fundamental to the protection of an organization's most valuable assets: its employees and clients. Personnel security and integrity are essential to organizational success, form the foundation for effective and ethical business practices, ensure the availability of human resources, and assist in the maintenance of high morale, economic stability, and fair and equitable treatment.

Protection of people involves the application of the principles and practices of physical security, the subject of Chapter 4, as well as the protection from violence in the workplace discussed in Chapter 11. In this chapter, attention is focused on protection *from* people, especially employees of the organization. Therefore, this chapter addresses personnel selection, supervision, and integrity. Clearly, the process of security management must assure that honest, dedicated, industrious people are employed by the organization. After the initial decision to employ an individual is made, the person's emotional, mental, and physical health must be maintained and the employee's trustworthiness and reliability evaluated continuously. Hiring the right people and maintaining their integrity is a management responsibility.

Personnel security is effectively maintained through the demonstrated ethical orientation and leadership capabilities of everyone within the organization. For this reason, the study and practice of ethics and leadership are critical to this chapter and to any progressive organization's personnel security program.

PERSONNEL RECRUITMENT AND SELECTION

Recruitment is the process of locating and attracting suitable applicants as candidates to fill job vacancies. **Selection** involves the process of evaluating and choosing the most appropriate and qualified person from a pool of applicants.

Recruitment

Recruiting candidates to fill a position vacancy is accomplished in a variety of ways. Internally, it may be accomplished through promotion or transfer. Externally, the recruitment process may involve newspaper and trade journal advertising, college and university career fairs, the Internet, former employees, friends and relatives of employees, applications on file, labor organizations, employment agencies, and community job fairs.

Recruiting acceptable candidates is critical and can be difficult. A low birth rate in the United States has limited the number of people available in the pool of qualified workers. During good economic times, organizations find it even more challenging to recruit new hires. In addition, lax attitudes and apathy toward drug use, theft, and loyalty often threaten the integrity of prospective employees. Numerous laws also regulate the employment procedure, making the recruitment and selection process elaborate and time consuming.

The recruitment process normally begins with a request for, or submission of, a **resume** and an **application**. The resume or application can be solicited by the employer or submitted on the prospective employee's initiative. A resume is a subjective account of a person's background, while an application is more objective. A comparison of the resume with the application may help to reveal any contradictions and inconsistencies.

Employment application instruments should be objective, uniform, consistent, and job-task related. Care should be exercised in the development of application forms to ensure that information is not requested in violation of any state or federal statute. Age, birthplace, race, citizenship, religious affiliation, and arrest information is often protected by antidiscrimination and privacy laws. In addition, some public organizations, such as law enforcement agencies, may request information that cannot be requested by a private organization. For example, as a general rule, private organizations have access to and may request conviction data but not arrest records. Conviction records are public information, whereas arrest records are not.

An application form should not contain questions other than those pertaining to the applicant's ability to perform the job for which application is made. An appropriately constructed application form, once completed by the applicant, provides a window into the candidate's past and assists in the candidate's background verification process. Signed and dated below a statement affirming to state the truth, the application becomes a legal document. It can be used by the employer as a defense in a subsequent legal proceeding if the employee is terminated due to false or misleading information presented in the application (American Society for Industrial Security, 1998; Bland & Stalcup, 1999; Cheeseman, 2010; Greer & Plunkett, 2007; Lewis, Goodman, & Fandt, 2008; Ortmeier & Davis, 2012; Pitorri, 1998).

Selection

The selection process begins with a preliminary **preemployment screening** of the applicants. Improper employee selection can result in devastating consequences, in the private as well as the public sectors (Moran, 2011). Preemployment screening involves a review of each resume and application package to ensure that the candidate meets the qualifications and specifications for the position. The preemployment screening process may involve preemployment aptitude, ability, psychological, and integrity (honesty) tests; appropriate physical agility tests; a medical examination; criminal history, driving record, and credit checks; a legally permissible polygraph examination; and an interview.

The applicant can be asked to authorize the disclosure of relevant background information by third parties. To release the prospective employer and the third parties from liability associated with disclosure of the information requested, the candidate should be required to sign an *authorization to release information document* as a condition for employment. Prospective employers should consult in-house or contracted legal counsel regarding the appropriate language to be included in the authorization to release information document.

Aptitude, knowledge, and skills tests determine suitability for the position and provide objective verification of the knowledge and skills claimed in the resume and application. The tests can help conserve resources and assist in determining the level and amount of training necessary to prepare the candidate for the position. A wide range of valid pencil and paper **psychological tests** are available that can be used to determine a candidate's emotional stability and mental health. The test procedures often include the use of staff psychologists to interpret the results.

Employers are cautioned that the use of any test designed to diagnose psychological disorders of a candidate may lead to an unintended violation of the Americans with Disabilities Act (ADA). The ADA prohibits the use of medical examinations to disqualify people from employment or promotion. In 2005, the 7th U.S. Circuit Court of Appeals ruled against an employer who used the results of a psychological test to deny promotion. The court reasoned that certain psychological tests, in this case, the Minnesota Multiphasic Personality Inventory (MMPI), is a medical test because it can diagnose psychiatric disorders, although the primary use of the MMPI may be for another purpose (*Karraker v. Rent-A-Center, Inc.*, 2005). Employers should consult with legal counsel prior to using a psychological test for employment purposes.

Integrity tests can be used to detect a propensity toward dishonesty, substance abuse, violence, or a high level of tolerance for such behavior in others. Similar in format and application to psychological tests, several integrity testing instruments are commercially available. Test producers should provide validity data for psychological and integrity tests (Jones & Arnold, 2003).

Using tests to identify attitudes toward substance abuse and theft, and to predict behavior based on these attitudes, is not always foolproof. Employers should not rely solely on the results of such tests when making hiring decisions. The tests should be viewed as complementary tools in a comprehensive preemployment screening arsenal. Additionally, organizations risk violation of federal and many state laws if tests discriminate against anyone on the basis of race, gender, or political views. Employers should not overlook the job application form itself as a tool for collecting information to predict behavior. If questions on an application form are presented properly, candidates often admit past misconduct.

A growing number of employers are requiring performance-simulation tests of job applicants. Especially useful in determining an applicant's potential, performance-simulation tests address actual job behaviors. Through work sampling and assessment centers, candidates demonstrate their skills or they are evaluated as they progress through exercises or scenarios intended to simulate problems they will confront on the job.

Simulation exercises may be used to rehearse responses to various security scenarios such as armed security personnel conducting a simulation at a nuclear power facility.
(Photo courtesy of Patrick Ortmeier.)

A physical agility test may be required if it relates to the tasks the candidate is required to perform in the position for which application is made. Subject to limited exceptions as outlined in the ADA as well as to limited exceptions for applicants for some government positions, medical examinations can be required only after an offer of employment has been made. Normally, the results of the medical examination are used to determine if a preexisting medical condition restricts the candidate's ability to perform the tasks in the position or if the candidate suffers from a disease that can be communicated to others (Anderson, 1999; Bland & Stalcup, 1999; Greer & Plunkett, 2007; Millwee, 2000; Robbins & Coulter, 2009).

Criminal history checks are imperative, yet current laws severely restrict a private employer's ability to access arrest data. As a general rule, conviction data is a matter of public record, accessible to anyone. Many county sheriff's departments, especially those in counties that contain major urban areas, have websites through which employers can obtain local conviction data as well as the identity of those who are in jail or have outstanding arrest warrants.

Although a criminal history is not an absolute disqualifier, the prospective employer should be aware of the nature and number of convictions. Recent theft, substance abuse, or violent crime convictions should disqualify a candidate. However, if the candidate is 45 years of age and the only conviction is for shoplifting at age 19, one could assume that the candidate has been rehabilitated. Driving record checks are also important if the employee is required to operate a motor vehicle as a condition of employment.

Technological advances combined with legal authority make background checks more accurate and efficient for some industries. Financial institutions currently use electronic systems to conduct criminal history checks and reduce employee prescreening and training costs. Federal laws require banks, brokerage houses, and insurers to conduct criminal history checks on all prospective employees who are required to handle cash or other financial assets. In the past, affected institutions fingerprinted individuals using traditional methods and submitted the fingerprint cards to the FBI, where the prints were classified manually and a felony records check was conducted. However, traditional processing methods took up to 3 months, and if the prints were not readable, a new set of prints was required. In many cases where the applicant was rejected, the prospective employee was already on the payroll and considerable time had been invested in training the new person. Utilizing the automated fingerprint identification system (AFIS), many institutions now scan fingerprints directly into a computer database that automatically classifies the prints and completes a criminal records check within minutes (Lushbaugh & Weston, 2012; Millwee, 2000).

A credit history check on the applicant should be conducted also. Late payments, nonpayments, bankruptcies, liens, and judgments against a candidate can be uncovered through a comprehensive credit reporting process. Most employees are placed in positions of trust and are charged with the responsibility for protecting assets. Although a poor credit history does not mean the new employee would steal to pay off debt, it may indicate inadequate self-management skills, poor judgment, and lack of responsibility, especially with respect to the management of financial assets. Most financial institutions will not employ individuals with poor credit histories. If they cannot manage their own money properly, they cannot be expected to manage another person's assets. Although some bad credit may be unavoidable, such as a catastrophic illness that leads to personal financial disaster, poor financial management is often linked to irresponsible behavior. A wise employer does not hire irresponsible people.

Employers who conduct credit history checks are well advised to protect a consumer credit history acquired during a background investigation. The Financial Modernization Act of 1999, also known as the **Gramm-Leach-Bliley Act**, includes provisions to protect consumers' personal financial information held by financial institutions. As defined in the regulations of the Act, financial institutions include banks, securities firms, and insurance companies as well as a wide array of other companies that provide financial services and products to consumers (tax preparers, consumer loan brokers, debt collection agencies, etc.). The law also applies to organizations, whether or not they are financial institutions, that *receive* consumer credit information (U.S. Federal Trade Commission, 2007).

A thorough background investigation on a prospective employee is not complete until personal references are checked and academic credentials and employment history provided by the applicant are verified. A high percentage of resumes, job applications, and employment interviews produce something less than the whole truth. Naturally, applicants prefer that derogatory information not be uncovered. Candidate-provided references rarely release any negative information about the applicant. Therefore, prospective employers must be diligent in the search for the truth. Since applicants provide references who will speak favorably of them, the prospective employer may do well to visit and interview coworkers and neighbors of the applicant, if time and resources permit. Additional information regarding background investigations is presented in Chapter 9.

With the advent and availability of sophisticated electronic databases, some organizations conduct post-hire, continuous screening of employees. Without an invasion of an individual employee's right to privacy, continuous screening permits an organization to extend its due diligence of employees from the initial contact with employee candidates through the complete life cycle of the employee–employer relationship.

Subject to limited exceptions discussed in Chapter 9, federal law prohibits private employers from using a polygraph or similar instrument as a preemployment screening tool. The law does permit the use of the polygraph for screening candidates for numerous government positions, including most public law enforcement occupations. Where appropriately used, the polygraph examination is a valuable tool for verification of information supplied by an applicant.

The interview is a face-to-face encounter between the candidate and the employer's representative or screening committee. The interview provides an opportunity to observe the candidate's appearance, demeanor, and response to questions designed to probe the candidate's abilities, honesty, dependability, judgment, and initiative. During an interview, questions that may be in violation of local, state, and federal statutes relative to marital status, lifestyle, and equal employment opportunity must be avoided (Anderson, 1999; Lewis, Goodman, & Fandt, 2008; Nixon, 2007). Ethical dilemmas as well as various types of situations may be presented to the candidate to evaluate the candidate's problem-solving skills under pressure and predict decision-making behavior.

SECURITY SPOTLIGHT

If you are employed by an organization, how does the organization conduct background investigations during the recruitment process? Consider the investigative techniques the organization used with you when you applied for an open position there. If you can, meet with someone in the human resources department to learn whether the organization's approach to background investigations has changed over the years and, if so, what prompted those changes.

Some interesting situations develop when private organizations employ off-duty public law enforcement officers to work in a private security setting. Although the reasons (more training and the ability to exercise public police powers) for employment of off-duty public law enforcement officers are legitimate and understandable, private employers should be aware of the potential legal implications that may arise when private security personnel have public police powers. Several court cases illustrate the legal tightrope walked by private organizations that employ public police officers as private security personnel.

On October 15, 1994, Robert Abraham and Dennis Redding were observed shoplifting in the men's department of the Macy's store at the Cherry Hill Mall in Cherry Hill, New Jersey, by store security personnel. The store security personnel followed the shoplifting suspects into the mall parking lot while radioing mall security personnel for assistance. Kimberly Raso, a Cherry Hill police officer working off-duty as a mall security officer, responded to the radio call. Suspect Abraham entered and started a vehicle and backed up abruptly toward Officer Raso. The officer avoided being hit by Abraham's vehicle. However, Abraham hit a parked vehicle and pulled forward toward Raso, despite Raso's repeated commands to stop. Raso again jumped out of Abraham's path, drew her weapon, and fired one shot through the driver side window. Abraham died after driving away and hitting another parked car, a parking island, and a tree. Subsequently, Abraham's widow filed a multicount lawsuit against Officer Raso, the mall, the Township of Cherry Hill, and Macy's department store for assault, battery, negligent hiring, and violation of Abraham's constitutional right against unreasonable search and seizure by using excessive force.

Regarding the violation of Abraham's constitutional right, his widow alleged that Raso violated Section 1983 of the U.S. Code, which prohibits persons acting under the authority granted to them by the state from violating another person's constitutional rights. Generally, private organizations cannot be sued under Section 1983 because their employees do not act under the authority of state law. However, when a private entity hires off-duty police officers, it can expose itself to liability under Section 1983. In this case, the private employer was fortunate. The court determined that Raso was not liable because she identified herself as a police officer, retained police authority while off-duty per state law, and was acting in self-defense. In a different but similar case, an off-duty Seattle, Washington, police officer, employed by Safeway as a private security officer, arrested a suspected shoplifter, although the suspect did not steal merchandise. A jury found the police officer and the store liable under Section 1983 of the U.S. Code.

Similar situations appear in case law throughout the United States. Although the respondents to a lawsuit may prevail, the cost of litigation increases the cost of doing business. Adequate training is one key to limiting liability. Off-duty police officers should be trained in the law as it relates to private security operations. Most important, private employers who employ off-duty police officers in a security capacity should be aware that unique legal issues arise in a public police officer–private employer relationship (Nemeth, 2005; Ortmeier & Meese, 2010; Peck, 1999).

Negligent Hiring and Retention

The hiring of an employee must be more than an intuitive guess. Although state and federal privacy statutes make preemployment screening challenging, failure to complete a diligent inquiry into the suitability of persons employed may constitute **negligent hiring** and can have devastating consequences. Poor hiring decisions result in losses due to theft, high attrition rates, increased insurance claims and premiums, vicarious liability, and negligent hiring lawsuits. A thorough background investigation on a prospective employee is not a luxury, it is a necessity. As numerous court judgments indicate, employers are held liable for the actions of employees when the employer failed to investigate properly and the investigation would have uncovered the risk.

The elements of negligent hiring liability include the following:

- The person in question was an employee of the organization.
- The employee was unfit for employment in the position.
- The employer knew or should have known the employee was unfit.
- The plaintiff was injured by the employee during a contact connected with employment.
- The employer owed a duty of care to the plaintiff.
- The hiring of the employee was the proximate (legal) cause of the injury to the plaintiff (Cheeseman, 2010).

A thorough background investigation can help an organization develop policies that support responsible hiring. For example, Con-Way Freight, headquartered in Missouri, has an unwritten policy of denying employment to applicants with theft-related convictions. One applicant pursued a racial discrimination lawsuit against the company because her prior theft convictions disqualified her from being hired. A federal appeals court ruled in favor of Con-Way Freight, suggesting that the court saw the organization's unwritten policy as reasonable (Anderson, 2011).

An employer may also be held liable for negligent supervision or retention of an employee. **Negligent retention** involves a situation in which the employer does not take disciplinary or remedial action after becoming aware of a risk factor. To avoid negligent retention lawsuits, the employer must thoroughly investigate claims of misconduct, such as sexual harassment and violent behavior on the part of any employee. **Sexual harassment** refers to a pattern of behavior that involves unwelcomed lewd remarks, offensive touching, intimidation, and other conduct or communication of a sexual nature that is offensive to a reasonable person. Violent behavior may involve threats as well as acts resulting in physical contact (Bland, 2000; Cheeseman, 2010; Kovacich & Halibozek, 2003).

In 2000, the Hawaii State Occupational Safety and Health Division cited Xerox Corporation for failure to have or enforce workplace violence policies that might have prevented Xerox employee Byran Uyesugi from shooting seven coworkers to death in 1999. Publicized as the worst mass killing in Hawaii's history, the state alleged that Xerox allowed Uyesugi to return to work after a 1993 on-the-job violent outburst. The state's citation also stated that Xerox did not have an effective workplace violence prevention program and did not properly train managers to recognize and deal with potential employee violence ("Hawaii cites Xerox in worker shooting," 2000).

If an investigation uncovers a foreseeable threat, the employer is legally obligated to take appropriate action to remove the threat through reassignment or termination of the employee. The elements of negligent retention include the following:

- The employee was hired by the employer.
- After hiring, the employer became aware that the employee is a potential threat.
- The employer retains the employee in the position, knowing the risk.
- The plaintiff's injurious contact with the employee was connected with employment.
- The plaintiff was injured during the contact.

Employer liability for the actions of an employee may extend beyond the employment relationship. If a former employee applies for a new position elsewhere, and the prospective employer contacts the former employer for a reference, the former employer should provide dates of employment only. A former employer may be held liable if a generally positive reference is provided for a former employee, despite knowledge that the person is a potential threat (American Society for Industrial Security, 1998; Cheeseman, 2010; Hess & Wrobleski, 2009).

PERSONNEL MANAGEMENT

Appropriate recruitment and selection procedures represent only the initial steps in the personnel security and management cycle. The protection of human beings also involves training and scheduling, supervision and leadership, performance appraisal, promotion, the development of policies and procedures, discipline, possible demotion or termination, adherence to employment law, and employee retention strategies.

Training and Scheduling

Employee training falls into three broad categories: **preservice training**, **in-service training**, and **career enhancement**. Some occupations require prescribed preservice training prior to employment. In most states, police, fire, corrections, and security personnel have specific preservice training requirements. In-service training involves apprenticeships, coursework, seminars, internships, or on-the-job training. Career enhancement includes educational experiences that focus on specific job-related training as well as those experiences that promote personal development of the individual. Substantial returns on the training investment may be realized if an organization focuses on individual career enhancement of employees. Benefits in terms of increased productivity, improved morale, and loyalty to the organization are positive by-products of an individualized career training program.

Employees are scheduled according to a plan that identifies need and productivity requirements. Employee work schedules are generally based on the assumption that individuals are willing to work at 100 percent capacity. However, all employees cannot be expected to work continuously at top speed. Therefore, adequate personnel must be assigned to a set of tasks to ensure that productivity needs are met (Johnson, 2003; Lenahan, 2000; Ortmeier, 1999; Slater, 2000; R. V. Smith, 2000). A comprehensive discussion of training and scheduling is presented in Chapter 8.

Supervision and Leadership

The management of human resources involves both **supervision** and **leadership**. Not all supervisors make good leaders. Not all leaders make good supervisors. Ideally, good supervisors are also good leaders. The concept of leadership is often misunderstood because definitions of leadership vary and the process for leadership development is vague. However, substantial evidence exists that leads progressive thinkers to believe that leadership skills are essential for all workers in contemporary society (Drucker, 1994). This notion seems to be garnering attention at many organizations. Indeed, a new survey by the American Management Association and the Institute for Corporate Productivity found that nearly one in 10 employers has a leadership-development program that is open to all employees—not just a few talented individuals whose status will likely rise within the reporting hierarchy.

Leadership is every person's responsibility, and each employee can assume a leadership role. The chief executive officer (CEO) of an organization is probably the most important strategic initiator. The CEO plays a significant role in defining the organization's philosophy, values, mission, and priorities. The CEO is instrumental in creating the climate conducive to successful change and positive outcomes. The CEO is also in the best position to assist with the creation of a vision for the future.

Upper and middle managers should lead as well as manage. Rather than insulate themselves from line supervisors and operations personnel, upper and middle managers should interact with subordinates, assisting the latter through mentoring, coaching, and team building. Upper and middle managers are in an excellent position to act as conduits, monitoring for and adjusting the pace of change. Some people are attracted to supervisory positions for the wrong reasons. They are attracted by the power and control that comes with a position of authority. However, true leadership is not so much the exercise of power as it is the empowerment of others. Leadership is service to others that requires tremendous commitment, energy, patience, humility, and selflessness.

Line supervisors are in a pivotal leadership position to facilitate the achievement of goals. These supervisors help line personnel achieve accountability and performance objectives. It has been stated that the quantity and quality of performance can be linked directly to the quality of supervision. Line supervisors are in the best position to assume a leadership role in reviewing individual productivity, making recommendations for improvement and taking corrective action when appropriate.

Finally, regardless of the size of an organization or the number of levels of authority or supervision, it is the line person who has the most direct role in serving the mission of the organization. The line person is in the best position to directly impact the lives of the people who are served. Thus, considerable training and education resources should be expended to develop ethical leadership competencies in line as well as senior personnel. Further, ethical leadership development should be viewed as a lifelong process, not an event (Baker, 2011; Johnson, 2009; Meese & Ortmeier, 2004; Ortmeier, 1997, 2003; Ortmeier & Davis, 2012).

The universal phenomenon called leadership has been the subject of a great deal of research from both the theoretical and the practical points of view. Leadership has been described variously as a trait, the focus of group process, the art of inducing compliance, an exercise of influence, a kind of behavior or act, a form of persuasion, a power relationship, an instrument in goal attainment, an effective interaction, a differentiated role, and an initiation of structure (Bass, 1990). Leadership has also been defined as acts or behaviors (Carter, 1953), an act that results in others acting or responding in a shared direction (Shartle, 1956), the process of arranging a situation to achieve common goals (Bellows, 1959), and the initiation and maintenance of structure through interaction (Stogdill, 1959). It has been defined as directing and coordinating work relationships while showing consideration (Fiedler, 1967), an activity that mobilizes people to do something (Heifetz, 1994), and a social meaning-making process that takes place as a result of activity or work in a group (Drath & Palus, 1994).

Leadership should not be confused with supervision or management. Leadership, a concept that is broader than supervision, occurs anytime one attempts to motivate, influence, or mobilize an individual or group. Supervision and management, on the other hand, involve directing people toward organizational goals (Hersey & Blanchard, 1982). Although supervision and leadership may be exercised or exhibited by the same individual, both represent distinct concepts. Leadership produces change by establishing direction, aligning people, motivating, and inspiring. Supervision and management bring a measure of order and consistency to organizations by planning and budgeting, organizing and staffing, and controlling (Kotter, 1990). In other words, supervision and management follow leadership (Covey, 1998). Bennis (1993b) distinguished leadership from management along numerous dimensions (see Table 5–1). As one author stated, the leader is the one who climbs the tallest tree, surveys the situation, and cries out, "Wrong jungle!" The manager responds with "Shut up! We are making progress" (Covey, 1998).

Throughout the twentieth century, numerous theorists attempted to define leadership. An important breakthrough in understanding the concept of leadership occurred with the publication of *Leadership* by James MacGregor Burns in 1978. Burns characterized leadership as either **transactional leadership** (when one person takes the initiative, making contact with others

TABLE 5–1 Management versus Leadership	
A manager	**A leader**
Administers	Innovates
Is a copy	Is an original
Maintains	Develops
Focuses on systems and structure	Focuses on people
Relies on control	Inspires trust
Has a short-range view	Has a long-range perspective
Asks how and when	Asks what and why
Keeps an eye on the bottom line	Keeps an eye on the horizon
Accepts the status quo	Challenges the status quo
Is the classic good soldier	Is not dependent on others
Does things right	Does the right thing

for the purpose of the exchange of valued things) or **transformational leadership** (when one or more persons engage with others in a way that the leader and nonleader raise one another to higher levels of motivation and morality). Examples of transactional leadership through a contingent reward approach can be found in *The One Minute Manager* (Blanchard & Johnson, 1992). The function of transactional leadership is to maintain the organization's operation rather than to change it (Burns & Becker, 1988). Transformational leadership, on the other hand, focuses on the three behavior patterns of charisma, intellectual stimulation, and individualized consideration (Bass, 1985). Tichy and Ulrich (1984) presented the transformational leader as the model for future leadership excellence. They cited three identifiable activities associated with transformational leadership: creation of vision (view of a future state, mobilization of commitment), acceptance of a new mission, and institutionalization of change (new patterns of behavior must be adopted).

Although leadership originally focused on traits or inbred qualities that a person possessed since birth, today it is believed that leadership skills can be acquired or modified extensively through learning. These skills include competence to keep communication channels open and functioning effectively, interact socially, solve problems, plan, initiate action, and accept responsibility. Such skills are not inherited; they are learned (McGregor, 1960). Also critical to the success of the leader are skills in facilitation of team interaction, effective team problem solving, and training (Miskin & Gmelch, 1985).

An effective leader is likely to demonstrate excellent communications and interpersonal skills. A leader is likely to be both relations-oriented and task-oriented, manage conflict successfully, and mobilize and direct individuals toward higher objectives (Bass, 1981). Orton (1984) cited the importance of quality decision making, commitment, and the ability to employ situational strategies. Motivational, or person-oriented behaviors, tend to promote follower satisfaction, although they may not contribute to group productivity (Bass, 1981). McGregor (1966) suggested that people already possess motivation and desire full responsibility.

Leadership competence has also been expressed in terms of the ability to plan, organize, and set goals. Leaders must create clear-cut and measurable goals based on advice from all elements of a community. Likert (1961, 1967) discovered that high-producing leaders make clear what the objectives are and give people freedom to complete the task. Argyris (1964) suggested that it is in an individual's nature to be self-directed and to seek fulfillment through the exercise of initiative and responsibility. Hersey and Blanchard (1982) suggested that leadership involves goal setting, organizing, setting time lines, and directing. Contemporary experts often focus on leadership competencies. Bennis (1984, 1993a) identified four competencies of leadership:

- Management of attention—the ability to attract followers
- Management of meaning—the ability to communicate one's viewpoint or vision
- Management of trust—reliability
- Management of self—the ability to know one's skills and use them effectively

Daniel (1992) identified 13 leadership competencies. They include a goal orientation, a bottom-line focus, the ability to communicate and enforce standards, initiative, strategic influence, communication of confidence, and interpersonal sensitivity. Good leaders also develop and coach others, give performance feedback, collaborate and build teams, problem solve, project a good image and reputation, and possess self-confidence. Kotter (1993) pointed out that good leaders articulate a vision, involve people in decision making, and recognize and reward success. Drath and Palus (1994) stated that leaders must be trained to participate in, rather than exercise, leadership by learning community-oriented, meaning-making capacities, such as the capacity to understand oneself as both an individual and a socially embedded being; the capacity to understand systems in general as mutually related, interacting, and continually changing; the capacity to take the perspective of another; and the capacity to engage in dialogue. Leaders must be flexible (W. Bridges, 1994) and demonstrate initiative, integrity, and the ability to empower others (Davids, 1995).

Essential leadership competencies can be grouped into five major categories. The communications and related interpersonal competencies category addresses one's ability to communicate with diverse populations. Through motivational competencies, a person demonstrates the ability to encourage others and build proactive relationships. Problem-solving competencies focus on problem identification, critical and analytical thinking, and situation analysis. Planning and organizing competencies are used to create a vision, prioritize, delegate, and define goals and objectives. Actuation-implementation competencies address the ability to implement a vision and evaluate results (Ortmeier, 1997, 2006).

In the final analysis, the real test of leadership lies in the performance of the groups being led (Bass, 1981). The competencies applied in a particular circumstance depend on the situation, the people involved, the action to be taken, and the desired results (Byrnbauer & Tyson, 1984). Leadership skills are especially important in an asset protection environment. As the primary protection officers for most organizations, security personnel must respond to threats against people and property and assume control in dangerous situations. The ability to communicate well, maintain integrity, exercise effective judgment, reduce hostility, promote safety, and restore normal operations requires ethical leadership competence (More, Vito, & Walsh, 2012; Ortmeier, 1997, 2006; Ortmeier & Meese, 2010).

SECURITY SPOTLIGHT

Think of someone you know whom you consider an effective leader. In your view, what makes this individual an effective leader? Consider the individual's personal characteristics, skills, behaviors, and impact on others.

Motivation and Management

Ultimately, what motivates others depends on the culture and situation at hand (Adler, 2008; Hellriegel & Slocum, 2011; Ortmeier & Davis, 2012). However, several theories that illustrate how individual differences affect motivation are useful to managers' understanding of the reactions of people with whom they come in contact.

Abraham Maslow arranged individual motivational factors according to a hierarchy of needs. Maslow identified five types of human needs: physiological (the most basic), security, affiliation, esteem, and self-actualization (at the top of the needs hierarchy). Physiological needs include those that are basic to human survival: food, water, shelter, and clothing. Security needs address the desire for stability, safety, good health, and the absence of threats or pain. In an employment situation, security needs may be satisfied if employment is stable and expands employee competence and confidence of long-term employability. Affiliation needs include the desire for friendship, belonging, and love. When a person's affiliation needs are not met, dissatisfaction may lead to low productivity, absenteeism, stress-related behaviors, and psychological problems. Esteem needs include the desire for self-respect, personal achievement, and recognition from

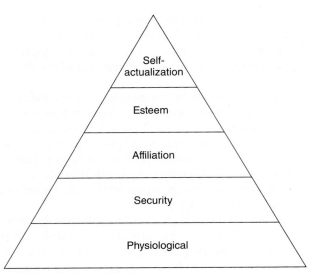

FIGURE 5–1   Maslow's hierarchy of needs.

others. To satisfy esteem needs, people desire prestige, status, and opportunities to demonstrate their competence and worth. Self-actualization needs, the highest level on Maslow's need hierarchy continuum, are achieved when one's desires for personal growth, self-fulfillment, and reaching one's full potential are realized. Maslow suggested that as one need is satisfied, motivation shifts to satisfying the next higher level of need (Maslow, 1987).

Clay Alderfer (1972) also viewed motivation from an individual needs perspective. In contrast to Maslow's five-level hierarchy of needs, however, Alderfer suggested three categories of need: existence, relatedness, and growth. Alderfer named his formulation Existence, Relatedness, and Growth (ERG) theory. Alderfer's ERG theory recognized Maslow's satisfaction-progression hypothesis, but the ERG theory also contains an additional dimension called the frustration-regression hypothesis. The frustration-regression hypothesis suggests that frustration (obstacles) encountered when seeking to meet higher-level needs leads to a reemergence of lower-level needs.

In his learned needs theory, David McClelland (1971) suggested that people develop needs through interaction with the surrounding environment. Thus, social contexts influence the learning of motivational needs. This theory contrasts with Maslow's theory that a needs hierarchy is inherent to human beings. According to McClelland, understanding the differences among individual motivators depends on the presence of three key motives: affiliation, achievement, and power.

According to expectancy theory, an individual, given choices, selects options that are perceived to provide the greatest rewards. Thus, the expectancy theory or model suggests that motivation to perform is based on an understanding of the relationship between performance and effort and the perception of the desirability of outcomes associated with different performance levels (Vroom, 1964).

Behavioral Assumptions and Leadership Style

Numerous factors and conditions operate to create behavioral assumptions that influence a person's perception of another individual or of specific circumstances (Adler & Towne, 2007).

Behavioral assumptions about people and how to motivate them influence leader behavior. If a leader harbors false assumptions about people, the beliefs can cause a leader to use inappropriate motivational techniques with followers. Correct behavioral assumptions can result in positive outcomes (Fournies, 2000). Although many of the assumptions and the accompanying models for direction and control of human beings were developed for managerial personnel, the concepts apply to leaders as well.

One of the most widely quoted models for recognizing and distinguishing assumptions about motivation was developed by Douglas McGregor in the 1950s. In his classic work, *The Human Side of Enterprise*, McGregor (1960) explored theoretical assumptions about human nature and human behavior as it relates to ethics, management, leadership, and motivation. McGregor proposed that two sets of leadership or managerial assumptions regarding human behavior appear to exist. He referred to the traditional view of leadership and managerial direction and control as Theory X and the view that leadership and management should be based on the integration of individual and organizational goals as Theory Y. Theory X includes the following leadership and managerial assumptions:

- The average human being has an inherent dislike of work and will avoid work if possible.
- Because of the dislike for work, most people must be coerced, controlled, directed, or threatened with punishment to get them to put forth adequate effort toward the achievement of objectives.
- The average human being is self-centered, prefers to be directed, wishes to avoid responsibility, has relatively little ambition, and wants security above all.

McGregor suggested that Theory X leaders and managers did not account for critical factors associated with motivation. These factors include a few simple generalizations about human beings. First, human beings are "wanting" animals. As soon as one need is satisfied, it is replaced with another. Second, human needs are organized in a hierarchy of importance. Third, a satisfied need is not a motivator of behavior. According to McGregor, Theory X leaders and managers ignore these generalizations. They direct and control through the exercise of authority.

Theory Y leaders and managers, on the other hand, operate with a different set of assumptions regarding human behavior. Theory Y assumptions include the following:

- The expenditure of physical and mental effort in work is as natural as play or rest.
- External control and the threat of punishment are not the only means for bringing about effort toward objectives. People will exercise self-direction and self-control in the service of objectives to which they are committed.
- Commitment to objectives is a function of the rewards associated with their achievement.
- The average human being learns, under proper conditions, to accept as well as seek responsibility.
- The capacity to exercise a relatively high degree of imagination, ingenuity, and creativity in the solution to problems is widely, not narrowly, distributed in the population.
- Under the conditions of modern industrial life, the intellectual potentialities of the average human being are only partially realized (McGregor, 1960).

Theory Y assumptions are dynamic rather than static and they represent significantly different implications for leadership and management than do Theory X assumptions. Theory Y assumptions focus on human growth. Theory X leaders and managers blame followers and workers for failure to achieve goals. Theory Y implies that poor productivity is more often the result of poor leadership and management. Theory Y focuses on the integration of goals: the creation of conditions through which members of a group or organization may achieve their own goals as well as the goals of the enterprise. Thus, motivation, the potential for growth, the ability to assume responsibility, and the readiness to work toward individual as well as group goals are present in all people. The leader's responsibility is to recognize, harness, and channel these characteristics toward common goals by creating a climate and methodology conducive to success (Gomez-Mejia & Balkin, 2012; Hellriegel, Jackson, & Slocum, 2005; McGregor, 1960).

An adaptation of Theory Y, called Theory Z, was created by William Ouchi in the early 1980s. Theory Z is a leadership and management style that advocates trusting followers and employees and creating an environment in which followers and employees feel as though they are an integral part of the group or organization. According to Theory Z, a relationship of trust promotes increased productivity and goal achievement (Ouchi, 1981).

The managerial grid developed by Robert Blake and Jane Mouton (1985) identifies five leadership styles that integrate varying degrees of concern for people with concern for production and goal achievement. Blake and Mouton's five leadership styles are arranged on a grid. The impoverished leadership style (1,1) demonstrates low concern for people, production, and goal achievement. Leaders utilizing this style exert minimal effort and wish to maintain the status quo. Through the country club style (1,9), leaders demonstrate high concern for people but low concern for production and goal achievement. Leaders create a secure and comfortable environment in the hope that followers will produce. Low concern for people and high concern for production and goal achievement characterize the produce or perish leadership style (9,1). Leaders use coercive powers to achieve results and show little concern for the personal needs of followers. Through the middle-of-the-road style (5,5), leaders strive to balance follower personal needs with a concern for productivity and goal achievement. Through the team style (9,9), leaders demonstrate high concern for people as well as productivity and goal achievement. Blake and Mouton believed that 9,9 was the optimal style. The 9,9 approach is consistent with McGregor's Theory Y. Leaders at 9,9 strive for teamwork and commitment to goal achievement among team members.

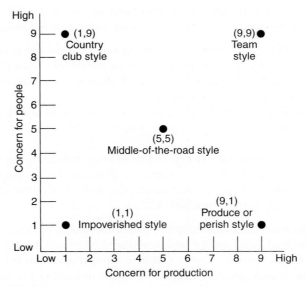

FIGURE 5–2 Managerial grid.

Paul Hersey and Ken Blanchard created a situational leadership model that suggests that supportive (people-centered) and directive (production- and goal-centered) leadership behaviors should be contingent on the readiness level of followers and workers. Supportive leadership behavior is consistent with open communication links between a leader and followers. Leaders listen, encourage, and involve followers in decision making. Directive leadership behaviors are consistent with situations requiring structure, control, direct supervision, and a reliance on one-way (leader-to-follower) communication. Follower readiness (maturity, experience, expertise) determines the follower's ability to set high and attainable task-related goals and willingness to assume responsibility for achieving the goals. The level of supportive or directive leadership behaviors is dependent on different levels of follower readiness. According to the situational leadership model, leaders use a delegating, participating, selling, or telling style, depending on follower readiness.

The leadership style with the highest probability of successfully and effectively inducing the desired behaviors of a follower who is skilled, competent, and motivated is that of delegating (S4). This involves monitoring and observing on the part of the leader. Keep in mind that this kind of empowering behavior should only be entered into with a follower who is in fact demonstrating at a sustained and acceptable level, otherwise the leader risks making followers feel abandoned. The participating leadership style (S3) is used to encourage, assist, and maintain communication between the leader and follower when the follower is performing at a sustained and acceptable level but may be feeling a little insecure yet about the leader completely backing off. They do not need to be told how to do the task anymore because the follower is performing, but they do need some help from their leader to build their confidence in their own ability. It is about getting the follower to admit that they have it. The selling style (S2) requires the most from a leader. It is used appropriately when a follower is starting to perform or is new to a task and is also willing, committed, or motivated to perform. The follower not only needs task direction from the leader like how and when to do the job but also support and encouragement for steps taken in the development direction. The telling style (S1) is used appropriately for those followers who not only are not performing but are either insecure about their ability to do so or downright unwilling to do the task. In this instance, followers need clear and specific instructions and possibly even consequences for nonperformance. Relationship or supportive behavior at this juncture could be misconstrued by followers as confirming their level of performance as acceptable if the leader is not careful to tie it incrementally and specifically with improvements in performance (Hersey & Blanchard, 1982; Hersey, Blanchard, & Johnson, 2008).

Although many leadership theories include motivation of others as an objective, the stated purpose of path-goal leadership is to enhance performance and satisfaction by focusing on motivation as a primary ingredient of leadership. The underlying assumption of path-goal leadership theory is that followers will be motivated if they believe that they are capable of performing tasks assigned, that their efforts will result in a certain result, and that the rewards for completing the tasks are worthwhile. Through the application of path-goal theory, the leader's challenge is to select and implement a leadership style that best meets a follower's motivational needs.

Although complex, the application of the path-goal theory of leadership achieves follower motivation through careful consideration of leadership behaviors, follower characteristics, and task characteristics. The theory suggests that each type of leader behavior (directive, supportive, participative, or achievement oriented) has a different impact on the follower. Which leadership behavior is motivating is contingent on follower and task characteristics (House, 1996; Meese & Ortmeier, 2004; Northouse, 2010).

Performance Appraisal

A **performance appraisal** is a systematic assessment of how well an employee is performing. It is used to establish standards, appraise employee performance, make objective human resource decisions, and provide documentation to support those decisions. An objective, well-documented performance appraisal, one conducted according to legally permissible human resource policies and procedures, may be the best defense against litigation arising from claims of inappropriate discipline or wrongful termination.

The appraisal focuses on performance, not on the person, and on strengths as well as weaknesses. The appraisal process should be designed to enhance performance. The ideal appraisal process includes the supervisor's evaluation of the employee and a self-evaluation made by the employee. In addition, some formal appraisal processes include peer evaluations and evaluations of the employee by clients or consumers of the employee's services (George & Jones, 2012; Ortmeier & Davis, 2012).

The appraisal meeting is one of the most important parts of the appraisal process. It is constructive, emphasizing strengths and pointing out areas for improvement, and is used as the means for achieving future goals. An appraisal meeting should be held in a trusting, private environment with adequate, uninterrupted time allotted for open, honest, and frank discussion. The content of the appraisal meeting is kept strictly confidential and shared with others on a need-to-know basis only, since the discussion may often include expressions of opinion and criticism.

Ultimately, good organizational reputation and successful achievement of an organization's goals are the result of excellent performance resulting from human effort. Regardless of the knowledge a supervisor possesses, operational success is measured through the line operator's performance. Thus, excellent performance by others is a primary goal of the supervisor (Sennewald, 2003). If an organization has a human performance problem, it probably has a supervision problem.

Promotion

Promotion serves as a means to fill job vacancies, as a reward and morale booster, and as an incentive for employees to perform better. Employees with the best records in production, quality of work, and cooperation should be the ones promoted. Due to financial constraints or the inability to measure performance objectively, salary increases or promotions may be difficult. Virtually all employees expect to be rewarded for a job well done. If promotion is difficult, even though a promotion is warranted, the progressive manager may choose to assist the employee with a transfer or new job search. If promotion from within is possible, it is accomplished through merit and ability to perform specific tasks. For those who are good candidates and seek promotion, the competition for promotion may be intense. Therefore, the promotion process should be fair, objective, and based on the candidate's ability to perform in the new position. A competitive process involves the use of standardized objective assessments of the candidate's qualifications and current performance as well as an evaluation of the candidate's strengths and weaknesses as predictions of future performance (Lewis, Goodman, & Fandt, 2008; Mosley, Megginson, & Pietri, 2005).

Failure to promote or reward employees appropriately can be extremely expensive. Arbitrary and discriminatory promotion practices can cost millions of dollars. On November 16, 2000, the Coca-Cola Company agreed to pay $156 million to settle a federal lawsuit brought by approximately 2,000 of its African-American employees. The largest dollar settlement ever in a racial discrimination lawsuit, the settlement also requires sweeping changes in, and outside monitoring of, Coca-Cola's promotion and compensation procedures. The changes were estimated to cost the company an additional $36 million. A $140 million cash settlement was agreed upon in a similar case involving Texaco and some of its employees in 1996 (Winter, 2000).

Discipline

The primary purpose of disciplinary action is to improve performance and behavior rather than punish or seek revenge. The disciplinary process serves to educate the employee. Except in rare instances when immediate termination may be warranted by policy or law, a system of uniformly applied **progressive discipline** should be used. Utilizing this system, corrective action progresses through the following steps: verbal warning, verbal warning noted in employee's record, written reprimand, suspension, demotion, or termination. The agency or business should also create a written policy that addresses uniform standards of behavior. The standards must focus on habitual tardiness and absenteeism, actual or attempted theft of company/agency property, fighting or bodily injury to others, malicious mischief and harassment, intoxication on duty, possession of illegal drugs or alcohol on duty, refusal or failure to comply with supervisory instructions, inattention to duties (sleeping, idleness), violation of published safety or health rules, unauthorized possession of weapons or explosives, and sexual harassment.

Failure to discipline appropriately can have far-reaching negative consequences, especially when illegal activities are involved. Obviously, theft of an organization's assets, liability associated with negligence, and settlements resulting from lawsuits exact a heavy toll from businesses and government operations. In some cases, losses result from extremely subtle activities. Even pilferage of employees' personal property, including lunch items from communal refrigerators in the workplace, impact negatively on employee morale. Low morale tends to reduce productivity, resulting in incalculable losses to an organization.

Discipline must be based on an objective standard. Several questions should be answered prior to any disciplinary action:

- Was the employee forewarned concerning consequences?
- Was the rule reasonable?
- Did the firm/agency verify the violation prior to disciplinary actions?
- Was the investigation thorough and fair?
- Is there substantial evidence of guilt?
- Were rules and penalties enforced uniformly?
- Was the disciplinary action appropriate to the situation?

If disciplinary action is warranted, employer reaction should be immediate, consistent, and fair. Disciplinary action is more likely to be viewed as fair if reasonable notice of rules of conduct is provided and employees are warned of the consequences for misbehavior. The employer representative should present the behavioral problem in specific terms by providing the date, time, and place of the incident as well as the organizational rule or policy violated. Due process requires that the employee be allowed to provide an explanation. Discussions should remain impersonal and agreement on the direction of behavioral change should be obtained (Certo & Certo, 2012; Slater, 2000).

Human Resource Policies and Procedures

Unique human resource situations arise that can be addressed with special policies and procedures. These situations involve problems associated with substance abuse, grievances, and claims of sexual harassment. All organizations should have written policies regarding substance abuse in the workplace. The policies must be communicated to each employee. Disciplinary procedures for policy violation must be consistent with applicable laws. Substance abuse issues are particularly sensitive, and related policies must be carefully crafted. Case law on the constitutionality of substance testing in the workplace generally is still inconclusive.

Clearly defined policies must also address employee grievances. Complaint procedures usually progress from informal to formal stages. In a nonunion organization, the procedure begins with the immediate supervisor and progresses through middle management to the CEO and, possibly, an outside arbitrator. In a unionized organization, a similar process is followed in liaison with union representatives. The complaint or grievance is filed by the employee with the union steward and progresses through a union committee and the union president toward outside arbitration if warranted and necessary.

By definition, sexual harassment involves any unwelcome sexual advances, requests, conduct, or actions motivated by hostility directed toward the victim's gender. A growing number of court cases address the subject of sexual harassment. The cases and decisions generally hold that an employer is liable if sexual harassment is unreasonably condoned, improperly investigated, or left uncorrected. All organizations should have a clear, written policy on sexual harassment and should train employees adequately on the policy. For assistance with creating policies of this nature, an organization can consult the policy guidelines established and published by the U.S. Equal Employment Opportunity Commission (EEOC).

The policy against sexual harassment should state that the tenets apply at the worksite as well as elsewhere during any other business-related activity, such as a business trip or office party. The policy should expressly provide that there will be no reprisals against any complainant, outline complaint procedures, and require all employees to sign and date a form acknowledging receipt of the policy statement. The policy should be conspicuously posted in at least two locations at the worksite. As an added precaution and protection against claims of sexual harassment, supervisors should obtain permission from a superior or the human resources (personnel) department before any adverse employment action is taken against a subordinate (Bland, 2000; George & Jones, 2012).

Employer–Employee Relations Laws

A great deal of legislation governs the relationship between employers and employees. Most of the laws address prospective, current, and former employee civil rights. The following summarizes the principal legislation in this area.

- Social Security Act of 1935. This Act established the social security system.
- Fair Labor Standards Act of 1938. This Act established minimum wages to be paid to employees, the 40-hour workweek, and regulations regarding child labor.
- The Equal Pay Act of 1963. This law provides for equal pay for equal work for individuals of different gender working in the same job classification.
- Title VII of the Civil Rights Act of 1964 (amended in 1972). This law prohibits employers of 15 or more persons from discriminating against any individual on the basis of race, color, gender, religious preference, or national origin. None of these factors may be used in any decisions with respect to hiring, promotion, discharge, compensation, training, or any other term, condition, or privilege associated with employment. Responsibility for enforcement of the law rests with the EEOC. Many state and local governments have similar legislation that parallels the federal law.
- Executive Order 11246 of the Civil Rights Act. This presidential order amended and added the requirement of affirmative action to Title VII of the Civil Rights Act of 1964.

- Age Discrimination in Employment Act of 1967 (amended in 1986). This law prohibits employment discrimination against a person because the person is 40 or older.
- Occupational Safety and Health Act of 1970. This law provides that employers must do everything possible to protect human resources by furnishing employees with a work environment that is free of recognizable hazards likely to cause serious injury or death. The Act is administered by the Occupational Safety and Health Administration (OSHA). The Act applies to virtually all private employers. It does not apply to local, state, or federal employees or workers covered by some other health and safety law, such as the Federal Coal Mine Safety and Health Act or the Atomic Energy Act of 1954.
- Pregnancy Discrimination Act of 1978. This law prohibits employers from discriminating against pregnant women.
- Worker Adjustment and Retraining Notification (WARN) Act of 1988. This law requires employers to notify workers of impending layoffs.
- Drug-Free Workplace Act of 1988. Covered employers under this law must implement certain policies to restrict employee drug use.
- Americans with Disabilities Act of 1990 (amended in 1991). The ADA prohibits discrimination against a disabled person with respect to employment, public accommodations and services, and services provided by private organizations. An employer may not discriminate against a disabled person because of the disability. The ADA also prohibits testing for or inquiring about a medical or physical disability until a job is offered. Preemployment inquiries regarding substance abuse must be limited to recent and current use. The Act prohibits any preemployment, promotion, or discharge test that is designed to disqualify persons with disabilities.
- The Employee Polygraph Protection Act of 1988. Subject to limited exceptions, this law prohibits or severely restricts the use of the polygraph or similar instruments by private employers. Under the Act, private employers cannot use a polygraph for preemployment screening. The Act further prohibits employers from requiring or requesting an employee to submit to a polygraph. A private employer cannot take any action against an employee for refusing to take a polygraph or for the results of such a test.
- Family and Medical Leave Act of 1993. This Act provides that employers must allow unpaid leave for childbirth, adoption, or illness.
- Health Insurance Portability and Accountability Act of 1996. This law contains mandatory national standards for electronic health-insurance transactions, including claims, enrollment, eligibility, payments, and benefits. Law also established standards to protect the privacy of personal health information (Cheeseman, 2010; Lee, 2003; Mann & Roberts, 2009; Ortmeier & Davis, 2012; U.S. Department of Health and Human Services, 2007).

A QUICK SURVEY

If you are, have been, or have considered being employed by an organization, have your civil rights as a current or potential employee ever been violated? Consider the following examples, and check any that apply:

- Denied employment because of your gender, age, religion, age, race, national origin, disability, or reproductive status (e.g., you were pregnant, recently gave birth, or adopted a child)
- Received wages that were below the minimum wage
- Required to work more than 40 hours in a week

- Paid less than someone else who was doing the same job
- Required to take a polygraph test during preemployment screening
- Privacy of personal health information was violated
- Not notified of an impending layoff
- Subjected to unsafe workplace conditions
- Other (describe)

If your civil rights as an employee were violated in any of these ways, how did you know a violation was occurring? (For example, were you familiar with employer–employee relations laws? Did you describe the situation to someone who informed you of the violation?) What (if any) actions did you take regarding the violation? What happened as a result of any actions you took?

Employee Retention

Much has been written about employee recruitment, selection, training, supervision, and evaluation. Yet little attention is directed toward **employee retention**, an issue in times of cost containment and a critical necessity when the unemployment rate is low. During periods of cost containment, retrenchment, or downsizing due to the need to contain or reduce expenses, decisions must be made regarding which employees to retain. Thus, organizations should have written reduction in force (RIF) policies in place. Even more critical is the need to recruit and retain capable employees when the economy is doing well and labor is scarce.

A new employee's adjustment to an organization and its culture is often difficult and stressful for both the organization and the individual. Existing employees also encounter stressful situations and demands. As a benefit to the organization and employees, a strategy for retention as well as recruitment of qualified personnel is necessary. Every effort should be made to retain the most productive people since the costs associated with recruitment and training of new employees can be considerable.

Employee retention begins with policies and open lines of communication designed to ensure realistic expectations on the part of new and existing employees. Preemployment interviews might be structured so the employer representative speaks first, describing the negative as well as the positive aspects of employment with the organization. This procedure provides time for the candidate to relax during the initial phase of the interview and presents a preview of what the applicant can expect if offered a position. The job description and specifications, compensation and benefits plan, and minimum activity requirements should be discussed. Negative aspects may include extensive travel requirements, long workdays, lack of support staff, and numerous time-sensitive projects. Honesty on the part of a candidate is expected. Employers should also be honest with job applicants. Lack of honesty and assurance of expectations at the beginning of an employee–employer relationship is a recipe for a costly disaster.

The next step in the employee retention process involves a proper orientation to the new employee's work environment. Prior to the new employee's start date, existing employees should be notified of the new person's impending arrival. Publication of a biographical statement and a photograph of the new employee is helpful. A staff member should be assigned as a peer guide, and the new employee should be introduced to other employees. Policies, procedures, worksite arrangements, and physical layout of the facility should be explained thoroughly.

Next, training of the new employee is absolutely essential, especially where skills are deficient. Initial training involves an orientation to the organization, its products or services, culture, and expectations. Ongoing in-service training is necessary to reinforce perishable technical skills, develop new skills, and review policies. Advanced training involves job specialization and management training, as well as personal and professional career development.

Although the retention of good employees cannot be guaranteed, proper orientation and training can assist with retention. Employees who demonstrate the knowledge, ability, and skills necessary to do a job well are difficult and expensive to replace. Encouraging good employees to remain with an organization should be one of management's highest priorities (Certo & Certo, 2012; R.V. Smith, 2000).

PERSONNEL INTEGRITY

Maintenance of personnel integrity involves more than effective preemployment screening procedures, periodic performance appraisals, and internal security controls. Personnel integrity also involves promotion of and adherence to a **code of ethics** and appropriate standards of professional conduct.

Ethics involves moral principles and focuses on the concept of right and wrong and standards of behavior. Unlike law or organizational policy, which are formally prescribed and enforced by a controlling authority, ethics is based on moral standards, whether illegal or not. These moral standards, or ethical **values**, are formed through the influence of others. These standards are concerned with the relationships between people and how they exist in peace and harmony.

Values are fundamental beliefs upon which personal decisions and conduct are based. Societal values are based on the norms of the community. Organizational values represent the beliefs of an organization. Professional values are reflected by an occupation or discipline. Personal values are based on individual beliefs. Values may be ethical or unethical. Gang members have values, but their behavior may be unethical. Behavior may be unethical, yet not illegal. Therefore, ethics assumes a special meaning and involves the systematic reflection on, and analysis of, morality. It takes on a specific form when someone assumes the role of a professional.

Ethical standards dictate behavior when law or precedent, which may prescribe behavior, does not exist. Whenever one possesses the power of discretional decision making, the decision should conform to what one ought to do even though law, policy, or precedent prescribing must-do behaviors is not available. The ends do not always justify the means. Conducting oneself according to an acceptable ethical standard, whether the profession has a code of ethics or not, means doing the right thing at the right time. Ethical conduct relates to qualities and actions that are morally correct, such as honesty and appropriate behavior. Unethical conduct refers to immoral behavior such as corrupt practices, dishonesty, and violation of acceptable standards.

In some cases, the law may permit or condone behavior that one might consider to be unethical. OSHA regulations, for example, establish minimum workplace health and safety standards. Yet, an employee's health and safety might be enhanced significantly if the employer sets standards that are higher than the OSHA-established minimums. Thus, the employer can adhere to the legal standard but it may be unethical to do so (Cheeseman, 2010).

Ethical behavior is based on virtues, values, morality, and appropriate choices. The premise of ethics is simple—people with high moral character make good moral choices. A genuine moral dilemma occurs in a situation from which the decision maker cannot emerge innocent, no matter what the decision. To what extent does a morally good end justify the use of an unethical, even illegal, means to achieve this end? Can falsifying a report to achieve a good end (convicting a known internal thief) be justification for using unethical, and possibly illegal, means to achieve this end? Could inaction lead to a lawsuit by the victim of the dangerous person who was not apprehended because ethical means were not available? Hopefully, when confronted with these types of decisions, people will make the morally correct choices (Johnson, 2009; Klockars, 1991).

The importance of choice in ethics is often confused with the notion that values are subjective and people merely choose their own set of values. This assumption is misleading because most ethical decisions involve a choice between already established possibilities. Personal values are rarely one's own values alone. By their very nature, values are shared and exist outside those who embrace the values. A person does not choose the alternative. Rather, the person chooses among alternatives.

Most people live in a pluralist society, an environment with no single code of ethics but several sets of values emanating from a variety of cultures and subcultures. Members of a criminal gang may subscribe to a particular set of values or code of ethics. They may not believe it unethical to kill a rival gang member. A security person may be reluctant to intervene to stop another's inappropriate behavior. Although it may be incorrect, this is the security person's choice. The individual challenge is to choose and follow an appropriate set of values.

Certain cognitive processes and socialization with others reinforce unethical conduct and influence the onset and proliferation of undesirable behavior. Thus, psychological and social forces help produce misconduct. However, one should not lose sight of the role of choice when engaged in unethical and unprofessional conduct. Given a security person's position of trust, unethical, even illegal, behavior results when the person makes a conscious decision to act in a way that is not appropriate to the situation. While circumstantial reasons, peer pressure, loyalties, social factors, or psychological problems may exist, the fundamental ingredient for unethical conduct is a conscious decision to abuse authority or engage in misconduct. Although the other factors may help perpetuate, justify, or excuse unethical conduct, it is an individual's conscious decision-making process that is ultimately determinative.

Potential ethical problem areas in security management include corruption, discrimination, violation of rights to privacy, violation of rights under the Constitution, negligence, use of excessive force, uncivil conduct, violation of organizational policies or procedures, and violations of the professional code of ethics. Each of these areas should be addressed in recruitment and in-service training programs.

Although real or imagined unethical behavior may involve a very small number of individuals, the negative impact of this behavior can be devastating. People engage in unethical conduct when they accept gratuities, practice racism and discrimination, misuse privileged communications and confidential information, misappropriate property, obstruct justice, engage in inappropriate behavior, and invoke a code of silence with respect to another person's unethical behavior (Byers, 2000; Foss, 2003; Ortmeier, 2006; Ortmeier & Meese, 2010; Solomon, 1996).

Morally correct values are at the core of ethical behavior. Doing the right thing at the right time, delivering what is promised, taking responsibility for one's own actions, and treating others with courtesy and respect lie at the heart of ethical standards. Most institutions, agencies, and professions have a code of ethics that prescribes ethical conduct. As exemplified by the ASIS International Code of Ethics, standards of ethical behavior must emanate from the organization as well as the individual.

ASIS International Code of Ethics

Preamble

Aware that the quality of professional security ultimately depends upon the willingness of practitioners to observe special standards of conduct and to manifest good faith in professional relationships, the American Society for Industrial Security adopted the following code of ethics and mandates its conscientious observance as a binding condition of membership in or affiliation with the Society:

ARTICLE I

A member shall perform professional duties in accordance with the law and the highest moral principles.

Ethical Considerations

I–1   A member shall abide by the law of the land in which the services are rendered and perform all duties in an honorable manner.

I–2   A member shall not knowingly become associated in responsibility for work with colleagues who do not conform to the law and these ethical standards.

I–3   A member shall be just and respect the rights of others in performing professional responsibilities.

ARTICLE II

A member shall observe the precepts of truthfulness, honesty, and integrity.

Ethical Considerations

II–1   A member shall disclose all relevant information to those having a right to know.

II–2   A right to know is a legally enforceable claim or demand by a person for disclosure of information by a member. Such a right does not depend upon prior knowledge by the person of the existence of the information to be disclosed.

II–3   A member shall not knowingly release misleading information nor encourage or otherwise participate in the release of such information.

ARTICLE III

A member shall be faithful and diligent in discharging professional responsibilities.

Ethical Considerations

III–1   A member is faithful when fair and steadfast in adherence to promises and commitments.

III–2   A member is diligent when employing best efforts in an assignment.

III–3   A member shall not act in matters involving conflicts of interest without appropriate disclosure and approval.

III–4   A member shall represent services or products fairly and truthfully.

ARTICLE IV

A member shall be competent in discharging professional responsibilities.

Ethical Considerations

IV–1   A member is competent who possesses and applies the skills and knowledge required for the task.

IV–2 A member shall not accept a task beyond the member's competence nor shall competence be claimed when not possessed.

Article V

A member shall safeguard confidential information and exercise due care to prevent its improper disclosure.

Ethical Considerations

V–1 Confidential information is non-public information, the disclosure of which is restricted.

V–2 Due care requires that the professional must not knowingly reveal confidential information or use a confidence to the disadvantage of the principal or to the advantage of the member or a third person unless the principal consents after full disclosure of all the facts. This confidentiality continues after the business relationship between the member and the principal has terminated.

V–3 A member who receives information and has not agreed to be bound by confidentiality is not bound from disclosing it. A member is not bound by confidential disclosures made of acts or omissions which constitute a violation of law.

V–4 Confidential disclosures made by a principal to a member are not recognized by law as privileged in a legal proceeding. The member may be required to testify in a legal proceeding to information received in confidence from the principal over the objection of the principal's counsel.

V–5 A member shall not disclose confidential information for personal gain without appropriate authorization.

Article VI

A member shall not maliciously injure the professional reputation or practice of colleagues, clients, or employers.

Ethical Considerations

VI–1 A member shall not comment falsely and with malice concerning a colleague's competence, performance, or professional capabilities.

VI–2 A member who knows, or has reasonable grounds to believe, that another member has failed to conform to the Society's Code of Ethics shall present such information to the Ethical Standards Committee in accordance with Article XIV of the Society's Bylaws (ASIS International, 2007).

Additional information regarding codes of ethics can be obtained by contacting the University of British Columbia's W. Maurice Young Centre for Applied Ethics at www.ethics.ubc.ca.

Summary

Personnel security involves the protection of, as well as protection from, individuals. Internally, personnel security begins with an effective recruitment, selection, and preemployment screening strategy. Externally, it involves the use of physical security and other measures to prevent human threats against personnel and property from materializing. Employers may be held liable for negligent hiring and retention of employees. This means that employers must complete a diligent inquiry into the suitability of persons to be employed and take appropriate action in cases of employee misconduct.

Personnel management involves training, scheduling, and effective supervision of employees as well as the development of leadership competency among all employees. Performance appraisal, promotion, and discipline of employees should follow established procedures and be consistent with applicable laws and rules promulgated by regulator agencies. Human resource management policies and procedures should be clearly defined and describe how employees should behave and what conduct is prohibited. Employers must also be thoroughly knowledgeable regarding laws that affect the employer–employee relationship. The maintenance of personnel integrity is vital to short-term and strategic individual and organizational success. All employees should adhere to a code of ethics and standards of professional conduct, and appropriate values should be promoted. Ethical behavior must emanate from the organization as well as the individual employee.

Key Terms

application
career enhancement
code of ethics
employee retention
ethical standards
ethics
Gramm-Leach-Bliley Act
in-service training
integrity tests
leadership

negligent hiring
negligent retention
performance appraisal
personnel integrity
personnel security
preemployment screening
preservice training
progressive discipline
promotion

psychological tests
recruitment
resume
selection
sexual harassment
supervision
transactional leadership
transformational leadership
values

Discussion Questions and Exercises

1. Describe the role of personnel security in the protective function.
2. Outline and describe the process for recruitment and selection of personnel.
3. Numerous federal and state statutes regulate the employer–employee relationship. Most statutes are designed to establish and protect employee rights, promote safety and health, and prevent discrimination. What impact do these laws have on the ability to manage human resources? Are statutory protections a hindrance or do they assist with achievement of organizational goals?
4. Human resource management requires effective supervision as well as leadership development for all personnel. Explain. Include a description of the difference between supervision and leadership in the explanation.
5. Distinguish ethics from law and policy. What role does maintenance of personal integrity play in the personnel security arena?

YOUR TURN: Demonstrating Ethical Leadership in the Face of Workplace Theft

Surveys indicate that many workers are reluctant to report unethical practices, including stealing, in the workplace. Although a federal law (Sarbanes-Oxley) was passed to counter unethical corporate behavior and protect workers who report unethical activities, many employees still face loss of their jobs or ridicule if they blow the whistle on corporate misconduct (Spherion, 2006).

Further, it has been reported that nearly 25 percent of young workers aged 18 to 24 do not believe that stealing office supplies for personal use is wrong. Many steal employer property, including pens, pencils, paper, self-adhesive notepads, and paper clips without regard to the activity's illegality. Employee theft costs American businesses over $40 billion each year (Wulfhorst, 2006).

Unethical behavior, dishonesty, and theft in the workplace often occur in a gradual incremental process. Theft, in particular, stems from a complex set of causes. Foremost among them is simply that an opportunity to steal arises, because the chances of getting caught are low. Additional causes include low workforce morale, employees' sense that they are being underpaid, and minimal consequences for getting caught stealing (Walsh, 2000).

As seemingly insignificant misconduct and theft go undetected, perpetrators often rationalize larger transgressions. Even high-level executives can become tempted to steal. Consider Dale Frantz, the former chief information officer of Auto Warehousing Company. Frantz embezzled more than $500,000 from his company during 2007–2009 and was sentenced to nearly 6 years in prison. He used a number of strategies to steal the funds, including writing up fraudulent invoices for expense reports and changing legitimate reports to maximize his reimbursements. In addition, he used company funds to buy computer equipment that he resold on the Internet (McMillan, 2010).

1. Do you believe that ethical behavior can be learned? If yes, who do you believe should take responsibility for teaching ethics?
2. If you observed a theft in your workplace, would you assume a leadership role and take action against the misconduct? If yes, what action(s) would you take?
3. Given your knowledge of the causes behind workplace theft, what steps would you advise organizations to take in order to discourage and minimize stealing by employees and thereby protect the organization's assets?
4. How would you go about strengthening your ethical leadership skills?

CHAPTER 6

Information, Communications, and Computer Security

LEARNING OBJECTIVES

After completing this chapter, the reader should be able to

- define critical and proprietary information as well as intellectual property.
- identify threats to critical information.
- explain the purpose of information security management.
- assess vulnerabilities to critical information.
- evaluate information protection strategies.
- develop policies, procedures, and systems for information protection.
- distinguish between government and business information.
- define and explain the four subfields of communications security.
- discuss the need for computer security policies, procedures, and systems.

INTRODUCTION

Information is a valuable asset and the lifeblood of almost every enterprise. As a basis for political power and societal defense, information and its protection are vital to national security. Information also represents one of the most important vehicles for survival within a competitive global economy. As a business resource, information is used for internal operations and strategic planning. Additionally, information provides the knowledge base necessary to identify risks and protect people and property. Information is extremely perishable and often costly to produce and protect.

Information critical to individuals and organizations surfaces in many forms. As defined by the **U.S. Economic Security Act of 1996**, the federal law relating to the protection of U.S. economic interests, **critical information** includes

> all forms and types of financial, business, scientific, technical, economic, or engineering information, including data, plans, tools, mechanisms, compounds, formulas, designs,

prototypes, processes, procedures, programs, codes, or commercial strategies, whether tangible or intangible, and however stored, compiled, or memorialized, if the owner has taken reasonable measures to keep such information confidential; and the information derives independent economic value, actual or potential, from not being generally known to, and not being readily ascertainable, acquired, or developed by legal means by the public (U.S. Congress, 1996).

Information may be defined and classified further in terms of its intended purpose and use. **Proprietary information** includes virtually any information belonging to an individual or organization. Proprietary information is identified through ownership or a possessory right. **Intellectual property** refers to information created through research and development, such as chemical formulas, software designs, and unique processes and procedures.

Threats to critical information come in numerous and varied forms. They include threats from environmental and natural disasters, fire, accidents, and intentional as well as unintentional human actions. Information can be physically or electronically damaged, destroyed, or stolen. Authorized as well as unauthorized persons can manipulate data, deny access to authorized users, conduct economic and political espionage, and improperly destroy critical information. Bribery and extortion as well as physical and electronic eavesdropping undermine efforts to safeguard proprietary information and intellectual property. Employees, guests, vendors, foreign nationals, and computer **hackers** (computer intruders) can sabotage databases. New vulnerabilities are created and discovered each day (American Society for Industrial Security, 1998; Boyce & Jennings, 2002; Jones, 2000; Maras, 2012; U.S. Department of Justice, Federal Bureau of Investigation, 2007). No longer confined to hard-copy recording and storage or oral exchanges, information can now be digitized through the use of computers. It can then be gathered, analyzed, stored, retrieved, intercepted, and manipulated electronically, without physical intrusion into the database. **Digitized information** is not distance-dependent or time-dependent. It can be transmitted around the globe in seconds. It can be transmitted or received without human presence; altered, destroyed, or removed without leaving a physical evidence trace; and transported on pocket-sized computer disks and drives.

Truly, the compromise of critical political and business information represents the greatest threat to governments and businesses today (Greenemeier, 2007; Moore, 2011; Raum, 1999; "Seven major U.S. agencies get 'F' in computer security," 2000). Yet, complacency and carelessness on the part of many individuals and organizations often leads to the unauthorized disclosure of information. Those concerned about unauthorized intrusion often overlook risks that emanate from activities such as cellular phone use and commerce on the **Internet**. In addition, many businesses engaged in the collection, storage, retrieval, and dissemination of personal financial information may disregard information protection guidelines mandated in the Gramm-Leach-Bliley Act and the **Fair Credit Reporting Act**. Both laws were created to protect consumer financial and credit information (Jesdanun, 2000; U.S. Federal Trade Commission, 2007).

In medieval times, forces attacking a castle had to overcome numerous obstacles before penetrating defenses and reaching the inner sanctum in the heart of the castle. As technology developed, the means for penetration became more sophisticated, but the primary targets were still people and tangible assets. In the information age, however, the manipulation, theft, or compromise of personal, business, and government data represents the primary threat to individuals and organizations. Thus, in today's environment, the database, likened to the coveted heart of the medieval castle, is the inner sanctum that requires protection (Aun, 2007; Lodin, 1999).

INFORMATION SECURITY RISK ASSESSMENT AND ANALYSIS

The purpose of **information security (INFOSEC)** is to protect information assets and systems against any internal or external threat that might endanger them. To accomplish INFOSEC goals, management utilizes **INFOSEC risk assessment and analysis** to determine the criticality of the information, its vulnerability, and the probability that a threat will materialize. Management must assess threats in terms of their seriousness, frequency, and immediacy. The cost of information replacement, waste, abuse, and liability associated with its unauthorized release must be evaluated. The cost effectiveness of the information safeguards recommended and implemented must also be determined.

Evaluating information assets and assessing the threats against them is not always an easy task. Such assets are often difficult to identify. In the early days of common law, information had no intrinsic value because it was not tangible. Today, the intangible asset identified as information does have value, but its worth can only be determined by calculating the political and financial impact of its loss. In addition, INFOSEC risk assessment and analysis is conducted within an environment full of uncertainty. Forecasts are often based on subjective evaluations as predictions of future events. There is no way to predict with any certainty how often an adverse event will occur or how severe the impact of the event will be.

In spite of the problems and challenges associated with INFOSEC risk assessment and analysis, the identification and safeguarding of critical information is imperative. Yet, security personnel are faced simultaneously with new threats, new technology, and new legislation. New information systems applications, software, and hardware are installed and implemented continuously. Changes in organizational structures and cultures also dictate the need for ongoing INFOSEC risk assessment and analysis. As the demand for enormous volumes of timely and accurate information increases, so do the responsibilities for threat identification and safeguards implementation (Anti-Phishing Working Group, 2007; Boyce & Jennings, 2002; Carroll, 1996; Gersh, 2000).

INFORMATION PROTECTION STRATEGIES

Virtually every individual or group is aware of the need to identify and protect vital information. Although most make an effort to safeguard data and systems, some enterprises are more diligent in their efforts than others. National governments have traditionally engaged in the protection of state secrets. Private businesses, on the other hand, have been slow to develop comprehensive policies, procedures, and strategies for the protection of proprietary information and intellectual property. Because of false assumptions about the nature and possibility of potential threats, businesses lose billions of dollars annually to poor and inadequate data protection.

Control Strategies

Discretionary and mandatory access control strategies govern approaches to information protection. Through **discretionary access control**, no one has an intrinsic right to view critical or sensitive information. Rather, access is allowed on a need-to-know basis. One is allowed to view only that which is vital to completion of assigned tasks. The problem with discretionary information access control is that the authorized user may inadvertently grant access to an unauthorized user. Discretionary access control is often used in private business enterprises.

Mandatory access control strategies can, on the other hand, trace their origins to restrictive legislation. The National Security Act of 1947, the Atomic Energy Act of 1954, and the National Security Decision Directive 145 of 1985 provide the foundation for mandatory access control policy. Two types of control structures, hierarchical and nonhierarchical, are established by the policy. The hierarchical structure includes four categories for classified information:

- **Top Secret.** Unauthorized disclosure of information in this category would cause *grave damage* to the United States.
- **Secret.** Unauthorized disclosure of information in this category could cause *damage* to the United States.
- **Confidential.** Unauthorized disclosure of information in this category would be *prejudicial to the interests* of the United States.
- **For Official Use Only.** Unclassified but sensitive. Unauthorized disclosure of this information would compromise trade secrets, give a contractor a competitive bidding advantage, or circumvent the Privacy Act of 1974.

Nonhierarchical INFOSEC falls within one of two categories: caveats and compartments. In government security operations, caveats refer to the nationality of the author or viewer of the classified information or object. Examples of caveats include NOFORN (no foreign access) and US/UK EYES ONLY (only U.S. and U.K. viewers allowed). Compartments refer to the subject matter of the information or object. Through background investigations, individuals are cleared to view material at different hierarchical levels based on a determination of the cleared person's reliability and loyalty to the government. The clearances correspond to the security categories assigned to the information or objects (Boyce & Jennings, 2002; Maras, 2012; U.S. Department of State, Overseas Security Advisory Council, 2007).

Despite efforts to protect government data, breaches still occur. In 2010, there were 662 breaches reported nationwide, according to the nonprofit Identity Theft Resource Center. Of that number, 15.7 percent comprised breaches of information managed by state and federal agencies or the military. One particular data breach exposed 207,000 records of army reservists in Colorado (Kalish, 2011).

A preoccupation with competition, maximizing net profit, increasing shareholder equity, or the process of juggling multiple tasks often relegate information protection to last place on most organizations' priority list. The prevailing attitude among many is that theft or inadvertent destruction of information cannot or will not happen to them. However, as has been demonstrated, substantial evidence suggests that lax INFOSEC can and does result in critical information loss. Consequently, many businesses, large and small, file for bankruptcy each year because they fail to anticipate the possibility of information loss and to implement adequate precautionary measures to protect this vital asset.

The business community might save itself considerable time, effort, and money by adopting information protection strategies that replicate those employed in government operations. Paralleling government efforts, **operations security (OPSEC)** involves information risk assessment and business intelligence activities in a process through which business operations are analyzed to identify potential intelligence indicators that competitors might scrutinize to gain a competitive advantage. OPSEC views operations from an adversary's perspective in an effort to seek out an organization's vulnerabilities and protect its critical information (OPSEC Professionals Society, 2007). This means that businesspeople must think like criminals, anticipating the threat. Private businesses seeking government contracts for classified projects are often required to submit OPSEC plans along with their bids. Ingredients to the development and implementation of an OPSEC plan include

- identification and valuation of the critical information.
- identification and analysis of a potential threat, including the threat's motivation and capabilities.

- evaluation of the organization's information vulnerabilities.
- assessment of the impact of a materialized threat as well as a cost–benefit analysis of any protective measure implemented.
- implementation of the most cost-effective protective measure options (countermeasures) (Jelen, 1994; OPSEC Professionals Society, 2007).

The rise of social networking media has presented businesses with yet another challenge related to INFOSEC: employees' increasing use of such media during the workday. Managers naturally are worried that when employees frequently check their Facebook page or use Twitter at their desks, productivity could suffer. But there is also the troubling possibility that employees could share confidential information about the company on these networking sites, or spread untrue information that could hurt the company's reputation or brand. To mitigate such risks, companies are considering developing policies governing when and how much employees can engage in social media during the workday (West & Bosley, 2011).

Aside from risks to businesses, the advent of social networking media also presents new dangers for individuals. The popularity of these services has made them a target for hackers and identity thieves. When individuals post too much personal information on a social networking site, they become susceptible to cyberstalking. The lesson for individuals is to be mindful of such dangers and carefully consider the kind of information posted on these sites.

Smart phones have only added to the security challenges facing users. Consider these anecdotes:

- In August 2010, Adam Savage, of the TV series *Mythbusters*, took a photo of his vehicle using his smart phone. The vehicle was in front of his home. He then posted the photo to his Twitter account and added the phrase, "off to work." The image contained metadata revealing the exact geographical location where the photo was taken. Anyone who saw the tweet now knew where Savage lived, what vehicle he drove, and what time he left for work.
- A 2009 article in *Wired* magazine contained the following story: "I ran a little experiment. On a sunny Saturday, I spotted a woman in Golden Gate Park taking a photo with a 3G iPhone. Because iPhones embed geodata into photos that users upload to Flickr or Picasa, iPhone shots can be automatically placed on a map. At home I searched the Flickr map, and score—a shot from today. I clicked through to the user's photostream and determined it was the woman I had seen earlier. After adjusting the settings so that only her shots appeared on the map, I saw a cluster of images in one location. Clicking on them revealed photos of an apartment interior . . . Now I know where she lives."

As these stories demonstrate, advancements in technology—including enhanced global positioning system (GPS) capabilities and smart phones with built-in GPS—have made management of privacy and security more difficult than ever (*Geotags and location-based social networking*, 2011) (see Table 6–1).

Information Security Legislation

In 1988, President Ronald Reagan signed National Security Decision Directive 298, which established the National Operations Security Program. The program is used to identify, control, and protect unclassified information associated with U.S. national security programs and activities. If not protected, the information could be used by adversaries or competitors against the interests of the United States. The directive names the director of the National Security Agency

TABLE 6–1 Tips for Securing New Devices

- Use strong discretion when storing, saving, or editing personal information on your smart phone or other device. Do not store passwords on devices or use them to store financial information such as credit card and bank account numbers.

- Recognize that a gaming console may represent a port of entry for cybercriminals into a household. Install antivirus software, two-way firewalls, antispyware, antiphishing, and safe search capabilities in Internet TV applications.

- Secure USB sticks by encrypting information, and install security software to protect portable hard drives.

- Guard against data loss by using a regular backup software program to ensure that all critical information and personal files from devices are safe in case of emergency.

Source: "Secure new devices in the new year," 2011.

(NSA) as the person in charge of interagency OPSEC training. The directive also includes a provision for the establishment and maintenance of the **Interagency OPSEC Support Staff (IOSS)**, which includes representatives from the NSA, FBI, CIA, U.S. Department of Energy, U.S. General Services Administration, U.S. Department of Defense, and other government organizations. The IOSS provides training to members of the security, intelligence, law enforcement, acquisitions, and research and development communities (Interagency OPSEC Support Staff, 2007).

The **National Industrial Security Program (NISP)** was established in 1993 by the President's Executive Order 12829. The NISP regulates private industry's access to classified government information. Although the National Security Council normally prescribes NISP policy, the U.S. Department of Defense and the U.S. Department of Energy as well as the CIA and Nuclear Regulatory Commission have equal NISP authority. The NISP publishes the NISP Operating Manual (NISPOM), a document that prescribes policies and procedures for all private contractors that have access to classified government information.

Learn more about the regulations governing protection of classified government information by accessing the NISPOM at www.fas.org/sgp/library/nispom.htm.

Information security countermeasure expenditures are easily justified when the cost–benefit ratio is calculated. Utilizing the guidelines associated with determining vulnerability to loss, coupled with the criticality and probability of loss as outlined in Chapter 7, the potential negative economic impact of the loss can be affirmed. The return on investment (ROI) or value-added contribution (VAC) is determined by comparing the cost of the countermeasure against the financial damage that could result if an information loss occurred.

Classification Systems for Business Information

As previously mentioned, business information may be classified utilizing a system that replicates government security classification systems. It takes little thought or effort to develop a protocol for classifying valuable business information that parallels a government system. Consider these classifications:

- *Company confidential, special control* is assigned to the business equivalent of top secret information. This classification is awarded to material with a loss value of 10 percent of the company's annual net profit.
- *Company confidential* information parallels government's secret classification. Compromise of company confidential information could result in a loss value of 1 percent of annual net profit.
- *Private confidential* information parallels government's confidential classification and refers to information that, if compromised, could embarrass an individual or damage the public reputation of the company.
- *Internal use only* (restricted) information refers to material that does not fit easily into one of the first three categories.

Access to information can be restricted through the use of **Sensitive Compartmented Information (SCI)** protocols. SCI refers to security systems, policies, and procedures designed to protect classified and sensitive information, not the information itself. Through SCI, access is restricted on a need-to-know basis.

A distinction must be made between government and private business information. At the government level, unclassified information falls within the public domain and must be released, upon request, under the conditions set forth in the U.S. Freedom of Information Act. Private businesses, on the other hand, subject to certain exceptions, retain ownership of or a possessory right to information. Thus, private organizations are not required to release proprietary information to the public (Carroll, 1996; U.S. National Archives and Records Administration, Information Security Oversight Office, 2007; Walsh, 2007).

Information protection goes beyond procedural controls involved in security classification systems. Complementary physical access controls, policies, personnel security, and computer logic protection are also necessary. Physical security, for example, is a basic first-line defense requirement for any information protection program. Security personnel, employee and guest identification systems, surveillance and alarm systems, automatic door controls, fences, lighting, signage, and crime prevention through environmental design (CPTED) all contribute to the protection of information.

Information Security Policies

Policies lie at the foundation of any information protection program. They serve to guide and inform employees and outsiders on how the program works and to whom it applies. Policies address minimum information protection standards and set forth procedures to be followed as information technology (IT) advances. Authorization policies establish permission levels for access to information. Special audit assignments describe provisions for information protection oversight responsibilities. Legal protection policies remind staff of special agreements in place to maintain confidentiality and rights to privacy (American Society for Industrial Security, 1998; Greer & Plunkett, 2007).

Policies should also address procedures for destroying or disposing of information that is no longer needed. Too often, critical information is discarded carelessly. In most jurisdictions, discarded materials placed in a trash can or dumpster are considered abandoned property, thus belonging to no one. An adversary may remove the discarded materials and use the information against its former owner. Shredding or pulping documents and appropriate deletion of information stored in an electronic medium helps to prevent adversarial access to information.

The Role of Personnel Security

Unauthorized persons often view or have access to intellectual property, trade secrets, and sensitive information. Therefore, personnel security is also an integral part of the information protection program. Effective preemployment screening is essential. Personnel integrity must be maintained, and minimum standards of professional conduct must be adhered to. Security managers, in conjunction with other personnel, can establish guidelines for classifying critical information. The guidelines should address the specific protection level associated with each classification and ensure that classification levels are conspicuously posted on critical material. Passwords, coding, and physically secured areas should be utilized along with a record of who possesses critical information and why. Such information is shared on a strict need-to-know basis.

Subject to certain exceptions discussed in Chapter 5, "Personnel Security through Leadership and Ethics," employees can be required to sign **information protection–related agreements**. Nondisclosure agreements, usually directed toward individuals with authorized access to critical information, prohibit disclosure of the information to individuals or organizations not specified in the agreement. Secrecy agreements are used to prevent release of information by those who inadvertently come into contact with the information. Noncompete agreements are used to prevent an employee from leaving the company and obtaining employment with a competitor. Noncompete agreements have some legal limitations. The agreement cannot deny an individual the right to earn a living, even with a competitor. However, such agreements may be enforceable if the competitor is nearby or the former employee transfers company information to the new employer. Those who wish to create information protection–related agreements are advised to consult with legal counsel regarding language appropriate for each agreement.

Other personnel security–related information protection tools include the use of seals, audiovisual equipment restrictions, and financial records controls. Tamper-evident seals and other indicative systems can be used as a deterrent and indicate when controlled access to information has been breached. The use of cameras and audio–video recording equipment on site can be restricted. Access to accounting, shipping, receiving, payroll, bank records, income, and similar financial information should be restricted to those who have an absolute need to view and use the information.

Copyrights, Patents, and Trademarks

Many types of proprietary information and intellectual property can be protected through the use of copyrights, patents, and trademarks. A **copyright** seeks to prevent unauthorized use of virtually any creative writing or expression that can be physically observed. Materials that may be copyrighted include items such as books, periodicals, lectures, videos, maps, musical compositions, drawings, and works of art. A copyright infringement occurs whenever one copies a substantial and important part of a copyrighted work without permission. However, under the fair use doctrine, the law does permit limited unauthorized use of copyrighted materials. Fair use applies to brief quotations of copyrighted material used in a news report, for review in a scholarly work, in a parody, or by a teacher or student to illustrate a lesson. For individuals, a copyright expires 70 years after the death of the creator. For business copyright registrants, a copyright expires 120 years from the date of creation or 95 years from the date of the first publication, whichever is shorter.

A **patent** protects a novel, useful, and nonobvious invention from unauthorized replication or use. The subject matter for patents includes processes, machines, compositions of matter, improvements to existing processes, machines, and compositions of matter, designs of articles for manufacture, living material invented by a person, and asexually reproduced plants. Patent infringement occurs when the replication or use of a patent is unauthorized. Under the public use doctrine, a patent may not be granted if an invention is used by the public more than 1 year prior to the patent's application filing. Twenty-year terms are granted to patents on processes and manufactured articles. Design patents have a 14-year life term.

A **trademark** protects against unauthorized use of a distinctive mark, name, word, symbol, or device that identifies the product of a particular commercial enterprise. In addition, trade names (service marks) and quality certification marks can be protected by trademarks. The term for the original registration of a trademark is 10 years. Trademark registrations can be renewed for an unlimited number of 10-year terms. However, once a trademark becomes a common term (generic name) for a product or service, it loses its federal trademark law protection (Cheeseman, 2010; Greer & Plunkett, 2007; Moore, 2011).

Although an appropriate integration of physical and INFOSEC is necessary to protect sensitive and critical information, most organizations still separate physical and INFOSEC operations. However, as organizations pass through the twenty-first century, many realize that the principal asset in need of security is the organization's information. Thus, the role of organizational security may change to reflect the need to integrate all aspects of security into a comprehensive asset protection program. Physical, information, and computer (logical) access will be controlled by a single entity. One large company is leading the trend toward this type of integration. Microsoft Corporation of Redmond, Washington, combined its physical, information, and corporate security groups under the chief INFOSEC director (Gersh, 2000).

SECURITY SPOTLIGHT

Consider the educational institution where you are enrolled or the organization where you are employed. What information do you think most needs to be protected at this institution or organization? Why?

Talk with someone in your institution's or organization's security department to gain insights into the following questions:

1. *What strategies does the institution or organization use to protect that information? Has your school or employer ever experienced damage to or theft of important information? If so, how did the breach happen? What were the consequences? And what steps did the institution or organization take to prevent a recurrence?*

COMMUNICATIONS SECURITY

Communications security (COMSEC) includes all efforts to protect information transmitted by voice, electronic impulse, wire, microwave links, fiber-optic lines, and satellite systems from unauthorized interception. An interception can be accomplished by wiretapping, through interception of electrical impulses radiated (emanated) from computer equipment, and by concealing audio or visual transmitters on the victim's premises (bugging).

Communications security subfields include line, transmission, cryptographic, emanations, and technical security. Communications line security involves protection of telephone cables, junction boxes, switches, modulator–demodulator sets (modem), local area networks (LAN), and telephone space radio. **Line security** is effective only on lines within an individual's or organization's control. **Encryption** of communications through **cryptography** is the best method for defeating an assault by unauthorized communications line interception (wiretapping). Additionally, communications lines and equipment should be inaccessible or secured within locked or guarded perimeters. Tamper-resistant telephones and communications apparatus are also recommended.

Wiretaps are difficult to detect. Most make no noise, and they consume very little detectable energy. Especially vulnerable are **space radio communications**, which include cellular phones, marine and mobile radio telephones, microwave radio relays, satellite radio, and high-frequency radio used in remote locations of the world. Although interception of microwave and satellite signals typically requires special equipment, cellular phone and radio telephone communications can be monitored with devices purchased at a local retail electronics store. Therefore, line transmissions and telephones should not be used for communicating extremely sensitive information. Meeting in person may be the best alternative.

Transmission security involves policies and procedures that place an adversarial interceptor at a disadvantage. Authentication of the parties to the transmission, communications logs, speech privacy equipment (scramblers), and access control are primary communications transmission protection mechanisms. No telephone number that provides direct access to a computer should be published. Computer hackers can capture telephone numbers from computers with dial-up service.

Cryptography is the science of secret writing, and **cryptographic security** involves a transformation (secret writing) of the data being transmitted to render it unintelligible to an unauthorized interceptor. Cryptography involves the use of nonexclusive codes and **ciphers**. A code can represent a complete message, such as the Associated Public-Safety Communications Officers (APCO) 10-code system used by most police and security dispatchers (Adams, 2007). A cipher is the one-to-one correspondence between the characters in the actual message (plain text) with the characters or symbols in the secret writing equivalent (crypto text). Converting plain text to crypto text is referred to as an **encryption**, while conversion of crypto text to plain text is referred to as a **decryption**. If the same character or symbol key is used for encryption and decryption, the cipher is symmetric. If different keys are used, the cipher is asymmetric. The only unbreakable cipher is a randomly produced cipher that is used only once. With time and perseverance, virtually any multiple-use cipher can be compromised (broken) by a knowledgeable and determined person.

A detailed explanation of cryptography and cryptographic security is beyond the scope of this book. The foregoing simply provides a brief explanation of the science and uses of secret writing. No security system, policy, or procedure is absolute. Cryptographic security is no exception. It must not be viewed as a substitute for other information protection procedures or good physical or personnel security. When part of the overall security package, cryptography can be an asset protection tool, but only when it is used infrequently and reserved for the most sensitive information. When purchasing crypto devices and software, the manager must realize that someone, at least the manufacturer, has a key to the cipher.

Cryptography is one of the most secure methods of preventing unauthorized interception of data communications. Therefore, the hostile attacker must resort to acquiring the data before it is encrypted. Since traditional methods, such as wiretapping, require some physical intrusion, the attacker can resort to interception of emanations (emissions) from electronic equipment. Acoustical (sound) and electromagnetic (electrical and mechanical parts interplay) emanations from equipment can be captured by the directional pickup devices available today. Utilizing **emanations security** to prevent compromise of information through the capture of acoustical emanations, rooms that contain computer and other radiating electronic communications equipment can be constructed with sound deadening materials such as acoustical tiles. Emanations security can also be enhanced if one uses nonradiating electronic equipment or equipment designed to shield radiating electronic equipment from outside emanations interception.

Technical security in communications involves prevention of adverse technical surveillance through the use of intrusion devices. Technical surveillance devices include microphones and wires as well as mechanical instruments used to listen through a heating duct or conduit. Carrier current devices, which capture voice communications by utilizing a facility's internal electric wiring system, visual-optical (CCTV) devices, and telephone bugging instruments are also used. COMSEC defenses against technical surveillance include physical inspection (search) for devices, electrical wiring and equipment inspections, metal and harmonic detectors for electronic bugs, and instruments that detect electronic emanations from bugging devices (Association for Computing Machinery, 2007; Maras, 2012).

A QUICK SURVEY

Which of the following COMSEC efforts are made at your educational institution or the organization where you are employed?

- Line security
- Transmission security
- Cryptographic security
- Emanations security
- Technical security

Why do you think your school or employer has invested in the particular COMSEC efforts you have identified? How effective have these measures been?

COMPUTER SECURITY

To understand computer security, it is valuable first to grasp threats to computers that have evolved since the technology was first developed, and then to examine protection strategies that have emerged.

Computer Crime and Cybercrime

Since the early 1970s, computer technology has dramatically changed the way information is acquired, transmitted, analyzed, stored, and retrieved. It has transformed the work world and is part of almost everyone's daily life. Computerized cash registers exist at most retail checkout counters. Onboard computers are used to detect problems in late-model vehicles. Sophisticated systems manipulate national defense information and manage global financial transactions.

Along with the increased use of computers has come a commensurate increase in computer-related crime. No longer limited to interference by a few high-tech hackers (unauthorized computer database intruders), numerous forms of computer-related crime are now common. Computer crime is limited only by the ingenuity of the criminal and the offender's knowledge of computer technology. With computers, funds can be stolen from financial institutions without physical intrusion. Business trade secrets and classified government information can be obtained without physical penetration of a business or country. Personal information stored in electronic databases can be manipulated, destroyed, or used for unethical or illegal purposes.

Computer crime is defined generally as any crime committed with computer technology. It may involve the actual destruction of computer hardware and software, or it may be used as a tool in a criminal enterprise. More commonly, it involves unauthorized access (or exceeding authorization) to a computer's database. Computers have been used to steal patient records ("Hacker steals patient records," 2000) as well as credit card and bank account numbers, and to commit fraud, theft, burglary, embezzlement, espionage, sabotage, and even murder. Computers are also used in support of criminal enterprises associated with child pornography, prostitution, gambling, illegal drugs, money laundering, identity theft, and organized crime. Misuse of computers in the workplace, such as computer game-playing and personal communications, divert and consume employee production time.

Internet access increases risk and threats to sensitive and proprietary information. **Cybercrime** (computer crime committed using the Internet) is increasing. As the Internet becomes the primary electronic vehicle for transmitting information throughout the world, thousands more new users log onto the World Wide Web each day. With the vast amount of information in transit and little thought given to its security, the opportunities for data theft and destruction increase. Studies indicate that nearly half of all computer software and equipment are prone to a computer virus (disruptive software infections) malware (malicious software), or web browser attacks. Many contain passwords that can be breached by a computer hacker in a few minutes. To gain access to computer databases, the hacker or cybercriminal searches for the path of least resistance, exploiting security-related weaknesses that provide unimpeded access to targeted networks (Adams, 2000b; Aun, 2007; Boni & Kovacich, 2000; Lam, Beekey, & Cayo, 2003; Maras, 2012; Moore, 2011).

The advent of **cloud computing**—the accessing of computing resources owned and operated by a third-party provider on a consolidated basis in data-center locations—has raised additional security challenges. Cloud computing promises to help companies achieve flexibility and agility as well as reduce costs associated with their use of IT. For instance, instead of owning the hardware and software necessary to operate a customer call center, a company can pay a vendor to manage the computers, code, and data involved in this business function. The company pays the vendor only for the number of "seats" (employees responding to customer calls) it needs at the time. It can thus scale that number up or down to reflect business cycles; for instance, scaling up during the holiday selling season. Despite these advantages, cloud computing has raised questions in some executives' minds about how secure and private their data (especially associated with customers) will be in the cloud. Vendors hosting the data centers and hardware, for example, may hire people without doing sufficient background screening. And when data goes into the cloud, a software bug could accidentally reveal it (Brenner, 2010).

As businesses and governments increase their reliance on IT-based networks, cyberattacks are a critical and growing threat. One study revealed that as much as 58 percent of executives polled across 19 countries say that their companies have lost control of sensitive personal information, and in almost 60 percent of cases this was not an isolated event. Indeed, cybercrime has become a global industry: 45 percent of financial services representatives believe that fraud attacks against their institutions have made use of card data stolen in bulk over communications networks. Over the next 6 years, the U.S. federal government expects to spend $55 billion on cybersecurity (*New waves of growth*, 2011).

Currently, the total indirect and direct costs associated with computer crime may approach hundreds of billions of dollars annually. One study put average losses from cybercrime incidents at $875,146, a number that encompasses a broad range of business impacts—including financial loss, intellectual property theft, compromising of a company's brand or reputation, loss of shareholder value, and lawsuits (Brenner, 2010).

Losses can be devastating, and the threat often originates with unknown sources. On March 2, 1998, the night before former Microsoft Chairperson Bill Gates was scheduled to testify at a congressional committee hearing, a computer hacker launched a massive attack against computers using Microsoft network software. The hacker targeted computers in government and universities running Windows NT software (Bigelow, 1998). On May 19, 1998, a group of seven hackers testified before a U.S. Senate Government Affairs Committee that they could destroy the foundation of the Internet within 30 minutes by interfering with the links between long-distance carriers.

According to the hackers, poor computer security can be blamed on the multitude of Internet networks, user ignorance, inadequate security measures in software programs, and lack of government regulation. According to the congressional General Accounting Office, U.S. State Department computers, the Federal Reserve System, individual credit and medical records, utilities, and stock exchanges are also at risk (Aun, 2007; Bigelow, 1998; Moore, 2011).

The personal computer, now found in most businesses and many homes, linked through cyberspace by the Internet, eliminates the need for an actual physical intrusion into a business, government agency, or personal residence. Advances in technology have created a virtual world with no physical boundaries or barriers. Virtual organizations, which exist mostly in cyberspace, have been created. These organizations exist but are not represented in a physical form. This phenomenon presents new challenges for security personnel.

Hackers

Hackers pose one of the greatest threats to computer systems. Kevin Mitnick, named to the FBI's most-wanted list, was captured in 1995 in Raleigh, North Carolina, after a nationwide hunt aided by Tsutomu Shimomura, a researcher at the University of California–San Diego (UCSD), Supercomputer Center. The Mitnick case highlighted the damage a single hacker can cause. Mitnick stole computer passwords, damaged UCSD and University of Southern California computers, allegedly pilfered software and product plans valued in the millions of dollars from high-tech companies, and installed programs that caused severe damage (Krasnowski, 1997). Other than UCSD, some of Mitnick's victims included Motorola, Novell, Nokia, and Sun Microsystems. Although it was never proven, Mitnick was alleged to have penetrated the computer system at the North American Air Defense Command. At sentencing, Mitnick was ordered to pay $4,125 to the companies that suffered millions of dollars in damages and ordered to serve 3 years and 10 months in prison. With credit for time served awaiting trial, Mitnick was released from prison on January 21, 2000, under the condition that he not use computers, software, cell phones, televisions, modems, or other computer system or Internet-accessible equipment for a period of 3 years.

The Mitnick case is by no means an isolated incident. Consider the following hacker attacks initiated in the ensuing years:

1996

- On March 29, federal authorities identified Julio Cesar Ardita, a 21-year-old Buenos Aires, Argentina, student as the person who tapped into sensitive research on satellites and penetrated computer systems in at least six countries. Ardita gained access to U.S. government computers, including the U.S. Navy's system, and to numerous university computer laboratories.

- On August 13, a computer hacker vandalized the U.S. Justice Department's Internet home page. The hacker posted obscenities and antigovernment graffiti on the Department's website.

1998

- In August, a security risk was discovered in Qualcomm's popular Eudora electronic mail software. By exploiting a flaw in the software, a hacker disguised a program to look like a harmless address on the Internet. Computer users who clicked on the address would inadvertently allow hackers access to the innocent user's own computer.

1999

- On August 30, a hacker gained access to millions of email messages by exploiting a flaw in the software program used by Microsoft to run its free Hotmail web service for 40 million people worldwide. The hacker revealed how access was gained and forced Microsoft to shut the service down to make necessary repairs.
- In October, computer security experts discovered an electronic reconnaissance program designed to infect Windows-based personal computers without the user's knowledge and to transmit the captured data to a Russian website.

2000

- In February, electronic vandals crippled some of the world's most popular Internet sites by using dozens of powerful computers to flood the sites with false data. The hackers created the virtual traffic jams by penetrating less secure computer workstations and servers with high-speed Internet connections and installing stealth programs on the hijacked computers. Next, the hackers activated the programs, flooding target sites with bogus requests, thus jamming the target sites. Buy.com, Yahoo!, eBay, ETrade.com, Amazon.com, and the Cable News Network (CNN) fell under the attack before computer security technicians were able to shield the computers from assault. Before service was restored, the companies lost sales to millions of customers. The attacks on the websites also caused stock prices to drop on some of the high-technology companies.
- In March, Max Butler, a computer expert working as an informant for the FBI, faced charges himself for allegedly hacking into U.S. Department of Defense, U.S. Air Force, NASA, and other sensitive computer databases.
- In May, Canadian police arrested a 15-year-old Montreal-area hacker for disabling CNN's website on February 8, 2000 (Koerner, 2000). The boy subsequently pleaded guilty to 56 computer crime-related charges. From his bedroom overlooking a golf course, the boy penetrated numerous websites, including those of Yahoo.com, Amazon.com, and eBay. com, causing an estimated $1.7 billion in damages (Brooke, 2001).
- Also in May, computer viruses swamped computer networks around the world. The viruses were spread through Microsoft Outlook email applications. The virus arrived disguised as a "joke" or "I LOVE YOU" email with an attached file. When the unsuspecting user opened the attachment, the virus emailed itself to everyone on the computer's address book and attacked music, graphics, and other files and programs on the computer's hard drive. The virus hit over 82 million computers and infected 2.6 million email sites, causing an estimated $6.7 billion in damage (Markoff, 2000).

- On September 21, a 20-year-old Mission Viejo, California, hacker was arrested by U.S. authorities for allegedly hacking into computers operated by the National Aeronautics and Space Administration's Jet Propulsion Laboratory in Pasadena, California, as well as computer systems in prestigious universities such as Harvard, Stanford, and Cornell. The man also allegedly penetrated hundreds of other computers throughout the United States and, in some cases, used stolen credit card numbers to purchase thousands of dollars worth of merchandise (Lota, 2000).

- On October 25, Microsoft security personnel discovered a computer system penetration that allowed access to source codes (software blueprints) under development. No software was compromised in this case. With source codes in their possession, however, competitors could write programs to challenge Microsoft products. The codes can also be used to identify software flaws, making database break-ins and virus infection easier (Johnson, 2000).

2001

- Antiglobalization computer hackers penetrated the computer systems of the World Economic Forum in Davos, Switzerland. More than 3,000 of the world's top executives, bankers, politicians, scholars, and journalists were in attendance. The hackers obtained the names, email addresses, and phone numbers of 27,000 people along with 1,400 credit card numbers and 3,200 passwords (Giussani, 2001).

- At the height of the energy crisis in the spring of 2001, a key computer system used to monitor electricity transmission throughout the state of California was targeted by hackers. Although the hackers experienced limited success, the incident exposed security weaknesses within the system ("Hackers target state's electricity," 2001).

2007

- An investigation in Florida revealed that thieves used data stolen from TJX, the parent company of T.J. Maxx and other retailers, to steal $8 million in merchandise from Wal-Mart stores. The thieves created fictitious credit cards and used the fake cards to purchase Wal-Mart and Sam's Club gift cards. Subsequently, the gift cards were used to buy goods in stores in 50 Florida counties (Greenemeier, 2007).

2011

- On January 28, two men were arrested and charged with being involved in a security breach targeting AT&T and Apple iPad users in 2010. According to prosecutors, the men created a computer script called the "iPad 3G Account Slurper" and used it to attack AT&T's servers over several days in June. They designed the script to imitate the behavior of an iPad 3G so it would trick AT&T's servers into thinking that they were communicating with an actual iPad. In addition, the script was designed to randomly guess the unique identifier for each iPad, which resulted in the iPad's email address being displayed on AT&T's website. The attack allegedly allowed the men to obtain email addresses and personal information of roughly 120,000 iPad users (Bray, 2011).

- In January, the FBI executed more than 40 search warrants throughout the United States as part of an ongoing investigation into coordinated cyberattacks against major companies and organizations. Britain's Metropolitan Police Service executed additional search warrants and arrested five people for their alleged role in the attacks (FBI National Press Office, 2011).

Email Wiretapping, Phishing, and Vishing

Utilizing an email wiretap, individuals and organizations can surreptitiously obtain business intelligence and proprietary information from another group. For example, if company A wants to acquire company B, company A can email a purchase proposal to company B. Included in the email is an invisible computer code designed to forward internal company B email to company A. As the target company's employees communicate with each other regarding the proposal, a copy of each email is sent to company A. According to one expert, such email wiretaps may become more common than computer viruses (Hopper, 2001).

Thieves use computer technology to steal someone's identity in a variety of ways. **Phishing** is a form of identity theft through which the perpetrator uses email and malicious websites to obtain personal information. Phishing has become the leading type of Internet-based fraud. In the typical phishing attack, the scammer sends an email message to the victim. The email message appears legitimate and requests that the victim update, or verify, personal information by clicking on a link in the email message. The link connects the victim to what appears to be a legitimate company web page such as EBay, PayPal, or Amazon.com. However, the web page is actually a well-designed fake that only appears authentic. When the victim supplies the personal information requested, the victim is actually supplying the information directly to the scammer.

A more recent version of phishing, named **vishing**, is similar to the traditional phishing scam. But instead of being directed by an email to an Internet site, the victim is asked to provide personal information via telephone, using Voice over Internet Protocol (VOIP), which enables telephone calls to be made over the Internet. Victims enticed to place the call are led through a series of voice-prompted menus that request account numbers, passwords, and other sensitive information. In another version of vishing, the victim is contacted by phone instead of email. The caller is a live person or a recorded message that directs the victim to take action to protect a personal account (U.S. Department of Justice, Federal Bureau of Investigation, 2007).

Employees often use their employer's computer system to shop online, thus providing an opportunity for the phishing criminal to penetrate an employer's database. In addition, many employees engage in employment-related work on personal as well as business computers. They transport data between the personal and organizational system with a computer disk or flash drive, increasing the likelihood of cross-contamination.

According to FBI statistics, the number of reported Internet fraud cases tripled during 2002. Nearly 50,000 Internet fraud complaints were referred to prosecutors. By the end of 2006, almost 100,000 complaints were referred for investigation or prosecution. The most common complaints involve online auction fraud, nondelivery of merchandise, credit card fraud, fictitious investment schemes, and Internet identity theft. The FBI's Internet Fraud Complaint Center, operated in cooperation with the National White Collar Crime Center, also received nearly 150,000 nonfraud complaints involving unsolicited email, child pornography, and computer intrusions (Anderson, 2003; U.S. Department of Justice, Federal Bureau of Investigation, 2007). From January 1, 2010, through December 31, 2010, the Complaint Center received 303,809 complaint submissions, the second highest total in the center's 10-year history (Internet Crime Complaint Center Annual Report, 2011).

The Challenge of Computer Security

Such disruptions illustrate how vulnerable computer systems are and how reliance on technology can be devastating. As individuals and organizations are enticed to place their personal, financial, political, planning, and medical information online and into computer databases, consideration must be given to the security of the systems and the data they contain. Unauthorized computer system intruders can easily falsify their digital fingerprints, thus making offenders difficult to trace and locate. In addition, the high-tech workplace itself is often an antisecurity environment. In an effort to promote ingenuity, industriousness, wealth, and a casual no-holds-barred workplace culture, many organizations are lax on computer security procedures development and enforcement. Even when computer security is a priority, experts trained to protect systems and software are often unavailable (McCollum, 2000; Volonino, Anzaldua, & Godwin, 2007).

The security of computer databases is probably one of the greatest challenges facing business and government in the twenty-first century. During testimony before the U.S. Congress in 1997, FBI Director Louis Freeh intimated that the greatest threat facing U.S. national security was economic crime, most of which could occur through the illegal use of computer technology. In a government computer security audit conducted in 2000, one-fourth of the U.S. government's 24 major agency computer systems failed the review. The U.S. Departments of Justice, Interior, Labor, and Health and Human Services were among the agencies cited for poor computer security. In one agency, all 1,100 computer users had access to sensitive information, while in another agency, 20,000 users without written authorization had access to one system ("Seven major U.S. agencies get 'F' in computer security," 2000).

Threats against government agencies and personnel do not always originate from likely sources. On December 4, 2000, a threatening email was sent to President Clinton via the Internet from a small town of about 4,000 in Nebraska. The email originated in the community's only parochial high school. A student was using one of the school's computers—against school policy—to check messages on his private email account. The student left the computer unattended for a few moments. In his absence, two other boys used the student's email account to send the threatening message to the White House. The Secret Service traced the email to the school's computer and the innocent student's email account. No charges were filed. However, the case demonstrates the seriousness and far-reaching implications of seemingly minor pranks. The expense associated with the U.S. Secret Service investigation and the harm caused by lax security measures on the innocent student's part illustrate the impact of poor computer security ("Threatening email traced to computer at CC," 2000).

Computer Protection Strategies

Security for computer systems and data must include strategies to protect the equipment, software, and information stored in the database. Examples of strategies follow:

- Physical security is used to prevent fire or access to computer terminals.
- Administrative controls can be implemented to maintain accountability for those who have legitimate access to the system and the database. Such controls can restrict employees' access to a company's computer network and/or software on a client computer. They can also be used to control employees' use of the Internet, their selection of websites visited, and the times when they can use the Internet. For examples, employees may be allowed to use the network only during specified hours.
- Logical controls may be used to restrict access to information stored in the database. **Passwords** (unique identifiers), biometrics (fingerprints and retinal scans), and data encryption are examples of logical controls. **Firewalls**, the electronic security tools that screen traffic before allowing access to computer networks, can be used to restrict access to databases. Intrusion by a **computer virus** (destructive software program) and **malware** (malicious

TABLE 6–2 Five Tips for Safe Computer Use

- Use an antivirus. Keep it updated so computers stay protected from the latest threats.
- Update computers. Patches and security fixes are vital to eliminating vulnerabilities that cybercriminals can exploit.
- Routinely scan systems and connected devices. Most antimalware products enable individuals and organizations to set up a daily scan that runs automatically.
- Strengthen and change passwords. Maximize password security by combining upper/lowercase letters, numbers, and symbols. Avoid expected combinations (such as birthdays and addresses), and change passwords every 3 months.
- Secure business interests. Protect business networks and sensitive data by investing in solutions that protect all threat vectors: endpoints, email, and the web.

Source: "Five tips for safe computer use," 2011.

software) can be prevented through the use of antivirus and malware-unfriendly software. Access by **spyware** (software that collects personal information without consent) or **computer worm** (a form of malware that exploits vulnerabilities in operating systems/ networks) can be prevented through the installation of antispyware programs. Backup duplicate files should be maintained to prevent total loss of data due to criminal activity, accident, or natural disaster. Internet privacy can be protected through appropriate technological advances, self-regulation by e-commerce organizations, and government regulation (Boyce & Jennings, 2002; Harley, 2000; Hutchinson & Warren, 2001; Lodin, 1999; Maras, 2012; Volonino, Anzaldua, & Godwin, 2007) (see Table 6–2).

One recent survey of 12,847 business and technology executives around the world indicated that computer security is very much on executives' minds. Responses revealed that in the 2011, businesses' top IT security priorities would include end-user firewalls, biometrics, data leakage prevention, encryption of removable media, and the provision of locks and keys for computer hardware. Yet the same survey showed that laws and regulations are the primary drivers— in a list of five drivers—that executives cited to justify IT security expenditures. Professional judgment came in as the third-most commonly cited driver, and potential liability or exposure came in fifth (last) place in the list (Brenner, 2010).

Well over a decade ago, Carroll (1996) suggested 10 principles for safeguarding sensitive computer information. These principles are still relevant today:

1. Simple security. No person shall view information that has a classification that exceeds the person's security clearance.
2. Nonaccessibility. No sensitive information will be released to any person or object except according to established procedures.
3. Lattice. The classification of an information item or clearance of a person or process shall consist of its (their) hierarchical classification or clearance plus the sum of all compartment classifications or clearances.
4. Star (*). No person shall write or submit classified information to another person or object whose classification is lower than the subject classified information.
5. First integrity. No computer program will accept information from a less privileged (lower level) computer program.

6. Second integrity. No computer program shall write into a higher privileged program.
7. Labeling. All classified information items are clearly labeled with their classification in human-readable and machine-readable formats.
8. Tranquility. The security classification of information can be changed only according to established procedures.
9. Audit ability. All relevant security-related actions performed on sensitive information items will be recorded in an indelible record.
10. Trusted software. Trusted software will be permitted to violate principles if necessary.

Identification of vulnerabilities and investigation of computer crime are often difficult because traditional criminal identification and investigative methods are inappropriate. Most law enforcement agency expertise focuses on street crime, not computer crime. Cyperspace and computer security and investigations require different skills. The computer "nerds" of today will be the sophisticated IT hackers of tomorrow. However, resources are available to security professionals and computer systems administrators. Some of these resources have been available for over a decade:

- the Computer Emergency Response Team (CERT)
- the Systems Administration, Networking, and Security (SCANS) and its Global Incident Analysis Center
- the FBI's National Infrastructure Protection Center (NIPC) (Sniffen, 2001).

Organizations and businesses may report Internet-related crime to their local law enforcement authority or the federal investigative authority responsible for enforcement of Internet crime–related statutes. The types of cybercrimes that can trigger involvement of federal agencies are shown in Table 6–3.

The FBI established Regional Computer Forensic Laboratories (RCFLs) to retrieve computer data that can be used as evidence (Hughes, 2000). RCFLs are nationwide resources that work in conjunction with local law enforcement. In 2002, President Bush signed the **Cyber Security Research and Development Act** into law. The legislation dedicated more than $900 million over 5 years to research and education programs designed to help secure the nation's technology infrastructure against terrorists and computer hackers ("Bush signs Cyber Security Act," 2002). In addition, information is available on several computer-security news websites, including Security Watch, Packet-Storm, Security-Focus, and DHS/Cybersecurity Outreach, News & Events. Purdue University maintains the computer security research–oriented Center for Education and Research in Information Assurance and Security (CERIAS) website. Princeton University's Secure Internet Programming Laboratory, the University of California, Davis' Computer Security Laboratory, and the NSA's Central Security Service are also valuable resources (Neeley, 2000; U.S. National Security Agency, 2011).

Computer security information sources:

U.S. Computer Emergency Readiness Team at www.us-cert.gov/federal

U.S. Department of Homeland Security, Information Analysis and Infrastructure Protection at www.whitehouse.gov/issues/homeland-security

The National White Collar Crime Center at www.nw3c.org

TABLE 6–3 Cybercrime Types and Federal Agencies	
Cybercrime type	**Federal agencies to contact**
Computer intrusion (hacking)	• FBI • NIPC • Secret Service
Password trafficking	• FBI • NIPC • Secret Service
Theft of trade secrets	• FBI
Internet harassment	• FBI
Counterfeiting	• U.S. Secret Service
Child pornography	• FBI • U.S. Customs and Border Protection, if imported
Trademark infringement	• FBI • U.S. Customs and Border Protection, if imported
Copyright infringement	• FBI • U.S. Customs and Border Protection, if imported
Internet fraud	• FBI • Federal Trade Commission • Securities and Exchange Commission, if securities fraud
Internet bomb threats	• FBI • Bureau of Alcohol, Tobacco, Firearms, and Explosives (ATF)
Illegal trafficking of explosives or firearms	• FBI • ATF

Sources: "How to report Internet crimes," 2000; Maras, 2012; Moore, 2011.

The training and education of cybersecurity professionals is also an essential element in protecting computer and information systems. To this end, the National Science Foundation (NSF), in collaboration with the American Association of Community Colleges (AACC), developed a plan to establish cybersecurity-workforce foundation-skill standards, certification assessments, and cybersecurity training programs. The plan proposed to establish and maintain comprehensive cybersecurity education programs as well as continue professional training for cybersecurity personnel (American Association of Community Colleges, 2002). Several community colleges have established cybersecurity professional training programs (The Chronicle of Higher Education, 2011).

SECURITY SPOTLIGHT

Think about the computers you own and use—desktop, laptop, mobile device. What steps have you taken to protect your computing equipment from threats? How effective have these steps been? What options are available to you for improving security for the computing equipment you own?

Summary

Critical information includes all forms and types of tangible and intangible information. The protection of critical information is vital to organizations, nations, and individuals. Threats to critical information include environmental and natural disasters, fire, accidents, and intentional and unintentional human actions. The purpose of INFOSEC is to protect information assets and systems. Through assessment and analysis techniques developed through OPSEC and COMSEC, threats to information can be evaluated and strategies implemented to protect critical information. Effective INFOSEC policies and procedures lay the foundation for information protection.

The introduction of computers dramatically altered the manner through which information is collected, transmitted, analyzed, stored, and retrieved. Crimes committed with computers are increasing for many reasons, not the least of which is that physical contact with a victim or actual intrusion into a protected area are not necessary. Protection of computer systems and databases includes the use of physical security as well as administrative and logical controls. Computer security breaches require nontraditional investigative skills.

Key Terms

ciphers
cloud computing
communications security (COMSEC)
computer crime
computer virus
computer worm
copyright
critical information
cryptographic security
cryptography
cybercrime
Cyber Security Research and Development Act
decryption
digitized information
discretionary access control
emanations security

encryption
Fair Credit Reporting Act
firewalls
hackers
information
information protection–related agreements
information security (INFOSEC)
INFOSEC risk assessment and analysis
intellectual property
Interagency OPSEC Support Staff (IOSS)
Internet
line security
malware
mandatory access control

National Industrial Security Program (NISP)
operations security (OPSEC)
passwords
patent
phishing
proprietary information
Sensitive Compartmented Information (SCI)
space radio communications
spyware
technical security
trademark
transmission security
U.S. Economic Security Act of 1996
vishing

Discussion Questions and Exercises

1. What is the purpose of INFOSEC?
2. Define and contrast critical information, proprietary information, and intellectual property.
3. Identify three threats to critical information and describe strategies to protect the information. What role does risk assessment play in the information protection function?
4. How should information protection strategies be evaluated?
5. What is COMSEC? Describe the four COMSEC subfields. How does COMSEC differ from other protection strategies?
6. What should be included in an OPSEC plan?
7. Outline and describe the strategies for protecting computer systems and databases.
8. Discuss methods for protecting *personal* information, including data that may be stored in one's personal computer.
9. Traditional criminal identification and investigation methods are inappropriate for computer-related crime. Explain.

YOUR TURN: Preventing Cyberstalking

Advances in GPS technology, the proliferation of smart phones with embedded GPS, and the increasing popularity of social networking media such as Facebook, Twitter, and Flickr have all made cyberstalking easier than ever. To protect yourself and your loved ones from this particularly dangerous form of cybercrime, learn as much as you can about these technologies. Next, consider the following questions:

1. How do these technological advances enable cyberstalkers to capture and use personal information about potential victims?
2. In what ways (if any) are you and your loved ones currently using such technologies that could make you vulnerable to cyberstalking?
3. What changes could you make in your own and your loved ones' use of these technologies to enhance your and your loved ones' safety from stalking?

PART THREE

Security Management

This part focuses on security management principles and practices. Chapter 7 examines the nature of risk and emphasizes the need for risk assessment, security surveys, and planning, providing techniques including crime prevention through environmental design (CPTED). Chapter 8 addresses the implementation and administration of action plans selected, providing insight into themes including the administrative process, ethical leadership, staffing, facilities management, contract services, and organizational performance assessment. Chapter 9 discusses and describes civil and criminal investigations; explains how to conduct business, criminal, and national intelligence operations; and provides suggestions for writing effective reports.

CHAPTER 7

Risk Assessment, Security Surveys, and Planning

LEARNING OBJECTIVES

After completing this chapter, the reader should be able to

- define risk and risk assessment.
- list and describe five distinct types of risk that threaten individuals and organizations.
- discuss management techniques associated with risk elimination, reduction, and mitigation.
- evaluate risks to determine vulnerability, probability, and criticality of loss.
- conduct a risk assessment utilizing subjective as well as objective measurements.
- conduct a security survey.
- analyze needs identified through a risk assessment.
- develop appropriate courses of action to eliminate, reduce, or mitigate risks identified in a risk assessment.
- discuss the importance of the budget process.
- demonstrate knowledge of crime prevention through environmental design.
- demonstrate knowledge of emergency planning.

INTRODUCTION

A major focus for security management is the concept of risk. Subjective information as well as objective measurement instruments (such as a security survey) are used in an essential first step of a planning process designed to identify and assess the threat posed by each risk source. As the planning process proceeds, security personnel make recommendations and determine the financial impact of any potential risk mitigation strategy. Planning activities also involve preparation for emergency situations and consideration of anticrime measures available through environmental manipulation.

THE CONCEPT OF RISK

Risk Defined

Risk may be defined as the possibility of suffering harm or loss, exposure to the probability of loss or damage, an element of uncertainty, or the possibility that results of an action may not be consistent with the planned or expected outcomes. A decision maker evaluates risk conditions to predict or estimate the likelihood of certain outcomes. From a security perspective, risk management is defined as the process involved in the anticipation, recognition, and appraisal of a risk and the initiation of action to eliminate the risk entirely or reduce the threat of harm to an acceptable level. A risk involves a known or foreseeable threat to an organization's assets: people, property, information, or reputation. Risk cannot be totally eliminated. However, effective loss prevention programs can reduce risk and its impact to the lowest possible level. An effective risk management program can maximize asset protection while minimizing protection costs (Fay, 2000; Fischer & Janoski, 2000; Kovacich & Halibozek, 2003; Robbins & Coulter, 2009; Simonsen, 1998; Sweet, 2006).

Types of Risk

Generally, risk is associated with natural phenomena or threats created by human agents. Natural risks arise from earthquakes, volcanic eruptions, floods, and storms. Risks created by human beings include acts or failures to act that lead to crime, accidents, or environmental disaster. As many as five distinct types of risk threaten individuals and organizations:

- **Pure risk** exists when there is a potential for injury, damage, or loss with no possible benefit. Potential medical claims resulting from accidents may be classified as pure risks. The threat of criminal attack and natural disaster are also examples of pure risk. These events increase operating costs, a form of loss.
- **Dynamic risk** exists when threat conditions fluctuate. Examples include areas of the world that are subject to weather extremes, communities that depend on seasonal tourism, or changing political conditions.
- **Speculative risk** exists when there is a potential for benefit or loss, depending on the consequences of an activity or inactivity. New product research and development as well as business ventures into new markets are examples of speculative risk.
- **Static risk** is constant and unchanging. If a critical component needed to manufacture a product is provided by a single patented source, the risk associated with the loss of the supplier is static. The risk is always present. Loss of the sole source means the product manufacturing process is stopped.
- Finally, some threats involve **inherent risk**. These risks are unavoidable because of the nature of the business, such as transportation and mining, or because the business is operating in an extremely competitive marketplace.

Failure to recognize and take action against a risk is potentially costly for any organization. Materialized risk increases the cost of doing business, may increase insurance premiums, and exposes the organization to criminal as well as civil liability. In addition to direct costs associated with a reduction in organizational assets, indirect costs are incurred when the organization experiences loss of market, reputation, or competitive edge. Losses in shareholder equity and reductions in productivity also result. A risk event may adversely impact profitability for private business and affect a public organization's ability to render services (American Society for Industrial Security, 1998; Collins, 2008; Fay, 2000).

RISK ASSESSMENT AND MANAGEMENT TECHNIQUES

Risk assessment and management involve processes that have been used by insurance companies for decades. They involve deliberate actions aimed at loss prevention and mitigation of risk. Through the use of **risk management techniques**, security professionals anticipate, recognize, and analyze potential risks and loss-creating threats, and implement strategies to mitigate loss and damage. A comprehensive risk management program involves

- the identification of risks and vulnerabilities through continuous threat assessment.
- analysis of the risks and vulnerabilities identified.
- optimization of cost-effective risk management alternatives designed to avoid, reduce, spread, or transfer identified risk (Fischer & Janoski, 2000; U.S. Department of Justice, Bureau of Justice Assistance, 2005a, 2005b).

Externally, a risk management program utilizes the society and its legal system to protect assets against threats. Internally, a risk management program incorporates administrative controls as well as physical, personnel, and information security policies and procedures to protect assets against threats and hazards.

Elimination, Reduction, Mitigation

Risk management techniques involve elimination of the risk if possible, reducing the probability that a loss will occur, and mitigating the damage if a threat materializes. Total elimination of risk is difficult, although mitigation of risk is possible in some cases, given the right circumstances. Removing all flammable materials from a facility will eliminate the threat of fire fueled by the flammable materials. It will not, however, eliminate the threat of fire fueled by a different source.

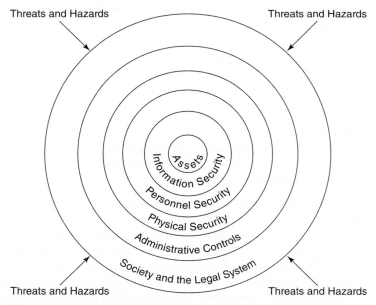

FIGURE 7–1   Risk Management/Asset Protection System

Implementing an effective access control system may reduce the possibility of criminal attack. Appropriate disaster planning may mitigate damage, minimize injuries, and save lives in the event of a hurricane, a tornado, or an earthquake.

Three Factors Influencing Risk Management Decisions

The security professional must consider three factors that influence risk management decisions: vulnerability (exposure), probability (likelihood), and criticality (impact). Each of these factors must be considered and the cost of asset protection balanced against the potential for loss.

VULNERABILITY   First, the security professional must consider vulnerability to loss. If an individual or organization is vulnerable, it is exposed to the possibility that the risk or threat will materialize. Little or no physical security certainly exposes physical assets, personnel, and information to attack. Factors to consider when calculating vulnerability include threat identification as well as location, accessibility, adequacy of security measures, and availability of response personnel and emergency equipment. A vulnerability scale may appear as follows:

- Highly vulnerable (3). Assets are open to unimpeded and direct access or are protected by security systems that are easily defeated.
- Moderately vulnerable (2). Assets are protected by access-resistant mechanisms such as patrols, remotely monitored alarm systems, and other physical security measures that can be defeated with the application of moderate force.
- Low vulnerability (1). Assets are difficult to access directly and are protected by adequate patrols, remote alarm sensors and reporting systems, physical barriers, and a response force sufficient to overcome perpetrator resistance.

PROBABILITY   Second, the probability of loss must be considered. The security manager must consider the likelihood a threat will materialize and pursue measures to prevent an incident or mitigate the negative impact of an event. A facility, because of a general lack of physical security, could be extremely vulnerable to criminal action. However, if the facility is located in an area that has experienced an extremely low crime rate, the probability of criminal attack may be negligible. In this case, the cost of additional physical security measures may outweigh the benefits.

A negative event probability scale may appear as follows:

- High probability (3). It is highly likely that a negative event will occur.
- Medium probability (2). A negative event may occur.
- Low probability (1). It is highly unlikely that a negative event will occur.

CRITICALITY   Finally, the security professional must consider the criticality of a loss if the loss occurred. In other words, one must foresee the likely impact and consequences associated with the loss. If a product research and development organization stores all of its data in a database at a single location and the database is completely destroyed during a flood, the loss to the organization would be devastating. If a subsidiary or vendor to a manufacturing firm is the sole supplier of a component critical to the manufacturing process, what impact would a personnel strike at the subsidiary's or vendor's facility have on the ability of the manufacturing firm to assemble product and service customers? If a terrorist group attacked a nuclear power facility, how might people and property be affected?

A criticality assessment involves an evaluation of each human, physical, and information asset to determine its value as well as prioritizing the allocation of security resources to protect the most critical assets. A five-level priority scale can be used as a guide to estimate criticality.

- Extremely critical (5). Substantial loss of life or irreparable, permanent, or prohibitively costly damage or repair is likely if asset is not protected. Loss could also provide invaluable advantage to an adversary (i.e., loss of intellectual property or government secrets).
- Highly critical (4). No loss of life. Serious damage to a facility or costly loss of information could occur.
- Medium criticality (3). No loss of life. Disruption of operation could occur and result in costly repairs.
- Low criticality (2). No loss of life. Minor disruption to operations. Does not materially advantage the competition or enemy.
- Negligible criticality (1). No loss of life. Insignificant loss or damage to operations or budget (Fay, 2000; Kovacich & Halibozek, 2003; U.S. Department of Justice, Bureau of Justice Assistance, 2005a, 2005b).

The overall risk level associated with asset loss or damage vulnerability, probability, and criticality can be expressed quantitatively, using numerical values ranging from 1 to 45. To calculate the overall risk level, the individual numerical values of vulnerability, probability, and criticality are entered into the following equation:

$$\text{Vulnerability} \times \text{Probability} \times \text{Criticality} = \text{Risk Level}$$

The higher the resultant number, the greater the risk. Loss prevention resources are allocated to protect resources exposed to the highest risk.

SECURITY SPOTLIGHT

Select two assets at the educational institution you attend or the organization where you are employed. For example, one asset could be a building and the other asset might be the institution's or organization's IT network. For each asset you selected, calculate the risk level associated with that asset, by assigning numerical values for vulnerability (1 to 3), probability (1 to 3), and criticality (1 to 5). Which of the assets has the highest risk level? What could be done to mitigate that risk level?

In summary, vulnerability to loss as well as the probability and criticality of loss must be considered when making risk management decisions. All three factors are equally important. The sophisticated security professional analyzes the risk and allocates resources for maximum benefit. Realistic asset protection and loss prevention can be achieved when limited security resources are allocated according to need and the potential consequences of a materialized threat. In some cases, a thorough risk assessment reveals a low probability that a breach of security or disastrous event will occur. However, the security manager should not disregard low-probability risks, because failure to protect against such risks can be a fatal error. The impact of the bombings at the World Trade Center in New York City in 1993 and the federal building in Oklahoma City in 1995 as well as the terrorist attacks of 9/11 provide ample evidence of the consequences associated with disregarding low-probability risk (Garcia, 2000; Jopeck, 2000; Oliver, 2007; Scalet, 2007).

New York City's World Trade Center under attack on September 11, 2001.
(Photo courtesy of Ken Tannenbaum/Shutterstock.com.)

RISK ASSESSMENT

As a method for identifying and evaluating risks, a **risk assessment** involves a critical, objective analysis of an organization's entire protective system. Continuous risk assessment enables the security professional to provide sound data upon which to solicit funding and make informed decisions regarding the allocation of scarce resources.

The Guidelines Commission of ASIS International developed a recommended practice advisory for conducting general security risk assessments. The following is a brief outline of the Commission's recommended approach. The approach is aligned with planning processes discussed later in this chapter.

- Develop an understanding of the organization and identify the human, physical, and information assets at risk.
- Specify loss risk events and vulnerabilities.
- Establish the probability of loss risk and determine the frequency of loss events.
- Determine the impact of loss events, including the financial, psychological, and other costs associated with a loss event.
- Develop options to prevent or mitigate losses.
- Study the feasibility of implementing each option.
- Perform a cost–benefit analysis (ASIS International Guidelines Commission, 2007).

Additional information regarding the guidelines can be obtained by contacting ASIS International at 703-519-6200 or www.asisonline.org.

The processes and instruments utilized during the risk assessment depend on the situation. It is necessary to collect and analyze relevant data. This data may be collected utilizing subjective as well as objective techniques. **Subjective (qualitative) measures** include the use of forecasting, employee surveys, expert opinion, and the **Delphi technique**. The Delphi technique involves a process through which several individuals or experts provide input on a given issue and ultimately arrive at a consensus on a prediction or list of needs and priorities. **Objective (quantitative) measures** include the use of audits, marketing, operations research, incident and statistical reports, threat assessment, investigations, risk analysis, inspections, and security (loss prevention) surveys (Bunning, 1979; Jacobson, 1997; Oliver, 2007).

SECURITY SURVEY

A **security survey** is used to evaluate an entire organization to identify risks and security deficiencies. The survey must be comprehensive, and it should identify

- assets (people, property, information) to be protected.
- anything (or anyone) that could adversely threaten the well-being of the assets.
- the vulnerabilities (weaknesses) that could conceivably be exploited by the threats (Fischer & Janoski, 2000; Oliver, 2007).

The results of the survey are used for risk assessment as well as safety and security planning.

A survey instrument (checklist) is often used to conduct a security survey. The security survey should assess several areas of concern. Every facility faces a multitude of security threats. Each potential threat must be analyzed in terms of its source (internal or external) as well as the goals, tactics, capabilities, and motivation of any criminal perpetrators. The nature of the organization and its activities as well as the country within which the organization is located must be considered. The availability of public services, utilities, and health care, along with political and economic conditions, must be evaluated. The general area or neighborhood surrounding the facility must be analyzed. Consideration must also be given to area crime rates, aesthetic qualities, and susceptibility to catastrophic events such as floods. The perimeter near the facility should be evaluated in terms of its parking, fencing, landscaping, and signage. The survey of the building itself should include points of entry, exits, access control, locks and keys, alarm systems and lighting, and vulnerability to intrusion.

Restricted areas within the facility must be identified. These include computer and data storage areas, key storage areas, mechanical and utility rooms, telecommunication rooms, mail rooms, and executive office suites. Alarm and surveillance systems, fire protection, personnel security, and information protection must be reviewed. The procedures for investigations and the collection of business and criminal intelligence, as well as reporting systems, operations, and liaison activities, must be evaluated.

A review of organizational policies includes an analysis of procedures used in the management of human resources and in the protection of property and information. A review of safety procedures should include mechanisms for prevention of accidents as well as fire safety and emergency plans. An assessment should be made of the number of security personnel required and of personnel responsibilities and training requirements. The survey should also assess the indoctrination and education of all employees regarding security and safety policies and procedures.

Some surveys uncover surprises that are really not unique. In one organization, a man posing as a repair person was caught attempting to steal proprietary information. He was able to escape without being identified. The incident was not reported when it occurred but was disclosed when employees were interviewed during the course of a security survey. The incident proved that the organization was the target of competitive intelligence operatives. The discovery led to the development of business counterintelligence procedures and counterintelligence training for employees.

As organizational stakeholders, all employees should be consulted during the security survey. Employees typically know where vulnerabilities lie and people are an excellent source of information. Input from employees also assists with the creation of employee ownership of the security program. Ownership, or buy-in, with employees is critical to program success.

At a minimum, the survey should address the general area or neighborhood surrounding the facility, as well as the perimeter, buildings, restricted areas, organizational policies, safety, personnel, and security education. The approach to a security survey may vary. Objective as well as subjective measures may be used to collect information. Emphasis should be placed on the physical environment, effectiveness of security personnel, policies and procedures, and management's attitude toward the loss prevention function. A comprehensive survey instrument should be used in the actual on-site survey. A sample safety and security survey instrument is included in Appendix B. Since each type of organization has special needs, it may be necessary to customize the survey instrument to accommodate organizational requirements (Collins, Ricks, & Van Meter, 2000; Craighead, 2009; Garcia, 2000; Ortmeier, 1999; Schaub & Biery, 1994).

The risk assessment and security survey processes are widely recognized and have been adopted by private industry, public law enforcement, and all levels of government. Therefore, the sources of information for determining the probability of loss and the actual frequency of risk events are extensive. Local police crime statistics, the Uniform Crime Report (UCR), the National Crime Victimization Survey (NCVS), and criminal intelligence reports are excellent sources. An organization's internal documents (e.g., incident reports, complaints received) and civil claims can provide critical risk assessment data. Information about general economic conditions, the threat of natural disasters, and industry trends are also vital to the risk assessment process (ASIS International Guidelines Commission, 2007).

PLANNING AND BUDGETING

Effective **planning** requires a definition of individual, group, or organizational vision and mission based on core values. Values are enduring yet changeable beliefs that certain conduct and goals are personally and socially preferable to opposite conduct and goals. Values such as integrity, honesty, compassion, respect, professionalism, and accountability represent the foundation upon which planning activity should be based. Values are used to create a **vision statement**, the articulation of an image of a better future. The vision statement, in turn, helps to formulate a **mission statement**, the language designed to help operationalize action plans.

Types of Plans

A plan involves the detailed formulation of a program for action. There are several types of plans:

- A **single-use plan** is used once and no longer needed when the objectives of the plan are accomplished. Budgets and special projects are examples of single-use plans.
- A **repeat-use (standing) plan**, on the other hand, may be used several times. Repeat-use plans are implemented each time a given situation or incident occurs. Unless modified,

repeat-use plans change little over time. Examples of repeat-use plans include policies, procedures, and methods for achieving objectives.

- A **tactical plan** is short range and scheduled to be implemented within a short time frame. An example of a tactical plan is an **operational plan**. Operational plans cover very brief periods of time such as a week or a month. They detail the steps and tasks to be accomplished by individuals, groups, or task forces.
- A **strategic plan** is long range and involves implementation over a period of years.
- A **contingency plan** is one that will be implemented only if a certain event, such as a natural disaster, occurs (Collins, 2008; Ortmeier & Meese, 2010; Perry, 1996).

Plans define an organization's goals, establish strategies for achieving those goals, and integrate and coordinate organizational efforts (Robbins & Coulter, 2009). Plans are developed and implemented to project revenue and expenses, control access, create security awareness among constituents, protect people and property, prepare for emergencies, and recover from unfortunate events (Collins, 2008; Fay, 1999; Haque, 2011; Peak & Glensor, 2008).

Elements of Plans

All planning processes include at least three common elements. The **elements of planning** include a needs (or risk) assessment, the development of alternative courses of action, and the selection of an action plan. Initial considerations in the planning process include the creation of vision and mission statements based on core values as well as the establishment of a need for a plan. In security practice, the risk assessment and analysis determines the need. A thorough examination of existing conditions as well as the prediction of potential threats will help determine if an actual need exists or if a perceived need is simply based on unnecessary desires or special interests. Assets requiring protection, potential threats, and vulnerabilities are identified and assessed. Thus, the practitioner must realistically identify the threats against the organization, its people, its property, and its information.

After needs are identified, objectives for meeting the needs are outlined. For the security manager, this involves qualifying and quantifying the risk and the development of action plan countermeasures that correspond to the threats identified in the needs assessment. Action plans must include measurable objectives. Decisions on courses of action and the selection of the most appropriate action plan will be based on an analysis of current and forecasted conditions. Each alternative must be analyzed and evaluated to determine probable undesirable as well as

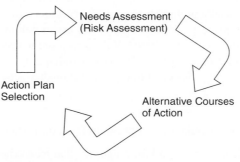

FIGURE 7–2   The Planning Process (common elements)

desirable consequences. This will involve conscious consideration and selection of a course of action among available alternatives to produce the best possible outcomes.

SECURITY SPOTLIGHT

Develop a disaster plan for your home. Start by interviewing everyone with whom you live—whether they are family members or housemates—to arrive at a consensus on the risks facing your home. According to the responses from everyone you interviewed, what is the worst disaster that could strike your home? What steps could you take to prevent that disaster, mitigate its impact, and enable your household to recover should the disaster strike?

Planning Tools

CompStat (computer-driven statistics) shows tremendous promise as a planning and management tool. CompStat was made famous through its application in the New York City Police Department (NYPD) during William Bratton's tenure as NYPD's commissioner in the mid-1990s. CompStat technology and management helped New York City reduce its crime rate significantly. Prior to CompStat's integration into NYPD's tactical and strategic planning processes, the department collected crime data, but the statistics were 3 to 6 months old before they were compiled and analyzed. CompStat technology, and the interactive managerial communications that accompanied it, provided current, almost real-time statistical information. The information provided a framework for more effective deployment of police resources and accountability for results.

CompStat is applicable in the private as well as the public sectors. Security managers may wish to develop and implement a CompStat-style incident tracking system. Coupled with a comprehensive data collection system (i.e., detailed reports that include when, where, who, what, how, and why an incident occurred), security-related incidents can be coded, automated, and analyzed quickly utilizing CompStat computer technology. Appropriately applied, CompStat planning and management processes increase efficiency and cost-effectiveness, and they can have a dramatic positive impact on profitability (Henry, 2002).

Other planning tools include mapping software such as **geographic information system (GIS) technology** and metrics-driven performance measurements. Commonly referred to as crime mapping, GIS software can be used to map reported safety- and security-related incidents and to predict future occurrences. GIS technology is capable of integrating multiple databases into one display so security personnel can isolate and address problems, manage resources efficiently, and evaluate results. Metrics-driven performance measurements are used to quantify and demonstrate the contributions security expenditures make to the goals of the organization, agency, or community (Campbell, 2006; Ortmeier, 2006). The metrics-driven process is discussed further in Chapter 8.

Learn more about mapping and analysis through the National Institute of Justice MAPS Program at www.ojp.usdoj.gov/nij/maps.

The decision-making process and the decisions made are not always popular. The impact a decision has on the organization, its people, its clients, and the community will require careful consideration. Change causes stress and anxiety. However, if well defined and communicated, each decision may be viewed as an opportunity for development, progress, and advancement of individual as well as organizational goals and objectives. The plan must project an implementation schedule, identify who is responsible for its implementation, monitor and evaluate its progress, and establish the criteria for evaluating results.

Budgeting

The financial impact of each action plan must also be determined. This requires a **budget** for each alternative action plan. Budget preparation is an integral part of the planning process. It is an essential planning tool tied to the established goals and objectives developed as alternative courses of action. The budget is a plan expressed in financial terms. An analysis must be made of the cost versus the benefit of each threat countermeasure. Industry standards indicate that the protection cost should be less than 2 percent of the value of the asset to be protected. Higher protection cost percentages are justifiable only if special circumstances exist. Countermeasure expenditures exceeding 5 percent of the value of the protected item are rarely justifiable (American Society for Industrial Security, 1998; Bassett, 2006).

COST–BENEFIT ANALYSIS A **cost–benefit analysis** provides a useful decision-making tool when one considers the commitment of funds or other resources. The analysis is a systematic process through which one attempts to determine the value of the benefits derived from an expenditure and compare the value with the cost. The cost–benefit analysis usually involves three steps.

- The identification of all possible consequences of an expenditure.
- The assignment of a monetary value to each consequence (cost and benefit) associated with the expenditure.
- The discounting of anticipated future costs and revenues accruing from the expenditure to express those costs and revenues in current monetary terms (ASIS International Guidelines Commission, 2007).

The cost–benefit analysis can assist with the calculation of the **return on investment (ROI)** of security-related expenditures and the **value-added contribution (VAC)** of the security program. ROI refers to the net savings that result when security measures are in place. The VAC refers to those anticipated threats that do not materialize because of the security program.

The ROI and VAC can be difficult to quantify unless one has a baseline for comparison. A reduction in the number of thefts after protective measures are placed in service is quantifiable. Savings can also be estimated in such diverse areas as illicit drug use and employee attrition. However, without a basis for comparison (i.e., how much overall crime is prevented), security's productivity can be questioned because its VAC is unquantifiable in specific terms. Thus, selling the security program and its budget can be challenging. To overcome the challenge, the security manager must be creative. The manager must also be assertive and pursue collaborative asset protection linkages and advocates with personnel in other organizational units, such as operations, sales, marketing, human resources, information technology, and community relations (Bragdon, 2006; Dalton, 1995; Harowitz, 2003; Johnson, 2003; Jones & Arnold, 2003; Sommer, 2003).

To justify security-related expenditures, asset protection and loss prevention must be viewed by budget decision makers as something more than an expense item. In addition, everyone in the organization must view the security function as vital and integral to agency or corporate strategy. In business, chief executive officers (CEOs) are driven by earnings before taxes, interest, depreciation, and amortization. The CEO is interested in profitability. Therefore, the security professional must present budget requests that are supported with quantifiable evidence that security expenditures will increase profitability. The sophisticated security manager speaks the language of business, and highlights how security improves earnings through efficiency and loss prevention.

Areas to consider in budget preparation include past operations, present conditions, and future expectations. Vulnerability to loss as well as the probability and criticality of loss must be considered. Revenue forecasts and projected expenditures are also useful ingredients to budget preparation. The budget process should be continuous, flexible, and responsive to the changing needs of the organization.

TYPES OF BUDGETS   There are several types of budgets:

- A **traditional budget** is a simple percentage increase over the last budget.
- A **line item budget** includes a description of items and the cost of each item. Line item budgets provide detail and clarity, and are easy to audit. Their disadvantages include inflexibility and isolation from the objectives.
- A **performance-based budget** includes measurable units tied to objectives that allow for a cost–benefit analysis by program type. The disadvantage to this type of budget is that some items, such as how many crimes or accidents are prevented as a result of money spent on a security system, are not easily measured.
- With a **zero-based budget (ZBB)**, each program within a budget period must justify its existence and expenditures.

Budgets are used to forecast expenditures and revenues, and as quantitative standards against which one can measure and compare resource consumption. The type of budget selected will depend on the circumstances, information needs, and organizational policy.

A QUICK SURVEY

Which of the following types of budgets is used by the educational institution you attend or the organization where you are employed? Check all that apply.

- Traditional
- Line item
- Performance based
- Zero based

What are the advantages of the types of budgets your educational institution or employer uses? What are the disadvantages?

BUDGET EXPENDITURES   Regardless of the type of budget used, the elements of a budget should include an accounting for personnel services, operating expenses, supplies and materials, capital outlay, and miscellaneous expenditures. The personnel services portion of the budget includes identification of the types and number of persons required as well as **personnel expenses** associated with salaries and wages, including statutorily mandated payroll taxes, discretionary personnel-related expenses such as health insurance and retirement, and overtime pay for hourly employees.

Operating expenses include items such as rent, utilities, contract services, training, insurance, leases, professional fees, preemployment screening, and memberships in professional organizations. **Supplies and materials expenses** include objects with an expected life of 1 year or less. This category includes office supplies, computer software, and fuel.

Capital expenditures are depreciable assets. They are objects with an expected life of 1 year or more. Large capital expenditures may require a separate capital budget and are usually amortized over a period of years. Examples include vehicles, computers, phones, and buildings. The **miscellaneous expense** category of the budget includes any item not appropriately placed in one of the other categories. Travel and depreciation of capital assets are placed in the miscellaneous category.

If a budget format is not provided by the organization, business, or agency, a budget request may be produced with a worksheet similar to that illustrated in Figure 7–3.

Selling the Plan

To select the most appropriate action plan, all stakeholders should be involved in the decision-making process. In other words, a determination of available resources must be made and consumers should be interviewed to solicit input before countermeasures are implemented. Support must be generated for the recommended plan. Effective implementation will depend on organizational support. Positive employee and constituent relations requires that they be involved in the decision-making process or, at the minimum, be informed of future plans. People often experience difficulty with change, whether the change is viewed negatively or positively.

When an entire community may be impacted by a plan, information should be disseminated, on a need-to-know basis, to generate public support. This can be accomplished through the media, through public-speaking engagements in community forums, and at meetings of professional organizations. Support from the persons responsible for approval of the budget is also necessary. A strategy must be developed to justify the budget to all the major stakeholders. They will want to know what value the proposed plan will contribute to the goals and objectives of the organization or agency.

Security professionals are always challenged to do more with less. Stakeholders and shareholders alike pressure senior management to survive, compete, and seek new ways to reduce expenses, increase revenue and profit, and improve the quality of products, personnel, and the workplace. Change in a competitive environment increases stress, the likelihood of uncivil behavior, and excuses for wrongdoing. The potential for workplace violence also increases. Simultaneously, organizations are faced with a complex web of environmental, health, safety, and security regulations, compliance issues, legal constraints and confrontations, increased risk exposure, and decreased employee morale and loyalty. Consequently, increased pressure is placed on the security professional to widen the span of control and accept more responsibility for the bottom line. The security manager's dilemma, however, can be transformed into a window of opportunity for growth and can lay the foundation for justification of security expenditures. If security managers expand their range of skills, embrace technology, and confront business issues in an intelligent manner, they can convincingly describe and demonstrate security's

Budget	
Item	**Amount Requested**
Personnel Expenses	
Salaries/Wages	
Payroll Taxes	
Health Insurance	
Retirement	
Overtime Pay	
Other	
Operating Expenses	
Rent	
Utilities	
Contract Services	
Training	
Insurance	
Leases (equipment, etc.)	
Professional Fees	
Preemployment Screening	
Memberships	
Other	
Supplies/Materials	
Office Supplies	
Software	
Fuel	
Other	
Capital Expenditures	
Building(s)	
Vehicle(s)	
Computer(s)	
Phone(s)	
Other	
Miscellaneous Expenses	
Travel	
Depreciation	
Other	
TOTAL EXPENDITURES	

FIGURE 7–3 Budget Worksheet

tremendous ROI (Bassett, 2006; Caldwell, 2000; Price, Haddock, & Brock, 2007; Robbins & Coulter, 2009).

If the plan involves other organizations and agencies, liaison should be established with them. For example, corporate security departments tend to be more effective when liaison is established with relevant public safety agencies. Similarly, if resources are to be shared through a consortium, the planning process must involve the other organizations impacted by the plan. Liaison with other agencies is a necessity. Given the reality of terrorism and the fact that the crime rate, although declining in recent years, remains relatively high, cooperation between and among law enforcement and security operatives is essential. Strong alliances have already developed between the public and private sectors in many areas of the United States (Operation Cooperation, 2001). Public–private partnerships such as the Virginia Police and Private Security Alliance (Bentley, 1997) and the East Bay Public Safety Corridor Partnership in San Francisco (U.S. Department of Justice, Bureau of Justice Assistance, 1997), and the use of private security on public transit systems are but a few examples of how cooperation and complementary relationships can benefit all citizens (Lyman, 2010; Moses-Schulz, 1997).

At a minimum, liaison activities, such as NYPD's Area Police–Private Security Liaison (APPL) project and communication with the U.S. Department of Homeland Security (DHS), allow security executives to share information and network to facilitate the distribution of intelligence alerts (Henry, 2002; U.S. Department of Homeland Security, Office of the Press Secretary, 2007). Truly, liaison activities help to create a foundation upon which the public police and security organizations can multiply their capabilities (Ortmeier & Meese, 2010).

CONTINGENCY PLANNING

A contingency plan addresses operational elements that are most likely to be adversely affected by change. The contingency plan includes alternative courses of action that may be implemented in the event an anticipated change actually occurs.

There may be several versions of each type of contingency plan. Some plans are simple, while others are complex. The response to an accident requiring basic first aid may be relatively simple, while a response to an environmental disaster may be very detailed and complex. Disasters can impact an entire community or region. Therefore, a contingency plan should address all conceivable variables and requirements. A chain of command designating authority relationships must be created. This includes command staff as well as a designated emergency coordinator. The plan must state its purpose, the types of emergencies covered, and the transition process from normal to emergency operations. Plan execution instructions and supporting information must be included. Maps and information on procedures, local resources, mutual-aid agreements, and liaison personnel are essential. The locations of the emergency control and operations center must be identified and communications channels should be described in the plan. Provision must be made to secure vital agency and organizational records and databases. This includes data files, incorporation certificates, bylaws, client lists, stock records, board meeting minutes, and financial records. Emergency shutdown procedures, personnel protection systems, the roles of supervisors, emergency evacuation routes, and shelter locations must be specified. All contingency plans should be contained in a manual, and employees must be trained regarding their response in the event of a disaster. Finally, the plan should be tested periodically to ensure organizational readiness and to assess the need for changes to the plan (Collins, 2008; Haddow & Bullock, 2010; Meese & Ortmeier, 2004; Papi, 1994).

Examples of contingency plans include business continuity plans as well as disaster and emergency plans.

Business Continuity Plans

A **business continuity plan** (or operations continuity plan) is designed to ensure that normal business operations are not disrupted by disasters, emergencies, crises, or other significant events. Failure to maintain continuous operations can negatively affect a business' revenue stream—a danger that seems to have captured executives' attention. In a survey of Fortune 1000 companies, respondents cited business continuity as among their top three concerns, behind cyber/communications security and workplace violence (*Top security threats and management issues facing corporate America*, 2010). A business continuity plan typically includes information on line of succession, notification of stakeholders, plan activation, recovery, and restitution (return to normal operation).

A form of business continuity plan is also essential for the public sector. Without an ability to restore public services to normal operations, property can be destroyed and lives may be lost. In the immediate aftermath of Hurricane Katrina, chaos and anarchy flared. Many who survived the storm died from neglect while trapped in the ruins of their homes or waiting for assistance on streets or at New Orleans' Superdome and convention center ("Lawlessness reigns as storm victims try to flee New Orleans," 2005).

Disaster and Emergency Plans

Disaster and emergency planning should occur at the individual and organization levels as well as the federal, state, and local community levels. Preparedness is everyone's job. Indeed, in October 2010, Federal Emergency Management Agency (FEMA) Administrator Craig Fugate challenged Americans to offer creative ideas for preparing communities for disasters. The challenge came during a time when explosives were found on cargo jets overseas. The explosives were planted by terrorists and intended for the United States. Fugate explained that responding to disasters takes an entire team, not just the U.S. government, and that planning for an entire community must be done before a disaster hits. Fugate invited all members of the public to submit ideas by January 2, 2011, after which FEMA personnel would begin the judging. The winning idea chosen by FEMA management would be highlighted on www.fema.gov (*FEMA challenge seeks innovative preparedness ideas*, 2010).

During the first few hours or days of a major disaster or emergency, essential public services may not be available. In preparation for a major event, individuals, families, groups, and organizations should familiarize themselves with local disaster and emergency plans, learn how to identify hazards that affect their area, create and maintain emergency communication systems, and collect and store disaster supplies. Evacuation procedures, emergency shelters, care of animals, and assistance for the elderly and persons with disabilities are also extremely important considerations.

Are You Ready? An In-depth Guide to Citizen Preparedness, a comprehensive resource for individual, family, and community disaster and emergency preparedness, is available through the FEMA at www.fema.gov/areyouready/.

Disaster and emergency planning is also critical to business survival. America's businesses form the backbone of the nation's economy. Thus, businesses must be prepared to survive and manage the consequences of and recover from natural and environmental disasters. Safe and secure businesses help to secure the economy and the nation. Businesses should plan to manage any abnormal event. Businesses must identify possible emergencies that might affect the business; develop plans to respond to those emergencies; involve, protect, and communicate with all stakeholders (employees, customers); establish liaison with public safety agencies; and safeguard the business' physical and information assets.

NATIONAL INCIDENT MANAGEMENT SYSTEM   While most emergencies are handled locally, major incidents often require the assistance of several jurisdictions, including the state and federal governments. The **National Incident Management System (NIMS)** was developed through the DHS to promote collaboration among first responders from different jurisdictions and public safety disciplines. Through NIMS, agencies are better able to respond to natural disasters and emergencies, including acts of terrorism. NIMS benefits include an emphasis on preparedness, mutual aid and resource management as well as standardized command structures, and a unified approach to incident response (Federal Emergency Management Agency, 2007).

In addition, the *National Response Plan* promotes an all-hazards approach to enhance the ability of the United States to manage major domestic incidents. The Plan incorporates best practices and procedures from incident management disciplines—law enforcement, firefighting, public works, emergency medical services, public health, emergency management, responder and recovery worker health and safety, homeland security, and the private sector—and integrates them into a unified structure. The Plan forms the foundation for private sector and federal, state, local, territorial, and tribal government coordination to prevent, respond to, and recover from major incidents.

> Learn more about the *National Response Plan* through the DHS at www.dhs.gov/nrp.

STATE-LEVEL STANDARDIZED EMERGENCY MANAGEMENT SYSTEM   State-level emergency services are provided through the state's **Standardized Emergency Management System (SEMS)**. Integrated with NIMS, a state's SEMS must comply with federal NIMS regulations. The SEMS is designed to coordinate state agencies' activities relating to the preparation and implementation of a state emergency plan. SEMS functions avoid duplication of effort and ensure maximum efficiency and effectiveness of response efforts. The SEMS also coordinates the integration of federal resources into state and local emergency response and recovery operations. SEMS guidelines address planning, finance, and logistics (procurement, maintenance, and transport of supplies, equipment, and personnel). The guidelines also address management and operations at the field, local government, operational area, and regional levels within a state (California Office of Emergency Services, 2007).

Disaster and emergency plans should be tested to identify weaknesses and assess their viability prior to an actual incident. Such plans are typically evaluated through the use of exercises designed to simulate, as closely as possible, a major disaster or emergency event. Discussion-based and operations-based exercises can be used to simulate catastrophic events and evaluate responses.

The most widely used discussion-based exercise is referred to as a tabletop exercise. An event scenario is presented to stakeholders in a roundtable format. Participants discuss how their functional areas would respond to the event. Facilitators provide basic information (place, time, magnitude, resource limitations) concerning the event, conduct the exercise, and guide the discussion. Facilitators also inject additional information, such as damage reports and changing conditions, as the exercise proceeds.

Operations-based exercises are more complex. Participants are required to role-play and act out their responses. Personnel with simulated injuries are treated, participants use emergency equipment, and criminal perpetrators (if any) are apprehended. In addition to the actual participants in the simulation, operations-based exercises typically employ an exercise director, controllers who inject new information, a group of people who represent external organizations and individuals interfacing with the exercise participants, actors who role-play as victims and bystanders, and exercise evaluators. The actions of the participants are the focus of the exercise. Discussion based- as well as operations-based exercises are assessed through after-action evaluations and reports (Gomez-Mejia & Balkin, 2012; Haque, 2011; Nason, 2007).

CRIME PREVENTION THROUGH ENVIRONMENTAL DESIGN

Crime prevention through environmental design (CPTED) is based on the theory that the environment can be protected, and crime prevented, through the proper design of facilities and communities. Emphasis is placed on effective use of architecture, building codes, and defensible space. Security and safety concepts are incorporated into the planning of the facility or community. In conjunction with community policing programs, CPTED may be applied to residential and business areas to increase public safety and reduce citizen fear of crime.

Risk assessment and security planning through CPTED have been very effective in preventing and deterring crime. Alternatively, poor security planning not only fails to prevent and deter crime, but also encourages it, because the facility design attracts criminal activity. Failure to design residential and business environments with effective safety and security measures also creates a liability connection between victims of crime and property owners, managers, organizations, and landlords.

History of CPTED

Crime prevention through environmental design is not new. In prehistoric times, cave dwellers cleared areas in front of their caves and stacked rocks around the perimeter to mask their space and warn intruders. During the early Greek empire, temple designers used environmental concepts to affect and control behavior. The temples were built of a type of stone that contained phosphorus and reflected a golden light shortly after dawn and just before dusk. During medieval times, height was used as a defensive tool. Sleeping quarters were high above ground level and whole communities were surrounded by high walls (Crowe, 2000).

Beginning in the 1970s, the National Institute of Justice sponsored research and promoted crime prevention strategies that use CPTED and community policing to make neighborhoods safer. Results indicate that proper design of the physical environment can control and prevent crime. Private individuals and businesses working in conjunction with the police have reduced fear of crime and deterred criminals. They have also used government building codes and agency inspection power to discourage illicit drug use and other criminal activity (Fleissner & Heinzelmann, 1996).

Crime prevention through environmental design supports the movement toward community- and problem-oriented policing. Alternately, community policing and problem solving reinforce the concepts of CPTED (Scott, 2000). Although long in coming to policing, when used in conjunction with community policing programs CPTED can increase public safety (Kroeker, 2001). Utilizing CPTED concepts, the police may actually be able to predict where crime is most likely to occur. After high-risk areas are identified, the police can work closely with individuals and businesses to prevent and control crime (Meese & Ortmeier, 2004).

Assumptions behind CPTED

The conceptual thrust of CPTED is that an environment can be manipulated to produce behavioral effects that prevent crime and improve the quality of life. The environment includes people and physical and social surroundings. The design includes all those activities, structures, and policies that seek to positively impact human behavior as people interact with the environment. CPTED focuses on the physical aspects of the environment as well as on what social scientists, public safety and security personnel, and community organizations can do to safely meet the needs of legitimate users of a space. Traditional target-hardening techniques, such as natural and artificial barrier systems, access control, and surveillance, are used to reduce the threat from criminal offenders. However, the CPTED concept is applied beyond the use of target hardening. It also involves strategies developed, implemented, and evaluated by security and law enforcement personnel, as well as by the community, to allow for the least restrictive human interface with the barrier systems (Harrell & Taylor, 1996; Oliver, 2007).

Crime prevention through environmental design is based on certain assumptions relating to how space is to be designed and used. First, all human space has a designated purpose that lays the foundation for the social, legal, cultural, or physical definitions that prescribe desired and acceptable behaviors. Second, facilities and communities are designed to support and control the desired behaviors. The basic concepts of territorial reinforcement, access control, and surveillance are inherent in the approach. These basic concepts are accomplished through any combination of the following:

- A clear border definition of the controlled space. Public and private spaces must be clearly delineated.
- Clearly marked transitional zones. The user must be forced to acknowledge movement into the controlled space.
- Relocation of gathering areas. The design must formally designate gathering areas in locations with good access control and natural surveillance capabilities.
- Safe activities in unsafe locations. Safe activities serve as magnets for normal users and communicate to abnormal users that they are at greater risk of detection.
- Unsafe activities in safe locations. Vulnerable activities should be placed within tightly controlled areas to help overcome risk and make normal users feel safer.
- Use of space to provide natural barriers. Conflicting activities may be separated by distance and natural terrain to avoid fear-producing conflict.
- Improved scheduling of space. The effective use of space reduces actual risk as well as the perception of risk for normal users.
- Appropriate space allocation and design. This increases the perception of surveillance.
- Reduction in isolation and distance. Design efficiencies and improved communication systems increase the perception of surveillance and control (Crowe, 2000).

One of the most significant shifts in modern thinking about crime prevention is that individual action in a vacuum often increases risks to safety and security. However, the mobilization of all stakeholders in a collaborative effort to prevent crime and disorder creates an environment in which success is more likely. From a CPTED perspective, this means effective communication and collaboration between and among business organizations, public agencies, security managers, architects, and others to engineer safe and secure environments.

Good planning will dictate the tactical implementation of CPTED concept design strategies. Risk and crime analyses, demographic and land use information, and resident or user interviews should be utilized to plan security controls. CPTED is not a substitute for a comprehensive loss prevention program. However, it can reduce the opportunity to commit crime when implemented in the context of a program designed to prevent crime while providing freedom from interference for legitimate users. CPTED concepts and strategies may be accomplished in a variety of ways. Since each situation is unique, CPTED design concepts should be applied as appropriate planning warrants (American Institute of Architects, 2003; Crowe, 2000; Fennelly, 2004; Jeffery, 1972; Ortmeier & Davis, 2012).

Summary

Risk is defined as the possibility of suffering harm or loss, exposure to the probability of loss or damage, an element of uncertainty, or the possibility that the results of an action may not be consistent with expected outcomes. Risk management techniques involve elimination, reduction, and mitigation of risk, as well as a determination of asset vulnerability and the probability and criticality of loss.

Risk assessments are accomplished using a variety of subjective and objective measures. Typically, a security survey is conducted utilizing a security survey instrument. The risk assessment and security survey represent the initial step in the planning process. The initial step is followed by the development of alternative courses of action and selection of the action plan. The potential financial impact of each plan must be determined through the creation of a budget.

Disaster and emergency planning, forms of contingency planning, should occur at the individual and organizational levels as well as the various levels of government. Disaster and emergency planning are critical to business and national survival. The NIMS and the state-based SEMS represent integrated emergency planning activities designed to prevent and manage major disaster incidents. CPTED methodology is used to design facilities and communities with safety and security in mind.

Key Terms

business continuity plan
budget
capital expenditures
CompStat
contingency plan
cost–benefit analysis
crime prevention through
    environmental design (CPTED)
Delphi technique
dynamic risk
elements of planning
geographic information system
    (GIS) technology
inherent risk
line item budget

miscellaneous expense
mission statement
National Incident Management
    System (NIMS)
objective (quantitative) measures
operating expenses
operational plan
performance-based budget
personnel expenses
planning
pure risk
repeat-use (standing) plan
return on investment (ROI)
risk
risk assessment

risk management techniques
security survey
single-use plan
speculative risk
Standardized Emergency
    Management System (SEMS)
static risk
strategic plan
subjective (qualitative) measures
supplies and materials expenses
tactical plan
traditional budget
value-added contribution (VAC)
vision statement
zero-based budget (ZBB)

Discussion Questions and Exercises

1. Describe five types of risk and discuss management techniques for eliminating, reducing, or mitigating each risk type.
2. How is an asset evaluated to determine its vulnerability, probability, and criticality of loss?
3. Contrast subjective with objective risk assessment measurements. Which is more appropriate in a security setting? Why?
4. Describe the process for analyzing needs identified through a risk assessment.
5. How many courses of action should be developed to eliminate, reduce, or mitigate risk? Explain your response.
6. What role does the budget assume in action plan development, selection, and implementation?
7. What is CPTED, and how is it applied?

YOUR TURN: Conducting a Safety and Security Survey

Conduct a safety and security survey of your home or a small business. To survey a small business, follow these steps.

1. Identify a small business and obtain permission from the owner (or responsible person in charge) to conduct the survey.
2. Utilizing the Safety and Security Survey Instrument located in Appendix B, conduct the survey. Disregard sections that do not apply and/or areas of the business to which access is denied.
3. Analyze the hazards and deficiencies identified and recommend corrective actions.
4. Based on the budget categories discussed in this chapter, prepare a budget to cover the cost of your recommendations. Contract security services.

CHAPTER 8

Program Implementation and Administration

LEARNING OBJECTIVES

After completing this chapter, the reader should be able to

- compare public and private administrative processes.
- discuss the principles of organization and management.
- articulate the importance of ethical leadership to the administrative function.
- discuss the procedure for protection plan implementation.
- assess the need for security personnel.
- demonstrate knowledge of security force management, principles, and techniques.
- design a training program for security personnel.
- develop policies and procedures.
- assess the need for contract services.
- evaluate protection systems and security programs.

INTRODUCTION

After selecting an action plan, an individual, group, or organization proceeds with the planned program's implementation, administration, and evaluation. Activities must be organized, assignments must be scheduled, and personnel must receive training and education appropriate to the assignments. Security professionals lead by example, demonstrating ethical leadership behaviors. Equipment and facilities are purchased or leased, policies and procedures are developed, and external services, if any, are contracted. Throughout the implementation and administration process, progress and outcomes must be evaluated to determine whether actions are achieving the desired results.

THE ADMINISTRATIVE PROCESS

The administrative process involves two or more people working collaboratively to accomplish a predetermined vision. The process emerges from the need to cooperate with others on complex, difficult, or multiple tasks to achieve common objectives of an organization, community, or society. Those engaged in the administrative process are simultaneously involved with activities such as planning, organizing, staffing, training, equipping, leading, and evaluating people and processes.

PUBLIC VERSUS PRIVATE ADMINISTRATION

To understand and appreciate the nature of security management, it may be helpful to review the general characteristics of public and private **administration**. Tables 8–1 and 8–2 shed light on these characteristics.

In some areas, the distinction between public and private organizations is blurred. Privatization of public services is one example. However, similarities as well as differences continue to exist. They differ because public agencies are usually financed through tax revenues, while private organizations are financed through profits from business operations. Private organizations may enforce regulations not under the authority of public governmental entities. The statutory authority granted to private individuals and organizations to arrest, search, and enforce the law also varies between and among government jurisdictions.

TABLE 8–1	Defining Characteristics of Public Administration
Characteristic	**Explanation**
Public affairs oriented	Public administration focuses on the management of public agencies and organizations.
Impartial and fair	All citizens are entitled to a particular government service and must be treated in a uniform manner.
Apolitical	The policies of government may be political, but the detailed execution of these policies is administrative.
Public service oriented	Public administration exists to serve the public, and profit is not a motive for its operations.
Publicly funded	Funds for public administration are appropriated by law and derived primarily from tax revenues.
Publicly documented	Administrative records and financial documents are public information that must be made available for review by all citizens.
Accountable to the public	Public administration is subject to legislative and judicial review at all times.
Selectively staffed (civil service)	Qualified personnel are selected on the basis of demonstrated merit through civil service examinations.
Hierarchical	Public agencies are official and formal and consist of levels of positions.

Sources: Cordner & Scarborough, 2010; George & Jones, 2012; Perry, 1996.

TABLE 8–2	Defining Characteristics of Private Administration
Characteristic	**Explanation**
Private enterprise	Private administration exists to fulfill a private rather than public obligation or interest.
Private or corporate ownership	Private individuals, groups, or stockholders own private organizations.
Competitiveness	The organization may be in competition with other enterprises engaged in producing the same product or service.
Profit incentive	Except for certain nonprofit private organizations, the incentive is to generate net profit.
Financing regulated by market price	Revenue is based on the ability to sell the product or service.
Privacy of information and records (within limits)	Information is proprietary and the property of the owner(s).
Accountability to owners and stockholders	The organization and its employees are held accountable to the organization's owners rather than the public.
Some freedom in selection and termination of employees	The organization is not bound by civil service rules related to hiring or termination of employees.
Freedom to regulate work methods and organization	The organization is not bound by civil service regulations.

Sources: Cordner & Scarborough, 2010; George & Jones, 2012; Perry, 1996.

PRINCIPLES OF ORGANIZATION AND MANAGEMENT

To **organize** is to create an orderly structure or arrangement. Organizing is designed to achieve maximum effectiveness, efficiency, and productivity, while reaching organizational goals and objectives (More, Vito, & Walsh, 2012). For any security enterprise, whether public or private, the following steps can help the enterprise apply important principles of organization and management.

Step 1: Establish an Organizational Structure

The first major step to the implementation and administration of an action plan is to organize operations according to the plan. The organizational structure, or framework, of a business or governmental agency unit will vary depending on its size, location, budget, and methods of operation.

From a structural perspective, the traditional principles of organization in the administrative process include the following:

- Similar tasks are grouped together.
- Specialized units or departments are created when necessary.
- Lines of demarcation between responsibilities are clearly established.
- Communication channels are established.
- Structure and common terminology are used.
- Unity of command is developed (one person, one boss).
- Span of control is exercised for effective supervision.
- Each task is assigned to someone (responsibility).
- Supervision for each person is required of someone.

- Authority is commensurate with responsibility.
- Individuals and organizational units are held accountable for tasks.

The level of complexity within an organization depends on the amount of horizontal and vertical differentiation that exists. Horizontal differentiation is usually based on activity. This activity may be associated with the type of clientele, style of service, geography, time, or process. Vertical differentiation is based on levels of authority.

Small departments, agencies, or businesses may be simple or very complex in organizational design. Some organizations have narrow spans of management control, with tall vertical structures and many managerial layers (see Figure 8–1). Other organizations increase the span of control and decrease the organization's vertical structure, thus reducing layers of management (see Figure 8–2). There is no one-size-fits-all structure, and there are advantages and disadvantages associated with each. For example, tall organizations with narrow spans of control place fewer demands on supervisors but may have more problems with vertical communication. The most appropriate organizational structure is the one that best facilitates organizational performance (Certo & Certo, 2012; Hodge, Anthony, & Gales, 2003; Lewis, Goodman, & Fandt, 2008; Swanson, Territo, & Taylor, 2008).

A QUICK SURVEY

Think of an organization where you worked in the past or an organization where you are currently employed. Which of the following types of structure does the organization use?

- Tall
- Flat

In what ways does the type of structure used by the organization you selected facilitate the organization's performance and help it achieve efficiency and effectiveness? In what ways does that structure present challenges?

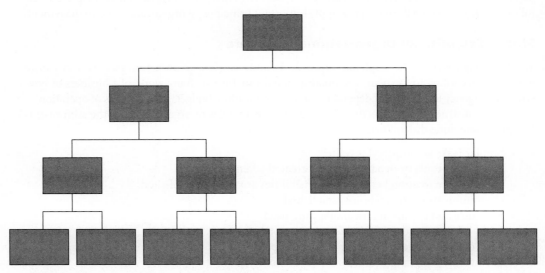

FIGURE 8–1 Tall Organizational Structure with Narrow Span of Control and High Vertical Complexity

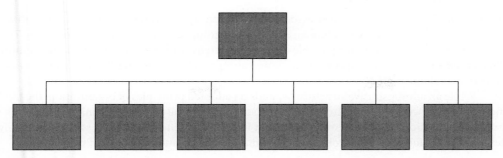

FIGURE 8–2   Flat Organizational Structure with Wide Span of Control and Low Vertical Complexity

Organizations may also be differentiated by line, staff, function, or project orientations:

- *Line activity* refers to those elements that perform tasks for which the organization was created.
- *Staff activity* refers to those elements that support the line, such as communications networks.
- *Functional structures*, although complex, improve communication between elements because delegation of management authority extends beyond normal spans of control. Business intelligence activities, for example, may cross all lines of authority.
- *Project structures* are characterized by the assignment of elements from various segments of the organization to task forces that address a specific problem. The task force is dissolved when the problem is solved.

The organizing process follows a logical sequence.

1. Managers determine tasks to be accomplished based on group or organizational goals and establish objectives in the planning process.
2. Major tasks are subdivided into individual activities and the knowledge, skills, and abilities (KSAs) to accomplish the tasks are identified.
3. Tasks are assigned to individuals who possess the appropriate KSAs. If personnel currently available do not possess the KSAs required, training of existing personnel or employment of adequately trained personnel is necessary.
4. Managers provide resources (physical, human, fiscal) necessary to accomplish the tasks.
5. Organizational relationships (arrangement of authority and responsibility) necessary to supervise the execution of tasks and completion of assignments are designed.

The structural component of an organization is often represented in the form of an organizational chart. However, the introduction of computer technology changed the way many institutions operate. Many organizations moved away from the hierarchical or military structure model to a flatter, more collegial organization built around shared information. As a result, middle management, which previously functioned as the conduit between higher management and line personnel, has been eliminated in many organizations. Each member of the organization becomes a member of a team that is more innovative, participatory, flexible, and adaptable (Greer & Plunkett, 2007; Hellriegel & Slocum, 2011).

After the September 11, 2001, terrorist attacks on the United States, many organizations reassessed the structure of their human operations. As a result, some organizations have distributed their workforces over wider areas, when appropriate, creating decentralized networks of workplaces in which human activities are grouped according to common tasks. This approach favors preparation for possible disasters, shortens worker commutes, and makes more efficient use of space. This organizational design also provides for greater flexibility in an era of environmental uncertainty.

While an administrative structure depends on adopted principles of organization, the fluid and dynamic process of administration is addressed through the principles of **management**. The traditional (classical) principles of management include planning, organizing, staffing, directing (leading), coordinating or controlling (evaluation), reporting, and budgeting (POSDCORB):

- *Planning* involves forward thinking and selection of courses of action based on an identified need.
- *Organizing* involves the collection and development of physical, financial, and human resources necessary to achieve the goals articulated in the planning process.
- *Staffing* is the process of hiring, training, and rewarding people for doing the organization's work.
- *Directing* (leading) involves guiding people to achieve the goals of the organization.
- *Controlling* (evaluation) involves comparing actual performance with planned performance.
- *Reporting* involves the dissemination of information and data according to organizational members' need to know.
- *Budgeting* entails planning expressed in financial terms. It is a process for determining expenditures versus revenue streams (Mosley, Megginson, & Pietri, 2005; Robbins & Coulter, 2009).

The traditional principles of management, as formulated in the POSDCORB model, provide a useful framework for describing the administrative process. However, the realities of modern administrative practice are not quite as simplistic as the descriptions of the POSDCORB management functions might lead one to believe. Simple, clear-cut steps to management do not exist. Realistically, managers often perform a little of each function simultaneously as they plan, organize, staff, direct, coordinate or control, report findings, and budget resources. Management functions may actually defy any sequentially ordered application. In a twenty-first century environment, management is usually a process, rather than a series of activities. Therefore, to effectively address issues of trust, ethics, accountability, work–personal life balance, and global changes, modern managers must be aware of and creatively utilize numerous management models (George & Jones, 2012).

Whether a business or agency conforms to traditional or more modern principles of organization and management, four common elements exist in all administrative processes. These include planning, implementation, ethical leadership, and evaluation:

- *Planning* uses the common elements as a focal point and involves need assessment, alternative action plan development, and selection of an action plan.
- *Implementation* and administration (operationalizing the plan) includes all activities designed to organize, staff, acquire equipment and facilities, develop policy and procedure statements, and allocate and deploy resources.
- *Ethical leadership* involves supervision and maintenance of ethical standards.
- *Evaluation* focuses on monitoring progress, control, and follow-up (Ortmeier, 1999; Ortmeier & Meese, 2010).

Step 2: Attend to Ethical Leadership

The concepts of ethics and leadership were introduced in Chapter 5 as essential ingredients to personnel security. These concepts are also relevant to the administrative process. As discussed in Chapter 5, leadership is every person's responsibility. Each person in an organization can and should assume a leadership role. The concept of leadership connotes a special meaning when one integrates ethics and applies ethical leadership to administration, supervision, and management. Ethical leadership is not simply what one does. Rather, ethical leadership refers to who a person is. At this juncture in the administrative process, many experts refer to the management of human resources as *controlling*. However, *controlling* is a negative term when applied to the administrative process. It implies that human beings cannot be trusted and must be manipulated to achieve organizational goals. The ethical leader does not control. The ethical leader activates others' desire to achieve (Ortmeier, 1996c; Robbins & Judge, 2010).

In the context of public and private administration alike, some observers have begun advocating a new model of leadership focused on managerial judgment and practice grounded in ethics. For example, according to Haque (2011), the primary force behind the recent worldwide global recession—marked by trillions of dollars of financial assets destroyed, trillions of dollars in shareholder value vanished, and stalling worldwide gross domestic product (GDP)—is overreliance on outdated Industrial Age leadership ideals. These ideals include rampant exploitation of resources and top-down command of resource allocations, as well as withholding of information from stakeholders to control them and a single-minded pursuit of profit for its own sake.

Haque maintains that adherence to these ideals has produced "thin value"—short-term economic gains that accrue to some people far more than others, and that have not made people happier or healthier. It has left resources depleted and has spawned conflict, organizational rigidity, economic stagnation, and nihilism. To reverse the situation, public and private organizations must adopt a new set of ideals:

- *Renewal*—Use resources sustainably to maximize efficiencies.
- *Democracy*—Allocate resources democratically to foster organizational agility.
- *Peace*—Practice economic nonviolence in business.
- *Equity*—Create industries that make the least well off better off.
- *Meaning*—Generate payoffs that tangibly improve quality of life.

While adopting these ideals requires ambitious and sustained changes in administration and management practices, some organizations (Haque cites Google, Wal-Mart, and Nike as examples) have begun making those changes and generating attention-getting results. The willingness and ability to change demonstrated by such renowned organizations suggest that more ethical models of leadership—models that create more value for more people than value created through Industrial Age ideals—are possible.

Step 3: Staff the Organization

The third major step in the implementation of the action plan is to staff the department, agency, or business. Regardless of the type of organization, basic elements exist in the management of human resources. These include the process of determining how many people the operation needs; what they will do; and how they will be hired, trained, led, and evaluated. Human resource management is discussed in detail in Chapter 5.

WORKFORCE PLANNING Determining personnel requirements necessitates careful assessment and planning. If designated security personnel are required, management must determine how many are needed, what knowledge they must possess, what tasks they are to perform, and how they are to be trained. Workforce planning is not an easy task. Budgetary constraints often limit payroll dollars. Security managers must be creative and use human resources wisely, thus avoiding unnecessary expenditures.

The first step in workforce planning is to determine how many people are required. The foundation for human resource recommendations is based on the needs assessment and security survey. The assessment will reveal where and when a human agent is necessary. After personnel assignments (posts) are determined, the number of coverage hours are calculated. For example, if a human agent is to be assigned to a workstation or post, 24 hours per day, 7 days a week, the result is the equivalent of 168 clock hours. An estimated 4.5 **full-time equivalent (FTE) persons** will be needed to cover this assignment. This accounts for vacations and sick leave without unnecessary overtime. The position could be filled with any combination of full-time or part-time employees.

There are 2,080 (52 weeks × 40 hours per week) working hours available per year for each FTE. However, this calculation is based on the assumption that the position is filled by a full-time person and no vacation, holidays, or sick leave time is taken. Therefore, adjustments must be made to reduce the number of hours a full-time person is available for work if vacation, holiday, and sick leave benefits are provided. To account for 2,080 working hours, two part-time workers could fill the assignment at 1,040 hours each. If a contract service provides security personnel, the client organization need only provide the number of workforce hours exclusive of any calculation for time off.

After the number of persons or employees required is determined, it is necessary to conduct an analysis of the tasks the person in this position is expected to perform. The **job task (occupational) analysis** can be accomplished through direct observation or by comparing this position with similar positions in or outside the organization. The tasks may also be identified by interviewing current employees or other employers. The purpose of the job task analysis is to identify the job functions (duties) a worker must perform. After job functions are identified, desired job behaviors are analyzed to determine future training needs. In addition, each behavior must be analyzed in terms of the actual performance of the behavior and how the behaviors will be measured.

People constitute the most significant protection resource.
(Photo courtesy of Irene Springer/Pearson Education/PH College.)

Next, a **job description** is created. Often referred to as a position description, it identifies the principal elements, scope of authority, and responsibilities involved in the job. The job description should be reviewed annually and revised as necessary. Closely aligned with the task analysis and job description are **job specifications**. Whereas the job description provides details on the major duties of a position, the job specifications outline specific skills, competencies, and personal qualifications that are necessary to perform the job adequately. The job description and job specifications may appear in the same document.

After the number and qualifications of people required have been determined, the workforce information as well as the job descriptions and specifications can be referred to the human resources department or other appropriate personnel to initiate the recruitment and selection process (see Chapter 5, "Personnel Security through Leadership and Ethics"). In some cases, the manager to whom the new employee(s) will report may prefer to initiate the process. If plans call for contract labor, the workforce planning information is made available to security personnel vendors who wish to submit bids for the services.

A careful risk assessment and security survey should reveal the times and locations where human resources are required. The results of this analysis are used to schedule working time. When a post must be staffed 24 hours per day, 7 days per week (continuous staffing), most organizations maintain at least three 8-hour shifts to ensure 24-hour service. Some organizations add a fourth shift for peak activity periods, as in the following example:

A Shift	2300 hours–0700 hours	(11:00 P.M.–7:00 A.M.)
B Shift	0700 hours–1500 hours	(7:00 A.M.–3:00 P.M.)
C Shift	1500 hours–2300 hours	(3:00 P.M.–11:00 P.M.)
D Shift	1900 hours–0300 hours	(7:00 P.M.–3:00 A.M.)
(optional)		

Organizations may also utilize what is commonly referred to as the 10 plan: three 10-hour shifts that overlap during peak periods. Fewer people are scheduled for each shift, but a greater number are available during peak periods. Ten plans also tend to improve the morale of employees. They work four 10-hour shifts and have 3 days off, as in the following example:

A Shift	2400 hours–1000 hours	(midnight–10:00 A.M.)
B Shift	0800 hours–1800 hours	(8:00 A.M.–6:00 P.M.)
C Shift	1600 hours–0200 hours	(4:00 P.M.–2:00 A.M.)
D Shift	1700 hours–0300 hours	(5:00 P.M.–3:00 A.M.)
(optional)		

To reduce overtime costs and sick leave abuse as well as improve morale, a few organizations are scheduling 12.5-hour shifts. Under the plan, employees work 3 or 4 days a week, alternating every 7-day period. The plan requires only two shift changes every 24 hours, instead of three, reducing the number of shift changes and resulting in more time for the actual work assignment. If employees work a shift in excess of 8 hours, state statutes should be researched to determine if state law requires overtime be paid for hours worked in excess of 8 hours per day.

Workforce schedule planning involves a comprehensive labor needs assessment, the calculation of the total number of work hours required, and a determination of the workforce's impact on the budget. The goal of workforce scheduling is to maximize coverage with minimum resources without sacrificing quality. Visually, a schedule might be presented as follows:

Position	Days	Hours	Total Hours/Week
Security Director	Vary	Vary	40
Supervisor 1	Mon–Fri	2300–0700	40
Supervisor 2	Tue–Sat	0700–1500	40
Supervisor 3	Wed–Sun	1500–2300	40
Supervisor 4	Vary	Vary	40
Assignment 1	24/72	400–2400	168
Assignment 2	Mon–Fri	0800–1600	40
Assignment 3	Mon–Fri	1600–2400	40
Assignment 4	Mon–Fri	1200–2000	40
TOTAL			488

Since salaries and wage rates vary among positions and individuals, the total hours indicated on this schedule cannot simply be multiplied by a flat hourly rate. Rather, the dollar amount budgeted for each position must be calculated separately. For example, if the wage rate for Assignment 2 is $15 per hour, the total direct labor cost for that position is $600 per week, or $31,200 per year. Statutorily mandated and related payroll costs, training, and discretionary benefit packages could account for an additional 40 percent in indirect labor costs for each position. Thus, a $31,200 position may actually cost $43,680 per year (Moran, 2010; Ortmeier, 1999; Payton & Amaral, 2004).

TRAINING AND EDUCATION Effective security depends, to a great extent, on the KSAs of the human beings who monitor security systems and respond to security breaches. Further, it is often the security manager or frontline security supervisor who is responsible for security training and education.

Training and education represent different approaches to learning. Training often refers to the development of specific skills or competencies related to tasks performed by an individual in a workplace environment. Education on the other hand encompasses general knowledge development. As a means for human resource development, emphasis should be placed on both education and training. Any personal or professional learning activity, whether education-related or training-related, designed to prepare or improve an individual or enhance performance is beneficial. Competence in leadership, human relations, written and oral communications, critical thinking, and problem solving are just as important as driving skills and dexterity in handling equipment. The success of an organization depends on its personnel. What employees know, how they perform, the values they possess, and the judgment they exercise determine outcomes for any enterprise. To ensure high productivity, quality performance, and adherence to ethical standards, education as well as training must be top priorities (Ortmeier, 1995, 1996a; Ortmeier & Davis, 2012).

As stated in Chapter 1, formal security management–related education programs are presented by numerous colleges and universities. As security education struggles to become a discipline, some experts argue that security management curricula must focus more on the business-related aspects of the occupation. It is no secret that the role of the security manager has changed. Security managers are expected to possess business, legal, and diplomacy skills. While some educational programs claim to prepare individuals for the multidisciplinary, business-related tasks required to function effectively as a security manager, existing curricula often focus on the reactive approach necessary in many public law enforcement functions (Davidson, 2003; Longmore-Etheridge, 2010; Nalla, 2001; Ortmeier, 1994, 1995, 1996b).

The author conducted a survey that involved approximately 200 security service providers in Southern California. The purpose of the survey was to identify, from a career perspective, the training and education needs of contemporary security personnel. The survey acted as the basis for the development of a focused, comprehensive strategy to promote security management as a distinct academic discipline and to legitimize the profession at all levels of education. The results were used to incorporate security management courses into a state university's business college curricula as well as develop a security officer academy and security management associate degree at a community college.

The survey revealed that all respondents favored seminars to address specific training needs, and 98 percent favored a career education pathway (see Figure 8–3). In addition, the respondents favored security-related training and education at all educational levels. Eighty-seven percent

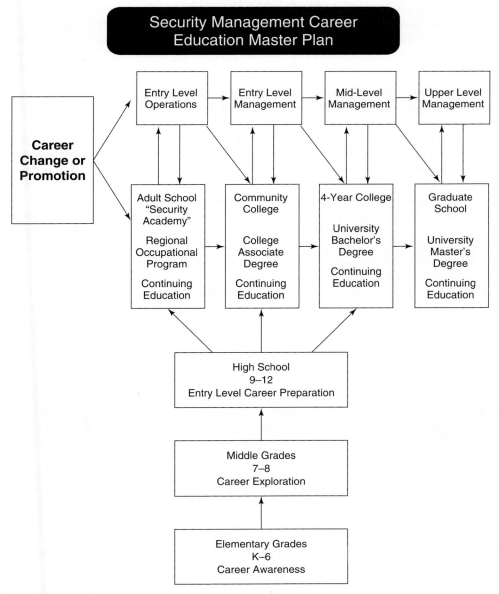

FIGURE 8–3   A Professional Education Plan for a Career in Security Management

thought high schools should include security occupations as part of their career awareness programs, and 85 percent said a security officer academy for basic training was needed. An associate degree at the community college level was favored by 95 percent of respondents, and 92 percent thought a bachelor's degree program at the university level was appropriate.

While the study produced no consensus as to what level of education security professionals should attain, survey participants largely agreed on what subjects should be studied at each level. Using a Likert scale, respondents were asked to rate the most appropriate educational level for delivering 177 subject areas identified by the Academic Program Committee of the San Diego Chapter of ASIS International.

The survey addressed four educational levels, including high school, security/protection officer academy, associate degree/lower division, and bachelor's degree/upper division. Lower division refers to the first 2 years and upper division refers to the second 2 years of a 4-year bachelor's degree program. The associate degree could, with an appropriate combination of courses, function as the first 2 years of a bachelor's program.

- High school. The respondents indicated that foundation coursework in government, history, applied math, written and verbal communications, computers, hygiene, and physical education were appropriate at this level.
- Security officer academy. At this level, the respondents identified a need for technique-oriented coursework associated with self-defense; cardiopulmonary resuscitation (CPR) and first aid; chemical weapons, baton, and firearms training (where appropriate); patrol procedures; and traffic regulation. Respondents recommended that instruction emphasize the legal aspects of security, public relations, and report writing.
- Associate degree/lower division. At the associate degree level, the competencies identified by the respondents were consistent with those of entry-level management. Here, emphasis was placed on accounting, general business practices, public and human relations, law, written communications, investigations, computer literacy, specialized security applications, public speaking, and social science.
- Bachelor's degree/upper division. At this level, the respondents indicated a need for the development of competencies appropriate to midlevel management. These competencies include business law and ethics, budgeting and finance, contracts, personnel management and labor relations, planning, organizational theory, communications, public relations, policy formulation, statistics, systems engineering, technical writing, and threat assessment and analysis.

Additional information regarding high school preparation for security careers may be obtained by contacting States' Career Clusters at www.careerclusters.org.

The respondents also indicated that working security professionals who wish to enhance policy formulation and systems integration skills may wish to pursue a master's degree in security management or business administration.

Overwhelmingly, the security professionals who responded to the study indicated a need for specialized training and education in security services. In addition, the study revealed a trend toward incorporating business-related rather than law enforcement competencies into a security management career education plan (Ortmeier, 1995, 1996b). Business-related skills are as relevant as ever (More, Vito, & Walsh, 2012; Ross, 2012).

When it comes to teaching and learning strategies, the methods used to teach children and teenagers are not appropriate for adults. Differences in experience, education, and levels of motivation require different approaches to adult learning methodologies. Malcolm Knowles (1970) was one of the first to acknowledge that adult learning strategy embodies five key principles:

1. Adults accept the material presented based on evidence, not blind faith. Learners must be aware of the credibility of the information and how it relates to the real world in which they operate.
2. Adults are active rather than passive during the learning process. Adults contribute thoughts and ideas and relate relevant personal experiences to the subject being taught.
3. Adults' individual needs must be addressed. Although experience and education levels vary, the instructor who facilitates discussions well can provide a valuable learning experience for the most knowledgeable individual.
4. Adult learners evaluate themselves. As learning progresses, individuals conduct an internal self-assessment of their understanding of the material and how it relates to their personal situation.
5. Instructional methods that promote effective adult learning must be used. Discussion, role-playing, and the demonstration method of instruction provide an opportunity for interaction and promote an effective learning environment.

For adults, learning is a process through which the student as well as the instructor assumes responsibility for what, when, where, and how learning takes place and to whom the learning process is directed (Certo & Certo, 2012; Pike, 1992).

SECURITY SPOTLIGHT

Consider the fact that adult learners, unlike children, assume responsibility for what, when, where, and how they learn. In your experiences so far with learning about security, in what ways have you taken responsibility for your own learning? In what ways (if any) could you take even more responsibility for your learning?

In terms of educational program development, professional development through appropriate training and education results in professional action. The ultimate goal of any **professional development** curriculum is to prepare individuals to perform well. To be effective, career education and training programs must be performance-based. Participants should demonstrate real-world, integrated job skills. According to the U.S. Department of Labor Secretary's Commission on Achieving Necessary Skills (SCANS), superior performance requires a three-part foundation: basic skills (reading, writing, computation, listening, and speaking); creative thinking and problem-solving skills; and personal qualities associated with responsibility, self-management, and integrity. Participants should also demonstrate the ability to identify, organize, plan, and allocate resources; work well with others; acquire and use information; understand complex relationships; and work with a variety of technologies.

Utilizing these competencies as a core, career education and training programs can be relevant to the workplace and promote critical thinking, problem solving, flexibility, teamwork, leadership, and communication. Instructional programs for the workplace should focus on employee response to security-related problems. Scenario-based instruction can assist in this effort. Evaluations of situational exercises provide valuable insight into employee preparedness.

Further, employees who participate in scenario-based situational exercises are more likely to translate lessons learned during training into effective response during actual events.

The development of a performance-based education or training program begins with a job-task (occupational) analysis. The job-task information collected and analyzed becomes the foundation for workforce training curriculum development. The analysis helps to identify general knowledge requirements, such as those articulated in the SCANS report cited previously, and specific job-related skills and desired employee qualities. The analysis will disclose what the trainees should know and be able to do, and how should they think and act.

Professional career program development can address psychomotor, cognitive, and **affective skill** development. Psychomotor skills are required to perform functions such as manipulation of tools and weapons. Cognitive skill development focuses on knowledge acquisition. Knowing the law, for example, is vital to success in security occupations. Affective skill development addresses desired values and attitudes consistent with those demanded of security personnel.

After job-related competencies (skills) and human behaviors are identified, the education and training program can be developed and implemented. The first step in this process involves the creation of **instructional goals** and **instructional objectives**. An **instructional goal** is the learning outcome expected at the conclusion of an instructional program. Instructional goals should

- translate job outcomes into instructional outcomes by reorienting the statement to the thinking skill required and the context in which the performance occurs.
- develop outcomes around the essential functions or problems of the discipline or job area.
- reflect the breadth of application that learners may face in specific job positions.
- include the personal interactions, communications, and basic skill requirements related to performance.
- be presented in a way that emphasizes, in relevant, authentic terms, the importance of each goal.

An **instructional objective** describes the skills and behaviors the learner is expected to exhibit to demonstrate competence. Instructional (enabling) objectives are measurable (performance-based) and enable the learner to achieve the instructional goal. Written tests, verbal presentations, projects, collaborative activities, and practical demonstrations are often used to measure performance and progress toward meeting instructional goals. Instructional objectives

- offer a balanced core of learning in each course.
- promote a belief that in-depth study of a limited number of important topics will have a more lasting effect than a course that tries to cover many disconnected topics.
- are designed to focus on results, with multiple indicators (assessments) of performance.
- utilize authentic assessments that encourage originality, insightfulness, and problem solving, along with mastery of important information.
- ensure active learner involvement.
- avoid tracking plans that assign students to a particular level and deny some students the opportunity to acquire knowledge and skills to succeed.
- get students *doing* early in the course rather than studying all the principles and *basics* prior to performing (Nicholson, 1997).

Perhaps the most widely accepted approach to developing and classifying instructional objectives is found in the classic *Taxonomy of Educational Objectives* (Bloom, Englehart, Furst, Hill, & Krathwohl, 1956). The taxonomy serves as a guide for specifying performance outcomes. It provides a hierarchy (levels) of thinking processes that enable learners to develop an understanding of complex material (see Table 8–3).

TABLE 8–3	Taxonomy of Educational Objectives (from simplest to most challenging)	
Level	**Explanation**	**Example**
Knowledge	This is the simplest level and represents a mere recall of facts or other memorized information. Verbs most commonly used in knowledge-level objectives include *define, state, repeat, locate, name,* and *recognize.*	Upon the completion of this course, the learner should be able to define *security management.*
Comprehension	Slightly broader than the knowledge level, comprehension-level performance standards require the learner to organize facts and select among available alternatives. Some verbs used in comprehension-level objectives include *describe, identify, discuss, estimate,* and *summarize.*	Upon completion of this course, the learner should be able to identify a situation in which asset protection is required.
Application	At this level, a learner should be able to apply skills or information learned to new and different situations. Some verbs used in application-level objectives include *solve, illustrate, demonstrate, translate,* and *interpret.*	Upon the completion of this course, the learner should be able to demonstrate asset protection techniques.
Analysis	At this level, the learner should be able to classify and sort information. Some verbs used in the analysis level include *differentiate, criticize, categorize, compare,* and *contrast.*	Upon completion of this course, the learner should be able to differentiate low from high loss probability.
Synthesis	At this level, the learner must combine ideas from previous learning to create new concepts and information. Some verbs that characterize the synthesis level include *create, design, develop, organize, compose,* and *construct.*	Upon completion of this course, the learner should be able to create a loss prevention program.
Evaluation	This is the highest level of the taxonomy, and it requires the learner to make decisions and exercise judgment based on previously known facts or opinions. Some verbs that characterize this level include *evaluate, appraise, assess, prioritize, justify,* and *recommend.*	Upon completion of this course, the learner should be able to justify the budget for a loss prevention program.

Evaluation of a trainee's progress and assessment of outcomes should be matched to the instructional objectives. Methods used to assess learner performance should replicate, as closely as possible, the actual performance standards in the workplace. Written tests should not be the only assessment tool. Projects, team activities, demonstrations, and simulations also help predict success in the actual work environment. The ultimate success of the program is measured against the individual's ability to perform and apply what was learned in accordance with the measurable standards identified in the occupational (job-task) analysis (Ortmeier, 1999; Ortmeier & Davis, 2012).

Step 4: Acquire and Maintain Equipment, Facilities, and Supplies

The fourth step in the implementation process is to acquire equipment, supplies, and facilities necessary to put a security plan into action. Equipment, supplies, and facilities represent high-dollar cost items in the budget. Careful planning may avoid the pitfalls of overextension. A lease arrangement may be a viable alternative to purchase. With respect to physical facilities, the location selection process should receive special attention. Area crime rates and availability of public services should be researched. Equipment typically utilized in a security environment includes communications hardware, alarm systems, firearms, and vehicles. The quality and expected life span of each item as compared to price should be a consideration. Competitive bidding, references, as well as the requirement for performance and service contracts are essential ingredients to successful equipment, facilities, and supply acquisitions.

EQUIPMENT An almost endless array of equipment is used to fulfill the security function. Vehicles, communications equipment, weapons, computers, emergency lights, alarm systems, cameras, uniforms, flashlights, and numerous other articles with a life expectancy of more than

Vehicles are an example of equipment.
(Photo courtesy of Marquis/Shutterstock.com.)

1 year are represented on equipment lists. Typically, the persons responsible for equipment are involved with its acquisition, installation, inventory, and disposal. They evaluate the equipment's performance and recommend new acquisitions. They must calculate equipment life span and submit plans for equipment replacement. Based on equipment specifications, they also establish bidding procedures and supervise the bidding process.

FACILITIES   The facilities task involves all aspects of real property (land and buildings) acquisition and use. Most security personnel are not well versed in architecture and engineering. Therefore, security managers should seek professional advice regarding land acquisition as well as building construction and retrofitting. Related activities should be grouped within a facility. Concepts of crime prevention through environmental design (CPTED) should be incorporated into every facilities plan.

SUPPLIES   Supplies include those items with a life expectancy of less than 1 year. Supplies include items such as paper, forms, pens, pencils, ammunition, batteries, software, fuel, medical supplies, printer cartridges, light bulbs, and training manuals. Typically, the personnel responsible for equipment are also tasked with the acquisition, inventory, and distribution of supplies.

Proper maintenance enhances equipment and facility life span and functionality. Alternately, malfunctioning equipment and dirty facilities negatively affect personnel safety, efficiency, and morale. In large organizational units, maintenance and custodial personnel may be employed full-time. Small departments may secure the services of outside vendors to supply maintenance and cleaning services on a contractual basis.

Step 5: Establish Policies and Procedures

The fifth major step to implementation of the action plan is the development of policies and procedures. Written policies and procedures provide uniform guidelines for handling various types of situations. A **policy** is a general statement describing how anticipated situations should be handled. A **procedure** outlines a series of steps to be followed consistently in a definite order.

POLICIES   Policy statements focus on a wide range of personnel issues, such as selection, discipline, promotion, and termination. They often address behavioral problems associated with substance abuse, sexual harassment, discrimination, as well as use of force. Thus, policies can be used to help create accountability for behavior. Policies can also be used to describe general goals. As exemplified by the following list, policy statements address a wide range of topics and issues:

- affirmative action
- conflicts of interest
- drug and alcohol abuse
- equal employment opportunity
- equal employment opportunity for the disabled, Vietnam-era veterans, and special disabled veterans
- ethics
- firearms
- general practices
- harassment
- health, safety, and the environment
- human resources
- information security

- Internet use
- investigations
- political contributions
- protection of assets
- security
- sexual harassment
- smoking
- special project security
- travel and entertainment
- use of force
- U.S. sentencing guidelines
- workplace violence

Most existing organizations have numerous policy statements in place. Existing policies may require periodic revision to accommodate new variables, and additional policies may be created as new situations arise.

Although policies and their presentation format may vary among organizations, each statement should include the title of the policy statement, the name of the issuing department, an effective date, the name of the persons responsible for approving the policy and the statement, and the purpose of the policy stated in clear, concise terms. The statement should also include the scope of the policy. In other words, to whom does it apply? This is followed by the policy statement itself, the procedure for implementing the policy, and a list of definitions if uncommon terminology is used.

PROCEDURES   Procedures outline specific operational protocol and describe detailed responses to incidents or events. As exemplified by the following list, procedures often cover a wider range of activities and are more specific than policies:

- AIDS contact
- antieavesdropping
- antistalking
- attack avoidance
- auto theft prevention
- background checking
- bank security officer
- bomb threats
- burglary prevention
- canine security
- civil process acceptance
- classification of sensitive information
- cleaning crew access control
- clear desk
- computer virus protection
- conference security
- driving safeguards
- duress alarm
- electronic information security
- electronic mail protection
- emergency calls

- employee access control
- executive protection
- fire responses by security officers
- flag etiquette
- guest security
- handling classified information
- hazards identification
- human resource management
- information protection at the office
- Internet protection
- intranet protection
- lost and found
- medical emergencies
- office building evacuation
- office inspections
- office security management
- password protection
- property removal
- rape avoidance
- repair crew access control
- security program auditing
- sexual harassment reporting
- substance abuse program audit
- telephone answering
- two-way radio

SECURITY SPOTLIGHT

Select five procedure categories that interest you from the list on pages 194–195. Research your educational institution's or employer's procedures regarding the categories you have selected. To conduct this research, you may need to talk with someone in your school's or company's human resources, legal, or security departments as well as review written resources such as procedure or employee manuals.

Procedures function as action plans for implementing policies. They describe specific methods of operation. Some procedures are extremely restrictive or legally binding. Procedural mandates of the U.S. Supreme Court are legally binding. For example, in its 1966 *Miranda v. Arizona* decision, the Court held that a suspect should be advised of certain rights under the Constitution when the suspect is in the custody of public police for purposes of interrogation.

Generally, procedures are exacting. They provide detailed instructions and limit individual discretion. However, precise guidance may not be appropriate in all situations. Security personnel often work alone in a setting that requires the exercise of independent judgment in individual situations. Thus, overreliance on standardized procedures can discourage critical thinking, problem solving, initiative, and imagination (Cordner & Scarborough, 2010; Dalton, 2003; Fay, 1999; Greer & Plunkett, 2007; Robbins & Coulter, 2009).

CONTRACT SERVICES (OUTSOURCING)   A contract vendor may be appropriate for certain types of security services. When a vendor is used, the contract should specify salaries and wages, insurance coverage, liability limits, employee screening procedures, audit rights for the contractee, performance standards, and procedures for compensation adjustments. A contract should also contain letters of authorization. If a premium wage rate (a rate above the prevailing wage) is specified, the contractor should be audited to ensure payment of the premium rate. The contractee should consult with an insurance expert to determine the type and amount of insurance required of the contractor. Some contractors are underinsured and underfinanced, and they do not have the resources to withstand a lawsuit. Indemnification permits the contractee to be reimbursed for expenditures incurred as a result of the contractual relationship. Through an **indemnity/hold harmless clause,** the contractee is held harmless in the event of a wrongful act by a contract employee. A preemployment screening procedure should also be specified in the contract.

The contractee should reserve the right to audit the contractor to prevent unscrupulous activities on the part of the contractor. Performance standards and training must be included in the contract. An adjustment of compensation clause allows the contractee to reduce compensation to the contractor for failure to meet obligations expressed in the contract. Letters of authorization should be included to specify what the contractor can do on the contractee agency's or corporation's behalf. The letters should detail contractor limits of authority (Cheeseman, 2010; Dalton, 1995; Johnson, 2003).

Outsourcing is common in manufacturing. Due to high domestic labor costs, many U.S. companies manufacture their products in countries where labor costs are substantially reduced. Computers, apparel, consumer electronics, and many other items are manufactured in foreign countries. Likewise, many business services are outsourced to foreign entities. Computer software development, accounting and insurance claim-related services, reservations services, and customer service hotlines may be outsourced to companies or subsidiaries in other countries (Collins, 2008).

One might question the viability of outsourcing any form of security service to an entity in a foreign country. Yet the possibility exists, especially with security services such as the monitoring of a central station alarm system. If outsourcing by a security contractor is a possibility, the contractee is advised to balance cost savings with the likelihood that a security system may be compromised or subject to an unauthorized electronic intrusion.

Step 6: Evaluate (Assess) Performance

Evaluation (assessment) consists of performance measurements and quality assurance.

PERFORMANCE MEASUREMENTS   Achieving excellent performance in any organization involves special attention to the **evaluation** process. Even carefully developed plans can fail without an evaluation of progress and outcomes. After a plan is implemented, the evaluation and control process begins. The process is exercised continuously throughout the life of the operation. Evaluation involves measuring performance, comparing performance with stated objectives, reporting results, and taking corrective action, if necessary. In essence, it involves a return to needs or risk assessment and planning and the completion of the administrative process (management cycle).

Evaluation has both predictive and after-the-fact aspects. Through predictions, the evaluator attempts to anticipate the possibility of undesirable outcomes and prevent deviation from established standards. Crime prevention is an example of predictive evaluation. After-the-fact evaluation analyzes an event or deviation from established standards to determine what corrective action is required. A determination of the cause of a theft is an example of after-the-fact evaluation.

The first step in the evaluation process is to measure performance based on the standards (objectives) established during the risk assessment and planning process. The standards are units of measurement that serve as reference points for evaluating results. There are several types of standards—tangible, numerical, and intangible:

- **Tangible standards** are quite clear, specific, identifiable, and generally measurable. They measure quantity and quality. They may be used to assess incident reduction efforts, appraise individual employee performance, or as an ingredient in the budget process. Tangible standards are expressed in terms of numbers, dollars, physical properties, and time.
- **Numerical standards** are quantifiable, such as the amount of crime reduction or number of personnel who successfully complete a training program. Examples of monetary standards include the impact of a budget or payroll and maintenance costs. Physical standards refer to quality, durability, and other factors related to physical composition. Vehicle durability can be determined with physical standards. Time standards refer to the speed with which a task might be completed.
- **Intangible standards** relate to human characteristics that are difficult to measure. They take no physical form, yet they are as important as tangible standards. Examples of intangible standards are a desirable attitude, high morale, ethics, cooperation, and the organization's reputation. In some cases, crime prevention cannot be measured utilizing a tangible standard. It is difficult, if not impossible, to measure the amount of crime that has been prevented unless a number of criminal incidents occurred before a prevention program was initiated. Thus, measuring a monetary return on investment (ROI) for security-related expenditures is often a challenge. Security's value-added contribution (VAC) to the organization is often incalculable. In many situations, security's VAC may be more qualitative than quantitative. Employees and clients may feel safer and experience less fear of crime. Thus, morale, productivity, and the quality of organizational life improve.

Methods for measuring performance include personal observation, written and oral reports of subordinates, automatic recording systems, inspections, tests, and surveys. Whatever method is used, performance standards should be based on realistic targets. Failure to meet a performance standard can result from a variety of causes. Identification of causes rather than the symptoms is extremely important if appropriate corrective action is to be taken. Those closest to the situation should be consulted to determine why the performance standards are not being met. Participation of all affected by the measurements is an essential ingredient in this process. The sooner a deviation from a standard is identified, the sooner the situation can be corrected. Evaluation and assessment, therefore, is a continuous process.

After a careful analysis of any deviation from a performance standard, corrective action may be necessary. Modifications to the original plan should not be viewed negatively. Objectives and standards stated in the original plan are often based on forecasts. If the deviation is extreme, it may be necessary to evaluate the planning process itself. There may be several reasons why a deviation from an established standard has occurred. It is possible that the standards could not be achieved because they were based on faulty forecasts or assumptions or because an unforeseen problem arose that distorted the anticipated outcome. Failure might have occurred in some other activity that supported the activity being evaluated. It is also possible that the employee who performed the task was unqualified, was not given adequate directions, was negligent, or did not follow required directions or procedures.

THE USE OF METRICS In recent years, the use of **metrics** has become popular as a means to evaluate performance. Metrics, as relates to performance, involves procedures designed to quantify and periodically assess processes that can be measured. The metrics (measurements) are compared to previous or similar assessments. Metrics are often used in management to track productivity, identify trends, and calculate resource consumption. The metrics tracked may be key performance indicators (benchmarks) against which similar activities are compared. In a security setting, metrics can be used to calculate ROI and VAC.

Well-managed security operations gather an enormous amount of information (e.g., traffic patterns, crime and accident incident reports, safety hazards). Utilizing a metrics-based performance measurement system, security information is quantified and aligned with organizational priorities (e.g., expense reductions, risk management, mitigation of liability, ROI, VAC, life safety, legal requirements).

Consider this simple example:

1. A review of incident reports reveals that nine minor vehicle collisions occurred within a month in the organization's parking lot.
2. The location and time of each incident is identified on a map of the parking lot.
3. An analysis reveals that most collisions occur at the end of the workday (5:00 P.M.) at a parking lot exit near a highway on-ramp.
4. A security officer is assigned to direct traffic at the relevant parking lot exit at the end of each workday.
5. Incident reports are reviewed periodically to assess collision reduction strategy.

Thus, metrics can be used to identify vulnerabilities and map risks, determine allocation of resources, and assess results. Sound metrics procedures and protocols are specific, measurable, attainable, relevant, and timely.

QUALITY ASSURANCE Quality performance standards are probably the most difficult to measure. Quality can be an elusive concept and it means different things to different people. Basically, quality means that the product or service meets or exceeds predetermined expectations. **Quality assurance,** continuous quality improvement, and total quality management (TQM) initiatives involve approaches to administration that attempt to maximize effectiveness of an organization through the continual improvement of the quality of its people, processes, products, and environment. To ensure quality performance, initiatives must be based on decisions founded on facts rather than on intuition. Participants must also take personal responsibility for quality, improve teamwork and commitment, and focus on the end user and service. Quality assurance is a way of life, not a program (Campbell, 2006; Dalton, 1995; Goetsch & Davis, 2010; Haberer & Webb, 1994; Lewis, Goodman, & Fandt, 2008; "Measuring up," 2011; Peters, 1987).

Quality assurance initiatives involve goal setting, trust, cohesiveness, increasing information flow, and resolving conflict. To succeed, quality assurance initiatives must incorporate an internal and external customer focus, an obsession with quality, long-term commitment, teamwork, employee involvement, and empowerment. They must incorporate education and training, freedom from control, and unity of purpose. The initiatives must also use the scientific approach to decision making and problem solving.

Some managers make errors when implementing quality assurance initiatives. They attempt a quality initiative by delegating responsibility to an outside expert rather than applying the leadership necessary to get everyone within the organization involved (Clemmer, 1992; Gomez-Mejia & Balkin, 2012). Employees must learn how to be team players. An organization must often undergo a cultural change before teamwork can succeed. Creating teams before learning about teamwork and quality assurance methods will be counterproductive and will create more problems than the teams will solve.

Organizations must develop quality initiatives concurrent with plans for integrating them into all elements of the organization. None of the approaches to quality management is truly a one-size-fits-all proposition. Quality programs must be tailored to fit organizational needs. According to Goetsch and Davis (2010), quality initiatives should include commitment, team building, training, vision and guiding principles, broad objectives, communication, a plan for implementation, project identification, feedback, and modification of the organizational infrastructure as necessary.

It is a long-established fact that human beings are resistant to change. Security personnel are no exception. The injection of quality assurance initiatives into the security function results in a major change in the way many agencies and firms conduct business. Attitudes do not change rapidly. Nor do they change without reasonable justification. Concrete evidence of the benefits of quality assurance initiatives can enlighten and convince security personnel that quality service is what helps gain public and consumer trust and support for the organization and the people in it. If not appropriately implemented, quality assurance initiatives become just another management fad that can damage, rather than assist, an organization.

Traditional organizational performance measures have focused on financial and statistical results. However, a consequence of a narrow focus on financial return and statistics is that it may encourage organizational leaders to lie, distort, or misrepresent data to demonstrate favorable results. This phenomenon is evidenced by the corporate scandals of the early twenty-first century. Investors and other stakeholders have learned, however, that numerical measures are only as accurate as the people who compile them. Ethical managers will ensure that adequate controls are in place to discourage attempts to distort or manipulate data (Dalton, 1995; Lewis, Goodman, & Fandt, 2008; Robbins & Coulter, 2009).

PRODUCT AND PROCESS QUALITY IMPROVEMENT: THE MALCOLM BALDRIGE NATIONAL QUALITY AWARD PROGRAM   In an effort to improve product and process quality and productivity in the public as well as private sectors, the Congress passed the Malcolm Baldrige National Quality Improvement Act of 1987—Public Law 100–107. The Act created the **Malcolm Baldrige National Quality Award** program. The Award is named for Malcolm Baldrige, who served as U.S. Secretary of Commerce from 1981 until his untimely death in a rodeo accident in 1987. Baldrige's managerial excellence contributed to long-term improvement in efficiency and effectiveness of government. The findings and purposes of the Act that created the Baldrige Award states that:

1. The leadership of the United States in product and process quality has been challenged strongly (and sometimes successfully) by foreign competition, and U.S. productivity growth has improved less than its competitors over the last two decades.

2. American business and industry are beginning to understand that poor quality costs companies as much as 20 percent of sales revenues nationally and that improved quality of goods and services goes hand-in-hand with improved productivity, lower costs, and increased profitability.

3. Strategic planning for quality and quality improvement programs, through a commitment to excellence in manufacturing and services, is becoming more and more essential to the well-being of U.S. economy and to the ability to compete effectively in the global marketplace.

4. Improved management understanding of the factory floor, worker involvement in quality, and greater emphasis on statistical process control can lead to dramatic improvements in the cost and quality of manufactured products and services.

5. The concept of quality improvement is directly applicable to small as well as large companies, to service industries as well as manufacturing, and to the public sector as well as private enterprise.

6. To be successful, quality improvement programs must be management-led and customer-oriented, and this may require fundamental changes in the way companies and agencies do business.

7. Several major industrial nations have successfully coupled rigorous private-sector quality audits with national awards giving special recognition to those enterprises the audits identify as the very best.

8. A national quality award program of this kind in the United States would help improve quality and productivity by:

   a. helping to stimulate American companies to improve quality and productivity for the pride of recognition while obtaining a competitive edge through increased profits;

   b. recognizing the achievements of those companies that improve the quality of their goods and services and provide an example to others;

   c. establishing guidelines and criteria that can be used by business, industrial, governmental, and other organizations in evaluating their own quality improvement efforts; and

   d. providing specific guidance for other American organizations that wish to learn how to manage for high quality by making available detailed information on how winning organizations were able to change their cultures and achieve eminence (National Institute of Standards and Technology, 2007).

The Baldrige criteria for performance excellence provide a systems perspective for understanding performance management. They reflect validated, leading-edge management practices against which an organization can measure itself. With their acceptance nationally and internationally as the model for performance excellence, the criteria represent a common language for communication among organizations for sharing best practices. The criteria are also the basis for the Malcolm Baldrige National Quality Award process.

Learn more about the Malcolm Baldrige National Quality Award criteria and quality self-analysis worksheets at www.quality.nist.gov.

Summary

Security program implementation involves the development and acquisition of an organizational structure, staff, equipment and facilities, and policy and procedure statements as well as the use of contract services when appropriate. Security workforce planning involves a determination of personnel requirements, job-task analyses, the creation of job descriptions and specifications, scheduling, training, and professional career education.

Human beings represent the most valuable resource in any enterprise. Enlightened management, supervision, and leadership of human resources are critical to organizational success. An organization must hire the right people, train them well, maintain their integrity, and treat them with respect.

Security program administration emerges as a mechanism to collaborate with others to achieve organizational goals. Quality products and services can be assured through a comprehensive evaluation process, coupled with a determination of the value an efficient and effective security program represents.

Key Terms

administration
affective skill
evaluation
full-time equivalent (FTE)
    persons
indemnity/hold harmless clause
intangible standards
instructional goal

instructional objective
job description
job specifications
job task (occupational) analysis
Malcolm Baldrige National
    Quality Award
management
metrics

numerical standards
organize
policy
procedure
professional development
quality assurance
quality assurance initiatives
tangible standards

Discussion Questions and Exercises

1. What are the major differences between public and private administrative processes?
2. What or who determines an organization's structure?
3. Explain the importance of ethical leadership to the administrative process.
4. List and describe the workforce planning process.
5. Appropriate preservice and in-service career education and training are essential for security personnel. How are training and education needs determined? Does training help to reduce civil and criminal liability? How?
6. How does a policy differ from a procedure?
7. Why is program evaluation important? Who should be involved in the evaluation process?

YOUR TURN: Evaluating a Mall or Business District Security Program

Five people in the Trolley Square Shopping Center in Salt Lake City died on Valentine's Day 2007 as a result of gunshot wounds inflicted by an 18-year-old man. The death toll could have been higher if the shooter had not been stopped by an armed, off-duty police officer who witnessed and responded to the attack.

While shootings in shopping malls and business districts are rare, mass killing is always a possibility in any public place. For this reason, it is valuable to evaluate security programs in such settings. For the purposes of this case study, you will evaluate the security program associated with a shopping mall or a business district of your choice. To do so, take the following steps:

1. Walk through a shopping mall or business district in your area.
2. Determine whether there is a visible security presence (police or security personnel, surveillance cameras) to deter criminal activity and reduce legitimate fears of assault on the part of shoppers or customers.
3. Based on your observations, evaluate the crime deterrent efforts of the mall or business district you visited. How effective are these deterrents? What (if any) additional efforts would you advise to improve security in the mall or business district you have examined?

CHAPTER 9

Investigations, Intelligence Operations, and Reporting

LEARNING OBJECTIVES

After completing this chapter, the reader should be able to

- list and describe the common elements of the investigative process.
- discuss the types of human resource investigations.
- describe elements of personal injury and property damage investigations.
- outline the procedure for collection and preservation of evidence.
- analyze evidence gathered in a civil or criminal investigation.
- describe situations in which surveillance and undercover assignments are warranted.
- identify business crime activity.
- describe business crime prevention techniques.
- locate and develop sources of information.
- discuss procedures for information gathering and analysis.
- evaluate information gathered from public and private sources.
- identify impermissible investigative conduct.
- describe industrial espionage techniques.
- compare and contrast business intelligence with counterespionage.
- outline procedures for documentation.

INTRODUCTION

Central to the tasks and functions of loss prevention, asset protection, and the security management process is the need to gather information and accurately document and report findings of fact. Thus, investigations, intelligence operations, and reporting are critical. An investigation should be conducted any time a loss occurs or a threat materializes. Intelligence is gathered to maintain a competitive edge and identify potential criminal activity. The results of an investigation or intelligence operation must be reported in a fashion that enhances organizational decision-making capabilities.

INVESTIGATIONS

The Basics

An **investigation** is a systematic process through which information is gathered, analyzed, and reported. It facilitates decision making (American Society for Industrial Security, 1998). It also involves an investigator who conducts an inquiry for a particular purpose (Walsh & Healy, 1987). The inquiry is a systematic gathering of the facts surrounding an event, condition, or situation (Ortmeier, 2006).

An investigation is warranted when an accident occurs, when unexplainable property losses are discovered, or when personal misconduct or criminal activity is observed or reported. In addition, an investigation is a necessary step in the process of gathering information on prospective employees and business partners. Background investigations are integral to business and criminal intelligence operations. Through a systematic inquiry, the investigator collects information, identifies and analyzes problems, determines facts, preserves evidence, and reports findings in an objective manner. Subsequent to an incident, the investigator must determine who was involved and what, when, where, how, and why the incident occurred. As a preventive tool, the investigator can use the systematic inquiry to identify potential problem individuals, predict behavior, and forecast events.

The investigative process is an art as well as a science. Through training, education, experience, and intuitive judgment, a good investigator re-creates events and facilitates decision making. Leveraging the personal qualities of honesty and open-mindedness, along with excellent human relations, communications, and critical thinking skills, a good investigator adds value for organizations (Lushbaugh & Weston, 2012; O'Hara & O'Hara, 2003).

Types of Investigations

Several types of investigations are conducted in a security and protective services environment. These investigations focus on noncriminal and criminal events as well as predictions of future behavior and activity. They may be conducted to ensure compliance with safety laws and regulations, support litigation activities, assess protective systems' vulnerabilities, follow up on consumer complaints, prevent accidents, trace and locate a criminal suspect, or identify the source of an unexplained loss. In a business environment, an investigation can focus on customer service, finance, purchasing, sales and marketing operations, human resources, or information systems protection, or it may be conducted in support of litigation activities.

HUMAN RESOURCE INVESTIGATIONS   In the personnel arena, typical **human resource investigations** include those related to employee backgrounds, workplace violence, employment discrimination, worker compensation claims, sexual harassment, substance abuse, and wrongful termination. Background investigations on prospective employees should be part of the preemployment screening process. As a due diligence requirement, an organization should verify information contained in a candidate's employment application. Failure to exercise due diligence could result in the development of a liability connection between the new employee and the organization. Criminal, credit, previous employment, academic, and other background history information must be authenticated. Untruthful statements and deceptive practices by the applicant provide clues to the job candidate's integrity, ethics, and propensity toward improper, even criminal, behavior. In some instances, it is also appropriate to update background information on those seeking promotion within the organization. Chapter 5 contains additional information regarding background investigations for employees.

Employers are required by law to investigate claims of sexual harassment and unlawful employment discrimination. Failure to conduct a thorough investigation and take prompt corrective action in a case of sexual harassment can have severe consequences. For example, inaction and inappropriate action on the part of employers have led to multimillion dollar civil judgments for plaintiffs in sexual harassment lawsuits.

Sexual harassment is a form of discrimination that is defined as requests for sexual favors, unwelcomed sexual advances, or verbal or physical conduct of a sexual nature when submission to such conduct is used as a basis for employment decisions. The definition also includes conduct that creates an intimidating, hostile, or offensive work environment. Petty annoyances and isolated incidents (unless extremely serious) do not constitute sexual harassment. The harasser can be an employee, an employer's agent (e.g., a contractor), or a nonemployee over whom the employer has control (e.g., a customer). Victims include the person harassed as well as anyone affected by the offensive conduct. Prevention of sexual harassment is the best strategy for any organization to adopt. If a complaint arises, employers should investigate and take appropriate action immediately (American Society for Industrial Security, 1998; U.S. Equal Employment Opportunity Commission, 2007).

Likewise, employers must investigate, and have been held civilly liable for, claims of unlawful employment discrimination. Such claims are based on alleged discriminatory practices in selection, promotion, retention, and working conditions of employees. Discrimination against a person because of age, gender, race, ethnicity, lifestyle, or disability is prohibited by law.

Employers must investigate threats of harm against employees as well as claims of unsafe working conditions. Employers have been held liable for injuries or deaths resulting from workplace violence and failure to correct safety hazards. Liability may attach if the employer is aware, or should know, that employees are in danger because of the possibility of violent acts perpetrated by other employees, by outsiders, or as a result of hazardous working conditions.

In the area of worker's compensation, the need for an investigation arises from two types of situations. The first involves injuries to employees that have arisen out of employment (AOE). Typical AOE injuries are those that develop over an extended period of time, such as stress or lung disease. The other type of injury that may give rise to a worker's compensation claim and investigation is an injury that occurs during the course of employment (COE). A COE injury is attributed to a single act or event, such as an accident or fall.

Individuals under the influence of alcohol, drugs, or other substances are less productive, show poor attendance, create hazardous situations, and do poor quality work. Those who abuse substances in the workplace are high risk and may have a propensity toward theft, injuries, and property damage. Consider these statistics:

- Substance abusers are 33 to 50 percent less productive than individuals who are not substance abusers.
- Substance abusers are absent an average of 3 or more weeks per year and are late for work three times more frequently than non–substance abusers.
- Approximately 40 percent of industrial fatalities and 47 percent of the injuries that take place in the U.S. workplace are associated with alcoholism and alcohol abuse.

- Substance abusers are three to four times more likely to have an accident on the job and five times more likely to file a workers' compensation claim.
- More than 40 percent of U.S. corporate chief executive officers (CEOs) who participated in a recent survey stated that the use of illegal drugs and alcohol costs them 1 to 10 percent of their annual payroll.
- An estimated 50 to 80 percent of loss regarding pilferage and theft is related to substance-using employees.
- Substance abusers, when compared with people who are not substance abusers, file 300 to 400 percent more costly medical claims (*Alcohol Test Info*, 2011).

A key to dealing effectively with substance abuse in the workplace is the ability to recognize the symptoms of abuse and take corrective action through counseling and appropriate discipline. However, even when a company offers employee assistance programs including drug and alcohol counseling, employees who want to get help often hesitate to take advantage of such programs because they fear that counseling is not confidential. To combat this situation, companies must dispel these myths and reassure workers that getting help will not endanger their careers (Fisher, 2011). Another challenge for companies is that the symptoms of chemical abuse are often subtle, and direct confrontation of the abuses can subject the employer to legal challenges. Often, the best evidence is produced through an undercover investigation or surveillance activity.

Investigations relating to claims of wrongful termination result from allegations of discriminatory action on the part of an employer or from a discharge arising out of a false accusation of dishonesty or substance abuse in the workplace. In the event of a lawsuit, the plaintiff will often claim that the employer's investigation of the allegation was inadequate or improperly conducted. As a defense, the employer must present proof of a proper investigation into the allegations, with sufficient cause for the termination, meticulous documentation of the history of the employee's wrongdoing, coupled with the warnings given and reasonable actions taken by the employer.

A timely human resource investigation, coupled with the action warranted, can reduce organizational liability for the inappropriate actions of an employee. In this regard, the education of, and support from, senior management is critical to success. Security personnel must strive to educate management regarding the human resource policies, procedures, investigations, and corrective actions necessary to mitigate liability. In addition, new employees as well as existing employees should be informed and reminded of behaviors that may trigger a human resource investigation.

Finally, information or evidence discovered during the course of a human resource investigation should be disclosed according to applicable laws and organizational policy. Unless legally required to disclose the information to an external agency, sound management practice may indicate that internal distribution, on a need-to-know basis, is preferable to any form of public disclosure.

PERSONAL INJURY AND PROPERTY DAMAGE INVESTIGATIONS   Personal injury and property damage can result from an unintentional accident, from a collision, or through the intentional act (or omission to act) of another human being. Personal injury involves physical harm to an individual. Property damage involves harm to or destruction of property. An investigation must be conducted if personal injury is involved. Injury or damage scenes should be approached with caution if hazardous materials are present, electric power lines are exposed, or natural gas lines are broken. After all injured parties at the scene have received necessary emergency medical treatment, the investigation of the incident may proceed. Witnesses should be interviewed separately to avoid cross-contamination of statements. The person conducting the interviews should avoid leading questions that imply an answer. Rather, witnesses should be asked what they observed and responses should be recorded verbatim if possible.

When interviews are complete, the investigator will examine the scene, record measurements, photograph the area, if appropriate, and prepare follow-up written reports on the incident. In some cases, it may be necessary to reconstruct the event to determine the exact cause of the injury or damage. Ultimately, the goal of any **personal injury investigation** or **property damage investigation** is to prevent similar occurrences in the future. Information collected during the course of the investigation can be used to improve procedures and protective systems.

CRIMINAL INVESTIGATIONS   The purposes of a **criminal investigation** are to determine if a crime was committed, identify and locate the suspect, and recognize, collect, and preserve evidence that may establish guilt or innocence of the accused. A criminal investigation is successful when all available physical evidence is collected and preserved properly, witnesses are intelligently interviewed, and the suspect, if willing, is effectively interrogated. All leads must be properly developed and the investigation must be documented.

Criminal statutes describe criminal behavior and prescribe punishments for conviction. Each element of an offense must be established in the incident under investigation to determine if a crime occurred. If a crime has been committed, the investigator must distinguish misdemeanors from felonies. The powers to arrest differ between felonies and misdemeanors and between private security personnel and the public police. Failure to arrest legally may result in civil and possible criminal liability for false arrest or false imprisonment.

A suspected perpetrator can be identified in a number of ways. The suspect may be apprehended at the scene, or an individual may provide the investigator with an admission or confession subsequent to the incident. Eyewitnesses to the crime may be available. Circumstantial evidence in the form of a motive, opportunity to commit the crime, or trace evidence that can place the suspect at the crime scene may also be available. If the suspect is not present at the crime scene, it will be necessary to trace and locate the perpetrator.

Crime suspects are rarely in hiding. Their identity or location is simply unknown. Before notifying authorities or launching a search for a fugitive, the investigator must ensure that the legal requirements for a possible arrest have been satisfied and all pertinent background information and identification data on the suspect have been gathered. The investigator should collect as much information as possible regarding the suspect's history. Criminal records, if available, provide information regarding aliases used, convictions, and the nature of previous offenses. Other forms of trace information include telephone, city, and crisscross directories, credit bureaus, motor vehicle records, identification data from the U.S. Immigration Service, passport or military records, informants, county assessors and recorders offices, and friends and acquaintances.

Evidence collected must meet certain legal tests to maintain its evidentiary value. The courts will examine the chain of custody of the evidence and will want to know where, when, and by whom the evidence was located and how it was preserved for in-court presentation. Therefore, evidence must be carefully collected, marked for future identification, and preserved. Investigators should wear latex gloves when collecting evidence to avoid possible contamination of the evidence. Without destroying the integrity of the evidence, small as well as large items should be permanently marked for identification wherever possible.

A crime scene forensic specialist gathers evidence.
(Photo courtesy of corepics/Shutterstock.com.)

All physical evidentiary items should be placed in appropriate containers and the containers marked with identifying information. Small delicate items should be wrapped in cotton and placed in an envelope, bottle, or box. The investigator who discovered the evidence should place an identifying mark or initials on the evidence as it is collected. All containers should be sealed and identified with the appropriate evidence or property tag. Each item should be logged into the investigative report. To maintain the chain of custody of evidence, items must be secured and transported properly.

Surveillance and undercover operations are usually necessary when conventional investigative methods fail to produce enough evidence. **Surveillance** involves the observation of a person, place, or object. It is time consuming, expensive, and requires tremendous patience, alertness, and resourcefulness. Surveillance is most successful when the surveillant's appearance and activities do not attract attention from the subject or the public. However, the type of surveillance conducted depends on the nature of the investigation and the circumstances. Stationary, or fixed, surveillance (stakeout) is used when the subject is at a specific location.

Observations may be made from a vehicle, natural hiding places, or areas within a building. Surveillance technology in the form of video cameras and recording devices can substitute for a human surveillant, provided legal requirements are met. A moving surveillance (tail) is used to maintain observation of a moving subject. A close (tight) tail is used when it is extremely important not to lose sight of the subject. Rough (loose) tails are used when keeping the subject under constant observation is not necessary.

Audio and video monitoring are common surveillance methods. This usually involves electronic monitoring of conversations through wiretap or use of video cameras. However, since wiretaps and similar activities are considered searches, court authorization and a search warrant is required if conducted by law enforcement (government) personnel. The courts are reluctant to issue warrants for electronic surveillance unless there is a demonstrated need and all other investigative procedures are exhausted. For private-sector personnel, electronic surveillance is not subject to restrictions under any government exclusionary rule. However, such nongovernmental surveillance activity may be subject to privacy laws, the criminal law, and lawsuits. In the private sector, electronic undercover surveillance is not legally appropriate if the subject has a reasonable expectation of privacy.

An **undercover investigation** is a surveillance through which the surveillant, using an assumed identity or cover, personally encounters a subject under investigation. Undercover surveillance is justified when criminal activity is suspected but no hard evidence of a crime exists. The surveillant gains the confidence of the subject in the hope of obtaining incriminating evidence. Undercover assignments are expensive and can be dangerous. Surveillants must exercise care to avoid detection. Criminals are paranoid and suspicious of people around them. Subjects of a surveillance may also be aware of possible undercover activity.

Surveillance may be conducted by internal security staff or through the use of personnel from external security and investigations firms. There are dozens of large contract firms and hundreds of small companies throughout the United States that provide undercover and surveillance services. Retail outlets, financial institutions, lodging establishments, restaurants, automobile dealerships, and manufacturers are among the types of organizations that often use contracted undercover operatives to identify internal criminal activity, monitor the quality of customer service, and verify product knowledge on the part of employees (Bennett & Hess, 2007; F. Green, 2000; Lewis, Goodman, & Fandt, 2008).

BUSINESS CRIME INVESTIGATIONS Crimes are committed by and against all types of organizations. Most organizations are for-profit business enterprises that produce and sell goods and services. None are immune from crime in the form of business asset theft or damage. A criminal investigation, whether conducted internally or by an external agency, is warranted whenever criminal activity is suspected or identified.

Criminal investigations in businesses and similar organizations can be viewed from at least three perspectives. Some crimes take the form of **fraud**, **embezzlement**, and theft committed against business organizations by employees. Other crimes such as arson, vandalism, robbery, burglary, and theft are committed against a business by outsiders. Still other crimes involving regulatory noncompliance, price-fixing, tax evasion, and commercial bribery are committed by employees and others on behalf of business organizations.

Many of the losses due to crime in a business environment result from a fraudulent scheme or activity. Business-related frauds are often perpetrated through the dishonesty of a party to a business transaction. The parties to the transaction may be employers or employees, buyers or sellers, financiers or borrowers, stockholders or corporations, principals or agents. Frauds are perpetrated through embezzlement, misrepresentations on financial statements, false claims and bankruptcy, bid rigging, inflation of expense accounts, feigned accidents and injuries, and numerous computer and Internet-related activities. Fraudulent schemes include charity, investment, personal improvement, business opportunity, and telemarketing scams. They also include identity theft and countless forms of misrepresentation.

In simplest terms, fraud occurs when someone uses a scheme or device to deceive another. Perpetrators of fraud utilize false suggestions, forgery, false pretenses, misappropriation, suppression of the truth, surprise, tricks, and lying. Fraudulent behavior can be civil or criminal, or both. It can be prosecuted in criminal court, rectified in civil court, or it may be unactionable, as when a buyer has no legal recourse (caveat emptor—let the buyer beware). Most criminal statutes on fraud specify certain types of fraudulent behavior, such as embezzlement, larceny by trick, false pretenses, defrauding an innkeeper, bad checks, forgery, and uttering (passing) a forged instrument (e.g., a check or other document). The uncommon characteristic of each of these offenses is the method used or the time frame wherein the perpetrator forms the intent to permanently deprive someone else of property. A common characteristic is the possessory right to whatever the subject of the fraud is. In an embezzlement case, for example, the perpetrator already has legal possession of the property because of a relationship of trust. Subsequent to the lawful possession, however, the embezzler breaches the trust and misappropriates the property. Bank officers, cashiers, and bookkeepers embezzle. On the other hand, if a person obtains property from another through a misrepresentation of the facts, lawful possession does not pass and the perpetrator commits the crime of false pretenses. A broker who knowingly sells worthless or nearly worthless stock at an inflated price commits the fraud-related offense of theft by false pretenses.

In an effort to consolidate fraud-related crimes and simplify prosecution, many states merge these offenses and larceny into the statutory offense of theft. Under such statutes, criminal liability is incurred when a court can establish that the perpetrator unlawfully took property from another and did not intend to return it. The fact that the intent to permanently deprive the possessor of the property was formed before, during, or at the time of the taking is immaterial under these statutes. This eliminates the need to prosecute under separate statutes dealing with the crimes of larceny, embezzlement, false pretenses, larceny by trick, and the like.

A common and likely fraudulent scheme involves some form of internal theft by an employee. An internal theft may be disguised to mask the criminal activity, giving it the appearance of legitimacy. Secreting merchandise or products in a purse or briefcase are examples of a disguise. Other common forms of internal theft involve **accounts payable diversions** as well as a **cash conversion**, **inventory conversion**, or **receivables conversion**. Accounts payable diversions are disbursement frauds committed by an employee who processes payroll information, refunds, discounts, rebates, or purchases. Flaws in accounts payable processing systems and poor controls provide the opportunity for personnel to convert practically anything into cash or negotiable instruments. A cash conversion involves theft of liquid assets such as currency and negotiable instruments such as checks. Cash conversions occur most often because there are too few controls on persons handling liquid assets or there is little separation of responsibility for the accounting function. They are common when the same person is responsible for receiving and recording incoming receipts, recording sales, making bank deposits, reconciling bank and financial statements, and issuing credit memos.

Inventory and product conversions are usually accomplished by the internal thief who does not have ready access to liquid assets or the accounting function. Inventory or products are stolen. Thus, thieves convert the items to their own use (conversion). Receivables conversion occurs when an employee steals a customer's cash payment and covers the amount stolen with a payment received from another customer. Typically, the scheme involves keeping cash from customer A and waiting until the next day to credit the company with receipts from customer B. Referred to as *lapping receivables*, the scheme requires an element of ingenuity and attention to detail. Computerized point of sale and inventory systems have done little to prevent receivables conversion, although patterns of illegal behavior on the part of the internal thief are easier to detect.

Embezzlement is another common form of internal theft. As compared to larceny, in which the intent to permanently deprive someone of property is formed before or at the time of the taking, embezzlement is the appropriation of property by a person to whom it has been legally entrusted. Embezzlers, therefore, hold positions of trust and have a fiduciary responsibility for property in their possession. Embezzlements often go undetected, and when detected, they are rarely prosecuted. When prosecuted, the penalty after conviction is often significantly less than for other fraud or theft-related offenses. Like most other crimes, embezzlement occurs when motive and opportunity to commit the crime are present, and a capable guardian for the property, such as adequate security measures, is absent. Embezzlers often rationalize their behavior as necessary because of their circumstances, as compensation for being underpaid, or as a loan to be replaced at some future date. They tend to have low self-esteem, compulsive personalities, or excessive lifestyles.

SECURITY SPOTLIGHT

Conduct research into trends in business crimes in the United States. What types of business crimes seem to be increasing? decreasing? To what do you attribute these trends? Given the forces shaping these trends, what one or two actions by business organizations would best enable them to combat such crimes?

Prevention of employee fraud and embezzlement goes beyond security systems and procedural controls. Appropriate organizational culture and values, codes of conduct, and management's creation of an environment of trust and cooperation also promote a climate that helps to prevent employee theft. Yet, even in the best environments, internal theft can and does occur. Usually, detection involves identification of an intentional financial irregularity or discrepancy. Sometimes, detection occurs because transactions and dollar amounts in transactions are at variance with norms, or expectations in the normal course of business. Most often, the internal theft of cash or negotiables is discovered through an audit.

Audits generally take two forms: **financial audits** and **fraud examinations**. Financial audits involve an evaluation of the accounting system. Transactions are examined to evaluate the timeliness, accuracy, and completeness of the transaction recording. Financial auditors do not examine each transaction. They sample transactions and confirm that the records are free of material (significant) errors. Fraud examinations, on the other hand, require the investigator to think in terms of how the financial controls could be compromised by an ingenious criminal mind (Bologna & Shaw, 1997; Cheeseman, 2010).

The fraud examiner searches each transaction for any discrepancy, whether significant or not. Although minor errors may be the result of an honest mistake, the discovery of a relatively insignificant misstatement may lead to a disguised criminal scheme. A cashier who is over or short by a small amount at the end of a shift may be prone to simple mistakes. Numerous over-ages and shortages over a period of weeks may be the result of inattention to detail. At the very least, the cashier has a cash-handling problem. At the most, the cashier is under ringing (or not ringing) merchandise, mentally recording the amount of excess cash in the register, and remov-ing the overage at the end of the shift.

Information Gathering and Analysis

Sources of information in an investigation include physical evidence, specialized databases, vic-tims, witnesses, suspects, records, informants, and the Internet. Records include statutes and local, state, and federal law enforcement and other government data. Public databases generally accessible to everyone include records associated with motor vehicles, driving, criminal convic-tions, worker compensation claims, diplomas, degrees, and credentials, credit history, military service, licenses issued, bankruptcy, and civil litigation. Private individual and business records as well as various publications may also be valuable sources of information. Access to records may be gained through permission, the legal process, the information's status as a public record, and through computerized databases.

Informants are an important source of information and are indispensable in many criminal investigations. When informants are utilized, care should be exercised to evaluate their motives, as well as the information provided, to ensure reliability. In a criminal prosecution, the reliability (veracity) of informant information is critical. Failure to test the reliability of informant-supplied information could result in the suppression of evidence derived from the informant's informa-tion. A basis for the informant's knowledge must also exist. In other words, the informant must be in a position to know the facts asserted (Acker & Brody, 2004; O'Hara & O'Hara, 2003).

The Internet is an excellent vehicle for gathering information. Search engines (tables of content for the World Wide Web) provide useful windows to view websites throughout the world. All search engines operate in a similar fashion. They run computer software programs that search the content of websites. They create an index in a large database consisting of key words from web pages they examine. When a user enters key words, the search engines compare the key words entered with the web pages in the database and deliver the results to the user in the form of links. The key words or phrase entered should be specific to narrow the search parameters and to allow the search engine to identify websites relevant to the purpose of the search. Popular search engines include the following:

- www.google.com
- www.yahoo.com
- www.excite.com
- www.lycos.com
- www.hotbot.com
- www.altavista.com
- www.askjeeves.com
- www.webcrawler.com
- www.dogpile.com
- www.infoseek.com
- www.multicrawl.com

Government agencies maintain websites that contain considerable resources and Internet links of interest to the security professional. In addition, government regulations and laws pertaining to security management can often be accessed through government agency websites. Noteworthy government websites include the following:

- www.fedworld.gov. This website is a clearinghouse for government information.
- www.fbi.gov. This is the FBI's website and it contains information about FBI programs, including the National Infrastructure Protection Center (NIPC), the Awareness of National Security Issues and Response (ANSIR) program, and the Uniform Crime Report (UCR).
- www.treas.gov. This is the U.S. Secret Service website that provides information about financial crimes such as counterfeiting and electronic fraud.
- www.ncix.gov. This is the website for the National Counterintelligence Center (NACIC) that provides information about trends in foreign and domestic espionage against American businesses.
- www.dss.mil. This is the home page for the Defense Security Service (DSS). This website can assist companies in search of government contracts.
- www.nsi.org. This is the website for the National Security Institute. The Institute posts travel advisories.
- www.travel.state.gov. This is the U.S. State Department's Bureau of Consular Affairs website. It also contains travel advisories.
- www.loc.gov. This is the Library of Congress website that contains valuable and timely information about pending legislation and statutes.

Each state government also has a website. A search engine may be used to locate a state's website.

Security professionals can obtain updated information on new computer viruses by accessing the websites of the major antivirus software producers. These include the following:

- www.symantec.com
- www.mcafee.com/us/
- www.sophos.com
- www.norman.com (Norman Data Defense Systems)

Current events information and news are available through news services such as Excite's NewsTracker at nt.excite.com and Yahoo!'s News Clipper at my.yahoo.com. In addition, ASIS International offers a security news and legal update service through ASISNET, located at www.asisonline.org. Free information regarding security-related topics can be found at www.securitymanagement.com. In addition to ASIS, several other professional security organizations have websites. They include the following:

- www.classmgmt.com. The National Classification Management Society.
- www.scip.org. The Society of Competitive Intelligence Professionals.
- www.ifpo.org. The International Foundation for Protection Officers.
- www.cfenet.com. The Association of Certified Fraud Examiners (Lushbaugh & Weston, 2012; Uttenweiler, 1999).

Role of Forensic Science

Traditionally, the term *instrumentation* has been applied to laboratory analysis of physical evidence found at the crime scene. Instrumentation evolved into the fields of forensic science and criminalistics. Instrumentation, forensic science, and criminalistics are terms that are often used interchangeably. However, forensic science involves the application of the physical as

Criminalists analyze evidence in a crime laboratory.
(Photo courtesy of Kevin L Chesson/Shutterstock.com.)

well as some social and business sciences to the investigation of crime. Sophisticated laboratory procedures and analyses are currently available, and more are being developed. Psychological profiling, anthropology, forensic accounting, spectrographic analysis, biology, chemistry, DNA analysis, and new ballistics testing technology are used in contemporary criminal investigations. The use of digital imaging as an investigative tool has also increased. Thus, forensic science may be defined as the application of science to the enforcement of law, and it has become extremely important to investigations in the twenty-first century.

One of the most significant advances in forensic science in the latter half of the twentieth century was the development of DNA (deoxyribonucleic acid) profiling technology. Contained within a gene, DNA is a molecule that is present in all forms of life. It is unique to the life form, determines the organism's traits, and assists with the development of a genetic fingerprint specific to the organism from which the molecules are taken. Blood, semen, and body tissues are good sources of human molecular cells containing DNA. Human biological samples collected at crime scenes can be used to develop a DNA profile. Comparison samples taken from victims and suspects can be profiled and analyzed to determine if both samples have a common origin. For example, the DNA profile developed from a semen sample taken from a rape victim can be compared to the DNA profile of blood taken from the rape suspect (Adams, Caddell, & Krutsinger, 2004; Blitzer & Jacobia, 2002; Lee, Palmbach, & Miller, 2001; Saferstein, 2011; Young & Ortmeier, 2011).

DNA tracing technology was used in one case in which three former executives at the French automobile manufacturer Renault allegedly engaged in corporate espionage. Prosecutors used DNA technology in an attempt to determine who sent a letter to several Renault managers saying that one of the fired executives had been observed negotiating a bribe. The letter had prompted the investigation into the alleged corporate espionage. Authorities had hoped to find the sender's DNA on the back of the postage stamp used to mail the letter. However, the stamp turned out to be self-adhesive, so no DNA was found (Gauthier-Villars & Moffett, 2011).

Impermissible Investigative Conduct

Several legal issues arise when investigations are conducted in private businesses and non–law enforcement settings. These issues focus on **impermissible investigative conduct** surrounding searches, **surreptitious investigative methods**, use of the polygraph, and arrest and detention of suspected law violators. Searches of desks, lockers, and other areas under the direct control of employees, for example, raise serious questions regarding the right to privacy. If work areas are subject to search, employees should be given clear, written notice that such searches may occur. The search policy should be contained in an employee handbook and posted prominently in work areas. It is inadvisable to search a locked desk drawer or locker of an employee without the employee's consent. To prevent claims of invasion of privacy, an employee may be asked to sign a release form documenting the employee's consent to a search. The physical search of a person is not permissible in private businesses.

Many statutory provisions severely restrict an employer's ability to use surreptitious (secret) investigative methods such as electronic monitoring (wiretapping), eavesdropping, and undercover investigations. Other than cases involving interception of telephone conversations, there are few definitive court rulings that describe the limits (if any) of any employer's monitoring of employees by electronic means. However, several invasion of privacy actions have been filed against employers who monitored electronic mail or similar messages transmitted between employees. The courts have consistently held that organizational email systems are the property of the organization and subject to unannounced searchers by employers.

Electronic mail has emerged as an extremely popular and useful communications tool, especially in the workplace. Yet, email systems and their ancillary Internet links are also subject to abuse by employees. As a result, many organizations restrict and monitor employee email communications and Internet usage, limiting communications to that which is related to the job. Some argue that the monitoring constitutes a violation of one's constitutional right to privacy. However, the U.S. Constitution does not grant private, nongovernmental employees a right to privacy. The Fourth Amendment to the Constitution restricts governmental intrusions. Nevertheless, private employers may, through their words or actions, create an employee expectation to privacy that can form the foundation for an invasion of privacy lawsuit. To reduce the probability of a privacy lawsuit, employers are advised to create, communicate, and enforce a written policy regarding use of organizational email systems. To decrease the expectation of email privacy, employers should use the policy to inform employees that computer systems, accompanying software, and email communications are organizational property, not the personal property of the employee. Employees should be informed that all email messages will be treated as business messages and that the employer reserves the right to review these email messages. Employers should also inform employees that personal passwords do not establish a right to privacy. The policy should thoroughly define what types of communication are considered impermissible. Discriminatory, obscene, derogatory, sexually explicit, and defamatory communications of any kind should be prohibited. The policy should also specify the consequences for email system misuse, and the policy should be uniformly enforced. Finally, the employee should be required, in writing, to acknowledge receipt of, and consent to, the organizational email communications policy (Aronsohn, 2003).

Federal legislation that impacts electronic monitoring in the workplace includes the Omnibus Crime Control and Safe Streets Act of 1968. Federal courts have held that an employer can violate the Act by secretly recording telephone calls made by employees on the employer's telephone system. A provision of the Act contains an exemption for "system providers," such as employers who provide and maintain electronic communication systems (U.S. Congress, 1968).

Some states prohibit eavesdropping on any confidential employee communication. A **confidential communication** includes any communication carried on under circumstances reasonably indicating that any party to the communication desires it to be confined to the parties involved in the communication. The term does not include communications made in a public gathering, such as an office party. Furthermore, it does not apply to any public utility engaged in the business of providing communication services. Generally, these statutes provide that the use of devices for purposes of eavesdropping constitutes an invasion of privacy. The statutes define eavesdropping as intentionally tapping or making any unauthorized connection, whether physically, electronically, or otherwise; or willfully and without the consent of one party to the communication; or in any unauthorized manner, read, or attempt to read or learn the contents or meaning of any message or report. In a few states, such as California and Maryland, all parties to the communication must consent to the eavesdropping or recording of the conversation. Furthermore, evidence obtained in violation of the law is inadmissible in any judicial, administrative, legislative, or other proceeding. Accordingly, even if an employer uncovers significant information about the employee, the employer will not be able to use such information if a provision of the eavesdropping statute has been violated.

Some statutes also place severe restrictions on an employer's ability to monitor employee performance. They often prohibit employers from conducting any monitoring of employee email, Internet movements, or computer file use without first informing employees of the employer-organization's policy. One suggestion is to give employees advance written notice that monitoring may occur. Employees must give their full and voluntary consent in writing prior to monitoring.

At present, there are no definitive reported court cases limiting an employer's right to conduct a legitimate undercover investigation. Undercover investigations are most appropriate when an employer suspects theft or substance abuse is actually taking place within the organization. When undercover operatives are used, the investigation must have an effective infrastructure. The investigations team must maintain good communication linkages. The case must also be managed to ensure that it remains focused and is executed properly. Appropriate participants in the undercover investigation include the undercover operative, the case manager, the client, an employment law attorney, and applicable public law enforcement personnel. Written, email, or v-mail (digitally transmitted audio-video via the Internet) reports should be submitted daily by the operative. Telephonic contact with the case manager should also be made on a daily basis to clarify and expand the written reports as necessary. All reports, materials, and evidence collected should be organized into a case file for possible courtroom presentation.

State and federal laws also place severe restrictions on the use of polygraphs or similar devices by private employers. The federal statute contains a general exception for ongoing investigations involving economic loss and exceptions for employers in specific industries. Significant provisions of state and federal law prohibit employers from demanding or requiring that any applicant or employee take a polygraph test, a "lie detector" test, or any other similar test or examination as a condition of employment or as a condition of continued employment.

Specifically, the federal **Employee Polygraph Protection Act** of 1988 prohibits employers from directly or indirectly requiring, requesting, suggesting, or causing any employee or prospective employee to take or submit to any lie detector test; using, accepting, referring to, or inquiring about the results of any lie detector test; or discharging, disciplining, discriminating against, or denying employment or promotion to, or threatening any such action against, any employee or prospective employee who refuses, declines, or fails to take a lie detector test. In addition, an employer may not base an employment decision upon the results of any lie detector test. Lie detectors do not actually exist. However, the term *lie detector* is often applied to instruments such as a polygraph, voice stress analyzer, psychological stress evaluator, or any other similar device.

Exemptions under the Employee Polygraph Protection Act include the following:

- Government exemption. The Act does not apply to the U.S. government or any state or local government. Further, the Act does not apply to the federal government in the performance of any counterintelligence function or any test given to employees of private employers who have contracts with the Department of Defense.

- Private employer/investigative exemption. A private employer may request that an employee submit to a polygraph test if all of the following conditions are met: The test is administered in connection with an ongoing investigation involving economic loss to the employer's business; the employee had access to the property; the employer has reasonable suspicion that the employee was involved; and the employer gives fair notice to the employee that a request for a test may occur.
- Security service exemption. The federal Act does not prohibit the use of a polygraph test by private employers whose primary business consists of providing armored car personnel, security system personnel, or other security personnel.
- Drug security, drug theft, or drug division investigations exemption. The federal Act does not prohibit the use of a polygraph test by an employer authorized to manufacture, distribute, or dispense certain controlled substances.

There are additional restrictions on the use of exemptions. The employer investigation exemption does not apply if an employee is discharged, disciplined, denied employment or promotion, or otherwise discriminated against in any manner on the basis of the analysis of a polygraph test chart or the refusal to take a polygraph test without additional supporting evidence. Under the exemption for security services, drug security, drug theft, or similar investigation, an employer may not use the results as the sole basis for an adverse employment action. Furthermore, during the actual testing phase, the examiner may not ask any questions that were not presented in writing for review to the examinee before the test. Finally, a private employer may disclose information from a test only to the examinee or any other persons specifically designated in writing by the examinee or any court (Cheeseman, 2010; Ferraro, 2000; Simonsen, 1998; U.S. Congress, 1988).

Finally, unlawful detention issues, such as false arrest and false imprisonment, often arise when someone's freedom of movement is restricted in a significant way. Unless placed under a criminal or civil (citizen's) arrest, it is unlawful to detain persons against their will. **Unlawful detention** could result in criminal as well as civil liability. Readers should consult their respective state statutes for specific detention requirements in their jurisdictions.

The legal restrictions placed on the investigative conduct of the public police, as agents of government, are distinguished from the legal restrictions placed on similar conduct of private security personnel. The Bill of Rights (the first 10 amendments to the U.S. Constitution) place restrictions on the conduct of representatives of government, not the behavior of private persons. Thus, the laws of arrest and rules of evidence, as well as the legal aspects of interrogation, search, and seizure, often vary between the public and private sectors. Additional information regarding these legal aspects is presented in Chapter 3.

INTELLIGENCE OPERATIONS

Business Intelligence

In a competitive environment, loss prevention goes beyond identification of and protection from obvious threats. The successful business cannot operate in a vacuum. The business must also protect against loss due to competition. In this vein, **business intelligence (BI)**, sometimes referred to as **competitive intelligence**, involves the process of collecting, analyzing, and disseminating competitive information and other data that can be used to meet business organization objectives.

Remaining in business and staying ahead of the competition are legitimate business objectives. Legally appropriate BI activities help to meet such objectives.

Sole proprietorships, partnerships, and corporations benefit from successful anticipation of the competition's tactics and strategies. Through tactical intelligence operations, one seeks to identify and analyze short-range activities of similar businesses. **Tactical business intelligence** focuses on actual rather than perceived or advertised schemes of competitors. Pricing policies and terms of sale, for example, must be in line with the competition and consistent with the marketplace.

Strategic business intelligence seeks to forecast the long-range implications of business activities. Long-range predictions of the competition's activities involve the identification of new target markets as well as the number of competitors available in the future. It involves an analysis of the competitors' capabilities, assets, methodologies, and skills. It provides information to assess the value of alliances and assists a business with the creation of a corporate vision.

Business intelligence also involves the use of counterintelligence to protect the organization from internal and external intelligence-gathering threats. BI is not **industrial espionage (IE)**. BI is a legitimate activity. IE, on the other hand, involves the use of illegal, unethical, and fraudulent means to obtain proprietary information and intellectual property.

The BI process involves the gathering and analysis of raw data about the competition. Illegal IE includes activities such as theft of a competitor's information through traditional methods or computer or Internet access, extortion, commercial bribery, or employment of the competition's personnel to extract information. Legitimate BI activities can be conducted without resorting to any illegal methods. Intelligence is gathered by observing the competition and by accessing other individuals and organizations external to the competition. Much of the information is actually hiding in plain sight.

Sources of information include a competitor's finance, accounting, and human resources personnel as well as marketing and sales executives, operations managers, and staff. They can be observed in an effort to discover information about sales promotions, employee recruitment campaigns, training programs, labor contracts, distribution channels, pricing practices, physical plant, warehouse, and distribution center utilization, advertising, customer service, employee morale, and corporate security operations.

> Learn more about business (competitive) intelligence by contacting the Society of Competitive Intelligence Professionals (SCIP) at www.scip.org.

Sources of information external to target competitor organizations include credit agencies, chambers of commerce, better business bureaus, distributors, industry experts and information brokers, market research organizations, trade associations, and competitor customers. If a competitor is a corporation with stock that is publicly traded, financial statements may be available. The U.S. Freedom of Information Act of 1966 requires public as well as many private corporations to disclose information about finances and operations. Information on patents or the development of items to be patented can be obtained from the U.S. Patent Office (Pitorri, 1998; Society of Competitive Intelligence Professionals, 2007).

After compiling data for a BI effort, an organization may initiate a field investigation to generate information not found through data compilation. It is during field investigation that an organization can cross the line from legal and ethical to illegal and unethical—from competitive intelligence gathering to IE. Potential pitfalls include trespassing, hacking, surveillance, pretexting, targeting employees, and wiretapping (DeKieffer, 2009). Table 9–1 shows examples.

TABLE 9–1	Field Investigation Pitfalls	
Pitfall	**Legitimate practice**	**Illegal or questionable practice**
Trespassing	Wandering in public areas, such as comparison shopping in a competitor's retail establishment	Entering locked areas without permission
Hacking	Accessing public areas of a target's website and reviewing registration data, archived web pages, and linked websites	Gaining unauthorized access to websites through hacking
Surveillance	Taking photographs of public areas without permission	Taking photographs of data that can be linked to personal information—such as photographing license plate numbers in a parking lot and matching them to owners by using public databases
Pretexting	Claiming that you are "with the media" to gain access to persons and property (legal since the line between journalist and citizen has blurred with the rise of blogging)	Impersonating law enforcement, military personnel, or anyone in authority to gain entry into otherwise restricted areas; assuming the identity of a contemporary person or company
Targeting employees	Obtaining information from employees who freely release it	Seeking information that is generally protected, such as trade secrets; getting information from employees recruited specifically to produce documents or to spy on the employer
Wiretapping	Obtaining a court order to wiretap or a search warrant to plant spyware in a target computer	Attempting to wiretap without a court order or to plant spyware without a search warrant; recording conversations without the knowledge of the other party

Source: DeKieffer, 2009.

SECURITY SPOTLIGHT

All organizations—from educational institutions to corporations to not-for-profit entities— have competitors, organizations striving to achieve the same goals and gain the same resources. What is the biggest competitor to the educational institution you attend, to a corporation that employs you, or to a not-for-profit entity in which you are involved? Draw on information readily available about this competitor to determine its strategic goals and advantages. Based on your findings, what is one step your school or employer could take to gain an advantage over this competitor?

Organizations that conduct business in the global marketplace, especially those with a physical presence in a foreign country, must consider local conditions to protect personnel and organizational assets. Several contract services provide up-to-date information on political conditions, criminal activity, and corruption as well as investing, licensing, and commercial trade in the international arena. Organizations can subscribe to database services that provide comprehensive guides to foreign laws and regulations, operating conditions, rules on foreign investment, labor availability, and price control policies. These services, some of which are available online or through U.S. government agencies, cover the latest business developments in major and emerging world markets.

> Information regarding political and economic conditions in foreign countries may be obtained by contacting the Northwestern University Library's Economist Intelligence Unit at www.library.northwestern.edu/reference/instructional_services.

Criminal Intelligence

Criminal intelligence involves gathering information about actual as well as possible criminal activity and threats to an organization and its assets. Whereas BI typically refers to information about competitors gathered legally, criminal intelligence focuses on the activities of individual criminals and organized criminal groups. Security personnel gather criminal intelligence information as part of risk assessment and analysis designed to prevent the criminal threat from materializing. Paramount among the criminal threats to information assets is the threat of IE.

In March 2002, law enforcement executives and intelligence experts met at the International Association of Chiefs of Police (IACP) Criminal Intelligence Sharing Summit to articulate an intelligence sharing plan designed to coordinate the collection, analysis, and appropriate dissemination of criminal intelligence data across the United States. The participants at the Summit called for the creation of a Criminal Intelligence Coordinating Council (CICC), composed of members representing law enforcement agencies at all levels of government.

To address past inadequacies in U.S. intelligence process, the U.S. Department of Justice, at the request of the IACP, authorized the formation of the Global Intelligence Working Group (GIWG) to develop a collaborative intelligence sharing plan. The result was the National Criminal Intelligence Sharing Plan, completed and endorsed by former U.S. Attorney General John Ashcroft in October 2003.

In addition to creating the intelligence sharing plan, the goals of GIWG include seamless sharing of intelligence information among systems, allowing for access to information throughout the law enforcement and public safety community. The GIWG is also active in determining standards for intelligence sharing, developing model policies, determining training needs, and creating an outreach effort to inform law enforcement of the result of this effort (Institute for Intergovernmental Research, 2011; U.S. Department of Justice, Office of Justice Programs, 2007).

National Intelligence

National intelligence operations focus on gathering information about foreign entities that may pose a threat to the nation. National intelligence is discussed in Chapter 12.

COUNTERESPIONAGE

Industrial espionage is a term often used to describe illegal activities that are designed to obtain trade secrets, proprietary information, and intellectual property. **Counterespionage** refers to those activities designed to prevent espionage from occurring. Generally, counterespionage involves the application of appropriate physical, personnel, and information security measures as well as a thorough investigation of all actual or attempted security breaches. IE awareness and prevention training programs should reach all staff. Security policies must also be enforced at all staff levels. Comprehensive risk assessments and periodic reviews of the assessment process greatly enhance the organization's ability to identify weaknesses in the security system. Persons responsible for the security function must be thoroughly knowledgeable regarding illegal espionage methodologies (American Society for Industrial Security, 1998; Friedman, 2011).

Industrial (economic) espionage threats stem from several sources. A business's own employees are possible, albeit improbable, sources. Employees who are disgruntled or experiencing financial difficulties may steal information and give or sell it to a competitor. In a highly competitive environment, other companies and their personnel may resort to crime to obtain vital information. Some nations, even allies of the United States, are possible perpetrators of IE. Heads of state in nations with crumbling economies (or no economic base at all) often promote state-sanctioned IE. Unhappy citizens may overthrow a government. If a country does not possess the technology to compete in the global marketplace, it could easily resort to IE to obtain the requisite technology to improve its economic position and keep its citizens from revolting.

Agents who participate in business espionage activities come from diverse backgrounds and numerous countries. Current and former employees, customers, competitors, contract vendors, business partners, and former government intelligence officers are involved with IE. Since the end of the Cold War in the early 1990s, many former Soviet Bloc intelligence agents shifted their focus from gathering political and military information to collecting U.S. and Western ally proprietary information and intellectual property. Secret economic data that has taken years of research to develop and millions of dollars to produce are typical targets of these former intelligence agents.

The current goals of the Russian intelligence service (KGB) as well as many other foreign nationals are to gather technical, scientific, and other forms of economic data from U.S. businesses. The U.S. Central Intelligence Agency (CIA) has identified several friendly and not-so-friendly nations as perpetrators of economic espionage activities. In addition to former Soviet Union countries, China, Iran, North Korea, and Cuba as well as Canada, France, Israel, Germany, India, South Korea, Japan, and Taiwan have been customers of stolen U.S. technology or have agents responsible for losses suffered by American businesses (see "Portrait of an Alleged Corporate Spy"). One former French official indicated that the United States and France are allies in political and military matters only, not in economic or technical environments.

Portrait of an Alleged Corporate Spy

A man named Huang Kexue was charged with economic espionage after he allegedly began sharing secrets gained from his work at a Dow Chemical lab in Indiana with Chinese researchers. Huang has a grant from the Natural Science Foundation of China. Though he grew up in China, he has lived legally in the United States and Canada since 1995. While working for Dow, he was also a visiting professor at a Chinese university and made numerous trips to China. In addition to sharing information, Huang was accused of trying to smuggle samples of a bacterial strain from Dow to China in his son's suitcase. Officials have said that the spying he is accused of is part of a trend of corporate spies working for foreign governments that are trying to obtain leading-edge technological advances (Drew, 2010).

Foreign competitors who criminally seek economic intelligence create and operate their spy networks utilizing one of three methods:

- Aggressively target and recruit susceptible people (often from the same national background) working for U.S. companies and research institutions.
- Recruit people to provide economic intelligence through bribery, computer disk theft, sorting trash (in search of discarded trade secrets), or wiretapping.
- Establish seemingly innocent business relationships with companies and industries to gather economic intelligence and classified information.

Whether the perpetrators of IE are employees or outsiders, domestic or foreign, they operate because businesses and organizations are vulnerable. Espionage agents take advantage of the vulnerabilities by identifying weaknesses in security systems and exploiting them. These agents utilize overt as well as covert (clandestine) avenues of attack. Almost 90 percent of an espionage agent's activity involves collection of information from and through overt sources. Trade publications and product shows, employment interviews, and online information services are excellent sources for overt information collection.

Common **covert operations** used to gather information include penetration of telephone and facsimile lines, examining trash, employee subversion, use of secret listening devices, secret insertion of an agent into the targeted organization, computer hacking through the Internet, and reverse engineering of a product. Conversations, computer modem transmissions, and facsimiles over telephone lines can be intercepted. Unshredded documents can be retrieved from trash. Employees can exchange information for money, sex, and other forms of value. Undercover agents, although costly, can surreptitiously penetrate an organization by posing as contractors, salespersons, or new employees. Agents have penetrated organizations by obtaining employment with the janitorial services vendor who holds the cleaning contract with the targeted enterprise. Once inside, the undercover agent, posing as a janitor, is free to roam the business, especially at night, collecting, examining, and analyzing documents, operations, and data visible on desks and available through open computer terminals. Undercover agents also frequent local gyms, restaurants, and bars where target company employees exercise, dine, and party. The agents eavesdrop on conversations and, in some cases, pose as employees of the target organization.

Virtually any organization or agency can be the target of industrial (economic) espionage. From a business perspective, the most frequent targets include companies engaged in global commerce, biotechnology, high technology, manufacturing of computers and electronics, and firms whose success is based on unique products, patents, or formulas. The Internet and other computer network information systems increase the risk of cyber-based threats.

To protect against industrial (economic) espionage, a business should

- recognize that real threats exist.
- identify and valuate trade secrets (intellectual property and proprietary information).
- implement a definable plan for safeguarding trade secrets.
- secure and limit access to trade secrets.
- confine knowledge of trade secrets to a limited number of people.
- provide continuous security training to employees.

(Boni & Kovacich, 2000; Pitorri, 1998; U.S. Department of Justice, Federal Bureau of Investigation, Economic Espionage Unit, 2007).

A QUICK SURVEY

If you are employed by a business organization, which of the following counterespionage measures does the organization use?

- Physical security
- Personnel security
- Information security
- Investigation of all actual or attempted security breaches
- Industrial espionage awareness and prevention training programs for staff
- Periodic review of risk assessment processes

How effective are the measures you checked? What additional measures or changes to existing measures do you think the organization should adopt? Why?

REPORTING

Many people dread the thought of note taking and report writing. They either do not understand the importance of **documentation** or appreciate the slow, deliberate process demanded by good writing. A security person's ability to document facts surrounding an incident, interview, accident, investigation, or criminal activity reflects on the writer's professionalism and the organization's ability to solve a problem. Probably no other single activity in loss prevention is more important than effective documentation and quality report writing.

Security personnel are required to perform writing tasks on a continuous basis. They must take notes, incorporate notes into reports, summarize statements of witnesses, record formal confessions, and enter information on report forms. Personnel must write in-depth narrative accounts containing complete sentences and paragraphs (investigative reports, supplemental/follow-up reports), and enter information into activity logs. They are often required to write press releases, memoranda, correspondence, and draft language for policy statement and training manuals.

Documentation Methods

Documentation can be accomplished through traditional note taking and report writing methods. If physical, technical, and legal requirements permit, documentation may also occur through the use of audiotape, videotape, stenography, computer-assisted recording devices, or any combination of methods. If computers are used, care must be exercised to ensure that confidentiality is maintained and access is restricted on a need-to-know basis. Computer disks and drives that have been erased still retain information that can be retrieved by technical experts skilled in this area. Additionally, other electronic media, such as email and the Internet, are not secure from message interception.

Notes

Notes are created in the normal course of business or in the field while investigating an incident. They are the primary source documents for a subsequent report. Notes should be made contemporaneous to an incident, during the course of the activity, or immediately after an incident occurs. These notes are often referred to as field notes because they are recorded on the job in the field. Since memories fade and are imperfect, notes must be written and maintained in the course of virtually every occupation. Notes are personal to the author and may be used to refresh one's memory, as the foundation for a report, and as supporting evidence in a judicial proceeding.

Reports

Reports become part of an official record and often form the foundation for the history of an incident. They may be viewed by other employees, supervisors, the media, attorneys, courts, insurance companies, and other organizations. They may be scrutinized in the judicial process, provide evidence for litigation against the report writer, support a petition, or lay the foundation for a defense against a lawsuit or criminal charge. Reports can help to determine future courses of action and are used as the basis for promotion, discipline, and evaluation. Report writing should be taken seriously. Reports with misspelled words, poor grammar, punctuation errors, inaccuracies, or omissions are potentially costly. Defective reports also cast doubt on the professionalism of the author. Although they vary in form and content, reports have one common purpose: to communicate information in a clear, concise, and accurate manner. They should always be written with the audience or potential readers in mind. Effective reporting is a matter of reducing to writing the pertinent facts concerning a problem or event.

Contact reports are used to document information acquired during an encounter with another person or persons. **Incident reports** and crime reports are used to document the occurrence of an event or reported criminal activity. **Narrative reports** and supplemental reports are used to narrate what happened, record witness statements, and document additional information acquired subsequent to an original report. Accident and traffic collision reports are used to document the circumstances surrounding an accident or vehicle collision. **Organization-specific reports** are written and completed in the normal course of business. The latter includes inspection reports, audit reports, and security surveys. Memoranda and letters are used for inter-departmental and other general correspondence.

The types of reports used by an organization depend on the nature of the organization's activity and its documentation requirements. Most existing organizations have reporting forms or formats in place. New organizations seeking to develop report forms and procedures should consult with existing organizations for information. Report form books and form tools in computer software packages are also commercially available.

General Writing Principles

Writing must be reasonably fluent, well developed, and organized, showing sufficient command of the language used to communicate the information. All essential information must be included in a report (who, what, where, when, how, why). The report must be free of errors in typing, grammar, punctuation, spelling, and word choice that diminish its value or usefulness. A writer should choose the correct language, use proper sentence structure, be completely accurate, include all facts, and distinguish facts from hearsay, conclusions, judgments, and personal opinions. A report writer should strive for clarity; be concise, fair, and complete; and record the sequence of events in chronological order. The writer should record the names, addresses, and if possible, social security numbers of all involved in an incident. Narratives should include an introduction, body, and conclusion.

At a minimum, investigative reports should contain information describing how the author became involved in the situation, the facts necessary to accurately describe what happened, identification of parties involved, statements of the parties involved, specifics relative to the scene of the incident, descriptions of physical evidence as well as property damaged or stolen, and actions taken by the personnel at the scene. To ensure that the report is complete, the report writer should strive to include the date of the report, file or case number (if applicable), subjects involved, type of report, and complainant (if any). Other necessary information includes the name and identification of the person writing the report; office or department of origin; report status (open, pending, supplemental, closing); individuals to whom the report is sent; a narrative, including all facts acquired and all developed leads; and conclusions and recommendations. If applicable, the report might also include undeveloped leads and photographs, sketches, copies of documents, evidence receipts, and computer disks.

In an attempt to sound official, personnel often adopt a writing style and use language that is elaborate, redundant, obscure, and full of jargon and legalese. Clear, concise, simple, commonly used vocabulary is best. In report writing, the author of the report should present accurate information with brevity and clarity as guides to readability. Writers should avoid using words of more than two syllables, and sentences should not exceed 10 words. Examples of jargon and wordy phrases (and their concise English counterparts) include the following:

- executed a stop (stopped)
- in the vicinity of (near)
- verbal confrontation (argument)
- inquired (asked)
- proceeded to the location (went to _____)
- terminate (end)
- approximately (about)
- initiated (began)
- related (said)
- party (person)
- in view of the fact that (because)
- for the purpose of (to)
- conducted an investigation (investigated)
- upon an individual basis (individually)
- pursued alleged perpetrator (ran after suspect)
- maintained visual contact (watched)
- exited the vehicle (got out of the car)

Correct spelling, word usage, punctuation, and capitalization are also essential ingredients to good report writing. Mistakes in these areas lead readers to believe that the writer is undereducated, poorly trained, careless, and unprofessional. The writer should not rely on computer spell-check programs, either. Inappropriate words that are not identified by a spell-check software program include those *italicized* (and the correct word in brackets) in the following sentences:

- He went to the *sight* [site] of the accident.
- The *breaks* [brakes] on the car did not work.
- It was a *miner* [minor] incident.
- He injured his left *feet* [foot].
- She did not *no* [know] where the suspect went.
- The item was found in the car's *truck* [trunk].
- He was unable to *here* [hear].

Reports should be written to express a thought accurately and clearly, not to impress the reader. The language used in normal conversation is the language of a report. The vocabulary and style used should approximate what and how the writer would communicate if telling a story. First-person rather than third-person voice is recommended in report writing. For example, the author should write "I asked to see the report" rather than "The supervisor asked for the report" (Adams, 2007; California Commission on Peace Officer Standards and Training, 2012; Guffey, 2005; Hess, 1997; Ortmeier, 2006; Parr, 1999; Thaiss & Hess, 1999).

Summary

An investigation is a systematic process used to determine the causes of accidents and losses as well as the facts surrounding personal misconduct and criminal activity. Investigations are also used to research the background of potential employees and business partners. Common types of investigations in a security setting include those associated with human resources, personal injury, property damage, and crime. Effective information gathering and analysis procedures are critical to any investigation. Impermissible investigative conduct emanates from invasions to privacy, improper use of the polygraph and similar instruments, and unlawful arrest and detention of suspected law violators.

Intelligence operations include the gathering of business and competitive intelligence as well as criminal intelligence. Counterespionage refers to those activities designed to prevent espionage from occurring. Utilizing numerous methods, current and former employees, business associates, and external agents are involved in business espionage activities.

Effective and efficient documentation is critical to the success of any security operation. Utilizing a variety of methods, security personnel document the circumstances surrounding incidents, interviews, interrogations, and continuous activities. As the primary source documents for the creation of a report, notes should be made contemporaneous to an event. Reports are part of an official record of an event or activity and form the foundation for the history of an incident. Report writers (authors) should practice generally accepted report writing principles to avoid suspicion and inquiries into the writer's professional capabilities.

Key Terms

accounts payable diversions
business intelligence (BI)
cash conversion
competitive intelligence
confidential communication
contact reports
counterespionage
covert operations
criminal intelligence
criminal investigation
documentation
embezzlement
Employee Polygraph Protection
    Act

financial audits
fraud
fraud examinations
human resource investigations
impermissible investigative
    conduct
incident reports
industrial espionage (IE)
inventory conversion
investigation
narrative reports
organization-specific
    reports
personal injury investigation

property damage investigation
receivables conversion
sexual harassment
strategic business intelligence
surreptitious investigative
    methods
surveillance
tactical business intelligence
undercover investigation
unlawful detention

Discussion Questions and Exercises

1. What elements are common to the investigative process?
2. Under what circumstances is a civil or criminal investigation warranted?
3. Describe the proper procedure for the collection and preservation of evidence in criminal investigations.
4. When are surveillance and undercover operations necessary?
5. Business crime often differs from traditional street crime. Describe the types of crime that businesses are most likely to encounter.
6. Discuss the procedure for developing, locating, evaluating, and analyzing information.
7. What constitutes impermissible investigative conduct?
8. What is BI? How does it differ from IE?
9. Documentation is vital to the success of every security operation. How can appropriate documentation be assured?

YOUR TURN: Investigating National Stability with Online Resources

Numerous business organizations and public agencies develop and publicize Internet websites that contain information of value to an investigation.

1. Suppose that you are employed by a multinational corporation that is interested in expanding its operations in another country. Executives at the organization know that the corporation will be most successful in this effort if the target country has a stable and favorable political, social, economic, and legal environment. Your supervisor assigns you the task of investigating the stability and favorability of two potential target countries and recommending one of the two countries for further consideration as a target for new operations. For the purposes of this exercise, select two countries to assess. Be sure that the two countries are in different regions of the world; for example, China and Brazil, or India and South Africa.
2. Using online resources identified in this chapter, explore Internet sites that might provide information on the *political* climate of the two countries you selected for investigation. For example, how frequently does political leadership change in each nation? What are the current political leaders' attitudes toward foreign investment and business activity in their countries?
3. Use the online resources to investigate the *social* climate of the two countries. For instance, how often do protests, riots, and labor strikes occur in these nations? What are the general populations' attitudes toward outsiders seeking to do business in their country?
4. Use the resources to examine the *economic* climate of the two countries. To illustrate, how wide is the gap between rich and poor in these nations? What is the unemployment rate? How high is the general population's standard of living? How stable and favorable are the countries' banking sectors and physical infrastructure (e.g., transportation and communication systems)?
5. Use the resources to assess the *legal* climate of the two countries. For example, do regulations exist to protect private and intellectual property? How strictly are laws and regulations enforced?

6. Based on your investigative research, which of the two countries you selected for analysis seems to offer the best potential for expansion of your company's overseas operations? Why?

7. Even countries that have relatively stable and favorable political, social, economic, or legal environments have inherent risks for organizations seeking to do business there. Given this fact, what do you see as the most serious inherent risks in doing business within the country you selected in Question 6? For example, is there enough social unrest to raise the threat of overthrow of the government? Do locals strongly resent the presence of foreign workers? Is physical infrastructure outdated and vulnerable to natural disasters? Are laws unenforced?

8. Given the risks you identified in Question 7, what security and safety advice would you offer your employer regarding the country you have selected as the most promising for expanding overseas operations?

PART FOUR

Security Applications and Solutions

The chapters in this section examine specific security applications and solutions to security problems. Chapter 10 concentrates on institutional security, disaster recovery, and executive protection. Chapter 11 focuses on industrial security, retail loss prevention, and workplace violence. Chapter 12 is devoted to homeland security, including coverage of terrorism, natural disasters, and security related to airlines, infrastructure, and utilities.

CHAPTER 10

Institutional Security, Disaster Recovery, and Executive Protection

LEARNING OBJECTIVES

After completing this chapter, the reader should be able to

- identify security threats unique to specific industries.
- describe asset protection priorities as well as loss prevention policies, procedures, and systems associated with the following:
- banking and financial institution security
- courthouse and courtroom security
- educational institution security
- health care security
- hospitality security
- entertainment security
- disaster recovery
- executive protection

INTRODUCTION

Although many threats and general security management principles apply across a broad spectrum of public and private environments, some threats as well as security services and practices are unique, with specific applications. Further analysis of unique and specific security requirements often yields even greater variance in loss prevention philosophy and practice among similar organizations and institutions. This chapter explores several unique security environments, applications, and services.

BANKING AND FINANCIAL INSTITUTION SECURITY

The nature of banking has changed dramatically. Gone are the days when states limited bank branches and financial transactions took place at a physical location. The personal computer, electronic fund transfers, automatic teller machines, debit cards, and the paperless money trail have revolutionized the banking and finance industry. The distinction between **financial institutions** such as commercial banks, savings and loans, credit unions, brokerage houses, and insurance companies has also become increasingly blurred.

Financial institutions provide attractive targets for the skilled (and unskilled) criminal. Robbery, burglary, embezzlement, loan fraud, manipulation of funds, computer hacking, and credit card and check fraud are major threats. Losses to financial institutions are direct, since the object of the theft is money, not goods or services. Losses from fraud alone are estimated to exceed $30 billion annually.

In an effort to reduce the vulnerability of financial institutions, the U.S. Congress passed the **Bank Protection Act of 1968**. The Act focused on minimum security measures at all federally insured financial institutions. It required

- a person to be designated as the bank security officer.
- the development of comprehensive security programs and implementation of protective programs that would meet or exceed federal standards.
- maintenance of bait money (currency with serial numbers recorded).
- periodic removal of excess cash from teller areas and bank premises.
- security-conscious opening and closing procedures.
- stringent security inspections.
- cooperation and liaison with the FBI and other law enforcement agencies.

The use of technology to commit crime against financial institutions represents a major threat to financial assets. Banks and other institutions have increased their risk exposure because they are connected internally and externally through online banking services and electronic fund transfers. Unauthorized use of an electronic database by an employee may result in invasions to privacy. Data manipulation through computers is particularly dangerous. Account and loan balances as well as credit lines can be altered or completely deleted. Financial institution websites can be penetrated (hacked) and the content altered to display false or slanderous information.

People constitute the most significant protection resource.
(Photo courtesy of Wackenhut Corporation.)

Through denial-of-service attacks, a hacker can electronically flood the institution's computer with email messages, collapsing the system. Insertion of computer viruses is always a concern, and confidential customer information can be obtained and redirected to different accounts or sold to illegitimate users. Some hackers offer to sell stolen information back to the financial institution or delete a virus for a fee, thus extorting money from the institution. Comprehensive personnel and physical and information protection strategies can help prevent these types of incidents and crimes from occurring in banks and other financial institutions (Hess & Wrobleski, 2009; Spivey, 2001).

SECURITY SPOTLIGHT

Do you conduct some or all of your banking activities online? If so, what steps are you taking personally to ensure security of your financial data and resources? What steps do the banking institutions you use take to keep customers' financial data and resources safe? If possible, arrange a telephone call with a security professional at an online banking institution you use. Ask the person about which security practices have been established by the bank to protect customers, and how (if at all) these practices have evolved over time to meet changing needs and challenges.

COMPUTER SECURITY

An in-depth examination of computer security is presented in Chapter 6.

CONTRACT SERVICES

Contract security services are discussed in Chapter 1.

COURTHOUSE AND COURTROOM SECURITY

The continuing growth of local, state, and federal judicial systems has forced existing court facilities to accommodate an increase in human activity. Expanding space requirements have pressured jurisdictions to construct new courtroom buildings, expanding the courts and increasing the number of judicial personnel, litigants, jurors, and a variety of ancillary activities associated with legal proceedings. In addition to litigation activities, courthouses contain other government agencies, receive deliveries, have adjacent or underground parking areas, are transfer points for defendants and convicted criminals, and function as venues for public ceremonial events.

In recent years, incidents of assault, bombings, and homicide have increased in American courthouses. Spectators become unruly, demonstrators may protest a judicial decision, defendants try to escape, witnesses are threatened, juries are tampered with, and judges, prosecutors, and courthouse staff receive death threats. The most vulnerable areas include courtrooms, judges' chambers, probation and parole offices, clerk of court offices, and areas where pro-defense and pro-prosecution witnesses may encounter one another. Courthouse building exteriors and perimeters must be protected against a possible bombing attack. After the bombing of the Alfred P. Murrah federal building in Oklahoma City in 1995, virtually all government buildings were identified as potential targets for terrorists (Thomas, 2001).

On March 11, 2005, Brian Nichols, 33, on trial for rape, was being transported through a courthouse in Atlanta, Georgia. Nichols overpowered his sheriff's deputy escort, took her fire-arm, and proceeded to the courtroom, where he fatally shot the presiding judge and a court reporter. Later, Nichols killed a sheriff's deputy outside the courthouse. In the course of his 24-hour escape ordeal, Nichols also hijacked three cars and a tow truck and shot an off-duty Immigration and Customs Enforcement agent to death, stealing the agent's car as well. Early the next morning, Nichols forced his way into a woman's apartment. Subsequently, he surrendered to the police without incident.

Bailiffs or court security officers keep order in most of the nation's courtrooms. In some states, county marshals or deputy sheriffs provide security for the courts. Security of federal courthouses and courtrooms is the responsibility of the U.S. Marshals Service. In an effort to increase the level of security, access control devices and metal detectors have been installed at entry points in many courthouses. Surveillance systems, duress alarms, security glass, contracted security officers, and armed courtroom security personnel provide additional protection. Many courthouses appear like fortresses, although access by the public and the media remain priorities (Champion, Hartley, & Rabe, 2008).

EDUCATIONAL INSTITUTION SECURITY

Statistically, educational institutions are safer than homes. Yet, private and public schools, colleges, and universities are not immune from the hazards and risks that threaten other types of institutions. Behaviors demonstrated in schools are typically reflective of the society and the com-munity a specific school serves. As a result, campus security departments have been formed to protect property, students, faculty, and staff. Local police agencies provide additional protection, and in some cases, an educational institution may create its own stand-alone police department.

Educational institution security is a relatively recent development. Most colleges and universities did not have formalized security or police departments prior to World War II. However, as student populations became more politicized in the late 1950s and throughout the 1960s, the threat of civil disorder became more evident. Anti–Vietnam War sentiment and the radical behavior of some during the civil rights movement led to violent demonstrations and riots on several college campuses.

During the 1970s and 1980s, enrollment in institutions at all educational levels increased dramatically. Violent crime, sexual assaults, unlawful homicide, and theft increased along with the increase in student populations. Gang and drug activity in elementary and secondary schools and escalating crime rates on college and university campuses created new challenges in learning institutions (Dunn, 1999; Simonsen, 1998; U.S. Department of Justice, Bureau of Justice Statistics, 2006).

Elementary and Secondary Schools

In kindergarten through twelfth grade institutions (K–12, elementary, and secondary schools), vandalism, burglaries, and arson are major problems. Many teachers report hearing violent words and observing aggressive behavior in children as early as kindergarten. Classroom teachers are spending more time helping students learn the social skills that young people previously learned from their parents. Schools have been successfully sued for failure to provide a safe and secure environment. In some cases, the suits arise because of the discovery of a sexually intimate relationship between a teacher and an underage student. The possibility of a terrorist incident in or near a school has become a concern as well.

Although reported violence in schools decreased in the 1990s, crimes in schools have increased overall in the last 40 years. The U.S. Bureau of Justice Statistics and the National Center for Education Statistics report an increase in gang activity and violent crime in schools. According to these reports, gang activity increased between 1989 and 1995. Students victimized by violent crime increased 25 percent (Arnette & Walsleben, 1998; Brummett, 2007; McQueen, 2000; U.S. Department of Justice, Bureau of Justice Statistics, 2006). Consider these alarming statistics for the 2008–2009 school year. Preliminary data shows that among youth ages 5 to 18, there were 38 school-associated violent deaths from July 1, 2008, through June 30, 2009. In 2008, among students ages 12 to 18, there were about 1.2 million victims of nonfatal crimes at school, including 619,000 thefts and 629,800 violent crimes (simple assault and serious violent crime). In 2009, 8 percent of students reported being threatened or injured with a weapon, such as a gun, knife, or club, on school property (U.S. Department of Education, Institute of Education Sciences, 2011).

Violence in schools can become deadly. On March 24, 1998, Andrew Golden, age 11, and Mitchell Johnson, age 13, killed four elementary school students and a teacher in Jonesboro, Arkansas. On April 21, 1998, 15-year-old Kipland P. Kinkel, wearing a trench coat and carrying three guns, ran through a crowded Springfield, Oregon, high school cafeteria firing a rifle from his hip. Twenty-three students were injured, 19 of whom were hit by gunfire. Two students died from their wounds. The bodies of Kipland's parents were later found in his home. He had shot them both. On the same day, a 15-year-old boy in Onalaska, Washington, ordered his girlfriend off a bus and took her to his home, where he shot himself in the head and died. In another incident on the same day, a 15-year-old student from Jersey Village, Texas, was shot in the leg in a high school classroom. The gunshot originated in another student's backpack containing a firearm that discharged accidentally.

In one of the worst and most publicized incidents of school violence to date, two students, Eric Harris, 18, and Dylan Klebold, 17, went on a lethal rampage at Columbine High School in Littleton, Colorado, on April 20, 1999. Harris and Klebold killed 12 fellow students and a teacher before taking their own lives. Other killings at schools by young people age 18 and under occurred at the following locations:

09-24-09	Mesa, Arizona
03-21-05	Red Lake Indian Reservation, Minnesota
05-02-99	Conyers, Georgia
05-19-98	Fayetteville, Tennessee
04-24-98	Edinboro, Pennsylvania
12-15-97	Stamps, Arkansas
12-01-97	West Paducah, Kentucky
10-01-97	Pearl, Mississippi
02-19-97	Bethel, Alaska
02-02-97	Moses Lake, Washington
11-15-95	Lynnville, Tennessee
10-23-95	Redlands, California
10-12-95	Blockville, South Carolina
02-01-93	Amityville, New York
01-18-93	Grayson, Kentucky

On March 5, 2001, Charles "Andy" Williams, a 15-year-old freshman at Santana High School in Santee, a suburb of San Diego, California, opened fire on fellow students, faculty, and staff on his high school's campus at 9:20 A.M. Reloading his .22 caliber revolver at least four times, young Williams fired about 30 shots, killing 2 boys and wounding 11 other students, a campus security supervisor, and a student teacher. Charles Williams was allegedly seeking revenge for being teased and bullied by students at Santana High School (McDonald, 2001a). On March 22, 2001, 18-year-old student Jason Hoffman opened fire with a shotgun at Granite Hills High School in El Cajon, California, injuring five people. Granite Hills is in the same school district as Santana High School and is located approximately 6 miles south of the Santana campus. Hoffman was angry with school officials. Richard Agundez Jr., an El Cajon police officer assigned to the Granite Hills High School, responded quickly to the incident and wounded and subdued Hoffman during a brief gun battle (McDonald, 2001b).

The shootings at Santana and Granite Hills high schools marked the first times since January 29, 1979, that such an incident occurred in a San Diego area school. Twenty-two years earlier, Brenda Spencer, a 16-year-old, used a scoped rifle her father gave to her for Christmas to shoot at employees and students outside San Diego's Cleveland Elementary School. From her home across the street from the school, she killed two and wounded nine because she said she did not like Mondays (Wolf Branscomb, 2001).

Violence in elementary and secondary educational institutions is not limited to U.S. schools. In Erfurt, Germany, in one of the worst school shootings of its type anywhere, an expelled student entered his former school on April 27, 2002, armed with a shotgun and a handgun. The student methodically killed 17 people before killing himself. Also in Germany, a teenager wielding a 9-millimeter pistol entered classrooms at his former high school on March 12, 2009, and killed 15 people, most of them female students and teachers, before taking his own life. In 2004, a school in Beslan, Russia, was the scene of enormous bloodshed. Terrorists took over the school and held the occupants. Fifty-two hours later, Russian authorities raided the school. In the aftermath, nearly 250 people—most of them students, teachers, and parents—lay dead. School violence can occur in the most unexpected places. In 2006, five girls were killed in a rural Amish school in Nickel Mines, Pennsylvania, by milk truck driver Charles Roberts IV.

According to a study conducted of 15 shooting incidents in schools, occurring since the early 1990s, the profile of the violent offender in schools includes the following characteristics:

- White male between 11 and 18 years of age.
- Product of a broken home.
- No symptoms of severe mental problems.
- No history of serious behavioral problems.
- Small in stature.
- Teased and bullied by student peers.
- Had access to firearms and often dressed in military-style clothing.
- Threatened violence before shooting (Washburn & Hasemyer, 2001).

As a result of a federal law passed in 1994, all 50 states enacted legislation that requires a 1-year suspension for students who take guns to school.

Successful strategies to reduce the incidence of crime and regulate noncriminal conduct in K–12 schools focus on behavior codes, graffiti removal, crisis management, conflict prevention, and more active parental and community involvement. Some school districts, especially in tough inner-city neighborhoods, have their own police or security departments. Many also use metal detectors and a few use high-tech options such as biometrics and finger scanning to identify

Laws prohibit firearms in school zones.
(Photo courtesy of Laura Bolesta/Merrill Education.)

authorized students and personnel (Michel, 2000). Crime prevention through environmental design (CPTED) has also been applied successfully in schools. Thousands of angry and disturbed young people enter school buildings every day and do not express their anger in a destructive way. Ultimately, the key to crime prevention in schools may rest with a process of identifying the symptoms and treating the causes of potentially violent behavior in young people. Apparently, violence occurs more often in schools where minor infractions of school policies are ignored. Order maintenance in schools sets the stage for a secure learning environment.

Legislation and several types of collaborative programs have been developed by national, state, and local governments to create a safe environment in schools.

- Most states have, through legislation, **created safe-school zones**. These zones include school transportation systems and off-campus school activities. The safe-school zones give rise to zero-tolerance policies focusing on weapons and drugs.
- Federal regulations enacted in 1994 require drug- and alcohol-use testing for all school bus drivers.
- School districts are collaborating with the courts, probation agencies, and youth-service professionals to share information and monitor students who have criminal records.
- School districts are developing crisis prevention and intervention policies and procedures.
- Many schools now have security personnel, security devices, and criminal background checks on prospective employees, and have enlisted parents and volunteers to monitor facilities and school activities.

Proposals to allow teachers to carry firearms in schools are met with opposition. Although teachers in a few countries, notably Israel and Thailand, carry weapons on campus, schools in the United States do not encounter enough serious crime to warrant arming teachers with firearms. However, in the aftermath of the April 16, 2007, Virginia Tech mass murder spree that left 33 dead, some suggest that armed professors and students on college campuses may prevent violence. Currently, Utah is the only state with a law that expressly permits the carrying of concealed firearms on public college and university campuses (Vergakis, 2007).

Police are assigned as resource officers in some schools.
(Photo courtesy of Liz Moore/Merrill Education.)

Chain-link fences are used to enclose some school campuses.
(Photo courtesy of Star Source International.)

Since 1999, the U.S. Secret Service and the U.S. Department of Education have collaborated to identify potential threats and prevent violence in schools. These federal agencies embarked on the Safe-School Initiative. Their efforts resulted in the development of a guide to managing threatening situations and creating safe school environments. The guide, *Threat Assessments in Schools*, is available through the U.S. Secret Service at www.secretservice.gov/ntac or the U.S. Department of Education at www.ed.gov/offices/OESE/SDFS (U.S. Department of Treasury, Secret Service, & Department of Education, 2002).

Numerous other resources are available to assist with the development of school safety and security programs. Some organizations and their accompanying websites relating to school safety include the following:

- Center for the Study and Prevention of School Violence, www.colorado.edu/UCB/Research/cspv
- Creating Safe and Drug-Free Schools: An Action Guide, www2.ed.gov/about/offices/list/osdfs/index.html
- Early Warning, Timely Response: A Guide to Safe Schools, www2.ed.gov/about/offices/list/oscp/gtss.html
- National Crime Prevention Council, www.ncpc.org
- National Resource Center for Youth Services (College of Continuing Education, University of Oklahoma), www.nrcys.ou.edu
- National School Safety Center, www.nssc1.org
- Office of Juvenile Justice and Delinquency Prevention, www.ojjdp.ncjrs.org/
- Partnerships against Violence Network, www.pavnet.org
- Safe and Drug-Free Schools Program Office, www2.ed.gov/offices/OSDFS/actguid/index.html
- The American Academy of Experts in Traumatic Stress, Comprehensive School Crisis Response Plan, www.schoolcrisisresponse.com
- The Safe Schools Coalition, www.safeschoolscoalition.org
- U.S. Department of Education emergency planning website, www.ed.gov/emergencyplan
- Youth Risk Benefit Survey, Centers for Disease Control and Prevention, www.cdc.gov/nccdphp

Colleges and Universities

Unlike K–12 schools, colleges and universities (**postsecondary institutions**) have longer instructional days and unique problems. Some are residential campuses with dormitories, apartments, and single-family residences. In addition to the types of crime problems that commonly occur on K–12 campuses, postsecondary institutions may experience muggings, sexual assaults, illegal drug use, domestic and child abuse, and homicides. On August 15, 1996, Frederick Martin Davidson, a 36-year-old engineering graduate student at San Diego State University, killed three professors. Apparently upset over the progress of his master's thesis, he hid a 9-millimeter handgun in a classroom first-aid kit before he methodically killed the professors who were members of his thesis review panel. On October 28, 2002, a man who was failing courses in the nursing school of the University of Arizona at Tucson shot three of his professors to death, then killed himself. On May 9, 2003, a gunman killed one and injured several others when he opened fire at the business school of Case Western Reserve University in Cleveland, Ohio. On September 13, 2006, a young man in a trench coat killed 1 person and wounded 19 others at Dawson College in Montreal, Canada. On February 12, 2010, biology professor Amy Bishop, possibly upset over being denied tenure, shot and killed three fellow faculty members and wounded three others at the University of Alabama in Huntsville during a faculty meeting. It was later revealed by police that she had fatally shot her brother more than 23 years ago, though the death was ruled an accident and Bishop was never charged. Other killings on college campuses include the following:

April 16, 2007—Cho Seung Hui killed 32 and committed suicide at Virginia Tech. For additional details, review the case study at the end of this chapter.

September 2, 2006—Douglas Pennington, 49, killed his two sons and himself during a visit to Shepherdstown University in West Virginia.

January 16, 2002—Peter Odighizuwa, 42, recently dismissed from Virginia's Appalachian School of Law, returned to campus and killed a dean, a professor, and a student.

August 28, 2000—James Kelly, 36, a University of Arkansas graduate student dropped from the program, shot one of his professors and committed suicide.

November 1, 1991—Gang Lu, 28, a graduate student in physics passed over for an honor, killed five employees and himself at the University of Iowa.

August 1, 1966—Charles Whitman opened fire with a rifle from the observation deck of the University of Texas at Austin's tower. The rampage lasted 96 minutes. Whitman killed 16 people, including 11 from the tower, his mother and wife earlier in the day, and three while ascending the tower. Several were also wounded before Whitman was killed by police.

Although killings on college campuses receive widespread attention, homicides on campus remain quite rare. The nation's approximately 4,200 college and university campuses—home to nearly 18 million students—report a total of about 15 homicides per year. Yet the publicity associated with campus killings can cause fear and anxiety among student populations.

Learn more about college campus security through Security On Campus, Inc. at www.securityoncampus.org.

Noncriminal problems and incidents occur at postsecondary institutions also. Nonpayment of dormitory and apartment rent, traffic and parking congestion, alcohol abuse, and suicide create challenges for campus-based protective services.

On college campuses, the professionalization and expansion of protective services coupled with increased student involvement in the preventive function have made a positive impact on crime and noncriminal problems. In addition, the **Crime Awareness and Campus Security Act** of 1990, otherwise known as the **Clery Act**, requires postsecondary institutions to collect and disseminate campus crime statistics to students, parents, faculty, and staff. The Act was passed through the efforts of many, including the parents of Jeanne Clery, a 19-year-old woman who was raped and killed in her residence hall room at Lehigh University on April 5, 1986. The law applies to all colleges and universities that participate in federal financial aid programs. Participating postsecondary institutions must file an Annual Campus Security Report with the U.S. Department of Education by October 1st of each year and they must issue timely warnings of potential crimes that threaten the safety of students, employees, and visitors.

On August 16, 1990, the U.S. Department of Education printed final regulations that implemented amendments to the Drug-Free Schools and Communities Act enacted by Congress on December 12, 1989. The amendments required each institution of higher learning, as a condition to participation in a federal financial aid to students program, to certify that it had adopted and implemented a program to prevent the unlawful possession, use, or distribution of illicit drugs and alcohol by students and employees (U.S. Department of Education, 2007). Published guides to colleges and universities also provide details on safety and security measures to prospective students and parents (*Peterson's guide to four-year colleges*, 2007; *Profiles of American colleges*, 2007). The Clery Act was amended in 1992 and 1998, expanding reporting requirements. The 1998 amendments also formally named the law in memory of Jeanne Clery. By October 17, 2000, colleges and universities throughout the United States were required to post their crime statistics on the U.S. Department of Education's website, www.ope.ed.gov/security. According to federal officials, postsecondary institutions traditionally underreported crime in spite of the 1990 federal law requiring submission of crime data. The Clery Act amendments closed a number of loopholes through which colleges could exclude some reported crimes. The amendments expand the definition of a campus to include city streets and other properties that meander through college campuses. Colleges and universities are also required to survey local police, dormitory leaders, and rape crisis centers for criminal allegations that may not have been reported to college officials. All criminal complaints, proven or not, must be documented and reported under the 1998 Clery Act amendments ("An education in crime stats," 2000; U.S. Department of Education, 2007).

SECURITY SPOTLIGHT

Arrange a meeting with someone from the security office at the educational institution where you are enrolled. Ask what security challenges the college or university has encountered during its history and what processes, systems, and practices the school has adopted to improve security of faculty, students, administrative personnel, facilities, and data.

HEALTH CARE SECURITY

As a profession, health care security developed gradually over the last 100 years. During the first half of the twentieth century, health care security was limited to the minor role hospital maintenance staff played in providing security. In the 1950s, off-duty police officers were used to provide security in emergency rooms and other sensitive areas. As police agency budgets stabilized (and, in some cases, shrank) during the 1960s and as off-duty police time became more constrained, hospitals assumed a more direct role in the provision of safety and security services. In 1968, the **International Association for Healthcare Security and Safety (IAHSS)** was established to provide a professional forum for health care security managers. Today, virtually every major urban hospital, as well as many other auxiliary **health care facilities**, has proprietary safety and security personnel.

Security in a health care environment is an absolute necessity, for these reasons:

- Hospitals and other health care facilities have a moral responsibility to serve the public. This obligation requires the provision of a safe and secure environment.
- Health care enterprises have a legal responsibility to protect persons and property. The legal duty to protect is even greater when patients are unable to care for themselves. Negligence on the part of hospitals has led to compensatory damage awards by juries as well as high punitive damage awards not typically covered by liability insurance carriers.
- Accreditation and regulatory requirements of the **Joint Commission for Accreditation of Healthcare Organizations (JCAHO)** and the Occupational Safety and Health Administration (OSHA), coupled with numerous other federal, state, and local statutes, require security in health care facilities.
- Health care organizations have a fiduciary responsibility to maintain a sound financial position. Thus, cost containment through the prevention of loss due to crime, waste, and natural phenomena is necessary.
- Good public and employee relations are maintained, in part, through the provision of a safe and secure environment.

Health Care Facilities

Health care is the fifth largest industry in the United States. More than 30,000 **health care facilities** administer care to millions of people. The health care facilities include about 6,000 hospitals in the United States, ranging from 25 to 2,500 beds, as well as public and private hospitals, clinics, medical offices, **nursing homes**, and extended care and outpatient facilities that must provide a safe and secure environment for patients, staff, and visitors. Since 2004, reports of assault, rape, and homicide in the health care setting have increased, with the greatest number of reports in the last three years: 36 incidents in 2007, 41 in 2008, and 33 in 2009 (The Joint Commission, 2010). The facilities must also prevent loss of assets. In fact, JCAHO requires minimum security standards for hospitals. As security-related problems in hospitals increase, the JCAHO stiffens and increases minimum standards for hospital security.

URBAN MEDICAL CENTERS Major urban medical centers function much like small cities. They never close. Each has retail outlets, pharmacies, restaurants, and offices, and many have multiple buildings. In addition, many patients are unable to care for themselves, much less protect themselves from dangerous situations. Theft, fire, natural disasters, accidents, personal attacks, and sexual assaults are constant threats. Shoplifting may occur in the gift shops, patients or visitors may become violent, and power failures may threaten life-support systems. Drugs are stolen from pharmacies, cars from parking lots, and babies from maternity wards ("University Health Care provides health, safety and security for patients," 2000). Rival gang members may pursue an injured gang member into an emergency room for revenge. Family planning clinics may be subjected to civil disturbances, forcible assaults, bombings, and homicides.

Access control is difficult in many health care facilities. Numerous entrances and exits coupled with busy medical staff and a constant flow of newcomers help create an environment where control and surveillance of pedestrian traffic is difficult. Hospitals and other health care

Access control is difficult in many healthcare facilities.
(Photo courtesy of Star Source International.)

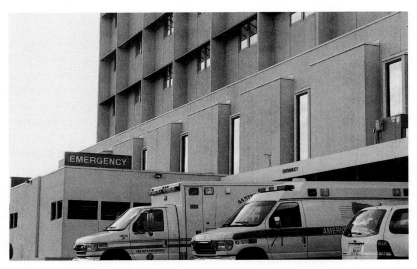

Numerous entrances and exits coupled with busy medical staff and a constant flow of newcomers help create access control difficulties in hospitals.
(Photo courtesy of Star Source International.)

facilities are also held liable when accidents and crime occur as the result of inadequate security. A safe environment reduces exposure to risks and limits liability.

Health care facilities, including hospitals and medical centers, tend to be a reflection of the environments within which they are located. If they are located in high crime rate areas, the threat of crime is great and the offense rate on or near facility property is also high. With the rapid growth of home health care, new, more diverse problems have developed. Health care professionals, working alone, must enter dangerous neighborhoods.

EXTENDED CARE AND ASSISTED CARE FACILITIES   Extended or assisted care facilities, the largest segment of which consists of nursing homes, face the same general threats that confront hospitals. Although usually smaller in size and scope than hospitals, nursing homes serve a segment of the population that is often physically or mentally incapacitated. Natural and environmental disasters, fire, theft of resident property, and patient abuse are common threats to safety and security in nursing homes. Medicare and Medicaid programs produced unique security concerns. Some facilities are alleged to have solicited kickbacks as a precondition for certain business arrangements. Some documented cases uncovered the involvement of organized crime with Medicare and Medicaid programs.

Since most nursing homes and assisted care facilities are small, the protective function is usually assigned to a nonsecurity professional, often the business manager for a facility. In addition, budgetary realities dictate the need for personnel multitasking in small health care facilities. Thus, the safety and security function is often given a low priority. However, through the use of alarms, closed-circuit television (CCTV), controlled access systems, policies, and procedures, increased protection of people, property, and information can be realized. Liaison with local, state, and federal public safety agencies as well as a thorough investigation of all injuries, losses, and security violations can help minimize protection problems (Colling, 2001; International Association for Healthcare Security and Safety, 2007; Simonsen, 1998).

Concerns about Cost

Cost has increasingly entered the health care facility security picture. Increasing and, in some cases, out-of-control costs associated with health care led to public outcry and subsequent regulatory controls in the late 1900s. The result was a trend toward cost containment and managed care. Traditional methods of financing health care were replaced with collaborative mechanisms to share resources and monitor health care expenses, income, and profit. Health maintenance organizations (HMOs) emerged to operate health care institutions as businesses rather than social service agencies.

This movement focused on cost reduction. As security requirements increased, the loss prevention manager was faced with the challenge of doing more with fewer resources. JCAHO and OSHA increasingly require security assessments and plans upon which a health care facility is evaluated. Yet, with fewer resources, the security manager may be faced with serious plan implementation constraints. Even more exacerbating is the situation in which the person normally responsible for the protection function is not a security professional but someone whose training and education has been in facilities management or human resources rather than protection services.

Strategies for Preventing Losses

Policies, procedures, equipment, and strategies for preventing losses in health care facilities are as numerous as the facilities are diverse. Photo identification badges for staff assist with access control. Electronic surveillance systems monitor patients, staff, and visitors. Security personnel patrol the buildings and parking lots and are part of emergency reaction teams.

Many health care facilities also provide Professional Assault Response Training (PART) to security and other emergency response employees. PART involves a comprehensive and systematic approach designed to minimize risks associated with assaultive behavior of patients, visitors, and others in a health care environment. PART emphasizes the roles of supervision, policy enforcement, and de-escalation of conflict. The training focuses on identification of the symptoms and motives of violent behavior, the development of alternative courses of action, a determination of levels of dangerousness, response techniques, and use of force. PART helps health care employees develop the skills necessary to manage risk associated with assaultive behavior, mitigate liability, maintain a safe environment, and conform to legislatively mandated training requirements (Professional Growth Facilitators, 2000).

Biometrics is being used to positively identify patients and staff. "Use of Access Control Technology at a Large Health System" sheds additional light on technological measures that some health care facilities are taking to strengthen security. Loss prevention and self-protection training is being provided to more staff, especially those who work alone in a community health environment. Health care security personnel conduct internal investigations, inspections, audits, and surveys. They provide other interdepartmental support, such as escort and mail services. They also develop safety and security plans, test emergency protection systems, and control access.

Health Care Data

Special security practices also protect electronic databases and computer-based information storage and transmission systems in health care settings. These practices are important, considering the increased use of computers and the sharing of patient and personnel data between

Use of Access Control Technology at a Large Health System

Christus Santa Rosa Health System (CSR) comprises more than 40 hospitals, inpatient and long-term care facilities, and dozens of clinics, physician offices, and health care services in more than 70 cities in Texas, Arkansas, Louisiana, Oklahoma, Utah, and Mexico. CSR decided to rethink the access control technology solution that it had been using, which had offered minimal potential to integrate its many facilities. The organization began by installing a new access control system at five of its hospital campuses spread throughout South-Central Texas, with the aim of managing about 210 doors spread among the campuses.

Rather than creating several different access control databases, CSR elected to keep all data and access management under one system, operated with a single graphical user interface. It also organized the nearly 9,000 users of the new system into 127 groups, each with different access privileges in terms of locations, days, and time periods of access. In addition, CSR created a single card that enables physicians to visit multiple locations—such as hospitals, pharmacies, labs, designated physician parking areas, secure locations in certain buildings, and their own offices. The card stores a physician's personal digital identity and can be accessed only by that physician ("Christus Santa Rosa Health System upgrades at five of its campuses," 2010).

departments and among health care organizations through electronic medical records (EMR) and electronic health records (EHR) technology. Data transmission interceptions and access to electronic mail and Internet connections threaten the privacy of countless individuals. The **Health Insurance Portability and Accountability Act of 1996** mandated national standards for the electronic storage and transmission of health insurance transactions, including information on claims, enrollment eligibility, payments, and benefits. The law also mandates strict standards to protect the privacy of personal health information (Dolan, 1999; U.S. Department of Health and Human Services, Office of Civil Rights, 2007).

HOSPITALITY SECURITY

The **hospitality industry** consists of bars and lounges, restaurants, lodging establishments, and similar facilities. Although bars and restaurants are subject to many types of crimes, especially robbery, burglary, and disruptive behavior, it is in the lodging industry where the crime rate has climbed most dramatically. Theft, both internal and external, prostitution, assaults, rape, drug activity, and in some instances, homicide have increased. Lawsuits against hotels and motels due to inadequate security have also increased.

In an effort to make lodging establishments more attractive and improve customer convenience and satisfaction, many hotel and motel operators sacrificed safety and security. Lack of internal controls has led to an increase in theft of hotel and motel property including cash, linen, supplies, dishes, and silverware. Guests and guest rooms are targets of the internal thief as well. Externally, professional thieves and burglars, prostitutes, drug dealers, rapists, and auto thieves find that lodging establishments make very attractive targets. Guests themselves steal ashtrays, towels, and linen for souvenirs and vandalize hotel and motel property. Credit card and check fraud, shoplifting, and nonpayment of room charges are also commonplace.

Losses are not always due to criminal activity. Accidents, fire, natural disasters, and poor inventory control also contribute to the depletion of lodging industry assets. Litigation costs and adverse judgments from lawsuits also affect the profitability of lodging facilities. Courts have held motels and hotels liable for theft of guest property and injuries and assaults on guests by employees as well as outsiders.

Surveillance and alarm systems in lodging establishments may reduce the need for human patrols.
(Photo courtesy of Wackenhut Corporation.)

Security measures in lodging establishments should focus on strict key control, comprehensive preemployment screening, CCTV and alarm systems, and safety programs to prevent injury to employees and guests. Guest room door locks should be rekeyed when keys are lost or not returned by a registered guest. Consideration may be given to the installation of a card-key access system to replace traditional keyed locks. When handing room keys to guests who have registered at a motel or hotel, desk clerks should avoid stating the guest's room number verbally, to prevent anyone within earshot from hearing the room number and possibly targeting that guest for theft or some other crime. Background checks on all prospective employees may uncover poor employment and criminal conviction histories, credit problems, and propensity toward chemical abuse. A well-planned and executed fire prevention strategy coupled with appropriate fire alarm and extinguishing equipment will reduce heavy losses, injuries, or deaths due to fire.

In many cases, a common response to an increase in criminal activity from outsiders against lodging establishments is to employ or add security personnel. In the long term, however, enhanced security may be achieved more inexpensively through incorporation of technology into a hotel or motel's security system. CCTV is an excellent complement to the security function. Surveillance and alarm systems reduce the need for human patrol and may be monitored continuously at or near the registration desk.

Some establishments incorporate contract interactive CCTV service to monitor lobby activity and deter or detect robberies and other violent activity. Contract service personnel located at a central station can view the lobby and front desk at regular intervals, usually about every 15 minutes. Lodging personnel can also notify the contract service by pressing an alert button located inside the front desk. This action immediately presents the establishment's front desk on the central station's CCTV monitor and notifies proper authorities. The event is also videotaped and stored as an aid to a subsequent investigation and possible prosecution (Stover, 2000; Walker, 2010).

ENTERTAINMENT SECURITY

As more individuals reach retirement age and the United States becomes more technologically advanced, the amount of leisure time available increases. As a result, people seek out media for entertainment. Sporting events, recreational facilities, theme parks, racetracks, movie studios and theaters, ocean liners, and casinos provide diversion venues for the leisure seeker. These venues also pose unique threats and provide opportunities for criminal activity. Organizations sponsor conventions, rock concerts, parades, festivals, and political rallies that draw large crowds and create problems related to order maintenance as well as crowd and traffic control. Theft, medical emergencies, and gate-crashing also create a need for security personnel, equipment, and procedures.

Sporting Events

Accidents, theft, assault, robbery, vandalism (during and after hours), bomb threats, and terrorism pose threats to persons and property at sporting events. Personnel, alarm systems, and CCTV surveillance equipment are the major sources of security at these events. Sporting events tend to draw fans who may become unruly and consume alcohol or drugs. Emotional highs may lead to aggressive behavior.

Some events draw huge crowds. The Olympic Games in Atlanta in 1996 drew an estimated 14,000 athletes and officials and over 2 million visitors. In 1998, Super Bowl XXXII in San Diego attracted over 100,000 ticket holders, concession workers, celebrities, party crashers, and media people along with intoxicated persons, thieves, car burglars, and ticket scalpers. A force of 1,000 police and security officers was assembled to deter criminal activity and arrest violators. Super Bowl XXXIV at the Georgia Dome in Atlanta on January 30, 2000, placed over 70,000 fans in the stadium. Security planning for the event began almost 2 years earlier. By the time of the game, systems were in place to prevent and protect against everything from accidents to biological and chemical attacks, terrorist bombings, sniper fire, and other types of violence (Adams, 2000a). Since 9/11, security at large public events has been expanded. The cost of security for the 2010 Winter Olympics in Canada was estimated at about $900 million. Security was organized through a special body, the Integrated Security Unit, of which the Royal Canadian Mounted Police (RCMP) was the lead agency; other government agencies such as the Vancouver Police Department, Canada Border Services Agency, Canadian Forces, police agencies across Canada, and Canadian Security Intelligence Service (CSIS) also played a role ("Olympic security estimated to cost $900M," 2009). This cost was radically higher than the cost of security at the 2002 Winter Olympic games in Salt Lake City, Utah, which approached $350 million, itself twice the cost of the entire 1980 Winter Olympics in Lake Placid, New York (Zeigler, 2002).

Recreational Areas and Theme Parks

Security problems in recreational areas and theme parks have increased in the past several years. Park rangers in national parks spend an increasingly disproportionate amount of time performing law enforcement duties. State, county, and city parks have also experienced an increase in security-related problems. Theft, illegal drug activity, vandalism, and assault have become more common. Theme parks such as Disneyland and Disney World, Busch Gardens, Sea World, and Universal Studios draw millions of people each year. The environment is designed so visitors feel a sense of security. Programs are also designed to anticipate trouble. Physical barriers and surveillance systems blend with the environment and go unnoticed by the average visitor. Security personnel focus on public relations, emergency response, shoplifting prevention, and traffic control.

Racetracks

Racetracks, particularly horse or dog racing tracks, face unique security problems. In addition to theft, robbery, auto theft, and assaults, animals must be protected and visitors must be protected from con artists, drunks, and pickpockets. Some racetracks employ proprietary security personnel while others use a contract service. Still others employ a hybrid security force with a permanent proprietary staff supplemented by contract security personnel during the racing season. Security personnel are used to protect cash in betting areas; control vehicular and pedestrian traffic; control crowds; prevent thefts from patrons; protect horse and dog owners, riders, and handlers; respond to medical emergencies; and prevent illegal gambling. Peculiar security and safety situations, although not necessarily criminal, may arise at racetracks. In 1998, the California House Racing Board investigated incidents in which an extraordinary number of horses sustained fatal injuries. The investigation focused on the physical condition of the horses as well as the condition of racetracks.

Movies and Music

The nature of entertainment has also changed dramatically. Television brought audiovisual entertainment into almost every living room in the country. The movie industry and the development of the Internet also provide means of entertainment. However, as a result of this expansion of technology, problems associated with the protection of celebrities and intellectual property have also increased. Celebrities have been stalked, even killed, by fanatical fans.

In addition, piracy (bootlegging or counterfeiting) of movies has become a problem. In February 2011, police in Salt Lake City and Ogden, Utah, arrested eight people in connection with the seizure of 29,000 pirated DVDs and CDs, which police said were worth a total of $345,000 (Falk, 2011). The **Motion Picture Association of America (MPAA)**, an entertainment industry professional organization, estimates that it loses $25 billion globally every year, owing to piracy, and that piracy is responsible for DVD sales falling in the United States from a high of $20.2 billion in 2006 to $14 billion in 2010 (Nakashima, 2011). Although inferior in quality, pirated videos are offered for sale at significantly lower prices at flea markets and through street vendors and fraudulent distributors. With new digital technology, the fake videos are easily copied. First-run movies are also copied by individuals who sit in movie theaters with video cameras when new films are released. The MPAA has offices in more than 70 countries, staffed with people who work to prevent piracy and to open legitimate distribution networks. Actual total losses due to pirating are difficult to estimate. Diminished consumer satisfaction due to low-quality pirated movies cannot be determined. Local, state, and federal sales and income taxes are also diverted (Lushbaugh & Weston, 2012; Motion Picture Association of America, 2007).

Piracy also occurs when movie studios send DVDs of movies still playing in theaters to voters of Oscar, Golden Globe, and other awards. Some of these disks are copied and the movies end up being shared online. To combat this kind of piracy, some studios are having voters view new movies through a free download from Apple's iTunes store. Downloads expire 24 hours after viewing and are not made available to the public. These virtual screenings are relatively inexpensive and simple to use, and they remove the risk that disks will go missing or be stolen. However, security experts note that such technology will not be a perfect solution: People determined to break the law will find a way to do it, even if they have to record a digital movie by pointing a standard video camera at the computer screen (Nakashima, 2011).

Ships and Boats

Cruise ships and riverboats also experience unique security problems. Ships and boats are usually in motion when operating, and steep, narrow passageways and stairwells create special hazards. Probably the greatest threat to cruise lines and riverboat operations is the potential for accidents, medical emergencies (such as an outbreak of a food-borne illness), slip-and-fall claims, and the resulting liability and lawsuits. In addition, although thieves cannot escape unless a ship or boat is in port, theft remains a major threat in marine entertainment.

Casinos

Gaming has also become a favorite pastime for many Americans. Wagering venues such as lotteries or casinos in some form are permitted and regulated in more than 60 percent of the states. Billions of dollars exchange hands each year in gaming environments. Theft, pilferage, cheating, and organized crime are constant threats in wagering establishments.

Although many courts have held that casino gamblers can use whatever mental tools they have at their disposal—intuition, memorization, even card counting—the courts draw the line at bribery and the use of devices for cheating (McDonald & Barfield, 2007). In May 2007, a federal grand jury in San Diego indicted 19 defendants on charges related to an alleged racketeering enterprise designed to cheat gaming casinos across the United States and Canada out of millions of dollars. According to the indictment, the defendants and their cohorts executed a false shuffle cheating scheme during blackjack and mini-baccarat games at nearly 20 casinos. The indictment alleged that members of the criminal organization bribed casino card dealers and supervisors to perform false shuffles during card games, thereby creating "slugs" of unshuffled cards. After tracking the order of the cards dealt in a particular game, a member of the criminal group signaled the dealer to perform a false shuffle, after which the gang member bet on a known order of cards when the slug appeared on the table. The indictment further alleged that the defendants used sophisticated mechanisms to track the order of cards during games, including hidden transmitter devices and software specially designed to predict the order in which the cards would reappear (U.S. Department of Justice, Office of Public Affairs, 2007).

In a casino, patrons may not pay close attention to their coins, tokens, handbags, or other personal items. Continuous surveillance, videotaping of suspicious people, and security personnel are used to monitor patrons and employees to identify thieves. **Casino security** consists of a three-pronged attack involving surveillance of patrons and employees, physical security, and investigations of potential employees as well as reports of theft, narcotics, gaming violations, and white collar crime. Armed and unarmed security officers, surveillance personnel, and gaming commission investigators are involved in the security and safety effort (Major, 1998; National Indian Gaming Commission, 2007).

The vast majority of gaming casinos are open 24 hours per day, 365 days each year. Customers can arrive at one of these casinos at any time, searching for a pleasurable experience. Legitimate patrons usually carry large sums of cash and have credit cards, travelers checks, jewelry, and luggage in their possession. They are extremely vulnerable and may become victims of theft. A determined thief does not limit targets to legitimate customers. Con artists working individually and in groups are a threat to all casino games. Some thieves insert slugs (a piece of metal the size of a coin or token) into gaming slot machines. Other thieves attempt to compromise slot machines by "stringing." This procedure involves the attachment of a very thin monofilament, such as fishing line, to a coin. The coin is inserted into the coin acceptor of a slot machine. The operator manipulates the line to activate the machine repeatedly with the same coin. Additionally, table card games and other games are subject to various types of theft.

Casinos use a five-part strategy to prevent or detect theft through the casino's games:

- Through the *command* component, casinos organize security and surveillance.
- Through the *control* component, casinos utilize security and surveillance to influence circumstances for a favorable outcome.
- Good *communication* is the component used to link elements and personnel.
- *Compliance* is the most vital component of the antifraud strategies. Compliance with house rules and agency regulations is a necessity. A significant portion of the losses to casinos results from irregular or minimal compliance with rules and regulatory agency policy.
- The introduction of *antitheft technology* to the gaming industry helps also. In addition to surveillance equipment, many casinos have installed automatic card-shuffling machines to prevent collaboration between criminals and bribed card game dealers (McDonald & Barfield, 2007; Nichter, 2000).

A QUICK SURVEY

Consider all the institutional settings with which you have interacted. In any of the settings with which you have interacted, have you become aware that a security breach occurred? If so, check any and all of the following settings in which this has occurred.

- Bank or other financial institution
- Courthouse or courtroom
- Elementary school
- Secondary school
- College or university
- Health care facility
- Hotel, motel, restaurant, bar, or other hospitality establishment
- Entertainment venue (concert, sports event, casino, theme park, etc.)
- Entertainment medium (movies, music)

In your view, what led to the security breaches in the settings you checked? What could security personnel have done differently to prevent the breaches?

DISASTER RECOVERY

Several types of natural and environmental disasters are potential threats to people and property—as the recent earthquake, tsunami, and resulting nuclear reactor leaks in Japan demonstrate. No place in the world is immune from the possibility of a catastrophic event that could result in injuries, loss of life, and destruction of property. For the security manager, prevention of loss due to a disaster is a critical responsibility. In addition, organizations must have policies, procedures, and protection systems in place that assist with the restoration of normal operations as soon as possible after a disaster.

Mitigating damages subsequent to a catastrophic event led to the development of **disaster recovery** as a new specialty within the field of security management. In some large organizations, such as international telecommunications companies, individuals may be tasked with the sole responsibility for developing and implementing disaster-management plans. Poor customer service and loss of market share are potential consequences of a failure to return to normal operations in a timely fashion.

Disaster recovery is part of a broader process known as operations (or business) continuity management discussed earlier in Chapter 7. In addition to natural and environmental (human-caused) disasters, other events such as employee strikes and downtime for equipment maintenance may disrupt normal operating activities.

Prevention of loss due to a disaster is a critical responsibility for security personnel.
(Photo courtesy of Wackenhut Corporation.)

For additional information on disaster recovery planning, contact the Disaster Recovery Institute International at www.drii.org.

Disasters can impact every aspect of organizational life, and each aspect must be addressed in the recovery effort. Public emergency responders must be assisted with traffic control and crowd management. The site must be secured and communications reestablished. Injured people may be trapped in the facility. Hazmat teams must isolate hazardous materials, and on-site crisis counseling may be necessary.

Unlike disaster response, disaster recovery requires balancing the need to return the affected area to normalcy with the strategic goal of reducing vulnerability. Because disaster recovery has long-lasting effects and is usually expensive, numerous stakeholders from the government, business, and the community should be involved in the recovery process (Haddow & Bullock, 2010).

EXECUTIVE PROTECTION

Executive protection (EP) encompasses all activities designed to maintain the safety, security, and health of a human asset, including executives, citizens, and political leaders.

Executive Kidnapping

Executive kidnapping is a potential threat in any part of the world, even in the United States. In some countries, it has become a criminal industry. The risk of kidnapping, injury, or death is not only possible, but may be probable in some areas of the world. Consider these examples of executive kidnappings in Mexico:

- On August 10, 1996, Sanyo executive Mamoru Konno was kidnapped in Tijuana, Mexico, and held for 9 days. Konno, in charge of a Sanyo factory in Mexico, was kidnapped from his car shortly after leaving a company-sponsored baseball game on the eastern edge of Tijuana. Fortunately, Konno was released unharmed after a $2 million ransom was paid.
- In August 1998, Daniel Arizmendi Lopez, when asked by a Mexican judge to state his occupation, allegedly identified himself as a kidnapper. Some authorities believe that Lopez abducted approximately 200 wealthy businesspeople and their family members over a 5-year period.
- On September 11, 1999, Chung Yin Ng, a 72-year-old Chinese-born businessman, was kidnapped in Tijuana and held for a $1 million ransom until he was rescued by Baja California state judicial police. Six men, including an associate of the victim, were arrested in connection with the kidnapping.
- A U.S. citizen who reportedly worked for a U.S.-based company with operations in Monterrey was kidnapped early on the morning of January 4, 2011, in Monterrey, Nuevo Leon state, in Mexico. The victim apparently was driving a company-issued armored luxury vehicle at the time of the kidnapping. The victim was severely beaten and was released later in the evening in the nearby city of Escobedo, Nuevo Leon state, just north of Monterrey. No ransom was demanded, indicating that the attackers' main objective was stealing the armored luxury vehicle ("U.S. executive kidnapped in Monterrey," 2011).

Organizations that assign human assets to work in foreign lands must ensure the health, safety, and security of personnel. Protection teams often accompany executives. In progressive security-conscious organizations, the human asset is briefed on potential dangers and trained to avoid high-risk areas and a conspicuous appearance. In addition to the threat of kidnapping and murder, health care services in many foreign venues are substandard. A failure to receive adequate medical care immediately after the onset of a sudden illness can be fatal. Some companies maintain, or establish contractual arrangements with, highly trained teams that specialize in medical evacuation of personnel from foreign countries.

Terrorism against Citizens

Since trends suggest that the United States and its citizens are preferred targets for terrorists, human assets will continue to be potential victims of terrorism. The possibility of terrorist activity demands precautionary measures. Cooperation between and among nations is also essential to counterterrorism operations. To this end, the globe's intelligence communities and criminal justice systems must assume additional responsibility for counterterrorism and personal protection (Martin, 2009; U.S. Department of State, Overseas Security Advisory Council, 2007).

Risks to Political Leaders

Political leaders constantly strive to strike a balance between protecting themselves from attacks by members of the public who disagree with their views or who are mentally unbalanced, and remaining accessible to their constituents. The consequences of underestimating the need for security made themselves tragically clear on Saturday, January 8, 2011, when Arizona Democratic Representative Gabrielle Giffords was shot in the head in Tucson during a political gathering held in the parking lot outside a supermarket. Jared Lee Loughner, the alleged shooter, killed six people, including a federal judge and a 9-year-old girl attending the gathering, and wounded 14 others, including Giffords.

The Tucson shootings initially sparked debate over whether the overheated political rhetoric that had begun characterizing public debate in the United States had impelled Loughner to take violent action against Giffords. However, as more information about Loughner came to light, it became clear that his actions more likely stemmed from mental illness rather than a clear-headed, if vicious, political agenda. Loughner had a history of run-ins with the law and had engaged in increasingly bizarre interactions with students, teachers, and school officials at Pima Community College the previous year, including writing disturbing poetry in a class and disrupting classes when he received criticism from teachers (Reston, 2011).

The shootings also prompted lawmakers to rethink questions about the benefits and costs of security. As Pima County Sheriff Clarence Dupnik explained, "there was no security at the political gathering in Tucson. At such events, there's never security unless there's advance intelligence that there may be a problem of some kind." He noted that Congresswoman Giffords often attended as many as eight events in a single day. While members of the House and Senate leadership have security provided by Capitol Hill, rank-and-file lawmakers like Giffords do not receive constant security detail. However, they can request security if they have safety concerns. All political leaders are subject to occasional threats, angry letters, and irate phone calls. But threats were heightened during the recent public debate over proposed new health care legislation. Giffords' district office in Arizona, for example, was vandalized, and a man went to trial for threatening to burn down the home of former Democratic Representative John Boccieri of Ohio (Keck, 2011).

As lawmakers returned to work after the Arizona shootings, partisan division emerged over their security needs. Democrats suggested that extra funding might be needed to strengthen security for themselves and their staff in districts where legislators felt particularly exposed. One proposal presented by some Democrats would provide funds for representatives who must reimburse local law enforcement that provide security at district events. Republicans sought solutions that would not require additional funding. Some lawmakers suggested that they might carry personal firearms for protection. Both parties discussed the possibility of having the U.S. Marshals Service play an expanded role in investigating threats made against members of Congress. Recent events suggest the importance of swiftly resolving the question of how political leaders can balance security with maintaining open access for their constituents: Soon after the Tucson shootings, the FBI arrested a Palm Springs man on suspicion of threatening Democratic Representative Jim McDermott of Washington. The 32-year-old suspect had left voicemail messages the previous month threatening to kill McDermott because of his position on the tax-cut debate (Mascaro, 2011).

Components of an Effective Executive Protection Program

The three essential components of an effective EP program include risk (threat) assessment, advance procedures, and protective operations:

- A *risk assessment* is used to examine an environment and attendant circumstances to identify threats that could harm a principal, predict the likelihood of a negative event, and assess the damage if a negative event materializes.
- *Advance procedures* involve touring the principal's intended route and coordinating security arrangements before, during, and after the principal's travel.
- Through *protective operations*, EP personnel accompany the principal, engaging in countersurveillance and defensive tactics (Gips, 2007).

Summary

Common threats as well as safety and security principles and practices apply across the broad spectrum of public and private enterprises. However, some threats and security measures are unique to specific environments. The nature of banking and financial transactions has changed dramatically, increasing targets of opportunity for the would-be criminal. Courthouses and courtrooms are no longer safe havens where adversaries can settle disputes without fear of disruption, injury, or death. Disaster recovery specialists develop and implement plans to assist organizations with resumption of normal activity after a major catastrophe.

Although educational institutions as a whole are safe environments, an increase in violent crime led to the development of safety and security programs in elementary and secondary schools as well as colleges and universities. The entertainment industry blossoms as more people seek leisure time activities. Sporting events, recreational facilities, theme parks, gaming casinos, and other entertainment venues serve millions of people. Computer technology and the Internet have created a need to prevent fraudulent appropriation of intellectual property.

The development of the global marketplace and an increase in international travel have led to a need to protect people in transit and those who visit unsafe areas of the world. Health care, the fifth largest industry in the United States, encompasses over 30,000 facilities. The sick, injured, and dying typically cannot care for themselves. Thus, the health care security business is expanding. Hospitality environments, especially lodging establishments, are targets for various types of crime committed by employees, guests, and unwanted visitors. Entertainment security focuses on many venues, including sporting events, recreational areas and theme parks, racetracks, movies, ships, and casinos. Disaster recovery involves mitigating damages and losses subsequent to a catastrophic natural or human-caused event. Executive protection includes all activities designed to maintain the safety, security, and health of a human asset.

Key Terms

bailiffs

Bank Protection Act of 1968

casino security

Clery Act

Crime Awareness and Campus
   Security Act

disaster recovery

executive protection

financial institutions

health care facilities

Health Insurance Portability
   and Accountability Act
   of 1996

hospitality industry

International Association for
   Healthcare Security and Safety
   (IAHSS)

Joint Commission for
   Accreditation of Healthcare
   Organizations (JCAHO)

Motion Picture Association of
   America (MPAA)

nursing homes

postsecondary institutions

safe-school zones

Virginia Tech

Discussion Questions and Exercises

1. Although commonalities exist, numerous unique hazards threaten specific types of industries and organizations. Explain.
2. Choose one specific security application from this chapter. List the types of crime and other hazards that threaten the operation, and design measures to prevent the threats from materializing.

YOUR TURN: Analyzing the Virginia Tech Incident

The deadliest single-perpetrator shooting rampage in the history of the United States occurred at Virginia Polytechnic Institute and State University (**Virginia Tech**) in Blacksburg, Virginia, on April 16, 2007. The shooter, Cho Seung Hui, killed 32 students and faculty and wounded 30 others before taking his own life.

The killing spree began shortly after 7:00 A.M. at West Ambler Johnson Hall, a dormitory on the Virginia Tech campus. The following is a brief summary of early morning events:

7:15 A.M.

Police receive a 911 phone call, reporting shots fired at Johnson Hall. Police find a female student and male resident advisor fatally wounded. Based on witness interviews, police believe the shootings are an isolated domestic incident. Police do not initiate campus-wide security measures. Police focus on the female victim's boyfriend, a student at nearby Radford University. Police later stop and interrogate the boyfriend on a highway in Blacksburg.

9:26 A.M.

Virginia Tech authorities issue first mass email, reporting the 7:15 A.M. shooting and warning students and staff.

9:45 A.M.

Police receive a phone call about a shooting at Norris Hall, a science and engineering classroom building, about 15 minutes walking distance from West Ambler Johnson Hall. After the perpetrator, Cho Seung Hui, chained the Norris Hall exterior doors shut, he killed 30 students and faculty in their classrooms before killing himself.

9:50 A.M.

A second mass email by Virginia Tech officials reports a gunman is loose on campus.

9:55 A.M.

A third mass email reports the shootings at Norris Hall and that the gunman is in custody.

Subsequent to the mass killing, it was learned that the killer, Cho Seung Hui, had been treated for mental illness.

1. In your view, were any or all of the killings at Virginia Tech preventable? If so, what could have been done to prevent them, and by whom?
2. Do you think that police and security measures and responses were appropriate? Why or why not? If not, what would have constituted more appropriate responses from police and university security personnel?
3. Are sufficient safety and security measures in place on school and college campuses in general?
4. Conduct research online or in your library to discover what actions the Virginia Tech massacre prompted key stakeholders to take. Consider actions taken by emergency services organizations, university administrators, Virginia's state government, families of the victims and shooter, and mental health professionals.
5. Research the news media's coverage of the Virginia Tech shootings and the shooters' mental state. Consider the benefits and risks of the press coverage. For example, a benefit might be that details about how events unfolded during the shootings could help other universities strengthen their security measures. A risk might be that the extensive attention given to the shooter could cause other mentally ill individuals to plan a similar massacre in hopes of getting media attention and a permanent place in history.
6. What impact did the Virginia Tech shootings have on the debate over gun control in the United States and on gun laws?

CHAPTER 11

Industrial Security, Retail Loss Prevention, and Workplace Violence

LEARNING OBJECTIVES

After completing this chapter, the reader should be able to

- identify security threats unique to specific industries.
- describe asset protection priorities as well as loss prevention policies, procedures, and systems associated with the following:
- industrial security
- library and museum security
- office building security
- privatization of public services
- residential security
- retail loss prevention
- workplace violence prevention
- zoo and aquarium security
- evaluate specific security environments, applications, and services.

INTRODUCTION

Although a comprehensive exploration of every unique security environment and service is beyond the scope of a single book, Chapters 10 and 11 are designed to introduce the reader to numerous security applications. This chapter continues with a discussion of specific security environments, applications, and services.

INDUSTRIAL SECURITY

Industrial security focuses primarily on the protection of the manufacturing process. Accidents, natural disasters, internal theft, sabotage, and espionage constitute the major threats to industrial complexes. Accidents may result in process downtime, property damage, personal injury, even death. Natural disasters can destroy an entire industrial facility.

Internal theft is a major contributing factor to losses in and around industrial manufacturing facilities. Theft of tools, raw materials, component parts, finished products, equipment, time, and technology are the primary means through which dishonest employees contribute to loss. Vulnerable areas include loading docks, shipping and receiving areas, warehouses, tool storage areas, trash containers, distribution points, and data systems (Fennelly, 1992; Johnson, 2005).

Although the Cold War is over, espionage and sabotage remain very real threats to manufacturing organizations. Industrial espionage occurs when trade secrets, proprietary information, or intellectual property are stolen. Sabotage occurs when the manufacturing process is intentionally disrupted or when machinery or products are intentionally destroyed. Likely suspects to espionage or sabotage are disgruntled employees, competitors, and in some cases, foreign governments.

Under contract to the U.S. government, many private organizations and numerous colleges and universities conduct classified research and produce classified material for government consumption. To ensure compliance with federally mandated security parameters, these private industries and academic institutions participate in the National Industrial Security Program (NISP). NISP security-compliance regulations apply to contractors performing for numerous government agencies, including the U.S. Department of Defense, U.S. Department of Energy, CIA, and Nuclear Regulatory Commission (Federation of American Scientists, 2007; Kovacich & Halibozek, 2003).

LIBRARY AND MUSEUM SECURITY

Due to the rare and sometimes irreplaceable nature of **library** and **museum** inventories, special attention must be given to criminal as well as noncriminal hazards. Theft, vandalism, fire, floods, leaking roofs, and the environment are common threats to library collections and museum pieces. Libraries contain a wide variety of out-of-print works, compact disks (CDs), audiovisual materials, and manuscripts. Museums contain rare, often irreplaceable, items. Irreplaceable and rare items and materials should be maintained in closed areas where access is easily restricted. Mutilation of books and periodicals may be reduced by providing copier machines to patrons. Unauthorized removal of library works may be prevented through the use of electronic markings in books and alarm sensors at exit points. Museum pieces can be monitored via closed-circuit television (CCTV) and through the use of security personnel in areas accessible to the public.

Theft of priceless rare items and works of art has been identified as second only to international drug trafficking in terms of dollar value per criminal transaction. In many cases, major thefts are the product of a contractual arrangement between the thief and the illegitimate consumer. The most frequently stolen works in museums and art galleries tend to be small items that can be concealed easily. As with libraries, most museum thefts occur while the facility is open to the public. Museums and art galleries must also be vigilant regarding purchases of additional pieces for the collection. Acquisitions should be authenticated to deter and detect criminals who specialize in the creation of fraudulent pieces or the disposition of stolen works.

In addition to protecting rare books and artifacts in the collection, such facilities are host to special events and are often visited by dignitaries. Libraries and museums host conferences, meetings, and parties. In addition, famous politicians, artists, authors, and celebrities visit libraries and museums.

Security personnel should be employed for office buildings.
(Photo courtesy of Wackenhut Corporation.)

Comprehensive physical security and access control programs, continuous inventory control procedures, and authentication and appraisal of new works can greatly reduce losses to museums and galleries. Maintaining appropriate air quality and temperature standards will help preserve rare items. In addition, emergency management planning and procedures, video surveillance, security personnel, and vigilant curatorial staff help to protect the contents of libraries and museums (Hough, 1999; Longmore-Etheridge, 2007).

OFFICE BUILDING SECURITY

Originally, the United States was an agrarian (agricultural) society. However, mass migration, immigration, and the industrial revolution in the second half of the nineteenth century and the early 1900s led to the development of cities and urban areas. In the latter half of the twentieth century, a technological revolution occurred. The United States, and most of the industrialized world, was transformed. Technologically advanced, service-related, information-based economies replaced industrial, labor-intensive, blue-collar economies. Today, white-collar workers comprise a substantial portion of the workforce. These workers are typically housed in offices and office buildings that may be scattered throughout metropolitan areas.

Most office buildings are open to the public and provide convenient entry and exit points. Unless one agency or company occupies an entire building, several tenants will occupy a single facility. As a result, during normal business hours, few office buildings restrict access to lobbies, different floors, individual business offices, or restrooms.

Major **office building security threats** include fire, poor or inadequate evacuation routes, terrorist activity, bombs or bomb threats, theft, burglary, robbery, sexual assault, and executive kidnapping. Office equipment, supplies, payroll checks, cash, proprietary information, copper from phone lines and cables, and even recyclable materials within office buildings are often the targets for thieves and burglars. Near-record prices for copper and other metals, for example, have spurred a resurgence in theft of such materials, especially from companies in industries that make extensive use of copper (such as utilities). In addition to theft, people may be assaulted in restrooms or parking areas, and corporate executives may be targeted for kidnapping.

The risk of loss or injury in office buildings can be minimized in several ways.

- Security personnel, contract or proprietary, should be employed.
- Liquid assets, such as cash and valuables, and sensitive proprietary information can be stored in vaults.
- Restrooms should be locked with passkeys restricted to tenants and their guests.
- Maintenance and custodial personnel should be properly screened prior to employment.
- Common areas and parking facilities should be patrolled regularly.
- Access control and surveillance systems may be utilized.
- Fire drills and inspection of fire prevention and protection equipment should take place on a regular basis.

Subsequent to the World Trade Center terrorist bombing in New York City in 1993, several high-rise office building management teams increased security. Measures implemented

High-rise office building security was increased subsequent to the terrorist attacks on New York City's World Trade Center.
(Photo courtesy of Wackenhut Corporation.)

or improved included access control, security patrols, staff awareness training, new policies and procedures, contingency planning, window glazing, and forms of perimeter fortification. During the 7 years subsequent to the 1993 incident, $60 million was spent at the World Trade Center to improve security and counter the threat of terrorism. However, it appears that only the high-profile facilities made measurable security improvements. In spite of the bombings at the World Trade Center in 1993 and the Murrah federal building in Oklahoma City in 1995, many office building security managers still believed their facilities were relatively safe from terrorism (Gips, 2000). The security measures in high-rise office buildings remained relatively loose during normal business hours. This false sense of security was shattered on September 11, 2001. Since the loss of New York's World Trade Center on 9/11, many high-rise facilities throughout the United States have improved security and safety measures dramatically (Craighead, 2009).

Ultimately, the type, amount, and cost of security measures employed in and around an office building will depend on the size, location, and nature of the facility. The number of tenants, the type of businesses involved, and crime rate within the area must also be considered when planning a safety and security program for an office building. Some businesses are banding together to provide their own security. For example, in 2009, more than a dozen businesses in Oakland, California, formed community-benefit associations in two sections of the city after Oakland reduced city services to close a $30 million budget deficit. The two associations eventually comprised about 100 member businesses. The associations have hired unarmed security guards who patrol the streets (White, 2010).

SECURITY SPOTLIGHT

Are you employed by an organization that rents or owns an office building? If so, identify the security measures that have been taken to protect the building as well as the people and assets within the building. In your view, could additional measures be taken? If so, which?

PRIVATIZATION OF PUBLIC SECURITY SERVICES

In principle, **privatization of public security services** in some cases may be in the best interests of society in general and taxpayers in particular. However, some experts express reservations about privatization, because the privatized activities are the responsibility of the criminal justice system (public law enforcement, courts, corrections). At issue is relegation of responsibility for two precious citizen possessions to private, for-profit organizations: personal liberty and life itself. Constitutionally, it may not be possible to delegate most crime-related law enforcement responsibilities to the private sector. However, many non–crime-related activities and services currently performed by the public police may appropriately be transferred, under contract, to private organizations through privatization of public services. In this regard, there appears to be a growing interdependence between the public and private sectors. Federal, state, and local government expenditures for private sector services have increased dramatically over the past several years. In many areas of the country, the private sector is involved in activities such as traffic and parking enforcement, preventive patrol, community policing, animal control, court security, prisoner transport, and corrections (Dempsey, 2011; Robinson, 1999).

As a result of stabilized and shrinking governmental budgets, some publicly provided services are being shifted to private providers who, through efficient business strategies and less bureaucracy, are able to reduce expenditures and provide equivalent services on a more effective basis. It is estimated that by 2035, private security companies will assume 50 percent of all public law enforcement responsibilities (Tafoya, 1994). Caution must be exercised to ensure the provision of quality public services by the private providers.

Some of the most visible efforts to privatize public services have been in the area of corrections. Private providers such as the Corrections Corporation of America, the GEO Group, Pinkerton, and the Wackenhut Corrections Corporation are involved in the construction and operation of jails and prisons throughout the United States. By the mid-1990s, approximately 80 privately run jails and prisons were operating within the United States. In addition, hundreds of private community-based corrections programs (halfway houses, drug treatment centers, small residential institutions, work and study release programs) operate throughout the United States. In most cases, the private companies meet or exceed the quality of government-provided services while reducing costs.

Many examples of public–private cooperation and effective privatization efforts exist. During the spring of 1997, the Dallas, Texas, police department, as part of a huge anticrime offensive, solicited assistance from the city's 15,000 private security officers. The police department asked the private forces to act as additional eyes and ears for the police. Rapport and a communications system was established between the public and the private sectors. Apparently, this collaboration was effective in reducing the crime rate, especially among juveniles. In addition, private security personnel, under contract to local, county, state, and national government, transport prisoners and provide security for courthouses in many areas of the United States. Private court security officers are also used quite extensively by the U.S. Marshals Service to secure federal courthouses and courtrooms. The sharing of information between private security and public law enforcement has also increased ("Operation Cooperation," 2001).

On the international scene, private U.S. corporations, under contract to the federal government, provide security services and personnel for U.S. embassies and missions throughout the world. These companies establish security programs that supplement U.S. Marines assigned to the U.S. government facilities in foreign countries. Typically, the private security operations are managed on-site by U.S. nationals with operations-level personnel recruited and employed from the host country's local labor market. Private contractors are also utilized in war zones, as demonstrated by security personnel employed by the U. S. government for the war in Iraq (Schmalleger, 2011; Simonsen, 1998).

RESIDENTIAL SECURITY

Individuals spend a majority of their time in a residential environment. People eat, sleep, socialize, and sometimes work in single-family homes, apartments, condominiums, and multipurpose facilities. The residence may be in a single- or multifamily dwelling. It may be located in the inner city, a suburb, or rural area. It may be part of a planned community or public housing facility. Residents often provide for their own security. Others, however, may employ contract or proprietary security personnel services.

Safety and security threats in a residence include accidents, medical emergencies, fire, theft, burglary, vandalism, assault, homicide, and damage or personal injury resulting from natural disasters. The home is actually a very unsafe place, and vulnerability increases when residents are asleep. Of all fire deaths each year, approximately one-half occur in the home. The residence is also an ideal target for burglars because the possibility of being caught is minimal. Nationally, only about 15 percent of all residential burglaries are solved. Most burglaries are committed when the home is unoccupied and the possibility of detection and apprehension is minimized.

In addition, many homicides are committed in the home, often as a result of a long history of domestic conflict (Barlow, 2000).

Most safety and security problems in a residence are preventable. Early warning fire detectors and adequate preplanned escape routes greatly reduce fire deaths. Physical security in the form of lighting, good locks on doors and windows, access control, and secure storage of valuables can deter or minimize the impact of an unauthorized intrusion. Some homeowners have also begun using web-based CCTV technology to view activities taking place in their home through the Internet while they are at work or on vacation outside the home. These pinhole cameras can be hidden anywhere within the home, and some digital alarm clocks have the minicameras built-in.

Residents should adhere to the following as a **residential burglary prevention strategy**:

- Ensure that the residence does not appear unoccupied.
- Maintain key control and keep doors and windows locked.
- Leave lights and a radio on while residents are away. Use timing devices to control lights.
- Do not admit strangers to the residence.
- Know the neighbors. Trusted neighbors may check on the home and retrieve mail and newspapers during an absence.
- Keep an inventory of valuables, and provide it to the police if a burglary occurs.
- Do not leave notes visible that indicate an absence.
- Do not broadcast travel plans.
- Consider installing an alarm system: the least expensive alarm is a dog that barks at strangers.

In an effort to create a more secure environment, many residential areas are supervised through neighborhood watch programs or are gated to restrict access. Some employ security patrols. In addition, multiunit buildings and housing facilities may utilize alarm systems, surveillance equipment, or interior and exterior patrols. They can be constructed, utilizing crime prevention through environmental design (CPTED) principles, with consideration given to security and safety. Through local community policing efforts, resources are often available to assist residential property managers in their efforts to secure property and deter illegal activity. A training program prepared by the U.S. Department of Justice, Office of Justice Programs, emphasizes cooperation among property owners, managers, tenants, and law enforcement agencies to help neighborhoods fight residence-related crime (U.S. Department of Justice, Bureau of Justice Assistance, 2000).

SECURITY SPOTLIGHT

Assess the risks to your residence, whether you live in an apartment, condominium, stand-alone house, or dormitory. What measures do you and others (e.g., campus security, a condo association, your family members, or an apartment building owner) currently take to ensure that your residence is secure? What additional measures (if any) would you recommend? Why?

RETAIL LOSS PREVENTION

Losses in retail operations may occur in several ways. Administrative errors and inaccurate record-keeping account for up to 20 percent of all retail losses. Natural disasters in the form of floods, tornadoes, and hurricanes certainly take their toll. Looting during civil disturbances and riots have also left their mark on history. Products developed for human consumption can be intentionally or unintentionally contaminated. However, losses due to theft, both internal and external, account for the greatest continuous economic drain on retail establishments. In 2006, retail losses due to theft were estimated at $41.6 billion, up 11 percent from 2005 (Davies, 2007; Nocella, 2000).

Theft-related losses may force a retail operation into bankruptcy. To compensate for actual losses, a retail outlet is required to generate, through additional sales, many times the amount of the loss. For example, if the store operates on a 5 percent net profit margin and experiences an actual loss of $50, it must generate additional sales of $1,000 to offset the loss and break even. Similarly, if the same store experiences a $500 loss, it must generate additional sales of $10,000 before profitability returns.

Inventory shrinkage is the major problem in retail environments. Shrinkage is defined as the reduction in inventories not accounted for through sales or other legitimate activity. It is the difference between the inventory that is on hand for sale and what the retail establishment indicates should be available for sale. The most significant causes of retail shrinkage are internal and external theft (Chan, 2003).

Internal Theft

The primary cause of inventory shrinkage to most retailers is internal theft. Over 40 percent of all retail losses due to theft is internal in nature. Approximately 30 percent is due to external sources, while 20 percent is due to administrative error (C. Bridges, 1994; Hollinger & Dabney, 1995; Kimiecik & Thomas, 2006). Employees have direct access to cash and merchandise, often work alone, and are familiar with retail loss prevention measures.

Employees may deplete the resources of a retail establishment in several ways. These include

- theft of cash.
- price alterations or switching.
- abuse of the refund system.
- undercharging of, or not charging for, merchandise to a friend or relative.
- theft of merchandise.
- kickbacks from vendors.
- damaging merchandise with the intention of purchasing it later at a discounted price.
- failing to record sales on the cash register and pocketing the cash from a customer.

Point-of-sale (POS) theft schemes are a particular problem for some retailers. Through this scheme, an offending employee under-rings a sale, manipulating the cash register into expecting a smaller amount than the customer is charged, then the employee pockets the difference. For Dunkin' Brands (which owns Dunkin' Donuts and Baskin-Robbins, chains of coffee shops and ice cream stores, respectively), POS theft was totaling millions in loss each year. To reduce loss from POS theft, the company's security team integrated video and POS data and used exception-reporting software to zero in on suspicious transactions. The team also implemented a third-party data-investigation service that can query Dunkin' Brands POS database in search of suspicious transactions, remotely access the corresponding video for confirmation, and report incidents of fraud to franchisees. Each transaction from the system flows into a sales-transaction database. The security team analyzes the data and then informs the franchisee of any suspected theft. The franchisee can then review the individual store's surveillance video to confirm the security team's suspicions. At one store, after several offending employees were discovered and fired, sales shot up 30 percent (Goodchild, 2010).

Internal theft can be prevented, or at least reduced, through the establishment of sound preemployment screening procedures, strict cash handling procedures and refund policies, cash register software that identifies suspicious transactions, random audits, a code of conduct for employees, and management's attention to employee behavior. In addition, independent honesty shopping services may be employed to test employee cash-handling procedures and customer service. The honesty shopper, posing as a customer, observes employee behavior and reports to management on sales personnel efficiency, courtesy, and violations of store policies and procedures (Davies, 2007).

External Sources of Loss

Most retail losses from external sources are due to vandalism, burglary, robbery, **credit card fraud** and **coupon fraud**, **bad checks**, and **shoplifting**. In addition, shopping centers and malls face unique challenges because they incorporate privately owned space where the general public gathers. Public demonstrations and disturbances can deter normal customer activity. Thus, shopping center owners and security personnel must balance private property interests with the public's right to gather and exercise constitutional rights such as freedom to associate and freedom of speech.

VANDALISM, BURGLARY, AND ROBBERY Vandalism and burglary may be prevented through the use of adequate exterior lighting, physical security, and subscription to a central station alarm service. When not preventable, losses due to robbery may be greatly reduced by limiting the amount of cash on hand in cash registers and other robbery targets. Stores that are open 24 hours are especially vulnerable to robbery. The Occupational Safety and Health Administration (OSHA) recommends that stores with late-night open hours take extra precautions. Improved lighting, increased staffing, video cameras, alarms, floor deposit safes, bullet-resistant glass, and employee training can prevent or at least reduce the impact of nighttime robberies.

CREDIT CARD AND COUPON FRAUD Credit card fraud resulting from the use of a stolen or fictitious credit card may be reduced through a careful examination of the credit card and the signature of the cardholder accompanied by verification of the signature and positive identification of the purchaser. Some form of photo identification is appropriate for this verification. Coupon fraud occurs when customers (or employees) redeem coupons for cash in lieu of the purchase of the item for which the coupon was issued (Nocella, 2000).

Most consumer card fraud occurs on existing debit and credit card accounts. In 2009, credit and debit card fraud accounted for 65 and 28 percent, respectively, of all existing card fraud that year. Merchants are fighting fraud by increasingly outsourcing transaction and customer profile databases to third-party risk management providers. They also are increasingly using POS authentication devices, Internet protocol address detection, rules-based filters, and tracking tools and online-purchase authentication systems (Bell, 2010).

BAD CHECKS Bad checks fall into four broad categories: forged or altered, insufficient funds, no account, and incorrectly completed checks. Postdated, out-of-town, second party, illegible, and counter checks are considered high risk. Since most checks are written and cashed in a retail environment, the potential for heavy dollar loss is great. Furthermore, only a small percentage of the dollar loss due to bad checks is ever recovered. Therefore, effective **check cashing procedures** are critical. Check cashing procedures include a thorough examination of the check and a positive identification of the check casher. Acceptable forms of identification for check cashing purposes include current photo, driver's licenses, government or military identification, passports, and state or national identification cards.

SHOPLIFTING   Shoplifting, by employees as well as outsiders, is considered to be the most frequent crime committed against retailers. It occurs whenever persons lawfully or unlawfully present on the retail premises misappropriate merchandise to their own use. It is one of the fastest growing theft-related crimes. Shoplifters fall into three broad categories: amateurs (the largest group), kleptomaniacs (compulsive thieves), and professionals. **Shoplifting methods** are limited only by the ingenuity of the thief. Common methods include:

- hiding items under or in clothing, purses, and briefcases.
- using a shopping bag lined with aluminum to thwart a store's sensor.
- switching price tags.
- placing items in another product's packaging.
- using a booster box (a box with a spring-loaded trap door) or shopping bag.
- wearing an item out of the store.

Some bold or desperate thieves simply grab items they want and run from the store. For example, armed robbers seeking opioid painkillers and other drugs to sell or feed their own addictions (e.g., OxyContin, Vicodin, and Xanax) have leapt over pharmacy counters to snatch the drugs or have threatened pharmacists (Goodnough, 2011).

If a retail establishment's policy is to apprehend shoplifters, at least one employee on duty should receive adequate training to handle shoplifters. The employee must be knowledgeable regarding state and local laws associated with a retail merchant's authority to detain, search, or arrest suspected shoplifters. Shoplifter apprehensions can easily result in a physical confrontation that should be avoided.

Apprehending shoplifters can also prompt them to file claims of malicious prosecution or defamation—either of which increases the retailer's liability and can damage the company's brand. Retailers can take steps to minimize their exposure to and damage from such claims. For instance, regarding malicious prosecution claims, retailers should conduct a thorough investigation following apprehension of a shoplifter and follow up on any reasonable explanations offered by the person to justify the actions the individual took. Retailers should never misrepresent, mischaracterize, or exaggerate evidence gathered regarding the alleged shoplifting. They should also immediately acknowledge any mistakes made in their investigation. Regarding defamation claims, retailers can mitigate their exposure by taking the following steps when apprehending a shoplifter:

- Be as discreet as possible when engaging with the person.
- Take reasonable steps to prevent situations from escalating.
- Escort the person out of public view as quickly as possible.
- Minimize use of handcuffs.
- Avoid parading the person through the store.
- Maintain the person's privacy to the extent possible.
- Discuss the case only with those who have a need to know (LaBruno, 2011).

An effective **shoplifting prevention strategy** includes deterrence and detection through the use of appropriate displays of merchandise, surveillance equipment and people, package

Electronic article surveillance devices are used to help secure high-value merchandise in a retail environment. These devices sound an alarm if their wires are cut or if they are removed from the store while attached to merchandise. *(Photo courtesy of Patrick Ortmeier.)*

and fitting room inspections, properly enforced refund procedures, locking devices, and alarms. Many apparel retailers also use electronic article surveillance (EAS) tags on clothing items, small devices that emit a signal if a shopper tries to remove an item from the store without paying for it. For items purchased properly at the cash register, the EAS tags are removed at point of sale (see "Improving EAS Tags at an Upscale Apparel Retailer"). However, the most effective deterrent is adequate, well-trained, and observant sales personnel. Shoplifting is an opportunity crime. If the potential thief suspects that detection and apprehension is a strong possibility, the shoplifter may not risk being caught.

REFUND ABUSE   Retail losses may also be prevented through an effective **refund policy**. Ideally, refunds should be tightly controlled and issued from a centralized service desk. To prevent refund abuse by customers as well as employees, retail merchants can develop a database of individuals who request refunds. Suspicious refunds are checked against the database to determine how often the person seeking a refund attempts to return merchandise. Additionally, when a refund is requested, a check of the inventory list may verify if the item returned was actually sold. **Transaction reports**, which include sales records, voided sales receipts, and other activity performed by the cash registers each day, may also be used where refunds are made from the cash registers and other points of sale. Loss prevention personnel should audit these reports to identify suspicious activity.

New Challenges and Opportunities for Retailers

Several challenges face those responsible for retail loss prevention. Rapidly evolving technology and its use, such as the Internet and retail sales online as well as mobile phone payments, present unique challenges to retailers. For example, merchants accepting mobile phone payments had

Improving EAS Tags at an Upscale Apparel Retailer

At apparel retailer bebe, older-generation, reusable hard tags applied to merchandise as it arrived in stores were not helping to discourage theft as much as they should have been. The tags were too easily removed by employees and customers. Also because the tags were applied in the stores, the risk of internal theft of newly arrived untagged items was high.

The company worked with a vendor to develop a new tag that featured a stronger locking mechanism, among other improvements. But it went beyond technological changes—identifying process improvements that would also help. Specifically, bebe persuaded its garment suppliers to apply the new tags to garments immediately after manufacture. When issuing a purchase order to a garment supplier, bebe now includes a specification for the tags in the same way that purchase orders also specify sewing style and style of shirt buttons. The tag supplier sends prespecified quantities of tags to the garment supplier's factories, which ship the tagged items to bebe distribution centers. From there, the items are shipped to the stores. After the tags are removed at point of sale, they are returned to the tag supplier, who sorts, cleans, tests, and repackages them for shipment back to garment makers to tag new merchandise.

These changes have paid big dividends. Since the program was implemented, tag "defeat" (removal) rates have declined significantly, as has shrinkage from internal theft and shoplifting. As a bonus, store employee productivity has improved, because employees no longer have to take time to tag newly arrived merchandise. Items can be displayed in the stores more quickly than before, which supports sales as well.

Source: Fahey, 2010.

---

the highest card-not-present fraud volume in 2009, according to one survey. The survey found that, on average, retailers faced about 3,400 attempts to perpetrate fraudulent transactions per month. Because of this high volume, 38 percent of counterfeit transactions go through undetected. Fraud losses as a percentage of total revenue were 1.13 percent for mobile merchants, versus 0.83 percent for online-only merchants, and 0.86 percent for merchants with both online and brick-and-mortar outlets (Bell, 2010).

Additionally, an aging consumer population will demand different types of products and increase the need for safety and possibly emergency medical response capability in physical retail outlets. New retail formats must address store layout, the use of television and the Internet as sales mediums, the ability to accept foreign currency, and the increased value of brand names and reputation. Crime will continue to be a major concern for retailers. Computer criminals are likely to take advantage of emerging technology and the new retail formats. Employee theft will continue to outpace theft due to external shoplifters. Organized groups of current and former employees are likely to steal merchandise in large volume. Merchandise warehousing and delivery systems may be particularly vulnerable. Effective retail personnel preemployment screening and on-the-job integrity training will significantly reduce losses due to internal employee theft.

In the future, retail merchants are more likely to rely on the use of technology as a means to prevent crime rather than apprehend shoplifters after the fact. Retailers will still apprehend shoplifters to recover merchandise. However, shoplifter apprehension is reactive, creates safety problems, and (as noted earlier) increases the probability of lawsuits associated with false arrest and false imprisonment. To avoid these problems, retailers are more likely to use technology in a proactive approach to asset protection. Increasingly, retailers will use EAS systems, merchandise alarms, access control, cash protection and transaction exception reporting systems, CCTV, as well as identification and recognition systems for customers and retail employees. Intelligent video systems are programmed to focus on suspicious behavior. Sensors can alert personnel when numerous items are in a fitting room or taken from a display. Radio-frequency identification chips can be embedded in price tags (Davies, 2007; Fickes, 2000; Fischer & Janoski, 2000; Hayes, 2000).

Other challenges face modern retail enterprises. Since 9/11, shopping center operators are increasing efforts to reduce risk associated with terrorism. The need for security must be balanced with customer convenience and sense of freedom. High priority is given to several security measures. Public information campaigns can encourage customers to report suspicious packages. Vehicle barriers can be placed at pedestrian entrances to inhibit suicide car bombers. Kiosks can be searched for bombs and weapons. Emergency exits can be clearly marked. In extreme situations, bags can be searched as people enter the shopping center (LaTourrette, Howell, Mosher, & MacDonald, 2007).

One of the most daunting problems facing retailers today is **organized retail crime** (ORC). Criminal organizations that focus on retail theft have developed lucrative illicit businesses. According to recent statistics, the total loss attributed to ORC in the United States exceeds annual losses due to automobile theft. Organized retail criminals work in teams, traveling across the country as they victimize retailers. Many techno-savvy ORC perpetrators engage in online schemes to defraud merchants (Talamo, 2007).

In response to the rise in ORC, the Retail Industry Leaders Association, the National Retail Federation, and the FBI collaborated to develop the Law Enforcement Retail Partnership Network (LERPnet). Traditionally, individual retailers reported thefts to their local law enforcement agencies, but retail crimes were not tracked across jurisdictions. With LERPnet, retail crime incidents are entered into a secure national database. The information can be shared among retail loss prevention personnel and public law enforcement agencies, allowing participants to track and hopefully apprehend ORC offenders (National Retail Federation, 2007).

WORKPLACE VIOLENCE PREVENTION

Workplace violence occurs on the job. It may occur between employees, may be the result of unsafe working conditions, or it may stem from a relationship that exists outside the workplace. Violence is identified as the third leading cause of injury or death in the workplace. According to available data, over 2 million U.S. residents are victims of violent workplace crime each year. A higher than average number of workplace violence victims are employed in retail sales, education, health care, transportation, private security, and law enforcement. In the first 25 days of 2011, 10 police officers had been killed in the line of duty. In 2010, 61 federal, state, and local officers were killed by gunfire—a 24 percent increase over 2009, according to the National Law Enforcement Officers Memorial Fund (Van Natta, 2011). The most common type of victimization is assault. Homicide results in over 1,000 cases annually. About 40 percent of victims of workplace violence report they were acquainted with the perpetrator, with women more likely than men to be victimized by someone they knew (Siegel, 2010; Warchol, 1998).

Workplace violence can occur in virtually any workplace and at any time. Often, incidents of workplace violence occur when and where they are unlikely or least expected. For example, in San Diego, California, on June 10, 1998, a 26-year-old man dressed as a woman fatally shot his female therapist and then himself. Apparently, the man was distraught because his therapist refused to write a letter endorsing his request for a sex-change operation. On February 3, 2011, a Domino's Pizza delivery man in New Orleans was robbed and attacked by an assailant who threw bleach in his eyes in order to steal the pizza. During interrogation, the suspect admitted to planning the attack. The delivery man was temporarily blinded by the bleach. The suspect faced charges of simple robbery and second-degree battery (Monteverde, 2011).

Spotlight on Workplace Shootings

Shootings in the workplace have occurred frequently in the United States over the years. The following are some examples.

On February 3, 2011, 38-year-old Alex Figueroa shot and killed his ex-wife, Guimmia Villia, at a small pharmacy in Queens, New York. Figueroa walked in the pharmacy carrying flowers and shot Villia, who had an order of protection against him. He later shot and killed himself. Domestic violence charges had previously been filed against him, but the charges were dismissed and the file sealed. One order of protection against Figueroa had expired on January 25; another was set to expire in April (O'Connor, 2011).

On August 3, 2010, Omar Thornton, 34, went on a rampage after being fired from a beer depot, Hartford Distributors, in the town of Manchester, Connecticut. Thornton pursued his victims as they hid in offices, closets, and the parking lot. Armed with two 9-millimeter handguns, Thornton killed eight people before turning a gun on himself. Police believed that Thornton, a warehouse driver, had gone to the depot to confront his bosses and union officials over allegations that he had been stealing alcohol. He was fired at the meeting. However, the shooting was apparently premeditated: Even before the meeting, Thornton had brought the two pistols into the facility hidden in a lunch box. According to police, a shotgun was also found in his car, but was not used. Police also believed that after the meeting, Thornton went to the kitchen area and retrieved the lunch box with the guns. The first two individuals killed by Thornton were the employees who had been assigned to escort him out of the building. After shooting them, Thornton ran inside and outside of the building seeking additional victims (Smith, 2010).

On July 8, 2003, Doug Williams, an employee at the Lockheed Martin aircraft parts factory in Meridian, Mississippi, killed five and wounded nine fellow employees before killing himself. Armed with a shotgun, Williams opened fire after attending a company meeting on workplace ethics. Prior to the shooting, Williams had several confrontations with management and other employees, and he had stated that he wanted to kill people. The shooting was the deadliest workplace violence incident in the United States in almost 3 years.

On February 5, 2001, 66-year-old William D. Baker, a former employee of truck diesel engine manufacturer Navistar International Corporation, walked into his former employer's plant in Melrose Park, Illinois, and began shooting with an AK-47 assault rifle. Baker had entered the facility carrying a golf bag used to conceal the assault rifle, a .38 caliber revolver, a Remington shotgun, and a .30 caliber hunting rifle equipped with a scope. When the incident was over, four people were killed, four injured, and Baker lay dead from a self-inflicted gunshot wound. Baker had worked at the plant for 39 years before being terminated amid allegations he was involved in a plot with two coworkers and three other men to steal diesel engines and parts from Navistar. In November 2000, Baker was convicted in U.S. district court of one count of conspiracy to commit theft of interstate shipments. Baker was scheduled to begin a prison term for the conviction the day after the shootings occurred (Rodriguez, Yates, & Marx, 2001).

On December 26, 2000, the day after the Christmas holiday, a 42-year-old Internet software tester, Michael McDermott, arrived at work at his usual time and spoke normally with several coworkers. At approximately 11:00 A.M., police responded to McDermott's workplace,

Edgewater Technology, Incorporated, and arrested him without incident. Apparently upset over U.S. Internal Revenue Service plans to garnish his wages for back taxes, McDermott used a semiautomatic assault rifle, a 12-gauge shotgun, and a pistol to kill seven of his coworkers. McDermott had caused a disruption in the accounting department a week preceding the incident. Most of the victims in the shooting worked in the accounting department ("Seven killed in office rampage," 2000).

On June 21, 2000, a sausage factory owner from San Leandro, California, was accused of killing three government food inspectors at his downtown facility. The factory owner was furious with the government's scrutiny of his operation.

On May 24, 2000, a Wendy's Restaurant in New York City became the scene of a blood bath. Two gunmen wrapped plastic bags around victims' heads and fatally shot five of them in the face at point-blank range. The killers, one believed to be a former Wendy's employee, fled the restaurant with $2,000 and two unopened safes.

Violence in Retail Outlets

Statistics indicate that retail sales workers have the highest risk of injury on the job. In fact, one-half of all occupational homicides occur at night in small retail outlets (U.S. Department of Labor, Bureau of Labor Statistics, 2007). OSHA released guidelines for workplace violence prevention in nighttime retail establishments. Rereleased to the public on April 28, 1998, the guidelines include the following suggestions for reducing homicides in small retail stores:

- Maintain video surveillance.
- Provide silent and personal alarms.
- Improve visibility through adequate lighting, installation of mirrors, and low-profile store fixtures.
- Install drop safes and signs indicating little cash is on hand.
- Establish emergency procedures, communications systems, and training and education programs.
- Restrict customer access by reducing store hours or closing portions of the store.
- Lock doors not in use.
- Increase staffing during high-risk periods.
- Install bullet-resistant enclosures for clerks.
- Take precautions when employees must access remote locations such as freezers and outside garbage containers.

Large retailers are also the scenes of violence sometimes. For example, two people were shot dead and two sheriff's deputies were wounded late Sunday afternoon, January 23, 2011, outside a Wal-Mart store in western Washington state. Three sheriff's deputies responded to the scene around 3:45 P.M. that day after getting a call about a suspicious person from a bystander who had concerns about a person inside the store. The deputies approached one man outside the store's south entrance, but he ran from the scene, turned around to face the deputies, and began shooting. The male shooter was shot and later pronounced dead in the Wal-Mart parking lot. A young female also was shot. Emergency personnel transported her to Tacoma General Hospital. She eventually died from her wounds. Authorities did not know if the female victim knew the male shooting suspect or if she was an innocent bystander. The two deputies who were wounded were sent to the same hospital for treatment for non–life-threatening injuries. The store was locked down for about 20 minutes immediately after the shooting with about 100 people inside ("Two dead, two cops hurt in shootout outside Washington state Walmart," 2011).

When the Perpetrator Is Not a Stranger

When workplace violence is committed by nonstrangers, the perpetrator may be a coworker, supervisor, client, or domestic partner. Workplace violence perpetrators tend to be loners, white males, 25 to 50 years old, and individuals with a history of violence. They are fascinated with weapons, antagonistic toward others, depressed, paranoid or psychologically imbalanced, self-destructive, and may be substance abusers. Often, the perpetrator is faced with job termination or layoff. In other cases, the offender may react violently to the leadership style of a supervisor. In some incidents, the perpetrator retaliates against a person who rejected romantic advances or reported the offender for sexual harassment.

Organizations should do everything reasonably possible to mitigate the opportunity for a violent episode. Employees should be trained to recognize the symptoms of workplace violence and the profile of potential perpetrators. Table 11–1 offers ideas. Organizations should also develop comprehensive plans to prevent or reduce the impact of workplace violence. Failure to do so may result in management liability for injuries or deaths to victims. A **workplace violence prevention plan** should include

- policies and procedures for prevention and response to workplace violence incidents.
- training of employees regarding the policies and procedures as well as the symptoms of potentially violent behavior.
- liaison with community resources.
- physical and personnel security.
- effective preemployment screening.

TABLE 11–1 Workplace Violence Warning Signs

The following behaviors may be warning signs that an individual known to the company may have potential to commit violence in the workplace:

- Blaming others whenever something goes wrong
- Acting impulsively
- Having difficulty controlling emotions
- Being fascinated with weapons
- Using drugs
- Being a loner
- Exhibiting a pattern of violent behavior or showing tendencies toward violence
- Being obsessed with death
- Experiencing feelings of worthlessness
- Having a deteriorating relationship with supervisors
- Having significant family, financial, and personal problems
- Perceiving or experiencing real discrimination
- Suffering psychiatric illnesses such as depression, paranoia, schizophrenia, or bipolar disorder

---

Source: Michelman, 2011.

- enforcement of codes of conduct.
- provision for assistance programs for employees with behavioral problems (Batza & Taylor, 2000; Berinato, 2007; Lynch, 2000; May, 2000).

Learn more about workplace violence prevention through the National Institute for the Prevention of Workplace Violence at www.workplaceviolence911.com.

There are several personal communication skills an individual can use to diffuse and reduce conflict that could lead to a workplace violence incident. Attitude is important, and one should treat an angry or verbally abusive person with respect. However, a potential victim must set limits on behavior, not tolerate verbal abuse, maintain personal safety, and seek assistance as soon as possible. Victims should attempt to remain calm, focus attention on the perpetrator, utilize delaying tactics, and accept criticism in a positive manner. They should also identify avenues of escape in the event a verbally abusive person becomes violent; place solid, bullet-resistant objects between themselves and the violent person; and comply with a violent person's commands if other options are not available (Albrecht, 2001; Dalton, 2003; Harwood, 1998; Siegel, 2010).

Cost and Causes of Workplace Violence

Workplace violence is very costly in terms of dollars as well as the potential for injury or death. Over 10,000 serious incidents each year cost organizations approximately $250,000 per incident. Approximately 30,000 medium severity incidents each year cost about $25,000 per occurrence. Tens of thousands of less severe incidents cost organizations about $10,000 for each incident. Over 5,000 fatal work-related injuries are reported annually in the United States (American Society for Industrial Security, 1998, U.S. Department of Labor, Bureau of Labor Statistics, 2007).

In 1992, the U.S. Centers for Disease Control (CDC) listed workplace homicide as a serious public health problem. The CDC, in collaboration with the National Institute of Occupational Safety and Health, cited six factors that increase the likelihood of workplace homicide:

1. contact with the public
2. working alone or in small groups
3. delivery of passengers, services, or goods
4. the exchange of money
5. working in high-crime-rate areas
6. working late nights or early morning hours

Stress also plays a major role in workplace violence. Although productivity appears to be increasing, physical and psychological stress in the workplace is increasing as well. Pushed by longer workweeks, larger workloads, and pressure to produce more, job-related stress can lead to depression, anxiety, and illness. During economic recessions, stress can translate into increased workplace violence—in the form of suicides, shootings sparked by layoffs, violent conflicts with shoplifters, and racially charged rampages (IOMA/IOFM, 2011). The trauma associated with the stress can result in harassment, verbal abuse, and physical violence events. Job-related stress should be a major concern for employers, especially since the courts are increasingly likely to hold organizations liable for hostile work environments. Even verbal abuse in the workplace can cost an employer hundreds of thousands of lawsuit judgment dollars if the behavior is tolerated (Fest, 2001; Ortmeier & Davis, 2012).

ZOO AND AQUARIUM SECURITY

A **zoological park** or **aquarium** is defined as any permanent cultural institution that owns and maintains wildlife that represent more than a token collection and, under the direction of a professional staff, provides its collection with appropriate care and exhibits them in an aesthetic manner to the public on a regularly scheduled, predictable basis (American Zoo and Aquarium Society, 2007). Zoos and aquariums also exhibit, conserve, and preserve the earth's fauna in an educational and scientific manner. Based on this definition, there are 172 zoos and aquariums in North America.

Facilities that house rare and exotic plants, animals, fish, and other wildlife have special security needs. Many plant and animal species are near extinction. Precautions must be taken to ensure their safety and good health. They must be protected from environmental disasters, mistreatment by human beings, and assaults from predators. Some zoological parks are small, while others cover hundreds of acres. The Zoological Society of San Diego, in addition to its world famous zoo, maintains a 1,800-acre wildlife preserve, The Wild Animal Park, that contains more than 2,500 animals comprising 250 different species.

Zoos open to the public are subject to vandalism, accidents, health-related emergencies, theft, and shoplifting. Ticket and credit card fraud, auto theft, and violence against persons are potential threats in zoological parks. Bus and tram rides require safety considerations. People undertaking close encounters with dangerous wildlife, users of automatic teller machines, and endangered species necessitate special protection, security, and safety precautions. Moreover, food service areas' compliance with health regulations must be monitored (Bagott, 2003).

In 1999, zoo officials from Atlanta, Georgia, faced several challenges in their 10-year quest to house giant pandas at the facility. Pandas in the wild are found only in the central region of China, and their fate is controlled by the Chinese government. However, since 1972, Chinese officials have lent pairs of pandas to zoos to conduct research. In addition to stringent health, safety, and habitat requirements, Chinese officials wanted the Atlanta zoo to provide continuous audio-video monitoring of the pandas and allow open access to the monitoring by Chinese

Facilities that house rare and exotic animals have special security needs.
(Photo courtesy of Star Source International.)

Some zoo animals require continuous monitoring.
(Photo courtesy of Star Source International.)

researchers. Through integration of CCTV and Internet technology, continuous monitoring of the pandas is provided and the Chinese can observe the pandas at any time (White, 2001).

On December 27, 2000, two female koalas, ages 7 and 15, were reported stolen from the San Francisco Zoo. Although the zoo has a 24-hour security operation, the koalas were discovered missing by an animal keeper. Apparently, the thieves stole the marsupials during the previous evening. The suspect(s) climbed onto the koala exhibit roof, penetrated a skylight, and entered the koala facility through a furnace door. Zoo officials were extremely concerned for the rare creatures' safety because the stress associated with improper care could be deadly. Koalas do not drink water. They require a specialized diet, consisting only of the freshest tips of eucalyptus buds, the bearlike creatures' main source of water. In addition, koalas have no body fat. Therefore, the temperature of a koala's environment must be maintained at a constant 65 to 70 degrees (Mason, 2000). On December 28, 2000, two teenage boys were arrested and charged with burglary, possession of stolen property, and felony theft in connection with the koalas' disappearance. Apparently, the two boys took the koalas to give to their girlfriends ("Two teens arrested in theft of koalas," 2000).

As zoos and aquariums seek to place visitors closer to wildlife in a natural habitat, traditional physical barriers, such as glass enclosures and cages, are being eliminated. As a result, the risk of improper interactions with wildlife as well as the possibility of wildlife theft increases. Birds and snakes are most vulnerable, especially as objects of theft, because they are easy to conceal and sell.

Many zoos and aquariums are accredited by the American Zoo and Aquarium Association (AZA). To be accredited, all aspects of wildlife care must be highly professional. In addition, the zoo or aquarium must demonstrate significant support through donations, volunteerism, and membership. Other factors that are heavily considered in the accreditation process include fiscal viability, educational activities, operations, strategic plans, physical facilities, visitor services, management of the collection, participation in conservation and research programs, safety and emergency procedures, and security measures.

Critical to the success of any zoo or aquarium security program is planning and personnel training. Contingency plans that can be activated quickly provide guidance for personnel in an emergency, especially in the event of an animal's escape. A comprehensive training program, for facility staff as well as security personnel, creates security awareness and helps promote rapid and appropriate responses to crime and emergency situations (American Zoo and Aquarium Society, 2007; Bagott, 2003).

A QUICK SURVEY

Which of the following settings are places where you have personally spent a significant amount of time and where security breaches have occurred? Check any and all that apply.

- An office building where an organization you work for is located
- A library that you use
- A museum that you frequently visit
- Your own residence, or that of a friend or relative
- A retail store where you have shopped

For each setting you checked, what was the nature of the security breach or breaches? What steps were taken to reduce the risk of additional breaches? Who took these steps? In your view, were these steps effective? Why or why not?

Summary

Internal theft is a major contributor to losses in and around industrial facilities. Libraries, museums, and art galleries require special security measures due to the rare and often irreplaceable nature of their contents. Most office buildings are open to the public, providing easy access for criminal offenders. The privatization of public services is expanding as private providers assume safety and security responsibilities under contract to public jurisdictions. Most safety and security problems in a residence are preventable, and since people spend most of their time in and around their home, residential security should be a priority. Retail establishments incur losses in a variety of ways, with internal theft identified as the primary cause of losses due to theft. Many workplace violence incidents can be prevented if workplace safety plans are developed and implemented, symptoms of violence are identified, preventive action taken, and disruptive behavior dealt with appropriately. Zoological parks and aquariums contain rare and exotic wildlife species requiring unique safety and security measures.

Key Terms

aquarium
bad checks
check cashing procedures
coupon fraud
credit card fraud
industrial security
inventory shrinkage
library

museum
office building security threats
organized retail crime
privatization of public security
   services
refund policy
residential burglary prevention
   strategy

shoplifting
shoplifting methods
shoplifting prevention strategy
transaction reports
workplace violence
workplace violence prevention
   plan
zoological park

Discussion Questions and Exercises

1. Security organizations within retail operations often differ in their approaches to loss prevention. Some focus most protection resources toward externally motivated crime prevention while others emphasize internal theft prevention. Is one approach better than the other? How should protection resources be allocated in any organization?

2. Choose one specific security application from this chapter. List the types of crime and other hazards that threaten the operation, and design measures to prevent the threats from materializing.

YOUR TURN: Managing Workplace Violence

Apollo Communications provides technical support services to several major companies engaged in landline, digital, and satellite communications. Due to the nature of Apollo's business, it employs numerous technical experts who are difficult to retain because of their high-demand status. During a hiring surge initiated after Apollo took on several large new customers, the company hired a new employee, Bob Jones. Before being offered the position, Jones interviewed well. Moreover, his criminal, credit, employment, and academic histories were subjected to Apollo's preemployment screening process. Although many of Jones' previous employment positions had lasted less than a year, Apollo hired Jones because managers believed that he had the technical expertise the company needed. However, within a few months, it became obvious to Apollo that Jones did not have the level and types of technical expertise his credentials had promised. Jones was terminated before the end of his probationary period.

Subsequent to his termination, Jones sent threatening emails to former coworkers. Further, employees often encountered Jones in the company's parking lot as they ended their workday. On several occasions, Jones confronted and verbally threatened his former supervisor in the parking lot.

1. In your view, could a defective preemployment screening process have led to Jones' hiring? If so, in what respects might the screening process have been defective?
2. If you had been involved in the process used to hire Jones, what warning signs would you have noticed and investigated?
3. Did Apollo exercise poor judgment when hiring Jones? If so, what may have led to the poor judgment? For example, could feelings of pressure to enhance staff quickly to serve new customers have caused hiring managers to overlook warning signs they normally would have noticed? If Apollo had successfully hired large numbers of new people in the past, could those involved in the hiring process become complacent?
4. In your opinion, how likely is it that Jones could become violent? Explain your reasoning.
5. How would you advise Apollo to respond to Jones' threats? Draw on what you learned in this chapter, including suggestions for securing office buildings, assessing the likelihood that someone in the workplace could become violent, and preventing workplace violence.
6. Who do you think should bear primary responsibility for preventing workplace violence—employers? local law enforcement? mental health professionals? Explain your thinking. In what ways (if any) could these and other stakeholders work together to prevent workplace violence more effectively?

CHAPTER 12

Homeland Security: Confronting Terrorism and Domestic Threats

LEARNING OBJECTIVES

After completing this chapter, the reader should be able to

- identify security threats unique to homeland security.
- describe protection priorities for government operations.
- create a definition for terrorism.
- develop a response plan to a report of a bomb, bomb threat, or weapon of mass destruction.
- contrast natural and environmental disasters.
- describe government security responsibilities, especially as they relate to the U.S. Department of Homeland Security.
- analyze the findings of the 9/11 Commission.
- articulate procedures for securing airlines, airports, ground transportation systems, and utilities (critical infrastructure).

INTRODUCTION

Prior to September 11, 2001, few Americans were familiar with the concept of homeland security. Since 9/11, however, homeland defense against terrorists has become a priority. Yet homeland security involves more than the prevention of terrorist acts. Broadly speaking, homeland security encompasses a wide range of activities designed to address transnational crime, recover from natural and environmental disasters, prevent pandemics, and protect the quantity and quality of life for all.

Major organizational changes have occurred within the federal government to address homeland security. Additionally, states, private businesses, and individuals are keenly aware of the need to prevent and respond effectively to catastrophic events. This chapter addresses major homeland security concerns and challenges the reader to identify appropriate disaster and disorder prevention and response techniques.

HOMELAND SECURITY: A HISTORICAL PERSPECTIVE

The concept of homeland security did not emerge in the aftermath of 9/11. Rather, the notion of homeland security in the United States has evolved throughout the nation's history. The U.S. Constitution (Article 4, Section 4) established a republic in which the primary responsibility for homeland security (maintenance of law and order) rests with state and local governments. The national government's role is secondary, spurred to intervene when state and local governments are unable to cope with disorder or disaster. In fact, the Constitution severely limits the national government's ability to intervene in criminal matters within the United States. As time has passed, the national government has become more actively involved with homeland security issues by asserting federal authority when incidents (1) threaten the unity principle of the federal system of government; (2) threaten national security and involve foreign nations; or (3) violate laws enacted by Congress.

Violence, terror, and disasters—as well as national government responses to these events—are not new to America. For example, the federal government responded in the aftermath of devastating fires in Portsmouth, New Hampshire, in 1803 and in Chicago, Illinois, in 1871; flooding in Johnstown, Pennsylvania, in 1889; and the San Francisco earthquake in 1906. The federal government aided cities and states during the Whiskey Rebellion of 1794; the Pullman Strike of 1894; and the riots of the 1960s. The federal government also intervened during the Great Depression of the 1930s.

Beginning with World War I, the federal role in homeland defense expanded greatly. The United States was no longer isolated from other countries. The emergence of globalism, the rise of corporate culture, and reduced emphasis on states' rights altered Americans' lives and the way they viewed the national government's role. There were 10 presidential cabinet positions in 1945, suggesting a relatively limited federal government. By 2006, there were 20. Further, the Vietnam War placed increased emphasis on international intelligence (information) gathering. In 1986, Congress authorized the FBI to investigate attacks against U.S. citizens occurring outside the United States. However, except for a few individuals in the FBI, Central Intelligence Agency (CIA), military, and other government agencies, international terrorism and its prevention did not appear in the public's consciousness until September 11, 2001.

Contemporary definitions of homeland security certainly include terrorism as an ingredient. Yet terrorism is not new. The assassination of Roman dictator Julius Caesar in 44 B.C. was an act of terrorism. Religious and political groups that took shape during the Middle Ages spread terror among their enemies in the form of mass murder. Hitler and his Nazi party were responsible for terrorism in the form of genocide in the first half of the twentieth century. Individuals, extremists, and special interest groups also committed acts of terrorism.

A review of the historical roots and patterns of homeland security and terrorism provides clues to predicting behavior and preventing or responding effectively to catastrophic incidents. However, one might question whether historical patterns are accurate predictors of behavior in the twenty-first century. High-tech communications, rapid modes of transportation, and the development of weapons of mass destruction (WMDs) create new challenges that differ markedly from their historical counterparts (Oliver, 2007; Simonsen & Spindlove, 2007; Ward, Kiernam, & Mabrey, 2006).

TERRORISM

There is considerable disagreement on the definition of *terrorism*, largely because a definition depends on an interpretation of the motivation of the participants. What is terrorism to one person may be a selfless act to another. Thus, defining terrorism is not a simple process. Broadly speaking, **terrorism** involves the use of violence or threats to intimidate or coerce others. Terrorism may be used by an individual or a group. Within this context, terrorists could include the following:

- idealistic and political groups
- economic opportunists
- urban groups, such as predatory, ethnic, and economic gangs
- career criminals
- domestic violence perpetrators
- some firearms rights, antiabortion, pro-choice, animal rights, and environmental activists.

In addition, drug cartels are involved in what has come to be known as narco-terrorism. Drug cartels terrorize politicians, kidnap and execute government officials and corporate executives, and extort services and economic resources from international business concerns. Within a narrow context, terrorism is defined as an act of violence committed against an innocent person, or noncombatant, for the purpose of achieving a political end through fear and intimidation (Barlow, 2000; Deutch, 1997). The definition of terrorism continues to evolve as terrorists and their motives, targets, and methods change. Domestic and foreign terrorists include individuals, street gangs, political and religious zealots, and highly organized national and international organizations (Maniscalco & Christen, 2002; Martin, 2009; Siegel, 2010; Simonsen & Spindlove, 2007; White, 2012).

Domestic Terrorism

In 1995, Timothy McVeigh bombed the Alfred P. Murrah federal office building in Oklahoma City. One hundred sixty-eight men, women, and children died. McVeigh was subsequently convicted in U.S. district court in Denver and executed for the killing of several federal law enforcement agents who were present in the building at the time of the bombing. A terrorist group in Japan, the Aum Shinrikyo cult, was responsible for a sarin nerve-gas attack in a Tokyo subway in March 1995. The attack killed 10 commuters and left nearly 5,000 ill (Deutch, 1997; Gaines & Miller, 2011).

Homegrown terrorism is attracting increased attention. Homeland Security Secretary Janet Napolitano acknowledged in 2010 that the terrorists who want to attack the United States are increasingly legal U.S. residents rather than individuals traveling to the United States from abroad. These individuals may have little or no formal connection to terrorist groups such as Al Qaeda, and can be radicalized by watching jihadist videos, listening to sermons, and reading training manuals on the Internet. This trend could present challenges for the nation's intelligence system, Napolitano said, because the system has traditionally been tailored to uncovering identities of foreign terrorists and disrupting specific plots. Combating this new trend will require the Department of Homeland Security (DHS) to continue building relationships with police and will require local law enforcement agencies to strengthen their skills in identifying indications of possible terrorist activities ("Napolitano warns police chiefs of homegrown terror threat," 2010).

To combat domestic terrorism, the Justice Department launched the Nationwide SAR (Suspicious Activity Reporting) Initiative (NSI). The program sets up **fusion centers**, where reports of suspicious activities made by citizens and local police are collected and analyzed. NSI establishes a standardized process for gathering and sharing information among federal, state, local, and tribal agencies, with the aim of detecting and reporting underlying patterns of "precursor conduct"—activities that may signal a potential terrorist attack. Precursor conduct includes the following:

- Surveillance. Individuals are recording or monitoring activities, taking notes, or using observation equipment near a key facility.
- Asset deployment. Abandoned vehicles, stockpiled suspicious materials, and suspicious persons are deployed near a key facility.
- Suspicious persons. A person who does not appear to belong is present in the workplace, neighborhood, business establishment, or near a key facility.
- Suspicious questioning. Someone is trying to gain information in person or by phone, mail, email, or other communication method regarding a key facility or its personnel.
- Supplies acquisition. Someone is attempting to improperly acquire explosives, weapons, ammunition, dangerous chemicals, uniforms, badges, flight manuals, access cards, or identification for a key facility or to legally obtain items under suspicious circumstances that could be used in a terrorist act.
- Practice runs. Behavior appears to be preparation for terrorist activity, such as mapping out routes, playing out scenarios with other people, monitoring key facilities, and timing traffic lights or traffic flow ("Calling all eyes," 2010).

In addition to collecting data about possible domestic terrorism plots, fusion centers also collect and distribute criminal intelligence. The intent is to develop a system that fosters efficient receipt, sorting, and sharing of vital information needed to uncover terrorist plots before they can be carried out. Though use of fusion centers has led to the discovery of dangerous individuals who would not otherwise have been found, some observers are concerned that the centers could violate citizens' privacy and civil rights. The centers take steps to protect these rights, including not running names through databases unless there is reasonable suspicion to do so and preventing the misuse of government and commercial databases that contain large amounts of personal information (Dilanian, 2010).

Some domestic terrorists do acquire terrorism skills abroad and return home to initiate attacks, further complicating the picture. A study by the Homeland Security Policy Institute of the George Washington University and the Swedish National Defense College's Center for Asymmetric Threat Studies described a growing threat from Westerners who leave home to train or fight jihad (holy war) and are then sent back to their home countries armed with terror expertise and tasked with launching domestic attacks. Because these terrorists have different reasons for turning to terrorism and come from different backgrounds and ethnicities, they are difficult to identify and track. The study's authors advise Western countries to share passenger data to improve travel security, highlight the harsh realities of foreign training camps in public communications, and give greater visibility to fighters who have turned away from jihad (Baldor, 2010).

International Terrorism

International terrorists do not confine themselves to a nation-state. Numerous examples of international terrorism activity surfaced over the past several years. On March 11, 2004, terrorists linked to Al Qaeda bombed four commuter trains during the morning rush hour in Madrid, Spain, killing 191 people and injuring hundreds more. In August 2004, two Russian passenger airliners crashed, killing a total of 89 people. Extremists in Chechnya claimed responsibility. On July 7, 2005, three subway trains in London were bombed, killing 56 and wounding 700. Islamic extremists were blamed for the London attacks. On July 11, 2006, explosive devices were detonated on seven trains in Mumbai (formerly Bombay), India, killing nearly 200.

Bin Laden Brought Down

Osama bin Laden was shot and killed after a small group of U.S. Navy SEALs attacked his compound in Pakistan. The SEALs team flew by helicopter to the compound, which is located about 60 miles north of Islamabad. Intelligence experts believed that bin Laden had been hiding at the compound, which was fortified with unusually high security walls, since at least the summer of 2010. The raid was reportedly carried out with the help of intelligence collected from detainees in U.S. custody who identified a courier as someone who may have been living with or protecting the Al Qaeda leader. On April 29, 2011, President Barack Obama gave the order to carry out the operation, which had been set in motion by mid-February, when the president determined that there was a sufficient intelligence basis for the raid (Rucker, Wilson, & Kornblut, 2011).

The United States buried bin Laden's body at sea reportedly to discourage the creation of a shrine to the Al Qaeda chief. President Obama said that he would not release any photographs of bin Laden's body or the video of his burial at sea, to prevent bin Laden's followers from using the images as propaganda to incite violent acts. The U.S. forces who conducted the raid gathered extensive intelligence from the compound in Pakistan, some of which suggested that Al Qaeda may have been considering attacking the U.S. rail system on September 11, 2011, to mark the tenth anniversary of the 9/11 attacks. The intelligence also indicated that bin Laden was not merely an inspirational figurehead for Al Qaeda, he remained actively involved in planning attacks, identifying targets, and communicating his ideas to other Al Qaeda leaders.

The now deceased Osama bin Laden, an exiled Saudi Arabian financier, is alleged to have been responsible for a worldwide terrorism conspiracy. He was shot and killed on May 2, 2011, by U.S. forces while he was hiding with others in a compound in Abbottabad, Pakistan (see "Bin Laden Brought Down"). Bin Laden and his Al Qaeda organization were implicated in the 1993 bombing of the World Trade Center in New York City, the 1998 bombings of the U.S. embassies in Tanzania and Kenya, as well as the attack on the USS *Cole* on October 12, 2000. The *Cole*, a U.S. Navy ship, was refueling in Aden, Yemen. The bombing of the *Cole* left 17 sailors dead (Sniffen, 2000).

Of course, the most devastating terrorist attacks to occur on U.S. soil took place on September 11, 2001. Terrorists connected with Osama bin Laden hijacked four commercial aircraft. Two of the planes were flown into the twin 110-story towers of the World Trade Center in New York City. One was flown into the Pentagon. The fourth crashed into the ground in rural Pennsylvania after passengers overcame the terrorists; the plane's target is not known, although it was suspected to be Washington, DC. Subsequently, the World Trade Center towers collapsed. Approximately 3,000 deaths resulted from the 9/11 terrorist attacks ("America under attack," 2001).

Responses by the U.S. Government

A year after the 1995 Oklahoma City bombing, Congress passed and the president signed the Anti-Terrorism and Effective Death Penalty Act of 1996. The law

- allows victims to sue countries that sponsor terrorism.
- establishes a special "removal court" to oversee the deportation of aliens suspected of terrorist activities.
- provides immigration officials with more authority to deport aliens convicted of any crime.
- forbids fund-raising activities in the United States by any foreign group identified by the U.S. Government as engaged in terrorist activities.

Although not included in the new law, the Clinton administration wanted to expand the power of federal authorities to increase their ability to surreptitiously monitor suspected terrorists through the use of electronic surveillance equipment.

According to the U.S. Commission on National Security, in the twenty-first century, a new national security structure is necessary to replace the institutions that combated the threat of terrorism during the 40 years of the Cold War. Emerging technology and expanding economic growth promote new and different threats. Computer technology allows hackers to penetrate American businesses and vital public safety infrastructure databases. A foreign or domestic hacker, utilizing a computer, could manipulate and destroy vital and top secret information, create havoc with air traffic control systems, deactivate public utilities, and slow emergency communications systems. The Commission predicted that people are more likely to die in large numbers on American soil if precautionary measures are not implemented. New-age terrorism requires government and military capabilities characterized by stealth, speed, accuracy, mobility, and intelligence—capabilities that differ from counterterrorism mechanisms used in the past. Private, nonmilitary counterterrorism strategies will also be required.

Most experts agree that, even with the vanquishing of Osama bin Laden and other high-level members of Al Qaeda, the threat of terrorism is escalating. However, a lack of preparedness to prevent terrorism or to mitigate the damage from acts of terrorism exists in many areas. Some fail to recognize that weapons are plentiful and prevention strategies are often inadequate. The weapons of terrorism range from traditional low-technology firearms and improvised explosive devices (IEDs) to information warfare and WMDs, sometimes referred to as weapons of mass effect (WMEs). The threat of the use of WMDs is particularly frightening. Many nation-states as well as non-state organizations possess or have access to nuclear, biological, or chemical (NBC) devices that have the potential to cause loss of life and property destruction on a scale never before experienced. In recent years, WMD classifications expanded to include the characteristics of chemical, biological, radiological, nuclear, and explosive (CBRNE) agents. As the threat of terrorism increases, organizations will find it necessary to implement terrorism prevention procedures and install CBRNE detection devices at or near facility perimeters (Gaines & Miller, 2011; Hutchinson & Warren, 2001; Kreisher, 1999; Maniscalco & Christen, 2002; Nason, 2000).

THE USA PATRIOT ACT   Owing to limited resources and poor intelligence capabilities, law enforcement agencies and security organizations have not been able to prevent many terrorist attacks. However, the events of 9/11 provided the catalyst to create more proactive terrorism prevention strategies. In response to the 9/11 attacks, Congress enacted the **USA PATRIOT (Uniting and Strengthening America by Providing Appropriate Tools Required to Intercept and Obstruct Terrorism) Act of 2001**. The law dramatically increased the criminal investigative authority of local, county, state, and federal law enforcement agencies. The law strengthens law enforcement's ability to jail suspects, broadens search and seizure authority, enhances prosecutors' power, promotes the sharing of intelligence, and provides for more restrictive border security (U.S. Congress, 2001). In 2003, the U.S. Senate voted to retain the USA PATRIOT Act's 2005 sunset provision and passed a limited version of the Act. Many lawmakers expressed concern that the 2001 law jeopardized civil liberties.

THE FOREIGN INTELLIGENCE SURVEILLANCE ACT   The civil liberties of foreigners within the United States were limited through the **Foreign Intelligence Surveillance Act (FISA) of 1978**. The Act created procedures for the physical and electronic surveillance and collection of foreign intelligence information, between or among foreign powers, that is necessary to protect the United States against an actual or potentially grave attack, sabotage, or international terrorism. The president may authorize up to a year-long warrantless surveillance of a foreign power (government) or its agents if it is unlikely that the surveillance will uncover any communication to which a U.S. person (citizen, resident alien, or corporation) is a party. Alternately, the federal government may seek a court order for surveillance through the secret Foreign Intelligence Surveillance Court (FISC), otherwise known as the FISA court. Based on probable cause, the FISC may authorize a surveillance of a foreign power or agent (including a U.S. person) of a foreign power (U.S. Congress, 1978). In 2004, FISA was amended to include non-U.S. persons working alone, who are engaged in international terrorism and are not agents of a foreign power.

Foreign Intelligence Surveillance Act came under scrutiny in late 2005 when it was discovered that the Bush administration was ordering warrantless domestic surveillance of suspected terrorists since 2002. In August 2007, Congress passed the Protect America Act of 2007, giving the Executive Branch expanded surveillance authority for a period of 6 months while Congress works on long-term legislation to modernize FISA.

THE USA PATRIOT ACT IMPROVEMENT AND REAUTHORIZATION ACT   On March 9, 2006, President George W. Bush signed the **USA PATRIOT Act Improvement and Reauthorization Act of 2005** into law. The 2005 legislation reauthorized expiring provisions of the USA PATRIOT Act of 2001, added dozens of additional safeguards to protect Americans' privacy and civil liberties, strengthened port security, and expanded mechanisms to combat the spread of methamphetamine.

The reauthorizing legislation made permanent 14 of the 16 sunsetted USA PATRIOT Act provisions and placed 4-year sunsets on the other 2 (USA PATRIOT Act, Sections 206 and 215, respectively) authorizing roving surveillance and the authority to request production of business records under FISA. Among the 14 USA PATRIOT Act provisions made permanent are the ability to

- facilitate enhanced information-sharing and coordination between national security and law enforcement personnel.
- add certain chemical weapons offenses, international terrorism, nuclear and WMD threats, and computer espionage offenses to the list of wiretap predicates.
- allow Internet service providers to disclose customer records voluntarily to the government in emergencies involving an immediate risk of death or serious physical injury.
- permit victims of computer trespass (hacking) crimes to request law enforcement assistance in monitoring trespassers on their computers (U.S. Department of Justice, 2007b).

In February 2011, President Barack Obama signed a 3-month extension of several surveillance provisions of the USA PATRIOT Act. The law extends two areas of the 2001 Act. One provision allows law enforcement officials to set roving wiretaps to monitor multiple communication devices. The other allows them to ask a special court for access to business and library records that could be relevant to a terrorist threat. A third provision gives the FBI court-approved rights for surveillance of non-American suspects not known to be tied to specific terrorist groups. Legislators are debating a multiple-year extension of the provisions, which have been criticized by defenders of privacy rights ("Obama signs temporary extension of Patriot Act," 2011).

ADDITIONAL INITIATIVES   Additional initiatives to combat terrorism include various laws passed to reinforce security in the United States and elsewhere. Major among these initiatives are the Aviation and Transportation Security Act of 2001 and the Homeland Security Act of 2002.

Difficult Trade-Offs

The terrorist attacks of 9/11 represent the most destructive criminal event perpetrated on U.S. soil to date. Experts suggest that the United States and its foreign interests will continue to be a preferred target for international terrorists. Despite the death of bin Laden, U.S. officials are still concerned about the threat from terrorism, and U.S. government facilities across the globe were put on a heightened state of alert following bin Laden's death. The State Department also warned travelers about the increased possibility of anti-American violence following bin Laden's demise. The United States' reactions to terrorist threats have been and will likely continue to be swift and certain. Yet such reactions present difficult trade-offs.

The emerging issue of individual rights and freedom versus collective security and crime prevention is one example of these trade-offs. Critics argue that public pressure to combat terrorism can result in measures designed to curtail civil liberties, such as the right to privacy, due process, and freedom from unreasonable searches and seizures. However, if current terrorism patterns continue, U.S. citizens may wish to sacrifice some liberties in exchange for safety and security (Gaines & Miller, 2011; Meese & Ortmeier, 2004).

Fighting terrorism is also costly. International terrorists may accomplish their goals with only one or two bombings every few years. Subsequent to each bombing, the United States tightens security and supports a new offensive against terrorists. The result is less freedom of movement for people and heightened security and intelligence gathering that costs millions, if not billions, of dollars. According to a report series published in the *Washington Post*, there are now more than 1,200 government organizations and more than 1,900 private companies working on counterterrorism, homeland security, and intelligence—in some 10,000 locations across the United States. About 854,000 people—nearly one and half times the number of people who live in Washington—have top secret security clearance ("Intelligence gathering unwieldy, report says," 2010). An internal report by the inspector general published in 2009 criticized the Office of the Director of National Intelligence for bureaucratic bloat and financial mismanagement; Washington now spends more than $45 billion a year to gather information abroad, conduct covert operations, and produce intelligence reports (Mazzetti, 2009). Such expenditures cause an economic drain on the nation's economy and lessen the quality of life for many Americans.

Leaders must also balance the need to provide useful, up-to-date information to the public with the need to protect sensitive information from being released. With an eye toward this challenge, the DHS has decided to phase out the color-coded terror-alert system that was put in place by the Bush administration after the 9/11 attacks. The system has been criticized as being too vague and thus not useful. It is being replaced by a new system called the National Terrorism Advisory System, which will be used to notify certain groups of people about specific threats. For example, the system can be used to send threat descriptions to law enforcement personnel to tell them what they should be doing to address the threat and to alert them about the federal government's efforts. The system will alert the public to threats through announcements distributed by news outlets and social media websites (Sullivan, 2011).

Learn more about terrorist methods and counterterrorism strategies through the National Counterterrorism Center at www.nctc.gov.

SECURITY SPOTLIGHT

Where do you stand on the question of how best to balance civil liberties and collective security? Are you willing to sacrifice particular civil liberties if doing so would mean greater collective security and prevention of terrorism? If so, which civil liberties would you be willing to sacrifice? Why? If you would not be willing to give up any civil liberties to ensure collective security, explain the reasons for your choice.

BOMB THREATS AND WEAPONS OF MASS DESTRUCTION

The development and illegal use of bombs and WMDs are not new. They have been used by individuals, drug traffickers, perpetrators of organized crime, dictators, and terrorist groups for some time. Relatively inexpensive to produce, these devices and agents are commonly used by perpetrators who wish to be far from the scene when the detonation takes place. The Unabomber sent pipe bombs through the mail to specific targets. The deaths resulting from the bombing of the World Trade Center in New York City in 1993, the Alfred P. Murrah federal office building in Oklahoma City in 1995, and a nightclub in Bali, Indonesia, in 2002 demonstrated the catastrophic nature of explosives assembled for mass murder in a single event. The Tokyo subway sarin nerve-gas attack in 1995 also enlightened the world about the damage that can be created through the use of NBC weapons.

Bomb Threats

Although the majority of bomb threats are a hoax, they should be treated seriously. In most jurisdictions, the threat itself is a crime. In the event a person has reported a suspicious package, it should be treated as an actual explosive device. Upon arriving at the scene where a suspicious package is reported, the initial responder should contact the person who reported the package so the person can direct emergency personnel to the location of the item in question. A safe distance around the package should be established. Personnel should not handle, touch, smell, or attempt to dismantle any suspected or known explosive device. Bomb disposal experts or explosive technicians should be summoned. Personnel should use landline telephones rather than cellular phones or radios for communication because of the possibility of a radio-activated device (California Commission on Peace Officer Standards and Training, 2012). Electric and gas utilities should be disconnected, a no-smoking policy must be enforced, and any inflammable combustibles in the vicinity of the device should be removed.

If a bomb threat call was received and no suspicious package has been located, a search for the device must be conducted. Contrary to early practices, the best people to conduct the initial search for a suspicious package are the people who live or work in the area. These people are familiar with the area and are more likely to observe something that is out of place or does not belong to an occupant. If a suspicious package is located, an evacuation is necessary.

It is also important to interview the person who received the bomb threat. If the threat was received via telephone, the interview should focus on what the caller said, the sound of the caller's voice, and any background noises apparent to the listener. If an explosive incident has occurred, personnel should treat the affected area as a crime scene unless determined otherwise.

Bomb searches should be conducted with extreme caution. Ideally, two persons familiar with an area should search for a suspicious package. After entering an area or room, the searchers should stand quietly with eyes closed and listen for clockwork devices or any unusual sounds. The area should be divided into two equal parts. Searchers will start at the perimeter, searching from the bottom and working up, from ground (floor) level to hip height, waist height to ceiling, ceiling area (light fixtures, air ducts), and any area behind a false or suspended ceiling. Searchers should work back-to-back, working toward each other, from the perimeter to the center of the area of room being searched. After the search is completed, the area (room) should be identified with a sign or marker indicating a search has been completed in the area. If a suspicious package is located, the area should be evacuated to a safe distance and bomb disposal experts summoned to remove the package (U.S. Department of Justice, Bureau of Alcohol, Tobacco, Firearms, and Explosives, 2007).

Nuclear Weapons

Atomic and hydrogen bombs are referred to as nuclear weapons. They are the most difficult weapons to construct because their nuclear elements—plutonium and/or highly enriched uranium—are expensive and difficult to obtain. Nuclear weapons can be delivered through gravity bombs or missiles or can be activated by malfunctions at nuclear power facilities. Even if victims do not die from the initial impact of a nuclear weapon's blast, they may exhibit symptoms including vomiting, weakness, burns, hair loss, cancer, and birth defects. Treatment protocols include removal and destruction of clothing, bathing, and the use of laxatives and other substances that inhibit the human body's absorption of radiation.

Biological Weapons

Substances that can be used to create biological weapons include anthrax, botulinum, toxin, ricin, smallpox, and viral hemorrhagic fevers. Biological weapons can be aerosolized into the air and inhaled, inserted into water and food supplies and ingested, or cause harm through contact with human skin. Symptoms include exhaustion, pneumonia, weight loss, stomach pain, diarrhea, respiratory failure, and shock. Treatments include antidotes, antibiotics, vaccines, and purging of the stomach.

Chemical Weapons

Major chemical weapons include mustard gas, sarin, soman, tabun, cyanide, hydrogen chloride, chlorine, and various irritants and toxic waste. They can be delivered through sprayers, gravity bombs, missiles, and water and food contamination. Symptoms include burning or blistering of the eyes and skin, coughing, dizziness, headache, convulsions, involuntary defecation and urination, and respiratory disease. Treatment methods used to relieve suffering include antibiotics, painkillers, dressings, and rinsing of eyes and skin.

Radiological Weapons

A *dirty bomb* is classified as a radiological weapon. Unlike nuclear weapons, radiological weapons spread radioactive material that contaminates the environment and acts as a toxic chemical. Although most radiological material is not soluble in water, it is the most likely choice of terrorists because it can be delivered through small dirty bombs and artillery shells to contaminate objects and food supplies. Symptoms range from mild effects, such as reddening of human skin, to cancer or death. Treatment for radiological contamination includes removal of clothes and bathing, using bleach if necessary (Porteus, 2006; White, 2012).

NATURAL DISASTERS

Security personnel are responsible for loss prevention and asset protection. Since human assets are the most valuable, systems must be in place to protect people from the negative impact of natural disasters. History is replete with numerous examples of the heavy toll natural disasters levy on human existence. In the United States alone, extreme heat, earthquakes in California, hurricanes in the Southeast, and tornadoes in the Midwest pose threats annually. In 1995, nearly 700 Chicagoans died as the result of exposure to extreme heat. In a 2-week period between July 19 and August 1, 2000, a heat wave was blamed for 149 deaths in the central plains and northeastern United States.

Tornados

A tornado touched down in Fort Worth, Texas, on March 28, 2000, killing 4 people and injuring 36. Although weather conditions indicated a tornado was possible, no one could predict if or where the storm would hit. Ultimately, downtown Forth Worth bore the brunt of the storm, which shattered windows in high-rise buildings, overturned vehicles, and uprooted trees (Hawkins, 2000). On December 16, 2000, unseasonable tornados killed 11 people and left numerous others injured in Alabama. May 2003 was one of the worst months for tornados in recorded U.S. history. From Colorado to Virginia over 300 twisters caused millions of dollars in damage, killed nearly 50 people, and injured hundreds more. On March 2, 2007, 20 people were killed when tornadoes raced through Alabama, Georgia, and Missouri.

Cold and Snow

During December 2000, severe cold and heavy snowfall covered much of the continental United States. Storms paralyzed ground transportation and caused considerable delays with air travelers during the preholiday season. Businesses were impacted negatively, since holiday shoppers were unable to reach retail establishments and shipping was delayed. Ice and snow across the southern plains of the United States damaged power lines and left almost 600,000 homes and businesses without electricity. A thick coat of ice stretching from New Mexico to Arkansas created massive traffic jams and stranded thousands of people. At least 37 deaths were attributed to the severe winter weather conditions (Barnes, 2000; Conlon, 2000).

That same month, a blizzard struck the northeastern United States. The storm created whiteout conditions and left 9 to 18 inches of snow between Delaware and Maine. The gigantic blizzard disrupted holiday travel and commerce, with major urban areas such as New York City hard hit by the storm (McFadden, 2000; Revkin, 2001).

On February 17, 2003, a blizzard in the Midwest and Northeast regions of the United States was blamed for at least 28 deaths (Petterson, 2003). And during the winter of 2011, uncharacteristic winter storms wreaked havoc throughout most of the United States. Hardly any portion of the country was spared. At one point, snow could be located in every state except Florida. As much as 2 feet of snow fell across a 2,000-mile path from the Southwest through Louisiana up to the northern plains and across to the eastern seaboard in New England. Airlines canceled nearly 2,000 flights during the week before Superbowl Sunday XLV, scheduled for February 6, 2011, in Dallas, Texas. The rate of airline cancellations for 2011 was calculated to be the highest in 15 years (Deanna, 2011).

Earthquakes and Tsunamis

On January 17, 1994, the Northridge earthquake in Los Angeles killed 72, injured 9,000, and caused $25 billion in property damage. A year later, an earthquake in Kobe, Japan, killed 6,000 people. On December 26, 2004, an undersea earthquake in the Indian Ocean triggered a series of devastating tsunamis, inundating coastal communities across Southeast Asia, including Sri Lanka, Indonesia, India, and Thailand. The tsunami was classified as one of the deadliest natural disasters in modern history. United Nations estimates placed the number of persons lost at nearly 187,000 dead and 43,000 people missing. On March 11, 2011, an 8.9-magnitude earthquake and resulting 13-foot tsunami struck Japan, killing an estimated 13,000 people and injuring about 5,000. Another estimated 14,000 people were missing. The earthquake and tsunami heavily damaged roads and railways as well as caused fires in many areas. A dam also collapsed. Roughly 4.4 million households in northeastern Japan were left without electricity and 1.5 million without water. Many electrical generators were destroyed, and explosions occurred in several nuclear reactors because of hydrogen gas that had built up within their outer containment buildings after cooling system failure (Foster, 2011). Japan experienced several strong aftershocks in the weeks following the original earthquake, and concerns about radiation leaking from the damaged reactors spread around the world.

Hurricanes

On August 29, 2005, **Hurricane Katrina**, one of the worst natural disasters in the history of the United States, hit the Gulf Coast. In its wake, Katrina left nearly 1,300 people dead, hundreds of thousands homeless, and billions of dollars in property damage. Most of the destruction occurred in Alabama, Mississippi, and Louisiana. In New Orleans, two major levees broke, a full day after Katrina struck, allowing water to gush into the city's streets. An estimated 80 percent of the city was flooded. New Orleans plunged into chaos as people drowned, looters ravaged businesses, health-related problems multiplied, public safety and security services disintegrated, and

Hurricane Katrina left nearly 1,300 deaths, hundreds of thousands homeless, and billions of dollars in property damage.
(Photo courtesy of Caitlin Mirra/Shutterstock.com.)

billions of dollars worth of property were damaged or destroyed. Subsequently, several reports cited flaws in planning for and response to major disasters as culprits leading to the deaths, injuries, and destruction (Jordan, 2006).

ENVIRONMENTAL DISASTERS

Environmental disasters are caused by the impact of human action on the natural environment and can take numerous forms, including oil spills, toxic waste spills, damage to ecosystems through use of pesticides, and air pollution—to name just a few. A recent example includes the BP oil spill in the Gulf of Mexico. Environmental disasters become more commonplace as the human population increases. Currently, the world's population stands at about 7 billion, and will reach roughly 9.3 billion in 2050.

Environmental legislation has been enacted in many jurisdictions in an effort to prevent damage to biological and ecological systems. The first recorded environmental legislation in America occurred in 1626, when the Plymouth Colony enacted ordinances that regulated harvesting and conservation of timber on colonial land (Rettie, 1995).

Numerous local, county, state, and federal statutes exist that are designed to protect the environment. In some cases, statutes provide for criminal prosecution as well as compensation under civil law. Under these laws, civil and criminal liability may be incurred for conduct resulting in air and water pollution, improper pesticide distribution and use, excessive noise, and possession or emission of regulated chemicals. Corporations as well as individuals may be held civilly and criminally liable for violations. The laws hold corporate officers and other employees liable if they know or should know environmental laws are being violated. Specific intent to commit a crime is not required (Epstein, 1998). Simply stated, an **environmental crime** is any human activity that violates an environmental criminal statute (Clifford & Edwards, 1998; U.S. Environmental Protection Agency, 2007).

Primary enforcement responsibility for federal environmental laws and regulations rests with the **Environmental Protection Agency (EPA)**. More than a dozen major laws form the basis for EPA enforcement. These laws focus on security and safety of chemicals, fuel, air, water, endangered species, insecticides, food and drugs, and toxic substances. The EPA also enforces laws relative to occupational safety and health, pollution, and resource conservation (U.S. Environmental Protection Agency, 2007). The U.S. Food and Drug Administration (FDA) is another government body responsible for preventing environmental disasters in the area of food and drug safety. For example, the FDA Food Safety Modernization Act (FSMA), signed by President Barack Obama in January 2011, is designed to build a new system of food-safety oversight, with an emphasis on prevention of outbreaks of food-borne illnesses. Such outbreaks have become more common with the globalization of food supply chains and consolidation of farms and food manufacturing plants. With globalization and consolidation, a food-safety failure at a single farm or in a single plant could threaten immense numbers of people. The FSMA has key provisions including increased FDA inspection frequency, expanded access to food companies' records, import certification authority, and mandatory recall authority.

Learn more about environmental laws and regulations through the U.S. EPA at www.epa.gov.

Although many countries may be environmentally conscious, activities in some countries create international environmental problems. A **transborder** flow occurs when an event in one country impacts the environment in another country. Transborder flows of toxic substances occur when pollutants originate in one country and move to other countries through water and air currents, living organisms, and deliberate transportation. Transborder flows of some economic decisions have produced devastating human and environmental consequences for almost 500 years. Through direct political and military control, such as colonialization, less developed areas of the world have been victimized when economic decisions originating in developed countries deplete resources in underdeveloped nations. Transnational corporations as well as powerful nations can penetrate international borders to exploit human and biological environments in host countries (Martin, 2009; Michalowski, 1998).

Occasionally, environmental disasters arise from unlikely sources. In May 2000, National Park Service personnel started a controlled burn to clear brush near the Bandelier National Monument near Santa Fe, New Mexico. As warm winds reached speeds of up to 55 miles per hour, the fire burned out of control. The wildfire caused the evacuation of nearly 25,000 area residents, including the entire population of 11,000 of Los Alamos, New Mexico. Over 200 homes and an unknown number of other buildings were destroyed by the fire.

Recently, concern has arisen regarding the possibility of an influenza (flu) pandemic. A **pandemic** (large-scale epidemic) occurs when a disease emerges for which there is little or no immunity in the human population. A pandemic strains health care systems and supplies and may cause widespread economic and social disruption. When a pandemic influenza virus emerges, its global spread is considered inevitable.

Government agencies as well as businesses are advised to develop contingency plans for coping with a pandemic, especially if the organization's personnel travel to foreign countries. The federal government develops and disseminates pandemic preparedness guidelines. The guidelines include planning checklists that address health and safety, continuity of operations, resources required, and emergency communications (U.S. Department of Health and Human Services, 2007).

> More can be learned about influenza pandemics and their control by contacting the U.S. Department of Health and Human Services at www.flu.gov.

Due to the threat of terrorism, new laws and government regulations have been promulgated to prevent environmental disasters. Notable are the Bioterrorism Act of 2002 and the U.S. DHS regulations for securing high-risk chemical facilities.

The **Bioterrorism Act of 2002**, otherwise known as the Public Health Security and Bioterrorism Preparedness and Response Act of 2002, seeks to improve the ability of the United States to prevent, prepare for, and respond to bioterrorism and other public health emergencies. As of 2007, the DHS requires owners of chemical facilities containing certain quantities of specified chemicals to complete a preliminary screening assessment that determines the level of risk associated with the facility. If a chemical facility preliminarily qualifies as high risk, its owners are required to prepare and submit a security vulnerability assessment and site security plan. Submissions are validated through audits and site inspections. DHS provides technical assistance to facility owners and operators as needed. Security standards are required to achieve specific outcomes, such as securing the perimeter and critical targets, controlling access, deterring theft of potentially dangerous chemicals, and preventing internal sabotage.

GOVERNMENT SECURITY

Security at and for government facilities and agencies is a large, yet less visible, asset protection function. Traditionally, security at local, county, and state government facilities has been provided by the police, sheriffs' departments, state police and highway patrol agencies, and local or county marshals. The U.S. Secret Service protects the president and numerous other officials. U.S. State Department security personnel provide protection to the U.S. Secretary of State, State Department personnel, and many foreign diplomats. In U.S. government facilities and courts, security is provided by Federal Protective Officers, Park Police, Capitol Police, and U.S. Marshals. Recently, a trend toward privatization of public services has led several agencies to outsource provision of many of their security personnel.

Security of personnel, property, and sensitive information is critical to a functioning government and, at the federal level, necessary to national security. Virtually all federal law enforcement agencies are involved, some to a greater extent than others, with the provision of security services. Protection of the president and presidential candidates as well as foreign ambassadors and dignitaries is always a requirement. Classified information must be protected against espionage (see "WikiLeaks: Making Secret Government Information Public"). Government facilities must be protected from sabotage and terrorism. National parks also require attention because they encounter a multitude of safety and security problems due to their increased use.

Serious damage and injury, even death, can occur in and around government facilities in spite of sophisticated security and police protection. The U.S. Capitol building in Washington, DC, has been the scene of random violence since the early 1800s. Crime in the Capitol building occurs even though security devices and armed Capitol Police are present. On July 24, 1998, two 18-year veterans of the Capitol Police force were killed and a visitor seriously wounded when a gunman opened fire after bypassing a metal detector at a Capitol building entrance. This was the first time the Capitol Police lost officers on duty since the inception of the agency in 1828.

Risks to government facilities are not confined to the boundaries of the United States or its territories. For example, Mexican drug cartels have targeted law enforcement officers on both sides of the border with the United States for kidnapping and death. U.S. military bases, embassies, and missions throughout the world are potential targets. In fact, the U.S. Department of State receives over 30,000 reported threats to its facilities each year. On June 25, 1996, a truck bomb exploded outside a housing complex near Dhahran, Saudi Arabia, killing 19 Americans and injuring more than 500 Americans and Saudis. On August 7, 1998, bombing attacks on two

WikiLeaks: Making Secret Government Information Public

U.S. investigators suspect that Bradley Manning, an army private stationed in the Persian Gulf, downloaded 250,000 secret State Department cables to compact disks from a computer terminal in Kuwait during 2010. Manning then allegedly provided the files to the antisecrecy group WikiLeaks, which shared them with newspapers and posted hundreds of them online. Observers call the leak the largest heist of sensitive U.S. government documents in modern times.

Several problems enabled the leak to occur. For example, owing to a design flaw, Net-Centric Diplomacy, an obscure database set up after the 9/11 terrorist attacks to foster information sharing among federal users, became an inadvertent repository for an immense range of State Department cables. Sensitive cables were often stored in the database regardless of whether they belonged there. Moreover, the system was unable to detect unauthorized downloading of data. Linked to a vast Defense Department system, the database was used by nearly half a million government employees and contractors with security clearance who could access the diplomatic cables from computer terminals anywhere in the world. Officials relied on end users of the data, primarily military and intelligence personnel, to guard against abuse, and the State Department was not equipped to assign individual passwords (Warrick, 2011).

Security of personnel, property, and sensitive information is critical to a functioning government.
(Photo courtesy of Wackenhut Corporation.)

U.S. embassies in East Africa occurred within 10 minutes of each other. A bomb blast was detonated at 10:35 A.M. in a parking lot adjacent to the U.S. embassy in Nairobi, Kenya, killing more than 240 people, 12 of whom were American, and injuring over 5,000. At 10:40 A.M., a second bomb exploded in Dar es Salaam, Tanzania, 450 miles from Nairobi. The second blast claimed the lives of 10 people and injured over 70. The bombings were believed to be the responsibility of a small, sophisticated, fundamentalist, Middle Eastern terrorist group, financed and led by Osama bin Laden, that targeted U.S. installations (Raum, 1999; Ross, 2012; Shenon, 1999).

On August 20, 1998, the United States used approximately 75 navy warship-based cruise missiles to retaliate against bin Laden by attacking a pharmaceutical factory in Sudan and a suspected terrorist training camp in Afghanistan. Both sites were believed to be facilities operated by the bin Laden terrorist group. Subsequently, the United States heightened security at U.S. airports and government facilities and warned U.S. citizens of the possibility of future terrorist attacks.

The bombing incidents in East Africa on August 7, 1998, did not represent the first time U.S. embassies were targeted by terrorists. Other major incidents include the following:

02-16-96	Athens, Greece: rocket-grenade attack; terrorist group suspected
09-13-95	Moscow: rocket-propelled grenade fired; minor damage
07-27-93	Lima, Peru: bomb exploded in bus outside embassy; one person killed
01-31-91	Lima, Peru: bomb attack from rocket launcher
03-23-88	Bogota, Columbia: rocket-propelled grenade launched by guerrilla group; causes minor damage
06-09-87	Rome: rocket fired on embassy by Japan-based Red Army terrorists; minor injuries
03-27-86	La Paz, Bolivia: dynamite exploded on roof of embassy
02-18-86	Lisbon, Portugal: car bomb exploded outside embassy

09-20-84	Beirut, Lebanon: suicide car bomb killed 16
12-12-83	Kuwait City: suicide truck bomb killed 6, injured 12; 17 pro-Iranian terrorists convicted
04-18-83	Beirut, Lebanon: suicide car bomb killed 63

Although the Cold War ended in the early 1990s, U.S. government officials learned that complacency can result in negative consequences. Lax security at the Los Alamos National Laboratory in New Mexico threatened to compromise U.S. nuclear secrets. Even the CIA is not immune from breaches in security. Revelations early in 2000 raised concerns that John Deutch, who directed the CIA from May 1995 to December 1996, used an unclassified computer in his home to work on highly secret classified material. A CIA inspector general's investigation also revealed that the home computer containing the classified material was used to gain access to unsecured Internet pornographic sites ("Security fears cited over prior CIA chief," 2000).

In another security breach in early 2000, undercover Government Accountability Office (GAO) investigators, using fictitious law enforcement identification credentials, were able to penetrate 19 secured federal facilities, including the Washington, DC, FBI building, the Pentagon, and the CIA headquarters in Langley, Virginia (" 'Cops' test security, get in CIA, other buildings," 2000).

Risks to government personnel and information can also take the form of potentially misguided actions by private citizens. In January 2011, the *New York Times* reported that Duane Clarridge, former head of the CIA's Latin America division, was running a stable of spies from his home. His network of field agents, funded by donors, had supposedly been operating in Pakistan and Afghanistan for 2 years, to support Clarridge's aim of gathering information about militant fighters, Taliban leaders, and Afghanistan's ruling elite. The Pentagon official who arranged a contract for Clarridge in 2009 is under investigation for possibly violating Defense Department rules. Sources describe the official as convinced that Washington bureaucrats and lawyers are impeding U.S. troops and that leaders rely too much on allies. Clarridge gave a statement maintaining that his private spy operation may be an effective model for providing information to officers and U.S. government officials. But a Pentagon spokesman expressed concerns about relying on unvetted and uncorroborated information from private sources. Such information, the spokesman explained, could endanger U.S. forces and taint information collected during legitimate intelligence operations ("Spy network reportedly based in Escondido," 2011).

THE U.S. DEPARTMENT OF HOMELAND SECURITY

In response to the threat of terrorism, the **U.S. DHS** was created by the **Homeland Security Act of 2002** (U.S. Congress, 2002). Representing the largest transformation of the U.S. government since the 1947 creation of the U.S. Department of Defense, the DHS consolidated 22 scattered domestic agencies with nearly 180,000 employees into one department on March 1, 2003. Originally, the DHS was organized into four major directorates.

The *Border and Transportation Security Directorate* consolidated major security and transportation operations. It included the following federal agencies:

- U.S. Customs Service (formerly in Treasury Department)
- Immigration and Naturalization Service (INS) (part) (formerly in Justice Department)
- Federal Protective Service (formerly in General Services Administration)

- Transportation Security Administration (TSA) (formerly in Transportation Department)
- Federal Law Enforcement Training Center (formerly in Treasury Department)
- Animal and Plant Health Inspection Service (part) (formerly in Agriculture Department)
- Office for Domestic Preparedness (formerly in Justice Department)

The *Emergency Preparedness and Response Directorate* consolidated domestic disaster preparedness training and coordinated government disaster response. Its agencies included the following:

- Federal Emergency Management Agency (FEMA)
- Strategic National Stockpile and National Disaster Medical Systems
- Nuclear Incident Response Team
- Domestic Emergency Support Teams
- National Domestic Preparedness Office

The *Science and Technology Directorate* sought to utilize all scientific and technological advantages to secure the U.S. homeland. The following agencies were consolidated as part of this effort:

- CBRN Countermeasures Programs (formerly in Energy Department)
- Environment Measurements Laboratory (formerly in Energy Department)
- National BW Defense Analysis Center (formerly in Defense Department)
- Plum Island Animal Disease Center (formerly in Agriculture Department)

The *Information Analysis and Infrastructure Protection Directorate* was established to analyze intelligence and information from other agencies (including the CIA, FBI, NSA) involving threats to homeland security and it evaluated vulnerabilities in the nation's infrastructure. It included the following:

- Federal Computer Incident Response Center (formerly in General Services Administration)
- National Communications System (formerly in Defense Department)
- National Infrastructure Protection Center (formerly in FBI, Justice Department)
- Energy Security and Assurance Program (formerly in Energy Department)

The Secret Service and the Coast Guard, both previously in the Treasury Department, were relocated to the DHS, remaining intact and reporting directly to the secretary. In addition, the INS adjudications and benefits programs reported directly to the deputy secretary as the Bureau of Citizenship and Immigration Services (U.S. Department of Homeland Security, 2003). The U.S. liaison to the International Criminal Police Organization (INTERPOL) is located in the U.S. National Central Bureau of INTERPOL in the U.S. Department of Justice (U.S. Department of Justice, 2007a).

On October 4, 2006, the president signed the **Post-Katrina Emergency Reform Act of 2006** into law. This Act established new leadership positions within the DHS, brought additional functions into the FEMA, created and reallocated functions to other components within the DHS, and amended the Homeland Security Act of 2002 in ways that directly and indirectly affected the organization and functions of various entities within the DHS. In addition, the DHS made other organizational changes outside of FEMA that complemented the changes mandated by Congress. The changes to the DHS became effective on March 31, 2007.

DHS Components

Currently, the major components of the DHS include the following:

- The Directorate for National Protection and Programs works to advance the Department's risk-reduction mission. Reducing risk requires an integrated approach that encompasses both physical and virtual threats and their associated human elements.
- The Directorate for Science and Technology is the primary research and development arm of the Department. It provides federal, state, and local officials with the technology and capabilities to protect the homeland.
- The Directorate for Management is responsible for Department budgets and appropriations, expenditure of funds, accounting and finance, procurement, human resources, information technology systems, facilities and equipment, and the identification and tracking of performance measurements.
- The Office of Policy is the primary policy formulation and coordination component for the DHS. It provides a centralized, coordinated focus to the development of Department-wide, long-range planning to protect the United States.
- The Office of Health Affairs coordinates all medical activities of the DHS to ensure appropriate preparation for and response to incidents having medical significance.
- The Office of Intelligence and Analysis is responsible for using information and intelligence from multiple sources to identify and assess current and future threats to the United States.
- The Office of Operations Coordination is responsible for monitoring the security of the United States on a daily basis and coordinating activities within the Department and with state governors, homeland security advisors, law enforcement partners, and critical infrastructure operators in all 50 states and more than 50 major urban areas nationwide.
- The Federal Law Enforcement Training Center provides career-long training to law enforcement professionals to help them fulfill their responsibilities safely and proficiently.
- The Domestic Nuclear Detection Office works to enhance the nuclear detection efforts of federal, state, territorial, tribal, and local governments, and the private sector to ensure a coordinated response to such threats.
- The TSA protects the nation's transportation systems to ensure freedom of movement for people and commerce.
- U.S. Customs and Border Protection (CBP) is responsible for protecting the nation's borders to prevent terrorists and terrorist weapons from entering the United States, while facilitating the flow of legitimate trade and travel.
- U.S. Citizenship and Immigration Services is responsible for the administration of immigration and naturalization adjudication functions and establishing immigration services policies and priorities.
- U.S. Immigration and Customs Enforcement (ICE), the largest investigative arm of the DHS, is responsible for identifying and confronting vulnerabilities at the nation's border as well as entities associated with the nation's economy, transportation, and infrastructure.
- U.S. Coast Guard protects the public, the environment, and U.S. economic interests in the nation's ports and waterways, along the coast, on international waters, and in any maritime region as required to support national security.

- The **FEMA** prepares the nation for disasters, manages federal response and recovery efforts following any major national incident, and administers the National Flood Insurance Program.
- U.S. Secret Service protects the president and other high-level officials and investigates counterfeiting and other financial crimes, including financial institution fraud, identity theft, computer fraud, and computer-based attacks on the nation's financial, banking, and telecommunications infrastructure.

Office of the Secretary

The Office of the Secretary (DHS) oversees activities with other federal, state, local, and private entities as part of a collaborative effort to strengthen U.S. borders, provide for intelligence analysis and infrastructure protection, improve the use of science and technology to counter WMDs, and to create a comprehensive response and recovery system. It includes multiple offices that contribute to the overall homeland security mission:

- The Privacy Office works to minimize the impact on the individual's privacy, particularly the individual's personal information and dignity, while achieving the mission of the DHS.
- The Office for Civil Rights and Civil Liberties provides legal and policy advice to DHS leadership on civil rights and civil liberties issues, investigates and resolves complaints, and provides leadership to Equal Employment Opportunity Programs.
- The Office of Inspector General is responsible for conducting and supervising audits, investigations, and inspections relating to the programs and operations of the DHS, recommending ways the DHS may carry out its responsibilities in the most effective and efficient manner possible.
- The Citizenship and Immigration Services Ombudsman provides recommendations to resolve individual and employer problems with the U.S. Citizenship and Immigration Services to ensure national security and the integrity of the legal immigration system, increase efficiencies in administering citizenship and immigration services, and improve customer service.
- The Office of Legislative Affairs serves as primary liaison to members of Congress and their staffs, the White House and executive branch, and other federal agencies and governmental entities that have roles in assuring national security.
- Other offices include the Office of the General Counsel, the Office of Counternarcotics Enforcement, the Office of Public Affairs, the Executive Secretariat, and the Military Advisor's Office.

Advisory Panels and Committees

The DHS advisory panels and committees include the following:

- The Homeland Security Advisory Council provides advice and recommendations to the secretary on matters related to homeland security. It is comprised of leaders from state and local government, first responder communities, the private sector, and academia.
- The National Infrastructure Advisory Council provides advice to the secretary of Homeland Security and the president on the security of information systems for the public and private institutions that constitute the critical infrastructure of the nation's economy.

- The Homeland Security Science and Technology Advisory Committee serves as a source of independent, scientific and technical planning advice for the undersecretary for Science and Technology.
- The Critical Infrastructure Partnership Advisory Council was established to facilitate effective coordination between federal infrastructure protection programs with the infrastructure protection activities of the private sector and of state, local, territorial, and tribal governments.
- The Interagency Coordinating Council on Emergency Preparedness and Individuals with Disabilities was established to ensure that the federal government appropriately supports safety and security for individuals with disabilities in disaster situations (U.S. Department of Homeland Security, Office of the Press Secretary, 2007).

In addition to creating the DHS, a subsection of the Homeland Security Act of 2002 created protections for those engaged in the development and sales of antiterrorism technology. The subsection is entitled, the **Support Anti-Terrorism by Fostering Effective Technologies Act (SAFETY Act) of 2002.** The SAFETY Act created certain liability limitations for claims arising from an act of terrorism when the antiterrorism technologies have been deployed. Those who sell antiterrorism technologies can apply to the DHS for SAFETY Act designation and certification. The Act's designation limits antiterrorism technology supply and distribution chain liability.

Learn more about the U.S. DHS at www.dhs.gov.

In September 2007, the U.S. GAO reported that the DHS made progress toward its mission of developing plans and programs. However, the GAO cited the DHS for lack of progress in DHS management and implementation efforts. Among the deficiencies cited, the GAO indicated that

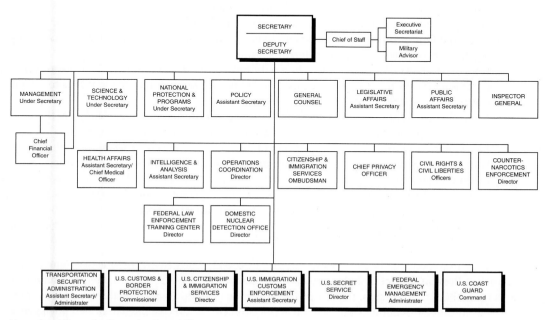

Homeland Security Organizational Chart.

the DHS has not yet fully adopted and applied a risk management approach to implementing homeland security concepts (U.S. Government Accountability Office, 2007).

THE 9/11 COMMISSION

The independent, bipartisan **National Commission on Terrorist Attacks Upon the United States,** also known as the **9/11 Commission**, was established in late 2002 to prepare a full and complete account of the circumstances surrounding the September 11, 2001, terrorist attacks, including events leading up to the attacks as well as the government's response. The Commission was also tasked with the responsibility to provide recommendations against future terrorist attacks. Created by an act of Congress and signed into law by President George W. Bush, the Commission comprised five Republicans and five Democrats. The Commission was cochaired by former New Jersey governor, Thomas Kean (Republican), and Lee Hamilton (Democrat), former U.S. Representative from Indiana's Ninth District. The Commission conducted hearings and interviewed numerous individuals.

On July 22, 2004, the 9/11 Commission issued a final report, culminating an exhaustive 20-month investigation of the 9/11 terrorist attacks. The Commission cited systemic failure and charged that elected and appointed government officials in the Congress, the administrations of Presidents Bill Clinton and George W. Bush, the CIA, and the FBI failed to grasp the seriousness of terrorism as an imminent threat. Although the Commission stopped short of stating that the 9/11 attacks could have been prevented, it noted many government missteps. The Commission's recommendations included the following:

- Create a single, high-level intelligence director to supervise and oversee 15 intelligence agencies of the United States.
- Create a National Counterterrorism Center to coordinate data collection and analysis among intelligence-gathering agencies, including the CIA and FBI.
- Develop a global diplomatic and public relations strategy to dismantle the terrorist network that Osama bin Laden created and to defeat the radical fundamentalist Islamic ideology that encourages and supports terrorist groups.
- Improve homeland security, including national standards for issuing driver licenses and other identification, terrorist watch lists, and increase use of biometric identifiers to screen travelers at seaports, borders, and airports.
- Improve oversight of intelligence gathering and counterterrorism activities by the U.S. Congress, especially during transitions between presidential administrations. This recommendation supports radical changes, including a proposal for either a single, joint House–Senate intelligence oversight committee or separate House and Senate committees, with direct budget authority over the U.S. intelligence function (National Commission on Terrorist Attacks Upon the United States, 2004). In response to the Commission's recommendations, President George W. Bush signed executive orders on August 27, 2004, that are designed to strengthen the CIA director's power over intelligence agencies and create a national counterterrorism center.

Also, in response to the Commission report, the president signed the **Intelligence Reform and Terrorism Prevention Act of 2004** into law on December 17, 2004. Fashioned after recommendations of the 9/11 Commission, the law provided for the creation of a national intelligence center as well as the appointment of a national intelligence director to oversee the nation's 15 intelligence agencies. Additional changes and restructuring of the U.S. intelligence function appeared likely.

The 9/11 Commission was criticized by some for not stating that the events of September 11, 2001, could have been prevented. A few years after issuance of the 9/11 Report, several members of the 9/11 Commission itself criticized the federal government for failing to implement several of the Commission's strongest recommendations, citing lack of priority and urgency being given to the prevention of terrorist acts. Although a national intelligence center and directorate were created, former Commission members stated that more could have been accomplished. Notable among the Commission's recommendations not implemented were improved communications channels among emergency responders, directing antiterrorism funds to states based on level of risk, and consolidation of airline passenger databases into a single terror watch list to aid screening at airports (Yen, 2005).

In July 2007, Congress enacted legislation designed to carry out the major recommendations of the 9/11 Commission. The law elevated the importance of risk factors in determining federal homeland security funding for states and cities. The law also funded a program to improve emergency communications systems. Further, the law requires screening of all cargo on passenger planes within 3 years and it set a 5-year goal for radiation scanning of all cargo containers bound for U.S. ports.

A CIA inspector general's executive summary released in August 2007 reinforced the 9/11 Commission's findings. Although the CIA report did not identify a single point of failure, it concluded that CIA resources devoted to counterterrorism were mismanaged prior to 9/11. The report faulted nearly 60 senior CIA administrators, including the director, for systemic failure to follow through with counterterrorism operations and properly share and analyze critical data (U.S. Central Intelligence Agency, 2007).

Learn more about the 9/11 Commission Report at www.9-11commission.gov.

AIRLINE AND AIRPORT SECURITY

The terrorist attacks of September 11, 2001, sharpened focus on airline and airport security. However, long before 9/11, other incidents illustrated the need for and the uniqueness of airline and airport security. For example, a 6-foot 2-inch, 250-pound, incoherent man shed his clothes and mumbled threats while he broke into an in-flight Alaska Airlines cockpit on March 16, 2000. The man attacked the crew and grabbed for the aircraft's controls before he was subdued by the copilot and some terrified passengers. On December 29, 2000, a deranged man tried to seize the cockpit controls of a British Airways 747 jumbo jet en route from London to Kenya. The man bit the captain's ear and finger, sending the aircraft into a dive of several thousand feet before he was subdued by passengers and crew (Fisher, 2000).

Deregulation of commercial airlines during President Reagan's administration led to increased competition, lower airfares, and increased air travel by the public. Competitive pressures forced many airlines to reduce meal portions and flight attendant crews, resulting in poor service and disgruntled passengers. Other cost-cutting measures led to poor aircraft maintenance, which resulted in reduced safety.

Many airports are similar to 24-hour cities. All of the approximately 450 commercial airports in the United States are considered high security risks, with the highest risk airports located in large urban areas. Large airports in other countries face similar risks—a fact made all too clear in January 2011 when a suicide bomber blew himself up in Moscow's busiest airport, killing 35 people. Airports accommodate millions of people annually, and aircraft typically cross numerous jurisdictional boundaries (Garbera, 1998; Ward, Kiernam, & Mabrey, 2006).

Airline and airport security developed primarily as a result of the skyjackings that occurred during the 1960s. The U.S. government's initial response was to place sky marshals (deputy U.S. Marshals) on commercial airline flights. Carry-on luggage and passengers were screened by metal detectors and security personnel contracted by the airlines. In addition, bomb threats, actual bombings, the taking of hostages, terrorist activities, even disruptive behavior from passengers created a need for increased security in the air travel and transport industry.

Air cargo theft, airline ticket fraud, theft of passenger luggage and items from vehicles in parking lots, traffic control problems, and the potential for fire and major disasters are commonplace in some airports. Not all criminal activity in airports originates with external sources. Theft, sabotage, and personal injury also result from employee actions. Disgruntled and terminated employees are responsible for much of the property damage and, in at least one documented case, the death of innocent people.

Although air travel is still one of the safest modes of human transportation, incidents such as the bombing of Pan Am Flight 103 over Lockerbee, Scotland, in 1989; the Atlantic Ocean crash of TWA Flight 800 in 1996; and the terrorist attacks on the United States in 2001 generated tremendous concern for airline passenger safety. Numerous other air disasters spotlighted the need for air security and safety:

- On August 6, 1997, 228 people aboard a Korean Air Boeing 747 were killed when the jetliner crashed in Guam.
- On February 2, 1998, 104 people were killed when DC-9 Cebu Pacific Air Flight 387 crashed into a mountain as it prepared to land in the southern Philippines.
- On February 16, 1998, 196 people aboard the aircraft and 6 people on the ground were killed when a China Airlines Airbus A-300–600R crashed while approaching the airport in Taipei, Taiwan.
- On September 2, 1998, 229 people were killed when Swissair Flight 111 crashed off the coast of Nova Scotia. The MD-1 was en route from New York to Geneva.
- On December 11, 1998, 101 people were killed when a Thai Airways Airbus A310–200 crashed during landing at an airport approximately 300 miles south of Bangkok, Thailand. Forty-five people aboard the aircraft survived.
- On February 24, 1999, 61 people were killed when a China Southwest Airlines plane crashed 250 miles south of China's Zhejiang province. The aircraft was a Russian-built TU-154.
- On October 31, 1999, 217 people were killed when EgyptAir Flight 990 crashed into the Atlantic Ocean 60 miles south of Nantucket, Massachusetts. The flight was en route from New York to Cairo.
- On January 30, 2000, 169 people were killed when Kenya Airways Flight 431 crashed into the ocean after takeoff from Abidjan, Ivory Coast. Ten people survived the crash of the Airbus 310.
- On January 31, 2000, Alaska Airlines Flight 261, a McDonnel Douglas MD 83, bound from Puerto Vallarta, Mexico, to San Francisco, crashed into the Pacific Ocean about 40 miles northwest of Los Angeles International Airport. Eighty-eight passengers and crew members were killed.
- On November 12, 2001, American Airlines Flight 587 crashed in the Rockaways section of New York City, killing all 265 aboard. The John F. Kennedy International Airport flight was bound for the Dominican Republic.

The Federal Aviation Administration

In 1972, the **Federal Aviation Administration (FAA)**, the federal agency responsible for regulating air transportation in the United States, began to require specific minimum security measures at major airports. These measures included

- screening of all persons and baggage entering aircraft departure areas.
- the availability of law enforcement support with the ability to respond to screening points within 5 minutes.
- the development of security plans by airlines and airport management.
- the development of airport disaster plans.

In 1987, the FAA assumed the responsibility for enforcing comprehensive safety and security standards and programs for airports and the airline industry. In 1988, with the enactment of Federal Aviation Regulation (FAR) 107.14, the U.S. government required heightened access controls at commercial airports and restricted access to commercial aircraft.

The White House Commission on Aviation Safety and Security

Subsequent to the TWA Flight 800 crash in 1996, the White House Commission on Aviation Safety and Security (the Gore Commission) was formed. It recommended uniform standards for the selection, training, certification, and recertification of airport boarding area passenger and luggage screening personnel and screening companies.

Congress reacted with the passage of Public Law 104–264 in October 1996. The law mandated additional security features and screening. The screening was designed to ensure that dangerous articles and explosive devices were not introduced into controlled areas. However, the wage rate and training provided to screening personnel was often minimal because many airlines responsible for screening did not wish to pay more than necessary. The airlines maintained they were in the transportation business, not the security business (Vincent, 2000). Concerns about the cost of providing security personnel persist today. Indeed, in January 2011, the mayor of

Security at U.S. airports was heightened, beginning in the 1960s.
(Photo courtesy of Marc Anderson/Pearson Education/PH College.)

Syracuse, New York, called for private security guards to replace most of the police officers who provided security at Syracuse Hancock International Airport. The mayor noted that the city was paying $3.1 million in overtime each year for police who provide security at the airport and that the amount was making it difficult to attract low-cost airlines to the facility (Knauss, 2011).

On February 7, 1997, the White House Commission on Aviation Safety and Security issued its report. The report included 57 recommendations, 31 of which dealt with improvements in security for the traveling public (Thomason, 2000). The Commission recommended that the federal government consider aviation security a national security concern. Subsequently, the president of the United States included $100 million in the fiscal year 1999 budget request for upgrades in civil aviation security. The FAA used the money to continue installation of explosive detection systems and devices as well as hardened cargo containers to control explosions that could occur in the baggage compartments of commercial aircraft.

In February 1998, the U.S. Department of Transportation (DOT) issued a status report on the Commission's recommendations. The report indicated that the following actions had been taken:

- The U.S. Department of Defense established a task force to assess the possible use of surface-to-air missiles against commercial aircraft.
- The U.S. DOT strengthened its relationship with other departments and agencies to assess the possible use of chemical and biological weapons against commercial airlines.
- The FAA gave cleared security personnel access to classified information regarding terrorist threats.
- The FAA collaborated with the U.S. State Department to provide airport security training to personnel in foreign countries served by U.S. airlines.
- The FAA proposed a program to improve compliance with international security standards at airports.
- The FBI increased the number of agents assigned to counterterrorism activities (Doherty, 1998).

Strategies for Passenger Screening and Explosives Detection

In the late 1990s, a trend to improve security at airports included the development of **passenger profiling techniques**. The techniques were used to identify smugglers and possible terrorists. Profiling came under attack by some as a violation of civil liberty and for being discriminatory in its application. This led the U.S. Justice Department to develop guidelines to prevent any future discrimination.

Airline security personnel and U.S. Customs agents with dogs trained to seek out passengers, luggage, and cargo that possess or contain drugs, and explosives became common at major airports. Additionally, some airlines initiated extensive security training programs for their employees. Positive identification of passengers, baggage/passenger matching, and random baggage searches became part of the preboarding passenger-screening procedure.

In spite of increased security, airport screening methods still appeared inadequate primarily due to low pay, high turnover, and minimal benefits and training for airline-contracted screening personnel. A U.S. GAO report issued in March 2000 indicated that many other countries, including Canada, France, Belgium, the United Kingdom, and the Netherlands, had better-trained screening personnel. The responsibility for passenger and luggage screening in these countries lies with the government or the airport, not the airlines. Thus, screeners were paid more, received better training and benefits, and experienced lower attrition. As a result, they possessed a higher

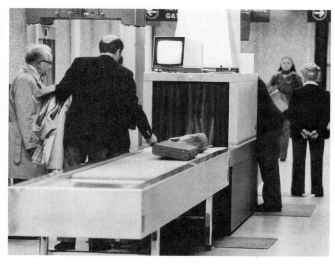

Passenger-screening checkpoint at O'Hare Airport in Chicago.
(Photo courtesy of Marc Anderson/Pearson Education/PH College.)

skill level and detected more suspicious objects than did their U.S. counterparts (Vincent, 2000). As screening technology advanced, many security personnel were replaced with screening equipment. The use of biometrics, automated scanners, and access control integration represented new airport security trends (Zunkel, 2000). Some experts expect biometrics to play an increasing role in security overall. While fingerprint technology currently dominates the biometrics market owing to significant cost advantages and mature technology, iris and facial recognition may fulfill a larger role in the coming years (*"New waves of growth,"* 2011).

Of the many initiatives designed to combat the threat of terrorism in the skies, one FAA project involved the installation of explosive detection equipment in airports. As the FAA upgraded safety and security regulations, new explosive detection technology was developed and implemented. The new equipment, installed in several unnamed airports, included FAA-certified explosive detection systems, automated dual-energy x-ray machines, and trace explosive detection devices. Other FAA initiatives included deployment of agency security personnel in foreign countries, research into making aircraft more resistant to explosive detonations, and expanded passenger bag matching (Major, 1999).

The Transportation Security Administration

A major problem at U.S. airports was the fragmentation of the responsibility for security. Apparently, no single entity, whether it be the airlines, the FAA, or the jurisdiction associated with the location of the airport facility, was able to assume overall responsibility for the security function. Although all domestic aviation activities were licensed, certified, or supervised by the FAA, the airport security duties were performed by the local police agencies and private security companies. In addition, domestic commercial airports are not federal facilities, despite the federal authority overriding their operations. Thus, lack of standard operating procedure at many airports added to the confusion. Recommendations for improvement included placement of the overall security function within the federal government, with uniform passenger, luggage, and cargo screening standards under the auspices of the FAA (Slepian, 2000).

The September 11, 2001, terrorist attacks changed the course of commercial aviation security in the United States. In response to the obvious need to improve airline and airport security, the federal government began to assume responsibility for the security function in November 2001. Congressional action on November 16 led to the passage of the **Aviation and Transportation Security Act of 2001.** The law federalized aviation security and centralized responsibility under the newly created **TSA.** The TSA officially assumed its duties on February 17, 2002. Currently, the TSA oversees U.S. airline and airport security. It provides trained federal employees for passenger and baggage screening and it supplies sky marshals (air marshals) for unnamed commercial flights (Salant, 2002; U.S. Department of Homeland Security, Transportation Security Administration, 2003).

Federalization of commercial aviation security resulted in the removal of contract private security personnel from passenger- and baggage-screening points. They were replaced with twice as many federal TSA employees, who earn almost double the salary of their private-sector counterparts. The impact of this transition has yet to be measured effectively. Some argue that federalized passenger screening has not delivered a noticeable improvement in air passenger safety (Dalton, 2003). In 2005, audits performed by the U.S. DHS inspector general revealed that federal passenger screeners at U.S. airports did not perform better than private-sector screeners did before 9/11 (Miller, 2005). The GAO also said that it did not notice any difference in private versus government screeners' performance during covert checkpoint testing in 2007. Both groups failed to find concealed bomb components, according to the GAO. TSA chief John Pistole decided to end acceptance of new applications for a private airport screening program in use at 16 airports (Ahlers & Meserve, 2011).

Without proper training, equipment, management, policies, and procedures, neither federal employees nor private security personnel can provide improved security. However, additional training is underway, and new weapon- and explosive-detection technology is under development.

Since 9/11, airline passengers are required to present government-issued photo identification—usually a driver's license—before entering airline passenger boarding areas. However, driver licenses issued in many states are easy to counterfeit. In response, Congress passed the **REAL ID Act of 2005.** The Act is contained in Division B of the Emergency Supplemental Appropriations Act for Defense, the Global War on Terror, and Tsunami Relief, 2005. The Act imposes prescriptive federal standards for driver licenses and identification cards. Specifically, the law requires that counterfeit-resistant security features be incorporated into each driver's license or ID card, verification of information provided by applicants be carried out to establish their identity and lawful status in the United States, and physical security measures be specified for locations where licenses and cards are issued (U.S. Congress, 2005). The law has been mired in controversy over potential implementation costs and privacy issues. As a result, the U.S. DHS extended the law's implementation deadline (Straw, 2007).

SECURITY SPOTLIGHT

Research airline security procedures used in the United States and compare them with those used in the United Kingdom. What similarities and differences do you find? Which procedures do you consider most effective? Why? What, if any, trade-offs do the procedures entail?

Tighter controls over intercountry air travel have been implemented as well. Effective January 23, 2007, all commercial air travelers, including citizens of the United States, Canada,

Mexico, and Bermuda are required to present a passport to enter the United States from another country, even when arriving from another part of the Western Hemisphere (U.S. Department of Homeland Security, 2007). A new screening program introduced by the TSA in October 2009 also aims to further strengthen screeners' ability to detect terrorists (see "The Secure Flight Program").

New security measures implemented by the TSA after a would-be terrorist was found to have explosives in his underclothing have also raised questions. These measures include the use of full-body scanners that produce detailed images of passengers' bodies. Some have expressed concern that images would be made available online, violating passengers' privacy. Others have protested supposedly dangerous levels of radiation emitted by the scanners. While passengers can opt out of the new scanning, those who choose to do so must submit to an "enhanced pat-down" by a TSA agent, which some passengers have decried as too invasive ("TSA chief likely to face lawmakers' questions on pat-downs, body scans," 2010).

Some security experts suggest augmenting use of scanning technology with careful observation and strategic conversation—in real time—to detect potential terrorists. Screeners, these experts say, should be able to access a more comprehensive database of government and law enforcement data, as well as information from airlines about "tells" (such as paying cash for a ticket and flying only one way). By combining such information with their own observations

---

The Secure Flight Program

Secure Flight is a behind-the-scenes program that streamlines the travelers watch-list matching process. It aims to improve the travel experience for all passengers, including those who have been misidentified in the past. Under the Secure Flight Final Rule, TSA requires airlines to collect and transmit to TSA the Secure Flight Passenger Data (SFPD) including the following:

- name as it appears on government-issued ID when traveling
- date of birth
- gender
- redress number (for inquiries or attempts to seek resolution regarding difficulties the traveler experienced during screening at transportation hubs while crossing U.S. borders) if available

The TSA determined that mandating the provision of date of birth and gender would reduce the number of passengers misidentified as a match to the watch list, particularly for individuals who have similar names to those on the watch lists.

The program's key goals are to identify known and suspected terrorists, prevent individuals on the No Fly List from boarding an aircraft, subject individuals on the Selectee List to enhanced screening to determine if they are permitted to board an aircraft, facilitate passenger air travel, and protect individuals' privacy.

By assuming watch-list matching responsibilities from the airlines, the TSA maintains that it is decreasing the risk of compromised watch-list data by limiting its distribution; providing earlier identification of potential matches, allowing for speedier notification of law enforcement and threat management; providing a fair, equitable, and consistent matching process across all airlines; reducing instances of misidentified individuals; and offering consistent application of an integrated redress process for misidentified individuals via the DHS's Travel Redress Inquiry Program.

Source: Transportation Security Administration, Frequently Asked Questions, 2011.

of passenger behavior, screeners could determine which passengers are more likely to present legitimate threats, and spend less time searching harmless travelers (Ron, 2010). In January 2011, TSA head John Pistole proposed a new risk-based screening method that calls for screeners to spend more time with passengers who are being assessed, using intelligence or information volunteered by the passenger or gleaned from a behavior detection officer who noticed something suspicious about the individual (Yager, 2011).

TRANSPORTATION AND CARGO SECURITY

Over a 3-year period, one major urban area's public transit system experienced losses estimated at between $160,000 and $1,000,000 due to employee theft. The losses resulted from thefts from bus fare boxes and black market sales of counterfeit and stolen public transit passes. Money was stolen from bus fare boxes when the transit system's buses were cleaned each day. In one case, a fare-box repair person confessed to using a key from the transit agency's accounting office to unlock fare boxes to obtain cash. The fare-box repair person worked honestly for the transit company for 6 years before becoming an internal thief. After the stealing commenced, the employee admitted to thefts totaling approximately $56,000 (Arner, 2000b).

The transportation of persons and goods by air, land, and sea represents one of the largest industries in the United States. Aircraft, railroads, trucks, buses, automobiles, ships, and barges transport millions of people as well as millions of tons of raw materials and finished products each year. The remainder of this section focuses on the threats to, and protection of, **cargo** transported for commerce.

Cargo-Related Threats

Cargo refers to any object that is moved through the transportation system. The system includes not only the aircraft, vehicles, and vessels used to move materials but also the facilities and equipment used to load, store, and unload the materials. Terrorist attacks in the form of explosives

The transportation of persons and property is one of the largest industries requiring special attention to security.
(Photo courtesy of Wackenhut Corporation.)

positioned in cargo have become threats. Smuggling is another concern. Indeed, according to the DHS, smuggling of heroin increased 200 percent from 2009 to 2010, as measured by prohibited-property border seizures. And smuggling of steroids has jumped 308 percent in the same period. Internal and external theft, burglary, vandalism, and truck hijacking are additional common threats.

TERRORIST ATTACKS   On October 29, 2010, two packages, each containing a bomb consisting of plastic explosives and a detonating mechanism, were found on separate cargo planes. The bombs were discovered as a result of intelligence received from Saudi Arabia's security chief. They were bound from Yemen to the United States, and were discovered at stopovers in England and in Dubai. The bombs were intended to blow up planes over the United States.

While the terrorism plot was thwarted, it revealed gaps in government intelligence gathering and information sharing as well as the need for a new approach to air cargo security. Some experts recommend applying security methodologies used with imports in maritime shipping containers. For example, the CBP unit of the DHS requires import shippers to submit data on containers and their contents 24 hours before the containers are loaded onto U.S.-bound ships at foreign ports. Containers are then assessed for risk. High-risk containers may be searched overseas or barred from import before departure.

Air carriers are required to submit their cargo manifests for U.S.-bound international flights just 4 hours before scheduled arrival. In many cases, this means that the flight is already airborne. CBP is talking with air carriers about extending the time requirement for submission of cargo manifests. However, questions remain regarding whether the parties involved will be forthright with manifest submissions and whether unusual tactics (something as unique as the printer-cartridge bombs) would raise suspicions or trigger the high-risk red flag.

Since the plot was discovered, the TSA imposed new cargo rules, including a ban on high-risk cargo in the bellies of passenger planes, a ban on air cargo from Yemen and Somalia, and a ban on toner cartridges larger than 16 ounces on passenger flights. However, these policies are reactive, and a more proactive solution is needed (Straw, 2011).

THEFT   Theft can occur anywhere within the distribution system. Shipping and receiving areas, containers in transit, warehouses, depots, terminals, and piers are common targets for the thief.

The U.S. DOT estimates that losses due to cargo theft may approach $20 billion annually. Globally, the losses are estimated at $50 billion. The Department also estimates that approximately 80 percent of the losses are due to internal theft, 15 percent to external sources, and 5 percent to hijacking. Only about 20 percent of stolen cargo is ever recovered. A vast majority of the losses occur in warehouses and distribution centers through theft by those who are authorized to be in the area. In some cases, organized gangs place part-time or temporary workers into target companies. Once inside, the gang's members provide information about shipments that leads to cargo thefts worth millions of dollars each. In addition, the increased use of computers and electronic documentation has made cargo a tempting target for thieves as well as domestic and international organized crime syndicates. Automated files contain sensitive shipping information that can be accessed electronically by hackers or through collusion with employees.

Most stolen cargo is returned illegally to the marketplace, where it is sold at a tremendous discount. Thus, product manufacturers incur a loss twice: once as a result of the theft and again when a legitimate sale is lost as the stolen goods are sold on the black market. Cargo theft reached epidemic proportions during the 1970s. This led the U.S. government to establish the Office of Transportation Security (OTS) within the U.S. DOT. Cargo theft decreased in the 1980s, largely

Transportation security measures include use of personnel, physical security, and a system of accountability.
(Photo courtesy of Wackenhut Corporation.)

due to the efforts of OTS. In 1983, the agency was dissolved and replaced with the **National Cargo Security Council (NCSC)**, a voluntary organization consisting of government and private industry representatives. The NCSC functions as a clearinghouse for cargo theft information. Cargo theft increased during the 1990s. Apparently, organized criminal groups were attracted to the low-risk, high-profit nature of cargo theft because tough law enforcement and conviction sentencing strategies focused on illegal drugs rather than cargo theft.

Cargo security measures that may prevent, or at least reduce, losses due to theft include personnel and physical security; a system of accountability and proper documentation through purchase orders, invoices, shipping documents, and receiving slips; secure packaging; policies and procedures; prosecution of criminal offenders; and the use of global positioning system (GPS) to track trucks. To combat cargo theft, liaison between carriers and collaboration among government and industry representatives is especially helpful. All interested and affected parties must work together to develop effective reporting systems, promote knowledge of cargo theft, support task forces, encourage the development of law enforcement expertise relating to cargo theft, use cargo security technology, increase prosecutions, and stiffen penalties for cargo theft (Badolato, 2000; Brandman, 2007).

Trucking Industry Security

The development of trucks in the early 1900s precipitated the decentralization of the manufacturing industry. Trucks permitted goods to be moved farther, faster, and less expensively than ever before. Economic development was no longer limited to regions serviced by railroads and commercial waterways. The trucking industry experienced tremendous growth after World War II. Low-fixed-cost trucks captured a large portion of the cargo transportation business. Today, trucks transport nearly 75 percent of freight shipped within the United States (Sweet, 2006).

The increased use of trucks necessitated improved safety and security measures. As a result, regulation of the trucking industry increased in the latter half of the twentieth century. Highway safety and cargo theft prevention became major concerns. For example, testing of all drivers for drugs and alcohol was required by federal law on January 1, 1996. Surveillance, undercover operations, access control, and a system of seals also serve preventive and detection functions.

In the late 1990s, concern developed over the quality and credentials of truck drivers. The FBI and investigators in several states uncovered a commercial driver's license bribery scheme. Apparently, hundreds of truck drivers licensed in Illinois and Florida bribed Department of Motor Vehicle officials and workers at truck-driving schools to falsify commercial driving exams. Most states allow drivers to exchange licenses without retesting. Many of the drivers with licenses obtained with a fictitious test score exchanged Illinois and Florida licenses for permits in several other states, making unsafe drivers difficult to locate.

The **Federal Motor Carrier Safety Administration (FMCSA)** was established as a separate administration within the U.S. DOT on January 1, 2000. The primary mission of the FMCSA is to reduce collisions, injuries, and fatalities involving large truck and buses. It develops, monitors, and ensures compliance with commercial licensing standards for drivers, carriers, and states. Secondarily, the FMCSA is involved with security, especially with regard to the safe and secure transportation of hazardous materials. Through enforcement of the federal hazardous materials regulations (HMRs), the FMCSA addresses hazardous materials classification and packaging, employee training, communications, and hazardous materials transportation operational requirements (Federal Motor Carrier Safety Administration, 2007).

In May 2003, as part of an effort to prevent terrorist incidents, the U.S. TSA began checking the backgrounds of 3.5 million truckers who haul hazardous materials. Trucks carry over 90 percent of the almost 1 million daily shipments of hazardous materials in the United States. Over 60,000 materials are listed as hazardous. The list includes a wide range of substances, from nail polish, gasoline, and corrosives to nuclear waste. Those who are deemed mentally incompetent, illegal immigrants, and those with recent convictions for possession of controlled substances may not transport hazardous materials (Brandman, 2007; Miller, 2003).

Railroad Security

A tremendous amount of cargo is transported by railroads. Responsibility for promulgation and enforcement of railway safety regulations rests with the **Federal Railroad Administration (FRA)**. The FRA also administers railroad assistance programs, conducts research in support of improved railroad safety, and consolidates federal government support of rail transportation activities (Federal Railroad Administration, 2007). Human cargo is also transported by railroad. In response to the threat of terrorism, TSA officers and federal marshals are assigned to some commuter railway lines and stations. The railroad industry also employs proprietary security officers and police. In some states, railroad security personnel are commissioned as peace officers with full police powers while on duty and on railroad property. Local, county, and state law enforcement agencies as well as the FBI and ICE provide assistance as well.

Railroads help to integrate countries and continents. They also contribute greatly to economic development and they function as an important strategic resource.

Maritime Security

The maritime component of the transportation industry includes the use of a vast network of canals, rivers, lakes, oceans, and ports to transport people as well as cargo. In the global economy, modern container ships transport tons of cargo in railcar-sized, preloaded, standardized containers that are easily transferred to and from trucks and railcars that provide land-based distribution of the freight. Each year, over 17 million cargo containers carrying nearly one-half of the nation's imports arrive by ship at U.S. seaports. Only a small fraction of the containers are inspected (Lindquist, 2007; Sweet, 2006).

In response to the terrorist attacks of 9/11, Congress passed the **Maritime Transportation Security Act (MTSA) of 2002**. The law is the United States equivalent of the International Ship and Port Facility Code (ISPS). The MTSA was fully implemented on July 1, 2004. The MTSA requires vessels and ports to conduct vulnerability assessments, develop security plans, and engage in activities designed to protect the nation's ports, vessels, and waterways. Specifically, the MTSA-required security plans must include provisions for passenger-, vehicle-, and baggage-screening procedures, security patrols, restricted areas, personnel identification procedures, access control measures, and installation of surveillance equipment.

Developed with risk-based methodology, the MTSA regulations focus on the elements of the maritime industry that are at a high risk for involvement in a transportation security incident. Thus, the MTSA regulations apply to large passenger ships, tankers, barges, cargo, and towing vessels, offshore oil and gas platforms, and ports that handle hazardous cargo and service the types of vessel identified in the MTSA. In addition, the MTSA requires Area Maritime Security Committees be located in all of the nation's ports to coordinate activities of relevant federal, state, and local agencies; industry; and the boating public (U.S. Coast Guard, 2007).

Subsequent to the passage of the MTSA of 2002, Congress enacted the **Security and Accountability for Every (SAFE) Port Act of 2006**. The Act is designed to make maritime commercial transportation more secure. It requires implementation of an international, multilayered approach to cargo-screening and security that includes automated container-tracking systems as well as deployment of nuclear and radiological detection systems at all U.S. ports. The SAFE Port Act works in conjunction with the Customs–Trade Partnership against Terrorism (C–TPAT), which is designed to enhance global supply-chain security under the supervision of CBP (Hammons, 2007).

CRITICAL INFRASTRUCTURE SECURITY

Critical infrastructure includes those publicly and privately controlled resources and assets that are deemed most critical to national public health and safety, governance, economic and national security, and maintaining public confidence.

Infrastructure Sectors

The U.S. DHS identified 17 critical infrastructure sectors that require protective actions to prepare for, or mitigate against, a terrorist attack or other hazards. These sectors are

- agriculture and food
- banking and finance
- chemicals
- commercial facilities
- commercial nuclear reactors, including materials and waste
- dams
- the defense industrial base
- drinking water and water treatment systems
- emergency services
- energy
- government facilities
- information technology

- national monuments and icons
- postal and shipping services
- public health and health care
- telecommunications
- transportation systems including mass transit, aviation, maritime, ground or surface transport, rail, and pipeline systems.

Sector-Specific Security Plans

The vast majority of the nation's critical infrastructure is owned and operated by private industry. In support of the National Infrastructure Protection Plan (NIPP), sector-specific plans (SSPs) define roles and responsibilities, catalog existing security authorities, institutionalize already existing security partnerships, and establish the strategic objectives required to achieve a level of risk-reduction appropriate to each individual sector. Each SSP also establishes a sector-specific risk-reduction consultative network to exchange best practices and facilitate rapid threat-based information sharing among the federal, state, local, tribal, and private sectors. Strategic objectives include the following:

- Protecting critical sector assets, systems, networks, and functions prior to a terrorist attack or natural disaster.
- Rapidly reconstituting critical assets, systems, and networks after an incident.
- Planning for emergencies and updating response plans.
- Ensuring timely, relevant, and accurate threat information sharing among the law enforcement and intelligence communities and key decision makers in the sector.
- Educating stakeholders on infrastructure resiliency and risk management practices.

The NIPP and SSPs were developed through a collaborative process involving federal sector-specific agencies; private-sector owners and operators; state, local, and tribal entities; and other security partners (U.S. Department of Homeland Security, Office of the Press Secretary, 2007).

A catastrophic event in Minneapolis, Minnesota, on August 1, 2007, highlighted the need to maintain critical infrastructure in the United States. During the evening rush hour, the Interstate 35W bridge in downtown Minneapolis collapsed into the Mississippi River, resulting in several deaths and nearly 100 injuries. As early as 1990, the bridge was rated as structurally deficient. The bridge collapse focused attention on aging infrastructure. Many bridges and dams as well as water, power, and sewer systems in the United States are aging and badly in need of repair or replacement.

Another disaster on September 9, 2010, revealed the dangers of gas pipelines. Early that evening, in San Bruno, California (a suburb of San Francisco), a 30-inch diameter steel natural gas pipeline owned by Pacific Gas & Electric (PG&E) exploded in a residential neighborhood 2 miles west of San Francisco International Airport. Some people initially believed that an earthquake had struck or that a large airplane from the airport had crashed. The explosion killed eight people and had an impact similar to a 1.1-magnitude earthquake. Those who witnessed the initial blast reported seeing a wall of fire more than 1,000 feet high.

On January 3, 2011, the National Transportation Safety Board (NTSB) issued urgent safety recommendations as a result of preliminary findings from its investigation of the San Bruno rupture. The NTSB directed PG&E to search for "traceable, verifiable, and complete" records relating to pipeline-system components for which hydrostatic pressure testing had not yet established maximum allowable operating pressure (MAOP) and to use these records to determine valid MAOP based on the weakest section of pipeline.

The NTSB also asked the California Public Utilities Commission (CPUC) and the DOT's Pipeline Hazardous Materials Safety Association (PHMSA) to immediately inform other pipeline operators of the circumstances of the San Bruno rupture so they can proactively implement corrective measures appropriate for their systems. In the wake of the pipeline rupture in San Bruno, such measures are critical to ensuring public safety, especially for pipelines that were grandfathered—allowed to remain in use as long as they met code for a previous time. Operators of systems with numerous grandfathered pipelines must now take steps to ensure that these lines can continue to be operated safely moving forward (Menzie, 2011).

A QUICK SURVEY

Which of the following infrastructure sectors has a significant presence in the state where you are currently living? Check all that apply.

- Agriculture and food
- Banking and finance
- Chemicals
- Commercial facilities
- Commercial nuclear reactors, including materials and waste
- Dams
- The defense industrial base
- Drinking water and water treatment systems
- Emergency services
- Energy
- Government facilities
- Information technology
- National monuments and icons
- Postal and shipping services
- Public health and health care
- Telecommunications
- Transportation systems including mass transit, aviation, maritime, ground or surface transport, rail, and pipeline systems

Select one of the infrastructure sectors that you checked. How vulnerable is this sector to terrorist attacks or other hazards? What is currently being done, by whom, to ensure security in this sector? In your view, what (if anything) could be done differently to improve security in this sector?

The Utility Industry

The utility industry faces extremely diverse security and access control challenges, especially in the aftermath of 9/11. Major urban utility administrative facilities, remote production and transfer facilities, massive infrastructure, and unprotected personnel in the field create enormous exposure. Administrative buildings must be protected because they house corporate offices, financial centers, data systems, human resources, and customer centers. Access control and protection of remote facilities, power lines, and gas and water pipes are difficult. In addition, most utility company personnel are in the field, installing, servicing, and maintaining the utility's infrastructure.

The field of utility security can be traced to World War II when the protection of utilities against sabotage and direct attack was considered vital to the war defense effort. Utility facilities were protected by armed troops. Today, even though government troops are not employed, utilities are considered vital to national security and comprehensive security programs have been implemented to protect this valuable infrastructure.

Without adequate water supplies, sewage systems, natural gas, and electric power, an industrialized society cannot function. Modern economies, and the people who live and work within them, depend on (and often take for granted) the services provided by private and public utility companies. Coal, oil, gas, and hydro- and nuclear-powered electricity-generating facilities, transmission lines and transformer substations, sewage treatment plants, reservoirs, pipelines, and gas wells make up an elaborate system a modern nation needs to survive.

Utility operations often cover vast areas and serve millions of people. In the lower 48 states, a national electric power grid is divided into three independently operated regions: east, west, and Texas. Each region is subdivided into smaller units and electric power is traded between units. The western power grid alone serves 65 million customers in 14 states, 2 Canadian provinces, and parts of Mexico.

Security threats to utility providers and their facilities include natural disasters, accidents, employee theft of tools and time, vandalism to substations, trespassing, robbery at utility payment collection centers, theft of copper wiring stripped out of overhead power lines, energy theft by circumventing meters, and terrorism. Human and animal attacks on field meter readers and collection agents are also potential problems. On October 24, 1997, sabotage was blamed for an outage that cut electric power to San Francisco's downtown area. The blackout stopped clocks, elevators, and traffic signals. Entire neighborhoods lacked public transportation because the city's bus system is powered by electricity.

Increased demand for electricity can strain power grids. More electricity is being consumed and few generating plants are under construction to keep up with the demand. During the summer of 2000, the national electric power system, already strained from increased demand to supply computers and the high-tech industry, became overloaded when a heat wave engulfed the United States. Beginning in the fall of 2000, the demand for electricity exceeded supply, forcing prices to increase and resulting in blackouts in some areas, especially California (K. Green, 2000; Mendel, 2001; J. N. Smith, 2000).

Operators of the 103 nuclear power facilities in the United States have been cautioned to remain especially vigilant to any suspicious activity that could signal the possibility of a terrorist attack. The FBI warned that people observed taking photographs or flying aircraft close to a nuclear facility could pose potential threats. The federal government, through the U.S. Nuclear Regulatory Commission, has also increased the training requirements for nuclear facility security personnel, and it has mandated additional classified security measures to protect facilities against sabotage and terrorist attacks ("FBI issues alert to nuclear plant operators," 2003; U.S. Nuclear Regulatory Commission, 2007).

Economic loss, injuries, and deaths may be prevented through the use of policies, procedures, and measures designed to protect utility company property, employees, and customers. Effective use of appropriate physical, personnel, and operations security techniques may also reduce the impact of a negative event. Specific **utility security measures** employed by utility providers include the following:

- Losses due to natural disasters are reduced through the establishment of emergency preparedness plans, the development of redundant systems and procedures for rapid recovery from a disaster.
- Accident prevention programs are developed and implemented. Employee training and protective equipment are necessary ingredients to an effective program.

Losses in the utility industry may be prevented or reduced through the use of appropriate policies, procedures, and measures designed to protect people and property.
(Photo courtesy of Wackenhut Corporation.)

- Company tools and equipment are subject to detailed inventory control. A major utility company was able to reduce losses due to employee theft by instituting a tool loan program for employees.
- Vandalism at substations is reduced through the installation of conspicuous surveillance cameras.
- Robbery at payment collection centers is reduced by limiting the amount of cash on hand and encouraging the use of the mail and electronic funds transfers from checking and savings accounts for bill payment.
- Energy theft is reduced or eliminated by monitoring energy usage and comparing the recorded usage at a specific site to comparable norms at similar sites.
- Meter readers are trained to avoid confrontational situations and are skilled in conflict de-escalation techniques.
- Terrorism may be prevented through increased vigilance, target hardening, and improved training for security personnel.

Effective utility security is critical to the protection of persons and property. In health care facilities as well as some critical industries and government operations, life can be preserved and property loss minimized when emergency backup utility sources are available. Loss of electric power and inadequate water supplies can lead to injuries, death, expensive downtime, and threats to national security, safety, and the environment.

Summary

The notion of homeland security encompasses a wide range of public and private organizational activities designed to prevent and respond to events such as acts of terrorism, disasters, and pandemics. The concept of homeland security evolved throughout the nation's history as the national (federal) government assumed an expanded role in homeland defense, especially since the terrorist acts of September 11, 2001.

Homeland security involves protection and recovery from transnational criminal acts, detonation of WMDs, natural and environmental disasters, major epidemics, and other catastrophic events. Subsequent to 9/11, increased emphasis was placed on the prevention of terrorism. A major overhaul of the federal government led to the creation of the U.S. DHS. A major focus of the DHS is the protection of airlines and airports, transportation systems, and cargo as well as the nation's critical infrastructure.

Key Terms

9/11 Commission
Aviation and Transportation
    Security Act of 2001
Bioterrorism Act of 2002
cargo
cargo security measures
critical infrastructure
environmental crime
Environmental Protection
    Agency (EPA)
Federal Aviation Administration
    (FAA)
Federal Motor Carrier Safety
    Administration (FMCSA)
Federal Railroad Administration
    (FRA)
FEMA
Foreign Intelligence Surveillance
    Act (FISA) of 1978
fusion centers

Homeland Security Act of 2002
Hurricane Katrina
Intelligence Reform and
    Terrorism Prevention Act of
    2004
Maritime Transportation
    Security Act (MTSA) of 2002
National Cargo Security Council
    (NCSC)
National Commission on
    Terrorist Attacks Upon the
    United States
pandemic
passenger profiling techniques
Post-Katrina Emergency Reform
    Act of 2006
REAL ID Act of 2005
Security and Accountability
    for Every (SAFE) Port Act
    of 2006

Support Anti-Terrorism
    by Fostering Effective
    Technologies Act (SAFETY
    Act) of 2002
terrorism
transborder
TSA
U.S. DHS
USA PATRIOT (Uniting and
    Strengthening America by
    Providing Appropriate Tools
    Required to Intercept and
    Obstruct Terrorism) Act of
    2001
USA PATRIOT Act
    Improvement and
    Reauthorization Act of 2005
utility security measures

Discussion Questions and Exercises

1. Define terrorism.
2. Discuss homeland security from a history perspective.
3. Identify threats to homeland security and develop a protection strategy for each threat identified.
4. Is counterterrorism the responsibility of public law enforcement? If so, to what extent?

5. Are organizations and individuals other than public law enforcement responsible for the prevention of terrorist acts?
6. What impact might centralization of the U.S. intelligence functions have on individual rights and civil liberties?
7. Analyze the findings of the 9/11 Commission.

YOUR TURN: Spotting Potential Terrorist Activity

The NSI sets up fusion centers where reports of suspicious activities made by citizens and local police can be collected and analyzed. Authorities depend on ordinary citizens to provide reports. With fusion centers in mind, consider the following scenario and questions.

Miguel works in an agricultural supply store. One day, he notices a young man purchasing a ton of ammonium nitrate fertilizer from the store. He has never seen this individual in the store. Later that week, Miguel is socializing at a bar with friends. Carla, a friend who works at a nearby raceway, mentions seeing someone purchasing large quantities of racing fuel. Carla's story reminds Miguel of the man he saw in the farm store, and he says, "I guess some people have big gardens, and some are really into racing." Carla says, "It's funny that we both saw someone doing something unusual." Another friend remarks, "Well, it ain't illegal to buy fertilizer or fuel."

The following week, while running errands in the city, Miguel walks by a used car sitting vacant near a large civic center. The building has a banner advertising an upcoming performance by a famous rock band. He makes a special note of the car because it reminds him of a model that his older brother owned several years ago. And he reminds himself to try to get tickets to the concert, because the band is so popular that he expects tickets to sell out. A few days later, Miguel is in the city again. He sees the same used car, still sitting in the same place.

1. Does any of the three activities Miguel has noticed and heard about strike you as indicating potential terrorist plans in the works? Why or why not?
2. If you learned that all three activities were carried out by the same individual, would you be more or less likely to conclude that Miguel and his friends have observed potential terrorist planning in action? Explain your response.
3. Is there anything in Miguel's conversation with his friends at the bar that suggests an opportunity for them to share knowledge and thus build more collective insight into the behaviors they have observed? (Hint: What information do Miguel and Carla possess in common that, if shared, could shed additional light on the situation?)
4. If you believe that one or more of the activities observed by Miguel and his friends suggest possible terrorist plans, how would you advise these individuals to report the activities in question? To whom should they report the activities?

Postscript: In 1995, a young man bought a ton of ammonium nitrate fertilizer from a farm supply store. Later, he went to a raceway and purchased large quantities of racing fuel. Still later, he bought a used car and left it parked for several days near a nondescript federal building. None of these activities was illegal, and each went unreported. The young man who carried out each of these activities was Timothy McVeigh—the domestic terrorist responsible for the April 1995 attack in Oklahoma City that killed 168 people and wounded hundreds more ("Calling all eyes," 2010).

PART FIVE

Trends and Challenges

This section considers critical developments in the realm of security as well as challenges facing the security profession.Chapter 13 provides practical suggestions for developing a resume and examines career opportunities for security professionals today in a wide range of disciplines. Chapter 14 looks ahead to the future, anticipating developments in key areas including the security profession, legislative trends, terrorism, and the march of globalization.

CHAPTER 13

Career Opportunities

LEARNING OBJECTIVES

After completing this chapter, the reader should be able to

- identify career opportunities in security.
- describe the preparation necessary for a career in security.
- explore career streams in security services.

INTRODUCTION

Numerous security disciplines and occupational specialties are discussed in this book. All provide career opportunities for entry-level workers as well as seasoned professionals. Salaries are competitive compared with those of other business-related and public safety occupations. The image and reality of the security officer earning minimum wage is destined to history. The growth of security services, coupled with increased awareness of the value of security, is a prescription for excellent career options.

Salaries for many security professionals can exceed $100,000 annually. The median compensation for security professionals in the United States increased 6 percent from 2009 to 2010, to $93,000. Those who have a Certified Protection Professional (CPP) certification can earn a median salary of $118,000. The year 2010 marks a continuation of a 5-year trend in which average compensation for salaried security professionals has risen 19 percent, from $88,000 in 2006 to the current $108,000 (ASIS International, 2010) (see "U.S. Security Salary Survey Results: 2010").

SECURITY SPOTLIGHT

Arrange an informational interview with someone who has established a career in a security discipline that interests you. Keep the interview short—no more than half an hour—to respect the person's time. During your conversation with the interviewee, get as detailed a sense as possible of the job. For instance, ask questions such as "What do you like most about the work? least?" "What steps would you recommend I take to build a career in this security discipline?" "What opportunities for growth does a career in this discipline offer?"

U.S. Security Salary Survey Results: 2010

Findings from the ASIS International 2010 "U.S. Security Salary Survey Results" include the following:

- Salaries of those at the bottom-rung of earners—those in the 10th percentile—rose from $46,000 in 2009 to $52,000 in 2010, and those at the top of the scale—the 90th percentile—saw their compensation increase from $163,000 to $180,000.
- The Mid-Atlantic region continues to offer the security jobs with the highest compensation ($105,000 median), up 5 percent from 2009. Conversely, the Mountain and East South Central regions offer the lowest rates of compensation, and unlike every other region in which compensation rose, these regions show stagnant or dropping wages.
- Information and Natural Resources and Mining tied for the highest average compensation. However, the Information sector saw the greatest increase with an average salary of $142,000, up 30 percent from 2009. Natural Resources and Mining, with an average salary of $142,000, suffered a 10 percent drop from 2009 average compensation levels of $151,000.
- Federal government and law enforcement employees report an average salary of $114,000, and the highest median salary of any sector at $101,000.
- Thirty-nine percent of this year's respondents are top-level security professionals at their organization; this group earns an average salary of $123,000 and a median salary of $100,000.
- Holding a core industry certification correlates to compensation substantially higher than the salaries of peers with no certification. Those holding the CPP certification, administered by ASIS, for example, report an average compensation of $118,000, 18 percent higher than 2009, and a median salary of $100,000. Those with no certification reported an average compensation of $100,000 and a median salary of $85,000.
- Education also correlates with compensation. Thirty-one percent of respondents hold a master's degree and report a median compensation of $122,000.

Source: ASIS International, 2010.

Employers seek individuals with clear records and excellent human relations and communications skills.
(Photo courtesy of StockLite/Shutterstock.com.)

Further, the number of opportunities in security-related employment far exceeds those in public law enforcement. In addition, positions in security are not subject to the same age and disability restrictions found in public policing. In security, employment is based on one's ability to perform, and most career specialties do not require performance of strenuous physical tasks. Value is attached to the employee's ability to think critically, identify and solve problems, and exercise effective judgment. Opportunities abound for women, minorities, and the physically challenged as well as those interested in fields such as business, health care, hospitality, public safety, computer science, sales, information protection, and human resources (see "Career Suggestions for Female Security Professionals" and "Portrait of a Female Security Professional").

Career Suggestions for Female Security Professionals

In October 2010, the ASIS International CSO Roundtable's Preseminar Intensive offered suggestions for how women in the security profession can succeed in their careers. The suggestions are applicable to men as well as women. Ideas included the following:

- Do not be afraid to engage in self-promotion. Accept that you need to broadcast your skills and accomplishments to get recognition and promotions.
- Be self-promotive in the company where you are employed and outside of it. Let people know about your contributions and skills.
- How you promote yourself is important. Do not present yourself in an overly aggressive or obviously self-serving manner. For example, rather than telling your boss's boss that "I worked all weekend to make sure that the company didn't end up on the front page of the newspaper," say, "We dodged a bullet the other day, but we became aware of the situation and we worked to correct it." In this way, you stress that you are a team player who is bringing value to the organization.
- Project confidence, say what you need to say, and then stop.
- Externally, take advantages of opportunities to network, volunteer, and make yourself a "thought leader" in the industry. Participate in LinkedIn's forums.
- Always project professionalism. It is the key element in getting noticed in a positive way. You give the impression that you are someone valuable who can add to the organization.
- Be confident, but not cocky. Be assertive but not aggressive. Stay composed under pressure; you will inspire confidence in others.
- Communicate effectively in writing and in presentations.
- Find a mentor within your company whom you can consult, and mentor others in return.

Source: Longmore-Etheridge, 2010.

Portrait of a Female Security Professional

Although security has not traditionally been a sector that most women considered for their careers, the landscape has shifted dramatically. Security is attracting a diverse population of employees today, including women. The following is a profile of a female security professional. Her experience and insights offer valuable insights for other women considering a career in security.

Bonnie Michelman, CPP, CHPA, Director of Police, Security and Outside Services for Massachusetts General Hospital, has over two decades of security management experience in diverse industries and oversees 300 security professionals. Although her male colleagues have been overwhelmingly supportive, Michelman says, "There are times being a woman in this particular field feels like being a minority." But she believes there's an upside to working in an industry where you have to prove yourself, however unfairly, to your colleagues: it can light a fire inside. "Anyone who is a minority in an industry—whether you are a male nurse working with female peers or a female security professional working among all males—tends to work much harder to be successful," she says.

She's also seen the makeup of the security profession change drastically during her career. "There are many more women in the security sector today, than when I entered the sector over 20 years ago," Michelman says. But nevertheless, she decided to see herself as an individual not as a woman. "When you demonstrate your credibility in your profession, whether you are male or female, young or old, minority or majority, people respond favorably," she says. However, there have been challenges along the way.

Michelman earned a master's in business administration as well as a master's in criminal justice and is a CPP and a Certified Healthcare Protection Administrator. She also served as president and chairman of the Board of ASIS International and currently serves as president of the International Association for Healthcare Security and Safety (IAHSS). An instructor at Northeastern University's College of Criminal Justice, Michelman cites a "strong education including ongoing specialized security focused education, networking, and willingness to take on additional responsibility" as key drivers for women looking to be successful in security.

Source: Lanfranchi, 2011.

CAREER PREPARATION

In terms of **career preparation**, employers expect applicants for security positions to be free of felony and most misdemeanor convictions, possess a good driving record and credit history, demonstrate excellent human relations and communications skills, and be clear of illegal drug use and substance abuse issues. Educationally, most entry-level operations positions require a high school diploma but many demand a college degree. As discussed in Chapter 8, entry-level management positions often require the possession of an associate degree. Most mid- to upper-level management positions require the applicant to hold a bachelor's degree or higher. Except for positions requiring specific technical expertise, degrees in security management and business are preferred.

Learn more about colleges and universities that offer security education programs through ASIS International at www.asisonline.org/education/academicresources.

Resume Preparation Dos

The resume is one of the most important documents in a job search. For the applicant, the resume is a self-marketing tool used to make a first impression worthy of a job interview. For the employer, the resume is a preemployment screening device that is reviewed in less than a minute. Consider the following guidelines when creating a resume.

- Review sample resume formats available at college career centers, in books, and online.
- Limit the resume to one page, if possible. Do not go beyond two pages.
- Use a simple resume design, with bulleted items that are reader-friendly.
- Include detailed contact information (full name, address, a phone number [e.g., cell phone number], email address).

- Include a summary of qualifications.
- List education and training in reverse chronological order with name of college/university/institution, city/state, degree/diploma earned, graduation year, if within the last 15 years. Do not list your high school.
- List your previous employers, within the last 15 years, in reverse chronological order and include the title/rank/position occupied, name of employer, city and state, and dates of employment. List your accomplishments rather than mundane job responsibilities.
- List technical skills (writing, computer, investigative).
- Emphasize transferable skills (leadership, problem solving, communications, research, human relations, language, computer, technical).
- List volunteer service/community activities/awards and honors received.
- Use action verbs (planned, directed, analyzed, collaborated, investigated, designed, authored, budgeted, facilitated) to describe skills and accomplishments.
- Proofread the resume yourself and obtain another person's critique of it.
- Print the resume on high-quality resume paper. Select a neutral color (white or ivory). Envelopes should match the paper.

Resume Preparation Don'ts

- Avoid the verb *work* when describing accomplishments. Everyone works. Use substitute verbs, that is, *developed*.
- Do not list too much experience. The last 15 years will suffice.
- Do not include age, weight, height, date or place of birth, marital status, gender, race, health, social security number, reasons for leaving previous employers, photos, names and contact information of former supervisors, salary information, religious or political affiliation, the title *Resume*, hobbies, or any other controversial or irrelevant information.
- Do not list references on the resume.
- Do not include the phrase *References available upon request*. It is understood that applicants will provide references if requested.
- Do not list an unprofessional email address. For example, an email address that contains sexually oriented language (e.g., hotbody) is not appropriate.
- Above all, the job seeker should not present false or misleading information in a resume. Employers search for honest people, especially in security and other public safety occupations. Common resume and application fabrications include degrees not earned, colleges never attended, inflated grade point averages, diplomas from nonaccredited institutions, inflated job titles and salaries earned, incorrect dates of employment, reasons for leaving previous employment, and exaggerated accomplishments (Challenger, 2007; Hansen, 2007).

SECURITY SPOTLIGHT

Identify an organization that interests you as a potential employer. Visit the organization's website to see whether the organization has any security-related job openings. Learn as much as you can about the requirements for the vacant positions. Identify strategies for structuring and formatting your resume in ways that could enhance your chances of being called for an interview for one or more of the vacant positions.

CAREER OPPORTUNITIES

As one of the largest and fastest growing occupations, security offers a wide range of employment opportunities in government and the private sector. Jobs in the public sector have grown tremendously in the aftermath of 9/11. Further, every private business, large or small, is concerned with the prevention of crime, accidents, fire, and damage from natural and environmental disasters. The security field encompasses a broad range of disciplines including but certainly not limited to physical, personnel, information, and homeland security as well as critical infrastructure protection. The following specialties represent a sample of security career opportunities. Annual salaries for most of the security specialties listed are entry-level. Salaries for mid-level and top managers are much higher.

Airport/Airline Security

Commercial aviation security has grown tremendously since the events of September 11, 2001. U.S. Transportation Security Administration (TSA) employees now screen passengers and luggage at over 450 airport locations nationwide. Entry-level qualifications for TSA jobs include a high school diploma or equivalent, basic aptitudes and physical abilities, a command of the English language, and U.S. citizenship. The entry-level salary range is approximately $25,000 to $44,000. Career opportunities within the TSA are excellent. Federal air marshals can earn $40,000 to over $84,000 per year, not including overtime pay. TSA directors of security at airports can earn over $150,000 annually. Security career opportunities also exist within the airlines themselves.

> Learn more about employment opportunities with the TSA at www.tsa.gov.

Banking/Financial Services Security

Security positions within the financial services industry (retail banking, credit companies, mortgage lending, insurance companies, stock brokerage firms) typically require a bachelor's degree in business, finance, or security management. Entry-level salaries range from $35,000 to $65,000. Mid-level managers earn $40,000 to $100,000 annually.

Contract Services

Almost any security service provided through a proprietary (in-house) security organization or unit can be provided through a contract security company. Security vendors offer a wide range of personnel, equipment, and services including security officers, patrol, armored car, alarm systems, surveillance, investigations, and consulting. Due to competition, entry-level wages for most unarmed contract security officers is $10 to $15 per hour. However, contract security managers earn higher salaries. Regional managers and contract service sales personnel can earn well over $100,000 per year.

Computer/Information Security

The advent of computer science, the Internet, and electronic data processing have created a need for computer and information security specialists. Entry-level positions typically require a bachelor's degree in computer science. The average annual salary is $125,000.

Casino/Gaming Security

Casino and gaming security personnel provide traditional security services such as the protection of people and property. They also engage in sophisticated surveillance activities within casino and gaming establishments. Entry-level salaries range from $17,000 to $32,000, depending on location and qualifications. The salary for management-level positions can exceed $100,000 annually.

Chief Security Officer

Many large corporations employ a **chief security officer (CSO)**. The CSO's position (rank) within the organization is similar to the corporation's chief financial officer (CFO). CSOs often hold the title of vice president for security, loss prevention, or asset protection. CSOs are responsible and accountable for a wide range of activities. They

- develop and implement loss prevention strategy.
- gather information and assess risk.
- engage in organizational preparedness.
- prevent and respond to major incidents.
- manage disaster recovery efforts.
- coordinate with those responsible for investor and government relations, public affairs, and core business activities.
- protect people, physical and information assets, and organizational reputation.

Chief security officer positions typically require a bachelor's degree or higher in security management or business. In addition, CSOs must possess broad-based knowledge, skills, and abilities. They must be able to

- develop and maintain professional relationships.
- demonstrate exceptional leadership and management abilities.
- provide security-related subject-matter expertise.
- function as a team member.
- anticipate, recognize, and appraise security-related risks.
- think creatively and solve problems, using high-quality analytical skills.
- effectively communicate recommended courses of action.
- demonstrate integrity.
- adjust and respond rapidly to changing conditions.

Compensation potential is high. As discussed in Chapter 1, CSOs may earn up to $400,000 annually.

Educational Institution Security

A wide range of employment opportunities exist in elementary, secondary, and postsecondary educational institutions. Most school and college campus security operations provide traditional security services. Others employ sworn peace officers. Salaries range from $20,000 to over $60,000, depending on training and licensing requirements.

Health Care Security

Health care is one of the largest industries in the United States. Employment opportunities exist in hospitals, clinics, long-term care facilities, nursing homes, and emergency medical services. The work environment focuses on patient protection, service, employee safety, securing controlled substances, emergency management, and disaster recovery. Entry-level salaries range from $30,000 to $50,000, depending on qualifications required and location. The average annual salary for health care security managers is over $80,000.

Hospitality Security

Hospitality is big business. Lodging establishments, restaurant chains, cruise-ship lines, and theme parks must protect guests, employees, and property. As baby boomers retire, career opportunities are likely to expand. The entry-level salary range is $35,000 to $50,000. The average annual salary for hospitality security managers is nearly $75,000.

Industrial Security

Industrial security professionals protect a wide range of manufacturing and government contractor facilities. Government contractors must protect classified information in accordance with the National Industrial Security Program (NISP). Entry-level industrial security managers typically possess a college degree and earn between $55,000 and $75,000. The average annual salary for executive-level industrial security managers is over $100,000.

Learn more about security careers with the U.S. government through the U.S. Department of Homeland Security at www.usajobs.opm.gov.

Investigations

Investigators are employed within large proprietary security organizations and under contract as private investigators. Entry-level qualifications for proprietary investigators typically include some experience and an associate degree in security or criminal justice. The salary range is $40,000 to $55,000 annually. A **licensed private investigator (PI)** or private detective may earn $50 to over $500 per hour, depending on location and the market for PI services. Licensing requirements differ substantially among the states. In California, a person is not eligible for a PI license until the applicant has acquired a minimum of 6,000 hours of investigative experience over a 3-year period, working as an intern under the supervision of a licensee. Interns are typically paid $10 to $30 per hour, plus expenses. In addition, the license applicant must successfully complete a written licensing exam.

Museum and Library Security

Museums and libraries contain works of art, historical artifacts, archives, rare books, and other valuable and culturally significant items. Many museums and libraries also host major events. Entry-level security management positions typically require an associate degree in security services and pay $30,000 to $45,000 annually, depending on location and type of property.

Learn more about security careers through ASIS International at www.asisonline.org/careercenter/index.xml.

Residential/Commercial Real Estate Security

Office facilities, high-rise buildings, apartment and condominium complexes, as well as gated communities provide ample career opportunities for the public relations–oriented security person. Real estate security professionals maintain liaison with public safety agencies, monitor security alarm and surveillance systems, and protect vulnerable people and assets. The salary range for entry-level positions is $20,000 to $35,000. Entry-level supervisors may earn $40,000 to $50,000.

Retail Loss Prevention

Retail loss prevention personnel perform a wide range of tasks. Contrary to common belief, they do not spend most of their time apprehending shoplifters. In fact, studies reveal that most retail losses due to theft are internal rather than external in nature. Loss prevention agents are involved with the prevention and investigation of shoplifting. However, they also focus on employee theft and accidents as well as losses from other sources. They conduct audits and investigations. Many corporate loss prevention directors begin their careers as part-time store detectives while still in college. Entry-level salaries range from $25,000 to $50,000 depending on location, duties, and qualifications. Corporate loss prevention directors of large retail chain store operations may earn in excess of $200,000 annually.

Learn more about careers in retail loss prevention at www.lpjobs.com.

Security Sales and Service

Sales of security products and services as well as the installation, service, and repair of security equipment can be financially rewarding. Sales personnel employed by large security equipment manufacturers and contract security companies can earn a combined base salary and bonuses well in excess of $100,000 per year. In addition, technicians who install, program, service, and repair sophisticated security alarm surveillance and access control systems are highly valued and well compensated.

Systems Design and Engineering

In the past, security concepts and systems were applied to facilities after buildings were constructed, a process often referred to as *retrofitting*. However, retrofitting can be extremely expensive. Using the concepts of crime prevention through environmental design (CPTED), wise facility planners design security features into a facility before it is constructed or renovated. As time passes, more engineers and architects trained in CPTED are incorporating physical and electronic security measures into new construction and renovation plans. Security **systems design and engineering** positions typically require a bachelor's degree or higher. Salaries are commensurate with other engineering and architecture professionals.

Transportation Security

Virtually all forms of transportation employ security professionals. In addition to airports and airlines discussed earlier, railroads, trucking and maritime companies, and public transit systems utilize security personnel to protect cargo, passengers, employees, and physical assets.

Many security managers are responsible for facilities management and are involved with security systems design. *(Photo courtesy of Andresr/Shutterstock.com.)*

The entry-level salary range is $30,000 to $50,000. The average annual compensation for transportation security managers is over $100,000.

Utility Security

As discussed in Chapter 12, utility security involves the protection of critical infrastructure such as oil, natural gas, water, electric and sewer lines, as well as conventional and nuclear electricity generation facilities. Nuclear power plants are protected by proprietary and contract security personnel who receive extensive training and are armed with a variety of weapons. Salaries range from $30,000 to $70,000 annually, depending on qualifications and level of responsibility. On average, utility security managers earn in excess of $100,000 annually (ASIS International, 2005; Fischer & Green, 2008; LPjobs.com, 2007; Moran, 2007).

A QUICK SURVEY

Which of the following disciplines seems most interesting to you in terms of building a career in security? Check all that apply.

- Airport/airline
- Banking/financial services
- Computer/information
- Casino/gaming
- Education
- Health care
- Hospitality
- Industrial
- Investigations
- Museum and library
- Residential/commercial real estate
- Retail loss prevention
- Security sales and service
- Systems design and engineering
- Transportation
- Utilities

What interests you most about the disciplines you checked? What do you see as the unique challenges presented by each of the disciplines you checked?

Summary

With the tremendous growth in security services, career opportunities have increased dramatically. No longer confined to near-minimum wage, security personnel earn salaries that are competitive with other technical and professional occupations. The security industry is interdisciplinary and multifaceted, with abundant employment opportunities available in a wide range of disciplines and specialties.

Key Terms

career preparation
chief security officer (CSO)

licensed private investigator

systems design and engineering

Discussion Questions and Exercises

1. Generally, what are the prerequisites for employment in security services?
2. Utilizing Internet resources identified in this chapter, explore a security career stream of your choosing.
3. What security employment opportunities are available in your area?
4. Using guidelines presented in this chapter, create a resume.

YOUR TURN: Analyzing Careers in Security

Brad, a college classmate of the author, had his heart set on a special agent's position with the U.S. Secret Service. A Vietnam veteran and former U.S. Army officer, Brad completed requirements for a master's degree, scored high on the U.S. Secret Service entrance exam, interviewed well, passed his government background investigation, and was placed on the agency's list of special agent hopefuls. Although Brad was preapproved for employment, the Secret Service was not hiring at the moment. To pass the time while waiting for his Secret Service appointment and academy start date, Brad obtained a part-time job as a loss prevention agent in a local department store. Within weeks, Brad was working full-time and was promoted to store loss prevention manager. Within months, Brad became a district loss prevention manager, overseeing security operations at several of the retail chain's stores. Then came the phone call from the U.S. Secret Service. Brad's appointment as a special agent arrived and his academy entrance date was set. Did Brad accept the U.S. government's offer? No. Within a few years, Brad was vice president and director of loss prevention for a major national retail chain, earning three times more than ever possible as a Secret Service agent.

Dillon, a senior border patrol agent, resigned his position with the U.S. Border Patrol long before retirement eligibility to become the vice president of a national contract security firm. Kelly, a seasoned FBI special agent, gave up his FBI position and his government retirement to become the corporate security director of a large multinational electronics manufacturing company. Salaries for Dillon and Kelly almost tripled when they discarded their government jobs in favor of private-sector security positions.

Although their names have been altered slightly, the brief account of the careers of Brad, Dillon, and Kelly are true. All three relinquished secure public law enforcement jobs and government retirement to pursue security management careers.

1. Would you consider a career in security? Why or why not?
2. If you are considering a career in security, select one discipline that you find particularly interesting.
3. What steps could you take to learn more about the opportunities in the security discipline you identified in Question 2?
4. What strategies would you use to pursue the most satisfying position in the security discipline you identified in Question 2?
5. As an occupation, how does security overall differ from public law enforcement?
6. What do you see as the advantages and disadvantages of building a career in security within the public sector? within the private sector? Given your assessment, which sector would interest you most as an area in which to build a career in security?

CHAPTER 14

The Future

LEARNING OBJECTIVES

After completing this chapter, the reader should be able to

- identify and discuss future trends and challenges in security.
- evaluate the impact of globalization on the provision of security services.
- discuss legislative trends in security.
- analyze security's role in counterterrorism efforts.

INTRODUCTION

The 9/11 Commission reported that the September 11, 2001, terrorist attacks revealed failures in imagination, policy, capabilities, and management. Security professionals, as agents of loss *prevention*, cannot afford such failures. Yet security personnel are responsible and accountable for preventing and mitigating damage from a multitude of loss events, doing so with limited resources. The security professional must use imagination to peer into the future to anticipate, recognize, and appraise risks, and to develop policies, capabilities, and management strategies to prevent negative events from materializing.

THE FUTURE OF SECURITY: GROWTH AND CHALLENGES

The security profession has grown tremendously over the last 40 years. Security personnel currently outnumber law enforcement officers by at least three to one. Expenditures for private security are more than double that of public law enforcement. This is in stark contrast to the early 1970s, when the number of personnel and the dollars spent on security services were roughly equivalent to public law enforcement. The growth trend is likely to continue well into the twenty-first century. Many organizations rely heavily on security services. In addition, the responsibilities assumed by asset protection personnel are expanding rapidly. Security person- nel provide vital and unique services to the progressive organization that go beyond traditional uniformed officer presence and enforcement of policies, rules, and regulations. They protect national interests. They gather and disseminate important information for an organization that is not available through any other source. In many organizations, the security professional's responsibilities are expanding to include facilities management. In these organizations, the security professional is responsible for maintenance, landscaping, food service, and numerous other functions that were not a part of the security manager's job description in the past. Thus, security's value-added presence is expanding and becoming more important to an organization's survival (American Society for Industrial Security, 1998; Dalton, 2003; Davidson, 2003; Fischer & Janoski, 2000; Siegel & Senna, 2008; U.S. Department of Justice, Bureau of Justice Assistance, 2005a).

The future holds great promise for security services and for those who wish to pursue a career in asset protection. However, the twenty-first century security professional will also face great **asset protection challenges**. The changing nature of the workplace, ethical considerations, advances in technology, increased diversity, privatization of public services, terrorist activities, and the globalization of business activities will perpetuate the evolution of the security field. Security personnel at all levels must acquire new, more sophisticated skills to compete and demonstrate the competencies necessary to prevent losses in the future. Specialized training, education, and experience in loss prevention will be a necessity rather than a luxury. Traditional security and safety methodology must be supplemented, and in many cases replaced, with radically redesigned loss prevention processes. Security professionals can no longer afford to be satisfied with the status quo, but must think strategically to meet new organizational demands. As part of the executive management team, security professionals are required to operate within an increasingly diverse workforce. Security managers must possess the multidimensional competencies of loss prevention expert, intelligence gatherer, investigator, administrator, visionary planner, financier, resourceful inventor, and effective communicator.

Rapid information exchange and cost effectiveness lie at the heart of all successful contemporary organizations. With many corporations entering the global marketplace, security managers must constantly reevaluate their function's ability to reduce costs, secure the exchange of critical data, and measure performance. Corporate cost-reduction pressures and management's desire to centralize or decentralize control exacerbate challenges to security. In response to these challenges, the security operation must function as other successful groups function in the global economy's information age.

In spite of the challenges, the prospects for growth of security services and products appear promising. The privatization of certain public services, such as jail and prison management, will continue to expand. Security systems integration, security management, and a global security marketplace represent other segments of security services that may experience tremendous growth. Increased use of technology will also be part of the future of security, as will increased collaboration and cooperation between and among business and governmental units. As the security profession becomes even more complex and sophisticated, security managers will be chosen from the ranks of those with specialized training, education, and experience in security services rather than retired law enforcement officers. Security managers are also likely to assume a broader range of responsibilities, as evidenced by position titles that reflect facilities, continuity of operations, and risk management functions. In light of a promising future, the security professional of the twenty-first century is extremely well positioned to make tremendous positive contributions to the world, community, organization, and the profession (Bailin, 2000; Friedman, 2011; Harowitz, 2003; Kovacich & Halibozek, 2003; Maurer, 2000c; Pearson, 2000).

In some security disciplines, organizations may face a challenge in recruiting sufficient numbers of security personnel with the required specialized skills. U.S. cyberspace is one example. Former U.S. Department of Homeland Security (DHS) Secretary Tom Ridge has calculated that there are only about 1,000 security specialists in the United States who have the skills needed to protect U.S. cyberspace. About 30,000 such experts are required. Computer hackers represent a possible source of talent for filling the gap. However, many hackers are unwilling to work for U.S. security agencies because of regulations limiting private individuals' engagement with the federal government. Policies may need to be revised in order to address the talent gap. Additional strategies by the DHS include accelerating university recruitment and attending hacker conventions to enlist talent and observe the latest hacker methods (Rashid, 2011).

IMPACT OF GLOBALIZATION

Technological advances and economic **globalization**—the growing interconnectedness reflected in the expanded flows of information, technology, capital, goods, services, and people throughout the world—have given rise to new challenges for security management. In many areas, economic competition has replaced political and military power. Industry is globalizing, with many American companies conducting business in numerous foreign countries. Approximately 70 percent of every new dollar earned by American corporations has global trade as its source. Competitive pressures have forced many businesses to decentralize, enter global markets, create virtual corporations, and collaborate in joint ventures. This trend creates new business vulnerabilities.

The safety and security of almost all aspects of an organization's property and personnel are affected by globalization. Businesses are threatened with economic espionage, foreign control, executive kidnappings, terrorism, and narcotics trafficking. Conducting business in foreign countries is challenging and can be hazardous. Special attention must be given to the political climate, currency exchange rates, availability of labor, compliance with local laws and international treaties, cultural and language differences, organized crime, personal and executive protection, physical security, and disaster preparedness.

Today's security manager must be able to function in a global, high-technology environment. The world is experiencing fast-paced human evolution as well as some revolutions. Societies are evolving as they confront and experiment with the concepts of terrorism, diversity, human rights, democracy, and commerce in a high-tech information age. With the demise of the Cold War, espionage activities have shifted from the theft of nation-state political secrets to theft of economically significant proprietary information and intellectual property. The political, economic, human, and technological revolutions of the twenty-first century have a tremendous impact on, and can pose tremendous threats to, business and governmental operations. To appropriately confront the ever-changing world order, the security professional must be knowledgeable and understand, appreciate, and manage new world implications and requirements (Badolato, 2000; Kovacich & Halibozek, 2003; Ortmeier & Davis, 2012).

Resistance to Corruption

American companies must mitigate risks as they conduct business in foreign countries. Security professionals in these companies must ensure that personnel do not violate the U.S. **Foreign Corrupt Practices Act (FCPA)**. This federal law prohibits payment of bribes by U.S. companies to foreign government officials. In some countries, bribes are encouraged, even solicited, by officials as a fee for doing business in that country. However, fines of up to $250,000 and/or imprisonment of up to 5 years may be levied against individuals prosecuted and convicted under the Act. According to the law, a bribe or corrupt payment is defined as the fee paid directly to a foreign official to obtain work permits for individuals not otherwise eligible, have a police officer ignore an infraction, win approval of a government contract, have illegal items distributed in the mail, or encourage an official to give special privileges to the American company. The FCPA does not prohibit administrative fees ("grease" payments) designed to expedite an approval or paperwork process.

Problems with the FCPA may be avoided through a strong compliance program. Accurate records must be maintained to document the company's transactions. Background checks on foreign officials and a program of internal controls help prevent violations of the FCPA.

In addition to the business-related challenges posed by globalization, the phenomenon creates numerous challenges for government security and law enforcement operations as well. Not only do commercial, travel, and communications activities span the entire globe, the spread of crime and disease are no longer controlled by international boundaries. Nations and their citizens have become increasingly interdependent. And, although globalization is advantageous in many respects, effectively confronting transnational criminality and numerous negative international political and social issues demands creativity and responses beyond those developed through conventional law enforcement and security means (Adler, Mueller, & Laufer, 2009).

Shifts in Market Trends

Globalization is an overarching mega-trend, a pervasive force that will substantially shape all the other major trends in the future. But the future of globalization is not fixed; states and non–nation-state actors—including private companies and nongovernment organizations—will struggle to shape their contours. Some aspects of globalization, such as the growing global interconnectedness stemming from the information technology (IT) revolution, almost certainly will be irreversible. Yet it is also possible, although unlikely, that the process of globalization could be slowed or even stopped, just as the era of globalization in the late nineteenth and early twentieth centuries was reversed by catastrophic war and global depression.

Barring such a turn of events, the world economy is likely to continue growing impressively: by 2020, it is projected to be about 80 percent larger than it was in 2000, and average per capita income will be roughly 50 percent higher. Of course, there will be cyclical ups and downs and periodic financial or other crises, but this basic growth trajectory has powerful momentum behind it. Most countries around the world, both developed and developing, will benefit from gains in the world economy. By having the fastest-growing consumer markets, more firms becoming world-class multinationals, and greater science and technology stature, Asia looks set to displace Western countries as the focus for international economic dynamism—provided Asia's rapid economic growth continues.

Yet the benefits of globalization will not be global. Rising powers will see exploiting the opportunities afforded by the emerging global marketplace as the best way to assert their great power status on the world stage. In contrast, some now in the First World may see the closing gap with China, India, and others as evidence of a relative decline, even though the older powers are likely to remain global leaders out to 2020. The United States, too, will see its relative power position eroded, though it will remain in 2020 the most important single country across all the dimensions of power. Those left behind in the developing world may resent China and India's rise, especially if they feel squeezed by their growing dominance in key sectors of the global marketplace. And large pockets of poverty will persist even in "winner" countries.

The Spread of Technology

The greatest benefits of globalization will accrue to nations and groups that can access and adopt new technologies. Indeed, a nation's level of technological achievement generally will be defined in terms of its investment in *integrating and applying* the new, globally available technologies—whether the technologies are acquired through a country's own basic research or from technology leaders. The growing two-way flow of high-technology brain power between the developing world and the West, the increasing size of the information computer-literate work force in some developing countries, and efforts by global corporations to diversify their high-technology operations will foster the spread of new technologies. High-technology breakthroughs—such as in genetically modified organisms and increased food production—could provide a safety net eliminating the threat of starvation and ameliorating basic quality-of-life issues for poor countries. But the gap between the haves and have-nots will widen unless the have-not countries pursue policies that support application of new technologies—such as good governance, universal education, and market reforms.

Those countries that pursue such policies could leapfrog stages of development, skipping phases that other high-technology leaders such as the United States and Europe had to traverse in order to advance. China and India are well positioned to become technology leaders, and even the poorest countries will be able to leverage prolific, cheap technologies to fuel—although at a slower rate—their own development.

The expected next revolution in high technology involving the convergence of nano-, bio-, information, and materials technology could further bolster China and India's prospects. Both countries are investing in basic research in these fields and are well placed to be leaders in a number of key fields. Europe risks slipping behind Asia in some of these technological developments. The United States is still in a position to retain its overall lead, although it must increasingly compete with Asia to retain its edge and may lose significant ground in some sectors.

More firms will become global, and those operating in the global arena will be more diverse, both in size and in origin, more Asian and less Western in orientation. Such corporations, encompassing the current, large multinationals, will be increasingly outside the control of any one state and will be key agents of change in dispersing technology widely, further integrating the world economy, and promoting economic progress in the developing world. Their ranks will include a growing number based in countries such as China, India, or Brazil. While North America, Japan, and Europe might collectively continue to dominate international political and financial institutions, globalization will take on an increasingly non-Western character. By 2020, globalization could be equated in the popular mind with a rising Asia, replacing its current association with Americanization.

Competition for Resources

An expanding global economy will increase the demand for many raw materials, such as oil. Probably, the total energy consumed will rise by about 50 percent by 2020 compared to a 34 percent expansion from 1980 to 2000, with a greater share provided by petroleum. Most experts assess that with substantial investment in new capacity, overall energy supplies will be sufficient to meet global demands. But on the supply side, many of the areas that are being counted on to provide increased output—the Caspian Sea, Venezuela, and West Africa—involve substantial political or economic risk. Traditional suppliers in the Middle East are also increasingly unstable. Thus, sharper demand-driven competition for resources, perhaps accompanied by a major disruption of oil supplies, is among the key uncertainties. China, India, and other developing

More offshore drilling for petroleum will provide new security challenges.
(Photo courtesy of markh/Shutterstock.com.)

countries' growing energy needs suggest a growing preoccupation with energy, shaping their foreign policies. For Europe, an increasing preference for natural gas may reinforce regional relationships—such as with Russia or North Africa—given the interdependence of pipeline delivery (National Intelligence Council, 2007a).

SECURITY SPOTLIGHT

To gain a firsthand sense of the impact of globalization, consider all the ways globalization has affected you personally, in the context of security. For example, have you worried about your personal safety while vacationing or working in a country characterized by political instability? Have you purchased a food product that was recalled because it contained unsafe ingredients or toxins originating from an overseas supplier? Has your computer become vulnerable to cyberattacks from distant sources around the world?

LEGISLATIVE TRENDS IN SECURITY

Numerous recent federal and state legislative initiatives address safety and security concerns. As exemplified by lawmaker activity in a number of states, critical issues are being addressed in the areas of security personnel, school security, the use of defibrillators, preemployment screening, identity theft, digital signatures, drug testing, computer security, workplace violence, private prisons, terrorism, closed-circuit television (CCTV), and privacy.

In recent years, legislatures in five states passed laws affecting the requirements, duties, and responsibilities of security personnel. Fifteen states enacted legislation relating to school security. Four of those states passed legislation allowing release of juvenile crime records to school officials. Many states established school security programs. Included were school safety centers that collect information on school-related crime and use the information as the basis for prevention efforts and safety plans. To encourage life-saving efforts, 28 states passed laws granting immunity from liability to individuals and organizations who administer or use defibrillators to revive persons suffering from cardiac arrest. Twelve states passed legislation requiring or expanding pre-employment screening efforts to those employed in public or private schools, day-care centers, and nursing homes. A Colorado law grants immunity to employers who provide derogatory, yet truthful, information to a prospective employer on a former employee's work-related abilities, habits, or grounds for termination.

Several states also enacted legislation criminalizing the use or attempt to use another person's identification or financial information. Seven states, as well as the U.S. Congress, passed laws authorizing the legal use of electronic (digital) signatures in lieu of physically handwritten signatures. New drug-testing laws provide for denial of worker compensation claims and support disciplinary efforts against employees who test positive for drug use. The employee must be given fair written warning of the policy and the drug test must be administered and evaluated according to statutory guidelines. Other laws enacted relate to computer crime, workplace violence, the administration of private prisons, and restrictions on the use of CCTV in areas where the subject has a reasonable expectation to privacy. Numerous other privacy-related laws restrict access to patient medical records and driver license information. Future legislative efforts will continue to focus on school security and workplace violence, as well as on electronic commerce and the future of copyrights, contract law, terrorism, and intellectual property in the electronic domain (Anderson, 2000; Oliver, 2007).

On the federal level, in February 2011, President Barack Obama signed a 3-month extension of several surveillance provisions of the USA PATRIOT Act. The law extends some provisions of the 2001 Act. One provision allows law enforcement officials to set roving wiretaps to monitor multiple communication devices. The other allows them to ask a special court for access to business and library records that could be relevant to a terrorist threat. A third provision gives the FBI court-approved rights for surveillance of non-American suspects not known to be tied to specific terrorist groups. Legislators are debating a multiple-year extension of the provisions, which have been criticized by defenders of privacy rights ("Obama signs temporary extension of Patriot Act," 2011).

The twenty-first century presents new legal challenges for the security management professional. The elimination of, and alterations to, nation-states and societies, the changing nature of the workplace, increased use of high technology, terrorism, and the expansion of global competition help to create an environment in which the legal aspects of security management constantly evolve (Kovacich & Halibozek, 2003; Simonsen & Spindlove, 2007). In response, numerous legislative initiatives, as evidenced by laws associated with subjects such as cybersecurity, counterterrorism, and homeland defense, have been proposed and passed. The progressive, informed, and visionary security manager takes advantage of any opportunity to learn about new laws and their implications.

TERRORISM

The international community's conflict with transnational terrorists will continue in the twenty-first century. To date, some counterterrorism initiatives have experienced relative success. Cooperative international efforts improved border and transportation security, enhanced document security, disrupted terrorist financing, and restricted terrorist activities. Some success with dismantling terrorist organizations and disrupting their leadership has been achieved as well—most notably with the killing of Al Qaeda chief Osama bin Laden in May 2011. Further, a less-permissive operating environment for terrorists has been created. Leaders are kept on the move or in hiding, degrading their ability to plan and launch attacks. Many countries and interagency representatives in key terrorist theaters of operation assess threats and devise counterterrorism strategies, action plans, and policy recommendations.

For example, in March 2011, the European Commission released a review of a U.S. counterterrorism program that aims to track the finances of terrorism suspects. Under the program, U.S. agencies can obtain access to European banking data held by the Society for Worldwide Interbank Financial Telecommunication (SWIFT), which is a cooperative that routes trillions of dollars in transactions between financial institutions, brokerage houses, and stock exchanges. The Commission asked the United States to:

- Make the benefits of the program more transparent, so the public would support it.
- Make other relevant aspects of the program known, such as how much data the United States will access through SWIFT.
- Provide more information about its justifications for requesting information from SWIFT and to make those requests in writing so that European officials can evaluate them.
- Post more information on the U.S. Treasury Department's website about what types of information in SWIFT's database can be corrected, erased, or blocked (Kanter, 2011).

Despite progress in combating terrorism, major challenges remain. For example, several nation-states continue to sponsor terrorism, providing weapons, training, advice, and funding. The appeal and spread of Al Qaeda and radical ideologies continues. As security improves in one area, terrorists target other venues or adapt their methodology to meet changing conditions.

Al Qaeda: From Expeditionary to Guerrilla Strategies

Al Qaeda appears to have made a transition from expeditionary to guerrilla terrorism strategies. In the past, the organization selected and trained terrorists in one country, then clandestinely inserted a team into another country to attack a preplanned objective. The attack on the USS *Cole*, in 2000, and the events of 9/11 are examples of expeditionary terrorist activities. As security improved, the terrorists adapted, and took to training target-country nationals in guerrilla tactics close to the objective. Through intermediaries, web-based propaganda, and subversion of immigrant expatriate populations, terrorist organizations now finance and inspire local groups to carry out attacks. Thus, border security and international funds transfers are circumvented. The Madrid bombing in 2004, the London terrorist attacks of 2005, and additional incidents since then illustrate the guerrilla approach adopted by terrorist organizations.

The new trend represents a shift in the nature of terrorism, from traditional international terrorist activities to transnational non–state-sponsored warfare that resembles a form of global insurgency. New tactics and strategies must be developed to combat this changed form of terrorism. In addition to targeting violent extremist networks and individual terrorists, the new threats demand the application of **counterinsurgency techniques** that focus on protecting, securing, and winning the support of populations at risk of radicalization. Trusted networks of private and government organizations and individuals, along with integrated civil–military measures, are keys to the success of this new approach (U.S. Department of State, 2007).

The National Intelligence Council (NIC) affirms the opinions of other experts regarding the threat of terrorism. The NIC is a center for strategic thinking within the U.S. government that reports to the Director of National Intelligence (DNI) and provides analyses on foreign policy issues to the president and senior policy makers. Periodically, the NIC produces a **National Intelligence Estimate (NIE)**, a forward-looking assessment on national security issues. NIEs are classified intelligence estimates (rather than predictions) that express the composite views of 16 U.S. intelligence agencies. They present intelligence analysts' judgment regarding the capabilities, vulnerabilities, and probable courses of action of foreign groups and nations.

On July 17, 2007, the DNI released an unclassified NIE that assessed the threat of terrorism in the near future. The NIE focused heavily on Al Qaeda, citing the terrorist organization as the most serious continuing threat to the United States. Although worldwide counterterrorism efforts since 9/11 constrained Al Qaeda's ability to attack the U.S. homeland, the group retained its central leadership, continues to plan high-impact events, joins with like-minded groups, and has protected or regenerated key elements of its attack capability. Notably, the NIE assessed that Al Qaeda will probably seek to leverage its contacts and the capabilities of Al Qaeda in Iraq (AQI), its most visible and capable affiliate. The latter helps Al Qaeda energize the broader Muslim extremist community, generate resources, and recruit and indoctrinate operatives for terrorist attacks on the U.S. homeland and elsewhere.

The NIE assessed that Al Qaeda's plots against the U.S. homeland will continue to focus on prominent political, economic, and infrastructure targets with the goal of producing mass casualties, visually dramatic destruction, significant economic aftershocks, and fear among the U.S. population. Al Qaeda is proficient with small conventional weapons and improvised explosive devices but will continue to seek and possibly employ nuclear, biological, chemical, or radiological weapons materials.

Other Terrorist Threats

Besides Al Qaeda, the NIE described other potential threats to the U.S. homeland. The NIE assessed that Lebanese Hizballah, a Shiite Muslim extremist group, will consider attacks against the U.S. homeland if Hizballah perceives the United States to be a direct threat to the group or

Single-issue group protests and terrorist activities may increase.
(Photo courtesy of Catherine Jones/Shutterstock.com.)

Iran. Further, the number of radical, self-generating Muslim extremist groups within the United States and other Western countries is increasing, fueled by anti-American rhetoric presented in the media and on Internet sites. Finally, non-Muslim single-issue groups such as white suprema-cists, anarchists, antiabortion activists, and animal rights groups will probably launch small terrorist attacks within the United States (National Intelligence Council, 2007b).

Experts agree that the shifting nature of terrorism overall presents a major challenge. Individuals and organizations that use terror are mobile and constantly mutating. Thus these enemies have no fixed and definitive identity. Moreover, their methods are blending with those of other organizations: Criminal organizations use terror, and terrorists use the means of criminal organizations. Under these conditions, it is difficult, if not impossible, to combat terrorism by simply compiling lists of individuals or organizations that must be captured, prevented from boarding airplanes, or eliminated. And data that is collected becomes out of date quickly, making it irrelevant even if it is processed by the best available computer. To move out of the current culture of reaction, retrospection, and data compilation, the intelligence community will need to master the art of early detection of the threats and dangers presented by the modern world. This transition will require expert observation—but in the context of what threats may emerge and how their nature may change. Such expert knowledge will hinge on day-to-day connection with the real world—by the entire law enforcement community, ranging from small towns to large cities (Bauer, 2011).

THE GLOBAL LANDSCAPE IN 2020

The NIC produced three unclassified reports that document long-term estimates of future events and conditions. Table 14–1 presents the NIC's view of world conditions in 2020.

At no time since the formation of the western alliance system in 1949 have the shape and nature of international alignments been in such a state of flux. The end of the Cold War shifted the tectonic plates, but the repercussions from these momentous events are still unfolding. Emerging powers in Asia, retrenchment in Eurasia, a roiling Middle East, and transatlantic divisions are among the issues that have only come to a head in recent years. The very magnitude and speed of change resulting from a globalizing world will be a defining feature of the world out to 2020. Other significant characteristics include the rise of new powers, new challenges to governance, and a more pervasive sense of insecurity, including terror-ism. As the future is mapped, the prospects for increasing global prosperity and the limited likelihood of great power conflicts provide an overall favorable environment for coping with what are otherwise daunting challenges. The role of the United States will be an important variable in how the world is shaped, influencing the path that states and non–nation-state actors choose to follow.

New Global Players

The likely emergence of China and India, as well as others, as new major global players—similar to the advent of a united Germany in the nineteenth century and a powerful United States in the early twentieth century—will transform the geopolitical landscape, with impacts potentially as dramatic as those in the previous two centuries. In the same way that commentators refer to the 1900s as the American Century, the twenty-first century may be seen as the time when Asia, led by China and India, comes into its own. A combination of sustained high economic growth,

TABLE 14–1	World Conditions in 2020	

Relative Certainties	Key Uncertainties
Globalization largely irreversible, likely to become less westernized	Whether globalization will pull in lagging economies; degree to which Asian countries set new "rules of the game"
World economy substantially larger	Extent of gaps between haves and have-nots; backsliding by fragile democracies; managing or containing financial crises
Increasing number of global firms facilitate spread of new technologies	Extent to which connectivity challenges governments
The rise of Asia and advent of possible new economic middleweights	Whether the rise of China/India occurs smoothly
Aging populations in established powers	Ability of European Union (EU) and Japan to adapt work forces, welfare systems, and integrate migrant populations; whether EU becomes a superpower
Energy supplies "in the ground" sufficient to meet global demand	Political instability in producer countries; supply disruptions
Growing power of non–nation-state actors	Willingness and ability of states and international institutions to accommodate these actors
Political Islam remains a potent force	Impact of religiosity on unity of states and potential for conflict; growth of jihadist ideology
Improved weapons of mass destruction (WMD) capabilities of some states	More or fewer nuclear powers; ability of terrorists to acquire biological, chemical, radiological, or nuclear weapons
Arc of instability spanning Middle East, Asia, Africa	Precipitating of events leading to overthrow of regimes
Great power conflict escalating into total war unlikely	Ability to manage flashpoints and competition for resources
Environmental and ethical issues even more to the fore	Extent to which new technologies create or resolve ethical dilemmas
United States will remain the single most powerful actor economically, technologically, militarily	Whether other countries will challenge Washington more openly; whether United States loses its science and technology edge

expanding military capabilities, and large populations will be at the root of the expected rapid rise in economic and political power for both countries. Consider these facts:

- Most forecasts indicate that by 2020 China's gross national product (GNP) will exceed that of individual economic powers in the West except for the United States. India's GNP will have overtaken or be on the threshold of overtaking European economies.
- Because of the sheer size of China's and India's populations—projected by the U.S. Census Bureau to be 1.4 billion and almost 1.3 billion, respectively, by 2020—their standards of living need not approach the levels of the West for these countries to become important economic powers.

Most forecasts indicate that by 2020 China's gross national product will exceed that of individual economic powers in the West except for the United Sates. *(Photo courtesy of BartlomiejMagierowski/Shutterstock.com.)*

Barring an abrupt reversal of the process of globalization or any major upheavals in these countries, the rise of these new powers is a virtual certainty. Yet, how China and India exercise their growing power and whether they relate cooperatively or competitively to other powers in the international system are key uncertainties. The economies of other developing countries, such as Brazil, could surpass all but the largest European countries by 2020; Indonesia's economy could also approach the economies of individual European countries by 2020.

By most measures—market-size, single-currency, highly skilled work force, stable democratic governments, and unified trade bloc—an enlarged Europe will be able to increase its weight in the international scene. Europe's strength could be in providing a model of global and regional governance to the rising powers. But aging populations and shrinking work forces in most countries will have an important impact on the continent. Either European countries adapt their work forces; reform their social welfare, education, and tax systems; and accommodate growing immigrant populations (chiefly from Muslim countries), or they face a period of protracted economic stagnation.

Japan faces a similar aging crisis that could crimp its longer-run economic recovery, but it also will be challenged to evaluate its regional status and role. Tokyo may have to choose between balancing against or bandwagoning with China. Meanwhile, the crisis over North Korea is likely to come to a head sometime before 2020. Asians' lingering resentments and concerns over Korean unification and cross-Taiwan Strait tensions point to a complicated process of achieving regional equilibrium.

Russia has the potential to enhance its international role with others due to its position as a major oil and gas exporter. However, Russia faces a severe demographic crisis resulting from low birth rates, poor medical care, and a potentially explosive AIDS situation. To the south, it borders an unstable region in the Caucasus and Central Asia, the effects of which—Muslim extremism, terrorism, and endemic conflict—are likely to continue spilling over into Russia. While these social and political factors limit the extent to which Russia can be a major global player, Moscow is likely to be an important partner both for the established powers, the United States and Europe, and for the rising powers of China and India.

With these and other new global actors, how the world is mentally mapped in 2020 will change radically. The "arriviste" powers—China, India, and perhaps others such as Brazil and Indonesia—have the potential to render obsolete the old categories of East and West, North and South, aligned and nonaligned, developed and developing. Traditional geographic groupings will increasingly lose salience in international relations. A state-bound world and a world of megacities, linked by flows of telecommunications, trade, and finance, will coexist. Competition for allegiances will be more open, less fixed than in the past.

New Challenges to Governance

The nation-state will continue to be the dominant unit of the global order, but economic globalization and the dispersion of technologies, especially information technologies, will place enormous new strains on governments. Growing connectivity will be accompanied by the proliferation of virtual communities of interest, complicating states' ability to govern. The Internet, in particular, will spur the creation of even more global movements, which may emerge as a robust force in international affairs.

Part of the pressure on governance will come from new forms of identity politics centered on religious convictions. In a rapidly globalizing world experiencing population shifts, religious identities provide followers with a readymade community that serves as a "social safety net" in times of need—particularly important to migrants. In particular, political Islam will have a significant global impact leading to 2020, rallying disparate ethnic and national groups and perhaps even creating an authority that transcends national boundaries. A combination of factors—youth bulges in many Arab states, poor economic prospects, the influence of religious education, and the Islamization of institutions such as trade unions, nongovernmental organizations, and political parties—will ensure that political Islam remains a major force. Outside the Middle East, political Islam will continue to appeal to Muslim migrants who are attracted to the more prosperous West for employment opportunities but do not feel at home in what they perceive as an alien and hostile culture.

Regimes that were able to manage the challenges of the 1990s could be overwhelmed by those of 2020. Contradictory forces will be at work. For example, authoritarian regimes will face new pressures to democratize, but fragile new democracies may lack the adaptive capacity to survive and develop.

The so-called third wave of democratization may be partially reversed by 2020—particularly among the states of the former Soviet Union and in Southeast Asia, some of which never really embraced democracy. Yet democratization and greater pluralism could gain ground in countries of the Middle East and North Africa that thus far have been excluded from the process by repressive regimes, as evidenced by the recent populist uprisings in Tunisia, Egypt, Libya, Syria, and other countries in these regions. This unrest could signal a trend toward democratization in many Islamic countries.

With migration increasing in several places around the world—from North Africa and the Middle East into Europe, Latin America, and the Caribbean into the United States, and increasingly from Southeast Asia into the northern regions—more countries will be multiethnic and will face the challenge of integrating migrants into their societies while respecting their ethnic and religious identities.

Chinese leaders will face a dilemma over how much to accommodate pluralistic pressures to relax political controls or risk a popular backlash if they do not. Beijing may pursue an "Asian way of democracy," which could involve elections at the local level and a consultative mechanism on the national level, perhaps with the Communist Party retaining control over the central government.

With the international system itself undergoing profound flux, some institutions charged with managing global problems may be overwhelmed by them. Regionally based institutions will be particularly challenged to meet the complex transnational threats posed by terrorism, organized crime, and WMD proliferation. Post–World War II creations such as the United Nations and the international financial institutions risk sliding into obsolescence unless they adjust to the profound changes taking place in the global system, including the rise of new powers.

Pervasive Insecurity

A more pervasive sense of insecurity is estimated, which may be as much based on psychological perceptions as physical threats. Even as most of the world gets richer, globalization will profoundly shake up the status quo—generating enormous economic, cultural, and, consequently, political convulsions. With the gradual integration of China, India, and other emerging countries into the global economy, hundreds of millions of working-age adults will become available for employment in what is evolving into a more integrated world labor market.

This enormous work force—a growing portion of which will be well educated—will be an attractive, competitive source of low-cost labor at the same time that technological innovation is expanding the range of globally mobile occupations. However, the transition will not be painless and will hit the middle classes of the developed world in particular, bringing more rapid job turnover and requiring professional retooling. Outsourcing on a large scale would strengthen the antiglobalization movement. Where these pressures lead will depend on how political leaders respond, how flexible labor markets become, and whether overall economic growth is sufficiently robust to absorb a growing number of displaced workers.

Weak governments, lagging economies, religious extremism, and youth bulges will align to create a perfect storm for internal conflict in certain regions. The number of internal conflicts is down significantly since the late 1980s and early 1990s when the breakup of the Soviet Union and Communist regimes in Central Europe allowed suppressed ethnic and nationalistic strife to flare. Although a plateau has been reached where one can expect fewer such conflicts than during the last decade, the continued prevalence of troubled and institutionally weak states means that such conflicts will continue to occur.

Some internal conflicts, particularly those that involve ethnic groups straddling national boundaries, risk escalating into regional conflicts. At their most extreme, internal conflicts can result in failing or failed states, with expanses of territory and populations devoid of effective governmental control. Such territories can become sanctuaries for transnational terrorists (e.g., Al Qaeda, in Afghanistan) or for criminals and drug cartels (e.g., in Colombia).

The likelihood of great power conflict escalating into total war in the next 15 years is lower than at any time in the past century, unlike during previous centuries when local conflicts ignited world wars. The rigidities of alliance systems before World War I and during the interwar period, as well as the two-bloc standoff during the Cold War, virtually assured that small conflicts would be quickly generalized. The growing dependence on global financial and trade networks will help deter interstate conflict but does not eliminate the possibility. Should conflict occur that involves one or more of the great powers, the consequences will be significant. The absence of effective conflict resolution mechanisms in some regions, the rise of nationalism in some states, and the raw emotions and tensions on both sides of some issues—for example, the Taiwan Strait or India/Pakistan issues—could lead to miscalculation. Moreover, advances in modern weaponry—longer ranges, precision delivery, and more destructive conventional munitions—create circumstances encouraging the preemptive use of military force.

Current nuclear weapons states will continue to improve the survivability of their deterrent forces and almost certainly will improve the reliability, accuracy, and lethality of their delivery systems as well as develop capabilities to penetrate missile defenses. The open demonstration of nuclear capabilities by any state would further discredit the current nonproliferation regime, cause a possible shift in the balance of power, and increase the risk of conflicts escalating into nuclear ones. Countries without nuclear weapons—especially in the Middle East and Northeast Asia—might decide to seek them as it becomes clear that their neighbors and regional rivals are doing so. Moreover, the assistance of proliferators will reduce the time required for additional countries to develop nuclear weapons.

SECURITY SPOTLIGHT

Take some time to learn as much as you can about the Cold War era; in particular, the national security approaches adopted by the United States during that era. Given the changes in the nature of the threats facing the United States today, what do you see as the one or two most important modifications that should be made in the country's approach to national security?

Shifts in International Terrorism

The key factors that spawned international terrorism show no signs of abating over the years leading up to 2020. Facilitated by global communications, the revival of Muslim identity will create a framework for the spread of radical Islamic ideology inside and outside the Middle East, including Southeast Asia, Central Asia, and Western Europe, where religious identity has traditionally not been as strong. This revival has been accompanied by a deepening solidarity among Muslims caught up in national or regional separatist struggles, such as Palestine, Chechnya, Iraq, Kashmir, Mindanao, and southern Thailand, and has emerged in response to government repression, corruption, and ineffectiveness. Informal networks of charitable foundations, *madrassas*, *hawalas* (informal banking systems), and other mechanisms will continue to proliferate and be exploited by radical elements; alienation among unemployed youth will swell the ranks of those vulnerable to terrorist recruitment.

By 2020, it is expected that Al Qaeda will be superseded by similarly inspired Islamic extremist groups. Indeed, Al Qaeda is no longer the nucleus of any worldwide terrorist conspiracy and has not been for some time. There is a substantial risk that broad Islamic movements akin to Al Qaeda will merge with local separatist movements. Moreover, other militant terrorist groups, stronger than Al Qaeda, are emerging in countries other than Afghanistan, such as Yemen.

Pakistan likely is and will likely remain a center for harboring Al Qaeda terrorists. After bin Laden's death, questions arose regarding whether Pakistan's leaders knew of the Al Qaeda leader's presence in their country and whether they actively protected him. The compound where bin Laden was found was located in relatively close proximity to a Pakistani military facility. Pakistan's Inter-Services Intelligence (ISI) implied that it had helped the CIA locate the compound where bin Laden was killed, claiming to have it under surveillance since construction of the facility started in 2003. ISI also said that it had searched the compound at that time but found nothing, and that it had shared information with the CIA in early 2009 that contributed to the finding of bin Laden. The Obama administration has confirmed that Pakistani intelligence sources provided some assistance. However, as planning of the bin Laden mission advanced, CIA Director Leon Panetta said that the United States decided not to alert Pakistan's government or intelligence because of fears that it would inform the targets of the plan. White House counterterrorism advisor John Brennan said that Pakistani officials were trying to determine whether certain individuals within Pakistan's government or military intelligence services knew of bin Laden's whereabouts (DeYoung & Brulliard, 2011).

In addition to fueling suspicions that Pakistan had protected bin Laden, the death of the Al Qaeda leader prompted retaliation by the terrorist organization in the form of suicide bombings that took numerous lives. It also sparked anger within Pakistan that the United States had conducted the operation on Pakistani soil without informing the nation's leaders or obtaining their approval. Pakistanis decried what they defined as a violation of their nation's sovereignty. Bin Laden's killing also prompted some observers to question the legality of the act; for example, asking why the Al Qaeda leader was not taken into custody and given a trial. U.S. officials said that although bin Laden was unarmed when the Navy SEALs found him in the compound, he resisted, and they were concerned that he was reaching for a weapon after they entered his room. They later found AK-47 assault rifles and side arms in the room. The SEALs were also concerned that a woman who charged at them inside bin Laden's room may have been wearing an explosives-packed vest. Because the SEALs viewed bin Laden as a threat, they killed him rather than taking him into custody ("Officials: SEALs thought Bin Laden threatening," 2011).

Information technology, allowing for instant connectivity, communication, and learning, will enable the terrorist threat to become increasingly decentralized, evolving into an eclectic array of groups, cells, and individuals that do not need a stationary headquarters to plan and carry out operations. Training materials, targeting guidance, weapons know-how, and fund-raising will become virtual (online).

Terrorist attacks will continue to primarily employ conventional weapons, incorporating new twists and constantly adapting to counterterrorist efforts. Terrorists probably will be most original not in the technology or weapons they use but rather in their operational concepts—that is, the scope, design, or support arrangements for attacks.

Strong terrorist interest in acquiring chemical, biological, radiological, and nuclear weapons increases the risk of a major terrorist attack involving WMD. The greatest concern is that terrorists acquire biological agents or, less likely, a nuclear device, either of which could cause mass casualties. Bioterrorism appears particularly suited to the smaller, better-informed groups. It is also expected that terrorists will attempt cyberattacks to disrupt critical information networks and, even more likely, to cause physical damage to information systems.

Policy Implications

The United States will play an important role in the international order in 2020. The country may increasingly confront the challenge of managing—at an acceptable cost to itself—relations with Europe, Asia, the Middle East, and others in the absence of a single overarching threat on which to build consensus. Although the challenges ahead will be daunting, the United States will retain enormous advantages, playing a pivotal role across a broad range of issues—economic, technological, political, and military—that no other state will match by 2020. Some possible trends include dramatically altered alliances and relationships with Europe and Asia, both of which formed the bedrock of U.S. power in the post–World War II period.

The EU, rather than NATO, will increasingly become the primary institution for Europe, and the role that Europeans shape for themselves on the world stage is most likely to be projected through it. Dealing with the U.S.–Asia relationship may arguably be more challenging for the United States because of the greater flux resulting from the rise of two world-class economic and political giants yet to be fully integrated into the international order. Where U.S.–Asia relations lead will result as much or more from what the Asians work out among themselves as from any action by the United States. One could envisage a range of possibilities from the United States enhancing its role as balancer between contending forces to its being viewed as increasingly irrelevant.

The U.S. economy will become more vulnerable to fluctuations in the fortunes of others, as global commercial networking deepens. Americans' dependence on foreign oil supplies also makes the United States more vulnerable as competition intensifies for secure access and as risks of supply–side disruptions increase.

While no single country looks within striking distance of rivaling the U.S. military power by 2020, more countries will be in a position to make the United States pay a heavy price for any military action they oppose. The possession of chemical, biological, and/or nuclear weapons by Iran and North Korea and the possible acquisition of such weapons by others by 2020 also increase the potential cost of any military action by the United States against them or their allies.

The success of the U.S.-led counterterrorism campaign will hinge on the capabilities and resolve of individual countries to fight terrorism on their own soil. Counterterrorism efforts in the years ahead—against a more diverse set of terrorists who are connected more by ideology than by geography—will be a more elusive challenge than focusing on a centralized organization such as Al Qaeda. A counterterrorism strategy that approaches the problem on multiple fronts offers the greatest chance of containing—and ultimately reducing—the terrorist threat. The development of more open political systems and representation, broader economic opportunities, and empowerment of Muslim reformers would be viewed positively by the broad Muslim communities who do not support the radical agenda of Islamic extremists.

Even if the numbers of extremists dwindle, however, the terrorist threat is likely to remain. The rapid dispersion of biological and other lethal forms of technology increases the potential for an individual not affiliated with any terrorist group to be able to wreak widespread loss of life. Despite likely high-technology breakthroughs that will make it easier to track and detect terrorists at work, the attacker will have an easier job than the defender because the defender must prepare against a large array of possibilities. The United States probably will continue to be called on to help manage conflicts such as Palestine, North Korea, Taiwan, and Kashmir to ensure that they do not get out of hand if a peace settlement cannot be reached. However, trends suggest the possibility of harnessing the power of the new players in contributing to global security and relieving the United States of some of the burden.

As 2020 approaches, the increasing centrality of ethical issues, old and new, has the potential to divide the public worldwide and challenge U.S. leadership. These issues include the environment and climate change, privacy, cloning and biotechnology, human rights, international laws regulating conflict, and the role of multilateral institutions. The United States increasingly will have to battle world public opinion, which has dramatically shifted since the end of the Cold War. Some of the current anti-Americanism is likely to lessen as globalization takes on more of a non-Western face. At the same time, the younger generation of leaders—unlike during the post–World War II period—has no personal recollection of the United States as its liberator and is more likely to diverge with the U.S. position on a range of issues. In helping to map out the global future, the United States will have many opportunities to extend its advantages, particularly in shaping a new international order that integrates disparate regions and reconciles divergent interests (Friedman, 2011; National Intelligence Council, 2007a).

A QUICK SURVEY

Which of the security-related trends and challenges described in this chapter would you like to learn more about? Check all that apply.

- Impacts of globalization
- Legislative trends in security
- Domestic terrorism
- International terrorism
- Governance challenges
- Policy changes
- The increasing pervasiveness of insecurity

What prompted you to select the item(s) you checked in this list? For example, if you are considering a career in security, would you like to focus your work on combating international terrorism? What steps could you take to learn more about the item(s) you checked?

Summary

Technological advances, globalization, legislation, and terrorism create new challenges for the security professional. As threats are mitigated or eliminated, new threats will develop. Thus, the expansion of security services appears inevitable. The security person of the future must be adaptable, well trained, and educated, and perform tasks consistent with professional standards.

The growing interconnectedness created by advancing globalization is a pervasive force that will substantially shape all other trends in the future. By 2020, the world's economy is expected to be 80 percent larger than it was in 2000. The greatest benefits of globalization will accrue to countries and groups that can access and embrace new technologies. More companies will operate globally and they will be more Asian than Western in orientation. As globalization alters the status quo, a pervasive sense of insecurity is predicted.

Key factors that spawned international terrorism show no signs of abating through 2020. Facilitated by global communications, radical ideologies, and alienated unemployed youth, terrorism will likely continue. It is expected that Al Qaeda will be superseded by similarly inspired extremist groups employing conventional weapons and new techniques. However, strong terrorist interest in acquiring nuclear, biological, chemical, and radiological weapons increases the risk of a major terrorist attack.

Key Terms

asset protection challenges
counterinsurgency techniques

Foreign Corrupt Practices Act (FCPA)
globalization

National Intelligence Estimate (NIE)

Discussion Questions and Exercises

1. What challenges lie ahead for the security professional?
2. Do you believe that security personnel can disregard globalization? Why or why not?
3. What legislative trends are likely in the future?
4. Will the nature of terrorism change? If so, how?

YOUR TURN: Assessing Worldwide Threats and Intelligence-Community Efforts

On February 10, 2011, James R. Clapper delivered remarks at an open hearing on the annual worldwide threat assessment to the House Permanent Select Committee on Intelligence. Clapper had been DNI for 6 months when he made these remarks. The following are highlights from his presentation to the committee:

- The intelligence community's first and foremost concern is terrorism. The community has weakened much of Al Qaeda's core capabilities and has engaged with foreign partners to detect and prevent terrorist actions. However, the community is particularly concerned about Al Qaeda's resolve to target Americans for recruitment and to spawn affiliate groups around the world. Self-radicalization among U.S. citizens is also a concern. While homegrown terrorists are numerically a small part of the global threat, they have a disproportionate impact, because they understand the U.S. homeland, have connections there, and have easier access to U.S. facilities.
- Owing to the increasingly free movement of people, goods, and information across borders enabled by globalization, WMDs can be shared more easily and quickly than ever. And because we live in an ever more interconnected, interdependent world, instability can arise and spread quickly beyond borders. The intelligence community has tracked unrest, demographic changes, economic uncertainty, and lack of political expression for decades.
- Additional concerns include cyberthreats (industry estimates the production of malicious software has reached an average of 60,000 new programs or variations identified each day), intellectual property theft, energy security, drug trafficking, emerging diseases, water availability, international organized crime, humanitarian disasters, and unauthorized disclosures of sensitive and classified U.S. government information.
- The Office of the DNI is working to change the paradigm about what has been a historically strained relationship between the offices of the DNI and the CIA.
- Based on an efficiencies review, the Office of the DNI is being reduced in size and budget. Functions not required by law or executive order that are not core missions of the Office of the DNI are being reduced or eliminated. Where the Office can provide value to the intelligence community is to ensure that intelligence is integrated across disciplines and agencies before being presented to its customers (Clapper, 2011).

1. In his remarks, Clapper spoke at length about the threat of terrorism and the security-related implications of globalization. Why do you think he sees these two themes as meriting particular attention in assessing worldwide threats?

2. Given the range and extent of the threats noted by Clapper in his remarks, how might his proposal to reduce the Office of the DNI in size and budget affect the Office's ability to fulfill its mission? What steps might the Office take to "do more with less"—a challenge facing more and more organizations?

3. Clapper notes a desire to integrate intelligence across disciplines and agencies. What steps could he and leaders from other organizations take to help foster this kind of integration and collaboration, and to heal historically strained relationships between members of the intelligence community?

4. Use the Internet to learn more about the House Permanent Select Committee on Intelligence. What are the Committee's responsibilities? What is its relationship to the Office of the DNI?

GLOSSARY

Accident   An unfortunate event caused unintentionally by a human agent.

Accounts payable diversion   Disbursement fraud committed by person who processes payroll information, refunds, discounts, rebates, or purchases.

Administration   Process through which two or more people collaborate to accomplish a predetermined goal.

Administrative law   The branch of public law created by administrative agencies and presented in the form of rules and regulations that dictate duties and responsibilities of individuals and organizations.

Affective skills   Desirable values and attitudes.

Alarm   Communicator designed to notify a receiver of impending danger.

Alarm point definition   Identified points through which an alarm system is connected to a security management system.

Alarm system circuit   Communication link between alarm sensor and annunciator.

Alarm system management   Alarm point definition (identification) and integration with facility operations, the development of effective alarm response procedures, and training of alarm monitoring and response personnel.

American Society for Industrial Security (ASIS)   ASIS International; international organization of security professionals founded in 1955.

Annunciator   Signaling device that notifies recipient of detected alarm condition.

Appellate court   Reviews cases and decisions appealed to it from a trial court or lower appellate court.

Application   Objective account of a person's background; used as a preemployment screening device.

Aquarium   Tank containing live fish, animals, and plants.

Arraignment   Generally, the pretrial judicial hearing at which a defendant enters a plea to a criminal charge.

Asset protection challenges   Issues facing the security professional such as the changing nature of the workplace, ethical considerations, advances in technology, increased diversity, privatization of public services, terrorist activities, and globalization.

Aviation and Transportation Security Act of 2001   Federal law that created the Transportation Security Administration.

Bad check   Forged, altered, or incorrectly completed check or a check drawn on a nonexistent account or an account with insufficient funds.

Bailiff   Court security officer.

Bank Protection Act of 1968   Federal legislation designed to reduce the vulnerability of financial institutions.

Basics of defense   Involves use of policies, procedures, people, equipment, architectural design, and strategies to prevent loss and deter, detect, deny, delay, or detain the person or agent that may cause harm to the enterprise.

Biometric system   An access-control system that must recognize a human biological feature before access to a protected area is granted.

Bioterrorism Act of 2002   A federal law designed to improve the ability of the United States to prevent, prepare for, and respond to bioterrorism and other public health emergencies.

Budget   A plan expressed in financial terms; list of possible expenditures.

Business continuity plan   A plan designed to ensure that significant events do not disrupt normal operations.

Business intelligence (BI)   Competitive intelligence; process of collecting, analyzing, and disseminating competitive information and other data to meet business objectives.

Capital expenditures   Refers to depreciable assets, such as equipment and buildings.

Card-operated lock   Utilizes cards with magnetic strips inserted into a card reader connected to a microcomputer that activates the locking device.

Career enhancement   Educational experiences that focus on specific job-related training as well as those experiences that promote individual personal development.

Career preparation   Drawing upon human qualities as well as knowledge, skills, and abilities for successful career in security services.

Cargo   Any object moved through the transportation system.

Cargo security measures   Security personnel, physical security, accountability, proper documentation, secure packaging, policies and procedures, prosecution of offenders, global positioning system (GPS).

Cash conversion   Theft of liquid assets, such as currency, and negotiable instruments, such as checks.

Casino security Surveillance, physical security, and investigations activities in the casino industry.

Causes of crime Although the exact causes of crime are not known, crime causation is generally explained in terms of psychological, sociological, physiological, economic, drug use, demographic, urbanization, cultural, and expectations theories.

Central processing unit (CPU) Receives, processes, stores, and transmits information detected by alarm sensors.

Central station alarm system Similar to a proprietary alarm system control center; however, the alarm system is monitored from a facility at a remote location. The central station may monitor several alarm systems simultaneously.

Certified Protection Professional (CPP) Security professional designation awarded by ASIS International.

Challenge for cause A challenge to a potential trial juror's qualifications that must be accompanied by a reason; there is no limit to the number of challenges for cause.

Check cashing procedure Thorough examination of a check and positive identification of check casher.

Chief security officer (CSO) High-level security management person, typically with the title of vice president for security, loss prevention, or asset protection.

Cipher One-to-one correspondence between characters in an actual message (plain text) with the characters in a secret writing equivalent (crypto text).

Civil disorder Occurs when an individual or group disrupts the normal peace and tranquility of a community or the operations of a business or organization.

Civil liability May occur when a person is harmed or injured through the action or inaction of another. The harm may or may not be the result of criminal activity.

Classification of fire Class A, ordinary combustible; Class B, flammable liquid; Class C, electrical; Class D, combustible metal.

Clery Act Named for Jeanne Clery, this federal law requires all colleges and universities that participate in federal financial-aid programs to collect, maintain, and disclose information about crime on or near their campuses.

Closed-circuit television (CCTV) Video surveillance system closed to external transmission.

Cloud computing Assessing the computer resources owned and operated by a third-party provider on a consolidated basis in data-center locations.

Code of ethics Standards of professional conduct.

Code of Hammurabi First written law (circa 2100 B.C.) designed to prescribe responsibilities of the individual to a group. The Code also specified punishment for offenses.

Combination lock Dial or push-button lock commonly used with safes, vaults, padlocks, and vehicle doors.

Common law Unwritten law based on custom or tradition.

Communications security (COMSEC) All efforts to protect information transmission from unauthorized interception.

Compensatory damages Designed to compensate a petitioner in a lawsuit for actual losses incurred.

Competitive intelligence Business intelligence.

CompStat Computer-driven statistics used in planning and management.

Computer crime Generally, any crime committed utilizing computer technology.

Computer virus A destructive software program designed to invade a computer system and alter stored information or modify the computer system's operations.

Computer worm A software program that replicates itself over computer networks. Unlike computer viruses that infect programs in a single computer, computer worms infect multiple computers by taking over computer memory and denying its use to legitimate computer programs.

Confidential communication Any communication carried on under circumstances reasonably indicating that any party to the communication desires it to be confined to the parties involved in the communication.

Conspiracy Criminal plan involving at least two people. In some states, requires an act toward the completion of the intended (planned) crime.

Contact report Used to document information acquired during an encounter with another person or persons.

Contingency plan Plan implemented only if a certain event, such as a natural disaster, occurs.

Contract Legally binding voluntary agreement between or among parties through which promises are made for a valuable consideration.

Contract security service Security organization that provides security services to individuals or other organizations for a fee.

Copyright Protects against unauthorized use of virtually any creative writing or expression that can be physically observed.

Cost–benefit analysis A systematic process through which one attempts to determine the value of the benefits derived from an expenditure and compare the value with the cost.

Counterespionage Activities designed to prevent espionage from occurring.

Counterinsurgency techniques Tactics and strategies designed to protect, secure, and win the support of at-risk populations prone to insurgency.

Coupon fraud Occurs when customers or employees redeem coupons for cash in lieu of the purchase of the item for which the coupon was issued.

Court of last resort A state's highest court; U.S. Supreme Court.

Courts of general jurisdiction Courts that can try any state case brought before them.

Courts of limited jurisdiction Courts that are limited in the types of cases they are authorized to try.

Covert operations Undercover, secret, or surreptitious operations.

Credit card fraud Economic crime utilizing a credit card or credit card accounts.

Crime Offense against a society; an intentional act, or omission to act, in violation of the criminal law, committed without defense or justification and punished by society as a felony, misdemeanor, or infraction.

Crime Awareness and Campus Security Act 1990 federal law requiring postsecondary educational institutions to collect and disseminate campus crime statistics.

Crime prevention strategies Education, treatment, diversion, rehabilitation, and deterrence through law enforcement and security.

Crime prevention through environmental design (CPTED) Theory and practice associated with protecting people and the environment through the proper design of facilities and communities.

Crimes against persons Offenses committed by physical contact with the victim, in the presence of the victim with the victim's knowledge, or by placing the victim in fear of immediate harm; violent crime.

Crimes against property Offenses committed when victim is not present or is unaware that the crime is being committed; nonviolent crime.

Crimes against the public peace Acts that disturb public peace and tranquility. Examples include disturbing the peace, unlawful assembly, and riot.

Criminal intelligence Gathering information about actual as well as possible criminal activity and threats to a society or to an organization and its assets.

Criminal investigation An investigation that focuses on actual or suspected criminal activity.

Criminal negligence A form of criminal intent; the actor can foresee the result and fails to exercise the degree of care that a reasonable and prudent person would exercise in similar circumstances.

Critical information All forms and types of information as defined in the U.S. Economic Security Act of 1996.

Critical infrastructure Publicly or privately controlled resources such as agriculture, food, water, telecommunications, financial services, transportation, energy, and utilities deemed most critical to national public health and safety, governance, economic and national security, and retaining public confidence.

Cryptographic security Transformation (secret writing) of data to render it unintelligible during transmission.

Cryptography Science of secret writing; transformation of data to render it unintelligible to an unauthorized interceptor.

Cybercrime Computer crime committed using the Internet.

Cyber Security Research and Development Act of 2002 Federal law that established computer security research centers; intended to create programs to defend against terrorists that may target vital communications networks.

Decryption Conversion of crypto text to plain text.

Degrees of proof Standards by which guilt or liability must be established in criminal and civil cases.

Delphi technique Process through which several individuals or experts provide input on an issue and arrive at consensus on a prediction or list of needs or priorities.

Digitization The conversion and electronic storage of an image or information to a computer's digital language.

Digitized information Information that is created, stored, manipulated, and transmitted electronically.

Disaster recovery Addresses ability to recover from a disaster in a manner that does not adversely impact continuity of operations.

Discretionary access control Access to information is allowed on a need-to-know basis.

Documentation Any medium used to create a record of an event or communication.

Dynamic risk   Exists when threat conditions fluctuate.

Economic crime   A violation of the criminal law designed to reward the offender financially.

Electronic lock   Remotely controlled electronic locking device typically used to control gates and access.

Elements of planning   Needs assessment, development of alternative courses of action, and selection of an action plan.

Emanations security   Prevents compromise of information through capture of acoustical emanations.

Embezzlement   Fraudulent appropriation of property by a person to whom the property has been entrusted.

Employee Polygraph Protection Act   1988 federal law that severely restricts the use of the polygraph or similar instruments by private-sector organizations.

Employee retention   Strategies to retain productive employees to avoid expenses associated with recruitment and training of new employees.

Employment law   Refers to common law and statutory provisions that regulate the employment relationship.

Encryption   Conversion of plain text to crypto text.

Environmental crime   Human activity that violates an environmental crime statute.

Environmental disaster   Term associated with exposure to hazardous materials, conventional and nuclear power failures, and gas line or water main breaks.

Environmental Protection Agency (EPA)   Federal agency responsible for enforcement of federal environmental laws and regulations.

Ethical standards   Standards that dictate behavior when law or precedent, which may prescribe behavior, does not exist.

Ethics   Involves moral principles and focuses on the concepts of right and wrong and standards of behavior.

Evaluation   Process used to measure performance, compare performance with stated objectives, report results, and take corrective action.

Evidence   Information used to make a decision. In a judicial proceeding, includes testimony, writings, material objects, and other items presented to prove or disprove the existence or nonexistence of a disputed fact.

Executive protection   Activities designed to maintain the safety, security, and health of a human asset.

Expressed contract   Written or verbal contract in which all terms are explicitly stated.

Facility plan review   Fire department review of plans during facility construction.

Fair Credit Reporting Act   Federal law designed to promote accuracy and ensure the privacy of the information used in consumer credit reports.

Federal Aviation Administration (FAA)   Federal agency responsible for regulating air transportation in the United States.

Federal Emergency Management Agency (FEMA)   The agency that manages federal response and recovery efforts following a major national incident.

Federal Motor Carrier Safety Administration (FMCSA)   The federal agency with a mission to improve security and reduce injuries and fatalities involving large trucks and buses.

Federal Railroad Administration (FRA)   The agency responsible for promulgation and enforcement of federal rail safety regulations.

Felony   A crime for which the potential penalty may be a fine and/or imprisonment of more than 1 year, or death.

Financial audit   Evaluation of an accounting system; transactions are sampled to confirm records are free of significant errors.

Financial institution   Bank, credit union, brokerage house, insurance company, or any other institution in which financial transactions are the primary focus.

Fire hazard abatement   Involves use of fire abatement codes typically established at the municipal government level.

Fire inspection program   Fire safety surveys, testing of fire systems.

Fire investigation   Involves fire cause determination and investigation of criminal actions.

Fire prevention   Policies and practices designed to prevent a fire from occurring.

Fire prevention enforcement   Adoption and administration of fire prevention codes, enforcement procedures, and notices.

Fire prevention inspection   Determines if reasonable life-safety conditions exist within a facility.

Fire protection   Procedures and fire suppression systems and activities designed to minimize harm to persons and property after a fire has started.

Fire safety education   Fire prevention and fire reaction training.

Fire triangle   Heat, fuel, and oxygen necessary for a fire to occur.

Firewall   In computer security, the electronic tool used to restrict access to computer databases.

First (initial) appearance   Nonadversarial proceeding before a magistrate (judge) to set bail.

Foreign Corrupt Practices Act (FCPA)   Federal law that prohibits payments of bribes by U.S. companies to foreign government officials.

Foreign Intelligence Surveillance Act (FISA) of 1978   This Act permits physical and electronic surveillance and collection of foreign intelligence between or among foreign powers without a court order (as per presidential directive) for 1 year or with a court order issued by the Foreign Intelligence Surveillance Court (FISC).

Fraud   Involves practically any scheme or device used by a person to deceive another.

Fraud examination   Search of accounting records for any error or discrepancy, significant or not, to determine if financial controls could be compromised.

Full-time equivalent (FTE) person   Equivalent to a person, or combination of persons, assigned to work full time (40 hours per week).

Fusion centers   Venue where reports of suspicious activities made by citizens and police are collected and analyzed. Aim is to detect activities that may signal a potential terrorist attack.

Geographic information system (GIS) technology   Used to map reported safety- and security-related incidents and to predict future occurrences.

Globalization   Internationalization of economic and business activities; decentralization; commercial, travel, and communications activities spanning the entire globe.

Gramm-Leach-Bliley Act of 1999   A federal law that prohibits disclosure of consumer credit information by financial institutions as well as organizations that receive such information.

Hacker   An expert at programming and solving problems with a computer; can refer to a person who illegally accesses restricted databases.

Hallcrest Report II   A study of private security published in 1990 that reaffirmed the need for training and regulation of the security industry.

Health care facility   Hospital, medical center, health clinic, nursing home, or similar facility.

Health Insurance Portability and Accountability Act of 1996   A federal law mandating national standards for electronic health insurance transactions, including claims, enrollment, eligibility, payments, and benefits. The law also mandates standards to protect privacy of personal health information.

Highway patrol   A state agency with primary responsibility for traffic law enforcement and safety.

Homeland Security Act of 2002   Federal law that created the U.S. Department of Homeland Security and consolidated 22 separate federal agencies from several departments into one, effective March 1, 2003. The purpose of the consolidation is to better coordinate the defense of the United States and improve liaison with state and local governments and the private sector.

Hospitality industry   Hotels, motels, restaurants, and similar institutions.

Human error   Unintentional, human mistake.

Human resource investigation   All types of investigations related to the management of human resources.

Hurricane Katrina   The devastating hurricane that hit the Gulf Coast of the United States in August 2005.

Hybrid security organization   A security operation that employs proprietary security staff as well as contract security personnel to supplement proprietary staff.

Identity theft   A crime committed when an imposter fraudulently uses another's personal identification information to obtain credit, merchandise, or services in the name of the victim.

Impeachment   In a judicial proceeding, refers to an attack on the credibility of a witness; possible result of cross-examination of a witness.

Impermissible investigative conduct   Illegal or unethical investigative conduct.

Implied contract   Contract resulting from the actions of the parties.

Incident report   Used to document an event or reported criminal activity.

Indemnity/hold harmless clause   Clause in a contract through which the indemnified person or organization is held harmless for the action/inaction of another.

Index crimes   Contained in Part I of the Uniform Crime Report (UCR): murder, forcible rape, robbery, aggravated assault, burglary, larceny (theft), auto theft, arson.

Indictment   Formal criminal charge issued by a grand jury.

Industrial espionage (IE)   Use of illegal, unethical, and fraudulent means to obtain proprietary information and intellectual property.

Industrial security   Focuses primarily on the protection of the manufacturing process.

Information   In a criminal proceeding, the formal criminal charge issued by a prosecutor in a state felony case.

Information protection–related agreements Nondisclosure, secrecy, and noncompete agreements designed to prevent unauthorized disclosure of information.

Information security (INFOSEC) Security of information creation, processing, storage, retrieval, transmission, dissemination, and disposition. The protection of information assets and systems against any threat.

INFOSEC risk assessment and analysis Used to determine the criticality of the information, its vulnerability, and the probability that a threat will materialize.

Infraction Minor civil or criminal offense not amounting to a misdemeanor or felony.

Infrared (IR) camera Detects changes in infrared light radiation from area covered by camera.

Inherent risk Unavoidable risk due to nature of activity.

In-service training Continuous professional training for employees.

Instructional goal Learning outcome expected at the conclusion of an instructional program.

Instructional objective Enabling objective; describes skill or behavior the learner is expected to exhibit to demonstrate competence.

Intangible standards Characteristics that are difficult to measure. Examples include attitude, morale, and reputation.

Integrity test Used to detect a person's propensity toward dishonesty, substance abuse, violence, or high level of tolerance for such behavior in others.

Intellectual property Information created through research and development, such as chemical formulas and software designs.

Intelligence Reform and Terrorism Prevention Act of 2004 Fashioned after the recommendations of the 9/11 Commission, this law provided for creation of a national intelligence center and a director to oversee 15 U.S. intelligence agencies.

Intentional torts Willful tort activity. Examples include assault, false imprisonment, and defamation of character.

Interagency OPSEC Support Staff (IOSS) Interagency group that provides OPSEC-related training to security, intelligence, law enforcement, acquisitions, and research and development personnel.

Intermediate appellate courts Appellate courts between trial courts and courts of last resort.

International Association for Healthcare Security and Safety (IAHSS) Professional organization for health care security managers.

Internet An interconnected system of computer networks.

Inventory conversion Unauthorized conversion of inventory to one's own use.

Inventory shrinkage Reduction in retail inventory not accounted for through sales or other legitimate activity.

Investigation A systematic process through which information is gathered, analyzed, and reported.

Ionization sensor Senses virtually all products of combustion, including heat, flame, smoke, and invisible toxic gases.

IR sensors Sensors that respond to infrared emissions in flame.

Job description Position description; identifies the principle elements, scope of authority, and responsibilities involved in a job.

Job specifications Outline specific skills, competencies, and personal qualities necessary to perform a job adequately.

Job task (occupational) analysis Identifies the job functions (duties) a worker is expected to perform.

Joint Commission for Accreditation of Healthcare Organizations (JCAHO) Requires minimum security standards for hospitals.

Key-operated lock Most common lock; utilizes notched key inserted into the lock's keyway.

Keypad lock Generally, a lock that utilizes microcomputer technology. Keypad similar to touch pad on Touch-Tone phone.

Law Enforcement Assistance Administration (LEAA) Now defunct federal program, established through the Omnibus Crime Control and Safe Streets Act of 1968, that provided federal monies to fight crime and improve the criminal justice system.

Law Enforcement Education Program (LEEP) Now defunct federal program that provided grants and interest-free loans to preservice and in-service law enforcement personnel to attend college.

Leadership Occurs anytime one motivates, influences, or mobilizes an individual or group.

Library Collection of books and other media.

Licensed private investigator Any individual licensed by a state to provide investigative services for a fee.

Line item budget Detailed budget that includes a description and the cost of each item.

Line security Involves protection of telephone cables, modems, local area networks (LANs), and similar communications systems.

Local alarm system   When activated, produces an alarm signal in the immediate vicinity of the protected premises.

Malcolm Baldrige National Quality Award   Established by an act of Congress in 1987, this Award and its criteria seek to improve product and process quality and productivity.

Malware   Malicious software used to inflict damage to, or insert a virus into, a computer database.

Management   The fluid and dynamic process of administration. Management focuses on organizational goal achievement.

Mandatory access control   Origins traced to restrictive legislation. Hierarchical and nonhierarchical classifications for information. Information requires clearance to view.

Maritime Transportation Security Act (MTSA) of 2002   This federal law requires vulnerability assessments as well as security plans, regulations, and activities designed to protect the nation's ports and waterways.

Mental disorder   A psychological pattern generally associated with a defect or disease of the mind.

Metrics   As relates to performance, metrics involves procedures designed to quantify and periodically assess processes that can be measured.

Metropolitan Police Act   1829 British law, promoted by Sir Robert Peel, that established first public, full-time police department in the world.

Microwave motion sensor   Similar in operation to ultrasonic motion sensor except microwave systems utilize high-end radio frequencies rather than sound.

Miscellaneous expenses   In a budget, those expenses not assigned to any other established expense category.

Misdemeanor   Crime for which the potential penalty may be a fine and/or confinement for up to 1 year.

Mission statement   The language designed to help operationalize an organization's action plan.

Motion Picture Association of America (MPAA)   An entertainment industry professional organization that seeks to prevent motion picture piracy.

Museum   Used to preserve and display artistic and historic objects.

Narrative report   Used to narrate what happened, record statements, and document additional information acquired subsequent to an original report.

National Cargo Security Council (NCSC)   Functions as a clearinghouse for cargo theft information.

National Commission on Terrorist Attacks Upon the United States (The 9/11 Commission)   An independent bipartisan commission established to investigate the events leading to the terrorist attacks of September 11, 2001, and recommend improvements to security and intelligence gathering capabilities.

National Crime Victimization Survey (NCVS)   Random-sample survey conducted to determine unreported crime and other information.

National Incident-Based Reporting System (NIBRS)   Enhanced UCR; requires and provides more detailed information than UCR.

National Incident Management System (NIMS)   A disaster and emergency plan that provides unified federal, state, county, and local approach to disasters with emphasis on preparedness, standardization, mutual aid, and resource management.

National Industrial Security Program (NISP)   This Program regulates private industry's access to classified government information.

National Intelligence Estimate (NIE)   Strategic assessment (not prediction) on national security produced by the National Intelligence Council.

National law enforcement agencies   Federal agencies; have broad territorial and narrow subject matter jurisdiction.

Natural disaster   Sudden, extraordinary misfortune caused by a force of nature.

Negligence   Generally, a lack of due care or diligence that an ordinary, reasonable, and prudent person would have exercised in similar circumstances.

Negligent hiring   Possible liability associated with failure to complete a diligent inquiry into the suitability of a person for employment.

Negligent retention   Possible liability associated with employer's failure to take disciplinary or remedial action after becoming aware that an employee is a risk factor.

Numerical standards   Quantifiable standards such as numbers, statistics, percentages.

Nursing home   Extended care facility for the elderly and infirm.

Objective (quantitative) measures   Used in risk assessment, planning, and evaluation. Include audits, inspections, surveys, marketing, and reports.

Obstruction of justice   Crime that obstructs or hinders the administration of justice process. Examples include perjury, subornation of perjury, and bribery.

Occupational Safety and Health Act   Federal law created to protect worker health and safety.

Office building security threats   Fire, poor or inadequate evacuation routes, terrorist activity, bomb threats, theft, burglary, robbery, sexual assault, kidnapping.

Operating expense   Expense incurred as a result of organizational operations. Examples include rent, utilities, contract services, training, insurance, and licensing fees paid.

Operational plan   A type of tactical plan that details the steps and tasks to be accomplished by an individual or group.

Operations security (OPSEC)   Risk assessment activities designed to identify potential vulnerabilities that an adversary may exploit to obtain critical information.

Organization-specific report   Written in the normal course of business; inspection reports, audit reports, security surveys.

Organize   To create an orderly structure or arrangement.

Organized crime   Refers to relatively permanent group of individuals that systematically engage in illegal activities and provide illegal services.

Organized retail crime   Criminal organizations that focus on retail theft and defrauding of merchants.

Pandemic   Large-scale epidemic. Occurs when a disease emerges for which there is little or no immunity in the human population.

Passenger profiling techniques   Used to identify smugglers and possible terrorists attempting to board commercial airline flights.

Passive IR sensor   Detects changes in infrared light radiation in protected area.

Password   Unique identifier necessary to gain access, as in a code inputted to access a computer file or program.

Patent   A novel, useful, and nonobvious invention protected by the Federal Patent Statute from unauthorized replication or use.

Peel, Sir Robert   The British Home Secretary credited with creating the first full-time police department in the world in London in 1829.

Peremptory challenge   A challenge to a potential trial juror's qualifications for which no reason need be given; limited in number.

Performance appraisal   Systematic assessment of employee performance.

Performance-based budget   Includes measurable units tied to objectives; allows for cost–benefit analysis.

Perimeter controls   Refers to barriers, illumination systems, and personnel used to monitor or control a facility's perimeter.

Perimeter lighting   Use of street lights, floodlights, search lights, and Fresnel lights to illuminate facility perimeter.

Personal injury investigation   Investigation focusing on event that causes harm to an individual.

Personal property   Refers to property other than real property (real estate).

Personnel expenses   All expenses associated with wages, salaries, payroll taxes, and employee benefits.

Personnel identification system   A system that typically includes use of a color-coded, tamper-resistant identification card, pass, or badge.

Personnel integrity   Refers to honesty and appropriate behavior.

Personnel security   Protection of persons associated with an organization as well as protection from individuals who seek to harm the organization.

Phishing   A form of identity theft through which the perpetrator uses email and malicious websites to obtain personal information.

Photoelectric sensor   Detects objects, including smoke, in an environment.

Physical security   Tangible objects, lighting, surveillance and alarm systems, and security personnel devoted to access control.

Pinkerton, Allan   Established the first national private security and investigations company in the United States in 1851.

Planning   The process of formulating a detailed program for action.

Policy   General statement that describes goals or states an organization's position on issues or topics.

Post-Katrina Emergency Reform Act of 2006   A federal law that added functions to FEMA and amended the Homeland Security Act of 2002, directly affecting the organization and various functions of the U.S. Department of Homeland Security.

Postsecondary institutions   Colleges, universities, and other post–high school education and training institutions.

Preemployment screening   Preemployment selection processes.

Preliminary hearing   In the pretrial stages of a criminal proceeding, hearing at which the judge determines if probable cause exists that a crime was committed and that the person charged committed the offense.

Preliminary (Preparatory) Crimes   Acts completed in preparation for some other intended crime. Examples include criminal attempt, solicitation, and conspiracy.

Preservice training   Training provided prior to an employee's assumption of duties.

Private citizen powers to arrest   Private person's powers of arrest, as compared with those of a public peace officer.

Private justice system   Rules, regulations, standards of conduct, and punishments established by private enterprises.

Private person's search authority   Refers to limitations placed on a private person's authority to conduct a search (as compared to a public peace officer).

Private police   Private security; protective services typically financed through private funding sources.

Private/public interdependence   Joint private and public ventures, investigations, emergency planning, crime prevention programs.

Private Security Officer Employment Authorization Act of 2004   A federal law that, within limits, permits private employers to conduct criminal history checks of security personnel.

Privatization of public security services   Public services provided by private organizations (contractors).

Procedure   Outlines steps to be followed consistently in a definite order.

Products of combustion   Flame, heat, smoke, and toxic gases.

Professional development   Training, education, and experiences designed to assist a person to perform well.

Progressive discipline   Corrective action progressing through several steps, that is, verbal warning, written reprimand, suspension, demotion, or termination.

Promotion   Services as a means to fill job vacancies, as a reward or morale booster, and as an incentive for employees to perform better.

Property damage investigation   Focuses on damage to property, rather than harm to a person.

Proprietary alarm system   Owned and operated on-site by the protected user.

Proprietary information   Virtually any information belonging to an individual or organization.

Proprietary security   Security program controlled and financed directly by the protected organization.

Proximate cause   Legal cause; the actor can foresee (anticipate) the consequences of an act or omission to act.

Psychological tests   Used to determine an individual's emotional stability and mental health.

Public administration   Refers to administration of public and quasi-public organizations.

Public alarm system   Typically, an alarm system connected directly to a public 911 emergency dispatch center or police department.

Public law enforcement   Generally refers to peace officers working with a city, county, state, federal, or other public police or law enforcement agency.

Punitive damages   Designed to punish a respondent in a lawsuit.

Pure risk   Potential for harm or loss with no possible benefit.

Quality assurance   Continuous quality improvement; initiative designed to promote and assure quality.

Quality assurance initiative   Collaborative effort that involves goal setting, trust, cohesiveness, increasing information flow, and conflict resolution designed to improve the quality of products and services provided.

REAL ID Act of 2005   A federal law that imposes minimum standards for driver licenses, including verification of personal information provided by license applicants and counterfeit-resistant security features incorporated into each license.

Real property   Land and anything permanently (or semipermanently) attached to land; real estate.

Receivables conversion   Occurs when employee misappropriates a customer's cash payment and covers the theft with a payment received from another customer.

Recruitment   Process of locating and attracting suitable candidates to fill job vacancies.

Refund policy   Refunds tightly controlled from central location; sales receipt required; audit refund procedure.

Repeat-use (standing) plan   Implemented each time a given situation or incident occurs. Unless modified, repeat-use plans change little over time.

Residential burglary prevention strategy   Residence should appear occupied; key control; doors and windows locked; lighting; strangers not admitted; inventory valuables; travel plans not broadcast; alarm system.

Resume   Subjective account of a person's background. Used as a preemployment screening device.

Return on investment (ROI)   Net cost savings that result from security measures employed.

Risk   Possibility of suffering harm or loss; exposure to probability of loss or damage; an element of uncertainty.

Risk assessment   Critical, objective analysis of an organization's entire protective system.

Risk management techniques   Strategies and tactics designed to eliminate risk, reduce the probability loss will occur, or mitigate damage, if threat materializes.

Roles of public law enforcement Keep the peace, maintain order, police public property, and respond to and investigate crime.

Roles of the security manager Managerial, administrative, preventive, investigative.

Safe-school zone School campus areas, transportation systems, and off-campus activity venues that give rise to zero-tolerance policies focusing on weapons and drugs.

Security Freedom from risk or harm; safety.

Security and Accountability for Every (SAFE) Port Act of 2006 A federal law that requires deployment of automated container tracking systems as well as systems designed to detect nuclear and radiological materials.

Security management Multifaceted and interdisciplinary management tactics and strategies designed to secure persons, property, and information and prevent losses from any source.

Security services Public and private security services designed to protect people, property, and information.

Security survey Risk assessment tool used to evaluate an organization to identify risks and security hazards/deficiencies.

Selection In preemployment screening, the process of evaluating and choosing the most appropriate and qualified person from a pool of applicants.

Sensitive Compartmented Information (SCI) Security systems, policies, and procedures designed to restrict access to information on a need-to-know basis.

Sensor Device that senses a specific condition, such as motion, sound, temperature, or vibration.

Sexual harassment Pattern of behavior that involves unwelcome lewd remarks, offensive touching, intimidation, and other conduct or communication of a sexual nature that is offensive to a reasonable person; a form of discrimination defined as requests for sexual favors, unwelcome sexual advances, or verbal or physical conduct of a sexual nature when submission to such conduct is used as a basis for employment decisions.

Sheriff Historically, the chief law enforcement officer of a county.

Shoplifting Misappropriation (theft) of retail merchandise.

Shoplifting methods Hiding items, thwarting sensors, switching price tags, use of a booster box, wearing stolen item, grab and run.

Shoplifting prevention strategy Deterrence, detection, surveillance, inspections, enforced refund procedures, locks, alarms, observant personnel.

Single-use plan A plan that is used once and no longer needed when the objectives of the plan are accomplished.

Solicitation A crime that involves requesting another to commit a crime.

Space radio communications Includes communications systems and equipment such as cellular phones, marine and mobile radio telephones, microwave radio relays, satellite radio, and high-frequency radio.

Speculative risk Potential for benefit or loss, depending on consequences of activity or inactivity.

Spyware A form of software that collects personal information without the victim's consent. The victim's personal data is secretly obtained using a variety of methods, including logging the victim's keystrokes or Internet browsing history, or by accessing documents on the victim's computer hard drive.

Standardized Emergency Management System (SEMS) A state-level disaster and emergency response plan; integrated with the National Incident Management System (NIMS).

State, county, and local law enforcement agencies Public police agencies with narrow territorial jurisdiction and broad subject matter jurisdiction (general police powers).

State police Police officers with general police powers employed by a state.

Static risk Constant and unchanging risk, as in the possibility of an earthquake or severe storm.

Statute Written law that is the product of legislative activity.

Strategic business intelligence Seeks to forecast the long-range implications of business activities.

Strategic plan Long-range plan.

Street crime Generally, refers to crimes such as murder, rape, robbery, assault, burglary, larceny (theft), auto theft, and arson.

Strict liability Liability attached even though the person liable was not at fault or did not intend any harm.

Subjective (qualitative) measures Used in risk assessment, planning, and evaluation. Include expert opinion, forecasting, and the Delphi technique.

Substance abuse Refers to the inappropriate ingestion of toxic and controlled substances into the human body.

Supervision Management; involves directing people toward organizational goals.

Supplies and materials expenses Refers to objects with a life expectancy of less than 1 year; includes office supplies, computer software, fuel, and so on.

Support Anti-Terrorism by Fostering Effective Technologies Act (SAFETY Act) of 2002 This is a subsection (subtitle) of the Homeland Security Act of 2002. It created liability protections for sellers of qualified antiterrorism technologies and others in the supply and distribution chain.

Surreptitious investigative methods Secret (undercover) investigative methods.

Surveillance Covert or overt observation of persons or property.

Symptoms of substance abuse Significant changes in personal appearance, sudden and irrational changes in behavior, or similar changes in human behavior.

Systems design and engineering Tools used by professionals such as architects and engineers to design security features into a facility.

Tactical business intelligence Focuses on actual rather than perceived or advertised schemes of competitors.

Tactical plan Short-range plan.

Tangible standards Standards that are quite clear, specific, identifiable, and generally measurable; typically expressed in terms of dollars, numbers, physical properties, and time.

Task Force Report on Private Security Published by the National Commission on Criminal Justice Standards and Goals in 1976, this Report recommended minimum training and licensing requirements for private security.

Technical security Term used to describe the development and implementation of countermeasures identified in risk assessments; prevention of adverse technical surveillance caused by the use of intrusion devices.

Terrorism Use of violence or threats to intimidate or coerce.

Thermal sensor Senses heat in a protected area.

Thief takers Forerunners of bounty hunters; provided for in British Highwayman Act of 1692.

Tort A civil, rather than criminal, wrong for which the law provides a remedy.

Trademark Protects against unauthorized use of a distinctive mark, name, word, symbol, or device that identifies the goods of a particular commercial enterprise.

Traditional budget A budget that includes a simple percentage increase over the previous budget.

Traffic control Use of physical security and facility design to control vehicular and pedestrian traffic patterns.

Transaction report Sales records, voided sales receipts, and other activities performed by cash registers each day.

Transactional leadership When one takes the initiative, making contact with another, for the purpose of the exchange of valued things.

Transborder Crosses borders; generally refers to event in one country that impacts the environment in another country.

Transcript A written record; typically refers to a written record of a judicial proceeding.

Transformational leadership When one engages another in a way that the leader and nonleader raise one another to higher levels of motivation and morality.

Transmission security Policies and procedures that place an adversarial interceptor at a disadvantage.

Transportation Security Administration (TSA) Federal agency with primary responsibility for commercial aviation and transportation security.

Trial court Court where criminal or civil trial takes place.

Ultrasonic motion sensor Transmits and detects extremely high (beyond a human's audible range) sound energy.

Undercover investigation A surveillance through which the surveillant, using an assumed identity or cover, personally encounters a subject under investigation.

Uniform Crime Report (UCR) Document published by the FBI that includes crime statistics reported voluntarily to the FBI by law enforcement agencies throughout the United States.

Unintentional tort Emanates from a situation in which person liable did not intend harm but the person failed to exercise the care of an ordinary, reasonable, and prudent person.

Unlawful detention Detention of one person by another without lawful authority.

U.S. court of appeals Intermediate appellate court in the federal court system.

U.S. Department of Homeland Security (DHS) A department of the federal government responsible for protecting the United States from and responding to terrorism, disasters, and other major national incidents.

U.S. district court Trial court in the federal (national) court system.

U.S. Economic Security Act of 1996 Federal law relating to the protection of U.S. economic interests, including the protection of critical information.

U.S. Supreme Court Court of last resort in the United States. The only court created by the U.S. Constitution.

USA Patriot Act of 2001 Officially titled the Uniting and Strengthening America by Providing Appropriate Tools

Required to Intercept and Obstruct Terrorism, this federal law broadens law enforcement criminal investigative authority.

USA PATRIOT Act Improvement and Reauthorization Act of 2005 The reauthorizing legislation that made permanent 14 of the 16 sunsetted provisions of the USA PATRIOT Act of 2001.

Utility security measures Emergency planning, security personnel, redundant systems, disaster recovery, accident prevention, training, protective equipment, inventory control, crime prevention, conflict resolution, physical security.

Value Moral standard; formed through the influence of others.

Value-added contribution (VAC) Value security contributes to the organization.

Vicarious liability Liability incurred as a result of situations in which organizations or third parties may be held liable for the intentional or unintentional actions of others with whom they have a relationship.

Victimless crime Participants enter into the activity voluntarily. Examples include illegal gambling and drugs, prostitution, and pornography.

Virginia Tech Virginia Polytechnic Institute and State University; site of deadliest single-perpetrator shooting rampage in U.S. history; where Cho Seung Hui killed 32, wounded 30, and killed himself.

Virtual security organization The security function is integrated with the entire operation or merged with another department.

Vishing Similar to phishing but, instead of being directed toward an Internet site, the victim is asked to provide personal information through a telephone system connected to the Internet.

Vision statement Articulation of an image for a better future.

***Voir dire* examination** "Speak the truth" examination of a prospective trial juror to determine juror's suitability for jury service. The prospective juror's qualifications may be challenged for cause or a party may exercise a peremptory challenge.

White collar crime Offense committed by a person or group in the course of an otherwise respected and legitimate occupation or financial activity. Generally refers to crimes such as corruption, bribery, tax evasion, embezzlement, industrial espionage, and other economic crimes.

Workplace violence Violence upon a person that occurs in the workplace.

Workplace violence prevention plan Policies, procedures, training of employees, liaison with community services, security, enforcement of codes of conduct, assistance programs.

Zero-based budget (ZBB) Budget process through which each program within a budget period must justify its existence and expenditures.

Zoological park Permanent cultural institution that owns and maintains wildlife that represent more than a token collection and exhibits the collection to the public.

APPENDIX A

Correlation of ASIS International Syllabus for Introduction to Security for Business Students with *Introduction to Security: Operations and Management*, 4th Edition

ASIS International Syllabus Module		Relevant Text Chapters
I	The Context for Security	1, 4, 10–14
II	Risk Assessment	7
III	Legal Aspects of Security Management in America	3
IV	Investigations	2, 9
V	Personnel Integrity and Protection	5
VI	Technical Management	7, 8
VII	Information Protection	6
VIII	Business Intelligence	9

APPENDIX B

Safety and Security Survey Instrument

A safety and security survey involves a critical and objective audit, assessment, and analysis of an entire organization to identify hazards and deficiencies. A survey instrument, such as this checklist, is typically used to identify the organization's vulnerabilities. Utilize the following nomenclature to evaluate each area.

S = Satisfactory

U = Unsatisfactory

N/A = Not applicable

GENERAL

Nature of business/agency: _____

Facility name: _____

Address: _____

Survey date: _____

Hours of operations: _____

Facility contact person: _____

Phone number: _____

Fax number: _____

Email address: _____

Environment: (check one)

Urban industrial _____ Urban residential _____ Suburban industrial _____ Suburban residential _____ Rural _____

Survey conducted by: _____

Surveyor's address: _____

Surveyor's phone: _____

Surveyor's email: _____

Country (where facility is located)	S	U	N/A
Political conditions	_____	_____	_____
Crime rates	_____	_____	_____
Personnel safety	_____	_____	_____
Availability of labor	_____	_____	_____
Economic conditions	_____	_____	_____

Country (where facility is located)	S	U	N/A
Medical treatment availability	_____	_____	_____
Public firefighting availability	_____	_____	_____
Public utilities	_____	_____	_____
Public transportation	_____	_____	_____
Public roadways	_____	_____	_____
Flood susceptibility	_____	_____	_____
Earthquake susceptibility	_____	_____	_____
Fire susceptibility	_____	_____	_____
Hurricane susceptibility	_____	_____	_____
Tornado susceptibility	_____	_____	_____
Severe weather susceptibility	_____	_____	_____

Comments

_____

_____

_____

_____

Community (neighborhood)	S	U	N/A
Crime rates	_____	_____	_____
Aesthetic qualities	_____	_____	_____
Public police protection	_____	_____	_____
Fire protection	_____	_____	_____
Emergency medical services	_____	_____	_____
History of civil unrest	_____	_____	_____
Graffiti/vandalism	_____	_____	_____

Comments

_____

_____

_____

_____

Risk Assessment, Security Surveys, Planning	**S**	**U**	**N/A**
Continuous risk assessment/analysis	_____	_____	_____
Security surveys conducted regularly	_____	_____	_____
Contingency/disaster plans	_____	_____	_____
Business/operations continuity plans	_____	_____	_____

Comments

_____

_____

_____

_____

PHYSICAL SECURITY

Facility Perimeter	**S**	**U**	**N/A**
Fencing	_____	_____	_____
Landscaping	_____	_____	_____
Parking	_____	_____	_____
Employee parking area illumination	_____	_____	_____
Visitor/guest parking area illumination	_____	_____	_____
Employee parking area monitoring	_____	_____	_____
Visitor/guest parking area monitoring	_____	_____	_____
Lighting (all areas properly illuminated?)	_____	_____	_____
Vehicular traffic pattern	_____	_____	_____
Pedestrian traffic pattern	_____	_____	_____
Trash removal	_____	_____	_____
Protection from adjacent occupancies	_____	_____	_____
Proper signage	_____	_____	_____

Comments

_____

_____

_____

_____

BUILDING

Describe type of construction, building design, number of entrances/exits, windows, roof construction, number of stories, adjacent occupancies. Photographs or video of building are helpful.

_____

_____

_____

_____

_____

_____

_____

	S	U	N/A
Common walls with adjacent occupancies	_____	_____	_____
Exterior door construction	_____	_____	_____
Exterior door locks	_____	_____	_____
Door lock operation	_____	_____	_____
Exterior window construction	_____	_____	_____
Window height above ground	_____	_____	_____
Window security	_____	_____	_____
Roof access restrictions	_____	_____	_____
Building exterior lighting	_____	_____	_____
Emergency lighting system	_____	_____	_____
Shipping/receiving area monitoring	_____	_____	_____
Emergency exits	_____	_____	_____
Emergency exits unobstructed	_____	_____	_____
Interior door construction	_____	_____	_____
Interior wall construction	_____	_____	_____
Antitheft systems/mechanisms	_____	_____	_____

Comments

_____

_____

_____

_____

Access Control   S   U   N/A

Intrusion detection   _____ _____ _____

Building entrances minimized   _____ _____ _____

Employee entrance monitoring   _____ _____ _____

Visitor/guest entrance monitoring _____ _____ _____

Interior door locks   _____ _____ _____

Key control system   _____ _____ _____

Key sign-out/assignment system _____ _____ _____

Keys accounted for   _____ _____ _____

Key safeguards   _____ _____ _____

Employee distinguishability   _____ _____ _____

Visitor/guest supervision   _____ _____ _____

Restricted access to sensitive/vulnerable areas _____ _____ _____

Computer/data storage area restrictions _____ _____ _____

Key storage area restrictions _____ _____ _____

Mechanical/utility room restrictions _____ _____ _____

Telecommunications room restrictions _____ _____ _____

Mailroom restrictions   _____ _____ _____

Executive office suite restrictions _____ _____ _____

Vendor access   _____ _____ _____

Vault/safe security   _____ _____ _____

Controlled substance security _____ _____ _____

Hazardous material security   _____ _____ _____

Cash/liquid asset protection   _____ _____ _____

Proper signage to direct visitors _____ _____ _____

Comments

_____

_____

_____

_____

Alarm and Surveillance Systems

Does facility have an alarm system?   Yes _____   No _____

If yes, type: Local _____ Central station _____ Police connected _____

	S	U	N/A
Alarm coverage	_____	_____	_____
Emergency power source	_____	_____	_____
Frequency of alarm tests	_____	_____	_____
Frequency of false alarms	_____	_____	_____
Penalties assessed by government for false alarms	_____	_____	_____
Alarm response	_____	_____	_____

Alarm response provided by _____

Does facility have surveillance cameras? Yes _____ No _____

	S	U	N/A
Lighting compatibility with cameras	_____	_____	_____
Surveillance camera monitoring	_____	_____	_____
Surveillance camera video recording	_____	_____	_____

Comments

_____

_____

_____

_____

Fire Protection

Fire alarm system: manual _____ automatic _____ none _____

	S	U	N/A
Sprinkler system	_____	_____	_____
18-inch clearance below sprinkler head	_____	_____	_____
Fire extinguishers	_____	_____	_____
Fire suppression in computer facilities	_____	_____	_____
Fire alarm system testing	_____	_____	_____
Fire suppression system testing	_____	_____	_____

Gas line protection	_____	_____	_____
Electric power cord protection	_____	_____	_____
Fire doors functional	_____	_____	_____
Flammable material storage	_____	_____	_____
Fire notification plan	_____	_____	_____
Fire evacuation plan	_____	_____	_____
Fire exits unobstructed	_____	_____	_____
Fire exits secured from outside	_____	_____	_____
In-house fire brigade	_____	_____	_____
Fire safety policy/procedures	_____	_____	_____
Street number/address prominently displayed	_____	_____	_____

Comments

_____

_____

_____

_____

Personnel Security	**S**	**U**	**N/A**
Employee background investigations	_____	_____	_____
Previous employer verification	_____	_____	_____
Personnel records security	_____	_____	_____
Exit interviews at employee termination	_____	_____	_____
Organization property retrieval at termination	_____	_____	_____
Employee/visitor safeguards against:			
Accidents	_____	_____	_____
Theft	_____	_____	_____
Assault	_____	_____	_____
Workplace violence	_____	_____	_____

Comments

_____

_____

_____

_____

Information Security	**S**	**U**	**N/A**
Critical information identification	_____	_____	_____
Critical information security	_____	_____	_____
Information hard-copy destruction	_____	_____	_____
Employee nondisclosure agreement in place	_____	_____	_____
Intellectual property identification	_____	_____	_____
Intellectual property security	_____	_____	_____
Client/customer list protection	_____	_____	_____
Access to computers restricted	_____	_____	_____
Access to computer transmissions restricted	_____	_____	_____
Portable personal computers/laptop security	_____	_____	_____
Email access restrictions	_____	_____	_____
Internet connection security	_____	_____	_____
Electronic document destruction procedures	_____	_____	_____
Software licensing	_____	_____	_____
Prohibition against installing software from outside without authorization	_____	_____	_____
Terminated employees immediately denied access	_____	_____	_____
Disaster recovery plan	_____	_____	_____
Duplicate data files maintained at remote location	_____	_____	_____
Password security	_____	_____	_____
Information security indoctrination/training	_____	_____	_____
Cellular phones used to access confidential proprietary information?	_____	_____	_____
Cellular phone communication protection	_____	_____	_____

Comments

_____

_____

_____

_____

INVESTIGATIONS, INTELLIGENCE, AND SECURITY

Background Investigations	S	U	N/A
Employees (new)	___	___	___
Employees (existing)	___	___	___
Vendors/contractors	___	___	___
Partnerships with other organizations	___	___	___
Security clearances	___	___	___

Comments

_____

_____

_____

_____

Incident Investigations	S	U	N/A
Investigation of any loss	___	___	___
Accidents	___	___	___
Safety hazards	___	___	___
Crime	___	___	___
Natural disasters	___	___	___

Comments

_____

_____

_____

_____

Intelligence	S	U	N/A
Competition counterintelligence	_____	_____	_____
Criminal intelligence	_____	_____	_____
Foreign travel intelligence	_____	_____	_____

Comments

_____

_____

_____

_____

Reporting Procedures	S	U	N/A
Background investigations documentation	_____	_____	_____
Background investigations confidentiality	_____	_____	_____
Security Activity Log maintenance	_____	_____	_____
Recording of incidents	_____	_____	_____
Incident reported to proper manager/authority	_____	_____	_____
Adherence to reporting procedures	_____	_____	_____

Comments

_____

_____

_____

_____

Operations	S	U	N/A
Audit procedures	_____	_____	_____
Employee locker/workspace inspections	_____	_____	_____
Accounting function separation	_____	_____	_____
Package control system	_____	_____	_____
Opening time ambush controls	_____	_____	_____
Closing time ambush controls	_____	_____	_____
Receiving area security	_____	_____	_____

Operations

	S	U	N/A
Shipping area security	_____	_____	_____
Delivery driver controls	_____	_____	_____
Shipping/receiving area separation	_____	_____	_____
Equipment inventory	_____	_____	_____
Contractor/vendor audits	_____	_____	_____
Customer/guest/visitor service	_____	_____	_____

Comments

_____

_____

_____

_____

Policies and Procedures

	S	U	N/A
Mission statement	_____	_____	_____
Vision statement	_____	_____	_____
Organizational goals	_____	_____	_____
Organizational values	_____	_____	_____
Quality improvement initiatives	_____	_____	_____
Employee code of conduct (ethics)	_____	_____	_____
Employee misconduct policies	_____	_____	_____
Disciplinary procedures	_____	_____	_____
Termination procedures	_____	_____	_____
Search/inspection policies	_____	_____	_____
Removal of organization property	_____	_____	_____
Bomb threat procedures	_____	_____	_____
Evacuation procedures	_____	_____	_____
Severe weather procedures	_____	_____	_____
Natural disaster procedures	_____	_____	_____
Contraband detection	_____	_____	_____
Chemical abuse policy	_____	_____	_____
Drug testing policy	_____	_____	_____

Comments

_____

_____

_____

_____

Security Indoctrination/Training	S	U	N/A
Indoctrination (new employees)	____	____	____
Training (existing employees)	____	____	____
Executive protection	____	____	____
Foreign travel training	____	____	____

Comments

_____

_____

_____

_____

Liaison Activities	S	U	N/A
Contact with local police maintained	____	____	____
Contact with sheriff maintained	____	____	____
Contact with state police/highway patrol maintained	____	____	____
Contact with fire department maintained	____	____	____
Contact with appropriate federal agency maintained	____	____	____
Articulation/collaboration with other security organizations	____	____	____

Comments

_____

_____

_____

_____

Counterterrorism Activities	S	U	N/A
Employee education/training	_____	_____	_____
Terrorism prevention strategies	_____	_____	_____
Response plans (bombs, bomb threats, weapons of mass destruction)	_____	_____	_____

Comments

_____

_____

_____

_____

APPENDIX C

Websites and Email Addresses for Additional Exploration

Chapter 1

www.asisonline.org (ASIS International, for information regarding training, education, and certification programs)

Chapter 2

www.nida.nih.gov (National Institute on Drug Abuse, to learn more about substance abuse prevention and treatment)

www.nimh.nih.gov/index.shtml (National Institute of Mental Health)

www.dea.gov (U.S. Drug Enforcement Administration, for information on substance abuse and its prevention and treatment)

www.fbi.gov (Federal Bureau of Investigation, offering information regarding crime statistics and trends)

www.ftc.gov/idtheft (Federal Trade Commission, containing information regarding identity theft, its prevention, and how to report it)

www.ssa.gov/pubs/idtheft.htm (Social Security Administration, containing information regarding identity theft, its prevention, and how to report it)

Chapter 3

www.uscourts.gov/about (Federal Judiciary, for information about the federal courts)

www.abanet.org (American Bar Association, for information on the judicial process and legal concepts and laws)

www.hg.org (Hieros Gamos Legal Directories, to learn more about criminal laws in all 50 states)

Chapter 4

communications@csaaul.org (for information on alarm systems)

www.alarm.org (Central Station Alarm Association)

www.gsa.gov/portal/content/104644 (U.S. General Services Administration portal on alarm systems and management)

Chapter 5

www.ethics.ubc.ca (University of British Columbia's W. Maurice Young Centre for Applied Ethics for information regarding codes of ethics)

www.ethicalleadership.biz (The Ethical Leadership Institute for information on ethical leadership competencies)

Chapter 6

www.fas.org/sgp/library/nispom.htm (National Industrial Security Program Operational Manual, for details on regulations governing the protection of classified government information)

www.us-cert.gov/federal (U.S. Computer Emergency Readiness Team)

www.whitehouse.gov/issues/homeland-security (U.S. Department of Homeland Security, Information Analysis and Infrastructure Protection)

www.nw3c.org (National White Collar Crime Center)

Chapter 7

www.ojp.usdoj.gov/nij/maps (National Institute of Justice MAPS Program)

www.fema.gov/areyouready (Federal Emergency Management Agency, for access to *Are You Ready? An In-depth Guide to Citizen Preparedness*, a resource for individual, family, and community disaster and emergency preparedness)

www.dhs.gov/nrp (U.S. Department of Homeland Security, for information on the National Response Plan)

Chapter 8

www.careerclusters.org (States' Career Clusters, for details on high school preparation for security careers)

www.quality.nist.gov (about the Malcolm Baldrige National Quality Award criteria and quality self-analysis worksheets)

Chapter 9

www.fedworld.gov (a clearinghouse for government information)

www.fbi.gov (Federal Bureau of Investigation)

www.treas.gov (U.S. Secret Service)

www.ncix.gov (National Counterintelligence Center)

www.diss.mil (Defense Security Service)

www.nsi.org (National Security Institute)

www.travel.state.gov (U.S. State Department's Bureau of Consular Affairs)

www.loc.gov (Library of Congress)

www.symantac.com, www.mcafee.com/us, www.sophos.com, www.norman.com (Norman Data Defense Systems) (major antivirus software producers)

www.classmgmt.com (National Classification Management Society)

www.scip.org (Society of Competitive Intelligence Professionals)

www.ifpo.org (International Foundation for Protection Officers)

www.cfenet.com (Association of Certified Fraud Examiners)

www.library.northwestern.edu/reference/instructional_services (Northwestern University Library's Economist Intelligence Unit, for information on political and economic conditions in foreign countries)

Chapter 10

www.drii.org (Disaster Recovery Institute International, offering information on disaster recovery planning)

www.colorado.edu/UCB/Research/cspv (Center for the Study and Prevention of School Violence)

www2.ed.gov/about/offices/list/osdfs/index.html (Creating Safe and Drug-Free Schools: An Action Guide) www2.ed.gov/about/offices/list/losers/oscp/gtss.html (Early Warning, Timely Response: A Guide to Safe Schools)

www.ncpc.org (National Crime Prevention Council)

www.nrcys.ou.edu (National Resource Center for Youth Services, College of Continuing Education, University of Oklahoma)

www.nssc1.org (National School Safety Center)

www.ojjdp.ncjrs.org (Office of Juvenile Justice and Delinquency Prevention)

www.pavnet.org (Partnerships against Violence Network)

www2.ed.gov/offices/OSDFS/actguid/index.html (Safe and Drug-Free Schools Program Office)

www.schoolcrisisresponse.com (The American Academy of Experts in Traumatic Stress, Comprehensive School Crisis Response Plan)

www.safeschoolscoalition.org (The Safe Schools Coalition)

www.ed.gov/emergencyplan (U.S. Department of Education Emergency Planning)

www.cdc.gov/nccdphp (Youth Risk Benefit Survey, Centers for Disease Control and Prevention)

www.securityoncampus.org (Security On Campus, Inc.)

Chapter 11

www.workplaceviolence911.com (National Institute for the Prevention of Workplace Violence)

Chapter 12

www.nctc.gov (National Counterterrorism Center)

www.epa.gov (U.S. Environmental Protection Agency)

www.flu.gov (U.S. Department of Health and Human Services, providing information about influenza pandemics and their control)

www.dhs.gov (U.S. Department of Homeland Security)

www.9-11commission.gov (The 9/11 Commission Report)

Chapter 13

www.asisonline.org/education/academicresources (ASIS International, for information on colleges and universities that offer security education programs)

www.tsa.gov (U.S. Transportation Security Administration)

www.usajobs.opm.gov (for information about security careers with the U.S. government)

www.asisonline.org/careercenter/index.xml (for information about security careers)

www.lpjobs.com (for information about careers in retail loss prevention)

REFERENCES

Abcarian, R., Reston, M., & Hennessy-Fiske, M. (2011, January 16). Descent into darkness. *Los Angeles Times*, pp. A1, A18–A19.

Access Control & Security Systems Integration. (1999). *1999 salary survey*. Atlanta, GA: Security Lock Distributors.

Acker, J. R., & Brody, D. C. (2004). *Criminal procedure: A contemporary perspective* (2nd ed.). Boston, MA: Jones and Bartlett Publishers.

Adams, C. (2000a, March). Super security: Preparing for the big game takes months of effort. *Access Control & Security Systems Integration, 43*(3), 14, 16, 18.

Adams, C. (2000b, November). The Internet and security: Survey reveals possible lapses in judgment. *iSecurity*, p. 22.

Adams, T. F. (2007). *Police field operations* (7th ed.). Upper Saddle River, NJ: Prentice Hall.

Adams, T. F., Caddell, A. G., & Krutsinger, J. L. (2004). *Crime scene investigation* (2nd ed.). Upper Saddle River, NJ: Prentice Hall.

Adler, F., Mueller, G. O. W., & Laufer, W. S. (2009). *Criminal justice: An introduction* (5th ed.). New York: McGraw-Hill.

Adler, N. J. (2008). *International dimensions of organizational behavior* (5th ed.). Cincinnati, OH: Thomson Learning.

Adler, R. B., & Towne, N. (2007). *Looking out/looking in* (12th ed.). Fort Worth, TX: Harcourt College Publishing.

Ahlers, M. M., & Meserve, J. (2011, January 29). TSA shuts door on private airport screening program. CNN.com. [Online]. Available: http://articles.cnn.com/2011-01-29/travel/tsa.private_1_tsa-government-screeners-screening-program?_s=PM:TRAVEL.

Ainsworth, B. (2000, December 19). Drug measure a challenge to carry out. *San Diego Union Tribune*, p. A3.

Albanese, J. S. (1996). *Organized crime in America*. Cincinnati, OH: Anderson.

Albanese, J. S. (2008). *Criminal justice 2000 update* (4th ed.). Needham Heights, MA: Allyn & Bacon.

Albrecht, S. (2001, January 3). Guns at work in the wake of Wakefield. *San Diego Union Tribune*, p. B7.

Alcohol test info. (2011). [Online]. Available: http://www.alcohol-test-info.com/Employee_Drug_and_Alcohol_Testing_Statistics.html.

Alderfer, C. P. (1972). *Existence, relatedness and growth: Human needs in organizational settings*. New York: The Free Press.

America under attack. (2001, September 11). *Newsweek Extra Edition, 88*(12-A), 1–64.

American Association of Community Colleges. (2002). *Protecting information: The role of community colleges in cybersecurity education*. Washington, DC: Community College Press.

American Institute of Architects. (2003). *Building security through design*. [Online]. Available: http://www.aia.org/security.

American Society for Industrial Security. (1998). *ASIS International presents introduction to security for business students*. Alexandria, VA: American Society for Industrial Security.

American Zoo and Aquarium Society. (2007). *Accreditation fact sheet 2007*. [Online]. Available: http://www.aza.org/dept/accred/accredfacts.htm.

An education in crime stats. (2000, November 15). *Law Enforcement News, 26*(543), 1, 10.

Anderson, C. (2003, April 10). FBI reports internet fraud tripled last year. *San Diego Union Tribune*, p. A15.

Anderson, T. (1999, June). Treading lightly through the hiring thicket. *Security Management, 43*(6), 35–36, 38–41.

Anderson, T. (2000, May). Taking stock of the states. *Security Management, 44*(5), 74–79.

Anderson, T. (2002, December). On the money. *Security Management, 46*(12), 49–50, 68–69.

Anderson, T. (2010, October). How Dallas does security. *Security Management, 54*(10), 56–62, 64–66, 68, 70–72, 74, 76.

Anderson, T. (2011, January). Legal report: Employment compliance. *Security Management, 55*(1), 64.

Anti-Phishing Working Group. (2007). *What is phishing and pharming?* [Online]. Available: http://www.antiphishing.org.

Argyris, C. (1964). *Integrating the individual and the organization.* New York: Wiley.

Armour, S. (2003, February 10). Wal-Mart takes hit on worker treatment: Lawsuits, unions slam megaretailer. *USA Today*, p. B01.

Arner, M. (2000a, October 16). Crime rate falling in this county and in U.S. for now. *San Diego Union Tribune*, p. A1.

Arner, M. (2000b, December 31). Worker thefts hit transit agencies. *San Diego Union Tribune*, pp. B1, B4.

Arnette, J. L., & Walsleben, M. C. (1998, April). Combating fear and restoring safety in schools. *Juvenile Justice Bulletin*. Washington, DC: U.S. Department of Justice, Office of Juvenile Justice and Delinquency Prevention, pp. 11–12.

Aronsohn, A. J. (2003, April). E-Snooping. *Loss Prevention & Security Journal, 3*(4), 36–37.

ASIS International. (2005). *Career opportunities in security.* Alexandra, VA: ASIS International.

ASIS International. (2007). *Code of ethics.* Alexandria, VA: ASIS International.

ASIS International. (2010). *U.S. security salary survey.* Alexandria, VA: ASIS International.

ASIS International Guidelines Commission. (2007). *General security risk assessment guidelines.* Alexandria, VA: ASIS International.

Association for Computing Machinery. (2007). *About ACM.* [Online]. Available: http://www.acm.org/about_acm/.

Aun, F. J. (2007, January 23). Cybercriminals favor web browser attacks. *Tech News World.* [Online]. Available: http://www.technewsworld.com.

Badolato, E. V. (2000, July). Smart moves against cargo theft. *Security Management, 44*(7), 110–112, 114–115.

Bagott, J. (2003, May). It's all happening at the zoo. *Security Management, 47*(5), 46–50, 52, 54, 56.

Bailin, P. (2000, November). Gazing into security's future. *Security Management, 44*(11), 60–63, 65, 67.

Baker, T. E. (2011). *Effective police leadership: Moving beyond management* (3rd ed.). Flushing, NY: Looseleaf Publications, Inc.

Baldor, L. C. (2010, October 1). Report: US, EU must join to stop homegrown terror. Associated Press.

Balint, K. (2000, September 8). Copyrights take a licking on Net Frontier. *San Diego Union Tribune*, pp. A1, A23.

Banerjee, N. (2011, January 14). A new focus on safety in oil production. *Los Angeles Times*, p. A10.

Barlow, H. D. (2000). *Criminal justice in America.* Upper Saddle River, NJ: Prentice Hall.

Barnes, S. (2000, December 29). Freezing weather's icy grip continues in Midwest, South. *San Diego Union Tribune*, p. A12.

Bass, B. M. (1981). *Stogdill's handbook of leadership: A survey of theory and research.* New York: The Free Press.

Bass, B. M. (1985). *Leadership and performance beyond expectations.* New York: The Free Press.

Bass, B. M. (1990). *Handbook of leadership.* New York: The Free Press.

Bassett, J. (2006, September). When your CEO says "show me the money." *Security Technology & Design, 16*(9), 84–86.

Batterton, B. S. (2011). Terry stops, frisks and duffel bags. *Public Agency Training Council.* [Online]. Available: http://www.llrmi.com/articles/legal_update/2011_6th_walker.shtml. Retrieved: January 18, 2011.

Batza, D., & Taylor, M. (2000, December). James got his gun. *Security Management, 44*(12), 74–79.

Bauer, A. (2011, January). War on terror or policing terrorism? Radicalization and expansion of the threats. *The Police Chief*, pp. 46–52.

Bell, S. (2010, October 13). In accepting mobile payment, merchants face higher fraud risk. *American Banker.*

Bellows, R. M. (1959). *Creative leadership.* Englewood Cliffs, NJ: Prentice Hall.

Bennett, W. W., & Hess, K. M. (2007). *Criminal investigation* (8th ed.). Belmont, CA: Thomson Higher Education.

Bennis, W. G. (1984, September). The four competencies of leadership. *Training and Development Journal, 38*(9), 14–19.

Bennis, W. G. (1993a). *An invented life: Reflections on leadership and change.* Reading, MA: Addison-Wesley.

Bennis, W. G. (1993b). Managing the dream: Leadership in the 21st century. In W. E. Rosenbach & R. L. Taylor (Eds.), *Contemporary issues in leadership* (3rd ed.) (pp. 213–218). Boulder, CO: Westview Press.

Bentley, S. W. (1997, October). An alliance is born. *Security Management, 41*(10), 77, 78, 80.

Berinato, S. (2007, February). How to prevent workplace violence. *CSO, 6*(2), 18.

Bigelow, B. V. (1998, March 4). Hacker attack hits computers across nation. *San Diego Union Tribune*, p. A1.

Blake, R. R., & Mouton, J. S. (1985). *The managerial grid.* Houston, TX: Gulf.

Blanchard, K., & Johnson, S. (1992). *The one minute manager.* New York: Morrow.

Bland, T. S. (2000, January). Get a handle on harassment. *Security Management, 44*(1), 62, 64–67.

Bland, T. S., & Harkavy, M. S. (2000, September). It's all in their heads. *Security Management, 44*(9), 92–94, 96.

Bland, T. S., & Stalcup, S. S. (1999, June). Accurate applications. *Security Management, 43*(6), 38–39.

Blitzer, H. L., & Jacobia, J. (2002). *Forensic digital imaging and photography.* Boston, MA: Academic Press.

Bloom, B., Englehart, M., Furst, E., Hill, W., & Krathwohl, D. (1956). *Taxonomy of educational objectives: The classification of educational goals. Handbook 1: Cognitive domain.* New York: David McKay.

Bologna, J., & Shaw, P. (1997). *Corporate crime investigation.* Woburn, MA: Butterworth-Heinemann.

Boni, W., & Kovacich, G. (2000). *Netspionage: The global threat to information.* Woburn, MA: Butterworth-Heinemann.

Boyce, J. G., & Jennings, D. W. (2002). *Information assurance: Managing organizational IT security risks.* Boston, MA: Butterworth-Heinemann.

Bragdon, B. (2006, July). What security's worth. *CSO, 5*(7), 10.

Brandman, B. (2007, January–February). Cargo theft: A costly epidemic. *Loss Prevention, 6*(1), 46–50, 52.

Bratton, W. J. (2011, February). Reducing crime through prevention not incarceration. *Criminology & Public Policy, 10*(1), 63–68.

Bray, C. (2011, January 19). Two arrested in iPad security breach. *Wall Street Journal*, p. 1.

Brenner, B. (2010, October). Sea change. *CSO, 10*, 26.

Bridges, C. (1994, July). A pound of prevention for a ton of merchandise. *Security Management, 38*(7), 22–23.

Bridges, W. (1994, September 19). The end of the job. *Fortune 130*, pp. 62–64.

Brody, D. C., Acker, J. R., & Logan, W. A. (2010). *Criminal law* (2nd ed.). Gaithersburg, MD: Jones and Bartlett Publishing.

Brooke, J. (2001, January 19). Web hacker pleads guilty to attacking huge sites. *San Diego Union Tribune*, p. A16.

Brown, S. E., Esbensen, F. A., & Geis, G. (2007). *Criminology: Exploring crime and its context* (6th ed.). Cincinnati, OH: Anderson.

Brummett, J. (2007, February). An advanced class. *Security Products, 11*(2), 22.

Bunning, R. L. (1979). The Delphi technique: A projection tool for serious inquiry. In *The 1979 annual handbook for group facilitators* (pp. 174–181). San Diego, CA: University Associates.

Burns, J. M. (1978). *Leadership.* New York: Harper & Row.

Burns, L. R., & Becker, S. W. (1988). Leadership and decision making. In S. M. Shortell & A. D. Kaluzny (Eds.), *Health care management: A text in organization theory and behavior* (2nd ed.) (pp. 142–186). New York: Wiley.

Burstein, H. (1996). *Security: A management perspective.* Englewood Cliffs, NJ: Prentice Hall.

Bush signs Cyber Security Act. (2002, December 5). *Government Security.* [Online]. Available: http://govtsecurity.securitysolutions.com.

Businesses unsure how to protect cloud data: Survey. (2010, December 27). *eWeek.*

Byers, B. (2000, September/October). Ethics and criminal justice: Some observations on police misconduct. *ACJS (Academy of Criminal Justice Sciences) Today, 21*(3), 1, 4–7.

Byrnbauer, H., & Tyson, L. A. (1984, September). Flexing the muscles of technical leadership. *Training and Development Journal, 38*(9), 48–52.

Caldwell, G. E. (2000, June). Selling security's mission in a corporate environment. *Security Technology & Design, 10*(6), 12–14, 16.

California Bureau of Security and Investigative Services. (2003). *Assembly Bill (AB) 2880: Increased training and fee increase for security guards.* West Sacramento, CA: Bureau of Security and Investigative Services.

California Commission on Peace Officer Standards and Training. (2012). *Regular peace officer basic course.* Sacramento, CA: Commission on Peace Officer Standards and Training.

California Department of Forestry and Fire Protection. (2009). *20 largest California wildland fires (by structures destroyed).* [Online]. Available: http://www.fire.ca.gov/communications/downloads/fact_sheets/20LSTRUCTURES.pdf.

California Office of Emergency Services. (2007). *Standardized emergency management system (SEMS) guidelines.* [Online]. Available: http://www.oes.ca.gov/operational/oeshome.nsf.

California State. (2010). *Penal code.* Sections 1–632.

Calling all eyes: Spotting potential terrorist activity. (2010, November). *Securitas Security Spotlight*, p. 80.

Campbell, G. K. (2006, August). How to use metrics. *CSO, 5*(8), 40–44.

Canton, L. G. (2003). *Guard force management* (updated edition). Boston, MA: Butterworth-Heinemann.

Carroll, J. M. (1996). *Computer security* (3rd ed.). Woburn, MA: Butterworth-Heinemann.

Carter, L. F. (1953). Leadership and small group behavior. In M. Sherif & M. O. Wilson (Eds.), *Group relations at the crossroads* (pp. 312–322). New York: Harper.

Center for developmental disabilities installs access control, CCTV, fire alarms. (2000, September). *Access Control & Security Systems Integration, 43*(10), 81–83.

Certo, C. C., & Certo, T. (2012). *Modern management* (12th ed.). Upper Saddle River, NJ: Pearson Prentice Hall.

Challenger, J. E. (2007, July 22). Job seekers: Don't lie on your resume. *San Diego Union Tribune*, p. P1.

Champion, D. J., Hartley, R. D., & Rabe, G. A. (2008). *Criminal courts: Structure, process, and issues* (2nd ed.). Upper Saddle River, NJ: Pearson Prentice Hall.

Chan, A. (2003, January). Web-based loss prevention: The fast track to controlling shrink. *Loss Prevention & Security Journal, 3*(1), 12–14.

Cheeseman, H. R. (2010). *Business law* (7th ed.). Upper Saddle River, NJ: Pearson Prentice Hall.

Chenkin v. Bellevue Hospital Center, N.Y.C., ETC, 479 F. Supp. 207 (1979).

China's piracy plague. (2000, June 5). *Business Week*, pp. 44–46.

Christus Santa Rosa Health System upgrades at five of its campuses. (2010, September). *Security Technology Executive*, pp. 66–67.

Chuvala, J., III, & Fischer, R. J. (Eds.). (1991). *Suggested preparation for careers in security/loss prevention.* Dubuque, IA: Kendall/Hunt.

Clapper, J. R. (2011, February 10). *Remarks as delivered by James R. Clapper, director of National Intelligence, at open hearing on the worldwide threat assessment to the House Permanent Select Committee on Intelligence.* Washington, DC: Office of the Director of National Intelligence. [Online]. Available: https//www.dni.gov/testimonies/20110210_testimony.hpsci_clapper.pdf. Retrieved: February 21, 2011.

Clemmer, J. (1992, April). 5 common errors companies make starting quality initiatives. *Total Quality, 3*, 7.

Clifford, M., & Edwards, T. D. (1998). Defining "environmental crime." In M. Clifford (Ed.), *Environmental crime: Enforcement, policy, and social responsibility* (pp. 5–30). Gaithersburg, MD: Aspen Publishers.

Cole, G. F., & Smith, C. E. (2011). *The American system of criminal justice* (12th ed.). Belmont, CA: Wadsworth/Thomson Learning.

Coleman, J. (2000, August). Trends in security systems integration. *Security Technology & Design, 10*(8), 38–40, 42–44.

Coleman, J. W. (1994). *The criminal elite: The sociology of white collar crime.* New York: St. Martin's Press.

Colling, R. L. (2001). *Hospital and healthcare security* (5th ed.). Burlington, MA: Elsevier.

Collins, K. (2008). *Exploring business.* Upper Saddle River, NJ: Pearson Prentice Hall.

Collins, P. A., Ricks, T. A., & Van Meter, C. W. (2000). *Principles of security and crime prevention* (4th ed.). Cincinnati, OH: Anderson.

Conlon, M. (2000, December 21). No letup seen as freeze menaces much of U.S. *San Diego Union Tribune*, p. A14.

"Cops" test security, get in CIA, other buildings. (2000, May 26). *San Diego Union Tribune*, p. A10.

Cordner, G. W., & Scarborough, K. E. (2010). *Police administration* (7th ed.). Newark, NJ: Matthew Bender & Company.

Counting the cost of employee misunderstanding. (2008). Framingham, MA: IDC.

Covey, S. R. (1998). *The seven habits of highly effective people*. New York: Simon & Schuster.

Craighead, G. (2009). *High-rise security and fire life safety* (3rd ed.). Boston, MA: Butterworth-Heinemann.

Crowe, T. D. (2000). *Crime prevention through environmental design* (2nd ed.). Woburn, MA: Butterworth-Heinemann.

Cunningham, W. C., Strauchs, J. J., & Van Meter, C. W. (1990). *The Hallcrest report II: Private security trends 1970–2000*. Boston, MA: Butterworth-Heinemann.

Cunningham, W. C., & Taylor, T. H. (1985). *The Hallcrest report: Private security and police in America*. Portland, OR: Chancellor Press.

Dalton, D. R. (1995). *Security management: Business strategies for success*. Boston, MA: Butterworth-Heinemann.

Dalton, D. R. (2003). *Rethinking corporate security in the post-9/11 era: Issues and strategies for today's global business community*. Boston, MA: Butterworth-Heinemann.

Daniel, T. (1992, March). Identifying critical leadership competencies of manufacturing supervisors in a major electronics corporation. *Group and Organizational Management: An International Journal, 17*(1), 57–71.

Davenport, A. U. (2012). *Basic criminal law: The Constitution, procedure, and crimes* (3rd ed.). Upper Saddle River, NJ: Pearson Prentice Hall.

Davids, M. (1995, January/February). Where style meets substance. *Journal of Business Strategy, 16*(1), 48–55, 57–60.

Davidson, M. A. (2003, June). It is what you know. *Security Management, 47*(6), 69–70, 72, 74–75.

Davies, J. (2007, June 13). Smoking out shoplifters. *San Diego Union Tribune*, pp. C1, C4.

Davis, K. (2011, January 16). Fewest murders in city in 42 years. *San Diego Union Tribune*, pp. A1–A2.

Deanna, B. (2011, February 4). Bitter cold, destruction in the wake of mammoth storm. *San Diego Union Tribune*, p. A4.

DeKieffer, D. (2009, April). Investigating the competition. *Security Management*, pp. 110–111.

Del Rossi, A. F., & Viscusi, W. K. (2009). The changing landscape of blockbuster punitive damages awards. National Bureau of Economic Research (NBER) working paper No. 15571.

Dempsey, J. S. (2011). *Introduction to private security* (2nd ed.). Belmont, CA: Thomson Wadsworth.

Deutch, J. (1997, September 22). Terrorism. *Foreign Policy*, p. 10.

DeYoung, K., & Brulliard, K. (2011, May 4). U.S. presses Pakistan for answers. *Washington Post*.

Dilanian, K. (2010, November 15). "Fusion centers" gather terrorism intelligence—and much more. *Los Angeles Times*.

Doherty, K. (1998, May). Beyond the Gore commission: What next? *Access Control & Security Systems Integration, 41*(5), 1, 42–43.

Dolan, T. G. (1999, August). Healthcare security: A very insecure profession. *Security Technology & Design, 9*(8), 10–12, 14.

Dorning, M. (2000, August 28). U.S. violent crime rate dropped again last year. *San Diego Union Tribune*, p. A2.

Drath, W. H., & Palus, C. J. (1994). *Making common sense: Leadership as meaning-making in a community of practice*. Greensboro, NC: Center for Creative Leadership.

Drew, C. (2010, October 17). U.S. companies are at risk of spying by their own workers. *New York Times*.

Drucker, P. F. (1994, November). The age of social transformation. *The Atlantic Monthly*, pp. 53–80.

Dunn, M. (1999). Critical elements in school security. In J. Agron & L. Anderson (Eds.), *Under siege: Schools as the new battleground* (pp. 13–14, 16). Atlanta, GA: Access Control & Security Systems Integration.

Dunphy, H. (2003, May 1). Terrorist attacks worldwide declined substantially in 2002. *San Diego Union Tribune*, p. A22.

East Orange leading the way in crime-fighting technology. (2010, June 10). *Lincoln Journal Star*.

End in sight. (2003, November 2). *San Diego Union Tribune*, pp. A1, A10.

Epstein, J. (1998). State and local environmental enforcement. In M. Clifford (Ed.), *Environmental crime: Enforcement, policy, and social responsibility* (pp. 145–168). Gaithersburg, MD: Aspen Publishers.

Fagin, J. A. (2007). *Criminal justice* (2nd ed.). Boston, MA: Pearson Allyn & Bacon.

Fahey, S. (2010, November–December). Hard tag recycling: Transparent, sustainable, and profitable. *Loss Prevention*, pp. 19–22.

Falk, A. (2011, February 14). Police seize 29,000 pirated CDs and DVDs. *Salt Lake Tribune.*

Fay, J. J. (1999). *Model security policies, plans and procedures.* Woburn, MA: Butterworth-Heinemann.

Fay, J. J. (2000, August). SICM: A risk management tool. *Security Technology & Design, 10*(8), 22–24, 26.

FBI issues alert to nuclear plant operators. (2003, May 6). *Security Beat, 3*(18). [Online]. Available: http://www. securitysolutions.com.

FBI National Press Office. (2011). *Search warrants executed in the United States as part of ongoing cyber investigation.* [Online]. Available: http://www.fbi. gov/news/pressrel/press-releases/warrants_012711. Retrieved: February 6, 2011.

Federal Emergency Management Agency. (2007). *Welcome to the National Incident Management System Integration Center.* [Online]. Available: http://www. fema.gov/emergency/nims/index/shtm.

Federal Motor Carrier Safety Administration. (2007). *About FMCSA.* [Online]. Available: http://www.fmcsa. dot.gov/about/aboutus.html.

Federal Railroad Administration. (2007). *About the FRA.* [Online]. Available: http://www.fra.dot.gov/us/ content/2.

Federation of American Scientists. (2007). *Project on government secrecy.* [Online]. Available: http://www.fas. org/sgp/library/nispom.html.

FEMA challenge seeks innovative preparedness ideas. (2010, October 28). [Online]. Available: http:// ohsonline.com/articles/2010/10/29/fema-challenge- seeks-innovative-preparedness-ideas.aspx.

Fennelly, L. J. (1992). *Security applications in industry and institutions.* Woburn, MA: Butterworth-Heinemann.

Fennelly, L. J. (2004). *Handbook of loss prevention and crime prevention* (4th ed.). Boston, MA: Butterworth-Heinemann.

Ferraro, E. F. (2000, July). Ordinary people. *Security Management, 44*(7), 48–50, 99–101.

Fest, G. (2001, January 22). Desk rage. *San Diego Union Tribune*, pp. C1, C2.

Fickes, M. (2000, November). Soapbox at the mall. *Access Control & Security Systems Integration, 43*(12), 1, 26, 28.

Fiedler, F. E. (1967). *A theory of leadership effectiveness.* New York: McGraw-Hill.

Fireline Corporation. (2003). *Inergen systems.* Baltimore, MD: Fireline Corporation. [Online]. Available: http:// www.fireline.com.

Fischer, R. J., & Green, G. (2008). *Introduction to security* (8th ed.). Burlington, MA: Elsevier.

Fischer, R. J., & Janoski, R. (2000). *Loss prevention and security procedures: Practical applications for contemporary problems.* Woburn, MA: Butterworth-Heinemann.

Fisher, A. (2011, February 3). Drug use at work: Higher than we thought.CNNMoney.com.

Fisher, I. (2000, December 30). Passengers save jet from attacker, deadly free fall. *San Diego Union Tribune*, pp. A1, A10.

Fitzhenry, B. (2007, February). An eye on it all. *Security Products, 11*(2), 26D–26E.

Five tips for safe computer use. (2011, January 6). *Security Products.* [Online]. Available: http://secprodonline. com/articles/2011/01/05/five-tips-for-safe-computer- use.aspx.

Fleissner, D., & Heinzelmann, F. (1996, August). *Crime prevention through environmental design and community policing.* Washington, DC: National Institute of Justice.

Foss, B. (2003, January 1). Pain of scandals may yield benefits. *San Diego Union Tribune*, pp. C1, C8.

Foster, M. (2011, March 11). 8.9 quake rocks Japan. *San Diego Union Tribune*, p. A4.

Fournies, F. (2000). *Coaching for improved work performance.* New York: McGraw-Hill.

Friedman, G. (2011). *The next decade: Where we've been… and where we're going.* New York: Doubleday.

Fuller, J. R. (2012). *Think criminology.* New York: McGraw-Hill.

Gaines, L., & Miller, R. L. (2011). *Criminal justice in action: The core* (6th ed.). Belmont, CA: Wadsworth/ Thomson Learning.

Gallagher, F. J., & Grassie, R. P. (2000, September). Alarm management: The key ingredient in effective security management operations. *Security Technology & Design, 10*(9), 12–14, 16, 18.

Garbera, D. (1998, May). Protecting airports from themselves. *Access Control & Security Systems Integration, 41*(5), 1, 48.

Garcia, M. L. (2000, June). Truth and consequences. *Security Management, 44*(6), 44–48.

Gauthier-Villars, D., & Moffett, S. (2011, March 3). Renault to yield in l-affaire d'espionnage. *Wall Street Journal.*

Gemeny, D. F. (2000, August). Performance-based design: An overview. *Security Technology & Design, 10*(8), 64–66, 68.

George, J. M., & Jones, G. R. (2012). *Understanding and managing organizational behavior* (6th ed.). Upper Saddle River, NJ: Pearson Prentice Hall.

Geotags and location-based social networking: Applications, OPSEC and protecting unit safety. (2011). Social Media Roundup report. Washington, DC: U.S. Army.

Gersh, D. (2000, November). Untouchable value. *iSecurity,* pp. 16, 18–20.

Gigliotti, R., & Jason, R. (1999). Approaches to physical security. In L. J. Fennelly (Ed.), *Handbook of loss prevention and crime prevention* (3rd ed.). Boston, MA: Butterworth-Heinemann.

Gips, M. A. (2000, May). Building in terrorism's shadow. *Security Management, 44*(5), 42–44, 46–50.

Gips, M. A. (2007, March). My short life as an EP specialist. *Security Management, 51*(3), 52–56, 58–60.

Giussani, B. (2001, February 5). Hackers hit blue-chip World Economic Forum. *San Diego Union Tribune,* p. A1.

Global crime cartels are tech-savvy, U.S. says. (2000, December 16). *San Diego Union Tribune,* p. A12.

Goetsch, D. L., & Davis, S. (2010). *Quality management* (6th ed.). Upper Saddle River, NJ: Pearson Prentice Hall.

Gomez-Mejia, L. R., & Balkin, D. (2012). *Management.* Upper Saddle River, NJ: Pearson Prentice Hall.

Goodchild, J. (2010, November). Donuts to dollars. *CSO, 9*(11), 28.

Goodnough, A. (2011, February 7). Pharmacies under siege from robbers seeking drugs. *San Diego Union Tribune,* p. A4.

Green, F. (2000, November 26). Workplace gumshoes. *San Diego Union Tribune,* p. H2.

Green, K. (2000, August 3). Weather, consumers help avert blackouts. *San Diego Union Tribune,* pp. A1, A19.

Greene, J. D., & Tappen, A. R. (2000, July). Designing retrofit fire alarm systems: Part 2. *Security Technology & Design, 10*(7), 60–63.

Greenemeier, L. (2007, March 26). TJX data shows up in massive credit card fraud at Florida Wal-Mart stores. *Information Week.* [Online]. Available: http://www.informationweek.com.

Greer, C. R., & Plunkett, W. R. (2007). *Supervisory management* (11th ed.). Upper Saddle River, NJ: Pearson Prentice Hall.

Guffey, J. E. (2005). *Report writing fundamentals for police and correctional officers.* Upper Saddle River, NJ: Pearson Prentice Hall.

Haberer, J. B., & Webb, M. L. W. (1994). *TQM: 50 ways to make it work for you.* Menlo Park, CA: Crisp Publications.

Hacker steals patient records. (2000, December 12). *San Diego Union Tribune,* p. A3.

Hackers target state's electricity. (2001, June 10). *San Diego Union Tribune,* p. A3.

Haddow, G. D., & Bullock, J. A. (2010). *Introduction to emergency management* (4th ed.). Boston, MA: Butterworth-Heinemann.

Hails, J. (2012). *Criminal evidence* (7th ed.). Florence, KY: Cengage Learning.

Hakim, S., & Blackstone, E. A. (1997). *Securing home and business: A guide to the electronic security industry.* Woburn, MA: Butterworth-Heinemann.

Hall, M. (2003, January 23). "Rent-a-cops" rarely trained or investigated. *USA Today,* p. 1A.

Halligan, M. R. (2000, September). Inevitable disclosure. *Security Management, 44*(9), 94.

Hammons, M. (2007, January). Right on track. *Security Products, 11*(1), 72–73. [Online]. Available: http://www.uscg.mil/hq/g-cp/comrel/factfile/factcards/MTSA2002.htm.

Hancock, B. W., & Sharp, P. M. (2004). *Criminal justice in America: Theory, practice, and policy* (3rd ed.). Upper Saddle River, NJ: Prentice Hall.

Hansen, K. (2007). *Quintessential careers: Resume preparation do's and don'ts.* [Online]. Available: http://www.quintcareers.com/printable/resume-dos-donts.html.

Haque, U. (2011). *The new capitalist manifesto: Building a disruptively better business.* Watertown, MA: Harvard Business Press.

Harley, D. (2000, August). Living with viruses. *Security Management, 44*(8), 88, 90, 92–94.

Harowitz, S. L. (2003, January). The new centurions. *Security Management, 47*(1), 50–52, 54, 56–58.

Harr, J. S., & Hess, K. M. (2006). *Careers in criminal justice and related fields: From internship to promotion* (5th ed.). Belmont, CA: Wadsworth/Thomson Learning.

Harrell, A. V., & Taylor, R. B. (1996, May). *Physical environment and crime.* Washington, DC: National Institute of Justice.

Harwood, E. (1998, June). Going to work on workplace violence. *Access Control & Security Systems Integration, 41*(6), 1, 31–33.

Hawaii cites Xerox in worker shooting. (2000, November 8). *San Diego Union Tribune*, p. A10.

Hawkins, S. (2000, March 29). Texas twister kills four people, hurts 36 in Fort Worth. *San Diego Union Tribune*, p. A8.

Hayes, R. (2000, April). An inventory of what's in store. *Security Management, 44*(4), 72, 74, 76.

Heifetz, R. A. (1994). *Leadership without easy answers.* Cambridge, MA: The Belknap Press of Harvard University Press.

Hellriegel, D., Jackson, S. E., & Slocum, J. W., Jr. (2005). *Management: A competency-based approach* (10th ed.). Cincinnati, OH: South-Western/Thomson Learning.

Hellriegel, D., & Slocum, J. W., Jr. (2011). *Organization behavior* (13th ed.). Cincinnati, OH: South-Western/Thomson Learning.

Henry, V. E. (2002). *The COMPSTAT paradigm: Management accountability in policing, business and the public sector.* Flushing, NY: Looseleaf Law Publications.

Hersey, P., & Blanchard, K. H. (1982). *Management of organizational behavior: Utilizing human resources.* Englewood Cliffs, NJ: Prentice Hall.

Hersey, P., Blanchard, K. H., & Johnson, D. E. (2008). *Management of organizational behavior: Leading human resources* (9th ed.). Upper Saddle River, NJ: Pearson Prentice Hall.

Hess, K. M. (1997, December). The ABCs of report writing. *Security Management, 41*(12), 123–124.

Hess, K. M., & Wrobleski, H. M. (2009). *Introduction to private security* (5th ed.). Belmont, CA: Thomson Higher Education.

Hodge, B. J., Anthony, W. P., & Gales, L. M. (2003). *Organizational theory: A strategic approach* (7th ed.). Upper Saddle River, NJ: Prentice Hall.

Hollinger, R. C., & Dabney, D. A. (1995). *1994 national retail security research project.* Gainesville: University of Florida.

Hopper, D. I. (2001, February 6). E-mail wiretaps drive privacy advocates buggy. *San Diego Union Tribune*, pp. C1, C3.

Hough, W. O. (1999). Proactive security is called for. In R. R. Robinson (Ed.), *Issues in security management: Thinking critically about security* (pp. 158–162). Woburn, MA: Butterworth-Heinemann.

House, R. J. (1996). Path-goal theory of leadership: Lessons, legacy, and a reformulated theory. *Leadership Quarterly, 7*(3), 323–352.

House to take up PATRIOT Act again. (2011, February 10). *United Press International.*

How to report Internet crimes. (2000, March). *Security Management, 44*(3), 34.

Hughes, J. (2000, November 15). FBI regional computer lab has new San Diego headquarters. *San Diego Union Tribune*, p. B3.

Hutchinson, B., & Warren, M. (2001). *Information warfare: Corporate attack and defence in a digital world.* Boston, MA: Butterworth-Heinemann.

Inbau, F. E., Farber, B. J., & Arnold, D. W. (1996). *Protective security law* (2nd ed.). Woburn, MA: Butterworth-Heinemann.

Inciardi, J. A. (2010). *Criminal justice* (9th ed.). New York: McGraw-Hill.

Institute of Financial Management. (2011). *Security law handbook: The essential guide for the corporate security department.* Greenwich, CT: Institute of Management and Administration.

Institute for Intergovernmental Research. (2011). *Global Intelligence Working Group (GIWG).* [Online].

Available: http://www.iir.com/Information_Sharing/global/GIWG.aspx?AspxAutoDetectCookieSupport=1. Retrieved: March 18, 2011.

Intelligence gathering unwieldy, report says. (2010, July 20). *San Diego Union Tribune*, p. A7.

Interagency OPSEC Support Staff. (2007). *About us.* [Online]. Available: http://www.ioss.gov/html/About.html.

International Association for Healthcare Security and Safety. (2007). *Mission and goals.* [Online]. Available: http://www.iahss.org/about_mission.asp.

Internet Crime Complaint Center Annual Report. (2009). [Online]. Available: http://www.ic3.gov/media/annual-report/2009_IC3Report.pdf.

IOMA/IOFM. (2011). *2011 report on workplace violence: Complete guide to managing today's and tomorrow's threats.* Greenwich, CT: Institute of Management and Administration.

Is LA's crime honeymoon over? Gangs blamed for surge in violent crime rate. (2000, July/August). *Law Enforcement News, 26*(537–538), 8.

Jacobson, R. V. (1997, September). Look through the risk management window to add up security costs. *Access Control & Security Systems Integration, 40*(9), 59–62.

Jeffery, C. R. (1972). *Crime prevention through environmental design.* Beverly Hills, CA: Sage Publications.

Jelen, G. F. (1994, October). OPSEC for the private sector. *Security Management, 38*(10), 67–68.

Jesdanun, A. (2000, August 21). Personal data, privacy concerns clash online. *San Diego Union Tribune*, p. A5.

Johnson, B. R. (2005). *Principles of security management.* Upper Saddle River, NJ: Pearson Prentice Hall.

Johnson, C. E. (2009). *Meeting the ethical challenges of leadership: Casting light or shadow* (3rd ed.). Thousand Oaks, CA: Sage Publications.

Johnson, D. L., Klehbauch, J. B., & Kinney, J. (1994, February). Break the cycle of violence. *Security Management, 38*(2), 24–28.

Johnson, G. (2000, October 25). FBI starts probe into Microsoft break-in. *San Diego Union Tribune*, p. C1.

Johnson, J. W. (2003, February). Get the most from your guard force. *Security Management, 47*(2), 73–74, 76, 79–80.

Jones, D. (2000, August 2). Businesses battle over intellectual property. *USA Today*, pp. 1B–2B.

Jones, J. W., & Arnold, D. W. (2003, February). Trends in personnel testing: A loss prevention perspective. *Loss Prevention & Security Journal, 3*(2), 14–16.

Jopeck, E. J. (2000, August). Five steps to risk reduction. *Security Management, 44*(8), 97–98, 100–102.

Jordan, L. J. (2006, February 24). White House's Katrina Report calls for fixes. *San Diego Union Tribune*, p. A3.

Judge dismisses Paul Allen's patent suit against Apple, Google, others. (2010, December 13). *ComputerWorld*.

Justice Research and Statistics Association. (2008). *Status of NIBRS in the states.*

Kakalik, J. S., & Wildhorn, S. (1971). *The Rand report on private security.* Santa Monica, CA: The Rand Corporation.

Kakalik, J. S., & Wildhorn, S. (1972). *Private police in the United States: Findings and recommendations.* Washington, DC: U.S. Government Printing Office.

Kalish, B. (2011, January). Military and government data breached 104 times in 2010. NextGov.com.

Kanter, J. (2011, March 18). Europe seeks transparency from U.S. on anti-terrorism program. *New York Times*.

***Karraker v.** Rent-A-Center, Inc.*, 411 F. 3d 831 (7th Cir. 2005).

Keck, K. (2011, January 9). Lawmakers rethink security after Arizona shooting. CNN.com.

Kimiecik, R. C., & Thomas, C. (2006). *Loss prevention in the retail business.* Hoboken, NJ: John Wiley & Sons.

Klockars, C. B. (1991). The Dirty Harry problem. In C. B. Klockars & S. D. Mastrofski (Eds.), *Thinking about police: Contemporary readings* (2nd ed.) (pp. 413–423). New York: McGraw-Hill.

Knauss, T. (2011, January 27). Syracuse mayor seeks to replace police officers at airport with private security to save money. *Syracuse Post-Standard*.

Knowles, M. S. (1970). *The modern practice of adult education: Andragogy versus pedagogy.* New York: Association Press.

Koerner, B. I. (2000, May 1). Finally, an arrest: But how much damage do cyberattacks cause? *U.S. News & World Report*, p. 48.

Kotter, J. P. (1990). *A force for change.* New York: The Free Press.

Kotter, J. P. (1993). What leaders really do. In W. E. Rosenbach & R. L. Taylor (Eds.), *Contemporary issues in leadership* (3rd ed.) (pp. 26–35). Boulder, CO: Westview Press.

Kovacich, G. L., & Halibozek, E. P. (2003). *The manager's handbook for corporate security: Establishing and managing a successful assets protection program.* Boston, MA: Butterworth-Heinemann.

Krasnowski, M. (1997, December 14). Jailed hacker asking for keys. *San Diego Union Tribune*, p. A3.

Krasnowski, M. (2000, November 10). Fraud charges against Keating dropped. *San Diego Union Tribune*, p. A3.

Kreisher, O. (1999, October 3). Panel warns of turmoil, terrorism. *San Diego Union Tribune*, p. A3.

Kroeker, M. A. (2001, September). Proper design helps stem crime. *Community Links, 7*(3), 15–16.

LaBruno, L. (2011, January–February). Risks from shoplifter apprehensions: Part II. *Loss Prevention*, pp. 72–73.

Laforte, C. (2010, October). Bridging the gap. *Security Technology Executive*, p. 52.

Lam, F., Beekey, M., & Cayo, K. (2003, February). Can you hack it? *Security Management, 47*(2), 83–84, 86, 88.

Lanfranchi, M. (2011, April). Women in the security sector. *Security Management*. [Online]. Available: http://www.securitymanagement.com/article/women-security-sector-006567?page=0%2C1.

LaTourrette, T., Howell, D. R., Mosher, D. E., & MacDonald, J. (2007). *Reducing terrorism risk at shopping centers.* Santa Monica, CA: The Rand Corporation.

Lawlessness reigns as storm victims try to flee New Orleans. (2005, September 9). *San Diego Union Tribune*, pp. A1, A5.

Lee, H. C., Palmbach, T., & Miller, M. T. (2001). *Henry Lee's crime scene handbook.* Boston, MA: Academic Press.

Lee, S. (2003, January). Drug testing brings rights and responsibilities. *California Chamber of Commerce Labor Law Update.* [Online]. Available: http://www.calchamber.com.

Lenahan, M. (2000, September). Training in tandem. *Security Management, 44*(9), 67–71.

Lewis, P. S., Goodman, S. H., & Fandt, P. M. (2008). *Management: Challenges for tomorrow's leaders* (5th ed.). Belmont, CA: South-Western/Thomson Learning.

Likert, R. (1961). *New patterns of management.* New York: McGraw-Hill.

Likert, R. (1967). *The human organization.* New York: McGraw-Hill.

Lindquist, D. (2007, April 23). Spotlight increases on port security. *San Diego Union Tribune*, pp. A1, A6.

Lodin, S. (1999, October). Firing up data defenses. *Security Management, 43*(10), 68–70, 72–73.

Lohr, S. (2002, May 27). In new era, corporate security looks beyond guns and badges. *New York Times*, pp. C1, C3.

Longmore-Etheridge, A. (2000, August). Long day's journey into knowledge. *Security Management, 44*(8), 61–64.

Longmore-Etheridge, A. (2007, April). All along the watchtower. *Security Management, 51*(4), 74–76, 78–80, 82, 84.

Longmore-Etheridge, A. (2010, October 12). CSO roundtable hosts "women in security." *Security Management.* [Online]. Available: http://www.securitymanagement.com/news/cso-roundtable-hosts-%E2%80%9Cwomen-security%E2%80%9D-007742.

Lota, L. (2000, September 22). Hacker, 20, accused of invading NASA, university computers. *San Diego Union Tribune*, p. A4.

LPjobs.com. (2007). *Welcome job seekers.* [Online]. Available: http://www.lpjobs.com/seekers.aspx.

Lushbaugh, C. A., & Weston, P. B. (2012). *Criminal investigation: Basic perspectives* (12th ed.). Upper Saddle River, NJ: Pearson Prentice Hall.

Lyman, M. D. (2010). *The police: An introduction* (4th ed.). Upper Saddle River, NJ: Prentice Hall.

Lynch, M. (2000, December). Go ask Alice. *Security Management, 44*(12), 68–70, 72–73.

Major, M. J. (1998, March). A casino's three-pronged approach to security. *Security Technology & Design, 8*(3), 27, 29–33.

Major, M. J. (1999, June). An explosive issue: Airports install high-tech explosives detectors to combat terrorism. *Security Technology & Design, 9*(6), 10–12, 14, 16.

Maniscalco, P. M., & Christen, H. T. (2002). *Understanding terrorism and managing the consequences.* Upper Saddle River, NJ: Prentice Hall.

Mann, R. A., & Roberts, B. S. (2009). *Smith and Robertson's business law* (14th ed.). Belmont, CA: Thomson Higher Education.

Mann, T. (1999, October). Seven steps to successful contracting. *Security Management, 43*(10), 46–48, 50–51.

Maras, M. H. (2012). *Computer forensics: Cybercriminals, laws, and evidence.* Sudbury, MA: Jones and Bartlett Learning.

Markoff, J. (2000, May 5). E-mail worm-virus sent messages worldwide. *San Diego Union Tribune,* pp. A1, A23.

Martin, C. G. (2009). *Understanding terrorism: Challenges, perspectives and issues* (3rd ed.). Thousand Oaks, CA: Sage Publications.

Mascaro, L. (2011, January 13). Lawmakers debate cost of own protection. *Los Angeles Times,* p. AA5.

Maslow, A. H. (1987). *Motivation and personality* (3rd ed.). New York: Harper & Row.

Mason, M. (2000, December 28). Koalas' lives at risk after theft. *San Diego Union Tribune,* pp. A3, A6.

Maurer, R. D. (2000a, January). The evolving role of the security director. *Security Technology & Design, 10*(1), 12–14, 16.

Maurer, R. D. (2000b, August). Outsourcing: An option or a threat? *Security Technology & Design, 10*(8), 12–14, 18, 20.

Maurer, R. D. (2000c, December). Where will security be in 2010? *Security Technology & Design, 10*(12), 12–14, 16.

May, J. (2000, October). A tragedy in the making. *Access Control & Security Systems Integration, 43*(11), 42–43.

Mazzetti, M. (2009, April 2). Intelligence office gets low marks in efficiency. *San Diego Union Tribune,* p. A4.

McClelland, D. C. (1971). *Motivational trends in society.* Morristown, NJ: General Learning Press.

McCollum, K. (2000, March 24). Colleges struggle to train experts in protecting computer systems. *The Chronicle of Higher Education,* p. A–45.

McDonald, J. (2001a, March 6). Two killed, 13 wounded in rampage; suspect smiled as he fired, witnesses say. *San Diego Union Tribune,* pp. A1, A6.

McDonald, J. (2001b, March 24). Five injured in teen's rampage at Granite Hills. *San Diego Union Tribune,* pp. A1, A22.

McDonald, J., & Barfield, C. (2007, May 26). Against all odds, cheaters persist. *San Diego Union Tribune,* pp. A1, A15.

McFadden, R. D. (2000, December 31). Blizzard snarls Northeast. *San Diego Union Tribune,* pp. A1, A20.

McGregor, D. (1960). *The human side of enterprise.* New York: McGraw-Hill.

McGregor, D. (1966). *Leadership and motivation.* Cambridge: Massachusetts Institute of Technology Press.

McMillan, R. (2010, December). CIO gets six years for embezzlement scheme. *IDG News Service.*

McQueen, A. (2000, October 27). School violence decreases, study finds. *San Diego Union Tribune,* p. A9.

Measuring up. (2011, March). *CSO: Business Risk Leadership, 10*(2), 26–33.

Meese, E., & Ortmeier, P. J. (2004). *Leadership, ethics, and policing: Challenges for the 21st century.* Upper Saddle River, NJ: Prentice Hall.

Mendel, E. (2001, January 27). Davis touts plan to end energy ills. *San Diego Union Tribune,* pp. A1, A20.

Menzie, M. (2011). *Pipeline components traceability: New regulations, new challenges for utilities.* New York: PRTM Perspective.

Meredith, R. (1997, January 9). VW will pay $100 million to GM, settle spying suit. *San Diego Union Tribune,* p. C1.

Michalowski, R. (1998). International environmental issues. In M. Clifford (Ed.), *Environmental crime: Enforcement, policy, and social responsibility* (pp. 315–340). Gaithersburg, MD: Aspen Publishers.

Michel, R. (2000, September). Learning curve: Access control ensures a safe educational facility. *Security Products, 4*(9), 30–32, 34.

Michelman, B. (2011, February). Preventing workplace violence. *Security Management, 55*(2), 48.

Miller, L. (2003, May 3). U.S. to check background of truckers who haul hazardous goods. *San Diego Union Tribune,* p. A7.

Miller, L. (2005, April 17). Two reports are expected to slam airport screeners. *San Diego Union Tribune,* p. A14.

Miller, M. (2000). *Police patrol operations* (2nd ed.). Belmont, CA: Thomson/Wadsworth.

Millwee, S. (2000, February). You have not because you ask not: Cost effective screening that works. *Security Technology & Design, 10*(2), 12–14, 16.

Mishra, R. (1998, March 18). Drug addicts need treatment, not punishment, doctors say. *San Diego Union Tribune,* pp. A1, A21.

Miskin, V., & Gmelch, W. (1985, May). Quality leadership for quality teams. *Training and Development Journal, 39*(5), 122–129.

Monteverde, D. (2011, February 10). New Orleans pizza delivery man blinded by bleach in robbery. *New Orleans Times-Picayune.*

Moore, R. (2011). *Cybercrime.* Cincinnati, OH: Anderson Publishing.

Moran, C. (2011, February 6). Agency behind in checking for corrupt border agents. *San Diego Union Tribune,* pp. A1, A2.

Moran, M. (2007, August). What are you worth? *Security Management, 51*(8), 66–68, 70–73.

Moran, M. (2010, August). Pay for performance. *Security Management, 54*(8) 86, 88, 90, 92.

More, H. W., Vito, G. F., & Walsh, W. F. (2012). *Organizational behavior and management in law enforcement* (3rd ed.). Upper Saddle River, NJ: Pearson Prentice Hall.

Moses-Schulz, D. (1997, April). Private security comes on board. *Security Management, 41*(4), 59, 60, 62, 63, 65.

Mosley, D. C., Megginson, L. C., & Pietri, P. H. (2005). *Supervisory management: The art of inspiring, empowering and developing people.* Belmont, CA: South-Western/Thomson Learning.

Most drug abusers have steady jobs. (1999, September 9). *San Diego Union Tribune,* p. A6.

Motion Picture Association of America. (2007). *Antipiracy.* [Online]. Available: http://www.mpaa.org/piracy.asp.

Nakashima, R. (2011, January 28). Studios take high-tech stab at piracy. *San Diego Union Tribune,* pp. C1–C2.

Nalla, M. K. (2001, Spring). Designing an introductory course in private security. *Journal of Criminal Justice Education, 12*(1), 35–52.

Napolitano warns police chiefs of homegrown terror threat. (2010, October 26). SecurityInfoWatch.com.

Nason, R. R. (2000, October). Threats for the new millennium. *Security Technology & Design, 10*(10), 12–14, 16, 18.

Nason, R. R. (2007, April). Ready for anything? *Security Technology & Design, 17*(4), 46–49.

National Advisory Commission on Criminal Justice Standards and Goals. (1976). *Task force report: Private security.* Washington, DC: U.S. Government Printing Office.

National Commission on Terrorist Attacks Upon the United States. (2004). *The 9/11 Commission report.* [Online]. Available: http://www.9-11commission.gov.

National Drug Intelligence Center. (2009). *National gang threat assessment, 2009.* [Online]. Available: http://www.fbi.gov/stats-services/publications/national-gang-threat-assessment-2009-pdf.

National Fire Protection Association. (2007). *NFPA 72 national fire alarm code.* Quincy, MA: National Fire Protection Association.

National Fire Protection Association. (2008). *NFPA fire protection handbook.* Quincy, MA: National Fire Protection Association.

National Indian Gaming Commission. (2007). *Minimum internal control standards.* [Online]. Available: http://www.indiangaming.org/cgi-bin/store4/commerce.cgi.

National Institute of Mental Health. (2011). *Statistics: Any disorder among adults.* [Online]. Available: http://www.nimh.nih.gov/statistics/1ANYDIS_ADULT.shtml. Retrieved: January 29, 2011.

National Institute of Standards and Technology. (2007). *Baldrige national quality program.* [Online]. Available: http://www.quality.nist. gov/improvement_act.html.

National Institute on Drug Abuse. (2007). *Principles of drug addiction treatment: A research based guide.* [Online]. Available: http://www.nida.nih.gov.podat/podat1.htm.

National Intelligence Council. (2007a). *Mapping the global future: Report of the National Intelligence Council's 2020 project.* [Online]. Available: http://www.dni.gov/NIC_2020_ project.html.

National Intelligence Council. (2007b, July). *National intelligence estimate: The terrorist threat to the U.S. Homeland.* [Online]. Available: http://www.dni.gov/press_releases/20070717_release.pdf.

National Retail Federation. (2007). *LERPnet.* [Online]. Available: http://www.nrf.com/lerpnet/press.htm.

Neeley, D. (2000, July). The hacker files. *Security Management, 44*(7), 124, 126, 128, 131.

Nemeth, C. P. (2001). *Law and evidence: A primer for criminal justice, criminology, law, and legal studies.* Upper Saddle River, NJ: Prentice Hall.

Nemeth, C. P. (2004). *Criminal law.* Upper Saddle River, NJ: Prentice Hall.

Nemeth, C. P. (2005). *Private security and the law* (3rd ed.). Boston, MA: Elsevier.

New waves of growth: Unlocking opportunity in the multipolar world. (2011, January). Accenture Institute for High Performance, Accenture Institute for Health and Public Service Value, and Oxford Economics. [Online]. Available: http://www.accenture.com/SiteCollectionDocuments/PDF/Accenture_Institute_High_Performance_New_Waves_of_Growth_Executive Summary.pdf

Newman, B. (Writer), & Kurtis, B. (Producer). (1997). *Investigative reports: The new face of crime* (Videotape). New York: A&E Television Networks.

Nicholson, L. G. (1997). *Instructor development training: A guide for security and law enforcement.* Boston, MA: Butterworth-Heinemann.

Nichter, D. A. (2000, September). The house rules. *Security Management, 44*(9), 74–82, 84–86, 88.

Nixon, W. B. (2007, January). Check mate. *Security Products, 11*(1), 56–59.

Nocella, H. N. (2000, December). Clipping coupon fraud. *Security Management, 44*(12), 40–42, 44, 46, 48.

Northouse, P. G. (2010). *Leadership: Theory and practice* (5th ed.). Thousand Oaks, CA: Sage Publications.

Obama signs temporary extension of Patriot Act. (2011, February 25). Associated Press. [Online]. Available: http://www.washingtonpost.com/wp-dyn/content/article/2011/02/25/AR2011022505562.html.

O'Connor, A. (2011, February 10). Holding flowers and gun, Queens man kills his ex-wife and, later, himself. *New York Times.*

Officials: SEALs thought bin Laden threatening. (2011, May 5). Associated Press.

O'Hara, C. E., & O'Hara, G. L. (2003). *Fundamentals of criminal investigation* (7th ed.). Springfield, IL: Charles L. Thomas.

Oliver, W. M. (2007). *Homeland security for policing.* Upper Saddle River, NJ: Pearson Prentice Hall.

Olympic security estimated to cost $900M. (2009, February 19). CBC News. [Online]. Available: http://www.cbc.ca/news/canada/british-columbia/story/2009/02/19/bc-olympics-cost-colin-hansen.html

Online access with a fingerprint. (2010, December 15). *Security Management Weekly.*

Operation Cooperation. (2001, January/February). *ASIS (American Society for Industrial Security) Dynamics* (157), 1, 4.

OPSEC Professionals Society. (2007). *About OPSEC.* [Online]. Available: http://www.opsecsociety.org/about.htm.

Ortmeier, P. J. (1994, September 22). *Address.* Speech presented at the annual conference of the American Society for Industrial Security, Las Vegas, NV.

Ortmeier, P. J. (1995, September–November). Security management: A career education master plan. *California Security, 1*(8), 8–9.

Ortmeier, P. J. (1996a, May). Placement in employment. *The Cohort of San Diego State University,* pp. 1–2.

Ortmeier, P. J. (1996b, July). Adding class to security. *Security Management, 40*(7), 99–101.

Ortmeier, P. J. (1996c). *Community policing leadership: A Delphi study to identify essential competencies.* Ann Arbor, MI: University Microfilms International.

Ortmeier, P. J. (1997, October). Leadership for community policing: Identifying essential officer competencies. *The Police Chief, 64*(10), 88–91, 93.

Ortmeier, P. J. (1999). *Public safety and security administration.* Woburn, MA: Butterworth-Heinemann.

Ortmeier, P. J. (2002). *Policing the community: A guide for patrol operations.* Upper Saddle River, NJ: Prentice Hall.

Ortmeier, P. J. (2003, February). Ethical leadership: Every officer's responsibility. *Law Enforcement Executive Forum, 3*(1), 1–9.

Ortmeier, P. J. (2006). *Introduction to law enforcement and criminal justice* (2nd ed.). Upper Saddle River, NJ: Pearson Prentice Hall.

Ortmeier, P. J., & Davis, J. (2012). *Police administration: A leadership approach.* New York: McGraw-Hill.

Ortmeier, P. J., & Meese, E., III (2010). *Leadership, ethics, and policing: Challenges for the 21st century* (2nd ed.). Upper Saddle River, NJ: Pearson Prentice Hall.

Orton, A. (1984). Leadership: New thoughts on an old problem. *Training, 21*(28), 31–33.

Ouchi, W. (1981). *Theory Z: How American business can meet the Japanese challenge.* Reading, MA: Addison-Wesley.

Papi, V. (1994, February). Planning before disaster strikes. *Security Concepts*, pp. 6, 19.

Parr, L. A. (1999). *Police report writing essentials.* Placerville, CA: Custom Publishing.

Path of destruction. (1992, May 10). *Los Angeles Times*, p. A31.

Payton, G. T., & Amaral, M. (2004). *Patrol operations and enforcement tactics* (11th ed.). San Jose, CA: Criminal Justice Services.

Peak, K. J., & Glensor, R. W. (2008). *Community policing and problem solving: Strategies and practices* (5th ed.). Upper Saddle River, NJ: Pearson Prentice Hall.

Pearson, R. (2000, September). Security's new golden rule: Automation, integration and consolidation. *Security Technology & Design, 10*(9), 20–21, 24, 26, 28.

Peck, D. H. (1999, October). When police walk the security beat. *Security Management, 43*(10), 38–40, 42, 45.

Perry, J. L. (Ed.). (1996). *Handbook of public administration* (2nd ed.). San Francisco, CA: Jossey-Bass.

Peters, T. (1987). *Thriving on chaos.* New York: Knopf.

Peterson's guide to four-year colleges. (2007). Lawrenceville, NJ: Nelnet.

Petterson, R. (2003, February 18). Blizzard causes havoc in Northeast; 28 dead. *San Diego Union Tribune*, pp. A1, A12.

Picture of drug use by young mixed. (2000, September 1). *San Diego Union Tribune*, p. A6.

Pike, R. W. (1992). *Creative training techniques handbook.* Minneapolis, MN: Lakewood Publications.

Pitorri, P. (1998). *Counterespionage for American business.* Woburn, MA: Butterworth-Heinemann.

Porteus, L. (2006). *Weapons of mass destruction handbook.* [Online]. Available: http://www.foxnews.com/story/0,2933,76887,00.html?spage=fnc.

President's Commission on Law Enforcement and Administration of Justice. (1967). *Task force report: Police.* Washington, DC: U.S. Government Printing Office.

Price, J. E., Haddock, M. D., & Brock, H. R. (2007). *College accounting* (11th ed.). New York: McGraw-Hill.

Professional Growth Facilitators. (2000). *Preparation for a violent emergency … It's not a choice.* San Clemente, CA: Professional Growth Facilitators.

Profiles of American colleges. (2007). (27th ed.). Hauppauge, NY: Barron's Educational Series, Inc.

Purpura, P. P. (2003). *The security handbook* (2nd ed.). Boston, MA: Butterworth-Heinemann.

Rand Corporation. (1999). *The benefits and costs of drug use prevention: Clarifying a cloudy issue.* Santa Monica, CA: Rand Corporation, Drug Policy Research Center.

Rashid, F. Y. (2011, March 3). DHS needs to change rules to recruit hackers into U.S. security agencies. *eWeek.*

Raum, T. (1999, February 5). U.S. found vulnerable to bombing attacks. *San Diego Union Tribune*, p. A11.

Raymond, W. D., & Hall, D. E. (1999). *California criminal law and procedure.* Albany, NY: West/Thomson Learning.

Reston, M. (2011, January 13). He was no stranger to police. *Los Angeles Times*, pp. A1, A12.

Rettie, D. F. (1995). *Our national park system.* Chicago: University of Illinois Press.

Revkin, A. C. (2001, January 6). November–December coldest such span in U.S. since 1895. *San Diego Union Tribune*, p. A9.

Robbins, S. P., & Coulter, M. (2009). *Management* (2nd ed.). Upper Saddle River, NJ: Prentice Hall.

Robbins, S. P., & Judge, T. A. (2010). *Essentials of organizational behavior* (10th ed.). Upper Saddle River, NJ: Pearson Prentice Hall.

Robinson, R. R. (1999). Privatization of services. In R. R. Robinson (Ed.), *Issues in security management: Thinking critically about security* (pp. 193–194). Woburn, MA: Butterworth-Heinemann.

Rodriguez, A., Yates, J., & Marx, G. (2001, February 6). Former employee opens fire, kills 4, self in Illinois factory. *San Diego Union Tribune*, pp. A1, A7.

Ron, R. (2010, December 6). Man versus machine. *Newsweek*, p. 12.

Ross, J. I. (2012). *Policing issues: Challenges and controversies.* Sudbury, MA: Jones & Bartlett.

Rucker, P., Wilson, S., & Kornblut, A. E. (2011, May 2). Osama bin Laden killed by U.S. forces in Pakistan. *Washington Post.*

Rutledge, D. (2000). *California criminal procedure* (4th ed.). Incline Village, NV: Copperhouse Publishing.

Saferstein, R. (2011). *Criminalistics: An introduction to forensic science* (10th ed.). Upper Saddle River, NJ: Pearson Prentice Hall.

Salant, J. D. (2002, February 18). Federal government takes over airport security. *San Diego Union Tribune*, pp. A1, A14.

Scalet, S. D. (2006, June). The salary reality. *CSO, 5*(6), 42–43, 45.

Scalet, S. D. (2007, June). Vulnerability assessment's big picture. *CSO, 6*(6), 32–36.

Schaub, J. L., & Biery, K. B., Jr. (1994). *The ultimate security survey*. Woburn, MA: Butterworth-Heinemann.

Schmalleger, F. (2010). *Criminal justice: A brief introduction* (8th ed.). Upper Saddle River, NJ: Pearson Prentice Hall.

Schmalleger, F. (2011). *Criminal justice today: An introductory text for the 21st century* (11th ed.). Upper Saddle River, NJ: Prentice Hall.

Schumacher, J. (2000, October). How to resolve conflict with proper systems integration. *Security Technology & Design, 10*(10), 36–40, 42–43.

Scott, M. S. (2000). *Problem-oriented policing: Reflections on the first 20 years*. Washington, DC: U.S. Department of Justice, Office of Community Oriented Policing Services.

Secure new devices in the new year. (2011, January 13). *Security Products*. [Online]. Available: http://secprodonline.com/articles/2011/01/13/tips-secure-new-devices-in-the-new-year.aspx.

Security fears cited over prior CIA chief. (2000, February 4). *San Diego Union Tribune*, p. A1.

Seivold, G. (2011). *Security law handbook: The essential guide for the corporate security department*. [Online]. Available: http://www.iofm.com/products/view/security-law-handbook#TOC.

Sennewald, C. A. (2003). *Effective security management* (4th ed.). Boston, MA: Butterworth-Heinemann.

Seven killed in office rampage. (2000, December 27). *San Diego Union Tribune*, pp. A1, A19.

Seven major U.S. agencies get "F" in computer security. (2000, September 12). *San Diego Union Tribune*, p. A8.

Seven of history's most terrifying sports riots. (2009, May 29). *Wall Street Journal*.

Shartle, C. L. (1956). *Executive performance and leadership*. Englewood Cliffs, NJ: Prentice Hall.

Shenon, P. (1999, January 8). Years of security lapses blamed in 2 embassy bombings. *San Diego Union Tribune*, p. A15.

Siegel, L. J. (2010). *Criminology: Theories, patterns, and typologies* (10th ed.). Belmont, CA: Wadsworth/Thomson Learning.

Siegel, L. J., & Senna, J. J. (2008). *Essentials of criminal justice* (6th ed.). Belmont, CA: Wadsworth/Thomson Learning.

Simonsen, C. E. (1998). *Private security in America: An introduction*. Upper Saddle River, NJ: Prentice Hall.

Simonsen, C. E., & Spindlove, J. R. (2007). *Terrorism today: The past, the players, the future* (3rd ed.). Upper Saddle River, NJ: Pearson Prentice Hall.

Simonton, G. M. (1998, May). Embracing officer authorization. *Access Control & Security Systems Integration, 41*(5), 40.

Slater, P. (2000, April 3). Thefts eat away at office morale. *San Diego Union Tribune*, p. C1.

Slepian, C. G. (2000, November). Security up in the air. *Security Management, 44*(11), 54–56, 58–59.

Smith, G. B. (2000, June 15). Mob families muscled in on Wall St., charges say. *San Diego Union Tribune*, p. A12.

Smith, J. N. (2000, November). Powering up access control. *Security Management, 44*(11), 68–70, 72–73.

Smith, R. V. (2000, December). Sheparding your resources: Retaining employees in the new economy. *Security Products, 4*(12), 36–39.

Smith, S. (2010, August 4). 911 calls reveal horror as US gunman ran down victims. *AFP*. [Online]. Available: http://www.google.com/hostednews/afp/article/ALeqM5gsJKTGz2jPBoFjkLIlrnUc41NylA.

Sniffen, M. J. (2000, November 18). FBI pleased with progress in Cole probe. *San Diego Union Tribune*, p. A9.

Sniffen, M. J. (2001, January 6). Companies cooperate with FBI in fighting computer crime. *San Diego Union Tribune*, p. A11.

Society of Competitive Intelligence Professionals. (2007). *About SCIP*. [Online]. Available: http://www.scip.org/2_overview.php.

Solomon, R. C. (1996). *A handbook for ethics*. Fort Worth, TX: Harcourt Brace College Publishers.

Sommer, C. J. (2003, March). Survival of the fittest: Corporate success is dependent on strategic synergy. *Loss Prevention & Security Journal, 3*(3), 16–17.

Southerland, R. (2000, June). Protected against the enemy within. *Access Control & Security Systems Integration, 43*(7), 29–30.

Spherion. (2006). *Spherion snapshot survey finds some workers hesitant to "Blow the Whistle" on unethical workplace activities.* [Online]. Available: http://www.spherion.com/press/releases/2006/blow_the_whistle_snapshot.jsp?

Spivey, J. (2001, January). Banks vault into online risk. *Security Management, 45*(1), 132–134, 136, 138.

Spy network reportedly based in Escondido. (2011, January 25). *San Diego Union Tribune*, pp. B1, B4.

Stogdill, R. M. (1959). *Individual behavior and group achievement.* New York: Oxford University Press.

Stover, J. B. (2000, May). When security doesn't add up. *Security Management, 44*(5), 80, 82–83.

Straw, J. (2007, May). Rule puts driver's license debate in high gear. *Security Management, 51*(5), 40–41.

Straw, J. (2011, January). Cargo vulnerabilities persist. *Security Management*, pp. 26, 28.

Sukiennik, G. (2001, January 8). Juries send message with damage case awards. *San Diego Union Tribune*, p. A1.

Sullivan, E. (2011, January 27). Color-coded terror warnings to be gone by April 27. Associated Press.

Sun Microsystems integrates access control worldwide. (2000, October). *Access Control & Security Systems Integration, 43*(11), 1, 30, 32, 34.

Sutherland, E. (1949). *White collar crime.* New York: Dryden.

Swanson, C. R., Territo, L., & Taylor, R. W. (2008). *Police administration: Structures, processes, and behavior* (7th ed.). Upper Saddle River, NJ: Pearson Prentice Hall.

Sweet, K. M. (2006). *Transportation and cargo security: Threats and solutions.* Upper Saddle River, NJ: Pearson Prentice Hall.

Tafoya, W. L. (1994, May/June). The future of law enforcement: A chronology of events. *Criminal Justice International*, p. 4.

Talamo, J. (2007, January–February). Organized retail crime. *Loss Prevention, 6*(1), 22–28, 30.

Taylor, M. (2000, November). Security in the strike zone. *Security Management, 44*(11), 38–40, 42, 44–45.

Tech gadgets help corporate spying surge in tough times. (2009, July 29). *USA Today.* [Online]. Available: http://www.usatoday.com/tech/news/computersecurity/2009-07-28-corporate-espionage-recession-tech_N.htm.

Thaiss, C., & Hess, J. E. (1999). *Writing for law enforcement.* Boston, MA: Allyn & Bacon.

The Chronicle of Higher Education. (2011). *Community colleges mobilize to train cybersecurity workers.* [Online]. Available: http://chronicle.com/article/What-Theyre-Reading-on/44503/. Retrieved: February 13, 2011.

The Joint Commission. (2010, June 3). Preventing violence in the health care setting. *Sentinal Event Alert* (45), 1–3.

The Loss Prevention Foundation. (2007). *Loss prevention certified (LPC).* [Online]. Available: http://www.losspreventionfoundation.org/LPC.html.

Thomas, L. (2001, January). Security measures for the Miami federal courthouse. *Security Products, 5*(1), 54.

Thomason, R. (2000, September). Airport security for the new millennium. *Security Technology & Design, 10*(9), 52, 54, 56, 60.

Threatening email traced to computer at CC. (2000, December 20). *West Point News*, pp. A1, A3.

Tichy, N., & Ulrich, D. (1984). The leadership challenge—a call for the transformational leader. SMR Forum. *Sloan Management Review, 26*(1), 59–68.

Top agency warns austerity riots could hit America. (2010, March 16). Prisonplanet.com.

Top security threats and management issues facing corporate America: 2010 survey of Fortune 1000 companies. (2010). Anaheim, CA: Securitas Security Services, USA, Inc.

Transportation Security Administration, Frequently Asked Questions. (2011). [Online]. Available: http://www.tsa.gov/what_we_do/layers/secureflight/faqs.shtm.

Trimmer, H. W. (1999). *Understanding and servicing alarm systems* (3rd ed.). Woburn, MA: Butterworth-Heinemann.

Truth, DARE and consequences: What impact is anti-drug effort having? (1998, April 15). *Law Enforcement News, 24*(487), 1, 10.

TSA chief likely to face lawmakers' questions on pat-downs, body scans. (2010, November 17). CNN.com.

Tsunami toll updated. (2005, March 24). SBS World News.

Two dead, two cops hurt in shootout outside Washington state Walmart. (2011, January 23). CNN Justice. [Online]. Available: http://articles.cnn.com/2011-01-23/justice/washington.walmart.shooting_1_deputies-parking-lot-male-shooting?_s=PM:CRIME.

Two teens arrested in theft of koalas. (2000, December 29). *San Diego Union Tribune*, p. A3.

Tyska, L. A., & Fennelly, L. J. (2000). *Physical security: 150 things you should know.* Woburn, MA: Butterworth-Heinemann.

U.S. Central Intelligence Agency. (2007). *OIG report on CIA accountability with respect to the 9/11 attacks.* [Online]. Available: http://www.cia.gov/library/reports/Executive Summary_OIG Report.pdf.

U.S. Coast Guard. (2007). *Maritime Transportation Security Act of 2002.* [Online]. Available: http://www.uscg.mil/hq/g-cp/comrel/factfile/factcards/MTSA2002.htm.

U.S. Congress. (1978). 50 U.S.C. Sections 1801–11, 1821–29, 1841–46, and 1861–62.

U.S. Congress. (1988). *Employee Polygraph Protection Act.* Washington, DC: U.S. Government Printing Office.

U.S. Congress. (1996). *Economic Security Act.* Washington, DC: U.S. Government Printing Office.

U.S. Congress. (2001). *USA PATRIOT Act of 2001 (Public Law 107–56).* Washington, DC: U.S. Government Printing Office.

U.S. Congress. (2002, November 25). *Homeland Security Act of 2002.* Washington, DC: U.S. Government Printing Office.

U.S. Congress. (2005, May 11). Pub. L. No. 109–113.

U.S. Department of Education. (2007). *Campus security.* [Online]. Available: http://www.ed.gov/admins/lead/safety/campus.html.

U.S. Department of Education, Institute of Education Sciences. (2011). *Indicators of school crime and safety: 2010.* [Online]. Available: http://nces.ed.gov/programs/crimeindicators/crimeindicators2010/index.asp.

U.S. Department of Health and Human Services. (2007). *Factsheets.* [Online]. Available: http://www.pandemic-flu.gov.

U.S. Department of Health and Human Services, Office of Civil Rights. (2007). *Fact sheet: Privacy and your health information.* [Online]. Available: http://www.hhs.gov/ocr/hipaa/consumer_rights.

U.S. Department of Homeland Security. (2003). *DHS organization.* [Online]. Available: http://www.dhs.org.

U.S. Department of Homeland Security. (2007). *Travel security and procedures.* [Online]. Available: http://www.dhs.gov/xtrv/sec/.

U.S. Department of Homeland Security, Office of the Press Secretary. (2007). *DHS completes key framework for critical infrastructure protection.* [Online]. Available: http://www.dhs.gov/xnews/releases/pr_1179773665704.shtm.

U.S. Department of Homeland Security, Office of the Secretary. (2007). *Office of Secretary.* [Online]. Available: http://www.dhs.gov/xabout/structure.

U.S. Department of Homeland Security, Transportation Security Administration. (2003). *Aviation and Transportation Security Act (ATSA) Public Law 107-7.* [Online]. Available: http://www.tsa.gov.

U.S. Department of Justice. (2007a). *U.S. National Central Bureau home page.* [Online]. Available: http://www.usdoj.gov.

U.S. Department of Justice. (2007b). *Fact sheet: USA PATRIOT Act Improvement and Reauthorization Act of 2005.* [Online]. Available: http://www.usdoj.gov.

U.S. Department of Justice, Bureau of Alcohol, Tobacco, Firearms, and Explosives. (2007). *Bomb threats and physical security planning guide.* [Online]. Available: http://www.atf.treas.gov.

U.S. Department of Justice, Bureau of Justice Assistance. (1997). *East bay public safety corridor partnership.* Washington, DC: U.S. Department of Justice, Office of Justice Programs.

U.S. Department of Justice, Bureau of Justice Assistance. (2000, March). *Keeping illegal activity out of rental property: A police guide for establishing landlord training programs.* Washington, DC: U.S. Department of Justice, Office of Justice Programs.

U.S. Department of Justice, Bureau of Justice Assistance. (2005a). *Engaging the private sector to promote homeland security: Law enforcement–private security partnerships.* Washington, DC: U.S. Department of Justice, Office of Justice Programs, Bureau of Justice Assistance.

U.S. Department of Justice, Bureau of Justice Assistance. (2005b, September). *Assessing and managing the terrorist threat.* Washington, DC: U.S. Department of Justice.

U.S. Department of Justice, Bureau of Justice Assistance. (2010). *2009 internet crime report.* [Online]. Available: http://www.ic3.gov/media/annualreport/2009_IC3Report.pdf.

U.S. Department of Justice, Bureau of Justice Statistics. (2006). *2006 indicators of school crime and safety.* Washington, DC: U.S. Department of Justice.

U.S. Department of Justice, Bureau of Justice Statistics, Office of Justice Programs. (1997, May). *Criminal victimization in the United States 1994.* Washington, DC: National Criminal Justice Reference Service.

U.S. Department of Justice, Drug Enforcement Administration. (2007). *Drug testing.* [Online]. Available: http://www.dea.gov.

U.S. Department of Justice, Federal Bureau of Investigation. (2007). *Uniform crime reports.* [Online]. Available: http://www.fbi.gov.

U.S. Department of Justice, Federal Bureau of Investigation. (2010). *Preliminary semiannual uniform crime report, January-June 2010.* [Online]. Available: http://www.fbi.gov/about-us/cjis/ucr/crime-in-the-u.s/2010/preliminary-crime-in-the-us-2009.

U.S. Department of Justice, Federal Bureau of Investigation, Economic Espionage Unit. (2007). *Focus on economic espionage.* [Online]. Available: http://www.fbi.gov/hq/ci/economic.htm.

U.S. Department of Justice, Office of Justice Programs. (2007). *Global intelligence working group.* [Online]. Available: http://www.it.ojp.gov/topic.jsp.

U.S. Department of Justice, Office of Public Affairs. (2007). *Nineteen indicted for conspiracy to commit racketeering, money laundering, and related offenses.* [Online]. Available: http://www.usdoj.gov/opa/pr/2007/may/07_crm_385.html.

U.S. Department of Justice, Private Security Advisory Council to the Law Enforcement Assistance Administration. (1977). *Reports to the LEAA.* Washington, DC: U.S. Government Printing Office.

U.S. Department of Labor, Bureau of Labor Statistics. (2007). *Census of fatal occupational injuries summary, 2005.* [Online]. Available: http://www.stats.bls.gov/news.release/cfoi.nro.htm.

U.S. Department of Labor, Bureau of Labor Statistics. (2010a). *Workplace injury and illness summary, 2009.* [Online]. Available: http://www.bls.gov/news.release/osh.nr0.htm.

U.S. Department of Labor, Bureau of Labor Statistics. (2010b). *Census of fatal occupational injury summary, 2009.* [Online]. Available: http://www.bls.gov/news.release/cfoi.nr0.htm.

U.S. Department of Labor, Bureau of Labor Statistics. (2010c). *Work stoppages summary, 2009.* [Online]. Available: http://www.bls.gov/news.release/wkstp.nr0.htm.

U.S. Department of State. (2007). *County reports on terrorism.* [Online]. Available: http://www.state.gov/s/ct/rls/crt/2006/82727.htm.

U.S. Department of State, Overseas Security Advisory Council. (2007). *About OSAC.* [Online]. Available: http://www.osac.gov/About.

U.S. Department of Treasury, Secret Service, & Department of Education. (2002). *Threat assessment in schools: A guide for managing threatening situations and to creating safe school climates.* Washington, DC: U.S. Department of Education.

U.S. Environmental Protection Agency. (2007). *Major environmental laws.* [Online]. Available: http://www.epa.gov/epahome/laws.htm.

U.S. Equal Employment Opportunity Commission. (2007). *Harassment.* [Online]. Available: http://www.eeoc.gov/types/harassment.

U.S. executive kidnapped in Monterrey. (2011, January 14). *Borderland Beat.* [Online]. Available: http://www.borderlandbeat.com/2011/01/us-executive-kidnapped-in-monterrey.html.

U.S. Federal Trade Commission. (2007). *Privacy initiatives.* [Online]. Available: http://www.ftc.gov.

U.S. General Accounting Office. (2001). *Combating terrorism: Selected challenges and related recommendations.* Washington, DC: U.S. General Accounting Office.

U.S. General Services Administration. (2011). *Alarm and signal systems: Security system management.* [Online]. Available: http://www.gsa.gov/portal/content/104644#AlarmSignal. Retrieved: January 23, 2011.

U.S. Government Accountability Office. (2007). *Department of Homeland Security: Progress report on* *implementation of mission and management functions.* [Online]. Available: http://www.gao.gov/docsearch/ abstract.php?rptno=GAO-07-1081T.

U.S. National Archives and Records Administration, Information Security Oversight Office. (2007). *Executive order 12958-classified national security information, as amended.* [Online]. Available: http://www.archives.gov/ isoo/policy-documents/eo-12958-amendment.html.

U.S. National Security Agency. (2011). *Central security service: Information assurance.* [Online]. Available: http://www.nsa.gov/ia/ia_at_nsa/index.shtml. Retrieved: February 6, 2011.

U.S. Nuclear Regulatory Commission. (2007). *Nuclear security and safeguards.* [Online]. Available: http://www. nrc.gov/security.html.

U.S. Securities and Exchange Commission. (2007). *The laws that govern the securities industry.* [Online]. Available: http://www.sec.gov.

United States v. Walker. (2010, August 12). 6th Circuit. [Online]. Available: http://www.llrmi.com/articles/ legal_update/2011_6th_walker.shtml. Retrieved: January 18, 2011.

University Health Care provides health, safety and security for patients. (2000, October). *Access Control & Security Systems Integration, 43*(11), 44.

Use of illegal drugs up 9 percent in 2009. (2010, September 16). *San Diego Union Tribune*, p. A11.

Uttenweiler, W. L. (1999, October). Working the web. *Security Management, 43*(10), 75–78.

Van Natta, D., Jr. (2011, January 25). Wave of violence strikes officers. *San Diego Union Tribune*, p. A5.

Vergakis, B. (2007, April 28). Utah allows guns at public colleges. *San Diego Union Tribune*, p. A6.

Vincent, B. (2000, May). Protection at $5.75 an hour. *Access Control & Security Systems Integration, 43*(6), 1, 47–48.

Volonino, L., Anzaldua, R., & Godwin, J. (2007). *Computer forensics: Principles and practices.* Upper Saddle River, NJ: Pearson Prentice Hall.

Vroom, V. H. (1964). *Work and motivation.* New York: John Wiley & Sons.

Wagley, J. (2010, November). Be smart about IDs. *Security Management*, pp. 91–92.

Wal-Mart loses overtime pay lawsuit. (2002, December 20). *The Olympian.* [Online]. Available: http://www.theolympian.com/home/news/20021220/ business/314505html.

Walker, J. R. (2010). *Introduction to hospitality management* (3rd ed.). Upper Saddle River, NJ: Pearson Prentice Hall.

Wallace, H., & Roberson, C. (2012). *Principles of criminal law* (5th ed.). Upper Saddle River, NJ: Pearson Prentice Hall.

Walsh, J. (2000, August). Employee theft. *International Foundation for Protection Officers.*

Walsh, K. (2007, May). Secure locations. *CSO, 6*(5), 32–34.

Walsh, T. J., & Healy, R. J. (1987). *Protection of assets manual.* Santa Monica, CA: The Merrit Company.

Warchol, G. (1998). *Workplace violence, 1992–1996.* Washington, DC: Bureau of Justice Statistics.

Ward, R. H., Kiernam, K. L., & Mabrey, D. (2006). *Homeland security: An introduction.* New York: LexisNexis/ Anderson Publishing.

Warrick, J. (2011, January 1). Leak illuminates in info-sharing tool. *San Diego Union Tribune*, p. A2.

Washburn, D., & Hasemyer, D. (2001, March 9). New threats raise alarm: Violence study shows Willams "fits the pattern." *San Diego Union Tribune*, pp. A1, A23.

Wasserman, G. A., Miller, L. S., & Cothern, L. (2000, April). *Prevention of serious and violent juvenile offending.* Washington, DC: U.S. Department of Justice, Office of Justice Programs, Office of Juvenile Justice and Delinquency Prevention.

West, A., & Bosley, J. (2011, February 16). *Social media policies: Managing risk, while acknowledging reality.* Tampa, FL: Thompson Interactive Employee Law Webinar.

White, B. (2010, September 30). The new presence on Oakland's streets. *Wall Street Journal.*

White, J. R. (2012). *Terrorism and homeland security* (7th ed.). Belmont, CA: Cengage/Wadsworth.

White, S. (2001, January). Nature watch. *Security Products, 5*(1), 50.

Wilberg Fitzsimons, E. (2000, September 28). False alarms trigger fines. *San Diego Union Tribune*, p. B1.

Wimmer, R. (2000, January). Assessing CCTV's roles in public venues. *Security Technology & Design, 10*(1), 32–34.

Winter, G. (2000, November 17). Black Coke employees to receive $156 million. *San Diego Union Tribune*, p. A2.

Wolf Branscomb, L. (2001, March 9). A fatal day in 1979. *San Diego Union Tribune*, p. A24.

Wulfhorst, E. (2006, June 23). Younger workers more likely to think theft is OK. *San Diego Union Tribune*, p. A2.

Yager, J. (2011, February 10). TSA head wants "risk-based," tailor-made airport screening. *The Hill*.

Yen, H. (2005, December 5). Experts warn U.S. failing in 9/11 follow-up. *San Diego Union Tribune*, p. A3.

Young, T., & Ortmeier, P. J. (2011). *Crime scene investigation: The forensic technician's field manual.* Upper Saddle River, NJ: Pearson Prentice Hall.

Zeigler, M. (2002, February 16). Olympic security sky-high. *San Diego Union Tribune*, pp. A1, A12.

Zuckerman, E. (2003, February 22). Nobody had a chance. *San Diego Union Tribune*, pp. A1, A16.

Zunkel, D. (2000, September). Maintaining secure airports: An evolutionary process. *Security Technology & Design, 10*(9), 62–64, 66, 68.

INDEX